MW01127075

THE COLLEGE PRESS NIV COMMENTARY

ROMANS

VOLUME 2

JACK COTTRELL

New Testament Series Co-Editors:

Jack Cottrell, Ph.D.
Cincinnati Bible Seminary

Tony Ash, Ph.D.
Abilene Christian University

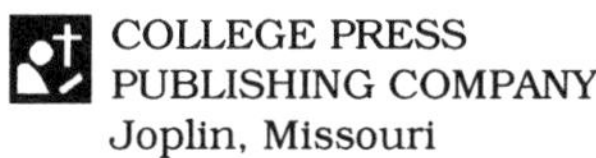

COLLEGE PRESS
PUBLISHING COMPANY
Joplin, Missouri

Printed and Bound in the United States of America

Library of Congress Cataloging-in-Publication Data

Cottrell, Jack.
Romans / Jack Cottrell.
p. cm. – (The College Press NIV commentary)
Includes bibliographic references.
ISBN 0-89900-647-7
1. Bible. N.T. Romans–Commentaries. I. Title. II. Series.
BS2665.3.C68 1996
227'.1077–dc21 96-46296
CIP

A WORD FROM THE PUBLISHER

Years ago a movement was begun with the dream of uniting all Christians on the basis of a common purpose (world evangelism) under a common authority (the Word of God). The College Press NIV Commentary Series is a serious effort to join the scholarship of two branches of this unity movement so as to speak with one voice concerning the Word of God. Our desire is to provide a resource for your study of the New Testament that will benefit you whether you are preparing a Bible School lesson, a sermon, a college course, or your own personal devotions. Today as we survey the wreckage of a broken world, we must turn again to the Lord and his Word, unite under his banner and communicate the life-giving message to those who are in desperate need. This is our purpose.

ABBREVIATIONS

AG . . . . *Arndt and Gingrich, Greek lexicon*
ASV . . . . *American Standard Version*
GC . . . . *God the Creator, by Jack Cottrell*
GRe . . . . *God the Redeemer, by Jack Cottrell*
GRu . . . . *God the Ruler, by Jack Cottrell*
JC. . . . . *Romans, by Jack Cottrell*
KJV. . . . . *King James Version*
KJII . . . . *King James II (New Testament translation)*
LB . . . . *Living Bible*
lit.. . . . . *literally*
LXX . . . . *Septuagint (Greek translation of the OT)*
MP. . . . . *McGarvey-Pendleton Romans commentary*
NAB. . . . . . . *New American Bible*
NASB. . . . . . *New American Standard Bible*
NEB. . . . . . . *New English Bible*
NIV . . . . *New International Version*
NRSV. . . . . . *New Revised Standard Version*
NT . . . . *New Testament*
OT . . . . *Old Testament*
RomDeb . . . . *The Romans Debate, by Karl Donfried*
RSV . . . . *Revised Standard Version*
SH . . . . *Sanday and Headlam Romans commentary*
TDNT. . . . . . *Theological Dictionary of the NT, ed. Kittel*
TEV. . . . . . . *Today's English Version*

For fuller titles and publishing information on books, see the Bibliography.

PREFACE

The introductory issues regarding the book of Romans have been discussed in Vol. 1 of this work (pp. 21-55). Also, the outline for chs. 1-8 of Romans is included in that volume (pp. 55-58).

References to passages in the book of Romans itself are usually limited to chapter and verse data only. For my policy regarding quotations from other sources, see the note at the beginning of the bibliography.

I wish to express my thanks to my wife, Barbara, for her patience in accepting my writing schedule while this work has been in production. My thanks go also to College Press for inaugurating this project, and especially to College Press editor John Hunter for adjusting to a writer who suffers from incurable prolixity. Another special word of thanks is due to my employers at the Cincinnati Bible College and Seminary who encourage my writing in many ways, especially through their regular sabbatical policy.

Above all, thanks be to God for his saving grace, for his Holy Word, and especially for the letter to the Romans with its incomparable beauty and power.

BIBLIOGRAPHY

The following bibliography includes commentaries, books, and articles cited in the text and footnotes of this work. Citations include a minimum of information; the reader must use this list for full titles and bibliographical data.

When commentaries are cited, only the author's name and page number are given. When other sources are cited, usually just the author's name and an abbreviated title (in **bold print** below) are given. Some sources are cited with an even more abbreviated reference (see list of abbreviations).

I. COMMENTARIES

Achtemeier, Paul J. *Romans*. Interpretation: A Bible Commentary for Teaching and Preaching. Atlanta: John Knox Press, 1985.

Barrett, C.K. *A Commentary on the Epistle to the Romans*. Harper's New Testament Commentaries. New York: Harper & Row, 1957; reprint, Peabody, MA: Hendrickson, 1987.

Black, Matthew. *Romans*. 2nd ed. New Century Bible Commentary. Grand Rapids: Eerdmans, 1989.

Bruce, F.F. *The Epistle of Paul to the Romans*. Tyndale New Testament Commentaries. Grand Rapids: Eerdmans, 1963.

Brunner, Emil. *The Letter to the Romans: A Commentary*. Trans. H.A. Kennedy. London: Lutterworth Press, 1959.

Calvin, John. *Commentaries on the Epistle of Paul the Apostle to the Romans*. Trans. John Owen. Grand Rapids: Eerdmans, 1947 reprint.

Cottrell, Jack. *Romans*, Vol. 1. The College Press NIV Commentary. Joplin, MO: College Press, 1996.

Cranfield, C.E.B. *A Critical and Exegetical Commentary on the Epistle to the Romans.* 2 vols. The International Critical Commentary, n.s. Edinburgh: T. & T. Clark, 1975 (1990 corrected printing).

Denney, James. "St. Paul's Epistle to the Romans." In *The Expositor's Greek Testament,* ed. W. Robertson Nicoll, II:555-725. New York: George H. Doran, n.d.

DeWelt, Don. *Romans Realized.* Joplin, MO: College Press, 1959.

Dodd, C.H. *The Epistle of Paul to the Romans.* New York: Harper & Brothers, 1932.

Dunn, James D.G. *Romans.* 2 vols. Word Biblical Commentary. Dallas: Word Books, 1988.

Earle, Ralph. *Romans.* Vol. 3 of Word Meanings in the New Testament. Grand Rapids: Baker Book House, 1974.

Edwards, James R. *Romans.* New International Biblical Commentary. Peabody, MA: Hendrickson, 1992.

Fitzmyer, Joseph A. *Romans: A New Translation with Introduction and Commentary.* The Anchor Bible. New York: Doubleday, 1993.

Godet, Frederic L. *Commentary on the Epistle to the Romans.* Trans. A. Cusin. Ed. Talbot W. Chambers. Grand Rapids: Zondervan, 1956 reprint of 1883 ed.

Griffith Thomas, W.H. *Romans: A Devotional Commentary.* 3 vols. London: Religious Tract Society, n.d.

Haldane, Robert. *An Exposition of the Epistle to the Romans.* MacDill AFB: MacDonald Publishing, 1958.

Harrison, Everett F. "Romans." In *The Expositor's Bible Commentary,* Volume 10, pp. 1-171. Ed. Frank E. Gaebelein. Grand Rapids: Zondervan, 1976.

Hendriksen, William. *New Testament Commentary: Exposition of Paul's Epistle to the Romans.* 2 vols. Grand Rapids: Baker, 1980-1981.

Hughes, R. Kent. *Romans: Righteousness from Heaven.* Preaching the Word. Wheaton, IL: Crossway Books, 1991.

Käsemann, Ernst. *Commentary on Romans*. Trans. Geoffrey W. Bromiley. Grand Rapids: Eerdmans, 1980.

Lard, Moses E. *Commentary on Paul's Letter to Romans*. Cincinnati: Standard Publishing, n.d.

Lenski, R.C.H. *The Interpretation of St. Paul's Epistle to the Romans*. Columbus, OH: Wartburg Press, 1945.

Lloyd-Jones, D.M. *Romans: An Exposition of Chapter 9 – God's Sovereign Purpose*. Grand Rapids: Zondervan, 1991.

Luther, Martin. *Luther: Lectures on Romans*. Ed. & Trans. Wilhelm Pauck. Vol. XV of The Library of Christian Classics. Philadelphia: Westminster, 1961.

MacArthur, John, Jr. *Romans*. 2 vols. The MacArthur New Testament Commentary. Chicago: Moody, 1991, 1994.

McGarvey, J.W., and Philip Y. Pendleton. *Thessalonians, Corinthians, Galatians, and Romans*. Cincinnati: Standard Publishing, n.d.

McGuiggan, Jim. *The Book of Romans*. Lubbock, TX: Montex Publishing Company, 1982.

Moo, Douglas. *The Epistle to the Romans*. The New International Commentary on the New Testament. Grand Rapids: Eerdmans, 1996.

Morris, Leon. *The Epistle to the Romans*. Grand Rapids: Eerdmans, 1988.

Moule, H.C.G. *The Epistle of Paul the Apostle to the Romans*. The Cambridge Bible for Schools and Colleges. Cambridge: The University Press, 1918.

Mounce, Robert H. *Romans*. Vol. 27 of The New American Commentary. Nashville: Broadman & Holman, 1995.

Murray, John. *The Epistle to the Romans*. 2 vols. New International Commentary. Grand Rapids: Eerdmans, 1959, 1965.

Newman, Barclay M., and Eugene A. Nida. *A Translator's Handbook on Paul's Letter to the Romans*. London: United Bible Societies, 1973.

Nygren, Anders. *Commentary on Romans*. Trans. Carl C. Rasmussen. Philadelphia: Fortress Press, 1949.

Sanday, William, and Arthur C. Headlam. *A Critical and Exegetical Commentary on the Epistle to the Romans*. 2nd ed. The International Critical Commentary, o.s. New York: Charles Scribner's Sons, n.d.

Shedd, William G.T. *A Critical and Doctrinal Commentary on the Epistle of St. Paul to the Romans*. Grand Rapids: Zondervan, 1967 reprint of 1879 edition.

Smith, Sherwood. *Thirteen Lessons on Romans*. Vol. 1 (1979). *Thirteen Lessons on Romans*. Vol. 2 (1981). Joplin, MO: College Press.

Stott, John. *Romans: God's Good News for the World*. Downers Grove, IL: InterVarsity, 1994.

Vanderlip, George. *Paul and Romans*. Valley Forge, PA: Judson Press, 1967.

Wuest, Kenneth S. *Romans in the Greek New Testament for the English Reader*. Grand Rapids: Eerdmans, 1955.

II. MISCELLANEOUS BOOKS AND ARTICLES

Arndt, William F., and F. Wilbur Gingrich. *A Greek-English Lexicon of the New Testament and Other Early Christian Literature*. 4th ed. Chicago: University of Chicago Press, 1957.

Bilezikian, Gilbert. *Beyond Sex **Roles***. 2nd ed. Grand Rapids: Baker, 1990.

Büchsel, Friedrich. "κρίνω [etc.]." *TDNT*. III:921-954.

Cottrell, Jack. ***Baptism**: A Biblical Study*. Joplin, MO: College Press, 1989.

_______________. "Baptism According to the **Reformed Tradition**." In *Baptism and the Remission of Sins*, ed. David W. Fletcher, pp. 39-81. Joplin, MO: College Press, 1990.

______________ . "The Biblical **Consensus**: Historical Backgrounds to Reformed Theology." In *Baptism and the Remission of Sins*, ed. David W. Fletcher, pp. 17-38. Joplin, MO: College Press, 1990.

______________ . *Faith's* ***Fundamentals****: Seven Essentials of Christian Belief*. Cincinnati: Standard Publishing, 1995.

______________ . ***Feminism*** *and the Bible: An Introduction to Feminism for Christians*. Joplin, MO: College Press, 1992.

______________ . "**1 Timothy 2:12** and the Role of Women." Four parts. *Christian Standard*, January 10, 1993, pp. 4-6; January 17, 1993, pp. 4-6; January 24, 1993, pp. 4-6; January 31, 1993, pp. 4-6.

______________ . "**Priscilla**, Phoebe, and Company." *Christian Standard*, December 12, 1993, pp. 4-5.

______________ . "**Response** to My Critics." Three parts. *Christian Standard*, November 21, 1993, pp. 5-6; November 28, 1993, pp. 4-6; December 5, 1993, pp. 4-6.

______________ . *Tough* ***Questions****, Biblical Answers*. Part Two. Joplin, MO: College Press, 1986.

______________ . *What the Bible Says about God the Creator*. Joplin, MO: College Press, 1983.

______________ . *What the Bible Says about God the Redeemer*. Joplin, MO: College Press, 1987.

______________ . *What the Bible Says about God the Ruler*. Joplin, MO: College Press, 1984.

Delling, Gerhard. "ὑπερέχω, ὑπεροχή." *TDNT*. VIII:523-524.

______________ . "τάσσω [etc.]." *TDNT*. VIII:27-32.

Donfried, Karl P., ed. *The Romans* ***Debate***, revised & expanded edition. Peabody, MA: Hendrickson, 1991.

______________ . "A Short **Note** on Romans 16." *RomDeb*, 44-52.

Forster, Roger T., and V. Paul Marston. *God's* ***Strategy*** *in Human History*. Wheaton: Tyndale House, 1974.

Fürst, Dieter. "**Confess.**" In *The New International Dictionary of New Testament Theology*, ed. Colin Brown, I:344-348. Grand Rapids: Zondervan, 1975.

Gaertner, Dennis. ***Acts***. The College Press NIV Commentary. Joplin, MO: College Press, 1993.

Hoekema, Anthony A. *The **Bible** and the Future*. Grand Rapids: Eerdmans, 1979.

Hübner, Hans. "ἄτιμος." In *Exegetical Dictionary of the New Testament*, ed. Horst Balz & Gerhard Schneider, I:177. Grand Rapids: Eerdmans, 1990.

Keil, C.F. and F. Delitzsch. *The Pentateuch*. Trans. by James Martin. Vol. 1 of Commentary on the Old Testament in Ten Volumes. Grand Rapids: Eerdmans, 1981.

Kittel, Gerhard, and Gerhard Friedrich, eds. *Theological Dictionary of the New Testament*. Trans. & ed. Geoffrey W. Bromiley. 10 vols. Grand Rapids: Eerdmans, 1964-1976.

Köster, Helmut. "τέμνω [etc.]." *TDNT*. VIII:106-112.

Lampe, Peter. "The Roman Christians of **Romans 16**." *RomDeb*, 216-230.

Lewis, C.S. *The Four **Loves***. London: Geoffrey Bles, 1960.

Michaelis, W. "μάχαιρα." *TDNT*. IV:524-527.

Nash, Donald A. "A **Critique** of the New International Version of the New Testament." Cincinnati: Christian Restoration Association, n.d.

Oepke, Albrecht. "ζέω, ζεστός." *TDNT*. II:875-877.

Pentecost, J. Dwight. ***Things** To Come*. Findlay, OH: Dunham, 1958.

Pinnock, Clark H. "From **Augustine** to Arminius: A Pilgrimage in Theology." In *The Grace of God, the Will of Man: A Case for Arminianism*, ed. Clark H. Pinnock, pp. 15-30. Grand Rapids: Zondervan, 1989.

Piper, John. *The **Justification** of God: An Exegetical and Theological Study of Romans 9:1-23*. 2nd ed. Grand Rapids: Baker, 1993.

Reicke, Bo. "προΐστημι." *TDNT*. VI:700-703.

Schreiner, Thomas R. "Does Romans 9 Teach Individual **Election** unto Salvation?" In vol. 1 of *The Grace of God, the Bondage of the Will*, ed. Thomas R. Schreiner and Bruce A. Ware, pp. 89-106. Grand Rapids: Baker, 1995.

Schüssler Fiorenza, Elisabeth. *In **Memory** of Her: A Feminist Theological Reconstruction of Christian Origins*. New York: Crossroad, 1987.

Shank, Robert. ***Elect** in the Son: A Study of the Doctrine of Election*. Springfield, MO: Westcott Publishers, 1970.

Sherlock, William. *A Discourse Concerning the Divine **Providence***. Pittsburgh: J.L. Read, 1848.

Spencer, Aida B. *Beyond the **Curse**: Women Called to Ministry*. Nashville: Thomas Nelson, 1985.

Spicq, Ceslas. *Theological **Lexicon** of the New Testament*. 3 vol. Trans. James D. Ernest. Peabody, MA: Hendrickson, 1994.

Stählin, Gustav. "φιλέω [etc.]." *TDNT*. IX:113-171.

______________. "σκάνδαλον, σκανδαλίζω." *TDNT*. VII:339-358.

Stendahl, Krister. ***Paul** Among Jews and Gentiles and Other Essays*. Philadelphia: Fortress Press, 1976.

Trench, Richard Chenevix. ***Synonyms** of the New Testament*. Grand Rapids: Eerdmans, 1958.

Walters, James. "'**Phoebe**' and 'Junia(s)' – Rom. 16:1-2, 7." In Vol. 1 of *Essays on Women in Earliest Christianity*, ed. Carroll D. Osburn, pp. 167-190. Joplin, MO: College Press, 1993.

Weiss, K. "φέρω [etc.]." *TDNT*. IX:56-87.

Wright, N.T. *The **Climax** of the Covenant: Christ and the Law in Pauline Theology*. Minneapolis: Fortress Press, 1993.

______________. "The **Messiah** and the People of God." Oxford University: D.Phil. dissertation, 1980.

OUTLINE OF ROMANS 9–16

PART FOUR: THE FAITHFULNESS OF GOD IN HIS DEALINGS WITH THE JEWS – 9:1–11:36

I. THE PROBLEM OF ISRAEL: THE AGONY AND THE ECSTASY OF THE JEWISH NATION – 9:1-5
- **A. Israel's Agony: They Are Accursed** – 9:1-3
- **B. Israel's Ecstasy: They Are Recipients of Unspeakably Glorious Privileges** – 9:4-5

II. THE DISTINCTION BETWEEN ETHNIC AND SPIRITUAL ISRAEL – 9:6-29
- **A. Israel's Situation and God's Faithfulness** – 9:6-13
  1. God's Word Concerning Israel Has Not Failed – 9:6a
  2. The Key to the Puzzle: the Existence of Two Israels – 9:6b
  3. Ethnic Israel Exists by God's Sovereign Choice – 9:7-13
     - a. The Choice of Isaac – 9:7-9
     - b. The Choice of Jacob – 9:10-13
- **B. God's Right to Choose and Use People without Saving Them** – 9:14-18
  1. God's Righteousness Is Challenged – 9:14
  2. God's Sovereignty in Election for Service – 9:15-16
  3. God's Purposes Can Be Served by the Unsaved – 9:17-18
- **C. God Used Ethnic Israel to Produce Spiritual Israel** – 9:19-29
  1. The Objection – 9:19
  2. Paul's Initial Rebuke of the Objector's Attitude – 9:20-21
  3. Beyond Ethnic Israel to Spiritual Israel – 9:22-24
     - a. The Calvinist View
     - b. Seeing Paul Through Non-Calvinist Eyes
  4. Prophetic Confirmation of God's Purpose – 9:25-29

III. ISRAEL'S CHOICE OF LAW RATHER THAN GRACE – 9:30–10:21
- **A. Personal Righteousness Versus the Righteousness of God** – 9:30–10:3
  1. The Reason for the Gentiles' Acceptance – 9:30
  2. The Reason for the Jews' Lostness – 9:31-33
  3. The Jews' Rejection of God's Righteousness – 10:1-3
- **B. Christ Alone Is the Source of Saving Righteousness** – 10:4-13
  1. An Either-Or Choice: Works-Righteousness, or Faith in Christ – 10:4
  2. The Futility of Law-Righteousness – 10:5
  3. Saving Righteousness Comes through Trusting Christ's Works, Not Our Own – 10:6-10
  4. God's Righteousness Is Available Equally to Jews and Gentiles – 10:11-13
- **C. The Jews Have Not Believed in Christ, and Their Unbelief Is Inexcusable** – 10:14-21
  1. The Necessary Prerequisites to Saving Faith – 10:14-15
  2. Most Jews Have Not Believed the Gospel Message – 10:16
  3. The Jews' Problem Is Not Ignorance but Stubbornness of Will – 10:17-21

IV. THE SALVATION OF GOD'S TRUE ISRAEL – 11:1-32
- **A. God's True Israel Is the Remnant Chosen by Grace** – 11:1-6
  1. God Has Not Rejected His People – 11:1-2a
  2. God Had a Remnant of Believers in the OT – 11:2b-4
  3. Those under Grace Are God's New Covenant Israel – 11:5-6
- **B. Unbelieving Israel Has Been Hardened** – 11:7-10
- **C. The Hardening of Unbelieving Israel Becomes a Blessing for Both the Gentiles and the Jews** – 11:11-16
- **D. The Olive Tree: A Metaphor of Judgment and Hope** – 11:17-24
  1. Words of Warning to Gentile Christians – 11:17-22
  2. Words of Hope for Hardened Jews – 11:23-24
- **E. God's Plan for Israel's Salvation** – 11:25-32
  1. The Mystery of Israel's Salvation – 11:25-27
  2. God's Continuing Love for Israel – 11:28-29
  3. God's Ultimate Purpose Is Mercy – 11:30-32

V. DOXOLOGY: GOD'S WAY IS RIGHT – 11:33-36

PART FIVE: LIVING THE SANCTIFIED LIFE – 12:1–15:13

I. A CATALOGUE OF VIRTUES – 12:1–13:14

A. Grace Demands a Transformed Life – 12:1-2

B. Using the Gifts of Grace for Unselfish Service – 12:3-8

C. Miscellaneous Moral Teaching – 12:9-16

D. Personal Vengeance Is Forbidden – 12:17-21

E. The Relation between Citizens and Government – 13:1-7

F. The Relation between Love and Law – 13:8-10

G. Walking in the Light – 13:11-14

II. CHRISTIAN LIBERTY IN MATTERS OF OPINION – 14:1–15:13

A. Do Not Judge Others in Matters of Opinion – 14:1-12

1. We Should Accept All Whom God Has Accepted – 14:1-3
2. We Answer to Our Lord and Not to Each Other – 14:4-9
3. Each of Us Will Be Judged by God – 14:10-12

B. The Stewardship of Christian Liberty 14:13-23

1. We Must Sacrifice Our Liberty for the Sake of the Weak – 14:13-15
2. Do Not Allow What You Consider Good to Be Spoken of as Evil – 14:16-18
3. We Must Do Only Those Things Which Build Others Up – 14:19-21
4. Each Christian Must Be True to His Own Convictions – 14:22-23

C. Living in Unity and Hope – 15:1-13

1. Selfless Service Produces a Unified Witness – 15:1-6
2. Through Christ's Selfless Service, Jews and Gentiles Glorify God Together – 15:7-12
3. A Prayer That All Believers May Abound in Hope – 15:13

PART SIX: PERSONAL MESSAGES FROM PAUL – 15:14–16:27

I. PAUL'S MINISTRY AS THE APOSTLE TO THE GENTILES – 15:14-33

A. Reflections on His Past Service – 15:14-22

B. His Plans for the Future – 15:23-29

C. His Request for Prayer – 15:30-33

II. PAUL AND HIS FELLOW WORKERS – 16:1-24
- **A. Commendation of Phoebe** – 16:1-2
- **B. Greetings to Individual Acquaintances** – 16:3-16
- **C. Warnings against False Teachers** – 16:17-20
- **D. Greetings from Paul's Companions** – 16:21-24

III. CONCLUDING DOXOLOGY – 16:25-27

9:1–11:36 – PART FOUR

THE FAITHFULNESS OF GOD IN HIS DEALINGS WITH THE JEWS

We now begin our consideration of one of the most difficult sections of the Bible, Romans 9–11. As N.T. Wright says, "It is as full of problems as a hedgehog is of prickles" (*Climax*, 231). It is a premiere example of the common hermeneutical challenge: how can we know the meaning of the parts until we first know the meaning of the whole? But how can we know the meaning of the whole until we first know the meaning of the parts?

We begin by examining the question of the meaning of the whole. The reader may correctly assume, however, that the conclusions set forth here have been preceded by a great deal of dialectical (back-and-forth) analysis of the parts and the whole together.

A. THE PRINCIPAL THEME OF THIS SECTION

As we read through these three chapters, a number of prominent themes leap to our attention. They are as follows, listed in the order of their initial appearance in the text.

a) *The Nation of Israel.* From beginning to end this section is dominated by references to ethnic or physical Israel, the Jews as a nation, those whom Paul calls "my brothers, those of my own race, the people of Israel" (9:3-4). Paul makes several points about their role in God's plan (9:4-5,22-23; 11:11-15,25-32), their historical destiny (11:1,11-15,25-32), and their salvation (9:30–10:3; 10:16-21; 11:7-32).

b) *God's Faithfulness.* Another subject introduced near the beginning of this section is the faithfulness of God, specifically, whether God has been faithful to his word concerning his people Israel (9:6a). Has he kept his promises to them? Has he been and is he being fair in his dealings with them? "Is God unjust?" (9:14). See also 9:19; 11:29.

c) *The Remnant.* Another key subject is the distinction between Israel as a whole and remnant Israel: "For not all who are descended from Israel are Israel" (9:6b). Membership in the former is determined by physical birth, but the latter is defined in spiritual terms as determined by God. See 9:23-29; 11:2-7. A key idea is stated in 9:27: "Though the number of the Israelites be like the sand by the sea, only the remnant will be saved." This is the "remnant chosen by grace" (11:5).

d) *God's Sovereignty in Election.* "God's purpose in election" is another important theme (9:11), especially his sovereignty in making the choices that he does. "For who resists his will?" (9:19). He has the same sort of sovereign authority that a potter has over his clay (9:21). See also 9:15-23; 11:5-10,28-29.

e) *The Gentiles.* Paul also raises the question of the relation between the Jews and the Gentiles. God's elect, he says, are drawn "not only from the Jews but also from the Gentiles" (9:24). See 9:24-31. How the two are related dominates chapter 11 (vv. 11-32).

f) *Law and Grace.* We are not surprised that the main subject in chs. 1–8, law and grace, comes to the surface again in 9:30-31 as the key to the question of why God saves some and rejects others. A major part of ch. 10 (vv. 3-17) is the point that salvation is by grace through faith in Jesus Christ, not by law or works of law. See also 11:6,20,23.

g) *The Church.* A final theme, discussed in 11:17-24, is the church. Though the word "church" itself is not used, this is clearly the point. The specific issue in this section is the relation between the church and Israel.

Having surveyed the various topics that arise in this section, we may now ask which of them is the *main point* of 9–11. What is Paul's purpose in writing this section? What is the underlying and unifying theme that ties it all together? What overall point is the author trying to establish?

1. Inadequate Answers

Several possibilities have been suggested as the main theme of these chapters, most of which are inadequate or off the mark. Three of these will now be briefly discussed.

God's Sovereignty in Election

A common idea is that Paul's main point here is the sovereignty of God in his election of individuals to salvation. Some see 9–11 as the *locus classicus* (main proof text) for the Calvinist doctrine of predestination. As Moo notes, Augustine taught that "Paul added these chapters to illustrate and expand on his teaching of predestination" (547, n. 1; see 548, n. 2).

In 1839 Robert Haldane said the same thing in his commentary on Romans. In earlier chapters, he said, Paul dealt mostly with justification and sanctification, but "now he proceeds to treat particularly of the doctrine of predestination, and to exhibit the sovereignty of God in his dealings both towards Jews and Gentiles." God's treatment especially of the Jews "furnishes the most ample opportunity for the illustration of this highly important subject" (438). "So," says Lloyd-Jones (*Chapter 9*, 2), "according to Haldane, the main object of this section is to deal with the doctrine of predestination and to illustrate it in that way."

William G.T. Shedd is another example of this view. Chs. 1–8, he says, show that the proximate cause of salvation is faith; but 9–11 are added to show that God is the ultimate and efficient cause. Here Paul "teaches that the ultimate reason why the individual believes, is that God elects him to faith, and produces it within him." Redemption thus rests upon "the divine sovereignty in the bestowment of regenerating grace." After touching on election in 8:28-33, Paul "now enters upon the full examination of it, together with the correlated doctrine of reprobation" (271-272).

This view must be rejected, however; neither election (predestination) as such nor God's sovereignty in election is the main point of 9–11. This conclusion has nothing to do with one's particular view of predestination, since scholars on both sides of this issue generally agree on this. Lloyd-Jones, a Calvinist, specifically rejects this view, saying that the subject matter here is "altogether bigger than predestination." Indeed, "for anyone to exalt predestination as the main theme in this section is almost to be guilty of blasphemy" (*Chapter 9*, 2,7). Godet, a non-Calvinist, agrees and declares that this view is refuted by "the entire course of this great exposition" (336). Nygren agrees: "If one uses chapters 9–11 as his point of departure in studying Paul's view of predestination, he ends with a false picture of it" (354). See also Moo, 548.

It is certainly true that the subject of God's sovereignty in election is present in these chapters, especially in ch. 9. It is not the main point, however.

Justification by Faith

Another view is that in 9–11 Paul is just continuing the theme of 1–8, that justification before God is by faith in the work of Jesus Christ, with a special emphasis on how this relates to Israel. For example, Fitzmyer sees Rom 1:16–11:36 as one unit in which the gospel is set forth. Part one (1:16–4:25) explains how the gospel reveals that the uprightness (or righteousness) of God justifies people by faith (253). Part two (5:1–8:39) explains that God's love further assures salvation to those justified by faith (393). Then part three (9:1–11:36), says Fitzmyer, discusses "the relationship of Israel to this mode of justification or salvation." He gives the following title to this section: "This justification and salvation through faith do not contradict God's promises to Israel of old" (539). Paul's main point is "to explain how the Jewish people fit into the new plan of God" (541).

Certainly the themes of law and grace are prominent in this section, especially in 9:30–10:21. Here Paul shows why God has rejected the Jews and accepted the Gentiles: the former have vainly sought justification by works of law, while the latter have accepted the free grace of Jesus Christ through faith. This theme appears also in ch. 11 (vv. 5-6,20-23). Thus there is a clear connection between this section of Romans and the first eight chapters. As Morris says, "Paul is not here proceeding to a new and unrelated subject. These three chapters are part of the way he makes plain how God in fact saves people" (344).

Nevertheless we must conclude that justification by faith is not the main point of 9–11. To be sure, the way the law-grace theme is presented in 1–8 indirectly leads to the question being dealt with here, as we shall presently see. But the main point is something else.

The Role of Israel in God's Plan

One other view, one that is quite common but still inadequate, is that Paul's purpose in writing 9–11 was to explain the role of the nation of Israel in God's redemptive plan. "God's Purpose for

Israel" is the heading given to this section by Matthew Black (122). "Chapters 9–11 are concerned with the place of Israel within the framework of God's redemptive purpose," say Newman and Nida (196). According to W.H. Griffith Thomas, this section "deals with the relation of the Jew to the Gospel of Righteousness treated of in chs. i.-viii." (2:112). "Chapters nine through eleven of Romans have as their theme *the destiny of Israel in the plan of God*," says Vanderlip (70). The subject here is "Israel herself," says Moo (548).

Many interpreters think this section is mainly concerned with the question of Israel's salvation. For example, MacArthur declares that "the major theme of chapters 9–11 is God's dealing with His elect nation" (2:17). In discussing this theme, he says, Paul addresses several basic questions. Has God forsaken his ancient people Israel, or does the gospel of grace apply to them, too? If it does apply, why have most Jews rejected it? Also, is there any hope for the *nation* of Israel (2:3-5)? The answer, of course, is in 11:26,29: "And so all Israel will be saved," since "God's gifts and his call are irrevocable."

Others believe that Paul's main point is to explain the relation between Israel and the Gentiles, or as Murray puts it, to "delineate for us the worldwide design in reference to Jew and Gentile." This is necessary in view of the fact that the gospel of grace is God's gift "to the Jew first and also to the Greek" (1:16, NASB; Murray, 2:xiii). The practical purpose of such an explanation would be to unite the squabbling Jewish and Gentile factions within the Roman church (see Moo, 553). It was especially crucial that they be united in their support of Paul's plan to preach the gospel in a new area, according to Wright (*Climax*, 252-253).

These chapters are obviously quite heavily focused on the nation of Israel. The Jews are involved in Paul's argument throughout the whole section. However, I disagree that Israel is the *main point* here, whether it be Israel and salvation, Israel and the Gentiles, Israel and the church, or national Israel and remnant Israel. Thus I would not entitle this section "The Problem of Israel," as Moo does (547).

2. The Faithfulness of God

The real focus of these chapters is not upon predestination as such, justification as such, or Israel as such. The focus is rather upon God himself (see Wright, *Climax*, 235). Specifically, the theme is *the faithfulness of God*. True, Israel figures heavily in this discussion. In fact, it is God's dealings with Israel that give rise to the question of his faithfulness. Has God been faithful to his chosen people? Has he kept his promises to them (9:6a)? Has he been fair to them? Because of Israel's involvement here one could probably say, as does Dunn, that "the true theme of chaps. 9–11 is God and Israel" (2:520). More specifically, though, it is God himself; and more specifically still, his faithfulness. As Piper says (*Justification*, 19), "What is at stake *ultimately* in these chapters is not the fate of Israel . . . . Ultimately *God's own* trustworthiness is at stake." Cranfield entitles this section, "The Unbelief of Men and the Faithfulness of God" (2:445).

What, specifically, has raised this issue? Two things: The Jews' rejection of the gospel, and God's consequent rejection of the Jews. First, it was a simple historical fact that most of the nation of Israel did not accept Jesus as the expected Messiah; they rejected the gospel of grace. Stott declares that in 9–11 "the dominant theme is Jewish unbelief, together with the problems which it raised" (262). I disagree that it is the dominant theme, but I agree that it helped to raise the problem that does dominate this section.

Second, it was also a fact that God rejected his people (9:3), the nation of Israel as a whole, when they rejected him. That is, he rejected them with respect to salvation. This fact in particular raised the issue of God's faithfulness. After all, God himself had chosen the Jews and showered them with covenant promises and covenant blessings. Is he now going back on his word? Piper speaks of "the tension between God's word and the fate of Israel" (*Justification*, 19). This indeed is a "key tension" (Moo, 548), and it raises what Godet calls "the greatest enigma in history: the *rejection* of the *elect* people" (336). "How, at a given point in time, can God reject those whom He has elected?" (337).

The issue, then, is whether or not God has been faithful with respect to his promises to the Jews. Has his word failed (9:6a)?

When he rejected his people, "*God's word of promise seems to have lost its validity*. . . . Does not that mean that God has revoked the promises He made to the fathers?" (Nygren, 356-357). "How stands his faithfulness in the face of Israel's unfaithfulness?" (Dunn, 2:530). As Wright puts it (*Climax*, 236), "The main subject-matter of Romans 9–11 . . . is the covenant faithfulness of God, seen in its outworking in the history of the people of God." This is *the* point. See Piper, *Justification*, 46.

Paul's intent in these chapters is to show that, in spite of the nation's unbelief and God's subsequent rejection of them, God has nevertheless been completely faithful to the Jews and has kept all his promises to them (9:6a). "All of Rom 9–11 is written with a view to showing that God has not been and will not be unfaithful to his word" (Piper, *Justification*, 217-218). See Moo, 550-551.

This section, then, is in effect an exercise in *theodicy*,[1] or an attempt to justify before men the ways of God. It is not, as some have thought, Paul's attempt to defend himself and his Gentile mission.[2] "No, it is not his mission, and still less his person, which Paul means to defend when he traces this vast scheme of the ways of God; it is God Himself and His work in mankind by the gospel. He labors to dissipate the shadow which might be thrown on the character of God or the truth of the gospel by the unbelief of the elect people" (Godet, 337).

One final point should be made in this connection. We are saying here that the theme of 9–11 is the *faithfulness* of God. Some interpreters identify it instead as the *righteousness* of God. "God's Righteousness Vindicated" is Mounce's heading for these chapters (193). "Chapters 9–11 discuss the subject of God's righteousness in view of his apparent rejection of the Jewish nation" (195). See also Harrison, 100; and Edwards, 228.[3]

---

[1]See Bruce, 183; Godet, 336-337. This is contrary to Nygren (354-355), who says, "Every theodicy is a blasphemy." But he then proceeds to explain the purpose of this section as if it were a theodicy.

[2]See Godet, 337; Piper, *Justification*, 18.

[3]Wright also identifies the theme as the righteousness of God, but he mistakenly takes this to be virtually synonymous with "covenant faithfulness" (*Climax*, 234). This modern attempt to redefine righteousness as covenant faithfulness has been discussed and refuted in GRe, ch. 4.

It is true that the concept of the righteousness of God appears in 9–11. It is also true that there is a close relation between righteousness and faithfulness. Also, the theme of divine righteousness figures prominently in 1–8. Nevertheless it is best not to speak of the righteousness of God as the main point of 9–11. The main reason is that the righteousness of God that may also be called his faithfulness is *not* the kind of righteousness that is at the heart of the gospel as explained in 1–8 (see 1:17; 3:21-22; 4:6,9,11; 5:17). In these first eight chapters the divine righteousness is primarily God's gift of righteousness to believing sinners, on the basis of which he justifies them. This kind of divine righteousness does appear in 9–11 (see 9:30-31; 10:3-6), but it is not the main point. The righteousness of God that is equivalent to his own internal integrity and self-consistency and faithfulness is also found in 1–8 (see 3:25-26), but there the issue is whether God can be righteous (i.e., true to himself) when he saves sinners. The answer is yes, he can, because of the cross. But here in 9–11, though this kind of righteousness is alluded to in 9:14, the issue is very different, namely, whether or not God is *un*righteousness when he does *not* save the Jews.

Thus, in order to avoid any confusion that might arise because of these different connotations of divine righteousness, and to avoid the misconception that the main point here is the same kind of divine righteousness that is prominent in 1–8, I believe it is better to speak here of the *faithfulness* of God.

B. PAUL'S ANSWER TO THE QUESTION OF GOD'S FAITHFULNESS

How then does Paul answer the question about God's faithfulness? The key to his answer is the distinction between service and salvation, with a corresponding distinction between utilitarian promises and redemptive promises. Being chosen for service is not the same as being chosen for salvation, and promises concerning the former do not necessarily entail promises concerning the latter. Thus it was concerning Israel: when God chose the Jewish nation to play a part in his great drama of redemption, he did not thereby guarantee the salvation of every individual Jew.

1. Chosen for Service

God did indeed choose Israel for a special role of unmatched service, which Paul spells out in detail in 9:4-5 (see 3:1-2). Their mission was filled with wonder and glory, leading up to the grand climax of bringing into the world the Messiah, the Savior of mankind. One cannot imagine a greater privilege.

The fact is, despite all her shortcomings, Israel did indeed accomplish this mission. Nursed along by God's patient and chastising hand, Israel at last yielded the Messiah. This is something in which every individual Jew can take pride: "Through *us*, through *our* nation, God brought the Savior into the world! What a wonder!" This, along with all the preparatory glories mentioned in 9:4-5, are privileges that will always belong to Israel and to Israel alone. These unique blessings have not been taken away from the elect nation, nor are they shared with anyone else, not even the church.

Thus Israel rendered to God and to the rest of the world the greatest possible service. But it was *service* nonetheless, and service is the *only* thing for which the Jews as a nation were elected or chosen. That God chose them to serve in even this exalted way did not include and was not even directly related to their salvation. Personal salvation – justification by faith – was never intended for nor guaranteed to any individual Jew just because he was a Jew (see Piper, *Justification*, 218).

Thus Schreiner is wrong when he declares that the crucial statement in 9:6a "*refers to God's promises to save his people Israel*," and when he links the list of privileges in 9:4-5 to "the salvation of Israel" ("Election," 91). Schreiner infers this conclusion from the fact that in 9:1-3 Paul does refer to Israel's salvation, or the lack of it. But to say that 9:6a, and the rest of ch. 9, must then be speaking of salvation promises is a *non sequitur*. In fact, it misses Paul's whole point, which is actually just the opposite: the nonsalvation of individual Jews does not negate God's promises to the Israelite nation, because those promises did not have to do with individual salvation in the first place.

Thus Israel's rejection of salvation in no way implies that God's plan for the Jews *as a nation* was a failure. The problem or challenge concerning God's faithfulness arises only when one misunderstands God's intended role for the Jews in the first place. This was in fact a major mistake that the Jews themselves had made. They assumed that their election for service automatically involved salvation; but this was never the point, as Paul has already shown in 2:1–3:8. In ch. 2 Paul addressed the Jews' assumption that their very Jewishness, symbolized by their possession of the Law and circumcision, guaranteed their personal salvation. Paul very clearly showed that this is false, and that the way of salvation for individual Jews, despite the privileges of the nation as a whole (3:1-2), was no different from the way Gentiles themselves are saved, i.e., not through law but through grace alone.

Paul's discussion in ch. 9 (vv. 1-29) presupposes that God has the perfect right to make this distinction between service and salvation. One might think (as did the Jews) that God surely cannot deny salvation to the people whom he loved and whom he chose and whom he used in such a marvelous way. Somehow this would just not seem fair! But that is the very point: it *is* fair; it *is* righteous for God to do this. He has the perfect right to make such a distinction, and to keep his choice for service completely separate from his choice for salvation. The fact that God used Pharaoh for his redemptive purposes did not require the latter to be saved (9:17-18). The same is true of Israel. If God wants to use the Jews in his service yet deny them salvation because of their unbelief, that is perfectly consistent with his nature and his promises. God is completely within his rights when he does this (9:19-21).

2. Chosen for Salvation

But what about the salvation of the Jews? If they are not necessarily saved, are they then necessarily condemned? Are they totally cut off from Jesus and from his saving grace? No, they are neither automatically included, nor are they automatically excluded from grace. The point is simply that the salvation of any individual Jew — and salvation is open to them all — is an issue that is separate from the nation's election to service. God in his sovereignty has set up a way of salvation according to his own choosing, and he has sovereignly established the conditions under which anyone may receive this salvation, whether Jew or Gentile. Any individual Jew is free to meet these conditions and to accept this salvation.

This way of salvation, of course, is the same that Paul has expounded throughout 1–8: grace, not law; and the means by which any Jew may receive it is just as Paul has explained in these earlier chapters: faith in God's promises concerning the death and resurrection of Christ. See 9:30–10:21.

It is true that most Jews are not saved (9:1-3), but the reason is that they are trying to be saved by a way of their own choosing rather than the way of God's choosing, i.e., by law and not by grace (9:30–10:3). When the Jews thus reject God's saving promises and are then themselves rejected, this is *not* a "defeat" for God's "redemptive word" (contra Achtemeier, 154), because this is completely consistent with what has always been God's way of redemption. Nor is it a defeat for God's utilitarian word, i.e., his promises to use Israel to bring salvation into the world, because these promises have been completely fulfilled apart from the salvation of any or all Jews.

Have any Jews actually believed and been saved? Of course they have! These are the "remnant" (9:27; 11:5) and the "descendants" (9:29, lit. "seed") of which Isaiah spoke. They are the seven thousand who did not bow to Baal (11:4). Though they be relatively few compared with the total number of ethnic Jews, they were the true Israel (9:6b) in OT times; and they along with believing Gentiles are in NT times the new Israel, the church (9:23-29). This way of salvation is still open to any and all Jews (11:17-24).

Paul emphasizes the point that it is possible for all Jews to be saved, but it will happen only "thus" or "so" (οὕτως, *houtos*, 11:26), i.e., only "in this way." The way of salvation for individual Jews is the same as for anyone else: grace, not law. Contrary to the speculations of many, God will not at some point in the future establish some totally different and special way of salvation for Jews (see Wright, *Climax*, 233). When we understand that God's utilitarian promises to Israel as a nation did not include salvation, and when we see that all these utilitarian promises have already been fulfilled, then we are able to see how God has been faithful in his promises to Israel without having to save every Jew. This also sets us free from an interpretation of ch. 11 that requires all physical Israelites to be saved in order for God to be true to his redemptive word.

C. THE RELATION BETWEEN 1–8 AND 9–11

Another introductory issue is the relation between 9–11 and the first eight chapters of Romans. How is this section related to Paul's overall argument thus far? What is the flow of his thought here? Is there a logical connection between 9–11 and 1–8?

1. Avoiding Extremes

In answering this question two extremes must be avoided. One is the view that there is no inherent connection, i.e., that chs. 9–11 are a kind of digression or parenthesis, or an appendix only loosely related to what has gone before. For example, C.H. Dodd sees this section as "a compact and continuous whole, which can be read quite satisfactorily without reference to the rest of the epistle" (148). He suggests that it may have been a sermon that Paul had written earlier and carried with him, which he would use when called upon to explain the role of the Jews, and which he decided to insert in his Roman letter at this point. Though its contents are not irrelevant to the material in 1–8, still, if he had omitted it, we would have had no sense of a gap between ch. 8 and ch. 12 (149-150).[4]

At the other extreme is the view that 9–11 is not just inherently related to 1–8 but is the logical climax to the argument being developed there. Viewed this way, 9–11 is then regarded as the heart and essence of the entire letter. Krister Stendahl, for instance, calls these chapters "the climax of Romans," the section to which everything else is leading (*Paul*, 4, 85). N.T. Wright also argues that 9–11 functions "as the climax of the theological argument. . . . The whole of Romans 1–11 is, in one sense, an exposition of how the one God has been faithful, in Jesus Christ, to the promises he made to

[4]See Fitzmyer, 540, for others who hold such a view.

Abraham." Rom 9–11 is the "climactic section" to the whole (*Climax*, 234, 255).[5]

Neither of these extremes is acceptable. On the one hand, chs. 1–8 do form a logically complete unit, to which 8:31-39 is a natural climax. These chapters deal with the question of personal salvation, affirming it to be by grace and not by law. But on the other hand, looking at it this way does not require us to regard 9–11 as a mere "aside or appendix, dealing with a different problem."[6] A more moderate view will now be explained.

2. The Nature of the Connection

What has happened in the writing of Romans is this. Throughout Paul's explanation of how we are saved by grace and not by law (1–8), a question comes repeatedly to the surface but is not dealt with in detail lest the flow of the argument be too greatly interrupted. But once the main argument has been completed, it becomes possible, even necessary, to return to this question and to address it more specifically and completely, which is what Paul does in 9–11. Thus 9–11 definitely has a thematic connection with 1–8, though it is not a part of the logical flow of the latter. It *is* a separate unit. The point of 1–8 would stand without 9–11, and we could understand the main point of 9–11 without 1–8. But we would not know *why* Paul wrote these three chapters without referring back to 1–8.

To be specific, the very point of the first eight chapters – that salvation is by grace and not by law – seems in itself to render the Jews irrelevant, to render God's 2000 years of dealing with them futile and pointless, and definitely to raise the question of God's faithfulness to them.

The argument of 1–8 is that one is saved not by his response to any law code, including the Law of Moses, but only by the grace of

---

[5]I am not comfortable with any outline of Romans that includes chs. 1–11 under a single heading, e.g., Fitzmyer (98-100).

[6]I am here disagreeing with Wright (*Climax*, 232). His complete statement is as follows: "If the letter is perceived as a treatise simply on individual salvation from sin, [9–11] cannot but be seen as an aside or appendix, dealing with a different problem, that of the Jews."

God made available to all through the saving work of Jesus Christ (see 3:28; 6:14). But since the Jews are so closely identified with law (in the form of the Law of Moses), and since the way of grace appears to some to disparage or even dismiss the law, the gospel thus appears to be dismissing the Jews from God's plan as well. What then has become of God's promises to the Jews and of God's faithfulness to his promises?

This problem is compounded by the many positive references to the Jews and to the OT in 1–8. Paul begins the letter by declaring that the gospel was promised by the OT prophets (1:2). He then declares that the gospel is actually intended for the Jews first (1:16). He says the Jews were given many advantages, especially their stewardship of the OT Scriptures (3:1-2). These very Scriptures testify to grace as the way of salvation (3:21). In fact, the gospel of grace actually upholds the law (3:31). The law is holy, and righteous, and good (7:12); and the believer agrees with it (7:16) and obeys it with his whole heart (7:25).

But all of these positive things about the Jews and about law seem to be overshadowed and negated by statements of another kind and by the general contrast with grace. This is especially true in the thematic statements, that we are justified by faith not by works of law (3:28), and that we are not under law but under grace (6:14). In addition, the entire second chapter is extremely critical of the Jews and their law. In the final analysis there seems to be no distinction between Jews and Gentiles (2:9-12,25-29; 3:9). The law is of no value for justifying sinners; such justification must occur "apart from law" (3:20-21). Anyone who believes is a child of Abraham, whether he be Jew or Gentile (4:9-16). We who are alive to Christ are dead to the law (7:4) and released from it (7:6).

The fact that the Jews and the law seem to be cast in such a negative light is what raises the question with which 9–11 deals. The message of grace in effect seems to make the 2000 years of Jewish history superfluous. Why did God focus his loving attention upon the Jews, and shower so many privileges upon them, if in the final analysis we are saved by grace, not by law? Has God changed his mind? Has he gone back on his promises to the Jews? Has he reversed his plan, and arbitrarily abandoned his people? As Moo (553) expresses it, "Does the gospel presented in the NT genuinely 'fulfill' the OT and stand, thus, as its natural completion [as the positive statements cited above would suggest]? Or is the gospel a betrayal of the OT, with no claim therefore to come from the same God who elected and made promises to Israel [as the negative statements would seem to suggest]?"

Thus "Paul's whole argument" in 1–8 "demands an examination of the Jewish question" (Morris, 343). There must be a "harmonizing" of the OT with the NT, says Lloyd-Jones (*Chapter 9*, 6).

Especially troublesome is the simple fact that most Jews rejected the grace of God and even their Messiah when he came. But if the gospel is so rooted in the OT, why did the Jews refuse it? As Calvin put it, "If this be the doctrine of the law and the Prophets [3:21], how comes it that the Jews so pertinaciously reject it?" (333). If it all began with Abraham and was even patterned after Abraham's faith-relation to God, "how came it, then, that it was pre-eminently Abraham's descendants who refused to believe the gospel?" (Bruce, 183).

These are the sorts of questions that are left hanging in 1–8, and which Paul's discussion of God's faithfulness to the Jews in 9–11 is intended to answer. In the earlier part of the epistle they are closest to the surface in 2:1–3:8. See especially 3:1, where Paul asks, "What advantage, then, is there in being a Jew, or what value is there in circumcision?" But at this point he gives only one positive answer to the question (3:2). Then in 3:3-8 the very issue of Israel's unbelief and God's faithfulness is raised, with Paul simply confirming the latter and quickly moving on in his argument. But now in 9–11 he comes back to these very questions and deals with them in more detail.

It is noteworthy also that Paul's basic *answer* to these questions has already been suggested in 2:1–3:8, where he addresses the Jews' assumption that the very fact that they were the "chosen people" guaranteed their salvation. In ch. 2 Paul explicitly denies that this is the case. No one, not even a Jew, is saved by his relation to God's law, and especially not by his mere possession of that law (as the Jews possessed the Law of Moses). In this earlier section, however, he makes only an abbreviated reference to the distinction between election to salvation and election to service (3:1-2). Now in 9–11 he presents this in detail as the solution to the problem.

3. The Immediate Contextual Connection: 8:31-39

The theme of 9–11 is God's faithfulness in his dealings with the Jews. We have seen that this discussion is necessary because the gospel of grace-not-law seems to be inconsistent with God's covenant promises to Israel. It looks as if he is relegating his chosen nation to the trash pile with a dismissive "Never mind!" To prevent such erroneous thoughts from taking root and becoming a stumbling block to many, Paul shows why this is not the case.

But there is another reason why it is appropriate if not necessary for Paul to defend God's faithfulness at this point in his letter to the Romans. He has just concluded his explanation of the gospel of grace with one of the greatest hymns of hope in the human language, 8:31-39. In this paragraph the Apostle sets forth the precious promises that are the essence of God's new covenant through Jesus Christ.

After reading these promises, however, some may be tempted to ask whether they are as wonderful as they seem to be at first glance. Certainly their *content* cannot be surpassed: God is on our side; he gave up his Son for us; he will give us all things; Christ even now is interceding for us at God's right hand; nothing shall separate us from the love of God that is in Jesus. What, then, is the problem? As some may see it, the problem is whether or not we can truly count on God to keep all these promises! In other words, will he be *faithful*?

Why should anyone raise such a question? Why should anyone dare to challenge the faithfulness of God? Here is where the question of Israel may possibly be raised. Someone may well ask, Did not God make equally great promises to the Jews under the Old Covenant? Did he not choose Israel as his special people and make them the special objects of his love and attention? But where are the Jews now? God seems to have abandoned them, and has even set aside the magnificent Law with which he entrusted them. So why should we count on him to keep all these high-sounding promises to us under the New Covenant? If his word has failed for the Jews, will it also fail for us Christians? The promises of 8:31-39 presuppose a faithful God. But if his faithfulness can be called into question concerning his promises to the Jews, how can we depend on him to keep his promises to us now?

Even if this is not the main reason why Paul wrote 9–11, it surely cannot have been absent from his mind as he constructed his careful argument concerning God's faithfulness in these chapters. Most interpreters[7] see such a connection, and conclude that 9–11 serves to reinforce the Christian's confidence in God's promises. God did not in fact go back on his promises to the Jews; neither will he fail to keep his promises to us.

D. THE QUESTION OF GOD'S SOVEREIGN ELECTION

A final issue that must be briefly discussed in this introduction is the question of God's sovereign election as it relates to human responsibility and free will. As we have noted above, some have drawn the conclusion that predestination is the main point of this whole section of Romans. Though this is not the case, this subject does figure prominently here, especially in ch. 9. Thus some preliminary remarks are in order before we turn to a detailed examination of the text.

Key affirmations of God's sovereignty are as follows. Even before Isaac was born, God chose him for his purposes (9:7), and he chose Jacob and rejected Esau in the same manner (9:11-13). God told Moses, "I will have mercy on whom I have mercy, and I will have compassion on whom I have compassion" (9:15). God's choice does not depend on man's efforts but on God's mercy (9:16). He chose Pharaoh for his purposes (9:17). "God has mercy on whom he wants to have mercy, and he hardens whom he wants to harden" (9:18). God is like a potter who has complete control over his clay (9:19-21). Some are prepared for destruction and some for glory (9:22-23). He calls individuals from among Jews and Gentiles (9:24). He has a remnant chosen by grace (11:5). The chosen obtained God's righteousness; the rest were hardened (11:7-8). God loves the Jews in accord with his purpose of election (11:28). His gifts and call are irrevocable (11:29).

These affirmations of God's sovereign election seem to be overwhelming, but at the same time there is considerable emphasis on human freedom and man's responsibility for his own fate. E.g., the

---

[7]E.g., Piper, *Justification*, 19; Morris, 344; Achtemeier, 154.

Gentiles obtained righteousness because they pursued it by faith, whereas the Jews did not attain it because they pursued it by works (9:30-32). The key is personal faith (9:33; 10:4,10). The Jews did not submit themselves to God's righteousness (10:3). The conditions for salvation are faith and confession (10:9-10). God saves all who call upon the name of the Lord (10:12-13). Faith comes through hearing Christ's word (10:17). Some whom God calls do not answer (10:21). Paul hopes his evangelism of the Gentiles will move some Jews to accept salvation (11:14). Jews are rejected because of their unbelief, and Gentiles are accepted because of their belief (11:20). God will save those believing Gentiles who continue in their belief, and reject those who do not (11:22). He will also restore those unbelieving Jews who do not continue in their unbelief (11:23).

How are we to assess these data? How may we harmonize the references to divine sovereignty on the one hand, with the references to human beings' responsibility for their own fate on the other hand? Some see the answer in the distinction between the election of groups and the election of individuals. It is often argued (by Calvinists and non-Calvinists alike) that the main point in ch. 9 is corporate election, especially the election of Israel as a nation. This is the view of Forster and Marston: "People often fail to understand that in this whole section the apostle is talking about nations and not about individuals." Even in 9:14-18, "the bearing of Moses and Pharaoh on the earthly function and destiny of the nation of Israel" is the issue (*Strategy*, 59, 75). See also Achtemeier: "Paul is addressing the problem of Israel as chosen people"; he "is *not* addressing the fate of some individual." In ch. 9 God is choosing the destiny "of peoples, not of individuals" (154-155). Fitzmyer also cautions us to remember that Paul's "emphasis is on corporate Israel despite the examples of individuals that he uses" (542). Cranfield agrees: "It is, in fact, with the election of the community that Paul is concerned in Romans 9 to 11" (2:450). See Morris: "We should bear in mind that Paul is here dealing with the community rather than with individuals" (345).

On the other hand, many deny that the main point is corporate election. In his book *The Justification of God* Piper believes he has shown that Rom 9 teaches "the predestination of individuals to their respective eternal destinies." At the same time he finds "the view that sees only *national* election in these verses" to be exegetically untenable (*Justification*, 218). Schreiner agrees, as he defends the typical Calvinist view "that Romans 9 teaches that God unconditionally elects individuals to be saved" ("Election," 89). He argues against the view that Rom 9 "relates to the salvation of groups, of corporate entities, and not of individuals" (90; see 98-105).[8]

What should we say about this? Surely, in our exegesis of 9–11 it is important to ask whether Paul is dealing with groups or with individuals. But actually this is not the key issue, and to approach this passage as if it were may cause us to miss its whole point. The key issue is the distinction between election for *salvation* and election for *service*.[9] Also significant is the distinction between physical or ethnic Jews – the *nation* of Israel, and those who are Jews spiritually – those described as the *remnant* (9:27; 11:5). Paul's main point, though, is the difference between service and salvation, and whether these refer to individuals or groups in the final analysis will not affect the main point.

One point on which almost everyone agrees is that, somewhere in Rom 9, Paul deals at least in part with God's election of Israel as a nation for a role of service, or what Moo calls "this general (and nonsalvific) corporate election of Israel" (559, n. 24). But the problem, the point at issue, is this: exactly *with what* is this corporate election for service being compared or contrasted? Some say the contrast is with election of individuals to salvation, and that this is really the main point of Rom 9. This is the view of Piper, Schreiner, and Moo, as cited above. Others say the contrast is with salvific corporate election, with the election of a *group*, not individuals, to salvation. Forster and Marston say, "The prime point is that the election of the church [which is comparable to the remnant in Israel] is a corporate rather than an individual thing" (*Strategy*, 136). "The election of grace is corporate rather than particular," says Shank (*Elect*, 157; see 114, 122).[10]

---

[8]Likewise Moo says, "It is important to distinguish between this [9:3] general (and nonsalvific) corporate election of Israel and the salvific individual election of 9:6-29 and 11:5-7" (559, n. 24).

[9]See GRu, 332-335; JC, 1:62, 178, 187-188, 219, 230.

[10]See also Pinnock, "Augustine," 20, though he does not specifically refer to Rom 9–11.

Which of these approaches is correct? In my judgment, neither of them. Does this mean that Paul is not concerned here with election to salvation at all? On the contrary, he is very much concerned with it *as a fact*, but especially in ch. 9 he is *not* concerned with any *details* relating to it. Again, the main point is the simple distinction between salvation and service. This is a distinction which the Jews themselves failed to make, and this very failure was the basis for questioning the faithfulness of God. "If God has chosen us, why is he now rejecting us and not saving us?" Because, says Paul, he did not choose you for salvation, but for service.

Election to service applies to the entire nation of Israel, and to every individual within it. Election to salvation applies only to the "Israel within Israel" – the remnant – and to every individual within it. Whether it be nations (groups) or individuals is not the point. This is contrary to the common Calvinist view, which tries to find individual election to salvation in this passage; it is also contrary to the view that salvific election is of groups, not individuals. The simple fact is that in Rom 9 it is not Paul's purpose to explain election to salvation at all.

Paul's discussion of Israel in Rom 9 in fact shows that God has the sovereign right to distinguish between salvation and service. The emphasis is on God's sovereign authority to choose unconditionally any group or any individual to fill any given role in the working out of his purposes, without being bound at the same time to guarantee their salvation. In this way God selected Israel from all the nations of the earth to perform the greatest act of service possible for an earthly agent.

At the same time God is sovereignly free to choose individuals for salvation in a way that is completely different from the way he chooses anyone for service. The fact is that he chooses to bestow salvation on the basis of grace and upon the primary condition of faith. This conditional election to salvation is established in 9:30–10:21. Certainly those unconditionally chosen for service can also be saved, but 9:30–10:21 shows that salvation is given only to those who through faith choose to relate to God in terms of grace instead of law. Those who put their trust in God's way of grace form another group within and distinct from ethnic Israel, namely, spiritual Israel, the remnant of believers.

This resolves the seeming paradox of divine sovereignty and human responsibility in 9–11. Many interpreters, especially Calvinists, are content to regard the presence of these two themes as a paradox, but this is totally unnecessary. God's sovereignty is exercised in his unconditional election of individuals and groups, Israel in particular, to roles of service in the working out of his redemptive plan. His sovereignty is also seen in the way he chooses to distinguish service from salvation, which allows him to choose and use Israel without guaranteeing the salvation of all individual Jews as part of the same package. Another expression of his sovereignty is his right to establish the system of salvation according to a way of his own choosing, in a way independent of works, namely, by grace. Those who accept this way to salvation become part of "the elect."

But it is made very clear from 9:30 onward that becoming a part of this grace category is the result of one's responsible choice to believe God's promises. In other words, salvation is *conditional*. This in no way contradicts the sovereignty of God, but rather upholds it, since it is perfectly consistent with the way God made human beings and configured his way of salvation in the first place.

E. AN OVERVIEW OF CHAPTERS 9–11

Romans 9–11 is divided into three main sections. After a prologue (9:1-5) that sets up the problem to be discussed, the first main section (9:1-29) discusses the fact that God has made a *distinction* within the nation of Israel so that there are in fact two Israels: (1) physical, ethnic, or national Israel, i.e., Israel according to flesh; and (2) remnant or spiritual Israel, i.e., Israel according to faith. The former was chosen for service, the latter for salvation. The second main section (9:30–10:21) explains the *criterion* for distinguishing between the two Israels, i.e., the choice between law and grace. The third section (11:1-32) shows that there is still *hope* for the salvation of all ethnic Jews. The passage closes with a doxology of praise to God (11:33-36).

I. THE PROBLEM OF ISRAEL: THE AGONY AND THE ECSTASY OF THE JEWISH NATION (9:1-5)

The transition from ch. 8 to ch. 9 is quite abrupt. No connecting word (e.g., "therefore," "however") links 9:1 closely with 8:39. There is an obvious shift in subject matter. Also, the tone changes dramatically. The spirit of joy and confidence characterizing the end of ch. 8 is replaced by a spirit of tension and sorrow.

The reason for this new direction in Paul's thought is the problem of his own kinsmen, the Jewish people. In view of the Jews' privileged role in God's plan, the logical expectation would be that they above all others should have been rejoicing in the hope Paul describes in 8:31-39. The shocking and tragic fact, though, was that most Israelites were rejecting the Messiah whose coming was their very reason for being. As a result, rather than celebrating their salvation, they were under God's curse.

Paul's reaction to the plight of the Jews took two forms. On a subjective, personal level his heart was filled with grief because of their lost state. On a more objective, theological level he was concerned that some might take Israel's rejection as an indication that God's word had failed. Though his personal grief was genuine, his greater concern was to show that the tragedy of the Jews in no way violated God's original promises and plans for them as a nation.

The main point of this section (9:1-5) is to set forth the contrast between the plight of Israel (1–3) and her privileges (4–5). How can these be reconciled? Has God's word somehow failed to come true? By raising these questions Paul thus prepares the way for his defense of the faithfulness of God in his dealings with his people.

A. ISRAEL'S AGONY: THEY ARE ACCURSED (9:1-3)

9:1 I speak the truth in Christ – I am not lying, my conscience confirms it in the Holy Spirit – With these introductory words Paul affirms in several ways the truthfulness of what he is about to say in vv. 2-3. In the Greek text of his positive statement, the word "truth" stands first, in the place of emphasis: "*Truth* I speak in Christ!" This point is reemphasized by saying the same thing negatively, "I am not lying."

To further confirm the veracity of his words, Paul invokes three distinct witnesses. One is his own conscience (see 2:15), which, he says, testifies or bears witness along with him. ("Testifies along with me" or "bears witness along with me" is a literal translation and is to be preferred over the NIV's "confirms it."[11]) In other words Paul has no inward reservations at all about what he is saying.

The other two witnesses are Christ and the Holy Spirit. Paul says he speaks the truth "in Christ." This could mean simply that he speaks as one who is conscious of being in union with Jesus Christ, and who thus as a Christian is always bound to speak the truth (see Moo, 555; Cranfield, 2:452). I believe, though, in view of the parallel idea in 1 Tim 2:7, that he is referring to his appointment by Christ to be an apostle; and thus "in Christ" is an invocation of his apostolic authority (see Dunn, 2:523).

Similarly "in the Holy Spirit" could be referring to the indwelling Holy Spirit, through whose moral power every Christian can resist the temptation to lie (see 8:13). More likely, though, Paul is here referring to his consciousness of the fact that he is writing under the inspiration of the Spirit and is thus divinely prevented from speaking falsehood (see 1 Cor 7:40).

Seldom does Paul go to such lengths to reinforce the truthfulness of his assertions. Sometimes he declares that he is telling the truth (2 Cor 11:10; Titus 1:13) and sometimes he denies that he is lying (2 Cor 11:31; Gal 1:20). In 1 Tim 2:7, as here, he does both. Such attestations do not mean that on other occasions he is not telling the truth. They are simply his way of underscoring the seriousness of what he is saying.

Paul's appeal to Christ and the Holy Spirit in addition to his conscience is an important lesson for us. We must remember that the conscience itself is not an infallible guide. Rather, it operates on the basis of a standard of truth and right that must be established on other grounds (see 2:15). Unlike Paul, we do not have personal apostolic authority and divine inspiration, but we do have the Spirit-inspired Bible to serve as the reference point for guiding our con-

[11]The same verb and the same construction appear in 8:16. The way it is used here in 9:1 gives support to the interpretation given to that verse above (JC, 1:483-484).

sciences. Thus what we believe and teach to be truth must pass not only the test of conscience but the test of biblical teaching as well.

9:2 Exactly what is the momentous truth solemnly introduced in v. 1? Strictly speaking, it is the fact that Paul is personally filled with tremendous grief and anguish: **I have great sorrow and unceasing anguish in my heart.** The cause of his grief is not actually stated in this verse, but is made clear in v. 3. It is the fact that his own natural kinsmen, the Jewish people, were under God's curse because of their unbelief.

That the Israelites were truly accursed will be established in the next verse, but Paul here certainly implies it by revealing the agony of his soul. The words "sorrow" and "anguish" refer to the emotional state of his heart, and their intensity is magnified by the adjectives "great" and "unceasing." Would Paul's spirit be filled with such deep suffering if he thought for a moment that the Jews as such were saved?

Just as Samuel "mourned for" the fallen King Saul (1 Sam 15:35), and Jeremiah wept for fallen Israel of old (Jer 4:19; 9:1; 13:15-17; 14:17), so was Paul in a state of constant grief because his own people would not accept the gospel and thus were not saved.

Why did Paul think it was so important to establish this fact in such an emphatic way? For one thing, he had already exposed the shallowness of the Jews (ch. 2) and consigned them to sin and condemnation (3:8-9). Also, in the discussion that is about to follow he is going to declare again that the Jews as such are lost, and that God is under no obligation to save them just because they are Jews. Thus Paul wants everyone, Jews and Gentiles alike, to know that he is not indifferent to Israel's plight nor does he take delight in it. This establishes his authenticity; it shows that his negative judgment against his countrymen is not just the result of some personal spite against them, but is the true word of God, a word that afflicted him so deeply that he would give anything if it were not true.

9:3 Just how deep are Paul's feelings for his fellow Jews? Just how far would he go to save them? This verse tells us: **For I could wish that I myself were cursed and cut off from Christ for the sake of my brothers, those of my own race, . . .**

Exactly what was Paul willing to endure on behalf of his brethren? To be "cursed and cut off from Christ." The word "cursed" translates ἀνάθεμα (*anathema*), used in other places for eternal condemnation (1 Cor 16:22; Gal 1:8-9). Literally this word refers to something delivered over to or consecrated to God, possibly for service but more often for destruction (see Deut 7:26; Josh 7:11-12, LXX). That the latter is its meaning here is made clear by the addition of the words "from Christ." There is no word for "cut off" in the Greek text. Literally it reads "accursed from Christ" (see 2 Thess 1:7-10). Most agree that this is a strong and clear reference to condemnation in hell (Lard, 294; MP, 377; Moo, 557).[12]

The verb translated "I could wish" is difficult, not in itself but in view of what Paul was wishing. This word (εὔχομαι, *euchomai*) can mean either "to pray" or "to wish"; either meaning conveys the notion of a sincere desire. The content of Paul's desire is that he himself might be sent to hell in the place of his fellow Jews.

What makes this difficult to translate is that although this is no doubt a continuing wish in Paul's heart, the verb form is a kind of past tense (i.e., imperfect). The straightforward meaning is "I was praying (wishing)," or "I used to pray (wish)"; but a past tense does not fit the context. Thus most agree that it should be treated as hypothetical, i.e., as a "potential imperfect" (Nash, "Critique," 31) or "the imperfect of wishes" (Lenski, 583). In other words, "I *would* pray or wish this *if* it could be done, but I know it cannot."[13]

But why is such a thing impossible? The Calvinist answer is that this would contradict the doctrine of the perseverance of the saints, or "once saved, always saved."[14] The more obvious answer, though, is that Paul knew that he as a sinful human being could not be an adequate substitute for even one other sinner, much less for the whole nation of Israel. Paul's words, "for the sake of my brothers," are the language of substitution (compare 6:6,8; see Moo, 559). But only the divine and sinless Messiah could be and was such a substitute (Gal 3:13).

---

[12]It means "to forfeit final salvation" (Cranfield, 2:457); "consigned to damnation or divine wrath" (Fitzmyer, 544); "devoted to destruction in eternal hell" (MacArthur, 2:11); "bearing the curse of God" (Morris, 347); "abandoned to perdition" (Murray, 2:3).

[13]See Godet, 339; Lard, 292; Cranfield, 2:455-457; Moo, 558.

[14]See Murray, 2:3; Hendriksen, 2:310; MacArthur, 2:11. See the discussion of 8:38-39 above (JC, 1:524-525).

What is unequivocally demonstrated by this statement is the reality of Paul's concern for his people, and the depth of his grief at their lost condition.[15] "Paul felt such love that he was willing to relinquish his own salvation and spend eternity in hell if somehow that could bring his fellow Jews to faith in Christ!" (MacArthur, 2:11). This seems to go beyond even John 15:13 and Rom 5:7. Maybe this is why Paul felt he had to multiply his assurances and witnesses in v. 1, "because it seems unbelievable that a man should want to be damned in order that the damned might be saved" (Luther, 261).

Another thing that is demonstrated by this statement is that Israel as a nation, i.e., the majority of the Jews, were in fact lost. The language "accursed from Christ" certainly refers to eternal lostness, and Paul's willingness to endure this state in Israel's place without a doubt implies that Israel herself was under such a curse (see Moo, 557-558; Piper, *Justification*, 45). The Jews "are really in this state," as Godet says (340). Though Dunn doubts this (2:525), he is on the wrong track. The whole discussion in 9–11 is predicated on the fact that God's chosen covenant people are in fact lost; anything less than this would negate the seriousness of the problem with which Paul is dealing here.

There is no question that Paul's concern is directed toward the nation of Israel. He calls them "my brothers, those of my own race." Paul often speaks of his fellow Christians as his "brothers" – 130 times, according to Moo (559, n. 24). Some conclude from this that Paul's calling his fellow Jews "brothers" implies that they are in fact saved. "That is, he recognizes them still, in spite of their unbelief, as fellow-members of the people of God." Indeed, "unbelieving Israel is within the elect community, not outside it" (Cranfield, 2:458-459). See Fitzmyer (545) for a similar view.

This notion must be rejected, however. Sometimes in the NT Jews spoke of their fellow Jews as "brothers." This is true often in the Book of Acts (e.g., 2:29,37; 3:17,22; 7:2; 9:17; 13:26). Even Paul addressed unbelieving Jews as his "brothers" (Acts 13:26,38; 22:1,5;

---

[15]This is similar to, but not the same as, Moses' despair over the sins of his fellow Israelites and the threat of their imminent doom (Exod 32:30-32). See Gen 44:33; 2 Sam 18:33.

23:1,5,6; 28:17). Thus no connotation of salvation is implied here by the term "brothers." In fact, one of Paul's main points in this very chapter is that membership in physical Israel is not equivalent to membership in the true spiritual people of God (9:6; see ch. 2).

In order to make it clear that he is talking here only about physical kinship, Paul adds "those of my own race," literally, "my kinsmen (relatives) according to the flesh." See 1:3 and 9:5 for uses of "according to the flesh" in the sense of physical lineage. Compare 11:14.

Despite the fact that Paul was "the apostle to the Gentiles," he never forgot his roots, his identity as a Jew. He never lost his sincere love for his original family, and his earnest desire for their salvation.

B. ISRAEL'S ECSTASY: THEY ARE RECIPIENTS OF UNSPEAKABLY GLORIOUS PRIVILEGES (9:4-5)

Paul now turns to the other side of the paradox called Israel. The same nation which is the object of God's curse is the one that he chose to receive some of the greatest blessings imaginable. These next two verses give a list of these privileges, a project begun in 3:1-2 and now continued in detail.

These verses also give us more insight into why Paul was willing to sacrifice himself for the sake of Israel's salvation. They were more than his relatives; they were the people who were next to God's own heart and who were at the very center of God's redemptive plan (Murray, 2:4).

One very important question regarding these privileges is whether they were related only to pre-Christian Israel, or whether they continue to apply to Jews in the Christian era and beyond. Some take the latter approach. Murray declares that the privileges enumerated here "have abiding relevance because 'the gifts and the calling of God are not repented of' (11:29)"; thus he sees them as applying to a future, restored Israel (2:xiv). Following Barth, Cranfield thinks this list of privileges indicates the "continuing fact" of Israel's election (2:459-460). Moo (560) argues that these blessings "relate not only to Israel's glorious past that she has forever forfeited; some of them, at least, relate also to Israel's present state and are pregnant with potential future significance (especially, 'adoption,' 'promises,' and 'patriarchs')." Piper agrees that these blessings will always apply, not to every individual Jew, but to the elect remnant at the end of the ages (*Justification*, 30). "In some sense," he says, they are "still the prerogative of historical Israel," and even have "saving implications" (40). That is, "the privileges taken as a whole are redemptive and eschatological" (46). Dunn even argues that the privileges are "the blessings brought to all believers, Jew and Gentile, through the gospel" (2:534).

I strongly disagree with this approach. It is true that everything in this list of blessings pointed beyond the OT era to this age and beyond, as did Israel's very existence. The single purpose of Israel's election, and of all the preliminary privileges listed in 3:2 and 9:4-5a, is the climactic privilege named in 9:5b, i.e., the first coming of Christ. By serving God's purpose of bringing the Christ into the world, all of these prerogatives have played a preparatory role in the eternal salvation of all believers, both Jews and Gentiles. And every ethnic Jew who ever lived and will live, whether saved or not, has a right to look at this list and take humble and grateful pride in the fact that God chose *his* nation to be the recipients of these blessings and thereby to prepare for the Christ and his saving work.

But this does not mean that these blessings in themselves are still actually being applied to and enjoyed by *anyone* today, whether Jew or Gentile. In fact, they are not. It is one thing to receive the intended *result* of these privileges, as does every saved person; it is quite another to receive the privileges themselves, which was true *only* of the nation of Israel (including every individual within it) up to the time of Christ's first coming. Here Paul is talking only about the latter circumstance. He is referring only to the privileges God bestowed upon the Jewish nation in the OT era, privileges that applied in that day to every Jew whether he was part of the saved remnant or not. But they no longer apply in any direct sense to *anyone*: not to Jews as Jews, whether individually or collectively; not to Gentiles as such; and not to Christians, whether Jews or Gentiles.

Herein lies the nature of the tragic irony of Israel's existence. They were so absorbed with the privileges themselves (and continued to be, in Paul's day), that they neglected and even rejected the intended result of these privileges, God's gracious salvation through Christ. They glorified the means, and ignored the end. The very people who were, by God's gracious choice, responsible for bringing the Redeemer into the world were themselves the object of his wrath.

9:4 At the beginning of v. 4 Paul refers to his brothers and kinsmen (v. 3) as **the people of Israel**. This can be taken in two possible ways. On the one hand, it may be in apposition to "brothers" and "kinsmen," bringing the thought of v. 3 to an end (as in the NIV). On the other hand, it may be the first item in the list of the privileges themselves, as the verse division suggests. I prefer the latter view, though this is not a serious issue.

Taking these words as the first blessing, we find a total of nine privileges bestowed upon the chosen people.[16] They are presented in four relative clauses relating back to the masculine plural nouns at the end of v. 3, "brothers" and "kinsmen." The first relative clause is this one, "who are Israelites" (NASB). This is a better translation than the NIV. The second relative clause begins with "of whom," and has six predicates: adoption as sons, divine glory, covenants, receiving of the law, temple worship, and promises (the verb "are" is understood). The third relative clause is "of whom [are] the fathers." The last relative clause is "from whom [is] the Christ according to the flesh." Schematically the list looks like this:

. . . my brothers and kinsmen –
– who are Israelites;
– of whom [are] adoption, glory, covenants, law, worship, and promises;
– of whom [are] the fathers; and
– from whom [is] the Christ.

The first privilege of the Jews, says Paul, is that they are *Israelites*. Most interpreters see this name as more than just a synonym for "Jews," and as signifying more than just ethnic identity. It seems to point back to the time of Israel's calling, to the period of their very formation as a people from the loins of Jacob, whom God renamed

[16]These nine are not totally distinct, since some overlapping occurs. E.g., the temple service is part of the law, and both the law and the promises are included in the covenants. In this paragraph the translations are literal.

"Israel" (Gen 32:28). Thus "Israelites" calls attention to the Jews' origin and to their unique covenant relationship with God. It is in itself a title of honor that embodies the totality of their God-given privileges.

Some think the present tense ("who *are* Israelites") is significant (Fitzmyer, 545). It shows that "this title has not been revoked," says Moo (561). This may be true in the sense described above, namely, that Jews may still take pride in the fact that theirs was the nation God used in a special way. However, this does not mean he is still using them thus, nor that he will ever do so again. Nor does being an "Israelite" today guarantee one's personal salvation, any more than it did in OT times.

Theirs is the adoption as sons . . . . Literally it says, "of whom is the adoption." This term, υἱοθεσία (*huiothesia*), is used in the NT to represent the individual Christian's relationship with God (8:15,23; Gal 4:5; Eph 1:5). As Christians we are his family, his adopted sons and daughters. Some see the term as applying here to the Jews in the very same way, with the "fullest saving significance" (Piper, *Justification*, 32). This saving sonship would then be a blessing possessed by present and future Israel.

I believe this view is quite mistaken. Here Paul is not talking primarily about individual Jews but about the nation as a whole. The term refers to God's sovereign choice of Israel collectively to be his son: "Israel is my firstborn son" (Exod 4:22). "I am Israel's father, and Ephraim is my firstborn son" (Jer 31:9). "When Israel was a child, I loved him, and out of Egypt I called my son" (Hos 11:1). In a derivative sense each individual born as a Jew enjoyed this status of adoptive sonship: "You are the children [sons] of the LORD your God" (Deut 14:1; see Deut 32:19; Isa 1:2; 43:6).

This concept of Israel's adoption emphasizes God's initiative and deliberate choice in establishing this relationship with Israel. It "helps bring out the sense of election more clearly" (Dunn, 2:526). Also, it indicates that God's relation with his people was one of fatherly affection (Deut 1:31; 8:5; Isa 46:3-4; Jer 3:19).

Though this adoption was extremely significant, its limitations must still be recognized. For one thing, it did not in itself entail the salvation (spiritual sonship) of any individual Jew. (See Lard, 294-295; Moo, 562; MacArthur, 2:13.) Also, this father-son relation with

Israel as a nation ended with the beginning of the New Covenant, under which adoption is now a saving relationship with all willing individuals, including both Jews and Gentiles (Gal 3:26–4:7).

[T]heirs is **the divine glory . . .** (literally, "and the glory"). Again some project this into the future history of Israel. They say that Paul is here guaranteeing that the Jews *as Jews* will participate in the messianic eschatological glory of Christ's second coming (Piper, *Justification*, 33-34; Dunn, 2:526-527, 534). In my opinion this is again a misreading of this text and of the whole section (9–11). "The glory" refers to the fact that God manifested himself to OT Israel and even dwelt among them in a glorious visible form (a theophany).

From the beginning of their exodus journey the people of Israel were blessed with the visible presence of God in their midst in the form of a pillar of cloud by day and a pillar of fire by night (Exod 13:21-22; 40:36-38). At least on some occasions "there was the glory of the LORD appearing in the cloud" (Exod 16:10). "The glory of the LORD settled on Mount Sinai" when God revealed the law to Moses (Exod 24:15-18). When the tabernacle was consecrated, "the glory of the LORD filled" it (Exod 40:34-35). "The glory of the LORD appeared to all the people" at times of sacrifice (Lev 9:23) and at times of judgment (Num 14:10; 16:19, 42). When Solomon's temple was dedicated, "the glory of the LORD filled the house of the LORD" (1 Kgs 8:11, NASB; see 2 Chr 7:1-3).

Later Judaism began to use the Hebrew term *shekinah* to refer to this glorious manifestation of God's presence. *Shekinah* means "dwelling" or "presence" (Cranfield, 2:462) and was thus a kind of shorthand for "the presence of God's glory." As a brightly shining radiance this visible entity marked the splendor of God's very presence among his people Israel. No wonder Paul included this in the list of Israel's privileges! Of course God is everywhere in the sense of his omnipresence, but to no other nation on the face of the earth has God displayed his special presence in glory as he did to his people Israel.

Today God is present in a special way within his church (1 Cor 3:16; Eph 2:22) and within individual Christians (1 Cor 6:19). Though this presence is not one of visible glory, it is even greater than the *shekinah* because it is part of our salvation.

The next privilege is **the covenants**. A major question is, why is this plural?[17] There are several possibilities. One is that Paul is speaking of the several *ratifications* of the Mosaic covenant – Exod 19:5-6, at Sinai; Deut 29:1, at Moab; and Josh 8:30-35, at Mt. Gerizim and Mt. Ebal (Barrett, 177-178). Another is that he is talking about all biblical covenants, including the New Covenant (Piper, *Justification*, 35; Dunn, 2:534; Bruce, 185). To include the New Covenant, however, violates the intent of this list, which is to name those privileges which are exclusive to Israel.

The third and most likely possibility is that "covenants" refers to all OT covenants specifically involving Israel. This would not include the covenant with Noah (Gen 9:9), since this was not with Israel *per se*. It would include the covenant with Abraham and the other patriarchs (Gen 12:1-3; 15:1-21; 17:1-14; 26:3-5,24; 28:13-15); the covenant at Sinai (Exod 19:1-6; 24:8), as ratified at Moab and at Gerizim-Ebal; and the covenant with David (2 Sam 23:5).[18] See Eph 2:12 for a similar use of the plural. In Gal 3:15-19 Paul treats the Abrahamic covenant and the Mosaic covenant as two *parts* of a single covenant, with the *promise* aspect given first to Abraham and the *law* aspect added later (v. 19) through Moses.

The main point is that Israel is the only nation on earth with whom God chose to enter a special covenant relationship. This is just one more indication of their status of exalted privilege.

The next blessing named by Paul is **the receiving of the law.**[19] This refers to the Law of Moses, and to the fact that being chosen to be the recipients of this law was an honor granted only to Israel. "He has done this for no other nation; they do not know his laws. Praise the LORD" (Ps 147:20). In ch. 2 Paul has shown that mere possession of this law did not guarantee salvation for any Jew, but still it was a unique privilege to receive it and to be granted stewardship of it (see 3:1-2).

---

[17]Some manuscripts have "covenant" (singular), but the plural seems to be the better reading. See Fitzmyer, 546.

[18]MP, 379; Cranfield, 2:462; Murray, 2:5; Morris, 348; Moo, 563.

[19]This word literally means "lawgiving" (NASB: "the giving of the law"), i.e., "legislation"; but it was also used for the *result* of the lawgiving, i.e., the law itself as possessed by the recipients. See Cranfield, 2:462-463.

In this and in the next two items we see examples of how these privileges overlap with one another at certain points. The law, the temple worship, and the promises are all included in the covenants to a certain degree.

Israel was also granted the privilege of **the temple worship**. This is the word λατρεία (*latreia*), which means "service," usually in the sense of worshiping the true and living God (see 12:1). This could mean Israel's general privilege of being able to serve the true God in a world of idolatry, but the NIV is probably correct to take it in the more narrow sense of the temple services. This would include "the entire ceremonial system" of the Law of Moses (MacArthur, 2:15), and especially the system of sacrifices that dealt with sin and foreshadowed the Messiah's atoning work. See Moo, 564.

The last privilege listed in v. 4 is **the promises.** This refers to all the promises included in God's covenants, as well as all the other promises made to Israel. This includes the promises given to the Jewish people generally,[20] and the promises given to individuals such as Abraham (Gen 12:1-3; Gal 3:16,21), Isaac (Gen 26:3-5), Jacob (Gen 28:13-14), Moses (Deut 18:18-19), and David (2 Sam 7:11-16; Acts 13:22-23). See Rom 15:8, "the promises made to the patriarchs."

All such promises ultimately pointed toward a single goal, the coming of the Messiah. Their fulfilment was the means to this one end. They are like individual notes that lead into the great symphony of messianic promises and prophecies themselves, e.g., Isa 7:14; 9:6-7; Jer 23:5; Ezek 34:23-24; 37:24-28; Micah 5:2; Zech 9:9-10; Mal 3:1. What is important to see is that all these promises made to Israel were fulfilled when Jesus came the first time; see Acts 13:32-34. Rom 9:5b is the goal and climax of them all. The promises made to Abraham and to the rest were fulfilled *through* Israel, *in* Christ, *to* us. These promises no longer apply to Israel today nor to Christians as such. We are not under these promises, but rather under their fulfilment. The promises of the New Covenant are different, and better (Heb 8:6).

9:5 Theirs are the patriarchs, . . . (literally, "the fathers"; see 11:28; 15:8). This refers especially to the "founding fathers" of the

[20]See Hendriksen's lengthy list of predictions and promises made to OT Israel (2:313-314).

Jewish people: Abraham, Isaac, and Jacob (see 9:6-13; Exod 3:15). From the perspective of the Jews, the fact that God chose these men to be the foundation of his chosen people made them not only national heroes but also the greatest figures in the history of the world (Deut 7:6-8). It was certainly a great privilege to be able to claim them as ancestors.

This leads to the climactic and most wonderful privilege of all: **and from them** [the Jews] **is traced the human ancestry of Christ . . . .** This is the blessing for which all the others were only means to an end, the one purpose for which the others existed in the first place, namely, to bring the Messiah, the Christ, into the world.

The emphasis here is on the human nature of Christ. The Greek text may be translated literally thus: "from whom is the Christ according to the flesh." Christ's saving work required that he have not only a divine nature but also a true and complete human nature. "Flesh" refers to the human origin of this human nature (body and spirit), in contrast with the divine origin of his divine nature. It was Israel's incomparable privilege to provide the former (see 1:3).[21]

The blessings mentioned earlier in the list are described as belonging to Israel: "theirs" (vv. 4a,5a), literally, "*of* whom." Here the expression changes to "*from* them." This shows that the relation between the Messiah and national Israel was one of origin or ancestry only. Jesus did not "belong" to Israel; he was not their Messiah in the sense of their personal Savior, since most Jews remained unbelievers. Although this did not contradict God's purpose for the nation, since their election was not meant to guarantee the salvation of individual Israelites (see 9:6-7), it was nevertheless a great irony and a greater tragedy. The very people granted the prerogative of bringing the Christ into the world rejected him when he came. Their greatest privilege was the very obstacle over which they stumbled.

What compounds the tragedy is the fact that by rejecting this climactic and teleological blessing, the Jews in effect repudiated the significance of all the others! As pointed out above, Paul is not here portraying Christian-era Jews as having a continuing and perpetual

---

[21]"Flesh" refers to human relationships also in 9:3, "kinsmen according to the flesh," and in 9:8, "children of the flesh" (NASB).

claim to the blessings listed here; these were privileges that belonged strictly speaking to pre-Christian Israel. But the tragedy is that whenever ethnic Jews hear the gospel of Christ and reject it, they are rejecting *everything* that has ever made their nation special from its very beginning.

This simple fact that *from Israel came the Christ* was the ultimate fulfilment of all God's promises to and covenants with the Jews as a nation. God's word thus did not fail, and his purpose for physical Israel was thus achieved.

The next clause – **. . . who is God over all, forever praised! Amen** – has been interpreted in two main ways. The basic question is whether the term θεός (*theos*, "God") refers to Christ or not. If it does, this verse is one of the strongest NT affirmations of the divine nature of Jesus.[22]

Since the original Greek text has no punctuation, every translation of this verse is actually an interpretation by virtue of the way the translators choose to divide and punctuate it. Those who deny that *theos* refers to Christ insert a period somewhere in the middle of the verse, usually after the word "Christ." Verse 5b then becomes a statement of praise to God, a doxology that is separate from the statement about Christ. The following are examples: From the Jews "according to the flesh, is the Christ. God who is over all be blessed for ever" (RSV). "Christ, as a human being, belongs to their race. May God, who rules over all, be praised forever!" (TEV). The NEB is similar.[23]

The other main possibility is to take the entire verse (after "the patriarchs") as a single statement about the Christ, which thus would be affirming that he is *theos*, or God. The NIV is an example of this view, as are the following: From the Jews "is the Christ according to the flesh, who is over all, God blessed forever" (NASB). "From them, according to the flesh, comes the Messiah, who is over all, God blessed forever" (NRSV).

---

[22]See the detailed discussions of this issue in Murray, 2:245-248; Cranfield, 2:464-470; Fitzmyer, 548-549; and Moo, 565-568.

[23]The order of the Greek words is as follows: "from whom is the Christ according to the flesh, the one who is over all, God, blessed forever." Thus it is possible to place the period after "over all," in which case *theos* would still not apply to Christ. See Stott, 265.

The evidence favors the latter interpretation.[24] The first three arguments have to do with the wording in v. 5b. (1) The Greek words at the beginning of the clause (ὁ ὤν, *ho ōn*) most naturally introduce a relative clause that refers to something in the immediately preceding context, i.e., "Christ." (2) Paul's doxologies of praise in other places do not stand alone but are attached to a word in the preceding context (1:25; 11:36; 2 Cor 11:31; Gal 1:5; 2 Tim 4:18). (3) In independent statements of blessing, the word "blessed" almost always precedes the word or words for God (e.g., 2 Cor 1:3; Eph 1:3; 1 Pet 1:3).[25] These first three arguments can be summed up together thus: if v. 5b were referring to God the Father and not to Jesus Christ, to be consistent with other biblical usage, the wording would have been different, as follows: "Blessed be God, who is over all forever."

Other arguments have to do with the context. (4) The reference to Christ's human nature in v. 5a calls for a complementary reference to his divine nature. (5) Taking the latter part of the verse as a doxology seems out of place in a paragraph "otherwise expressing sorrow and regret" (Fitzmyer, 549). (6) Taking v. 5b as affirming Christ's deity is compatible with the climactic nature of this last and highest privilege bestowed upon Israel. "Without some predication expressive of Jesus' transcendent dignity there would be a falling short of what we should expect in this climactic conclusion" (Murray, 2:247).

Over against these arguments from wording and context it is argued that Paul nowhere else refers to Christ as *theos* ("God"). It is true that Paul's usual title for Jesus is κύριος (*kyrios*, "Lord"), and that *theos* is usually reserved for God the Father (e.g., 1 Cor 8:6; 12:3-6; Eph 4:5-6; Phil 2:11). But Paul certainly attributes deity to Christ elsewhere (see Gal 1:1; Phil 2:6; Col 2:9), and a strong case can be made that he calls Jesus *theos* in Titus 2:13 and 2 Thess 1:12 (see Murray, 2:247-248). The title *kyrios* is itself a title of deity (see 1:4; 10:9-13).

Moo is therefore correct in concluding that Paul is calling Jesus *theos* in this verse, thus "attributing to him full divine status." This

[24]For good summaries of the arguments see Murray, 2:245-248; Cranfield, 2:467-468; Fitzmyer, 549; and Moo, 567-568.

[25]The only exception is Ps 67:19 (LXX), on which see Fitzmyer, 549.

view, he says, is "exegetically preferable, theologically unobjectionable, and contextually appropriate" (568).

The other descriptions of Christ in v. 5b are also indicative of his divine nature. He is the one who is "over all," an expression of his universal Lordship (Acts 10:36), which belongs only to God. He is the "blessed" one (NIV, "praised"), a term which elsewhere in the NT refers only to God (Mark 14:61; Luke 1:68; Rom 1:25; 2 Cor 1:3; 11:31; Eph 1:3; 1 Pet 1:3). He is blessed "forever," indicating his eternality.

This concludes our discussion of 9:1-5, where Israel's "ecstasy" (4-5) stands in sharp contrast with her "agony" (1-3). This paragraph certainly reveals Paul's own deep love and concern for his kinsmen, as he contemplates their lost state. But an even deeper consideration is his love for God and his concern for the integrity of God's faithfulness to his words of promise. How can Israel's accursedness be reconciled with all these glorious privileges? This is the question he begins to address in 9:6.

II. THE DISTINCTION BETWEEN ETHNIC AND SPIRITUAL ISRAEL (9:6-29)

The main theme of 9–11 is God's faithfulness in his dealings with Israel. The issue is summarized in 9:1-5 thus: in view of the privileges for which Israel was chosen (vv. 4-5), how is it possible for a faithful God to reject them and curse them (vv. 1-3)? Does this mean that God's purpose for Israel has in fact failed? "Have not God's promises to Israel ended in nothing as far as the Jews are concerned?" (Fitzmyer, 558).

Paul's answer, of course, is that God's purposes and promises have not failed (9:6a; see 3:4). The apparent paradox of 9:1-5 is easily resolved by seeing that there is not just one Israel, but two (9:6b), and by discerning the proper nature and purpose of each. National, ethnic, physical Israel was chosen by God to play a primary role in his plan of redemption. This entitled them to all the blessings of 9:4-5, but these blessings did not include the guarantee of personal salvation. Every covenant promise God made to Israel as a nation was completely fulfilled, irrespective of the salvation status of any individual Jew. God has the sovereign right to choose and use any individual or group in this manner. This is the point of 9:6-18.

Is it true, then, that every individual Israelite is actually lost? In 9:3 Paul implies that physical Israel, his "kinsmen according to the flesh," are indeed "accursed" (NASB). But he does not say this applies to every Jew without exception. Yes, some (most) Jews are lost, but some are saved! Those who are saved are still part of national Israel and participate in all the covenant blessings bestowed upon the nation as a whole, but they constitute an "Israel" of a different sort, an "Israel within Israel," one that is defined not just in terms of physical descent from Jacob but also in terms of a saving relationship with God. This is the point of Paul's key statement in 9:6b, "For not all who are descended from Israel are Israel." God's sovereign right to make this distinction within the larger body of ethnic Israel is the point of 9:19-29. He can use the entire nation for his redemptive purposes, while limiting salvation only to spiritual Israel, the remnant. "It is the remnant that will be saved" (9:27b, NASB).

It is extremely important to understand how the issue of salvation figures into the discussion in 9:6-29. Some points are accepted by almost everyone. It is agreed that *election* (choosing, making distinctions) is a key theme in this section. It is agreed that Paul is stressing God's sovereign *freedom* to make distinctions and choices in whatever way he pleases.[26] It is also agreed that belonging to physical Israel was not in itself a guarantee of personal salvation.[27]

But there is sharp disagreement, usually (but not always) along Calvinist vs. non-Calvinist lines, as to which parts of vv. 6-29 refer to God's election to *service*, and which refer to his election to *salvation*. This disagreement occurs in view of the fact that Calvinism generally teaches unconditional election to salvation,[28] and because (especially) vv. 7-23 seem to be affirming unconditional election. Thus it is quite common to see Calvinists use this passage as a proof text for the doctrine of the unconditional election of individuals to salvation

---

[26]Morris's title for this section is "God's Sovereign Freedom" (351), while Godet speaks of "the principle of divine liberty" (351). See MP, 392.

[27]"The privileges given to Israel can never be construed to guarantee the salvation of any individual Jew" (Piper, *Justification*, 24).

[28]Non-Calvinists usually teach conditional election. See GRu, 336-352.

(and usually, the unconditional reprobation of all others to hell). Examples are Murray (2:15-24), Schreiner ("Election," 89-106), Moo (584-588), and Piper (*Justification*, 50-73).

Non-Calvinists of course disagree, and usually take one of two approaches to this passage. Some say the election described therein does have to do with individual salvation, but it is conditional rather than unconditional. Even though the conditions (such as faith) are not specifically named in the text itself, they are taken to be implicit in view of other biblical teaching. A common form of this view is that God made his choices, e.g., of Jacob over Esau, based on divine foreknowledge of the lives and character of each. Examples of this view are cited in Piper (52, n. 13). Many are from ancient writers such as Philo[29] and Chrysostom.[30] A later example is Godet, who speaks of "God's prevision of the power of faith" in the case of Jacob (350). Foreseen faith is not at all the same as foreseen works, he says (348). See also Smith, 2:16-17.

Since the text itself does not mention foreknowledge and seems to exclude human conditions as such, others have taken the approach that Paul is here talking about unconditional election to *service*, not salvation.[31] Piper (57) cites several examples. Speaking of 9:12, Morris declares, "It is election to privilege that is in mind, not eternal salvation" (356). In my judgment this is the correct view.

Piper (58) argues that this view does not fit the context, that it "cannot successfully explain the thread of Paul's argument as it begins in Rom 9:1-5 and continues through the chapter." Especially, it does not address the problem of Israel's unbelief and rejection, and it is not a logical follow-up to Paul's statement about the two Israels (9:6b).

One reason Piper says this, is his erroneous view of 9:4-5, in which he takes these benefits as having *saving* implications for Israel (49). Thus, he says, since these blessings "imply the eschatological,

---

[29]See his *Allegorical Interpretation of the Laws* 3.88, quoted in Moo, 583, n. 60.

[30]See his homilies on Romans, 16.6 (PG 60.557), mentioned in Fitzmyer, 562.

[31]Some also say he is talking about the election of groups only (i.e., Israel as a nation) and not individuals, but this may be disputed and in the final analysis is irrelevant. The crucial point is the distinction between service and salvation.

eternal salvation" of the people of Israel, the line of thought developed in the following context "*must* address the issue of individual, eternal salvation" (65).

But Piper is wrong to include saving content in 9:4-5 (see above), and he is wrong to say that the concept of election for service is inconsistent with the problem as set forth in 9:1-5 and the solution as summed up in 9:6b. The following summary of the argument in 9:1-29 shows this to be the case.

First, Paul expresses his grief over the fact that most Jews are accursed – the very Jews who were chosen to receive the greatest of privileges (9:1-5). But how is this possible? Is this some kind of contradiction? Has God's word failed? No! God's purposes and promises have *not* failed (9:6a), basically because there are *two different kinds* of "Israel" (9:6b). One is national Israel, which was unconditionally chosen by God to be a party to the covenant made with the fathers, and thus to receive the blessings of 9:4-5. This was an election and a call to service only, and it was a matter of God's sovereign and unconditional choice with no requirement for saving faith on the part of any individual Israelite. Israel's founders were chosen apart from any decisions, qualifications, faith, or works on their part; and God kept his promises to the nation and carried out his purposes for them not because of their belief but in spite of their frequent unbelief (9:7-13).

The other Israel is composed of those individuals within the ethnic body which do in fact have a saving faith in the God of Abraham, Isaac, and Jacob. Salvation is promised and given not to the nation as a whole, but only to this *spiritual* Israel, which is in a sense the "true" Israel (see 2:28-29), the redeemed remnant. The fact that God has withheld salvation from the majority of Jews is not a violation of his covenant with them, for that covenant as such did not include a promise of automatic salvation based on ethnic heritage alone.

Paul's key point in v. 6b is in effect that God has *made a distinction* within the nation of Israel, using all Jews to serve his saving purpose but giving salvation only to some. This is his solution to the problem raised in vv. 1-5. But his following discussion shows that he anticipates that this solution to the original problem will itself be seen as a problem, namely, its fairness will be questioned (see v. 14).

Does God have the *right* to make this kind of distinction within his chosen people, a distinction resulting in two kinds of Israel?

In defense of his statement in 9:6b and in anticipation of such an objection, in 9:7-13 Paul makes a point that no Jew can deny, namely, that in the very events that gave rise to the nation of Israel, God had already made some unconditional distinctions within the progeny of Abraham. These verses are not talking about the distinction within Israel as affirmed in v. 6b, which is a distinction between service and salvation. Rather they describe divine choices whereby some were chosen for service and others were passed by, choices by which Israel as a nation was created in the first place.

This has two applications. The first refers to the distinction specified in v. 6b. To those who might suggest that such a distinction is unfair, Paul is simply pointing out that making such distinctions is nothing new for God; he did this sort of thing in the very beginning when he brought Israel into existence. Granted, that was a matter of selecting certain individuals and a certain people for service rather than for salvation, but it set a precedent showing that God was not acting out of character or contrary to established patterns when he made the distinction between the two Israels as such.

The second application of 9:7-13 relates directly to the problem of Israel's lostness raised in vv. 1-5. The point is that this lostness does not negate God's promises because his original choice of the founders of Israel had nothing to do with their works, character, merits, faith, or salvation status in general. It was simply his sovereign will to use these individuals (Isaac and Jacob) rather than the alternatives (Ishmael and Esau), and the purpose for which he chose them was such that they did not have to be personally saved to carry it out. God could and did choose to use them just as they were. The same is true for the entire nation of Israel that sprang from their loins. God intended to use them for his service whether or not they believed and were saved. Thus there is no conflict between vv. 1-3 and vv. 4-5.

In 9:14-18 Paul specifically raises the problem of fairness that some are bound to see in such divine distinguishing. Doesn't it seem unjust for God to choose people for service in this way? Shouldn't individuals have the right to volunteer, or at least consent to being thus used? And if they are going to be conscripted into service, as it were, shouldn't they at least be rewarded with salvation?

In response Paul simply *declares* that God has the right to choose whomever he wills to use for his purposes, whether they be saved or not. The subject is election for service, not salvation. The mercy and compassion of which Moses spoke is not saving grace, but God's selection and appointment of a person (or a nation) to have the privilege of serving him (see below). That such a person does not have to be saved to serve God's redemptive purposes is perfectly illustrated by Pharaoh, upon whom God had mercy by choosing him for a vital role in his plan, but who at the same time was hardened in order that he might fulfill that role. In like manner God chose the nation of Israel for his grand redemptive purpose, and he used them for it even though most individual Jews (like Pharaoh) were hardened.

In 9:19-29 Paul turns specifically to the original distinction set forth in 9:6b, the distinction between national Israel as a whole (used for service) and the spiritual Israel existing within it (blessed with salvation). Does God have a right to make this distinction? The objection is put into the mouths of those Israelites who are lost, as they try to blame God for their lost state (9:19). They say, if God is orchestrating this whole thing, how can he hold us responsible and condemn us for our unbelief? Hasn't God made us the way we are?

Paul's primary answer at this point is that the lost person (specifically, the unbelieving Jew) has no right to complain to God at all, since God is indeed the sovereign Lord who has by decree created this single "lump of clay" known as Israel (9:21). It is *his* plan and *his* clay, and he (like a potter) can do with it what he wills. Since it is his to begin with by right of creation (9:7-13), it is also his right to divide it as he chooses and to make different kinds of vessels from it. Some are vessels of wrath and are under the curse of v. 3; others are vessels of mercy and will be saved. These vessels of mercy are the remnant of which the prophets spoke, i.e., the true believers, or spiritual Israel, to which in this church age are added all true believers from among the Gentiles.

This main section comes to a close with this point, but in itself it does not resolve the issue of divine faithfulness raised in 9:1-5. It simply establishes the *fact* that God has made a distinction between the two Israels, only one of which is saved. It shows clearly that ethnic Israel's role of service had no essential connection with personal salvation. It also asserts God's sovereign right to make this distinction between the serving and the saved (9:19-29), but it does not go into detail as to the *nature* of such a distinction. In particular, this section does not raise the question as to the basis, or conditions, upon which God distinguishes the remnant from the larger group of Israelites according to the flesh.

Those of a Calvinist bent will insist that this is an improper question to begin with, since they are convinced that election to salvation is unconditional. But this conclusion is invalid in view of the fact that the language of unconditionality in 9:7-18 applies only to election to service. Election to salvation is a completely different issue. The divine distinguishing that separates the saved from the lost is conditioned upon the free human choice either to accept or to reject the saving promises of God. This is the point of the next main section, 9:30–10:21. Only when this point has been made is the issue of divine faithfulness regarding Israel completely resolved.

A. ISRAEL'S SITUATION AND GOD'S FAITHFULNESS (9:6-13)

The relationship of this section to Paul's overall argument has been discussed just above. It is clear that these verses deal with divine election. Morris's title for this paragraph is, appropriately, "God Works by Election" (351). But the question is, election *to what*? There are, as Cranfield says (2:471), "different levels or forms of election." The relevant choices are election to *service* and election to *salvation*. This distinction relates to the two Israels named in 9:6b: ethnic Israel, chosen for service; and spiritual Israel, chosen for salvation. But which of these two is the main subject of 9:6-13?

Many simply assume that spiritual Israel is the main subject, and that God's choice of Isaac and his choice of Jacob are prime examples of how God distinguishes the true spiritual Israel (the saved) from ethnic Israel as a whole.[32] They argue that the terminology used in these verses can only be salvation language: seed or children

[32]E.g., see Achtemeier, 156; and Hendriksen, 2:320.

of Abraham, children of God, children of promise, God's purpose, God's call as opposed to human works, God's love.[33]

A brief reflection upon the individuals and incidents being discussed in these verses will show, however, that Paul is *not* talking about how God makes distinctions *within* Israel (between the ethnic and the spiritual, as in v. 6b), but how he established ethnic Israel in the first place. Ishmael and Isaac as a pair were not the original "ethnic Israel" from which God elected only Isaac to be the first member of "spiritual Israel." Ishmael was never a part of Israel in either sense; he was chosen neither for service nor for salvation (as far as we know). The same is true of the twins Esau and Jacob.

The point of these verses is that Isaac and Jacob were chosen to be the first representatives of *ethnic* Israel (after Abraham himself). Whether they were saved or not, i.e., whether they were also part of spiritual Israel, is not relevant. In fact, the nonrelevance of their salvation status is the key to Paul's argument: Isaac and Jacob, like ethnic Israel as a whole, could be chosen and used for God's service whether they were saved or not. This is the key to v. 9:6a, "It is not as though God's word had failed." God's promises to physical Israel have not failed, even though most Jews are unbelievers, because these promises did not include salvation as such.

But what about the language used in this section? Is it not the language of salvation? This depends solely upon the context. In other NT contexts the terminology does refer to salvation and the saved, but it is not inherently limited to this. It is covenant language, to be sure, but covenant language is not always salvation language. A common error in modern theology is to erase the proper distinction between the Abrahamic covenant and the New Covenant, and to project the salvation content of the latter back into the former. This is common among Calvinists, and it is why someone such as Murray or Piper cannot separate the covenant realities of 9:4-5 from salvation, and why they cannot see anything but salvation in the language of 9:7-13.

The point of the Abrahamic covenant, though, was not the salvation of its recipients. Its point was rather that *through* Abraham and his (physical) seed the means by which all peoples could be

[33]See Piper, *Justification*, 67-68; Moo, 572.

saved would be brought into the world. This was a covenant of service; and the recipients of this covenant, i.e., ethnic Israel, were chosen to render this service and to experience its accompanying temporal privileges and rewards (vv. 4-5). Fitzmyer is simply wrong to say that "the OT promises were not made to the ethnic or historical-empirical Israel, those of physical descent or of flesh and blood, but to the Israel of faith" (559-560).

The language of 9:7-13 is perfectly consistent with the role played by ethnic Israel in God's plan. God had a definite purpose for choosing this nation (9:11), which he did by choosing its forefathers, Isaac and Jacob. He called them into his service without regard for any meritorious qualifications on their part and without even asking for their own conscious participation in the choice (9:11-12). It was all a matter of God's choice and promise, i.e., his covenant promise to bless and to use these individuals and their physical descendants for the purpose of bringing the Savior into the world. In this context "children of Abraham," "children of God," and "children of promise" (9:7-8) are perfectly consistent with God's purpose for ethnic Israel, and perfectly applicable to Isaac and Jacob and their natural descendants in contrast with Ishmael and Esau and their descendants. Isaac and Jacob were the progenitors not just of spiritual Israel, but of ethnic Israel as a whole.

Thus I agree with Lenski (597-598), that Isaac and Jacob are not types of election to salvation: "Paul's two illustrations have nothing to do with an eternal election or predestination of Isaac and of Jacob to salvation and with a reprobation of Ishmael and of Esau to damnation."

Shall we say, then, that 9:6-13 has no bearing at all upon the election of individuals to eternal salvation? Not necessarily. The error is to take the references to Isaac and Jacob as *examples* of election to salvation and therefore as *exact models* for the way God saves any individual. In other words, according to this erroneous view, just as God unconditionally chose Jacob and rejected Esau, so he unconditionally predestines some to heaven and some to hell. But this is not Paul's point. At the most, we may possibly say that God's choosing Isaac and Jacob for service is *analogous at some points* with his electing of individuals to salvation. For one thing, members of spiritual Israel are "children of promise" and not "children of the flesh," even though the promises that apply in this case are not the same promises that set ethnic Israel apart from the rest of the world. Members of spiritual Israel are also chosen and called, though not in the same way that God chose and called ethnic Israel. "Not by works" (9:12) is likewise a key ingredient in being chosen for membership in spiritual Israel, though such membership does require the precondition of faith, as Paul goes on to show in 9:30–10:21 and 11:20-23.

In other words, there are some similarities between election to service and election to salvation, but they are not the same in every detail. To assume that they are would defeat Paul's whole purpose in this section (9:6-13), which is to answer the charge that God is somehow being untrue to his word unless all ethnic Israel is saved. The very essence of his answer is that being chosen for service is *different* from being chosen for salvation. The two Israels are constituted differently, or are established on different bases. The process by which God established ethnic Israel, i.e., through the unconditional choosing of Isaac and Jacob, did not in itself involve their personal salvation, which requires a specific decision of faith.

Thus we must strongly disagree with Piper when he says that this sort of distinction between election to service and election to salvation goes against the point of chapter 9. Referring to the unconditional election of Isaac and Jacob "apart from all human distinctives," he says it is "an unwarranted leap to infer *against the context of Rom 9* that this principle applies when the promised blessing at stake is 'theocratic blessing' or a 'historical role' but does not apply when the promised blessing is personal, eternal salvation" (*Justification*, 64). On the contrary, the fact is that the context *demands* this very distinction, the distinction between unconditional election to service and conditional election to salvation. The one thing that Piper wants to find in this paragraph – the "*ongoing principle*," "the *principle* of unconditional election" to salvation (66, 69) – is the one thing that would undermine Paul's whole argument.

1. God's Word Concerning Israel Has Not Failed (9:6a)

9:6 It is not as though God's word had failed. This statement presupposes an unstated implication that someone might try to draw from vv. 1-5. In spite of the impressive list of covenant blessings bestowed upon the people of Israel (vv. 4-5), the majority apparently are "cursed and cut off from Christ" (v. 3). Has something thus gone wrong with God's plan for Israel? Has he failed to keep his word to his people?

Paul immediately rejects these unspoken suggestions. His response begins with a strong negative expression, "But it is not as if" or "But this does not mean."[34] He is saying that the seemingly conflicting circumstances described in vv. 1-5 do not mean that "God's word has failed."

The word "failed" is ἐκπίπτω (*ekpiptō*), literally, "to fall from" or "to fall off of" (see Acts 12:7; Jas 1:11; 1 Pet 1:24). In Gal 5:4 and 2 Pet 3:17 it is used metaphorically for "falling from" grace. Here it has the more general meaning of "fail, come to nothing, be annulled." This is parallel to its meaning in (some manuscripts of) 1 Cor 13:8, "Love never fails."

Paul declares that "God's word" (ὁ λόγος τοῦ θεοῦ, *ho logos tou theou*) does not fall away or fail. What is meant by "God's word"? Certainly what the Apostle says here is true of "the Word of God" in the most general and inclusive sense. *Every* word of God, including the entire Bible, is true, passes every test, will accomplish its purpose, will be fulfilled, cannot be broken. (See Ps 12:6; Prov 30:5; Isa 55:11; Matt 5:17-18; John 10:35; 17:17; Rom 3:4.) It is "the living and enduring word of God," says Peter; "the grass withers and the flowers fall [*ekpiptō*], but the word of the Lord stands forever" (1 Pet 1:23-25).

In this text, though, "God's word" means something more specific. "The declared purpose of God" (SH, 240) is still too broad. So is Barrett's suggestion that it refers to "the whole plan and intention of God in salvation," including messianic promises and "the gospel" as preached by Paul (126-127). The context shows rather that "God's word" here refers specifically to his words of *promise*, i.e., the promises he made to and about OT Israel (Dunn, 2:539). These "promises made to Israel and its patriarchs" (Fitzmyer, 559) are the word of God that has not failed.

[34]The NIV fails to translate the adversative δέ, "but" or "however."

2. The Key to the Puzzle: the Existence of Two Israels (9:6b)

But in view of Israel's lostness and the apparent inconsistency between vv. 1-3 and vv. 4-5, how can it be said that God's promises to Israel have never failed? The answer, says Paul, lies in the fact that there is not just one Israel, but two. **For not all who are descended from Israel are Israel.** This statement clearly affirms the existence of two groups, both called "Israel" but in two different senses: ethnic Israel and spiritual Israel. The former includes all those who bear Abraham's genes through physical descent from Isaac and Jacob, i.e., the Jews; the latter is composed only of those Jews who also share Abraham's faith in the God of salvation.

The literal sense of the Greek sentence is thus: "For all the ones who are from Israel – these are not Israel" (see Moo, 573, n. 19). The first group is called "the ones of [or from] Israel." This expression may mean simply "the ones who belong to the *nation* of Israel," or it may mean (as the NIV suggests) "the ones who can trace their physical lineage back to the *man* Israel," i.e., to Jacob whom God renamed Israel. The second group is simply called "Israel," but it is usually (and rightly) referred to as *spiritual* Israel or even as the *true* Israel, to distinguish it from the former.

These two Israels are not two totally distinct groups, with some Jews belonging to one and some to the other. In fact, *all* Jews belong to the first group, and only *some* to the second. I.e., those in the latter group actually belong to both. The relationship between the two Israels may be depicted not by two side-by-side circles, but by two concentric circles, thus:

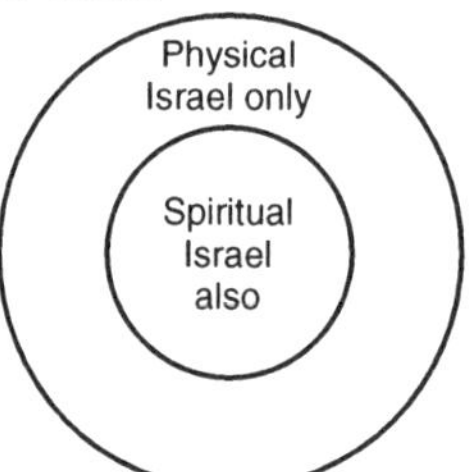

We should note that this passage has in view Jewish people only, and thus the "spiritual Israel" in this verse includes only Jewish believers (as the concentric circles indicate). Other NT teaching warrants the conclusion that in this dispensation the church as a whole, including believing Jews and believing Gentiles, may be called the true Israel or spiritual Israel. See Rom 9:23-30 and 11:17-24, where Jews and Gentiles together constitute the remnant and the one olive tree. Together they are called "the Israel of God" (Gal 6:16). This may be depicted thus:

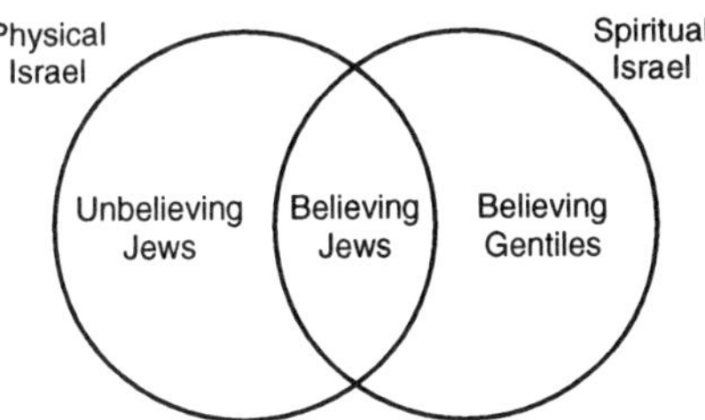

This is not the point of 9:6b, however. See Moo, 573-574.

A key word in this second sentence in 9:6b is γάρ (*gar*), "for" or "because." This word indicates that 6a is explained by 6b, i.e., the latter is the *reason why* the former is true. God's promises concerning Israel have not failed, *because* there are really *two* Israels.

Everyone seems to agree that this is how the two parts of the verse are meant to be connected. There is a serious disagreement, though, as to the *nature* and *recipients* of the promises included in the phrase "God's word." Some take God's word (of promise) to be referring specifically to his promises of *salvation*, or "all his promises relative to the salvation of Israel" (Lard, 298). How can one say, then, that this promise of salvation has not failed, in view of the *lostness* of most Jews (v. 3)? Here is how the point about the two Israels enters in, according to this view: the promises of salvation were made not to ethnic Israel as a whole, but only to spiritual Israel, the remnant (Lard, 298). As Murray puts it, "The purpose of this distinction is to show that the covenantal promise of God did not have respect to Israel after the flesh but to this *true* Israel and that, therefore, the unbelief and rejection of ethnic Israel as a whole in no way interfered with the fulfilment of God's covenant purpose and promise" (2:10). See also Hendriksen (2:317), Nygren (361-362), and Fitzmyer (559-560).

In my judgment this misses Paul's point completely. "God's word" does indeed refer to "the promises made to Israel and its patriarchs" (Fitzmyer, 559), but the main reference is to the promises made to ethnic Israel as a whole, especially the covenant promises[35] made to the patriarchs regarding God's messianic purpose for the nation collectively and including the accompanying privileges that served as a means to this end. In other words, God's promises to ethnic Israel included everything named in vv. 4-5, and every one of these promises was kept.

But did not God's OT promises include forgiveness and eternal life? Certainly, but here is where the distinction between the two Israels is crucial. Personal salvation was not among the unconditionally guaranteed promises enjoyed by the entire nation of Israel. This blessing was promised only to *spiritual* Israel, the believing remnant. The existence of the two Israels thus resolves the dilemma of vv. 1-5. "All who are descended from Israel" experience the covenant blessings of vv. 4-5, but only the true Israel escapes the curse of eternal damnation. The promises of salvation applied only to the latter. This had always been God's plan; this is the way it happened; thus his word did not fail.

3. Ethnic Israel Exists by God's Sovereign Choice (9:7-13)

The subject of these next seven verses – this is very important – is not spiritual Israel but ethnic Israel. In them Paul is responding to a possible objection that might be raised by what he has just said in v. 6. There he affirmed, contrary to the beliefs of practically every Jew at that time, that just because a person was a Jew did not necessarily mean that God would save him.[36] In other words, Paul has said that God could use the nation of Israel for service without giving them salvation.

This paragraph responds to expected resistance to this idea. Paul simply points out that this has been God's *modus operandi* from the very beginning. That is, Israel's existence as a nation is the result of God's sovereign, unconditional choice of Isaac over Ishmael and Jacob over Esau. God elected them (and the entire nation through

[35]We must remember that the word "covenant" does not necessarily have saving connotations, as many seem to assume (e.g., Murray, 2:9-10; Hendriksen, 2:317).

[36]Most Jews believed that all nonapostate Jews would be saved. See Moo, 569 n. 2, 573.

them) for service – apart from any salvation promises on his part or any salvation responses on their part – just because that was the way he wanted it. Because of God's sovereign "purpose in election" (v. 11) Israel would fulfill God's plan for the Messiah and God would thus fulfill his promises toward them, whether they as individuals entered into a saving relationship with him or not.

Thus we must not interpret vv. 7-13 as further elaboration upon the distinction between the two Israels in v. 6, as if these verses are describing *how* or *why* God made that distinction. Nor are these verses somehow meant to *justify* this distinction, contrary to Moo's view (570-571). They are in fact making a point that is separate from 9:6b. The progression of thought from 6b to 7a is thus: Not all members of physical Israel are also members of spiritual Israel; *neither* are they called the children of Abraham just because they are physically descended from Abraham. Thus v. 7 begins a separate thought. The paragraph through v. 13 focuses on the origin and role of ethnic Israel as such, explaining the manner in which God called them into his service. The main point is that this is *different* from the way he calls individuals to salvation. Only when the two are confused do questions about God's faithfulness to Israel arise.

The Choice of Isaac (9:7-9)

9:7 Nor because they are his descendants are they all Abraham's children. This verse begins with the negative particle οὐδέ (*oude*), which joins concepts that are related but not identical. Thus it introduces another consideration in answer to the charge that God has treated Israel unfairly. The erroneous assumption to which Paul is responding is the Jews' mistaken idea that just because they were descendants of Abraham, God was obligated to treat them in a certain way. Paul's point is that this is not true even with regard to Israel's role of service in God's historical plan of redemption, much less their participation in eternal life.

There has been much debate as to the respective meanings of "descendants" (lit., σπέρμα, *sperma*, "seed") and "children" (τέκνα, *tekna*). This debate is usually waged with the assumption that Paul is simply repeating his distinction between physical Israel and spiritual Israel (9:6b). Assuming this, a few proceed to identify the former with Abraham's "children" and the latter with his "seed" or "descendants."[37] Most, however, take the reverse approach, equating "seed" with physical Israel and "children" with spiritual Israel.[38]

The fact is that the terms "seed" and "children" seem to be used interchangeably in vv. 7-8, as they are in John 8:33-39 (vv. 33, 37, "seed of Abraham"; v. 39, "children of Abraham").

The most common error here is the assumption that v. 7 is parallel to v. 6b, which it is not. Spiritual Israel is not in view in v. 7, thus neither term ("seed," "children") applies to it in this context. The distinction rather is between *all* the physical descendants of Abraham, including those born to Hagar (Gen 16:15) and Keturah (Gen 25:1-5) as well as to Sarah, and *only* those physical descendants of Abraham born through Sarah and Isaac (Gen 21:1-3). Only the latter may be called Abraham's true seed or children. Just being physically descended from Abraham did not establish someone as the "seed of Abraham" named in the Abrahamic covenant (Gen 15:5, 18; 17:6-8; 22:17-18).[39] Something more than physical descent is required, as v. 8 specifies.

On the contrary, "It is through Isaac that your offspring will be reckoned." This is an exact quotation from the LXX translation of Gen 21:12. God made this promise to Abraham as he was explaining to him why the patriarch should not hesitate to sever his connections with his son Ishmael (Gen 21:8-21). The sense of it is, "Through Isaac *alone*, not through Ishmael or any other possible progeny, will come the seed specified in my covenant with you."

The word translated "reckoned" literally means "called." Here it does not have the theological connotation of "called unto salvation," as it does in 8:28-29; 9:24-26.[40] At most it may refer to God's call to

---

[37]E.g., Barrett, 180-181; Lenski, 591; Moo, 575. See the NRSV, "and not all of Abraham's children are his true descendants."

[38]E.g., Fitzmyer, 560; Morris, 353; Murray, 2:10. See the NIV.

[39]The concept of "descendants of Abraham" appears in both the OT and the NT in both the physical and the spiritual senses. The physical descendants who constituted the covenant line were called children of Abraham (John 8:39), seed of Abraham (2 Chr 20:7; Ps 105:6; Isa 41:8; Jer 33:26; John 8:33,37; Rom 11:1; 2 Cor 11:22), son of Abraham (Luke 19:9), and daughter of Abraham (Luke 13:16). Spiritual descendants are called both sons of Abraham (Gal 3:7) and seed of Abraham (Gal 3:29).

[40]Contrary to Moo, who sees in it "overtones of the notion of God's sovereign, creative summons to spiritual blessing" (576, n. 28).

service, i.e., only children born to Isaac will be called upon to continue the covenant responsibilities and receive the covenant blessings given to Abraham. Only those connected with Isaac will be called (named, counted as, recognized as, acknowledged as, reckoned to be) Abraham's true covenant seed. Dunn is correct: "God had told Abraham that his promise of seed and land applied only to the line of descent through Isaac, that so far as his covenant with Abraham was concerned only Isaac and his offspring would be recognized as Abraham's seed" (2:547). The only thing to remember is that this covenant did not include the promise of salvation as such; "Abraham's seed" in this context is not the same as spiritual Israel.

As the next two verses will show, Paul's main point in bringing up the "divine distinguishing" between Isaac and Ishmael is to emphasize the sovereign, unilateral way in which God established the nation of Israel and enlisted it into his service.

9:8 In other words, it is not the natural children who are God's children, but it is the children of the promise who are regarded as Abraham's offspring. "In other words" ("this is to say," "this means") introduces the basis upon which God chose Isaac. Though this may well be a general principle that God applies in the context of salvation, that is not how the statement functions here. In this case it relates to the choice of Isaac and thus to the manner in which Israel came into existence.

"The natural children" is literally "the children of the flesh," or children born by purely natural means. It is similar to the expression in 1:3 and 4:1 (κατὰ σάρκα, *kata sarka*, "according to the flesh"), where "flesh" is used in a morally neutral sense. "The children of the promise" refers to God's promise to Abraham and Sarah concerning the birth of Isaac, as v. 9 shows. They are "children of promise" because they owe their existence to this promise; they are "born as a result of a promise" (Morris, 354). These children of the promise are identified as "God's children" and as "Abraham's offspring." The latter expression is a loose but accurate paraphrase for one word, "seed" (*sperma*). "Regarded" is λογίζομαι (*logizomai*), the same word used for the concept of imputation almost a dozen times in Rom 4. Here it simply means "considered to be, counted as, looked upon as." It is equivalent to "reckoned" ("called") in v. 7.

It is easy to see why many take this verse to refer to the distinction between physical Israel and spiritual Israel, and thus take it as referring to the way God elects some to salvation while rejecting others. "God's children" and "children of the promise," as well as the verb *logizomai*, all have salvation connotations in other contexts. (See Moo, 577.) Indeed, we may agree that there is a significant analogy between the way God chose Isaac for service and the way he chooses individuals for salvation. The concept of *promise* is the main similarity. See Gal 3:14, 16-22, 29; 4:23.

We must remember, though, that such terminology does not always connote the eternal salvation of individuals. The covenant made with Abraham (and Isaac and Jacob) was primarily a series of promises, culminating in the promised coming of the Messiah (Acts 13:23,32; 26:6; Rom 15:8; Heb 8:6; 11:9). Thus it is appropriate to think of Israel as a whole as "children of the promise." The expression "children of God" is surprisingly rare in Scripture. Sometimes it refers to those in a saving relationship with God (Rom 8:16,21; Phil 2:15); at least once it refers to the Jews as a nation (John 11:52; see also Deut 14:1 and Ps 82:6, "sons" of God). It is not inappropriate to see the latter sense here.

We conclude, then, in accord with the present context, that it is ethnic Israel that is here identified as "God's children" and "children of the promise," and that these terms describe Israel's role as the special family through whom God brought the Messiah into the world. This is consistent with 9:4, which says that the Israelites received "the adoption as sons" and "the promises."

What is Paul's point? He is simply reminding Israel that their status as God's children and Abraham's seed was not something they possessed by an accident of nature, by inherent right, or by meritorious acquisition. It was theirs only by God's gracious choice and promise. God alone controls the selection process and the terms of selection. In this case God demonstrated his sovereign control by specifying that Abraham's covenant family would come into existence through one whose own existence was dependent upon nothing except the promise and power of God.[41]

---

[41]"Had it depended on *sarx* [flesh] alone, Isaac would never have been born to barren Sarah" (Fitzmyer, 561).

9:9 For this was how the promise was stated: "At the appointed time I will return, and Sarah will have a son." Paul's statement of the promise concerning Isaac is a combination of thoughts from Gen 18:10 and 18:14. God spoke these words during a glorious visitation (a theophany) to Abraham and Sarah (Gen 18:1-15). "At the appointed time" is usually taken to mean "about this time next year." "I will return" is literally "I will come." This does not necessarily mean that God was promising another visible manifestation of himself to Abraham and Sarah a year later; no such theophany is recorded in Genesis. It means only that God would come upon Abraham and Sarah in his providential power, opening Sarah's barren and "dead" womb (Gen 11:30; 18:11; Rom 4:19; Heb 11:11-12) and causing her to conceive contrary to all natural means.

This verse is important because it shows us that Paul's main concern here is not the general promise of salvation made to all who will believe in God's mercy, but rather the specific event of the choice of Isaac rather than Ishmael as the one who would carry on the covenant line of his father Abraham – which was a call to service, not to salvation. In fact, v. 8 says that the Israelites were "the children of *the* promise," meaning the specific promise identified in v. 9.

The first part of this verse specifically reads, "For the word [λόγος, *logos*] of promise is this." The term *logos* ties this in with 9:6a, where Paul says, "It is not as though God's word [*logos*] has failed." This shows that he is mainly concerned here with the charge that somehow God's words of promise to the *nation* of Israel had failed. The promises are those which establish Israel as the covenant nation, and as words of *promise* they establish God as the one who is in complete control of Israel's tenure as the covenant people.

Thus there is no reason for anyone to think that God has lost control of the situation with respect to Israel. Though most individual Israelites are accursed, God has still kept every promise he ever made to them as a people, as is evidenced by the way he kept one of the very first promises that brought them into existence in the first place.

The Choice of Jacob (9:10-13)

These next four verses show how God chose a particular son of Isaac to be the one who would carry on his covenant purposes. The debate continues, of course, as to whether this incident is intended to describe the way God chooses individuals for salvation. Does God's choice of Jacob demonstrate the way he distinguishes true spiritual Israel from ethnic Israel as a whole, or does it tell us how he chooses those who will serve him in the carrying out of his redemptive purposes? In my judgment *only the latter point is being made here.* The focus is exactly the same as in vv. 7-9, namely, the sovereignty of God in establishing the nation of Israel.

9:10 Not only that, but Rebekah's children had one and the same father, our father Isaac. This truth does more than simply repeat the lesson from Isaac and Ishmael; it strengthens it and clarifies it. Regarding the earlier example, someone might try to argue that the natural circumstances surrounding the births of Abraham's (first) two sons were so different that the choice of Isaac was no surprise. After all, the boys had different mothers, and Ishmael's mother was not even Abraham's true wife. But this cannot be said of Jacob and Esau. As twins, they were the product not only of the same mother, but of the same pregnancy. In addition, Esau was the first-born twin. Thus according to every natural expectation, Esau should have been selected as the covenant seed. The fact that God chose Jacob for this role shows unequivocally that his election of those who will serve his purposes need not be conditioned upon any human circumstance or qualification.

The grammar and syntax of this section are notoriously difficult, but the NIV generally sorts it out quite well. Literally v. 10 does not speak of Rebekah's children but of Rebekah herself. It says that she conceived "from one." The use of the Greek word κοίτη (*koitē*) leads to some rather graphic interpretations. The word basically means "bed," but was also used as a euphemism for sexual intercourse and even the emission of semen. Thus some say the verse means that Rebekah conceived "by the one act of sexual intercourse" (Dunn, 2:542) or even "from one seminal emission" (Hendriksen, 2:319). Thus "from one" is given a dual force: not only were Jacob and Esau conceived from *one father*, namely, "our father Isaac," but also from just *one act of intercourse.* The point is to minimize any natural distinctions between Esau and Jacob.

9:11 Yet, before the twins were born or had done anything good or bad . . . . This is a participial phrase. The subject ("the twins") is not in the Greek but is properly supplied by the NIV. The whole phrase modifies the main verb in v. 12b, "she was told." The participles themselves may be expressing simple temporal priority in relation to the main verb ("*Before* the twins were born . . . , she was told," NIV), or they may express a contrary or unlikely circumstance ("*Even though* the twins were not yet born" – see the NASB). The NRSV captures the meaning very succinctly: "Even before they had been born."

The point is that God had already made his decision as to his choice between Jacob and Esau, and had already announced it to Rebekah (v. 12), before anything had happened from the human side that might have any possible bearing upon that choice. "Before the twins were born" indicates that the birth order would be irrelevant. Before they "had done anything good or bad" shows that their future conduct was not a factor in the selection.

To introduce divine foreknowledge into the picture here, as some non-Calvinists do, misses the point. Certainly the omniscient God had a complete foreknowledge of the entire lives of both the twins, including which would be born first (v. 12b). But that is not only irrelevant; it tends also to obscure the very point Paul is making, namely, that the choice had nothing to do with either the works or the faith of either twin, whether foreknown or not. God wanted Jacob and not Esau, and that's that.

But someone will say that this sounds a lot like unconditional election, which is a main doctrine of Calvinism, and that we need the concept of foreknowledge here in order to avoid it. I will reply that the choice of Jacob over Esau *was* a case of unconditional election. But this is not a concession to Calvinism, because Paul is not talking about election to *salvation*, but to *service*.

Calvinists themselves usually fail to understand this point. They assume that God's choice of Jacob and his rejection of Esau had to do with the twins' eternal destinies, thus seeing this passage as biblical proof of the Calvinist doctrine of unconditional election. Murray says it indicates "the pure sovereignty of the discrimination which the covenant promise implies" (2:13). Cranfield says it shows that a key characteristic of the "divine distinguishing" is "its independence of all human merit" (2:477). Moo says it implies "that it was God's will alone, and not natural capacity, religious devotion, or even faith that determined their respective destinies" (578).

Such statements are true as they apply to God's selection of Jacob for covenant service, and they may be true of election to service in general; but the context does not warrant applying them to election to salvation, as these writers do.

– in order that God's purpose in election might stand. This is the first part of a parenthetical comment (vv. 11b-12a), separated from the rest of the sentence in the NIV by dashes. In this comment Paul is explaining why ("in order that") God's choice of Jacob (and thus of the nation of Israel) was unconditional (v. 11a), namely, so that his purpose according to election might not fail. What was God's purpose for choosing one or the other of these twins? It was the same purpose he had for choosing Abraham in the first place, then Isaac. It was the purpose expressed when God first made his covenant with Abraham: "All peoples on earth will be blessed through you" (Gen 12:3). This purpose was fulfilled with the birth of the Messiah (9:5b; Acts 13:32-33).

This redemptive purpose was too important to be allowed to depend on the vicissitudes of human behavior. Thus God made it clear from the very beginning that he was going to accomplish his purpose through this particular family regardless of their individual decisions and the direction of their personal piety. He showed this by the very way in which he chose Jacob over Esau, i.e., unconditionally. This means that even if he had chosen Esau over Jacob, he would still have accomplished his purpose.

How this applies to the issue under discussion should be clear. At stake is God's faithfulness in his dealings with the Jews. How could he shower them with the covenant blessings of 9:4-5 and allow them to be lost at the same time? The answer is that the covenant did not include a promise of individual salvation for all Jews; it was limited to God's special use of the nation of Israel as the conduit for bringing Christ into the world. From the beginning God determined that he was going to do this, regardless of whether any individual Jews were saved. Just as "God's purpose in election" did not depend upon the spiritual status of the twin he chose from

Rebekah's womb, so it did not depend upon the salvation status of the Jews in Paul's day.

Again it is an error to see in this expression, "God's purpose in election," any reference to God's general method of saving individuals. "God's purpose in election" is roughly parallel to "God's word" in 9:6a, i.e., to his covenant promises to the nation as a whole. In 9:6 Paul says these covenant promises have not failed; here in 9:11 he says that God's purpose for choosing Israel will "stand" or remain firm. These are basically the same idea stated first negatively then positively.

9:12 . . . not by works but by him who calls. Like many others, Schreiner says that the phrase "not by works" always is used in the context of individual salvation; thus that must be the subject here ("Election," 93). But the present context is different. It is clear that "not by works" simply explains or restates "before the twins . . . had done anything good or bad" (9:11), and (as we have seen) this refers to Jacob's unconditional election for service, not salvation. God's choice of Jacob had nothing to do with any superior qualifications he might have possessed, and it was in spite of any of his potential weaknesses or character flaws. It was simply God's sovereign decision to choose him and use him, and this was a paradigm representing his choice of the nation of Israel as such.

This entire phrase modifies 9:11b; it tells us why it is that God's purpose in election will stand, namely, *not* by virtue of the accomplishments, faith, or faithfulness of the ones called to fulfill that purpose, but solely by the invincible power of the God who called them.

Many of a Calvinist bent insist that the concept of *calling* must mean "the effectual call to salvation" (Murray, 2:19), or "the call to faith and obedience" (Cranfield, 2:478-479). Others rightly see it as a call that has "exclusive reference to time, and with no reference to eternity" (Lard, 301-302). "It is election to privilege that is in mind, not eternal salvation," as Morris says (356). The terminology of calling is not used exclusively for calling to salvation in the NT, but on several occasions refers to calling to service. Abraham was called to inaugurate God's covenant plan (Heb 11:8), and Aaron was called to the high priesthood (Heb 5:4). Jesus called James and John to apostleship (Matt 4:21). Paul was called to be an apostle (Rom 1:1; 1 Cor 1:1; Gal 1:15).

In Jesus' statement, "For many are called, but few are chosen" (Matt 22:14, NASB), the "many" who are called are probably the nation of Israel as a whole, which was called into God's service; and the "few" who are chosen are probably the spiritual Israel of Rom 9:6b. This verse from Matthew, especially in its context of the parable of the wedding feast, definitely helps us to understand the nature of the calling to which Paul refers here in 9:12.

– she was told, "The older will serve the younger." This picks up the thought from v. 11a: before the twins were even born or had done anything good or wrong, God had already told Rebekah which one he was choosing for his covenant purposes. The quote is directly from Gen 25:23 (LXX). The "older" is Esau, who was born first; "the younger" is Jacob.

Commentators argue over whether this divine decree refers to Jacob and Esau as individuals or to the two nations established by each. From Jacob, of course, came Israel; and from Esau came the Edomites. God's full statement to Rebekah, recorded in Gen 25:23, shows that he originally had the two nations in mind: "Two nations are in your womb, and two peoples from within you will be separated; one people will be stronger than the other, and the older will serve the younger." That is probably the main point here. The OT does not record any instance where Esau personally assumed the role of a servant to Jacob, but it does refer to times when the Edomites were in a kind of servitude to Israel or Judah (see Num 24:18-19; 2 Sam 8:14; 1 Kgs 11:15-16; 2 Kgs 14:7).

This is not a serious issue except for those who want to read election of individuals to salvation into this context; they may be inclined to limit Paul's reference to Jacob and Esau to these men as individuals. Even if this is the case, though, election to service (not salvation) is Paul's point. The language of servanthood is simply a way of indicating which of the twins would be favored by God and chosen to be the covenant son, and which would not.

9:13 Just as it is written: "Jacob I loved, but Esau I hated." This quotation, from Mal 1:2, continues the thought already elaborated in vv. 10-12 and carries it a step further. By introducing it with the formulaic "it is written," Paul presents it as a proof text for the point he is making. The main idea is that God's choice of Jacob and his rejection of Esau were based not on something within these men but upon something within God himself, i.e., his own love and hate.

Two main issues arise here. One is the common question of whether God's love and hate relate to Jacob's and Esau's temporal fortunes or to their eternal destinies. Consistent with their approach to the passage as a whole, many see God's love as the basis for his unconditional election of Jacob to salvation, and God's hatred as the basis for his unconditional reprobation of Esau to hell. This is then generalized into the Calvinist doctrine of unconditional election as such (see Moo, 585-586).

As we have already seen, however, the subject here is not individual salvation but election to service. This election is unconditional to be sure, but it is election to *service* nonetheless. In reference to this verse we can see this is the case by examining the context of the quotation as it appears originally in Malachi. There it is clear that the main point is not God's attitude toward and treatment of the two brothers themselves, but of the two nations springing from them. Even more significantly, the consequences of these contrasting attitudes are not eternal destinies but different earthly fortunes.[42]

The other main issue is the meaning of "Esau I hated." In what sense did God "hate" Esau? Some say Paul is merely employing a semitic hyperbole, in which the strong term "hate," when used in comparative conjunction with "love," sometimes simply means "to love less"; see Gen 29:33 (cf. v. 30); Deut 21:15; Luke 14:26 (cf. Matt 10:37); John 12:25 (MP, 389; Fitzmyer, 563). Others agree this is a valid meaning of "hate," but say that it does not apply here. They equate love with election, and see "hatred" as God's nonemotional decision to reject Esau (decline to choose him) and just set him aside (Moo, 587; Morris, 357; Dunn, 2:544-545). Still others believe, and I agree, that neither of these explanations is strong enough. Murray correctly observes that the treatment of Esau (Edom) in Mal 1:1-5 can hardly be called just a less intense love or even nonselection. It is "a positive judgment, not merely the absence of blessing." It is "disfavour, disapprobation, displeasure," a true "holy hate" (2:22-23).

---

[42]Others who take this view include Bruce, 193; Fitzmyer, 563; MacArthur, 2:27; and Morris, 356-357.

It is difficult to think of this "holy hate," even in the form of temporal destruction as described in Mal 1:1-5, as unconditional and in no sense related to Edom's conduct – or as Dunn puts it (2:544), "without any reference to Esau's (Edom's) deeds." Here is where I believe the thought of 9:13 goes a step beyond the basic point of 9:10-12. The main point throughout is God's sovereignty in his selection of those who will carry out his purposes. His initial choice of Jacob over Esau stresses this sovereignty, even to the point of unconditionality. This quotation seems to show, though, that God's subsequent historical treatment of their respective nations *was* conditioned to some extent upon their conduct.

This can be seen in other OT references to God's wrath upon Esau's people, Edom (Isa 34:5-15; Jer 49:7-22; Ezek 35:1-15; Obad 1-21). In these and other texts it is made clear that this wrath is divine vengeance against Edom because of its wicked treatment of Israel (Ps 137:7; Isa 5:8; Jer 49:12; Ezek 25:12-14; 35:5,11-15; Obad 10-16). Thus even if God's original choice of Jacob and rejection of Esau were totally unconditional, his subsequent treatment of them did have respect to their conduct. This does not contradict Paul's basic premise regarding the manner of God's original choice of Jacob (and the people of Israel); it simply adds another dimension to his continuing historical relationship with this nation.

The overall main point of this section (vv. 7-13) is still the sovereign freedom of God to set up his plan of redemption as he chooses. He can choose whomever he pleases, whether individuals or nations, to carry out his redemptive purposes, apart from their own choice or cooperation if necessary. His chosen servants do not have to be a part of "spiritual Israel" to be of service to him, and he is not obligated to reward them with eternal life just because they have played their intended part in the messianic drama. There is no inherent connection between service and salvation.

Such is Paul's reply (in part) to those who would accuse God of unfaithfulness in his dealings with the Jews. He appeals, as Godet says, to "the great truth of God's liberty." Godet (351) makes these perceptive comments:

> The two examples of exclusion, given in the persons of Ishmael and Esau, have served to prove a fact which Israel embraced with their whole heart: God's right to endow them

with privilege at the expense of the Arab (Ishmael) and Edomite (Esau) nations, by assigning to them in the history of redemption the preponderating part to which the right of primogeniture seemed to call those excluded. Now, if Israel approved the principle of divine liberty when it was followed in a way so strikingly in their favor, how could they repudiate it when it was turned against them!

B. GOD'S RIGHT TO CHOOSE AND USE PEOPLE WITHOUT SAVING THEM (9:14-18)

As we have said earlier, Paul's main purpose in Rom 9 is to affirm God's sovereign right to choose any individual or group for *service* without at the same time choosing them for *salvation*. The emphasis is not simply upon God's right to choose some while rejecting others; it is also upon the *manner* in which God makes his choices.

The bottom line is that God's distinction between physical Israel and spiritual Israel is based upon his freedom to choose in whatever way he wishes. There is indeed a spiritual Israel which enjoys the blessings of salvation, and God has determined to bestow these blessings on the condition of faith (9:30–10:21). But at the same time he has reserved the right to choose and use people for service with no strings attached, as in the case of physical Israel. If it suits his purposes, he can choose them unconditionally, and use them without saving them or rewarding them in any way.

This present paragraph lies at the heart of this argument. In the previous paragraph Paul demonstrates that this is the way God works by citing the concrete examples of Isaac and Jacob. Now in vv. 14-18 he affirms the general principle of divine sovereignty that underlies all such specific examples: "I will have mercy on whom I have mercy, and I will have compassion on whom I have compassion" (v. 15).

This is not an argument in the sense that Paul is attempting to justify God's actions before the bar of reason. He is not trying to defend God by appealing to some cosmic code of conduct that is independent of God and to which God himself is bound. Rather, by citing the general principle as stated in OT Scripture, Paul is simply showing that God's choices of Isaac and Jacob – and therefore of the nation of Israel – were consistent with his own nature and with his own plainly stated principles of action. This is the only sense in which this paragraph may be called a theodicy.

Throughout this study of Rom 9 we must keep in mind that the main issue is *the status of physical Israel*. I.e., if they have been chosen for covenant service, why are they not saved? Thus in 9:14 the question ("Is God unjust?") is not about those whom God has *not* chosen (such as Ishmael and Esau), but about those whom he *has* chosen, i.e., Isaac and Jacob – as forerunners of the nation of Israel. Like Isaac and Jacob, physical Israel did not receive its role in God's plan through personal achievement but solely through God's unconditional choice (vv. 15-16). Therefore it does not have any claim on God's saving grace, and can be chosen *and hardened* at the same time, like Pharaoh (vv. 17-18).

Again we must insist that the issue here is not how God chooses individuals for salvation, contrary to the common Calvinist effort to use this text as a proof for unconditional election. Achtemeier (163) is correct: "Paul is dealing in this passage with the place of Israel in God's plan of salvation. He is not dealing with the fate of individuals." Dunn (2:562) warns against "generalizing too quickly from this passage. . . . Paul is thinking solely in terms of salvation-history, of God's purpose for Israel. . . . A more extensive doctrine of election is not to be found here."

1. God's Righteousness Is Challenged (9:14)

9:14 What then shall we say? Is God unjust? Not at all! Paul dialogues thus with himself when he knows he has just said something that is likely to be misunderstood or to raise objections or false conclusions in the minds of his hearers. "What then shall we say?" is parallel to 3:5; 6:1,15; 7:7. "Not at all!" is μὴ γένοιτο (*mē genoito*), the very strong negative expression frequently used by Paul; see 3:4 above. The question itself, "Is God unjust?" is stated in such a way in the Greek (using the negative particle *mē*) that a negative answer is implied and expected. Also, "unjust" is actually a noun, ἀδικία (*adikia*). The NASB has a literal translation: "There is no injustice with God, is there?"

The term *adikia* has been used several times already, always for human unrighteousness or wickedness (1:18, 29; 2:8; 3:5; 6:13). It is the opposite of righteousness, the essence of which is conformity to the proper norm or standard (JC, 1:116-117). That God is righteous does not mean that he conforms to some norm outside himself, since such a norm does not exist. God's essence is itself the highest and ultimate norm, even for his own actions. To say, then, that God is righteous means that his actions always conform to his own essence. He never goes against himself and never acts in a way that is inconsistent with or contradictory to his own nature. He is always faithful to himself.

Thus to say that God is unrighteous or unjust is to accuse him of doing something that violates his very nature – which is impossible. Since it is his nature to be true (3:4) and never to lie (Titus 1:2), his righteousness thus requires that he always be faithful and true to his word. In the context of Rom 9, to suggest that God may be unrighteous or unjust is simply to raise the question again as to whether or not God's word of promise to Israel has failed (9:6a). "The question is – Is God *righteous?* – i.e., has he been true to his covenanted word?"[43]

We must remember that the issue here is the status of national Israel. Thus the objection stated in 9:14 is one that would most likely be raised by the Jews regarding God's treatment of them as a nation. It is a mistake to see this question as something that relates only to the immediately preceding section, and especially to limit it to the rejection of Ishmael and Esau.[44] It relates rather to everything Paul has said in vv. 1-13. "What then shall we say – about the way God chose and has been using Israel? Has his treatment of the nation been unjust? Has his word failed, as some seem to think? No! Absolutely not!" Paul's answer has the intensity and the content of Abraham's conviction in Gen 18:25, "Will not the Judge of all the earth do right?"

---

[43]N.T. Wright, "Messiah," 211; cited in Dunn, 2:551.

[44]As opposed to Dunn, who says Paul "intended to set up this question" by "introducing the thought of a deliberate choice against Esau." In this light, "if God chooses some and rejects others without reference to anything they do, surely that is unjust?" (2:561). See also Piper, *Justification*, 96.

Why is God's treatment of Israel not unjust? Because, as 9:6b says, there really are *two* Israels, and God is not obliged to treat them in the same way. Specifically, he is free to use the nation as a whole for his covenant purposes, while limiting salvation only to those who trust his saving promises. The unconditional nature of God's choice of the larger group is illustrated in vv. 7-13. These verses in themselves show that God's use of Israel has not been unjust. The question in v. 14 is not so much an objection to the content of vv. 7-13 as it is a statement of the implied objection that underlies the whole chapter. And Paul's answer to the question in vv. 15-18 is not different from what he has already said in vv. 7-13, but is a generalized restatement of it. He simply shows, as Lard says (304), "that God acted according to his own avowed principles of conduct."

2. God's Sovereignty in Election for Service (9:15-16)

9:15 For he says to Moses, "I will have mercy on whom I have mercy, and I will have compassion on whom I have compassion." The connecting word "for" (*gar*) has several possible meanings. Ordinarily it introduces the cause or reason for the preceding statement. In this case the idea would be, "No, God is *not* unjust, *because* . . . ." This would then raise the question as to how God's statement to Moses shows that God is not unjust. The best answer is that Paul believes that the *quoting of OT Scripture* is sufficient to establish his point. (See also v. 17.) Since the main source of the objection in v. 14 would be the Jews, refuting it from their own Scripture would be especially effective. This would also be indicative of Paul's high view of the authority of Scripture. See Murray, 2:25.

Gar suggests, then, that in these verses Paul is confirming his affirmation of God's justice or faithfulness. He confirms it by quoting Scripture, and especially by citing the general principle or general divine prerogative that embraces all the specific cases at issue. No, God has not acted unjustly in his choice of Isaac, in his choice of Jacob, and especially in his choice of the nation of Israel, because Scripture itself records his sovereign right to choose anyone he pleases according to his own terms. He has simply acted in accord with his established word.

The divine statement cited by Paul was spoken "to Moses." It is an exact quote from the Greek version (the LXX) of Exod 33:19b and is very close to the Hebrew. The general occasion for the statement was Moses' intercession for Israel following their unfaithfulness with the golden calf. Specifically it was part of God's reply when Moses requested to see the very essence of God: "Then Moses said, 'Now show me your glory'" (Exod 33:18).

Paul's citation of this statement by God raises several questions. First, does it apply to the eternal salvation of individuals, or to temporal election for service? Second, how does it relate to the overall argument of ch. 9? Third, why is the statement only *positive*, with no corresponding negative reference to exclusion from God's mercy?

The most crucial (and by now, most familiar) issue, of course, is whether the statement applies to God's choice for salvation or for service. Many, such as Murray, argue for the former: "In this context we may not tone down the soteric import" (2:26). Others declare that salvation is not the point here. For instance, DeWelt states that the choices of which this text speaks "never involve salvation of a man's soul" (148).

Either way we must show that our view fits into the overall context. But since this statement in 9:15 is a quotation from the OT (Exod 33:19b), this raises the question as to which context should be used to determine whether Paul is referring to salvation or service: Exod 33 or Rom 9? Lenski (611) says it is best to stay with the NT context, to take the words as Paul quotes them, "and not to consider the whole episode with regard to Moses, his prayer to see God's face, etc." DeWelt, on the other hand, declares that it is imperative to see "that this free reign of God's mercy and compassion is all related as occurring in the Old Testament and must not be carried over into the New Testament dispensation" (148). Such extremes are inadequate, however; both contexts are important, and in the end they yield the same result regarding the issue of salvation or service.

The OT context is important here and definitely must be considered. Why did God originally make this statement? It was addressed to Moses, but for what purpose? What was its intended application? To ask the question another way, *to whom* was the statement originally intended to apply: to Moses himself, or to the nation of Israel? Many have concluded the former, i.e., that God was telling Moses that he would be the recipient of God's blessing. This would happen not because of any meritorious accomplishment on Moses' part, however, but solely because of God's sovereign choice.

Fitzmyer says it refers to "how God called Moses" (565). This hardly fits the context, however. Others say it refers to God's decision to answer Moses' request, "Now show me your glory" (Exod 33:18). In response to this request, God says first of all that he *will* grant it: "I will cause all my goodness to pass in front of you, and I will proclaim my name, the LORD, in your presence" (33:19a). Then he says immediately, "I will have mercy on whom I will have mercy, and I will have compassion on whom I will have compassion" (33:19b).

Why did God make the latter statement immediately after declaring that he would answer Moses' request? Piper tries to make the case that it is a paraphrase of God's name as later revealed in the theophany in 34:6-7 (*Justification*, 84-89). Verse 19b is just "a brief, preliminary declaration of the verbal theophany," he says (88). This understanding does not fit the flow of the conversation between Moses and God, however. Verse 18 states Moses' request, "Now show me your glory." God's reply is threefold: the statement of his intention to grant the request (19a); the *reason* for his decision (19b); and the one qualification (20a), "'But,' he said, 'you cannot see my face.'"

This latter view is most consistent with the context and is held by many. Keil and Delitzsch (*Pentateuch*, 237) say v. 19b expresses "the reason why Moses' request was granted, viz. that it was an act of unconditional grace and compassion on the part of God." It definitely refers to Moses' request, according to Godet (352): in Exod 33:19 God, "when condescending to grant the bold request of Moses that he might behold His glory with his bodily eyes, gives him to understand that nothing in him . . . merited such a favor." See also DeWelt, 148; GRe, 364.

In my judgment the view just described is correct, being true to the context and to the terminology used (as will be explained shortly). But I have concluded that this is not the whole picture, and that the statement in 33:19b must be taken also in the broader context of the immediate crisis concerning Israel, and thus also applies to the nation as a whole. Only then is it relevant to Paul's argument in Rom 9.

Israel's episode with the golden calf, as an act of great sin and even apostasy, certainly raised the question of the salvation of those who were involved (Exod 32:25-35). But it also raised the question of Israel's preservation as the people chosen to serve God's covenant purposes. Moses was very concerned with the latter, especially when God told the people that from that point on he would not be personally present among them on their journey (33:3-5). The visible presence of God had up to that time been a crucial factor in their lives (33:7-11), and Moses argued before God that without his continuing visible presence among them they would not really know if they were still God's unique people, nor would anyone else know (33:12-16).

At this point in the narrative the issue is not the eternal salvation of individual Jews, but Israel's preservation as a nation and her continuing role in God's plan. In reference to God's threat to withdraw his presence, Moses reminds him, "Remember that this nation is your people" (33:13). Certainly it is true that Moses' prayer is "for the salvation of the whole people," to use Calvin's words (356), but the point is not the eternal salvation of individual Jews but the temporal preservation of the nation as such. See Fitzmyer, 566.

In the face of Moses' intercessory prayer God relents and tells Moses that he will indeed once more bestow his personal presence upon them (33:15,17). This is the point at which Moses makes his bold request, "Now show me your glory" (33:18), i.e., as an assurance that he and Israel had been restored to God's favor. What follows is the marvelous event of God's unique revelation to Moses, both visibly and audibly (33:19-34:7). Moses' response is a final and humble plea for the nation's reinstatement as God's "inheritance" (34:8-9), though they obviously did not deserve it. God concludes the matter by reestablishing his covenant with Moses and with Israel (34:10-28).

The point is that the critical statement in 33:19b refers not only to God's sovereignty in his choice of which prayers to answer (according to which he granted Moses' request), but also to his sovereignty in his choice of those who will serve him in the accomplishment of his plan of redemption. That God answered Moses' prayer and showed himself to Moses in a unique way was symbolic of his intention to relent and once more to grace the nation with his presence.[45] His ultimate answer to Moses' prayer was in "His sparing the people and continuing to guide and protect them" (MacArthur, 2:32).

In this light we can see why Paul chose to quote Exod 33:19b in support of his own argument that God's word toward Israel has not failed and therefore that he cannot be accused of injustice in his treatment of them. The issue in Exod 33 and Rom 9 is very much the same: not the salvation of individuals, but the role of the nation in God's plan. The point is that God is free to choose whomever he will, according to whatever conditions he pleases.

One main problem that many will have with this interpetation is the meaning of the terms "have mercy" and "have compassion."[46] Do not these terms refer to eternal salvation? Not necessarily. These terms and their Hebrew counterparts have a variety of uses, depending upon context.

The second word in God's statement is "have compassion": רחם (*racham*) in Exod 33:19b and οἰκτείρω (*oikteirō*) here. This verb and its cognates (words with the same root) refer to the attitude of compassion, mercy, or pity upon someone in any kind of need. It can refer to God's compassion upon the lost, leading to salvation (see Isa 55:7; Rom 12:1), but it can also refer to divine or human compassion expressed in temporal ways (see Luke 6:36; Heb 10:28). In the OT, *racham* is frequently used for God's temporal blessings upon his people, either as bestowed or as withheld (see Isa 14:1; Jer 13:14; 21:7; 33:26; 42:12; Zech 10:6). As Ezek 39:25 says, "Therefore this is what the Sovereign LORD says: I will now bring Jacob back from captivity and will have compassion [*racham*] on all the people of Israel."

---

[45]An incident parallel to this is in Num 14:1-25. God is once more ready to renounce his covenant with Israel, but Moses intercedes, citing Exod 34:6-7 as a reminder of how the Lord had once before forgiven his people and reinstated them into his favor.

[46]These terms are basically parallel in meaning, or "essentially synonymous" (MacArthur, 2:32). It is a case of repetition for emphasis. See Lenski, 607; Moo, 592; Morris, 359; Piper, *Justification*, 83.

The first word in God's statement, "have mercy," is used much more often in both testaments. The Hebrew word in Exod 33:19b is חָנַן (*chanan*). Because it is sometimes translated "be gracious" (as in the NASB in Exod 33:19b), and because its noun form (חֵן, *chēn*) is often translated "grace," some just assume that it refers to saving grace in this text. The word does have that meaning in some contexts; but saving grace is actually one of its lesser meanings. Basically it means to do someone a favor, to show favor, to be merciful and kind, or to bestow a blessing. Human beings are said to be merciful (gracious) to other people, and God is said to be merciful (gracious) to various people.

The word is often used as a preface to prayer, as in Ps 27:7: "Hear my voice when I call, O LORD; be merciful to me and answer me." Thus in Exod 33:19b, when God says, "I will have mercy on whom I will have mercy," he could very well be simply saying to Moses, "All right, Moses; I will answer your prayer this time; but remember that it is my sovereign prerogative to determine which prayers I will answer and which I will deny."

God's mercy (grace, favor) is sometimes the grace of forgiveness and salvation for individuals (Ps 51:1), but more often it refers to some temporal blessing (Gen 33:5,11; 2 Sam 12:22). The nation of Israel as such is often the recipient of such temporal mercy (favor, grace). For example, Ps 102:13 says, "You will arise and have compassion on Zion, for it is time to show favor to her." See also 2 Kgs 13:23; Isa 30:18-19; Amos 5:15. Thus it is completely consistent with the meaning of the word *chanan* to interpret Exod 33:19b as referring to God's sovereign choice to spare the people of Israel and to continue to use them as his servant nation.

In Rom 9:15 the Greek word used to translate *chanan* is ἐλεέω (*eleeō*), and it, too, has a range of meanings other than saving mercy (as does its noun form, ἔλεος, *eleos*). A few times it does refer to salvation (1 Tim 1:13,16; 1 Pet 2:10). More often, though, it refers to showing compassion to the poor, sick, or needy (Rom 12:8; Phil 2:27). Thus it is used as a prelude to a request for such mercy: "Have mercy on me, and help me" (e.g., Matt 9:27; 15:22; 17:15; 20:30-31; Luke 16:24). Most significantly, it is sometimes used to refer to God's choosing or calling someone for service, specifically,

Paul's call to apostleship: 1 Cor 7:25; 2 Cor 4:1.[47] This last meaning is the one Paul intends in 9:15, I believe; and it has special reference to God's choice of the nation of Israel to play a crucial role in his covenant purposes. In other words, when God chooses anyone for service, it is the bestowal of a great favor upon that person (or nation), whether that person (or nation) is saved or not.

The next question is how Paul's citation of Exod 33:19b relates to his overall argument in Rom 9. The answer should be obvious. At stake is the righteousness or faithfulness of God in relation to Israel. Does not his choosing of Israel for covenant service imply that all Jewish people should be saved? No, says Paul; as in his choice of Isaac and Jacob, God chooses as it pleases him. He is free to choose *whomever* he likes.[48] He can choose and use people, including the whole nation of Israel, whether they are saved or not. Salvation is neither a prerequisite for nor a necessary result of such a choice. The quote from Exod 33:19b states this as a general principle; the example of Pharaoh in 9:17-18 is a specific example.

The last question about v. 15 is, why does the statement refer only to a positive choice, i.e., one grounded in mercy and compassion? Why is there no reference to God's sovereign rejection of others? This question is meaningful only when one concludes that the passage is talking about the eternal salvation of individuals rather than election to service. For those who hold the former view, the issue is whether or not there is such a thing as double predestination, i.e., both election to salvation and reprobation to damnation.

Some see such a double predestination in vv. 7-13,18,21-24; thus they accept it as an inference in v. 15. Others see v. 15 as softening the negative side of predestination elsewhere in the chapter. It "shows that God is out to secure mercy, not condemnation," says Morris (359). A "symmetry between grace and wrath . . . is missing here," says Achtemeier, since Paul "speaks exclusively of God's decision to be merciful." Indeed, "the whole discussion is marked

---

[47]The similar word "grace" (χάρις, *charis*) is often used in reference to God's calling someone to a role of service: Luke 1:30; Rom 1:5. See JC, 1:77-78.

[48]The emphasis in the statement, says Godet, is not on the two verbs but on the pronoun, "whom," or more appropriately, "whomever." Here, "the idea of God's free choice reappears" (352).

rather by the asymmetry of a dominating grace" (162). See Cranfield, 2:483-484.

This whole discussion is meaningful, however, only if this chapter is dealing with the eternal destinies of individuals. If it is, the double-predestination folks are correct. To say that God is free to show saving mercy unconditionally on whomever he chooses definitely implies that he is free to withhold saving mercy unconditionally from whomever he chooses, and his decision to do the former necessarily entails his decision to do the latter. Such a decision to withhold mercy is in effect a decision to send these nonrecipients to hell, with all the resulting negative implications for the nature of God.

This is why it is so important to see that the issue is not a kind of sovereignty by which God chooses some for salvation and condemns others to hell. Rather, the issue in vv. 7-13 is his sovereignty in choosing one (Isaac, Jacob) *rather than* another (Ishmael, Esau) for a role of service, and the issue in the chapter as a whole is his sovereignty in choosing and using the nation of Israel apart from the promise of individual salvation. Such choosing of Isaac, Jacob and national Israel was a matter of (temporal) mercy and favor, but the nonchoosing of Ishmael and Esau was not *ipso facto* an act of eternal condemnation. Those who were not so chosen are just no longer relevant to the discussion. Thus to have added, "I will condemn whomever I will condemn" would have been irrelevant and beside the point, not to mention untrue. Even the references to Pharaoh and hardening in 9:17-18 are not about condemnation as such.

9:16 It does not, therefore, depend on man's desire or effort, but on God's mercy. Since the issue in this context is not the eternal salvation of individuals, the considerable amount of rhetoric that attempts to extract Calvinist unconditional election from this verse is wasted. Since the subject is the election of individuals and groups for service, all conclusions concerning divine sovereignty and unconditionality in election must instead be applied thereto. Further argument on this point is unnecessary.

The main point is that God's final decision to select someone for his covenant service is based not upon anything in the person himself, but entirely and only upon the divine purpose. If it is God's purpose to choose someone, he will do so, whether that person is willing or unwilling, or whether he is prepared or not. Of course, God would rather use a willing person who will devote his entire strength to God's cause. Also, for those tasks that require someone who is especially gifted and trained, God will prepare such a person through his providential control of life circumstances. Examples are Moses and Paul. But for other tasks he can use those who are unwilling and even hostile toward him. Examples are Balaam (Num 22–24) and, of course, Pharaoh (9:17-18). Many in Israel were in this last category.

The thought of this verse is not different from that of v. 15, and is set forth as a logical conclusion ("therefore") from it. The subject of v. 16 ("it") is not stated but must be supplied from the context. "Mercy" is the choice of many (e.g., SH, 254; Cranfield, 2:484; Moo, 593), and those who interpret the entire passage in terms of election to salvation naturally take this to be saving mercy, eternal life, or being a child of God (e.g., Hendriksen, 2:325; MacArthur, 2:32; Stott, 269). It is best not to take "mercy" as the subject, however, since whatever the subject is, it *depends* "on God's mercy." In keeping with our overall interpretation, I believe the subject is simply "being chosen for God's service."

Being thus chosen does not depend upon human desire or willing. Jacob is a perfect example; he was chosen before he was born and contrary to the will of his father Isaac (Gen 27). Nor does it depend on human effort. "Effort" is literally "the running one" or "the one who runs." This refers to "moral attainment" (Piper, *Justification*, 153), or vigorous, purposeful striving as in the running of a race. Paul uses this metaphor often, sometimes for the work of his apostolic ministry.[49] These two terms together "sum up the totality of man's capacity," his motivation and his action (Dunn, 2:553; see Phil 2:13). Sometimes this motivation and this action are good, sometimes bad. Either way, as Dunn says, "they are not factors in election, neither in the initial choice nor in its maintenance" (2:553). This applies, of course, to election to service in general, and specifically to God's purpose for Israel. As Dunn says, "God's purpose is not conditioned on Israel's good will and effort" (2:562).[50]

[49]On the latter see 1 Cor 9:24-26; Gal 2:2; Phil 2:16; 2 Tim 4:7. See also Gal 5:7; Phil 3:12-14; Heb 12:1.

[50]Dunn warns against generalizing this statement beyond God's purpose for Israel in salvation history (2:562).

Such election for service is a matter of "the one who shows mercy, namely, God," as the text literally says. This simply repeats v. 15, where we saw that "showing mercy" refers to the mercy God bestows in choosing someone to serve his covenant purposes.

3. God's Purposes Can Be Served by the Unsaved (9:17-18)

9:17 For the Scripture says to Pharaoh: "I raised you up for this very purpose, that I might display my power in you and that my name might be proclaimed in all the earth." Paul takes this quote directly from Exod 9:16. Obviously "the Scripture" did not say this to Pharaoh. God himself, through Moses, spoke these words to him. By thus personifying Scripture and thinking of it as interchangeable with God himself, Paul shows us his very high view of the nature of the Bible. This phenomenon is "a graphic illustration that Paul thinks of scripture as the word of God," says Dunn (2:553). "The Scripture says" is essentially the same as "God says." A similar equation is seen in Gal 3:8.

How are vv. 17-18 related to the preceding verses? This depends on how we understand the word "for" (*gar*) at the beginning of v. 17. Some say that *gar* ties this verse sequentially to v. 16, making vv. 17-18 an *example* of the principle in v. 16 (Achtemeier, 162), or "a development of v 16" (Dunn, 2:553). This is possible, but I believe it is more likely that the *gar* in v. 17 is parallel to the *gar* in v. 15, each relating equally to v. 14. Thus vv. 15-16 and vv. 17-18 are two distinct points, each confirming that God's treatment of the Jews is not unjust (v. 14) by citing data from the OT. See Lenski, 613; Cranfield, 2:485; Moo, 593-594.

What, then, is the progression of Paul's argument? First, God's treatment of the Jews is not unjust because he has complete sovereignty in the way he chooses those who will serve his purposes. The way he chose Isaac and Jacob demonstrates this by example (vv. 7-13), and this is further confirmed by the citation of the general principle from Exod 33:19b (vv. 14-16). All of this together shows that God is free to choose whomever he pleases for roles of service.

But this by itself does not fully address the issue of the Jews. The question specifically is whether God is unjust because he called the nation of Israel into his service while at the same time condemning many if not most individual Jews to hell. If God is going to use them, is he not thereby obligated to save them? This is the point addressed in vv. 17-18. Here Paul shows from the OT that God's sovereignty in election for service includes the prerogative of choosing and using someone without saving them. His premiere example is Pharaoh. Not only was he chosen ("shown mercy"), but he was also hardened (confirmed in his unbelief).

A very common approach to this text is to take Pharaoh as an example of *reprobation* (condemnation to hell), in contrast with Moses, who is an example of election to *salvation*. Verses 15-18 are taken as parallel to the two parts of v. 13. "Jacob I loved" is equivalent to the positive example of Moses in vv. 15-16, while "Esau I hated" corresponds to the negative example of Pharaoh in vv. 17-18 (Moo, 593; Morris, 360). According to Pendleton (MP, 398), Moses and Pharaoh are a pair between whom God chooses, just as he chose between Isaac and Ishmael, and between Jacob and Esau. And in this "third case he granted favor to Moses, and *meted out punishment* to Pharaoh."

I believe this approach is a very serious error, not only because the context is not dealing with the question of eternal destinies, but also because it is not warranted by what the text specifically says about Pharaoh and the others. For one thing, Moses is not introduced here as the object of election, whether for service or for salvation. He is simply the one to whom God spoke the statement in 9:15 and is not being used as an example of anything. Thus it is not proper to speak of a "contrast between Moses and Pharaoh." For another thing, there is no parallel between Esau and Pharaoh. Esau was not chosen for anything; but Pharaoh *was* chosen for a significant role, a fact that is crucial for Paul's point. (This is contrary to Dunn's assertion that Pharaoh "filled the same sort of antithetical role" toward Israel that Esau did [2:563].)

God's rejection and punishment of Pharaoh are indeed significant, but *not* as a parallel with Ishmael and Esau, and not even as a contrast with Isaac, Jacob, or Moses. They are significant only insofar as they make Pharaoh an exact parallel of the nation of Israel itself. God chose both Israel and Pharaoh for a role of service, and he used both of them not only *despite* their hardness of heart, but even *because* of it. Pharaoh is not an example of God's freedom to *reject* whom he will, contrary to Godet (352-353). Rather, he is an example of God's freedom to elect some for service while at the same time withholding salvation from them. Thus Pharaoh is a special kind of example of "God's freedom and sovereignty in the choice of instruments to achieve his end" (Fitzmyer, 568). The pagan King Cyrus is another such example (Isa 44:28-45:7).

In Exod 9:16 the LXX translates the Hebrew word for "raised up" with διατηρέω (*diatēreō*), "to keep, to preserve." Thus some, following the LXX, interpret God to be saying in Exod 9:16 that he has preserved Pharaoh alive or spared his life, in contrast with Exod 9:15. The NASB translates v. 16, "But, indeed, for this cause I have allowed you to remain." Hendriksen (2:325) says it means "spared you" both in Exodus and here in 9:17. The majority of interpreters, however, rightly take the Hebrew verb (literally, "I have caused you to stand") in a more general sense, as referring to God's causing Pharaoh to appear on the stage of history at this particular time for this particular purpose. See Cranfield, 2:486; Godet, 353; Moo, 595; Morris, 360; Murray, 2:27.

Thus in the affirmation "I raised you up," God is saying that he exercised his sovereign prerogative to choose Pharaoh for a very specific role in his redemptive plan. "For this very purpose" stresses the fact that Pharaoh was being used by God, even when it seemed that he was most emphatically opposing God. He was carrying out the divine purpose in and through his hardened heart.

God's purpose for Pharaoh was twofold: to be an instrument for displaying God's power and for proclaiming God's name in all the earth. The power to which God refers is not the power to save individuals from their sins (1:16), but the power to overthrow opposing earthly rulers and their so-called deities, and thereby the power to deliver his people from Egyptian slavery and oppression. How did God display this power "in" or "through" Pharaoh? By hardening his heart so that he continued to refuse to let the people go, thereby giving God the opportunity to add plague upon plague all the way to the climactic death of the Egyptian firstborn. What God needed from Pharaoh was not his immediate acquiescence but his continuing resistance. This he achieved by his providential power to harden the Egyptian's heart (GRu, 203), thus providing the occasion for the public and overwhelming display of his might.

The second part of God's purpose for Pharaoh (a direct consequence of the first) was the proclamation of the name of the true God in all the inhabited earth. "My name" does not have to refer to any one particular name, such as Exod 3:14, or Exod 33:19 or 34:6-7. The point is simply that God intended his utter defeat of Pharaoh's gods (via the plagues) and Pharaoh's forces (in the Red Sea) to be trumpeted abroad, so that everyone would know that Israel's God was the one true God, and that all other so-called "gods" are nothings.

In fact, thanks to the way God used Pharaoh through the whole episode of the Exodus, God's name and power *were* magnified in all the nations. The Song of Moses included these words: "The nations will hear and tremble; anguish will grip the people of Philistia. The chiefs of Edom will be terrified, the leaders of Moab will be seized with trembling, the people of Canaan will melt away" (Exod 15:14-15; see vv. 16-17). See Joshua 2:9-11; 9:9; 11:1-4 for the fulfillment of these words.

The display of power in Egypt was a continuing testimony to God's omnipotence for the Israelites themselves (Deut 6:22; 7:18-19; 11:1-4), and it continued to be celebrated throughout their history (Ps 78:12-13; 105:26-38; 106:9-11; 135:9; 136:10-15; Acts 7:36).

The main point is that God is free to use as his instruments even hardened unbelievers; this is not contrary to his justice (v. 14). That God was justified in using Pharaoh thus was something any Jew would have granted. Paul simply wanted the Jews to see that the same principle applied to them as a nation. They could serve God's purposes, whether as individuals they were believers or not.

9:18 Therefore God has mercy on whom he wants to have mercy, and he hardens whom he wants to harden. "Therefore" indicates this is the logical conclusion or summarized result, not just from vv. 15-17, but from the whole discussion in vv. 6-17.

Two errors must be avoided from the outset. One error is the common assumption that this statement applies to eternal destinies, and that it therefore confirms the Calvinist concept of unconditional election (see, e.g., Moo, 596-599). But as we have stressed repeatedly, the subject of this section is not eternal salvation but election to service. That is true of this verse also. Cranfield (2:489) is correct: "The assumption that Paul is here thinking of the ultimate destiny of the individual, of his final salvation or final ruin, is not justified by the text."

The other error is the assumption that the objects of the two verbs, "have mercy on" and "harden," are exclusive and cannot refer to the same individual or group. This error naturally follows from the first, and is accepted without question by those who think the subject is eternal destinies.

Once these two errors are accepted, it is extremely difficult to avoid the conclusion of double predestination. The parallelism between the two sides of Paul's statement would seem to make the condemnation as unconditional as the salvation. Yet sometimes even the most ardent Calvinists interject qualifications. Moo, for example, while acknowledging the "strict parallelism" here (597), nevertheless declares that the showing of mercy and the hardening "are not equivalent acts" (599-600). Likewise Murray, who says the divine sovereignty is "as ultimate in the negative as in the positive" (2:27), softens the negative by saying that the hardening was "judicial," or "presupposes ill-desert" (2:29). However, such qualifications are inconsistent with the parallelism of this verse and with the references to the irrelevance of works in other verses (9:11-12,16). They are introduced in order to avoid the harsh conclusion that unconditional reprobation is equally ultimate with unconditional salvation.

Both of the errors mentioned above, along with their necessary implication of double predestination, are easily avoided by understanding that the sovereign choices to which Paul refers in 9:18 are for historical roles of service, not eternal destinies. As Achtemeier says, "Paul is dealing in this passage with the place of Israel in God's plan of salvation. He is not dealing with the fate of individuals" (162-163).

The divine sovereignty in this matter is the main emphasis: "on whom he wants." This verb is θέλω (*thelō*), "to wish, to will." God's choice of the one to receive mercy and the one to harden is purely a matter of his own will. He does not have to justify his choices; his sovereignty is grounded in the very fact that he is, after all, *God*. Just because he is God, he "is free to choose whom he will for what he will" (MP, 400).

The common approach to this verse, whether seen as dealing with salvation or service, is that 18a refers to Moses and 18b to Pharaoh. Murray's statement is typical: "As Moses, in this context, exemplifies mercy, so Pharaoh hardening" (2:28). The verse means that "Moses was redeemed and Pharaoh was not," says MacArthur (2:35). Cranfield generalizes the disjunction as it refers to service: God gives some a positive role in which they serve consciously and voluntarily; he gives others a negative role in which they serve unconsciously and involuntarily (2:488).

In my judgment, though, this is not the point of v. 18. The mercy and the hardening are not exclusive, but may be bestowed upon the *same person* (or group). We have already seen that "having mercy" in this context refers not to saving mercy[51] but to the favor of being chosen by God to play some role in the working out of his redemptive purposes (see v. 15). Whether one is conscious of being chosen and used is irrelevant; even whether one is saved or not is irrelevant (see Isa 45:4-5, concerning Cyrus). "God has mercy on whom he wants to have mercy" refers thus to God's sovereign choosing of whomever he pleases to serve his purposes. It is an all-inclusive statement, embracing all who are selected for whatever roles they will play in his plan – even Pharaoh.

The second half of v. 18 thus does not refer to individuals or a group of individuals that are separate and distinct from those in 18a. It refers rather to certain individuals *within* the first, inclusive category. God has mercy on whom he wants to have mercy, i.e., he calls into his service whom he wants to call into his service; *but* some of these can serve his purposes only by being hardened. Thus it was with Pharaoh. God bestowed favor upon him by selecting him for a key role, but he could fill that role only by being hardened.

Only when we understand v. 18 thus can we see how this discussion really speaks to the issue raised in 9:1-5: how can God use Israel for his covenant purposes and at the same time condemn them? Is he being untrue to his word? No, because his original covenant with the nation did not guarantee salvation for individual Jews; *and* there is no inherent connection between service and salvation, as the example of Pharaoh shows. Thus the obvious and intended application of this whole section, 9:14-18, is to the nation

[51]"The mercy he shows does not determine salvation" (Lard, 308).

of Israel. God bestowed a temporal mercy upon them when he chose to use them in his redemptive plan, but he also hardened at least some of them (11:7,25) in reference to the role he wanted them to play. There is no inconsistency or contradiction here, either with Pharaoh or with Israel.

What is the nature of the *hardening* of which Paul speaks? This is obviously a reference to the OT teaching about Pharaoh, and to the fact that God used him in his service specifically by hardening his heart. The Greek word is σκληρύνω (*sklērynō*),[52] which means "to make firm, to harden." It can refer to something physical but is more often used figuratively for a hardened attitude or state of mind. In Scripture it usually refers to a hardened attitude toward God, an attitude of resistance and rebellion toward God's will. Also, in Scripture it is something that a person does to himself; hence the warnings in Hebrews to "not harden your hearts" (Heb 3:8,15; 4:7, quoting Ps 95:8). In the OT the Israelites are often accused of being stiff-necked, i.e., hardened in their hearts; and they are considered responsible for being in this state. See Deut 10:16; 2 Kgs 17:14; Neh 9:16-17,29; Jer 7:26; 17:23; 19:15.

The Exodus narrative refers to the hardening of Pharaoh's heart in various ways: (a) his heart "became hard" or "was hardened" (7:13,14,22; 8:19; 9:35; 13:15); (b) he hardened his own heart (8:15, 32; 9:34); (c) God promises to harden his heart (4:21; 7:3; 14:4); (d) God did harden his heart (9:12; 10:1,20,27; 11:10; 14:8). God also hardened the hearts of other Egyptian officials and soldiers (9:34; 10:1; 14:17).

Much is made of these different ways of speaking. It is assumed from them that the occasions when Pharaoh hardened his own heart are somehow distinct from those occasions when God hardened it. Then it is usually declared that Pharaoh's self-hardening preceded God's action. For example, Lenski says, "Ten times Exodus reports that Pharaoh hardened himself; then, only in consequence of this self-hardening, we read ten times that God hardened this self-hardened man" (617). Morris says that nowhere in Scripture "is God said to harden anyone who had not first hardened himself"

---

[52]A different but similar word, πωρόω (*pōroō*), is used in 11:7, and its cognate, πώρωσις (*pōrōsis*), in 11:25.

(361). "Harden your heart against God, and He will harden your heart," says Smith (2:19).

I believe this analysis is unnecessary and misleading. Throughout the series of encounters between Moses and Pharaoh, from beginning to end, God was working providentially to harden Pharaoh's heart. On every occasion where his heart was hardened, the hardening was accomplished by *both* God *and* Pharaoh. On each occasion it was Pharaoh who made the conscious and deliberate decision to not let the people go. But prior to this moment I suggest that God was working within Pharaoh's mental processes, causing such thoughts to enter his consciousness that he could not bear to grant or follow through with permission to let the people go. The following observation by Sherlock is relevant:

> Let a man be never so much bent upon any project, yet hope or fear, some present great advantage or great inconvenience, the powerful intercession of friends, a sudden change of circumstances, the improbability of success, the irreparable mischief of a defeat, and a thousand other considerations, will divert him from it; and how easy it is for God to imprint such thoughts upon men's minds with an irresistible vigour and brightness, that it shall be no more in their power to do what they had a mind to, than to resist all the charms of riches and honours, than to leap into the fire, and to choose misery and ruin (*Providence*, 51).

How did God harden Pharaoh's heart? Perhaps by flooding his mind with the kinds of thoughts to which Sherlock refers, i.e., what a great loss of free labor it will be to lose these Israelites! or what a laughing-stock the king of Egypt will be when other nations hear how a bunch of slaves had their way with him! Such thoughts would have great validity in the mind of Pharaoh, and God could have pressed them upon his consciousness at just the right time, i.e., when he was weakening and about to let the people go (GRu, 203).

While it is true that Pharaoh's heart was already self-hardened toward God in a general way before God hardened his heart, this was not in fact the *reason* why God worked this specific hardness upon him.[55] Many emphasize such a cause/effect connection, though,

[55]To declare that Pharaoh's self-hardening justified God's act of hardening, says Dunn, is a "rationalizing expediency" (2:555).

because they think God's hardening of Pharaoh's heart had something to do with his *salvation*. But the two are not causally related. Like any pagan unbeliever, Pharaoh had a heart that was self-hardened toward the true God (1:18-32), and God may already have confirmed him in that unbelief according to the principle implied in 1:24,26,28. But the divine hardening of Pharaoh in 9:18 is of a different kind. It is not about salvation as such; it is about how someone whose heart is already self-hardened by sin can in fact be fitted into God's cast of characters for working out his redemptive plan.

Thus we do not have to think of God's hardening of Pharaoh's heart as some kind of *punishment* for his sins. Such a view is very common, though. Morris says, "God's hardening follows on what Pharaoh himself did. His hardening always presupposes sin and is always part of the punishment of sin" (361). Murray says divine hardening always "presupposes ill-desert," i.e., a person so hardened deserves it because of his prior sin. "Hardening may never be abstracted from the guilt of which it is the wages" (2:29-30). Godet calls it "retribution" and "punishment" (355). See also Stott, 269; Lenski, 616.

This sort of thinking, however, is a serious misunderstanding of Paul's concept of hardening. It confuses the general self-hardening of rebellious unbelief with God's providential hardening in order to accomplish a specific temporal purpose. The hardening of Pharaoh, both in Exod 4:14 and here in 9:18, is of the latter type, not the former. It in fact had only one specific goal: to cause Pharaoh to oppose God's demand that he set the Israelites free. God expressed his purpose clearly: "I will harden his heart so that he will not let the people go" (Exod 4:21).

This particular hardening was not a natural consequence of Pharaoh's already rebellious heart, nor an act of divine retribution against him because of this rebellion. It did not cause him to be lost, nor did it somehow intensify his lostness. It simply brought him to a state of mind that resulted in his decision to forbid the Israelites to leave. This occurred over and over, which in turn allowed God to send plague after plague, which in turn accomplished the purposes stated by Paul: "that I might display my power in you and that my name might be proclaimed in all the earth" (9:17).

What this shows, in reference to Paul's overall point in Rom 9, is that God can call into his service someone who is lost (by his own choice), and can use him in a significant way even if that person's heart must be divinely hardened in some special manner. The ultimate application of this truth is to the nation of Israel. It demonstrates how God could take Israel, a nation comprised mostly of self-hardened sinners, and use them in their lost state to carry out his purposes. Paul's point is not to explain *why* such people are lost, but simply to affirm that God can use them even though they *are* lost.

The hardening of Pharaoh in 9:18 must not be equated with the general self-hardening that characterizes the lost state of every sinner. Nor is the hardening of Pharaoh necessarily the same as the hardening of Israel mentioned later (11:7,25), though they are of the same general type (i.e., a providential hardening that helps God carry out his purposes, rather than a hardening that causes them to be lost). That *God* has hardened Pharaoh, and even Israel, as part of his use of them, does not imply in any way that he has a hand in the hardening of sinners unto condemnation.

C. GOD USED ETHNIC ISRAEL TO PRODUCE SPIRITUAL ISRAEL (9:19-29)

We must remember that the main point in Rom 9–11 is the issue of God's faithfulness in his dealings with the nation of Israel. Despite their covenant privileges (9:4-5), the nation as a whole stands "cursed and cut off from Christ" (9:3). What does this imply, then, concerning God's commitment to Israel, and concerning his faithfulness to his word? Has he failed to keep his promises (9:6a)?

The reason why first-century Jews saw this as a problem was that they assumed that God's calling them into his covenant service guaranteed their final salvation. Paul is in the process of pointing out that this is a false assumption. Godet declares (373) that the Apostle's main concern in ch. 9 "is to destroy the false conclusion drawn by Israel from their special election, their law, their circumcision, their ceremonial works, their monotheism, their moral superiority. These were in their eyes so many bonds by which God was pledged to them beyond recall." But such was not the point of God's relation to Israel, says Paul.

But is not God the God of *salvation*? And is not salvation the inherent and ultimate purpose of the covenant with Israel? So how can God be true to his word and at the same time cut Israel off from this very salvation? The basic answer is that there are *two Israels* (9:6b). Israel the *physical* nation was God's main historical instrument or means for making salvation a reality (9:5); the Israel whose origin and essence is *spiritual* is the actual recipient of the salvation.

Paul develops this thought in two stages. First, in 9:7-18 the subject is physical Israel, Israel the nation. The Apostle sets forth the manner in which God elected this nation, and separated them from all the other nations of the world. By reminding them of the free and sovereign choices used to bring them into existence, he establishes God's sovereign right to choose and use them as he pleases. I.e., their election to covenant service was unconditional. God can use even the unbelieving and the hardened, as the example of Pharaoh shows.

But now in the second stage of this explanation, of which 9:19-29 is a part, the focus of attention is *spiritual* Israel, the group which is the recipient of God's saving mercy. A major point of this section is the fact that the calling and saving of spiritual Israel was all along a part of the very purpose for the existence of ethnic Israel. In other words, it has always been God's sovereign purpose to distinguish between the two Israels, as the remnant prophecies show (9:27-29). The *means* by which God distinguishes between them is explained in 9:30–10:21.

In summary, just as 9:7-18 explains how God separated physical Israel from the rest of the world, so does 9:19–10:21 explain how God separates spiritual Israel from physical Israel.

Here is how the present section (9:19-29) unfolds. First, by way of transition, Paul words an objection he anticipates from his Jewish readers (v. 19). His immediate response (vv. 20-21) is to issue a stern generic warning about how presumptuous it is for the creature (the clay) to challenge the ways of the Creator (the potter).

Applying the potter-clay analogy to the particular issue at hand, Paul then begins his specific reply to the objection in v. 19 by succinctly summing up God's purpose and intention for the two Israels (vv. 22-24). Like a potter, God has the right to take one lump of clay (the original nation of Israel) and make two completely different kinds of vases from it. One consists of those individuals who are Israelites by physical birth only. Like Pharaoh, they are unbelievers and will ultimately suffer the wrath of God. This is actually the bulk of Israel. So why does God put up with these "vessels of wrath"? Because only through them can he bring into existence the "vessels of mercy," i.e., spiritual Israel, which is the *church* – a group composed not only of believing Jews but of believing Gentiles as well.

In these three verses (22-24) is summed up one whole major aspect of the history and purpose of Israel. It is a supplement, as it were, to vv. 4-5.

To show that this is not some new and alien concept that he has hatched out of his own brain, Paul then cites prophecies from Hosea and Isaiah. These biblical texts show that this has been God's intention for Israel – and the Gentiles – all along (vv. 25-29). Dunn (2:575) points out that these verses turn on its head "Israel's belief that others were rejected in order that Israel might be chosen and redeemed." As the quotes from the prophets show, God's ultimate purpose was never physical Israel as such.

This does not end Paul's reply to the objection in v. 19, "Why does God still blame us?" Actually it only prepares the way for the main response to this question, which is given in 9:30–10:21. The curse upon physical Israel (9:3), and upon the individual Jews of which it is composed, is *not unconditional,* as if God were arbitrarily assigning some to eternal wrath. Nor are the individuals within spiritual Israel unconditionally elected to salvation. As 9:30–10:21 shows, the difference between the two Israels is *justification by faith.* Physical Israel, the vessels of wrath, are those who seek to be justified by their own righteousness, while spiritual Israel, the vessels of mercy, accept Christ's salvation through faith. This connection between 9:19 and 9:30–10:21 must not be missed.

This point *is* missed, of course, by those who think ch. 9 is a fundamental proof text for unconditional election. They find this doctrine especially in vv. 19-23, which they see as simply repeating the point of vv. 7-18. For example, speaking of vv. 14-23, Moo declares that "this text . . . gives further support (see Rom. 8:28-30) to the doctrine of unconditional election," and to some extent to the doctrine of reprobation as well (609). As Piper sees it, 9:14-23 deals specifically with unconditional election (*Justification,* 184). However, this approach hopelessly confuses two entirely distinct acts of God: one, his dealing with physical Israel in terms of unconditional election to service; and two, his way of distinguishing between physical Israel and spiritual Israel by the condition of faith.

It is important to see that in this present section (9:19-29), unlike in vv. 7-18, eternal destinies are now an important part of the picture, since the distinction between the two Israels has eternal consequences. But we must be careful not to apply the affirmations of God's sovereign, unconditional choice of the nation as such (vv. 7-18) to the respective eternal destinies of the individuals within the two groups.

In this paragraph, for the first time in this major section (chs. 9–11), Paul introduces the issue of the Gentiles. For some, the incorporation of the Gentiles into spiritual Israel is the key point of the paragraph. For example, Achtemeier (165) says, "The passage is therefore about the enlargement of God's mercy to include gentiles, not about the narrow and predetermined fate of each individual. We gentiles can now be part of his gracious purpose, we can be part of his people, chosen by grace through Christ Jesus. *That* is the point of this passage." Morris (363) says that this passage shows that God's work of showing mercy and hardening (v. 18) has been done "to extend his mercy to the Gentiles."

It is true that believing Gentiles are here identified as being included within the new Israel. Nevertheless, in my opinion, this is not a major point of the paragraph. The main emphasis here is still God's faithfulness in his dealings with physical Israel. I.e., his use of them has been in every way consistent with his stated purposes.

1. The Objection (9:19)

9:19 One of you will say to me: "Then why does God still blame us? For who resists his will?" At this point Paul anticipates an objection and directly addresses a representative of his audience, literally, "You [singular] will say to me therefore, 'Why does he still find fault?'" We immediately ask, find fault with whom? To whom is the objector referring?[54] To Pharaoh? Piper calls the objector Pharaoh's

[54]"Us" (NIV) is not in the original.

"advocate" (*Justification*, 186; see Lenski, 618). But this application seems too narrow. But Pharaoh might be seen as a representative of sinners in general, especially those who are thought to be unconditionally condemned to eternal hell. MacArthur applies it thus: "How can human beings . . . be blamed for their unbelief and sin, when their destiny has already been divinely determined?" (2:36; see Murray, 2:31). But this application is probably more inclusive than the questioner intends.

Who, then, is the objector? He is probably a typical first-century Jew. Forster and Marston say he is "obviously Hebrew" and call him "Paul's Pharisee critic" (*Strategy*, 80-81). These questions come from "the prejudiced mind of the Jew," says DeWelt (155). "It is an in-house Jewish argument," says Dunn (2:555). See also Fitzmyer, 568; Moo, 600.

The context supports this conclusion. In v. 20 Paul addresses the objector as "O man," using exactly the same Greek phrase with which he addressed the Jewish objector in 2:1 (see JC, 1:180). Also, the Greek word οὖν (*oun*, "then, therefore") shows that the objection grows out of the preceding discussion, especially what was said in vv. 15-18.[55] But these verses cannot be isolated from the total context, where the issue is the status of the Jewish nation as such. In 9:3 Paul clearly implies that the bulk of his physical brethren were under eternal condemnation, "cursed and cut off from Christ." He recognizes that the intervening references to God's unconditional decisions regarding mercy and hardening may cause some Jews to conclude that this explains why they were lost, even though this is not his point. This in turn generates their objection, which "runs thus: But, Paul, if God shows mercy to whom he will, and if he hardens whom he will, then it is he who has hardened us Jews in unbelief against the gospel. Why, then, does he still find fault with us, since he himself, according to your argument, has excluded us from blessedness, and made us unfit for mercy?" (MP, 402).

The word for "blame" (μέμφομαι, *memphomai*) includes the idea of "finding fault with" or "holding responsible for." I.e., how can God hold us responsible for our unbelief and therefore condemn us to hell (v. 3), if our hardening and therefore our unbelief are his

[55]See, e.g., Lenski, 619; Piper, *Justification*, 185; Stott, 270; Murray, 2:30-31.

own doing? Does this not all the more suggest that he is unjust (v. 14)?

In his second question – literally, "For who has resisted his will?" – the objector seeks to justify his first question by appealing to what seems to be an unassailable theological axiom: no one can resist the will of the sovereign God.[56] Has not Paul himself appealed to this very axiom in vv. 15 and 18? The word for "resist" is ἀνθίστημι (*anthistēmi*), which in the middle sense means "to resist, to oppose, to withstand, to go against, to set oneself against" (AG, 66). His "will" is βούλημα (*boulēma*), a word which means "counsel, intention, will, purpose."

But is it not possible for a free-will creature to resist or oppose God's will? Is this not the very essence of sin? Yes, if by "will" we mean God's *preceptive* will, i.e., his laws, his commandments, and even his desires. God's preceptive will can be rejected and thwarted by human beings. (See Matt 7:21; 23:37; Luke 7:30; Rom 2:18; 1 Tim 2:4; 2 Pet 3:9.)[57] But if we are talking about God's *purposive* will, i.e., his deliberate purposes and determinative decisions, then the answer is no, it is *not* possible for any human being to oppose, violate, or resist his will in this sense (Ps 33:11; Prov 19:21; Isa 14:27; John 6:40; Acts 2:23; 4:28; Eph 1:11).[58]

In 9:19 the objector's questions seem to have the latter aspect of God's will in mind, and so the objection does involve a valid theological truth, i.e., no one has ever truly resisted God's purposive will. But if this is the case, then why is God blaming *us* for our sin and rebellion against him? If "he hardens whom he wants to harden" (9:18), then our sin and rebellion are actually *his* will, are they not? So why is he punishing us as if we were *resisting* his will, when in reality we are not – since no one can? (See Cranfield, 2:489; Piper, *Justification*, 186).

A crucial issue at this point is whether or not the objection is valid in the sense that it correctly and accurately represents the

[56]The verb is in the perfect tense and literally reads "has resisted," but it is usually taken in the present sense,"resists." See Cranfield, 2:490. The implication, though, is that such resistance is impossible: no one *can* resist his will.

[57]See GRu, 310-313.

[58]Ibid., 304-310.

meaning of Paul's teaching in the previous verses. Is this a legitimate conclusion to draw from vv. 15-18? Many say that it is. Piper declares, "I have assumed with most commentators that the objection in Rom 9:19 is based on a sound interpretation of 9:18. That is, Paul agrees with the objector that no one can resist God's will and that nevertheless God still finds fault" (*Justification*, 189). Certainly if the objection was based on a misunderstanding, then "Paul would very simply have set the objector straight and removed the bogus stumbling block" (190). But as it is Paul "does not give the slightest trace of disagreement with the objector's interpretation of Rom 9:18" (191). Dunn agrees: "The question is a legitimate one, and Paul's response indicates that he does not dispute its logic: the objector has not misunderstood the thrust of vv. 17-18 . . . , and Paul does not attempt to deny its force" (2:555-556).

I have concluded that this approach is incorrect. As Lard says, "God does not do what is here ascribed to him" (309). I agree with Forster and Marston that "the question of Paul's critic . . . is based on a flagrant misrepresentation of Paul's teaching" (*Strategy*, 80).

Wherein lies the error? First, we should emphasize that it does not lie in the objector's second question, "For who has resisted [resists, can resist] his will?" As noted above, there is such a thing as God's *purposive* will, his eternal purpose which is irresistible and immutable, and which therefore cannot be opposed by mere creatures. This is God's "deliberate purpose" (SH, 259), his "determinate purpose" and "irresistible decree" (Murray, 2:31), his "effectual will" or "will of decree" (Piper, *Justification*, 192).

Wherein, then, is the error? The objector's misunderstanding was in assuming that this purposive will of God applied to Israel's salvation status (9:3) as well as to the nation's historical role in accomplishing God's redemptive plan. To say it another way, the objector took Paul's statements in vv. 15-18 as explaining why most Israelites were hardened to the point of rejecting their Messiah and thus being cursed. However, as we have seen, this is not Paul's point. In these verses he is affirming God's right to sovereignly choose and use anyone, even sinners, to serve his covenant purposes, and even to harden them with regard to certain decisions if this is necessary.

Calvinist interpreters and theologians commit the same sort of error. While correctly distinguishing between God's preceptive and purposive wills, they err in assuming that the latter is *all-inclusive*. I.e., they conclude that everything that ever happens, *period*, has been decreed to happen by God's purposive (secret, determinative, decretive, efficacious) will. This especially includes every individual's choice to believe or not to believe in God's saving promises. See my explanation and critique of this in GRu, 169-173, 301-310, especially the section on Eph 1:11 (306-309). This concept of an eternal, comprehensive, efficacious, unconditional, irresistible decree is simply not a biblical teaching; it finds no support in Rom 9.

One reason why interpreters assume that the objector must have understood Paul correctly is that they conclude that the Apostle does not try to refute the objection; he simply rebukes the objector for his presumptuous attitude.[59] But this is simply not true, as I have explained in the introduction to this section. Paul does rebuke the questioner (20-21), and he does reaffirm and explain God's inviolable purposive will for Israel the nation (22-29). But then (9:30–10:21) he sets forth a lengthy reply to the objector's first question, "Then why does God still blame us?" The reply, in effect, is simply this: "Because you refused to believe in your own Messiah." The attempt to excuse such unbelief by illegitimately applying God's purposive will to this circumstance is thereby repudiated.

2. Paul's Initial Rebuke of the Objector's Attitude (9:20-21)

These two verses are not a specific response to the objection worded in v. 19, nor are they meant to preclude such a response. They are only a preface to the more detailed response which follows. As a rebuke, they are directed more toward the tone of the objection than its content. The rebuke is actually generic and may be applied to many a presumptuous and misguided complaint against God's purposes and providence.

---

[59]See the statements by Dunn and Piper, above. "Paul anticipates the questions his reader will ask, but he does not answer them," says Morris (364). Even non-Calvinists sometimes think this is so: Paul "takes no notice of the man's question" (Lard, 309); the "untrue misrepresentation" is "passed over without detailed refutation" (Forster and Marston, *Strategy*, 81).

9:20 But who are you, O man, to talk back to God? In the NIV, "but" translates a much stronger Greek expression better rendered "on the contrary," as in the NASB. This indicates that Paul is about to correct the erroneous thinking by which the objector seeks to justify himself: "Hey, it's not *my* fault! God made me do it. So why should I be blamed?" "On the contrary," says Paul; "you have missed the whole point. Let me explain it to you."[60]

In view of this expression – "on the contrary" – it is strange that Dunn should say that Paul does not dispute the objector's logic (2:555), and that Piper should say that Paul "does not give the slightest trace of disagreement with the objector's interpretation of Rom 9:18" (*Justification*, 191). If 9:19 embodied a misunderstanding, says Piper, then "Paul would very simply have set the objector straight" (190). Well, the fact is that this is exactly what Paul *is* doing in the rest of ch. 9 and in all of ch. 10!

The first part of Paul's correction (vv. 20-21) is directed toward the objector's presumptuous attitude; the Apostle rebukes him for arguing with God. We must realize that the objector is not portrayed as simply raising a sincere question concerning God's ways as does Habakkuk (1:1-4,12-13), and as 9:14 seems to do. Rather, the man is described as arrogantly taking a debater's stance against God; he is "talking back" to God, says Paul. The word for "talk back" has strongly negative connotations, including "to make unjustified accusations," "to dispute" (Büchsel, "κρίνω," 945). It has a "nuance of contention," as Moo says (602). Compare 3:1-8.

The objector is addressed as "O man." This seems to be a way of emphasizing his mere creaturehood, in contrast with the all-powerful and all-knowing Creator. "Who are you, a mere *human being*, a 'feeble morsel of sinful dust' (MP, 403), to argue against *God*?" "By thus setting man over against God, Paul is certainly putting man in his place" (Cranfield, 2:490).

"Shall what is formed say to him who formed it, 'Why did you make me like this?'" The NIV puts this question in quotation marks because it represents the thought of Isa 29:16 and Isa 45:9, where the clay and the vessel made from it are likewise depicted as

[60]The same expression (μενοῦν γε, *menoun ge*) is used in 10:18 to introduce a correction. There the NIV translates it, "Of course they did."

sitting in judgment on the potter. As Paul uses the metaphor in v. 20b, the complaint comes not from the clay as such but from the piece of pottery formed from it. The scene is almost comical: a finished pot is lifted from the potter's wheel and, personified, looks upon itself with disappointment. It then glares accusingly at the potter and reprimands him thus: "Why did you make me to look like this? I'm a mess! Is this the best you could do? Haven't you made some sort of mistake?"

The potter-clay analogy can be used to teach many lessons (see Job 10:8-9; Isa 64:8; Jer 18:1-12), and we are rightly warned to stick to the point Paul is making here and not to try to apply all the details indiscriminately (Cranfield, 2:491). What is Paul's point? Just this: in a potter-clay relationship it is obviously the potter who decides how the clay will be used. Once his decision is made and the vessel has been formed, it is the height of absurdity and arrogance for the vessel to criticize the potter.

Why does Paul use this metaphor here? To what or whom does it specifically apply? Not to the original creation event (contra Achtemeier, 161; Dunn, 2:564-565); not just to individuals such as Pharaoh; and especially not to "the destinies of individual men" (contra Piper, *Justification*, 193). Its specific application is to the nation of Israel. This is how the analogy is used in Jeremiah: "Then the word of the LORD came to me: 'O house of Israel, can I not do with you as this potter does?' declares the Lord. 'Like clay in the hand of the potter, so are you in my hand, O house of Israel'" (Jer 18:5-6). Even the thought in Isa 29:16 and 45:9-10 is "that God formed Israel into a nation," says Morris (365).

Thus Paul is rebuking the objector of v. 19 not in the latter's role as a creature nor as a condemned sinner as such, but in his role as a representative of Israel who is complaining that God's treatment of the nation is basically unfair. To such an objection Paul simply says, "Whoa! Let's not forget who we are, shall we? Remember: God is the potter; you (Israel) are just clay in his hands. Who do you think you are, to challenge the one who formed you in the first place?"

9:21 Does not the potter have the right to make out of the same lump of clay some pottery for noble purposes and some for common use? While Paul's reference to the potter and the clay in

v. 20 was somewhat general, here he gets more specific. He refers to the potter's right and authority to do with the clay (Israel) whatever he chooses, particularly to his right to make from the same lump the two Israels of 9:6b.

This verse begins with the word "or" (ἤ [*ē*], untranslated in the NIV). Here it has the force of "to put it another way." Whereas the question in v. 20b has the Greek particle that shows a negative answer is expected ("Shall what is formed say . . . ? Of course not!"), v. 21 has the particle indicating that the answer is "Yes!" Thus it is the same as an affirmation.

The basic affirmation is the potter's authority over the clay. He, not the clay, has the right to decide how the latter will be used. And since this is where the authority lies, the clay itself has no basis for uttering a complaint such as "Why did you make me like this?" (v. 20b). And if a mere potter has this right, how much more does the sovereign God!

It is obvious that the potter here represents God, but to whom does the "same lump" refer? A common assumption is that it refers to the human race in general (Lard, 310; MP, 404), the "mass of humanity" (Moo, 603), "the same mass of human beings" (Hendriksen, 2:327), the "same human clay" (Lenski, 621; Dunn, 2:565). Understood thus, this verse is often taken as confirming the Calvinist concept of predestination, especially the twofold predestination of some sinners to heaven (election) and others to hell (reprobation). As Lenski says (620), "Calvinism assumes that the whole story as to why some are saved and others are lost is figuratively described in this verse." An example is this statement by Hendriksen (2:327):

> The main idea Paul is putting across is this: If even a potter has the right out of the same lump or mass of clay to make one vessel for honor, and another for dishonor, then certainly God, our Maker, has the right, out of the same mass of human beings who by their own guilt have plunged themselves into the pit of misery, to elect some to everlasting life, and to allow others to remain in the abyss of wretchedness.

Thus this "same lump" would refer not to the dust from which God made the two kinds of human beings, but to the mass of "fallen humanity" (Stott, 271), some of whom God chooses to save and others he chooses to condemn.[61]

In my judgment this approach is a serious error. In keeping with the overall context, the "same lump" here refers not to the mass of human individuals as such but to the totality of Israel, from which God makes the two derivative groups, physical Israel and spiritual Israel. As Smith rightly says (2:20), "Israel as a nation, is in the hand of God as a potter holds clay." Smith reminds us of Jer 18:1-12, where the clay in the potter's hand is the people of Israel.

From the same lump of clay, says Paul, the potter has the right to make pieces of pottery that are very different in their nature and disposition. On the one hand he can make from it a vessel εἰς τιμήν (*eis timēn*), "unto honor"; on the other hand he can make from it a vessel εἰς ἀτιμίαν (*eis atimian*), "unto dishonor."

This statement raises some key issues. First, how are these terms – honor and dishonor – related to each other? One approach is to take them in a comparative sense: one vessel is given more honor, the other less honor. This is the point of the NIV: some "for noble purposes and some for common use." It is the difference between exalted use and menial use, says Fitzmyer (569). As Lenski says (620), one vessel might be a beautiful ornamental vase, and the other "a slop jar" (a chamber pot). Both are useful, but for very different purposes (see 2 Tim 2:20).

The other approach is to take the terms *timē* and *atimia* in their more natural sense as *opposites* rather than as comparatives. Though the latter sense for these terms is possible (as in 2 Tim 2:20), such a relationship would more naturally be expressed with the comparative adjectival form, as in 1 Cor 12:23 (ἀτιμότερα, *atimotera*, "less honorable"). Also, if the vessels unto honor and unto dishonor in v. 21 are equivalent to the vessels of mercy and vessels of wrath in vv. 22-23, then they must be taken in an opposite and not just a comparative sense. This is also more in keeping with the actual meaning of the words. *Timē* means "honor, value, respect, worthiness"; *atimia* means "dishonor, contempt, shame, disgrace" (On the latter see Hübner, "ἄτιμος," 177.)

[61]"Paul is not now dealing with God's sovereign right over men as men but over men as sinners" (Murray, 2:32).

In my opinion the terms should be regarded as opposites, and the NIV is thus misleading.

This leads to the second and more overriding issue, namely, do these terms refer to God's creation of all individuals for the specific purpose of saving some ("for noble purposes") and sending the rest to hell ("for common use")? Or do they refer to God's preparation of some individuals and even some nations for specific uses in the accomplishment of his historical plan of salvation? Those taking the former view naturally see the terms *timē* and *atimia* as opposites; advocates of the latter view see them as comparative.

Calvinists argue for the former view. The terms refer to "the eternal destinies of individuals," says Moo. "Honor" means the eternal glory of the saved; "dishonor" means the eternal wrath suffered by the lost (603). God deliberately designs and forms individuals for these purposes. The evidence shows that v. 21 is "a reference to the predestining of individuals to their respective eternal destinies," says Piper (*Justification*, 202; see 200-204). The emphasis of the verse is upon God's sovereign right (as a potter) to do this.

Others, especially non-Calvinists, argue for the latter view, i.e., that God like a potter has prepared various vessels to be used in comparatively more honorable and less honorable ways for his covenant purposes. The emphasis is on God's sovereign right to form and use individuals and nations – particularly the latter – in this way. According to Dunn, "the more natural sense of the metaphor is of vessels put to differing uses within history" (2:557). "The vessels are nations" (MP, 404).

Those who take this latter view especially insist that eternal destinies are not in view, and that "dishonor" does not mean destruction or damnation (Fitzmyer, 569; Lard, 310; DeWelt, 156). Vessels "unto dishonor" are simply those chosen or appointed by God to carry out certain lesser tasks involved in salvation history. Just as a potter "never makes pots simply in order to destroy them" says Morris, so also "it would not be right for God to create sinners simply in order to punish them." But with regard to "the working out of the divine purpose," God certainly has the right to make certain vessels, such as Pharaoh and unbelieving Jews, for menial or "dishonorable" uses (366).

Cranfield agrees that the proper conclusion to be drawn from this verse is that God is free "to appoint men to various functions in the on-going course of salvation-history for the sake of the fulfilment of His over-all purpose" (2:492). See Moo, 602-603.

I cannot accept either of these two views. I do agree that the main reference here is to the nation of Israel, and not to the human race as such. But at the same time I believe Paul is referring not to how God used this nation in his historical plan, but to the eternal destinies of individuals within it.

It is unlikely that the point here is simply God's right to prepare and use individuals and nations – especially Israel – for his covenant purposes, because Paul has already made this point in vv. 7-18. An even more convincing reason, though, is the use of the word *atimia*, or "dishonor." The source and nature of the objection worded in v. 19 indicates that Paul is addressing here in vv. 20-21 the status of unbelieving Jews; thus the terms "honor" and "dishonor" must apply in some way to this group. Most who take the latter view outlined above would see unfaithful Israel as an example of a "vessel of dishonor" (e.g., Morris, 366).

My contention, though, is this: if this verse applies only to the way God *uses* nations, especially Israel, for his historical redemptive plan, there is *no way* that the role of Israel – believing or unbelieving – can be described as dishonorable or even menial. The term *atimia*, however interpreted, simply does not fit the use God made of the nation of Israel. Theirs was indeed the most exalted and honorable role imaginable, apart from that of the Messiah himself (9:4-5). Thus this interpretation of v. 21 cannot stand.

What, then, is the alternative? I believe Calvinists are right to see "honor" and "dishonor" as referring to eternal destinies, heaven and hell. But I believe they are wrong on two counts. First, they are wrong to assume that the "clay" refers to the human race in general. The clay is not the mass of humanity, but the nation of Israel only. Second, Calvinists are wrong to think that God made two separate vessels from this clay for the express purpose of sending one to heaven and the other to hell. "Unto honor" and "unto dishonor" do indeed refer to the eternal destinies of individuals within Israel, but these respective destinies are not determined by God himself. The next main section, 9:30–10:21, shows that individuals determine their own eternal destinies according to whether or not they put their trust in God's saving promises.

This distinction applies even to the people of Israel. God used the nation in its totality to accomplish his exalted redemptive purposes, and this honor belongs to believing and unbelieving Jews alike. But with regard to eternal destinies, God has exercised his sovereign right, like a potter, to make an internal separation among the individuals of whom this nation is composed. He makes from the one lump a vessel of honor, *spiritual Israel,* whose distinguishing characteristic is faith in God's gracious promises. Also from this same lump he makes a vessel of dishonor, the majority of the original nation, whose distinguishing characteristic is that, even though they are Jews physically, they have never given their hearts to God. As Forster and Marston say, "God obviously has the right to make from the nation of Israel two vessels rather than one, just as a potter can divide one lump and make two pots. This is, in fact, what God has done. The unrepentant portion of Israel has become a **vessel unto dishonor**, and the faithful part a **vessel unto honor**" (*Strategy*, 82).

A key point here is that this distinction between the vessel of honor and the vessel of dishonor, though decreed by God, is ultimately the responsibility of the individuals placed within each group. As Forster and Marston say, "The basic lump that forms a nation will either be built up or broken down by the Lord, *depending on their own moral response*" (ibid.). This view is supported by Jer 18:1-12, where God compares his relationship with Israel as that of potter to clay. "'Like clay in the hand of the potter, so are you in my hand, O house of Israel'" (18:6b). But God makes it clear that this potter-clay relationship does not mean that he arbitrarily determines the destiny of the nation. He declares that he tailors his final decision regarding any nation or kingdom to the way it responds to his warnings (18:7-12; see Smith, 2:20). In his role as a potter, God's method of dealing with nations must surely also apply to his dealing with individuals.

We should remember that the main point of vv. 20-21 is to rebuke the objector in v. 19 for his presumptuousness in talking back to God. The metaphor of the potter and his clay is a generic warning applicable to anyone who presumes to do the same in any sort of circumstance. We know that Paul intends that it be applied to Israel in the way explained above because of the way he himself continues the metaphor in vv. 22-24.

3. Beyond Ethnic Israel to Spiritual Israel (9:22-24)

In these next three verses Paul begins his specific response to the objection in v. 19. Basically he grants the objector's second point, that no one truly resists God's purposive will. This is surely true regarding Israel. Undeterred by massive unbelief, yea, even enduring it, God used this nation to accomplish his intended purpose for them.

That purpose first and foremost was to bring the Messiah himself into the world (9:5). But that is not the whole story. In these three verses Paul reveals another purpose for which God was using the nation of Israel: through them he brought into existence the other Israel, the true Israel, spiritual Israel, the remnant (9:6b). And here he mentions for the first time in this chapter the fact that believing *Gentiles* are also included within this spiritual Israel, the entity for which it was the glorious purpose of physical Israel to prepare.

In its fulness, then, spiritual Israel is no less than the church of Jesus Christ, which is composed of believing Jews and believing Gentiles, i.e., of anyone who accepts Jesus as Savior and Lord. It was God's *purposive* will to use ethnic Israel as an instrument for bringing forth the church. In this respect the objector is correct: no one could have resisted God's purpose to do this.

But the objector erred in thinking that this same principle ("Who resists his will?") was the explanation for Israel's state of accursedness (9:3). As Paul will explain in the next section (9:30–10:21), the reason for their condemnation was their resistance to God's *preceptive* will, i.e., that believing submission to Jesus Christ is a requirement for salvation.

The tragic irony of this, of course, is that most Israelites were lost because they refused to become a part of the very group whose origin was a major reason for their own existence.

As the following discussion will show, the Calvinist attempt to use these verses in their effort to find unconditional election in Rom 9 is futile. These verses are not, contrary to Piper, "Paul's final insight into the whys and wherefores of unconditional election" (*Justification*, 187).

This section is difficult to understand and translate because, even though the syntax is quite extended and complicated, it does not form a complete sentence. Verse 22 begins with the word "if," seemingly introducing a protasis, or first part of a conditional sentence. The problem is that the expected second part of such a sentence, the "then" part (apodosis), never appears. This sort of construction does occur occasionally in classical Greek and in a few other places in the NT, and it requires that the overall sense of the sentence be discerned from the context. (See Cranfield, 2:492-493.)

There is a fairly general agreement that the NIV captures the intended sense very well: "What if . . . ?" (See KJV; NASB; NRSV; Dunn, 2:558, 566; Moo, 604; Morris, 367.) The main clause following the "what if" is "God . . . endured" (v. 22; NIV, "bore"), which is then followed by a purpose clause, "in order that" (v. 23; NIV, "to"). I.e., Paul asks, "What if God endured this, in order that he might accomplish that?" Specifically, "What if God endured the vessels of wrath, in order that he might bring forth vessels of mercy?"

In any case the "if" does not mean that Paul is expressing an uncertain hypothesis here; he is stating a fact (Cranfield, 2:493). How does this relate to the objection in v. 19? The thought seems to be this: "What if it is so, in accordance with his role as a potter, that God sovereignly forms the nation of Israel and bears with their unfaithfulness in order to accomplish his purpose for them? So what if it is true, as you say, that no one can resist his will in this matter? Does this explain and excuse your sin? Does this shift responsibility for your condemnation to God? No!"

9:22-23 What if God, choosing to show his wrath and make his power known, bore with great patience the objects of his wrath — prepared for destruction? What if he did this to make the riches of his glory known to the objects of his mercy, whom he prepared in advance for glory . . . ?

Verse 22 begins with a particle, δέ (*de*), which the NIV does not translate. Here it introduces not a contrast but rather a more specific explanation and application of the potter-clay illustration (Moo, 604). It can be rendered "Now," in the sense of "Now, what does this mean?"

These verses form a single unit of thought, a thought which can be discerned only by working through a series of very difficult exegetical questions: Who are the "objects of his wrath"? In what sense are they "prepared for destruction"? In what sense does God *choose* to show his wrath? The word for "choosing" is a participle; what is its sense? What are the nature and purpose of God's patience? Who are the "objects of his mercy"? How are they "prepared in advance for glory"?

The Calvinist View

As is the case with most of chapter 9, there is a way of interpreting these verses and answering these questions that can only be called the Calvinist view. Unfortunately this Calvinist approach, though widely represented in the commentaries, is at odds with Paul's meaning at every step of the way. I will show this by first setting forth the Calvinist view in some detail, and then by explaining what I believe is the correct understanding of these verses. The exegetical issues will be discussed in detail in the latter part of this process.

The Calvinist interpretation is as follows. As to the scope of Paul's remarks, it is assumed that he is dealing here with the human race in general. The "objects of wrath" are the reprobate, the total number of lost human beings (Calvin, 367; Hendriksen, 2:328), the "world of sinners" (MacArthur, 2:40). Pharaoh may be particularly in mind, "yet he serves as the type of all other vessels of wrath" (Piper, *Justification*, 187).[62]

The reprobate are lost because they were from the beginning "prepared for destruction" by God himself; they were "made and formed for this end" (Calvin, 368). "Before they are born they are destined to their lot" (Calvin, 370), and so destined by "the divine agency" (Piper, *Justification*, 213). Moo agrees: "Paul considers the 'vessels on whom God's wrath rests' as prepared by God himself for eternal condemnation"; those who reject God's mercy "do so ultimately because God himself hardens them" (607-608).

God determines to create a certain amount of human beings as objects of wrath simply as a decision of his secret, purposive will (which is the implication of the word "choosing" in the NIV). Calvinists usually speak of two types or levels of God's will: his

[62]Non-Calvinists may occasionally take the "objects of wrath" to be "all the wicked" (Lard, 312); so this is not an exclusively Calvinist view, though I believe it is incorrect.

revealed, expressed will and his secret, ultimate will. Things do not always happen according to the former, but the latter is all-inclusive and all-determinative (see GRu, 301-310). That some are "prepared for destruction" is simply the result of "the secret and inexplorable counsel of God" (Calvin, 369).

This determinative counsel by which God fixes "the perdition of the reprobate" is "secret" and "incomprehensible," says Calvin (367). God is simply "silent as to the reason, why they are vessels appointed to destruction"; "the reason is hid" in his secret counsel (368-369). But it seems that it is not hidden very well, because Calvin and others believe that in v. 22 Paul is telling us the reason why God prepares some for destruction, i.e., "to show his wrath and make his power known." Because he wants to display his wrath and power in punishing the wicked, God assigns some to eternal condemnation in hell. These unfortunate ones are "vessels of wrath, that is, made and formed for this end, that they may be examples of God's vengeance and displeasure" (Calvin, 368; see Murray, 2:33; Cranfield, 2:494). This is why God "determined to allow sin," says MacArthur, "because it gave Him the opportunity to display His wrath" (2:39).

Even God's *patience*, i.e., his delay in exercising his wrath, is designed to make the ultimate expression of that wrath all the more powerful and glorious. Calvin says that "the Lord bears patiently for a time with these, not destroying them at the first moment, but deferring the judgment prepared for them, and this in order to set forth the decisions of his severity, that others may be terrified by so dreadful examples" (368). That is, the very reason for this "patience" is to magnify his wrath. Moo favors this interpretation: "In the case both of Pharaoh and of the vessels of wrath, God withholds his final judgment so that he can more spectacularly display his glory" (605). As Stott says, "His forebearance in delaying the hour of judgment" is designed to "make the ultimate outpouring of his wrath the more dreadful" (272). In Piper's words, "God sustains and tolerates vessels of wrath" so that his "sovereign power and terrible wrath can be demonstrated even more vividly" (*Justification*, 187).

But this is not the whole story. Verse 23 adds another reason why God "bore with great patience the objects of his wrath." He did it in order "to make the riches of his glory known" to the elect, which are chosen unconditionally for salvation. As Calvin interprets it, this means that God delays punishing the reprobate, thus increasing their punishment, because the greater the punishment poured out upon the reprobate, the greater will appear the mercy bestowed upon the elect. God wants his wrath to appear dreadful so "that the amplitude of his mercy towards the elect may hence be more fully known and more brightly shine forth" (368). "The glory of God" is manifest "in the destruction of the reprobate, because the greatness of divine mercy towards the elect is hereby more clearly made known" (369). "The infinite mercy of God toward the elect must appear increasingly worthy of praise, when we see how miserable are all they who escape not his wrath" (369). See Hendriksen, 2:329; and Piper, *Justification*, 188-189, for variations of this view.

Seeing Paul Through Non-Calvinist Eyes

Since Calvinists tend to see this entire chapter in terms of the unconditional predestination of individuals to their eternal destinies, it is not unexpected that they interpret these two verses as outlined above. But as we have seen, unconditional individual election and reprobation are not the point of this chapter. It deals rather with God's faithfulness in all his dealings with the nation of Israel. That is the subject of these two verses as well.

One point that Paul has stressed throughout this chapter is that God has the sovereign right to choose and use both individuals and nations in whatever ways he pleases for the accomplishment of his covenant purposes. No one "resists his will" in such matters (v. 19). These verses are simply reaffirming God's right, like a potter, to manipulate his clay in any way he chooses.

The "objects of his wrath" in v. 22 are not the total mass of lost human beings, but rather the nation of Israel, specifically the ethnic Jews who rejected God's promises of grace and were thus accursed (9:3). (The word translated "objects" is actually the word "vessels," as in v. 21, where the NIV translates it "pottery".) I.e., these unbelieving Israelites, viewed collectively as a nation, in spite of their indispensable role in God's plan, are nevertheless indeed the objects of his wrath (see Godet, 360). While allowing that pagans such as Pharaoh may be included, Dunn declares "that the 'objects of wrath' are the covenant people themselves, or more precisely, the bulk of the covenant people who have rejected the continuity/fulfillment of the covenant in the gospel" (2:567).

What is the "destruction" for which Israel has been prepared? It is possible that Paul is thinking about some sort of temporal destruction, such as the termination of Israel's special role in the plan of God as signified by the destruction of Jerusalem in A.D. 70 (Godet, 360). This may be the case, but it is also likely that Paul is referring to the final, eternal destruction of sinners in hell, since its counterpart of "glory" in v. 23 also likely includes eternal life (see Dunn, 2:560; Moo, 607, n. 96; Godet, 362, 372; MP, 406). "Clearly it stands for the ultimate loss," says Morris (368).

Who, then, is the agent by which these vessels of wrath, these unbelieving Jews, are "prepared" for such destruction, whether temporal or eternal? The difference between the term used here in v. 22 and the comparable term in v. 23 ("he prepared in advance") makes it very likely (contrary to Calvinism) that *they prepared themselves* for such destruction (Godet, 361; MP, 406). The verb in v. 23 is active and has the prefix *pro-*, and clearly means that God himself prepared in advance the vessels of mercy for glory. But in v. 22 the verb seems to be deliberately different. It is either passive voice: "they were prepared," or (more likely) middle voice: "they prepared themselves" (AG, 419). I.e., they are responsible for their own destruction; by their sin and unbelief and refusal to repent, they sealed their own doom. Even if the agent of preparation were God himself, the lack of the prefix *pro-* ("in advance, beforehand"),[63] unlike the verb in v. 23, would suggest that God prepared them for destruction only after they manifested their adamant unbelief. The more likely meaning, though, is that they prepared themselves.

The "objects [vessels] of his wrath," then, are ethnic Israel, viewed in terms of its unbelief. Like a potter God made the nation as such for his glorious purposes, which they did indeed fulfill. But in reference to their individual eternal destiny, the Jews' personal unbelief makes them the objects of divine wrath. Thus they ultimately become vessels of dishonor and shame (v. 21).

---

[63]This same verb does appear with the prefix *pro-* in 2 Cor 9:5.

Exactly what is Paul saying about these vessels of wrath prepared for ultimate destruction? He says that God "bore" or "endured" them "with great patience." This refers to God's relationship with his chosen people throughout OT history, especially to the fact that he refrained from completely destroying them despite their blatant and repeated idolatry. As Dunn says (2:558), "God's patience with his chosen people was one of Israel's most common refrains." See Exod 34:6; Num 14:18-20; 2 Kgs 13:23; Neh 9:16-19,29-31; Ps 86:15; 102:8.

This next point is crucial to our understanding of this whole section. The question is, what is meant by the expression, "choosing to show his wrath and make his power known"? As we have seen, Calvinists usually take this as referring to God's infallible, purposive will: because God has determined (chosen) to display his wrath and power upon the objects of wrath whom he has prepared for destruction, he patiently withholds this wrath until the time comes when it can be exhibited in its most spectacular intensity. I.e., he exercises patience in the interests of greater wrath. In my judgment this interpetation is atrociously inaccurate and is an insult to the mercy and grace of God. What does the expression mean, then?

First of all, "choosing" is an unacceptable translation for the verb θέλω (*thelō*), used here by Paul. Basically it means "to will, to be willing, to want, to desire, to wish." The object of the desire may become a reality (9:18), or it may not (7:15-21; Matt 23:37a). It certainly does not have the inherent connotation of the purposive will of God, contrary to many Calvinists. Also, Lard's "determining" is too strong a meaning (313). At this point Paul is simply saying that God *was willing* or *wanted* to show his wrath and power against Israel.

A second point is that the form of *thelō* is a present participle, indicating that this "wanting" is simultaneous with the action of the main verb, "bore." But the very nature of a participle requires that we determine from the context just how it relates to the main verb. Here it appears that the participle has either a *causal* or a *concessive* relationship with "bore." I.e., it means either, (1) "*Because* he was willing to show his wrath and make his power known, *therefore* he bore with great patience the objects of his wrath"; or, (2) "*Although* he wanted to show his wrath and make his power known, *nevertheless* he bore with great patience the objects of his wrath." For the latter, see the NASB.

In general, Calvinists accept the causal view; see Cranfield, 2:493-494; Murray, 2:34-35; Piper, *Justification*, 187; Moo, 605 (see also Dunn, 2:558). I.e., *because* God wants to display his wrath as impressively as possible, he patiently withholds it until he can do this. Likewise in general, non-Calvinists accept the concessive view; see Godet, 359-360; Lard, 312; Fitzmyer, 569 (see also SH, 261). I.e., *even though* God actually wanted to go ahead and abolish the nation of Israel and send unbelieving Israelites to hell, still he bore with them in order to achieve his ultimate saving purposes.

Is it possible to tell from Scripture itself which of these two views is correct? Yes. The key to the right understanding here is the reference to "patience" ("forebearance, longsuffering"; Greek, μακροθυμία [*makrothymia*]). Paul says that God bore (endured, put up with) the vessels of wrath – not with just a little patience, but with *great* patience. Why? According to the causal interpretation of *thelō*, accepted by Calvinists, God exercises his patience toward the vessels of wrath for the express purpose of being able to heap even greater wrath upon them.[64] On the contrary, however, I must insist that such a purpose is contrary to the very nature of patience. At the very heart of patience is the desire to decrease or even eliminate wrath, and to increase salvation.[65] The Calvinist (causal) view thus violates the very essence of divine patience.[66] The concessive view does not, as will be explained below.

This theological weakness of the Calvinist view was pointed out long ago by Godet. He says (359), "The connection expressed by *because* . . . would signify that God's long-suffering had no other

---

[64]Other purposes may be identified in addition to this, but this is the one specifically named in the *thelō* clause, according to Calvinists.

[65]Piper asks whether there is "any evidence that *makrothymia* could mean patiently holding back judgment with a view to a greater display of wrath and power." The only examples he can cite are from the Apocrypha (4 Ezra 7:72-74; 2 Macc 6:12-14). See *Justification*, 209-210.

[66]Some try to identify both increased wrath *and* opportunity for repentance as the dual purpose of patience (see Stott, 272; Moo, 606). But these are contradictory as *purposes*. If the former is a purpose for patience, then the latter may be a result but not an accompanying purpose.

end than to bring about an accumulation of wrath; but would such long-suffering deserve the name?" Sanday and Headlam (261) likewise point out that God's "great patience" is simply not consistent with the causal view. (See also Fitzmyer, 569.) Romans 2:4 expressly says that God's kindness and patience are designed to lead to repentance. Second Peter 3:9 says that God is patient because he does not want anyone to perish but for everyone to come to repentance. The Calvinist view of 9:22 makes a travesty of such texts.

Thus the *cause* of God's great patience cannot be found in v. 22. This verse simply asserts the reality of this patience: *even though* God many times wanted to pour out his wrath upon idolatrous and unbelieving Israel, and bring upon them the destruction they deserved, he bore with them with great patience. *Why* he did so is stated only in v. 23.[67]

The terse syntax in vv. 22-23 causes most translators to add a few words at the beginning of v. 23 in order to clarify the connection between the two verses: "And He did so . . ." (NASB); "What if he did this . . ." (NIV); "And what if he has done so . . ." (NRSV). These words are added to show that, while v. 22 states God's action (he "bore with great patience"), v. 23 sets forth the *purpose* for this action, as indicated by the Greek word ἵνα (*hina*; "in order that," NASB; "to," NIV).

What is this purpose? "To make the riches of his glory known to the objects [vessels] of his mercy." In continuity with everything we have seen in ch. 9 thus far, we take these vessels of mercy to be the spiritual Israel alluded to in 9:6b; and in view of the reference to the Gentiles in v. 24, we take this specifically to refer to the NT church. For hundreds of years God endured with great patience the unbelieving multitudes of ethnic Israel because it was his purpose to produce through them, in the fullness of time, the true Israel.

It was certainly the case that any of these unbelieving Israelites along the way could have "circumcised their hearts" (Jer 4:4) and turned in pentitent faith toward the gracious God; and many did so. But strictly speaking God did not exercise his great patience

[67]This is contrary to those who say that the purpose for God's patience was threefold: to show forth his wrath (v. 22), to make his power known (v. 22), and to make his glory known (v. 23). See Cranfield, 2:494; Piper, *Justification*, 188; Moo, 608.

toward OT Israel just for the purpose of allowing time for individual Jews to repent. The fact is, according to v. 22, he actually *wanted* to wipe them all out. What prevented him from doing so, and what caused him to be patient, was his determination to accomplish his final historical purpose for them as a nation: the establishment of the church of Jesus the Messiah.

The vessels of mercy are thus the individuals (Jews and Gentiles, v. 24) who respond in faith to the preaching of the gospel of Jesus Christ and receive within themselves the outpouring of God's saving mercy, the double cure of forgiveness through the blood of Christ and regeneration through the indwelling Holy Spirit. Collectively they form the church, which is the new and true Israel, or the Israel which is identified by spiritual rather than physical criteria.

How shall we understand "the riches of his glory" which he makes known to these vessels of mercy? Some take this to mean that God's purpose is to display *his own* glory by bestowing salvation upon the elect (Murray, 2:35). The NIV might be taken in this sense in that it refers to making the riches of God's glory "*known to* the objects of his mercy." I believe it is better, though, to interpret "the riches of his glory" to mean the riches of salvation as bestowed "*upon* vessels of mercy" (NASB, emphasis added). The preposition *epi* is better translated "upon" than "to." Thus it is God's purpose to manifest the glorious riches of his salvation by lavishly bestowing them upon the new Israel.

Does this "glory" refer to eschatological glorification, the final blessings of heaven itself? It certainly must include this, since "glory" most often has this specific reference (e.g., 2:7,10; 5:2; 8:18,21,30; Col 1:27). But it must not be limited to the glory of the end times; from the very beginning of the Christian life God pours "the riches of his glory" into the vessels of his mercy. This exact phrase is used in Eph 3:16 to refer to the sanctifying work of the Holy Spirit within us. See also 2 Cor 3:18; Eph 3:13; Phil 4:19; Col 1:11; 1 Thess 2:12.

In what sense are the vessels of mercy "prepared in advance for glory"? Here the verb "prepared in advance" (προετοιμάζω, *proetoimazō*) is different from the verb translated "prepared" (καταρτίζω, *katartizō*) in v. 22. Because the latter is middle or passive voice, we may conclude that the vessels of wrath prepared themselves for destruction. But in v. 23 the word is active voice and no doubt means that God is the one who has prepared the vessels of mercy for glory. Also, unlike v. 22, the verb in v. 23 has the prefix *pro-*, which means that God prepared them "in advance" or "beforehand."

If "prepared in advance for glory" refers to the final glory of heaven, then this statement is no different from 8:28-30. I.e., whom he foreknew would respond favorably to his gracious promises, he predestined to be in heaven (see JC, 1:502-514).

But it is possible that "prepared in advance" refers to the plan that God had begun to work out from the time he called Abraham and Isaac and Jacob, the plan whereby he would use the ethnic people of Israel to lay the groundwork for the establishment of the church. That he prepared them "for glory" would then mean that he had already determined that he would pour out the riches of salvation upon all who accepted the Messiah, whether Jew or Gentile. See Eph 2:10; 1 Pet 1:2.

The reference to Gentiles in v. 24 makes it likely that the latter is the main point, since one fact that caused Paul to offer frequent praise to God was God's "mystery plan" to include the Gentiles as well as the Jews in his new covenant people, the church. See 16:25-26; Eph 2:11-3:11. "This mystery," he says in Ephesians, "is that through the gospel the Gentiles are heirs together with Israel, members together of one body" (3:6). Even though this was God's "eternal purpose" (3:11), it "was not made known to men in other generations," but is now revealed through prophets and apostles, like Paul (3:5), who was given the privilege of preaching "to the Gentiles the unsearchable riches of Christ" (3:8). This mystery, long kept hidden, is now revealed "through the church" (3:9-10), which is spiritual Israel.

In other words, the church is the ultimate objective of God's advance preparation; its members are the vessels of mercy God "prepared in advance for glory." Every time a sinner is converted, God "make[s] the riches of his glory known" by pouring them out upon the convert.

We must not lose sight of Paul's main point, which is to declare God's faithfulness in his dealings with the Jews. As he has insisted all along, the members of ethnic Israel did not have to be personal believers as a prerequisite for being used to carry out the divine plan. Even as vessels of wrath, they were used collectively as an instrument for bringing the church into existence. This was God's purpose, and as the objector in v. 19 rightly observes, no one can resist his purposive will.

It is important to see that the ultimate purpose of God is not wrath, but mercy. He used vessels of wrath (unbelieving Israel) to accomplish this purpose, but the purpose itself is to make known the riches of his glory on vessels of mercy. And here is the most glorious truth of all: no unbelieving Jew – no individual vessel of wrath – needs to remain as such. Though the nation in general remains under God's curse because of unbelief, any individual Jew can respond to the gospel of Jesus Christ and *become* a vessel of mercy! After all, the gospel is "first for the Jew" (1:16).

9:24 . . . even us, whom he also called, not only from the Jews but also from the Gentiles? The main point of this verse has already been set forth in the above discussion, namely, that the vessels of mercy for which God had long been preparing would include not only Jews but Gentiles as well. The two together constitute "an expanded chosen people" (Achtemeier, 160).

Once the advance preparation through ethnic Israel was completed, God "called" (καλέω, *kaleō*) from the larger masses of Jews and Gentiles those who would receive his mercy. This is not the Calvinist "effectual call," which is identical with the doctrine of irresistible grace;[68] it is rather the call that is extended to all sinners through the preaching of the gospel, though it is accepted by only a few (see 1:6-7; 8:28, 30; see JC, 1:83-84, 500-501, 512-513).

The word "from" is ἐκ (*ek*), which can be more forcefully translated "out of." Thus Paul is here identifying the vessels of mercy as "called-out ones," which is etymologically related to the NT word for "church," which is ἐκκλησία (*ekklēsia*). This comes from the same two words used here in v. 24, *ek* and *kaleō*. This is completely consistent with what was said above, that Paul's whole point in this chapter is the way God used ethnic Israel to produce spiritual Israel, the church.

In view of this glorious and merciful purpose of God, how can anyone seriously complain against God and accuse him of unfaithfulness? As Lard says, he calls both Jews and Gentiles alike, and is

---

[68]Contra Murray, 2:37; Hendriksen, 2:329; Cranfield, 2:498.

willing to make them all into vessels of honor and mercy. Those who accept the call will be treated with equal mercy, but "on all the rest he will one day pour out his wrath" (312).

4. Prophetic Confirmation of God's Purpose (9:25-29)

This section does not add any new content to Paul's argument. It is a series of quotations from Hosea and Isaiah, cited to provide prophetic confirmation of God's purpose for Israel as it culminates in the birth of the NT church. The citations from Hosea (vv. 25-26) include the prophet's original application to exiled Israelites but are here also applied to the calling of the Gentiles into the people of God. The verses from Isaiah (vv. 27-29) show that God all along knew that only a small number, a remnant, of the Jews would accept the gospel and be saved.

This latter point speaks directly to the issue with which this chapter began, namely, the seeming paradox of Israel's position and privileges as the chosen people of God on the one hand, and her general condition of unbelief and accursedness on the other hand. To the Jewish mind, this appeared to be a contradiction. Especially, it seemed as if God's word and plan and promises had failed. Did not God's purpose for and use of the Israelite nation guarantee their personal salvation? Did God change his mind and go back on his word?

The answer, of course, is no; and this chapter shows why this is the case. God's use of Israel to work out his plan neither required nor guaranteed that every individual Jew would be saved. Any and all Jews could have been saved; if they were not, the cause was their own failure and refusal to believe and repent. In any case God's covenant purpose was not contingent upon it.

These OT quotations, especially those from Isaiah, show that the present state of Israel's unbelief and accursedness was no surprise to God, and that his original purpose had not failed. The quotations show, as Dunn says, "that God's purpose never had Israel as a people solely in view and never Israel as a whole or Israel the nation as such" (2:575). The nation itself was always intended to be a means to an end; the end itself is spiritual Israel, which consists of both the believing remnant from old Israel and all believers from among the Gentiles. This end, and therefore God's purpose for Israel, have been accomplished, in fulfillment of these prophecies.

9:25-26 As he says in Hosea: "I will call them 'my people' who are not my people; and I will call her 'my loved one' who is not my loved one," and, "It will happen that in the very place where it was said to them, 'You are not my people,' they will be called 'sons of the living God.'" A major question is whether or not Paul really intends to apply these quotes from Hosea to the calling of the Gentiles. This is problematic because Hosea's prophecy was originally addressed to Jews, specifically to the ten tribes of the northern kingdom. Because of their persistent unbelief God rejected them and caused them to be overrun and taken into permanent exile by the Assyrian forces. But Hosea's words gave them hope: though God rejected them as "not loved" and "not my people," a day would come when they would once again be God's loved ones and God's people (Hos 1:6-10; 2:21-23). The question now is this: how can Paul apply these prophecies to the Gentiles, when they obviously originally referred to the Jews?

One answer is that Paul does *not* apply them to the Gentiles, but is thinking only of the Jews in all the quotes from both Isaiah and Hosea. Lenski is an example of this view. He asks, "But why quote passages such as this [from Hosea] to establish the admission of the Gentiles when many passages speak of Gentiles directly? The passages quoted from Hosea show how God's word was fulfilled even in the case of the ten Israelite tribes" (627).

Most interpreters disagree with Lenski, however, and believe that Paul is indeed applying the Hosea texts to the evangelization of the Gentiles. One reason for saying this is that v. 24 ends with a reference to the Gentiles, and v. 25 begins with "as he says in Hosea." The word "as" seems to tie the quote to the Gentiles. Also, following the Hosea references Paul turns to Isaiah (v. 27), and he specifically mentions Israel: "Isaiah cries out concerning Israel." This suggests he was *not* referring to Israel in the previous quotes, says Moo (613).

But how could Paul justify applying the Hosea prophecies to the Gentiles? The consensus seems to be that the ten "lost" tribes' permanent exile has so intermingled them with the Gentiles that the evangelization of the one group will necessarily involve the evangelization of the other (Godet, 365). These Jews had become "not loved" and "not my people" through the judgment of the exile; the Gentiles were "not loved" and "not my people" by nature, so to speak. Thus in the NT age, when the church goes into all the world, the gospel appeal reaches Jew and Gentile alike, and the words of Hosea take on a new and expanded meaning. Hosea's prophecy specifically promises the restoration of the Jews, but because of their scattered status "Paul takes this promise as a proof of God's purpose to include the Gentiles in His salvation" (Cranfield, 2:500; see Morris, 370). Bruce's analysis is a fair one (196):

> What Paul does here is to take this promise . . . and extract from it a principle of divine action which in his day was reproducing itself on a world-wide scale. In large measure through Paul's own apostolic ministry, great numbers of Gentiles, who had never been "the people of God" and had no claim on His covenant mercy, were coming to be enrolled among His people and to be the recipients of His mercy. The scale of the divine action was far wider than in Hosea's day, but the same pattern and principle were recognizable.

First Peter 2:10 seems to apply Hosea 2:23 in a similar way.

In view of these considerations, in my judgment it is proper to apply the Hosea prophecies to both Jews and Gentiles.

In v. 25 Paul introduces the quotation from Hosea 2:23 thus: "As he says in Hosea." The "he" is God; this is Paul's testimony to the divine origin of these "oracles" (see 3:2). The quotation itself is more of a paraphrase than an exact quote; the two main clauses are reversed.

For God to punish Israelites by stripping them of their status as "my people" was a severe blow; being the people of God was their greatest treasure. Thus the messianic promise that God would one day bestow this title upon them again would have special meaning for Jews. Gentiles who have never had this status to begin with may not at first realize what a great promise this is. To be "God's people" means to come into a special family relationship with him (see 8:14-17). God loves all human beings (John 3:16), but his most special love is reserved for those whose hearts and lives are surrendered to him (John 14:21). Through unbelief and idolatry Israel forfeited this special love and became like Gentiles to God, but the gospel of Jesus Christ makes this love-relationship available once more to fallen Jews and fallen Gentiles alike.

The word "call" in both v. 25 and v. 26 does not refer to the gospel call but to the giving of a new name or title. "I will call them" means "I will name them" or "I will give them this name" (Lard, 314; Murray, 2:39).

Verse 26 is a citation of Hosea 1:10; its main point is the same as v. 25 and Hos 2:23. In this verse the "not my people" are renamed "sons of the living God." To a once-fallen but now-converted Jew, this is the restoration of a name once proudly worn by all Israelites. That it is now a name applied not just to believing Jews but also to believing Gentiles shows that mere physical descent from Abraham, Isaac, and Jacob does not suffice for true sonship. Today we are all – men and women, Jews and Gentiles, slaves and free men – sons of God through faith in Jesus Christ (Gal 3:26-29).

Paul says, citing Hosea, that this calling (naming) will happen "in the very place where it was said to them, 'You are not my people.'" This probably refers to the Gentile world. As applied to exiled and scattered Jews it means that they do not have to return to their "homeland" in order to become God's sons once again. Through the preaching of the gospel adoption into God's family takes place in whatever nation one is found, whether one be Jew or Gentile.

9:27-28 Isaiah cries out concerning Israel: "Though the number of the Israelites be like the sand by the sea, only the remnant will be saved. For the Lord will carry out his sentence on earth with speed and finality." Paul takes this quote from Isa 10:22-23 and specifically applies it to Israel. He says that Isaiah "cries out" this prophecy, indicating that the words were spoken with fervent emotion.

Though his message surely applies to the whole of Israel, Isaiah's ministry, unlike that of Hosea, was to the southern kingdom. The tenth chapter of Isaiah is mainly an oracle about Assyria, whom God used to punish unbelieving Israel and who then received God's punishment in return. The prophet is assuring Israel that even though they must suffer conquest and captivity, at least a remnant will survive and return to the Lord. But at the same time, the fact that only a remnant will be saved means that the rest will be destroyed.

Isaiah 10:21 says, "A remnant will return, a remnant of Jacob will return to the Mighty God." This does not mean that this remnant of the exiled northern tribes would return to their homeland, in the way that a remnant of the southern kingdom returned from Babylonian captivity to rebuild Jerusalem and the temple. Isaiah speaks rather of a *spiritual* return – a returning to the Lord. This is the way Paul understands it; thus in v. 27b he words the promise, "The remnant *will be saved.*" He sees Isaiah's prophecy as being fulfilled through the preaching of the gospel and the entry of many Jews into spiritual Israel, the church, through their conversion to Christ. As Fitzmyer says, "Paul applies the words to Jews called to accept Christ, and the remnant becomes those who actually did accept him, viz., Paul and fellow Jewish Christians" (574).

That the prophet Isaiah himself declares that only a remnant would thus be saved is a primary vindication of Paul's main point, "that the covenant promise did not contemplate or guarantee the salvation of all ethnic Israel" (Murray, 2:39). Everything that God promised to Israel as a nation *was* fulfilled, including the assurance that the number of Israelites would "be like the sand of the sea" – a promise spoken to Abraham in Gen 22:17 (see Gen 32:12). But the remnant prophecy shows that this great nation was chosen only for service, not for salvation; and the fact that only a small proportion were saved was in no way contrary to God's promises and God's faithfulness. See Dunn, 2:575.

Paul's use of the remnant concept in this way sheds important light on two other texts. One is 9:6b, "For not all who are descended from Israel are Israel." Ethnic Israel is the numerous-as-sand nation physically descended from Jacob; but only the remnant, those who accept salvation through Jesus Christ, are the true Israel, the true "sons of the living God." The other text is 11:26, "And so all Israel will be saved." The remnant doctrine, along with 9:6b, shows that "all Israel" does not have to refer to the nation as a whole.

The remnant doctrine is both a promise and a judgment. As a promise, it is an assurance that *at least* a remnant of Israel will be saved. There will always be an Israel, at least a spiritual Israel. But as a judgment, it is a solemn recognition that *only* a remnant will be saved. The NIV emphasizes this latter sense by translating *ean* as "though" and by adding the word "only" (both here and in Isa 10:22). Cranfield (2:502) says that the word translated "remnant" in itself implies "only a remnant." This necessarily means that the great majority of Israel will *not* be saved.

This note of judgment is emphasized in v. 28. It has the particle γάρ (*gar*, "for, because"); thus it "explains how it will come about that only a remnant of Israel will be saved" (Cranfield, 2:502). The verse seems to be a summary of Isa 10:22b-23, "Destruction has been decreed, overwhelming and righteous. The Lord, the LORD Almighty, will carry out the destruction decreed upon the whole land." In 9:28 the word λόγος (*logos*), translated "sentence" in the NIV, probably refers to the decree of destruction of which Isaiah speaks. This is the sentence of judgment or destruction upon the nation of Israel as a whole, which is implicit in the promise that *only* a remnant of them will be saved.

The Lord himself will carry out this decree of judgment upon the nation "with speed and finality." These last words are an attempt to translate two participles, forms of the Greek words συν–τελέω (*synteleō*, "to complete, to carry out, to accomplish, to fulfill completely") and συντέμνω (*syntemnō*, "to cut short, to cut off, to end, to shorten").[69] These words indicate that God carries out this sentence with thoroughness and completeness and finality. The former word (*synteleō*) looks to the past and means that in carrying out this sentence God is accomplishing an existing purpose, bringing it to completion, and fulfilling it completely. The latter word (*syntemnō*) looks to the future and means that in carrying out this sentence God is cutting something off and bringing it to an end; it will not continue to exist in the future. In my opinion this means that the establishment of the remnant (spiritual Israel) marks the end of God's dealing with Israel as a nation; his purpose for ethnic

[69]No objects are given for these verbal forms. Some take the sentence or decree itself to be the object, i.e., God completes and abridges the sentence (Cranfield, 2:502; see Lard, 315; Fitzmyer, 574). This is by no means certain, since in the text the word λόγος ("sentence") is the object of the verb ποιέω (*poieō*, "to make, to carry out"). I believe it is better to discern the objects from the flow of Paul's thought in the context as a whole.

Israel is now completed, and they are cut off as his special people. From this point on his focus is upon spiritual Israel.

The words translated "on earth" probably should be translated "upon the land," i.e., upon the land of Israel. In Isa 10:23 "upon the whole land" no doubt has this connotation, as it refers to "the devastation wrought by the destruction of Samaria by the Assyrians under Shalmaneser" (Lenski, 631). A similar devastation of "the land" was the destruction of Jerusalem in A.D. 70; Lenski thinks this is the sense of it for Paul's time (631). This may be so, but in any case we should understand "upon the land" as referring to the land of Israel, with the word "land" standing for ethnic Israel or physical Israelites as such.

9:29 It is just as Isaiah said previously:[70] "Unless the Lord Almighty had left us descendants, we would have become like Sodom, we would have been like Gomorrah." This last quotation, from Isaiah 1:9, reemphasizes both the seriousness of God's judgment upon unbelieving Israel and the divine provision for preserving at least a remnant of his people. In Scripture the destruction of Sodom and Gomorrah is a type of final and decisive judgment.[71] Thus without the remnant, Israel would have become like these two cities: extinct. By preserving only the remnant, God brought a judgment just short of this upon Israel.

But he did leave a remnant, as Isa 1:9 says and as Paul emphasizes. "The Lord Almighty" preserved this remnant. Both Isaiah and Paul actually say "the Lord of Hosts," but for some reason the NIV changes "hosts" to "Almighty." As "Lord of Hosts" God is the ruler of all the heavenly or angelic hosts; he is the King of kings and Lord of lords.

The word "descendants" definitely connotes the remnant idea in this text. Isa 1:9 says the Lord left "some survivors" (NIV), or "a few survivors" (NASB, NRSV), or "a very small remnant" (KJV).

---

[70]The word "previously" comes from the prefix *pro-* on the verb "he said." It probably just indicates that Isaiah's words were a predictive prophecy, spoken in advance of the event. See Fitzmyer, 575; Morris, 372. The NASB translates it "foretold."

[71]This is the sense in Isa 1:9. See also Deut 29:23; Isa 3:9; 13:19; Jer 23:14; 49:18; 50:40; Lam 4:6; Amos 4:11; Zeph 2:9; Matt 10:15; 11:23-24; Luke 17:28-30; 2 Pet 2:6; Jude 7; Rev 11:8.

The LXX uses σπέρμα (*sperma*, "seed") instead of survivors. Since he quotes the LXX verbatim, Paul also uses *sperma*, which the NIV translates "descendants." This is not a good translation, since "seed" here connotes not a relationship to what is past (i.e., to one's ancestors), but a preparation for the future, or (as Morris says) "the potential for new growth" (373; see Cranfield, 2:503). The purpose for leaving behind a few survivors is to reseed and replant for the future. The "new growth" that springs forth from this seed is the new spiritual Israel, the church.[72]

The Lord "left us" this remnant. The verb used here can mean "to leave behind" in the sense of "to forsake, to abandon"; but it can also mean, as here, "to allow to remain" (AG, 214-215). Though the Lord carried out his sentence of destruction upon the nation in general, he allowed this seed-remnant to remain. This is definitely a note of promise and hope, or as Dunn says, "a gasp of gratitude" (2:576).

In what sense did *the Lord* leave this remnant? He left it in the sense that he "bore with great patience the objects of his wrath" (v. 22) until the time that he was ready for the spiritual Israel to come into existence. As Lenski says (632),

> If God had made his final reckoning with the Jews in Isaiah's time or even prior to this, no godly remnant could have been obtained from them at any future time, certainly not at Paul's time. Judaism would have become a second Sodom, would have been made like to Gomorrah, not a soul would have been left after the cataclysm of punishment. But God restrained his wrath so that seed was left.

This brings the first main section of Rom 9–11 to a conclusion. Paul has shown that God has not been unfaithful to Israel nor treated them unfairly. He has kept every promise he made to them, and fulfilled every purpose he had for them as a nation.

---

[72]The term *sperma* in v. 29 does not point us back to the *sperma* ("offspring") in vv. 7-8, contra Murray, 2:41; Moo, 616; Dunn, 2:574. In vv. 7-8 the *sperma* of Abraham are ethnic Israel; in v. 29 the *sperma* are spiritual Israel. This distinction is crucial to the whole point of Romans 9.

The one question raised in this section that has yet to be addressed is the lost state of the great majority of the Jews, or more specifically, who is responsible for their lostness? The objector raised the question in v. 19a, "Then why does God still blame us?" The implication is that somehow God is responsible for the Jews' rejection of their Messiah; therefore they should not be blamed and punished. This is the issue that Paul will address in the next section.

III. ISRAEL'S CHOICE OF LAW RATHER THAN GRACE (9:30–10:21)

There is considerable agreement that 9:30–10:21 forms the next major section of 9–11, but how it relates to the previous section is a matter of dispute.[73] A common view is that ch. 9 explains Israel's lostness in terms of God's sovereign decision, while ch. 10 explains it as the result of Israel's own unbelief. For Calvinists especially, ch. 9 presents the picture of a sovereign God who unilaterally and unconditionally chooses which individuals he will save and which he will send to hell, while ch. 10 presents him as giving human beings the choice of whether to believe or not to believe, with salvation being conditioned on this choice. This seeming contradiction between divine sovereignty and human responsibility is a paradox with no ready explanation.

For example, Moo says that according to Paul in ch. 9, Israel's plight "is due to the sovereign determination of God. But in 9:30–10:21, he argues that it is also the result of human response." Though Paul simply presents both sides without attempting to reconcile them, it is likely that Israel's unbelief "is simply the result of God's prior decision" (617).

In my judgment the point of these two sections is something quite different. Paul's main purpose in 9–11, as discussed earlier, is

[73]The break between these two sections does not correspond with the chapter division in our Bibles; 9:30-33 is directly related to the content of ch. 10. As a matter of convenience, though, we will sometimes speak of the previous section as "ch. 9," though technically it includes only vv. 6-29; and of this present section as "ch. 10," though it includes the last four verses of ch. 9.

to vindicate God's faithfulness in view of (a) his promises to Israel and (b) Israel's lostness. Chs. 9 and 10 present two separate but related reasons why this situation does not violate God's faithfulness. First (ch. 9), his faithfulness is not violated because his promises to the nation as a whole involved only their role of service and not their salvation. God elected them to serve a special purpose in his redemptive plan, and he patiently accomplished this purpose through them. With reference to salvation, however, God has distinguished between two Israels: the physical nation and the spiritual remnant. This distinction explains the apparently contradictory way God has treated Israel according to the flesh. His sovereign election for covenant service, including his covenant promises, applies only to the former; salvation belongs only to those Jews who are also a part of the latter. Thus God's promises to ethnic Israel – all of which were kept – are consistent with their lostness.

The second reason (ch. 10) why God's faithfulness is not violated by this situation is because Israel's lostness (their exclusion from spiritual Israel) is the result of their own free choice of law rather than grace as the way of salvation. This is the main point of this present section, which stresses very clearly the fact that Israel is responsible for its own fate. As Fitzmyer rightly says, "The cause of Israel's failure is not to be found in God, but in Israel itself. . . . Its situation is derived from its own misstep" (576). Paul makes it clear that any and all Jews could have been saved if they had accepted God's gift of righteousness on his gracious terms instead of trying to attain salvation through their own works or personal righteousness. Such saving grace had always been available to individual Jews, based on God's loving offer of forgiveness of sins; but the offer was usually spurned, as the gospel of Christ itself came to be. In other words, it is the Jews themselves, not God, who have been unfaithful.

Herein lies the connection between 9–11 and 1–8, as well as between this section and the overall theme of the letter, which is the contrast between law and grace as ways of salvation (JC, 1:53). In 1–8 Paul has explained why it is impossible for anyone to be saved by the law system, and how God has therefore provided the alternative system of grace. Now he shows that the only reason most Jews were lost is that they persisted in trying to be accepted by God on the basis of their own righteousness, i.e., by the impotent system of law (see 1:18–3:20). Thus the responsibility for being accursed must be laid at their own feet, not God's.

Spiritual Israel, on the other hand, consists of those who have accepted the way of grace, in which God offers a divinely-established righteousness based on the death of Jesus Christ to all who put their trust in him (see 3:21–5:21). The reason some Gentiles are included in this new Israel is that they have trusted God's righteousness rather than their own, and the only reason the remnant of the Jews are included is that they do the same.

A. PERSONAL RIGHTEOUSNESS VERSUS THE RIGHTEOUSNESS OF GOD (9:30–10:3)

This paragraph presents the essence of this section in terms of the concept of righteousness, i.e., the righteousness on the basis of which one is accepted by God. The Jews were lost, says Paul, because they sought acceptance by God through their own personal righteousness or law-keeping, which can never be good enough. They rejected the gift of God's righteousness, which is the only hope for salvation.

"God's righteousness" (10:3) in this context is the same as the "righteousness from God" that is revealed in the gospel (1:17). It is not the attribute of God by which he is personally righteous, but rather a gift of righteousness that God offers to sinners, thus allowing him to accept them as righteous even though in reality they are not. Specifically, it is Jesus Christ's payment of the penalty of the law in our place (JC, 1:116-120).

Though the Jews are the main focus of this section, the Gentiles are mentioned here by way of contrast. The very thing the Jews were seeking but failed to attain, the Gentiles attained even though they were not seeking it (9:30-31). DeWelt paraphrases Paul thus: "It is strange, isn't it, that the Gentiles who were not looking or searching for justification, found it, and you Jews who were diligently seeking for a means of justification failed in your search?" (159). This is certainly tragic but also extremely ironic; indeed, it is "the most poignant irony in the whole of history" (Godet, 367).

1. The Reason for the Gentiles' Acceptance (9:30)

9:30 What then shall we say? Sometimes when Paul asks this question, he does so to introduce a false inference or idea, which he then proceeds to refute (e.g., 6:1; 7:7; 9:14). But here it serves simply to introduce the new section. What follows is not an objector's question but Paul's own teaching (as in 8:31; 11:7).

"What then shall we say" – about what? What has triggered this question? No doubt it is the whole of the previous section that is in view. I.e., what shall we say about the lostness of most Jews (9:3,22, 28), especially in view of the fact that even some Gentiles (!) are being saved (9:25-26)?

This is Paul's answer, **That the Gentiles, who did not pursue righteousness, have obtained it, . . .**[74] This refers not to all Gentiles, but only to those who accept the gospel. What is the righteousness they have obtained? Most agree that Paul is not speaking of moral righteousness or righteous character, but rather a "righteous status in God's sight" (Cranfield, 2:506), or a right standing with God (e.g., Hendriksen, 2:333; Morris, 374). It is not the same as justification (contra Lard, 317; DeWelt, 159), but is rather the result of it. On the basis of his gracious act of justifying (declaring or counting righteous), believing Gentiles obtain their right standing before God.

Whether righteousness be taken as right moral character or as a right standing before God, it was characteristic of the Gentiles that they sought for neither. Regarding the former, there were no doubt some exceptions, but in general the pagan world was noted for its wickedness (1:18-32; Acts 14:16; 17:30; Eph 4:17-19). But this very fact shows that the Gentiles were not striving for the latter, either. This is true because without special revelation the only known means of being right with God is earnest moral striving; but as just noted, this was not typical of the Gentile world.

But even though they were not pursuing a right standing before God, they obtained it anyway! The words "pursue" and "obtain" go

---

[74]This is sometimes taken as a second question after "What then shall we say?" (KJII; NAB). But if this is a question, then so is v. 31. But this cannot be, since v. 32 asks "Why not?" presupposing that what precedes is a statement of fact.

together. Literally they can refer to pursuing a quarry and catching it, or running after a prize in a race and winning it. Figuratively they refer to seeking after or pursuing a goal, and attaining it. What is so unusual is that the Gentiles attained this goal or prize without even seeking it. This refers to the fact that under the New Covenant God is actively seeking Gentiles to be his people through the worldwide preaching of the gospel. By accepting the gospel when it is presented to them, Gentiles obtain this right standing before God.[75]

Specifically, Paul says, the Gentiles obtained **a righteousness that is by faith . . . .** That is, they obtained a right standing with God based on the free gift of God's own righteousness, a gift which they received by putting their trust in Christ's saving work (1:17; 3:21-22; Phil 3:9). "Righteousness by faith" is a shorthand expression for the grace system as a whole and is similar to "justified by faith" in 3:28 (JC, 1:267-268).[76]

2. The Reason for the Jews' Lostness (9:31-33)

9:31 [B]ut Israel, who pursued a law of righteousness, has not attained it. Here is the tragic irony. The Gentiles did not pursue righteousness but obtained it anyway; Israel pursued it but did not attain it. "Israel" refers to the physical nation in general. "Pursued" is a present participle (literally, "pursuing"), to which both the NASB and the NIV give a purely descriptive meaning. Grammatically it could be causative ("*because* they pursued"), but this does not fit the context, as the following discussion shows. Another possibility, which I favor, is that the participle is concessive: "*although* they pursued." Although Israel, unlike the Gentiles, vigorously pursued a law of righteousness, they did not attain it.

The difficult part of this verse is the expression, "a law of righteousness" (νόμον δικαιοσύνης, *nomon dikaiosynēs*). Why didn't Paul

---

[75]This is not the same as 9:16 (contra Moo, 622), since v. 16 is speaking of election to service, while this verse speaks of salvation.

[76]This point is similar to the comment in MP (413), that "faith" is "the leading and initiatory part of the conditions of justification," a "synecdoche, employed to designate the whole of the conditions."

just say "righteousness," making the language parallel with v. 30? Why did he say "*law* of righteousness"? Some say "law of righteousness" is equivalent to "righteousness of law," and just turn it around: Israel "pursued the righteousness which is based on law: (NRSV; see Lard, 318; Fitzmyer, 578). This would suggest that the object of their pursuit was in itself a false goal, since righteousness based on law-keeping is impossible for sinners to attain.

This view is unacceptable, however, because v. 32 suggests that the Jews' problem was not the *goal* they were seeking but the *manner* in which they sought it:[77] they pursued it by works rather than by faith. Thus we should take Paul's expression at face value. The Jews were pursuing a law of righteousness, which in itself is a proper pursuit.

What, then, is this "law of righteousness"? Murray (2:43) says the word "law" (*nomos*) here is not used in the sense of a law code, i.e., the Law of Moses. Rather, it "means principle or rule or order," as in 3:27 (see JC, 1:267). I.e., Israel was pursuing the principle of righteousness. If so, then Paul is not really adding anything to the concept of righteousness as such. This, however, is just the problem with this view. To use the loaded term *nomos* in this context in such an inconsequential way would be very confusing, especially in light of the way it is used in 10:4. I deem this approach unacceptable.

The best understanding is that "law" here refers to the Law of Moses, which the Jews obviously pursued and after which they hastened with the greatest of zeal (2:17-20; 10:2). Moo agrees that the *nomos* here is the Mosaic Law, and that in principle it was not wrong for Israel to seek it; yet he says that in the final analysis it was the wrong goal, since they should have sought Christ instead (625-627). I disagree with this last point. It is true that once Christ has come, it is wrong to continue to pursue the Law of Moses in even the best sense, since the law itself points everyone to Jesus Christ (Gal 3:24) and is obsolete now that he has come (as Hebrews teaches). But Paul's lament in 9:31 applies not just to the Jews who were contemporary with Christ and the birth of Christianity (cf. 9:32b-33), but also to preceding generations of Israelites who would

[77]Cranfield, 2:507-509; Dunn, 2:581-582; Morris, 375.

not have known Christ as such. Hence throughout the OT era it was proper for the Jews to pursue the Law of Moses as a "law of righteousness."

In what sense is the Law of Moses a law of *righteousness*? We should remember that righteousness as such means "conformity to the proper and relevant standard or norm" (see JC, 1:116). Thus any form of God's law for mankind (heart-engraved [2:15], Mosaic, New Covenant) is a law of righteousness in the sense that it is the norm or standard to which all human beings in their respective contexts are obligated to conform. The Law of Moses was the norm by which the righteousness of the Jews was to be measured, or as Dunn says, "a standard which defines what God requires of his covenant people" (2:581). As such it was meant to be meticulously and sincerely obeyed, which was the professed goal of every Israelite (see Ps 119).[78]

Paul's lament is that, although the Jews pursued their law of righteousness, they did not attain it.[79] "Attain" here is not the same Greek word as "obtain" in v. 30, but the concept is similar. Contrary to the Gentiles, who did obtain righteousness, the Jew did not arrive at their goal. They did not "catch up with" it; it "always left them far behind" (Lenski, 636).

Exactly what did the Jews hope to gain by pursuing the law of righteousness, i.e., by conforming their lives and conduct to the Law of Moses? Not just righteousness in the sense of perfect moral character, but righteousness in the sense of right standing before God – the very thing the Gentiles attained without seeking it. But why did the Jews not attain it?

9:32 Why not? Because they pursued it not by faith but as if it were by works.[80] Here is a point that must not be overlooked: it was possible for the Jews to obtain a right standing with God by pursuing the Law of Moses, their "law of righteousness," as long as

---

[78]Stott says the "law of righteousness" was "Torah viewed as a law to be obeyed" (276).

[79]Paul specifically says that Israel "did not attain unto [the] law," i.e., the law of righteousness they were pursuing. The NIV replaces "law" with "it," making the object of "attained" ambiguous.

[80]The words "they pursued it" are not in the original but are the intended sense and are correctly supplied by the NIV.

they pursued it in the right manner. Of course, if anyone had obeyed it perfectly, he would have been justified before God for that very reason; but Paul has already shown that no Jew ever accomplished this (2:1-3:20), and he is not just repeating that point here. Rather, Paul says the reason the Jews did not succeed was that they did not pursue their law "by faith." This implies that they *could* have pursued it by faith; and if they had done so, they *would* have obtained the same righteous standing with God that the Gentiles did. In fact, we must assume that a large number of Jews throughout OT history *did* in fact follow after the law by faith and attain righteousness thereby (11:4), though most did not.

But how is it possible for the Jews to follow after the Law of Moses *by faith*? The most obvious way is that the Jews living in the Christian era can put their trust in the very one to whom their law points, namely, Jesus. But what of those who lived in pre-Christian generations? How could they pursue the *law* of righteousness *by faith*? Doesn't this sound like a contradiction?

It is not a contradiction. The Law of Moses as a law code was unique, in that it contained not just moral and legal precepts to be obeyed, but also religious provisions that embodied the very essence of grace (i.e., forgiveness of sins). Pre-Christian Jews did not know Jesus as such, but they knew that they were sinners and law-breakers as measured by all the moral and legal requirements of their law, and they knew from the laws of sacrifice the principle of atonement via substitution. Thus they knew that their sin and idolatry could be forgiven when God's promises of mercy displayed in the sacrifices were embraced by faith (see 3:21). Those Jews who trusted in the gospel aspects of the Law of Moses rather than its legal aspects are the ones who obtained a righteous status before God.

In this sense the Jews' law was not an enemy of faith, but was in fact designed to engender faith. As Achtemeier says, that law was intended to uphold a righteous relationship with God based on trust in him; its very purpose was to help the Jews achieve such trust (167). Cranfield (2:508) says it thus:

> . . . The law is the law of righteousness because it was intended and designed to show the people of Israel how they could be righteous before God, to show them that the way to

> this righteousness is – faith. In the law which they were pursuing so zealously they had that which was all the time pointing out the way to the possession of a status of righteousness in God's sight.

How then was it possible to pursue the law by faith? Again Cranfield's answer (2:510) is on target:

> . . . The answer must be, surely, that it is to respond to the claim to faith which God makes through the law, and must include accepting, without evasion or resentment, the law's criticism of one's life, recognizing that one can never so adequately fulfil its righteous requirements as to put God in one's debt, accepting God's proffered mercy and forgiveness and in return giving oneself to Him in love and gratitude and so beginning to be released from one's self-centredness and turned in the direction of a humble obedience that is free from self-righteousness; that it is to allow oneself to be turned again and again by the forgiving mercy of God in the direction of loving Him with all one's heart and soul and mind and strength and of loving one's neighbor as oneself.

A biblical example of one who pursued the law by faith is the publican or tax collector in Jesus' parable in Luke 18:9-14. In the temple as he prayed for acceptance by God, he was overwhelmed by his unworthiness and cried simply, "God, have mercy on me, a sinner." Jesus declared that this man went home "justified before God." Though this story may have been fictional, it shows how any Jew at any time in OT history was able to attain by faith a righteous standing with God, as guided by the law. As Hendriksen says, "The law, with its uncompromising demand of perfect love and obedience, should have driven each Israelite to God with the fervent prayer, 'Oh, God, be thou merciful to me, the sinner'" (2:334).

Many were thus driven, but most were not. Indeed, most were like the Pharisee in the same parable. Instead of pursuing the law of righteousness by faith, Israel as a whole pursued it "by works."[81]

---

[81]Lit., "as from works." The word "as" (ὥς, *hōs*) has the sense of "as if it were possible," i.e., as if it were possible to successfully pursue the law of righteousness by works.

Instead of simply trusting the law's manifested grace as the source of their righteous standing before God, they trusted that their own ability to obey its precepts would make them worthy of acceptance by God. "They thought that the law pointed to the contribution they had to make" toward that acceptance, "and hence lost the point of the law, which was to engender trust in the God who had chosen them" (Achtemeier, 167). Instead of depending on God's forgiving grace, they trusted that they had achieved a satisfactory degree of personal righteousness, "as if the accumulation of works-righteousness were God's way of salvation" (Stott, 276).

What Israel did, in effect, was to transform their law *code* into a law *system*. As a law code, the Law of Moses was a simple set of commands to which the Israelites were obligated to conform their lives and conduct. To use it as such was to use it properly (3:31). But the moment they began to regard such obedience as the means or basis for gaining acceptance by God, their law code became the centerpiece in the law system as a way of salvation (JC, 1:128). But this is exactly why Israel was lost: the law system cannot save sinners (1:18–3:20).

They stumbled over the "stumbling stone." This is a reference to Yahweh's warning to Israel in Isa 8:13-15. "The LORD Almighty," he said, "is the one you are to fear, he is the one you are to dread." Though he will be a sanctuary or place of safety, at the same time "for both houses of Israel he will be a stone that causes men to stumble and a rock that makes them fall." Many of the Jews "will stumble; they will fall and be broken."

Though 9:33 as well as other NT references show that the "stumbling stone" ultimately applies to Jesus Christ, originally the stone was Yahweh as such. To Jews in Old Covenant times, God presented himself as a sanctuary, i.e., as the holy place where one could find refuge from all his enemies (see 1 Kgs 1:50-51; 2:28-29). As such he placed himself squarely in the path of his people (Isa 65:1-2). Thus if they refused to take shelter in his grace, they ran headlong into him and crashed against him and fell. As Lenski says, "This is not a stone over which one may merely stumble and recover oneself but one against which one runs with his entire body and smashes it entirely; it is like knocking one's brains out" (637). Thus it was with all Jews throughout OT history who pursued the law of righteousness by works instead of by faith.

Thus it is no surprise that when Yahweh came in the flesh, the Jews of that generation stumbled against him as well. As Dunn says, their confusion regarding the law and righteousness "came to eschatological expression and climax in their refusal to recognize Christ as Messiah" (2:577). They were conditioned to do so by the chronic misuse of the law by their ancestors, which, in Achtemeier's words, "had as its inevitable outcome the result that when Christ came as the one who personified the call contained in the law to trust in God, the chosen people rejected him" (167).

9:33 As it is written: "See, I lay in Zion a stone that causes men to stumble and a rock that makes them fall, and the one who trusts in him will never be put to shame." This verse expands the "stumbling stone" concept and implicitly applies it to Christ. I say "implicitly" because Christ is not specifically mentioned in the verse, yet these same OT quotes are applied to him elsewhere in the NT.[82] In fact, the second part of this verse, a quote from Isa 28:16b, is explicitly applied to Christ in 10:11.

"Stone" and "rock" are two different Greek words. The "stone" of stumbling (also in v. 32) is λίθος (*lithos*), which refers to a loose stone of any kind, large or small. The "rock" of falling is πέτρα (*petra*), which generally refers to firm, immovable bedrock or rock-mass, whether underground or protruding from the ground (such as a cliff).

"As it is written" is a common NT way of introducing material from the OT, which in this case is a composite of two passages from Isaiah. "See, I lay in Zion a stone" is from Isa 28:16; "a stone that causes men to stumble and a rock that makes them fall" is from Isa 8:14; and the rest of the verse is from Isa 28:16 again. The way Paul combines them is an ingenious blending of the two texts. Isa 8:14 presents Yahweh as both a refuge (sanctuary) and a stone of judgment, with the emphasis being on the latter. Isa 28:16 concentrates on the stone as a place of refuge and safety. Paul simply combines the two and presents the one stone as the source of both judgment and promise.

---

[82]In 1 Pet 2:4 Peter calls Jesus "the living Stone," then applies three OT stone passages to Jesus: Isa 28:16 (v. 6), Ps 118:22 (v. 7), and Isa 8:14 (v. 8). Matt 21:44 (Luke 20:18) applies Isa 8:14 to Jesus; and Matt 21:42 (Mark 12:10; Luke 20:17) cites Ps 118:22 as referring to Jesus, as does Acts 4:11.

One reason for saying v. 33 refers to Jesus is that, while in Isa 8:14 Yahweh himself is the stone, in Isa 28:16 Yahweh is the one who lays the stone. That the latter is a messianic prophecy is indicated by the fact that Matt 16:16-18 is clearly based on Isa 28:14-19. Christ's person and work as summed up in Peter's confession are the foundation stone on which the church is built, and all the forces of Hades (=Sheol in Isa 28:15, 18) cannot overpower it. Thus most scholars agree that the stone of stumbling in 9:32-33 is Jesus, especially in his role as the crucified Messiah (see 1 Cor 1:23).

But how can Paul apply both Isaiah texts to Jesus? In Isaiah 28:16, to be sure, the stone does appear to be the Messiah, but in 8:14 the stone is Yahweh himself. So how can they both refer to Jesus? The answer is simple: "Christ is God!" (Hendriksen, 2:335). The Messiah-Stone "is therefore Jehovah in His final manifestation" (Godet, 369; see Rom 10:9,13). This does not mean that God the Father and Jesus Christ are one and the same person; it means only that Yahweh in the OT revelation is the entire Trinity: Father, Son, and Holy Spirit.

Jesus is "a stone that causes men to stumble and a rock that makes them fall." This does not mean that God *wants* anyone to stumble over him or that he *intended* the Jews to fall because of him (Lard, 319). Based on Paul's use of the Isaiah verses where Yahweh says that *he* is laying "in Zion a stone that causes men to stumble," Dunn draws the conclusion that "Israel's fall was intended by God" (2:584). But the stumbling is a *result*, not a purpose. The stone is intended as a refuge; but because he has been rejected, "what was meant to be a basis of security has become a stumbling block" (Fitzmyer, 580). We can agree with Moo, however, that "Israel's stumbling over Christ was predicted in the OT" (630).

In what sense does anyone stumble or fall over Jesus? The verb for "stumble" (v. 32) is προσκόπτω (*proskoptō*); it means literally "to strike or bump against, to stumble against or over"; figuratively it means "to give offense, to take offense at, to reject." The noun, πρόσκομμα (*proskomma*), is used in this verse. It can refer to the object over which someone stumbles, but here refers to the act of stumbling as such. The word for "fall" is the noun σκάνδαλον (*skandalon*), which can be defined as "that which gives offense or causes revulsion, that which arouses opposition" (AG, 760). This definition does not capture the entire meaning, though. In the LXX the word often means "cause of ruin," and is often used in the sense of a snare or trap or temptation, i.e., a cause for sin and punishment. In Paul the gospel about Jesus is a *skandalon* in a similar sense; it is an "occasion of guilt" and a "cause of destruction" (Stählin, "σκάν-δαλον," 342, 353). Thus a *skandalon* is something which one opposes or to which one takes offense only to his ruin and destruction. In this light it is easy to see how Jesus is a stumbling stone. Those who oppose him or who take offense at the gospel of the cross fall into eternal ruin and death. This is what happened to the Jews (1 Cor 1:23), and it can happen to anyone else.

But this is not the whole story. God lays in Zion a stone; some fall over him, but "the one who trusts in him will never be put to shame." This part of v. 33 is based on Isa 28:16b, where the Hebrew verb in the latter clause seems to be "will not be in haste," or "will not be in a hurry" (NASB margin). Other interpretations of the word are "will not panic" (NRSV), "will not fuss and rush around but trust in God" (Bruce, 200), will not be "fleeing away in confusion" (MP, 416). The passive verb used by Paul means "to be disgraced, to be put to shame," and speaks more of the reason for such panic or hasty flight than the fleeing itself. The idea is that those who take refuge upon the Rock by trusting in him will never have to slink away in shame for having made a humiliating decision.[83] As Bruce says, "Those who trust in God need never fear that their trust in Him will prove to be ill-founded. God vindicates His people's faith" (200). Those who do not believe will exist in "shame and everlasting contempt" (Dan 12:2).

In these three verses (31-33), then, Paul vindicates the faithfulness of God by declaring that Israel as a whole is responsible for its own lost condition. The essence of their failure was that they trusted in themselves rather than in God's promises and in their own Messiah; they pursued acceptance with God by works rather than by faith; they chose law rather than grace.

Such a path to perdition is not limited to the Jews, of course. Anyone living in the New Covenant era can respond to the New Covenant revelation in exactly the same way, i.e., by zealously

[83]The same word and idea appear in 5:5 (JC, 1:318).

pursuing its commands in an effort to win God's approval on the basis of such works. The fate of those who do so will be the same as Israel's.

3. The Jews' Rejection of God's Righteousness (10:1-3)

These three verses expand further the reason for the Jews' lostness, namely, they rejected the gift of God's own righteousness, preferring to stake their claim to heaven on the worthiness of their own works.

10:1 Brothers, my heart's desire and prayer to God for the Israelites is that they may be saved. Paul addresses his "brothers" (ἀδελπηοί, *adelphoi*), which are his fellow Christians (not just Jewish Christians, contra MP, 418). In general Greek usage *adelphoi* was often inclusive of men and women and thus could be translated "brothers and sisters" (AG, 15).[84]

Paul's sentiment here is directed toward his fellow Jews: his prayer is "for the Israelites."[85] It reminds us of 9:1-3, where the Apostle expressed his grief over Israel's lostness and declared his willingness to take their place if only they could be saved. Here he echoes that desire for their salvation.

"Desire" is εὐδοκία (*eudokia*), which is basically a feeling of good will toward others out of which a desire for their well-being naturally arises. Morris (378) calls it "warm affection" and favors Goodspeed's translation, "My heart is full of good will toward them." Paul's reference to his "heart" (the spirit, the inner man) expresses the depth and sincerity of his desire. Phillips' translation says, "From the bottom of my heart I long . . . that Israel may be saved."

"Prayer" is δέησις (*deēsis*), which is a petitionary prayer, an entreaty, a supplication, a request. Here Paul is following his own

---

[84]As a form of address in Romans ἀδελπηοί appears here and in 1:13; 7:1,4; 8:12; 11:25; 12:1; 15:14,30; 16:17. Moo translates it "brothers and sisters" in every case except 8:12, where he uses just "brothers." The NRSV does likewise except for 7:4, where it uses "friends." The reasons for these exceptions are unclear.

[85]The Greek text has only the pronoun "them," but the context clearly shows this refers to Israel (see 9:31).

instruction in Phil 4:6, "In everything, by prayer and petition, . . . present your requests to God." He lays his request before God on behalf of Israel "unto [εἰς, *eis*] salvation," i.e., for the purpose of their salvation.

Here is the situation: the Jews as a whole were lost, and Paul says he prays for them to be saved. What are the implications of such a prayer? Cranfield says it is "clear proof that he did not think of their present rejection as final and closed" (2:513). But how can this be, since he has already declared on the basis of divine prophecy that only a remnant will be saved (9:27-29)? On the basis of the remnant reference I believe Cranfield is wrong; Paul knows that no more than a remnant will be saved. Yet at the same time he does not know the exact number of this remnant, so he can pray for all Israel in the hope that as many as possible will be included in that number.

How to justify praying for the lost is an enigma for both Calvinists and non-Calvinists. For the former, if God's eternal decree has already inviolably fixed the number and identity of the elect, what is the use of praying? The prayer will surely change nothing. At this point Calvinists usually appeal to their concept of the two wills of God: the number of the elect is indeed fixed according to God's secret will, but his revealed will still enjoins us to pray for all and to seek the salvation of all (see Murray, 2:47; MacArthur, 2:58).

On the other hand, non-Calvinists believe that human beings have free will and that God does not coerce anyone into salvation. So in what way do we expect God to answer our prayers for the salvation of the lost? What do we expect him to do? In another place (GRu, 199-208) I have explained how God may seek to influence human decisions through his providential control of external circumstances and his intervention in our mental processes, but such influences are resistible (Amos 4:6-11; Hag 1:1-11). In any case, because God surely loves all men infinitely more than we are even capable of, surely he is already doing all he can to influence all men to salvation. So what possible difference can it make when we pray for the lost? Lard's comment on Paul's prayer is relevant for such prayer in general (322):

> . . . From the scope of prophecy and the obstinacy of the Jews, the Apostle must have felt sure that they would be lost. Yet he

prayed for their salvation. Did he pray for what he felt certain would not be? He might very consistently have done so. The loss of the Jews was not fixed by irrevocable decree. It was determined by their own wilful rejection of Christ, and although morally certain, it was not unalterably so. Hence the Apostle could very properly ask God to avert it. No one knows, not even Paul, the resources of the infinite Father.

10:2 For I can testify about them that they are zealous for God, but their zeal is not based on knowledge. This is a partial explanation of why Paul earnestly desires and prays for Israel's salvation, i.e., because they did seem to be genuinely sincere in their efforts to honor God. Literally Paul says "I bear witness" or "I do solemnly testify" that they have such zeal. How did Paul know this? Because this was his own state of mind prior to his conversion. He was truly zealous for God even while he was opposing Christ and his church in ignorant unbelief (Acts 22:3; Gal 1:13-14; 1 Tim 1:13).

To be zealous for a cause is certainly in itself an admirable trait, indicating sincerity and enthusiasm and passion. To be zealous "for God" is surely the most virtuous form of zeal. Thus this part of Paul's statement is probably a compliment: "I'll say this for them; I'll give them credit for this." As Dunn puts it, "Paul does honor to his fellow Jews for the fervor of their devotion to God and his law" (2:594). The problem is that one can be zealous, sincere, and enthusiastic and at the same time be deadly wrong. This was true of the Jews, whose zeal, says Paul, "is not based on knowledge" (see Prov 19:2). Unfortunately, where zeal serves the cause of error and ignorance, it is not a virtue but a vice. As Lenski says, "The greater the intensity of zeal devoid of true knowledge, the more damage it does to itself and to others" (643).

Paul's testimony concerning the Jews' uninformed zeal is a good corrective for those who think that sincerity is the deciding factor in one's relationship with God. If that were true, then the Jews would surely have been saved. But Paul makes it crystal clear that they are lost in spite of their sincerity. They are lost not because of their lack of knowledge as such, but because they refused to accept the knowledge that was available to them (see 10:16-21; see 1:18-25, about the Gentiles). One is not held responsible for knowledge that is actually unaccessible to him (4:15), but willful ignorance is inexcusable.

The Jews' zeal was blameworthy not because of its ultimate object, which was God, but because of the *way* they sought to honor him. This is explained in the next verse.

10:3 Since they did not know the righteousness that comes from God and sought to establish their own, they did not submit to God's righteousness. As we saw in our discussion of 1:17 (JC, 1:115-121), "the righteousness that comes from God" is the very heart of the gospel of grace. It is the same as "the righteousness that is by faith" in 9:30. The Greek uses the simple genitive construction, "the righteousness *of God*," but it is clear from the context and from the message of Romans in general that the NIV translation is correct. The righteousness of which Paul speaks is not God's righteous nature as such (contra Fitzmyer, 583), but the gift of a right standing before him which he offers to bestow on believing, penitent sinners. See 1:17; 3:21-22; 4:6; 2 Cor 5:21; Phil 3:9.

This is the righteousness by which God has always saved sinners, even before its basis was not specifically known. The actual basis for it is the propitiatory sacrifice of Jesus Christ; the righteousness of God is literally Christ's satisfaction of the penalty of the law (eternal punishment in hell) in our place (JC, 1:119). This is the gift of righteousness which God offered to all of Israel throughout OT history, through their humble acceptance of the gospel provisions of the law. This is also the gift he offered to them in the very person of their Messiah, Jesus.

But, says Paul, the Jews *did not know* this righteousness. They did not know it when it was initially offered to them in God's promises in OT history, and especially they did not know it when it was offered to them in Jesus himself. This is the climax of their not-knowing: the rejection of Jesus of Nazareth as their Messiah and Savior (DeWelt, 164). Their "chief ignorance" was their "failure to see that there is no other way to justification and salvation save by faith in Christ Jesus" (MP, 419). "The basic error of Israel was misconception respecting the righteousness unto justification" (Murray, 2:48).

To say that the Jews did not *know* this righteousness of God does not mean that they had never been exposed to it and were somehow ignorant of the very existence of the promises of God and the reality of the gospel facts. Rather, it means that they did not *acknowledge* the good news of God's righteousness; they did not accept it and welcome it and submit to it (Hendriksen, 2:342).

Instead, they continued to seek acceptance with God on the basis of their own righteousness, i.e., "as if it were by works" (9:32). They sought to use their law code as if it were a law system; they sought to achieve a level of personal obedience that would make them deserving of heaven. Rejecting the gift of the "robe of righteousness" (Isa 61:10), they relied on their own "filthy rags" (Isa 64:6). Or as one writer says, "Refusing to 'put on Christ' (Gal. 3:27), they clothed themselves with a garment of their own spinning, which they, like all other worms, spun from their own filthy inwards. . . . Refusing to accept Christ as the Rock for life-building, they reared their crumbling structure on their own sandy, unstable nature . . . (MP, 420)."

"Their own" righteousness means the personal self-righteousness achieved by each individual, not the national or corporate righteousness of the Jewish nation as compared with other nations. (See Moo, 634-635, contra Dunn, 2:587, 595.) Only if we take this in the former sense does it have universal application. I.e., every one of us, not just Jews living under the Mosaic Law, must fight the temptation to plead our case before God based upon our own moral and spiritual accomplishments rather than upon the blood of Christ.

The last part of the verse, "they did not submit to God's righteousness," is the main clause; the two verbs in the first part of the verse ("not knowing" and "seeking") are participles that modify or explain the main clause. That is, the Jews did not submit to God's righteousness in the sense that they ignored it and set forth their own as a substitute for it.

The word for "submit" is ὑποτάσσω (*hypotassō*), which is commonly used for submission to law or persons in authority (8:7; 13:1, 5). In what sense is a rejection of grace a refusal to submit to authority? It is so in the sense that grace is the way of salvation established by God himself and declared by him to be the only possible and acceptable way; thus to reject God's way by refusing his gift of righteousness is an act of rebellion against God. It is so also in the sense that accepting the gift of God's righteousness requires a humble and submissive attitude along with a repudiation of personal worthiness, to which human pride stubbornly clings. As Cranfield says, the Jews' rejection of God's righteousness involved "their refusal to humble themselves to accept it as an undeserved gift," and "the refusal to let grace be grace, the refusal to give God alone the glory" (2:515).

How, then, does one submit to the righteousness of God? By accepting *God's* way as the only way, thereby abandoning all claims to salvation based on self-righteousness. The only way to do this in the Christian era is to accept Jesus as the only Messiah and Savior, and to do so by fulfilling the gracious conditions for receiving God's righteousness as spelled out in the Word of God (JC, 1:108-115, 268-271). Chief among these conditions is faith (9:32a,33b; 10:4-17), the very essence of which is in part the act of submitting or surrendering oneself into the hands of God (JC, 1:108).

B. CHRIST ALONE IS THE SOURCE OF SAVING RIGHTEOUSNESS (10:4-13)

The main point of chs. 9–11 is to explain why God must still be regarded as faithful even though most Jews are lost (while many Gentiles are saved!). One key consideration is the distinction between *ethnic* or national Israel, and *spiritual* Israel, the remnant who along with many Gentiles are "vessels of mercy" (9:6, 23-29). Another key factor is the distinction between being chosen for *service* and being chosen for *salvation*.

In 9:1-29 Paul has shown that God is faithful to his promises to ethnic Israel, even though most of them are lost, because these promises had to do with the nation's service, not salvation. In 9:30–10:21 he is giving another reason why the Jews' lostness does not violate God's faithfulness, namely, it is the result of their own choice, not God's. The saved remnant does not owe its existence to a secret, unconditional choice on God's part; their salvation is the result of their free acceptance of God's free offer of grace, a grace that is now known to be possible only because of Jesus Christ. Anyone can choose to accept this grace – certainly the Jews, and Gentiles as well.

In other words, ch. 9 shows that ethnic Israel was unconditionally elected to service, and ch. 10 shows that spiritual Israel is conditionally elected to salvation.

The point Paul is making in this section presupposes the law/grace distinction spelled out in 1–8, especially the nature and role of the righteousness of God in justification (JC, 1:115-120; 250-265). Here Paul is simply applying what he has already taught on the subject to the question at hand, i.e., the question of God's faithfulness in view of the Jews' lostness. The bottom line is that the law/grace distinction, and more specifically the distinction between God's righteousness and personal righteousness, is the key to why God saves some (even Gentiles) and rejects others (even Jews).

In 9:30–10:3 Paul has shown that the Jews are lost because they deliberately chose to trust their own personal righteousness rather than God's righteousness (10:3). Many Gentiles, on the other hand, have chosen to accept the gift of God's righteousness through faith (9:30), and thus are saved.

Now in 10:4-13 Paul goes into more detail about the distinction between the two kinds of righteousness. Speaking especially about the present era, he gets specific about "the righteousness that comes from God." How can it be said that the Jews have rejected God's righteousness? Have they not cherished God's law and been zealous in their attempts to obey it? Yes, but the point is that righteousness according to law is *not* God's righteousness, the righteousness that saves. God's saving righteousness is to be found in Jesus Christ alone. So when the Jews rejected Jesus of Nazareth as their Messiah, they were rejecting the only source and basis for saving righteousness.

The content of this section unfolds thus. First Paul simply states the choice that anyone must make regarding his salvation: either law-righteousness, or faith in Jesus (10:4). The typical Jew chose the former, using his relationship with the Law of Moses as the basis for his claim to salvation. But Moses himself said that the only way to be saved by law is to obey it completely, which is a futile pursuit (10:5).

But the grace of Jesus Christ can set anyone free from the futility of this universal tendency to pursue righteousness via law-keeping. The gospel of grace is readily available to all. The key to receiving it is to trust in the mighty works of Jesus Christ, not in our own works (10:6-10). Saving faith understands that Christ's works alone are the basis for salvation.

This way of trust is open to all, to Jews and Gentiles alike. When it comes to salvation, God makes no distinction between these groups. Whoever calls on the name of the Lord will be saved (10:11-13).

1. An Either-Or Choice: Works-Righteousness, or Faith in Christ (10:4)

10:4 Christ is the end of the law so that there may be righteousness for everyone who believes. Most writers do not see a break between v. 3 and v. 4. They either see v. 4 as concluding the previous section beginning with 9:30, or see 10:1-13 as a unit.

I believe, though, that v. 4 begins a new paragraph. How then does this verse relate to the preceding paragraph? Verses 2, 3, 4, and 5 all begin with the particle *gar*, a word that usually introduces an explanation, a confirmation, or a reason for what precedes. (The NIV translates it only in v. 2). Thus the point is that something in the previous verse or context is true, because v. 4 is true. The key is the reference to the Jews' ignorance of true righteousness in v. 3 ("not based on knowledge") and v. 4 ("they did not know"). Their pursuit of righteousness via law was zealous, but it was ignorant and futile *because* (*gar*) Christ has shown once for all that law-keeping cannot make one acceptable before God.

The distinction between law and grace as contrasting ways of salvation is central to this paragraph (Moo, 644). This distinction has existed from the very moment sin entered the world, but it has now come into sharpest focus with the coming of Jesus the Christ. It is clear beyond the shadow of a doubt that the choice between works-righteousness and faith in Christ is an either-or choice. Jesus is the definitive end to all attempts to use the law as a way of being accepted by God.

This verse is without question "one of the fundamental theses of Pauline theology as a whole," as Cranfield says (2:515), and thus its interpretation is crucial. But how shall we interpret it? Exegetes are sharply divided over this question, and it cannot be answered easily. Four issues must be resolved: (1) What is the meaning of "end" (τέλος, *telos*)? (2) To what "law" is Paul referring? (3) What is the meaning of the connecting word (εἰς, *eis*) between "the end of the law" and "righteousness"? And finally, (4) is this a statement about an event in the overall history of redemption, or about each individual's experience of salvation?

As we analyze these questions, two principal interpretations will emerge. The first can be summarized thus: "Christ is the goal and fulfillment (and thus the termination) of the Law of Moses, so that now, in the NT era, there is righteousness for all who believe." The second is this: "Christ is the termination of the law-system as a way of righteousness for each individual who puts his trust in God's gracious promises." Here I will defend the latter view.

Regarding the first issue, what does it mean to say that Christ is the "end" of the law? The Greek word *telos* has many meanings, but only two or three are relevant here. One possibility is that it means "goal." That is, Christ is the very goal or purpose for the law's existence, or "that at which it was aimed or for which it was intended" (Fitzmyer, 584; see Hendriksen, 2:342). See Gal 3:24. Another possibility is that *telos* means "fulfillment," that Christ came to fulfill the law in the sense of Matt 5:17. Cranfield (2:519) rightly points out that these two nuances (goal and fulfillment) are not really distinct but are correlative: since Christ was the goal of the law, when he came he fulfilled the purpose for which it was given. Cranfield defends this view and shows that it has been held by many writers throughout Christian history (2:516-519). As Calvin says, this "remarkable passage . . . proves that the law in all its parts had a reference to Christ" (385). Lard agrees, declaring that Christ is not the "extinction" of the law, but its "ultimate object" and "final purpose" (325).

The other relevant meaning of *telos* is "termination." Christ is the end of the law in the sense that he terminated it or brought it to an end. Dunn argues for this meaning as primary here (2:597), as does Lenski (645).[86] Moo says this is the better option, though the nuance of "goal" is also present (641). Achtemeier argues for both goal and termination (168).

In my judgment "termination" is the correct view, as the following discussion will show.

---

[86]See also Godet, 376; MP, 421; SH, 284-285; Murray, 2:50; Bruce, 201, 203; Morris, 380-381; and Stott, 281.

The second issue, closely intertwined with the above, is the meaning of "law." Christ is the *telos* of the law – but which law? One main view is that this means the Law of Moses (see 9:31). "The Torah is clearly in view," says Dunn (2:591). Others agree; see Cranfield, 2:516; Fitzmyer, 584-585; Moo, 636. If this is what Paul means by "law," then either or both meanings of *telos* could apply. I.e., Christ was the goal and fulfillment of the OT law, and he also brought it to an end.

The other main view is that Christ is the end of all forms of law or law in general, as a way of attaining righteousness before God. This would apply certainly to the Law of Moses, but also to the law written on the heart as well as to the law-commandments of the NT. In other words, Christ is the end not just of this or that or all law *codes*; he is the end of any form of law as a *system* of salvation. Sanday and Headlam argue thus (284-285), as does Lenski (645).[87] If this is the meaning of "law," then *telos* must mean "termination," since it does not make sense to say that Christ is the aim or purpose or fulfillment of all law.

I accept the latter view of "law" in this verse, and thus take Paul as saying that Christ is the termination of any form of law as a way of righteousness or acceptance with God. It is certainly true that Christ is the *telos* of the Law of Moses. He both fulfills it[88], and brings it to an end; thus what Paul says is surely intended to apply to the Jews and to their law. But his point is not restricted to this. Indeed, Paul says Christ is the end of law for righteousness to *every* person who believes. This reference to "every person" (παντί, *panti*) shows that Paul is thinking not only of those to whom the Law of Moses applied but to those who have other forms of law as well (see SH, 284). The following conclusion concerning *eis* also confirms this view.

---

[87]Moo rejects this view because, he says, νόμος (*nomos*) is not used in this sense elsewhere in this context (636). But in this context (9–11) the word appears only here and in 9:31 and 10:5, which does not establish an overwhelming pattern. Also, in Romans as a whole, *nomos* is certainly used in this sense several times (e.g., 3:19-20, 28; 6:14-15) and as such is an element of the main theme of the letter (JC, 1:52-54).

[88]See Moo, 638-639, n. 39, for an explanation of the fact that Christ is indeed the goal and purpose of the OT law. See also Morris, 381.

The third issue in exegeting 10:4 is the connection between "the end of the law" and "righteousness." In the Greek text the connecting word is the preposition *eis*, and there are two main views as to its meaning here. One view takes "Christ is the end of the law" as being a complete thought in itself, with the rest of the verse (introduced by *eis*) expressing the goal or result of that fact. *Eis* would thus be translated "so that" or "therefore." This is what it means, says Moo: "Christ is the *telos* of the law, with the result that there is (or with the purpose that there might be) righteousness for everyone who believes" (636-637).[89] The NIV follows this view.

According to the other interpretation, *eis* should be connected only with the word "law," introducing a simple prepositional phrase (εἰς δικαιοσύνην, *eis dikaiosynēn*) that modifies that word alone. Thus the verse would be saying that Christ is the end of "law for righteousness" or law "as a means toward righteousness" (Dunn, 2:596). This is how the NASB translates it: "For Christ is the end of the law for righteousness to everyone who believes."

In my judgment the former view, represented by the NIV, is wrong; and the latter view is correct. This latter view is acceptable grammatically[90] and is theologically consistent with the theme of Romans in general and with Paul's point in this context (9:30–10:21). Also, there are two problems with the alternative. One is that the second part of the verse does not logically follow from the first part, as this interpretation of *eis* requires. To say "Christ is the *telos* of the law; *therefore* righteousness is there for all who believe" is a *non sequitur*: it does not follow. This is true whether *telos* be taken as "termination" or as "goal." Regarding the former, to say that doing away with the law (whether Mosaic or general) somehow leads to a righteousness-by-faith situation implies that before this happened, the law itself was somehow a proper means to righteousness – a

[89]See also Cranfield, 2:519-520; and Fitzmyer, 585.

[90]Moo rejects this view because he does not find any other place in the NT where an *eis*-phrase modifies a noun but is separated from that noun by the subject of the sentence, as would be the case here. I.e., in the Greek v. 4 begins with *telos nomou* ("end of law"), and is followed by the subject ("Christ"), then *eis dikaiosynēn*. In response I would say that the reason for this arrangement is that *telos nomou* is obviously placed at the beginning of the sentence for the sake of emphasis and is thus not in its normal position.

conclusion few will accept. Regarding the latter, there is no clear causal connection between the two parts of the verse, contrary to Fitzmyer's statement: "Because Christ is the goal of the law, a status of uprightness is available to all who believe in him" (587). Both these clauses are true, to be sure, but they are not logically connected as cause and effect.

The second problem with interpreting *eis* as "so that" (as in the NIV) is that this makes the first part of the verse say that Christ is the end of the law in an absolute, unqualified way. If "law" here means the Law of Moses, there is surely a sense in which Christ brought it to an end (see Hebrews), but not absolutely. Christ himself said he did not come to abolish the law (Matt 5:17). But as we have seen, "law" here does not refer to the Law of Moses anyway, but to law in general. And certainly Christ has not brought an end to law in general. Though we are not under law as a way of salvation, we are still under full obligation to obey its relevant commandments (6:14-15). Thus Paul must be saying that Christ has brought an end to law only in a qualified sense, and that qualification is spelled out in 10:4b. Christ has terminated the law "unto righteousness," or as a means of achieving a status of righteousness before God.

One final issue must be discussed, namely, what sort of event is this τέλος νόμου (*telos nomou*, "end of law")? Is it a one-time event accomplished by Christ in the process of salvation history? Or is it an ever-recurring event that takes place in each individual's experience when he comes to trust in God's saving grace? Those who take "law" as referring to the Law of Moses say the former. For example, Dunn declares that 10:4 "refers to the once-for-all transition in God's saving purpose effected by the life, death, and resurrection of Christ. It does not denote a timeless sequence which subsequent generations may expect to find constantly repeated in their own lives – as though everyone had to go through a 'law' phase before coming to Christ" (2:597; see 2:611). See also Moo, 641; MP, 421; and Bruce, 203.

I totally disagree with this view, and defend instead the very view that Dunn describes (above) only to reject. Jesus Christ is the termination of the law-system as a way of righteousness, as a way of acquiring God's favor, for everyone who comes to believe in him.[91]

[91]See Bruce, 201; Lenski, 645; Murray, 2:50; MacArthur, 2:67.

Even before Christ came, and not just in this new era, his planned and foreknown atonement was the basis for God's offer of righteousness to those who accepted his loving promises. As Lenski says, this verse "does not mark a date in history as though from that date forward all law was ended while before that date law was the means for righteousness . . . . Christ was 'an end of law for righteousness' from the beginning, for Abraham as much as for us" (645). Moses himself implies this in the statement from Lev 18:5 quoted in the very next verse (10:5). I.e., Moses taught for his own time the very truth that underlies what Paul is saying in 10:4.

It is important to see that ever since sin entered the world there has never been a time when law was an actual way of righteousness before God. Thus to say that Christ is the end of law for righteousness means that he is the end of all false and futile attempts to base righteousness on law-keeping. When we understand the work of Jesus Christ as the embodiment and source of grace, we understand that our righteousness is in him alone (2 Cor 5:21).

2. The Futility of Law-Righteousness (10:5)

10:5 Moses describes in this way the righteousness that is by the law: "The man who does these things will live by them."[92] This and the next five verses set forth in more detail the contrast between law-righteousness and God's righteousness, explaining why Christ has ended the former and established the latter. Verse 5 explains the way law-righteousness works,[93] with the implied conclusion that it is futile for anyone to attempt to actually achieve a right status before God by this method. This is in essence the same message as 1:18–3:20.

To make his point Paul cites a statement by Moses from Lev 18:5, which reads, "Keep my decrees and laws, for the man who obeys them will live by them. I am the LORD." Paul paraphrases it thus: "The man who does [the righteousness of the law] will live by it." See also Luke 10:28 and Gal 3:12.

---

[92]The beginning of the verse literally reads, "For Moses writes." "For" is γάρ, untranslated in the NIV.

[93]"Keep the commandments and escape the penalty," with the implied corollary, "Break the commandments and suffer the penalty." See JC, 1:128.

This statement has two levels of application. Its immediate application in Lev 18:5 was to the covenant responsibilities God imposed on the Jews as his special people. Contrary to the evil behavior of the Egyptians and the Canaanites, Israel was commanded to keep God's laws and decrees (Lev 18:1-4). Their relative righteousness[94] was a condition for their continued enjoyment of the blessings of the promised land. The words "will live" thus referred to peaceful and prosperous longevity in the land of Canaan.[95] Unfortunately, most of the time Israel was not able to fulfill even this requirement of relative righteousness, and thus ultimately forfeited its claim on the promised land. See Ezek 20:11,13,21.

But Paul, guided by the inspiration of the Holy Spirit, sees a deeper level of application in these words of Moses, one that is not limited to the Jews and to the Mosaic Law and to relative righteousness as a covenant condition. He sees therein a reference to law in general, and to the necessity of absolute obedience as a condition for eternal life. Thus the statement by Moses is presented as a terse summary of law as a way of salvation. When one chooses the law-system as his way of gaining acceptance by God, the only way to gain such acceptance is to obey the requirements of the law without exception. Thus Paul takes the statement from Moses to read, "*Only* the man who does these things *perfectly* will live *eternally* by them."[96]

In the background, however, lies the fact that "all have sinned" (3:23; see 1:18–3:20). Thus law as a way of righteousness is tragically futile; this is why it is so important to see that Christ has brought an end to all attempts to establish righteousness by law (v. 4).

3. Saving Righteousness Comes through Trusting Christ's Works, Not Our Own (10:6-10)

10:6a But the righteousness that is by faith says . . . . The next five verses set forth a contrast between law-righteousness and faith-

---

[94]On this concept see GRe, 202-209.

[95]See Dunn, 2:601, 612; Moo, 648; MP, 422.

[96]See Lard, 326-327; Lenski, 647-648. In Gal 3:10 Paul gives the negative side of this same coin, citing Deut 27:26, "Cursed is everyone who does not continue to do everything written in the Book of the Law." See Jas 2:10.

righteousness, a contrast indicated by the word "but" (Greek, *de*).[97] The main point seems to be that whereas law-righteousness depends on human works and accomplishments (which can never be adequate), faith-righteousness depends on the all-sufficient works of Christ. What is left for us to do is to humbly acknowledge these works and rest our hope of heaven on them.

Much of the content of vv. 6-8 consists of statements drawn from the words of Moses in Deut 30:12-14. Since these verses are in contrast with v. 5, which also cites Moses, it might at first seem that Moses is inconsistent. Stott opines that Paul "thus sets Moses against Moses, that is, Moses in Leviticus against Moses in Deuteronomy" (282). This is a faulty understanding of Paul's use of Deut 30, however.

Some declare that Paul in vv. 6-8 is quoting the Deuteronomy text. Bruce says that Paul "quotes verses 11-14" (201). Moo says that certain features in the text "imply that Paul is here applying a text he is quoting" (652). "Paul almost certainly does intend to cite Deut 30:12-13, or more precisely, to explain and expand it," says Dunn (2:603).

This assumption that Paul is *quoting* Moses raises some serious questions, though, since in v. 6 Paul specifically applies the words of Moses to "the righteousness that is by faith," while in Deuteronomy Moses is clearly talking about the law and obedience to it. This leads to some rather strained interpretations of Paul's use of the words of Moses. One of the most common is the idea that law as Moses refers to it in Deut 30 actually includes the message of Christ and his grace; thus Paul is only stating what is implicit in the Deuteronomy text. As Cranfield says, "it is in the law itself, in Deuteronomy, that Paul hears the message of justification by faith" (2:522). Thus 10:6-8 is Paul's "true interpretation in depth" of Deuteronomy (2:524). Paul's purpose, says Godet, is "to bring out the element of grace contained in the passage" in Deuteronomy. This "element of grace . . . is here disentangled by Paul from its temporary wrapping" (379). Moo's view is similar (645, 653-654).

This approach, I believe, is incorrect. It is true that the Law of Moses taken as a whole has an element of grace (see 9:32), but that

---

[97]See Moo's discussion and refutation of the view that vv. 5 and 6 are not antithetical but complementary (645-646).

is not the subject of Deut 30:11-14. In this text Moses speaks of the law as law, as commandments that must be obeyed. His main point is that the Jews had no need to mount a heroic search for God's law, since it was conveniently revealed to them in Moses' own words. Thus "Moses assures the Israelites that God's law is truly accessible to them" (Achtemeier, 169). His point was "to prevent the Israelites from evading their responsibility for doing the will of God by pleading that they do not know it" (Moo, 651).

What is Paul doing, then? He is simply taking the *form* of Moses' statements about the law, including some of the same wording, and applying it to grace instead. He is not attempting to quote Moses or interpret Moses. He simply wants to say the same thing about grace that Moses said about the law: we do not have to do something heroic to know about it and receive it; it has already been made available to us, namely, through Jesus Christ. As DeWelt says, "What Moses said of 'the commandment' . . . can be applied to justification by faith" (166). "St. Paul uses the same words to express exactly the same idea, but with a completely different application" (SH, 287).

We should note that in this verse, unlike in v. 5, Paul does not say "*Moses* says" or "*Moses* writes." This shows that it is not his intention simply to repeat Deut 30:12-14. Instead, Paul says that "the righteousness that is by faith"[98] is the one who speaks the words that follow. He thus personifies faith-righteousness. That faith-righteousness *says* these things means simply that it is *characterized* by them.

The first words of the personified faith-righteousness are in the form of an exhortation, **"'Do not say in your heart . . . .'"** "Heart" refers to the entire spiritual side of man's nature, including the intellect and the will as well as the emotions. According to Lenski, "'To say in the heart' is a Hebraism for 'to think secretly' and is used especially regarding some unworthy thought which one fears to utter aloud" (650). See especially Deut 8:17; 9:4, where this expression is used to warn against "presumptuous boasting in one's own merit" (Cranfield, 2:523).

---

[98]The expression "righteousness that is by faith" (ἐκ πίστεως, *ek pisteōs*) is Paul's shorthand reference to the entire grace system, just as "righteousness that is by the law" (ἐκ νόμου, *ek nomou*, v. 5) is his shorthand for the law system.

10:6b-7 What does Paul warn us not to say? Do not say **". . . 'Who will ascend into heaven?'" (that is, to bring Christ down) "or 'Who will descend into the deep?'" (that is, to bring Christ up from the dead).** This is certainly an allusion to Deut 30:12-13, where Moses says this concerning God's law: "It is not up in heaven, so that you have to ask, 'Who will ascend into heaven to get it and proclaim it to us so we may obey it?' Nor is it beyond the sea, so that you have to ask, 'Who will cross the sea to get it and proclaim it to us so we may obey it?'"

Moses' emphasis is clearly on the accessibility and understandability of God's law. It is not an esoteric message hidden in some secret place or located at some far corner of the universe. Possession of it is not dependent on some act of Herculean proportions, such as ascending into the heavens or crossing the sea. As Moses explains in v. 11, "What I am commanding you today is not too difficult for you or beyond your reach." You already have it; all you have to do is obey it.

By wording his questions in much the same way as Moses, Paul makes the same point about grace that Moses does about law, except he refers not just to the *knowledge* of saving righteousness, but to the actual *possession* of it. How can one be accepted as righteous before God? Not by personal obedience or "doing" ("the man who does these things," v. 5), but only by the works of Jesus Christ! So do not ask yourself, what great work must I do to be justified before God? Do not ask, "Must I ascend into heaven?" – as if you could! and as if Christ has not already been there and has not already come down to us, bringing salvation with him. Do not ask, "Must I invade the empire of death and Satan himself?" – as if you could! and as if Christ has not already done that and returned from the dead in triumph. Do you think you can match what Christ has done, or somehow participate in his work or improve upon it?

Paul's reference to ascending into heaven is the same idea and has the same force as Deut 30:12. As Moo points out, in the OT this act was "almost proverbial for a task impossible for human beings to perform" (654). The reference to descending into the deep makes the same point, using the figure of extreme depth rather than extreme height. In the second question Paul does not follow Deut 30:13; Moses speaks of crossing the sea while Paul speaks of descending into "the deep" (ἄβυσσος, *abyssos*, "the abyss"). In the Greek OT this word was often used for the depths of the sea, and the concept is sometimes paired with the heavens (Ps 107:26; see Ps 139:8, which has *hades* instead of *abyssos*). In either case, crossing the sea or descending to its depths, along with ascending to the heavens, to the Jews represented the most extreme effort imaginable.

Paul's reference to the abyss, though, probably has significance beyond the fact that it is simply the opposite vertical extreme compared with the heavens. In the OT the abyss is sometimes comparable to *sheol* (*hades*), the abode of the dead (Ps 71:20), and in the NT it is elsewhere depicted exclusively as the proper abode of Satan and his demonic angels (e.g., Luke 8:31; Rev 9:1,2,11). Thus descending into the abyss means coming face to face with man's greatest enemies, death and Satan. Fitzmyer is probably correct to say that Paul switches to this figure because this allows him to refer specifically to the resurrection of Christ (590).

What is the significance of Paul's christological comments appended to these questions? They are not meant to be a commentary on or an interpretation of Moses' questions in Deut 30:12-13. They are meant rather to point out that the only one who is capable of performing mighty works of salvation is Jesus Christ, and he in fact has already done them. There is no need to ask, "Who will ascend into heaven?" as if such an act on man's part would merit his salvation. In the first place, no human being can do this by his own effort. In the second place, even if he could, the only purpose for doing so would be to come before God and beg for a Savior. But this is unnecessary, because the Savior has already by his own initiative come down out of heaven for us, in the incarnation.

At the same time there is no need to ask, "Who will descend into the deep (the abyss)?" as if by this act we could in some way forge our own deliverance from sin. In the first place it would be futile, since the lords of the abyss, death and Satan, are both stronger than we are. In the second place, the Christ who came down from heaven has already through his death invaded the abyss, and he has defeated its inhabitants and been victoriously raised from the dead. He has done this by his own glorious power; he needs no help from us.

These questions are not meant to represent an attitude of denial and disbelief with respect to Christ's incarnation and resurrection (contra Godet, 381; Lard, 327-328; and Hendriksen, 2:344). Rather, they represent either an attitude of self-righteousness, as if a man could actually do works great enough to save himself – in which case the references to Christ are a rebuke; or (more likely) they are a cry of despair at the impossibility of saving ourselves – in which case the references to Christ are a comfort and a relief. Morris sums it up thus: "'The righteousness of faith' does not demand that we be supermen; it does not set some impossible task before us. God has done all that is necessary, and we receive his gift of righteousness by faith" (383-384). See MP, 424; Lenski, 650-651.

10:8 But what does it say? The subject of the verb "say" is the same as in v. 6, "the righteousness that is by faith." What does faith-righteousness say to us? **"The word is near you; it is in your mouth and in your heart". . . .** This statement closely follows part of Deut 30:14, "No, the word is very near you; it is in your mouth and in your heart so you may obey it." This completes the thought begun in Deut 30:11, where Moses tells his people that God's commands are not beyond their grasp, as if they could find them only by ascending to heaven or crossing the sea (30:12-13). On the contrary, his word is as close to you as your own mouth and heart. You already have God's law; all that remains is for you to obey it.

Though Paul in 10:8 is obviously echoing key elements of this verse in Deuteronomy, he is not just repeating it but is adapting it to his own purposes. When Moses said, "The word is very near you," he meant the word of command. Deut 30:11 speaks literally of "[this command which] I am commanding you today"; v. 14 says this word (of command) must be *obeyed*. But to show that he is not speaking of the same word, Paul adds this specific qualification: **. . . that is, the word of faith we are proclaiming . . . .** Moses spoke a word that must be obeyed; Paul proclaimed a word that must be believed.

The term for "word" is ῥῆμα (*rhēma*), not *logos*, probably because the LXX uses *rhēma* in Deut 30:14. It refers to the message Paul proclaimed or preached, the message of the gospel of Jesus Christ.

Why is it called "the word of faith"? One reason is that the proper and natural response to the word (message) of the gospel is to *believe* it (as contrasted with the proper and natural response to the word of law, which is to *obey* it). Another reason is that this word is what stimulates and evokes faith (10:17). Finally and primarily, as is often the case for Paul, the term "faith" stands in contrast with "works" (9:32) and with the "doing" required by law (10:5). Thus "the word of faith" is another shorthand expression for the entire way of grace.

The main point is that the word of faith is *near* you. This simply reinforces what was said in vv. 6-7, that the source of our salvation is not works that we do but the saving work of Jesus, which is made known to us through the word of the gospel. This means, as Lard says (329), "that what justification by belief requires is easy," as compared with the impossible requirements of salvation by law.

Just how near is this "word of faith"? It is so close that it is "in your mouth" and "in your heart." Deut 30:14 says the same thing about the word of law. The Israelites had heard the word of the law spoken by Moses; thus they were fully able to repeat it with their own mouths and understand it in their hearts. Likewise, through the proclamation of the word of faith, the saving righteousness of God is immediately present to the hearing sinner, so near and familiar to him that he can talk about it and mull it over in his mind.

10:9 It may be that in the original reference (Deut 30:14) the mouth and heart were mentioned simply because they are the epitome of nearness. I.e., what could be closer to the center of a person's being than something in his mouth or in the deep recesses of his heart? But Paul is not content to let these figures stand as simple symbols for nearness. In the next two verses he gives them a spiritual or theological application, showing that the mouth and the heart are both involved in receiving for oneself what the close-at-hand "word of faith" promises.

Moses declared that the word of command was very near to the Israelites, but it still had to be obeyed: "The word is very near you; it is in your mouth and in your heart *so you may obey it.*" Paul likewise tells us that the word of faith demands a response. The gospel may be in someone's mouth in the sense that he can repeat it, and it may be in his heart in the sense that he knows about it and understands it. But such a person is not actually saved unless he believes the gospel message to be true and both internally and externally surrenders himself to the Lordship of Jesus Christ.

Paul sums up this response in v. 9: **That if you confess with your mouth, "Jesus is Lord," and believe in your heart that God raised him from the dead, you will be saved.** This verse begins with the Greek word ὅτι (*hoti*), which the NIV and others translate as "that." Taken thus, v. 9 would be the content of the word of faith that Paul proclaimed. Others take *hoti* as meaning "because" (e.g., Moo, 657; NRSV). I.e., the word of faith is as near as your mouth and heart, because the simple hearing of the word puts one in the position of immediately being able to use his mouth and heart to receive salvation.

The Greek for "confess" is ὁμολογέω (*homologeō*), which literally means "to say the same thing, to agree," and thus to acknowledge the truth of something. Of course such a confession could be hypocritical, but the very sense of the word implies sincerity,[99] and in this context Paul ties it to sincere heart-belief.

Paul says that this confession is "with your mouth," which shows that he is referring to an oral, public confession of one's faith. In 1 Tim 6:12-13 Paul reminds Timothy that he confessed the "good confession in the presence of many witnesses," and notes that even Jesus "made the good confession" before Pontius Pilate (see John 18:37).

The essential content of our confession is specified: "Jesus is Lord." The Greek is κύριον Ἰεσοῦν (*kyrion Iēsoun*), literally "Lord Jesus." The KJV speaks of confessing "the Lord Jesus." It is generally accepted, though, that this double object of the verb "confess" has the sense of confessing "Jesus [to be] Lord." The NASB puts it "Jesus *as* Lord." The NIV gives the correct sense of the statement. (See 1 Cor 12:3, where the same formula, *kyrios Iēsous*, obviously means "Jesus is Lord.")

The confession of Jesus as Lord early became the standard way of acknowledging oneself to be a Christian. It was "the earliest . . . Christian creed" (Bruce, 202), "an established confessional formula" (Cranfield, 2:527), the "slogan of identification" that marked one as

---

[99]It was used by Greeks for confessing guilt in a court of law, confessing sin to a deity, and binding oneself with an oath to a treaty. See Fürst, "Confess," 344.

a believer (Dunn, 2:607). See John 20:28; Acts 2:36; 10:36; 1 Cor 12:3; 2 Cor 4:5; Phil 2:11.

What does it mean to confess Jesus as *Lord*? It ascribes to him two things: ownership and deity (see Cranfield, 2:529). The basic connotation of the word is that of the owner or master of something (cf. the English "landlord"). To confess Jesus to be our Lord is thus to confess that he is our owner and we are his slaves. It is the external expression of an internal spirit of complete submission to every aspect of his word and will.

In accord with the religious significance attached to the title *kyrios* in biblical times, it is clear also that confessing Jesus as Lord is to confess that he is deity, that he is fully divine, that he is God the Son, equal with God the Father and God the Holy Spirit in essence and power and honor. "Lord" is the name above every name (Phil 2:9-11); it is Paul's trinitarian title for Jesus (1 Cor 8:6; 12:4-6; Eph 4:4-6). It is also the Greek word used by Greek-speaking people to represent the holy name of God – Yahweh – in the OT, orally at first and then ultimately in copies of the Septuagint (see Moo, 660, n. 77; see GRe, 121).

There is still no greater and no more significant confession than "Jesus is Lord." To confess him as "the Christ" and "the Son of the Living God" (Matt 16:16) is accurate and appropriate, but to omit the central confession of his Lordship is to ignore the fundamental pattern of NT Christianity. MacArthur points out (2:74), "In the book of Acts, Jesus is twice referred to as Savior but ninety-two times as Lord. In the entire New Testament, He is referred to some ten times as Savior and some seven hundred times as Lord. When the two titles are mentioned together, *Lord* always precedes *Savior*."

The other necessary response to the word of faith mentioned by Paul in this verse is to "believe in your heart that God raised him from the dead." To "believe that" (πιστεύω ὅτι, *pisteuō hoti*) is to acknowledge or assent to the truth of some statement. This is a necessary aspect of saving faith,[100] but must be accompanied also by "believing in/on" Jesus, which is the element of trust. (See JC, 1:107-108.) Here the element of trust is not specifically mentioned but is

[100]"It matters that we believe, but it also matters what we believe" (Morris, 385).

implied in the confession of Lordship, by the phrase "in your heart," and by association with "trusts in" (πιστεύω ἐπί, *pisteuō epi*) in v. 11.

To "believe in the heart" means not only to accept the bare facts about something but also to accept its full meaning and significance and to be committed to applying its implications to one's own life. It is comparable to being "obedient from the heart" (6:17, NASB).

It is significant that believing and confessing are linked together; it shows that in the Christian life they cannot be separated. "Inward belief and outward expression of the word [are] inextricably linked, the two sides of one coin" (Dunn, 2:609). Confession without faith is of no value for salvation (Matt 7:21-23), and faith without confession is simply unthinkable: "True faith is never silent; it always confesses" (Lenski, 655).

It may seem strange that Paul mentions confession before faith, since the logical order would seem to be the reverse. The order in v. 9 is dictated, however, by the order of "mouth" and "heart" in Deut 30:14 as reflected in v. 8. In v. 10 Paul recapitulates v. 9, using the reverse (expected) order.

Exactly *what* must be believed in the heart about Jesus as a means to salvation? We must believe "that God raised him from the dead." In view of the centrality of the atonement in God's provision for our justification (JC, 1:118-120), it may seem strange that Paul should here omit any reference to the cross and mention only the resurrection. The resurrection is not unrelated to our justification, however (see 4:24-25). Also, we should not jump to the conclusion that Paul's list here in 10:9 is meant to be exhaustive (see below). Also, he focuses specifically on faith in the resurrection because in the NT the resurrection of Christ is directly related to his Lordship (see below).

That Jesus actually died and came back from the dead are two of the most firmly attested facts in the NT, and are completely indispensable to the gospel (1 Cor 15:1-4). Faith in the resurrection is the keystone (the top wedge of an arch) that gives legitimacy to all the other elements of our belief about Jesus. We cannot believe in his incarnation, virgin birth, deity, propitiatory sacrifice, and Second Coming if we deny his resurrection.

We must believe not just that he came back from the dead, but more specifically that *God raised him* from the dead. As such we acknowledge that his resurrection is not just some isolated and unexplained accident of nature, nor a part of some sinister hoax by an unidentified but malevolent power. No, his resurrection was an act of *God,* the God of the Bible, the God of the Jews, the God of our Lord Jesus Christ himself. Thus the resurrection establishes the entire biblical worldview, especially its claim that our justification before God is not by our own righteousness but by his righteousness alone.

Belief in Christ's resurrection is naturally linked with confession of his Lordship, since in the NT his resurrection and Lordship are inseparable. As the final and victorious stage in his battle against death and Satan, the resurrection is the supreme and conclusive expression and validation of the Lordship of God the Son in his incarnate form as Jesus of Nazareth. Because of the resurrection there can be no doubt that this man is, in Thomas' words, "my Lord and my God" (John 20:28). There are many others for whom deity and lordship are claimed (1 Cor 8:5), but the claims of Christ and Christ alone are vindicated once for all by his resurrection. See Matt 28:18; Acts 2:36; Rom 1:4; Eph 1:20-22; Phil 2:9-11; Rev 1:17-18.

This brings us to Paul's main point. Grace as a way of salvation is simple and relatively easy (compared with law), because the message has already been proclaimed to you, and the reality of which it speaks can be appropriated without delay by the activity of your own mouth and heart. You must respond as instructed, to be sure; but if you do respond, you can be assured that "you will be saved." This salvation includes the present down-payment of the "double cure" for sin (JC, 1:248), followed by the full inheritance of eternal life (8:17-25).

This verse clearly states that salvation is conditional: "*If* you do these things, you will be saved."[101] This is in keeping with Paul's main point in this chapter, namely, that the Jews' lostness is not the result of some action (or lack of action) by an unfaithful God, but is the result of their own refusal to meet the gracious conditions for receiving salvation.

---

[101]If salvation were unconditional, as Calvinists claim, Paul would have to say, "If you are saved, you will confess with your mouth that Jesus is Lord and believe in your heart that God raised him from the dead."

Regarding the specific conditions named here, v. 9 presents a dilemma for those committed to a faith-only view of salvation. On the one hand, the verse omits any reference to baptism, and thus seems to refute the claim that baptism is somehow a condition for salvation. On the other hand, it does speak of deliberate oral confession as a condition for salvation, and thus seems to go against the common view of justification by faith alone.

At the same time, this verse presents a problem for those who do believe that baptism is a condition for salvation. Paul seems to be saying that the *only* conditions for salvation are faith and confession; he makes no specific mention of baptism.

Regarding the former dilemma, some faith-only advocates simply ignore the implications of this verse for their view; others openly deny the parallel significance given by Paul to confession and faith. Moo (657) says it is surprising, "in light of Paul's stress on faith in this context," that he should list two conditions as our expected response to the word of faith. Moo's explanation is that Paul did this just for rhetorical purposes, i.e., to maintain a parallelism with the references to both mouth and heart in Deut 30:14. He then discounts the reference to confession thus:

> . . . Paul's rhetorical purpose at this point should make us cautious about finding great significance in the reference to confession here, as if Paul were making oral confession a second requirement for salvation. Belief in the heart is clearly the crucial requirement, as Paul makes clear even in this context (9:30; 10:4, 11). Confession is the outward manifestation of this critical inner response.

Murray's explanation is similar: "We are not to regard confession and faith as having the same efficacy unto salvation," he says (2:55). Like any other good work, confession "is the evidence of the genuineness of faith" (2:56). Lenski says the same thing: "The instant a sinner believes, righteousness results . . . . This is justification by faith alone. . . . One who believes and is thereby justified confesses and shows that his faith is genuine" (657).

Such attempts to discount the significance of confession in order to preserve a concept of "faith only" that has been around only since Zwingli (16th century)[102] are unfair to Paul's teaching, however. The references to confession and faith are grammatically parallel; the two verbs are identical in form and are related to "if" in exactly the same way, i.e., as equal conditions for salvation. If faith is a condition for salvation, then so must confession be. This is not to say that these two acts are related to salvation in the same way. I.e., both are conditions for salvation, but they do not play the same role in bringing the sinner to that point.

This verse shows the folly of taking any passage regarding the way of salvation in isolation from others that address the same subject. It especially shows the fallacy of drawing faith-only conclusions from texts such as John 3:16; Acts 16:31; and Rom 3:28. I have commented several times that when Paul uses expressions such as "righteousness by faith" (9:30; 10:6) and "word of faith" (10:8), these are shorthand expressions that stand for the entire grace system as contrasted with the law system. (See JC, 1:266-271, on 3:27-28.) Just as works are the central element in the law system, so is faith the central element in the grace system. The frequent reference only to faith is due to this centrality, and the absence of a reference to other acts (such as repentance and baptism) cannot be taken as ruling them out as conditions, as this verse shows.

Lard notes that Hodge says, "The two requisites for salvation mentioned in this verse, are confession and faith." Lard then comments, "But the reader may ask, Do you regard this condition [confession] as indispensable? I will answer the reader by asking, Are you ready to assume the responsibility of dispensing with it? I at least am not" (330).

The bottom line is that Paul's teaching about faith and confession is inconsistent with the prevalent Protestant understanding of salvation by faith alone. (See v. 14 below for a further problem with this view.)

But what about the absence of any reference to baptism here? Even if we grant that faith is not the only condition for salvation, the only other one mentioned here is confession, not baptism. How can we explain this?

---

[102]See Cottrell, "Consensus" and "Reformed Tradition."

The same cautions explained above apply to this concern as well. We cannot assume that any one NT passage includes the entire list of conditions for salvaiton – not even this one. In fact, this very verse contains something that shows us that it was not intended to include all the conditions necessary for salvation, namely, the limited nature of the content of the faith specified here. Paul says if you believe "that God raised him from the dead," you will be saved. But virtually all Christians agree that the content of faith must include more than this; it must especially include "faith in his blood" (3:25). Thus the abbreviated content of the faith described here shows this verse is not intended to be a comprehensive, exclusive list of conditions.

Compiling such a list requires looking at all that Scripture has to say about the way of salvation. (See JC, 1:112-115.) In Romans, Paul has already explained the saving significance of baptism (6:3-4); he need not repeat it here. Many other texts do the same. (See Cottrell, *Baptism.*)

One thing about this verse suggests that baptism may not have been absent from Paul's thinking after all, even though it is not specifically mentioned. That is the fact that the verbs "confess" and "believe" are aorist tense, which suggests that Paul had in mind a specific past act that was associated with the sinner's initial and decisive confession of faith.[103] In early Christian practice, this act was baptism. Bruce says, "If we are to think of one outstanding occasion for such a confession to be made, we should more probably think of that first confession – 'the answer of a good conscience' (I Pet. iii.21) – made in Christian baptism" (205). Also, Cranfield (2:527) notes that the confessional formula "Jesus is Lord" was probably "used in connexion with baptism (the present verse – perhaps also the fact that baptism was in, or into, the name of Jesus – would seem to point in that direction)." This confession, says Dunn, was "a public confession of a solemn nature," and "would no doubt be used at baptism" (2:607). The confession of Jesus as Lord is also referred to as "calling on the name of the Lord" in 10:13; and this is something associated with Christian baptism as a saving event (Acts 22:16; see Joel 2:32; Acts 2:21).

---

[103]Paul uses the aorist tense "of the act of Christian commitment for the first time," says Dunn (2:608).

10:10 For it is with your heart that you believe and are justified, and it is with your mouth that you confess and are saved. Literally this reads, "For with the heart one believes unto [εἰς, *eis*] righteousness, and with the mouth one confesses unto [*eis*] salvation." The NIV equates "unto righteousness" with being justified, which is probably accurate.

Do "justified" and "saved" refer to two different things in v. 10? MacArthur (2:72) says the former is the positive side of grace, i.e., what we become and receive (eternal life), while the latter is the negative side, i.e., what we escape (sin, eternal punishment). This distinction is completely artificial, however, and has no basis in the text. Godet makes a more reasonable distinction. He says justification is specific and depends only on faith, while salvation is more general, including sanctification and glory, and thus requires "persevering fidelity in the profession of the faith" (383; see MP, 427). But this is not Paul's point either, as the aorist tense for both verbs suggests. In other contexts such distinctions may be appropriate, but not in this verse. As Dunn says, here the words "could be reversed without loss of meaning" (2:609). "There is no substantive difference here," says Stott (283). Hendriksen (2:345) and Moo (659) also see them as synonyms in this verse.

The two parts of the verse are strictly parallel in form. In each case Paul is talking about how a sinner initially receives the gift of God's righteousness, which is the same as entering into the state of salvation. Thus this verse does not add anything to v. 9, in which being saved (the only term used there) is conditioned on both confession and faith.

One problem with the NIV is that it obscures the precise relation shown in the Greek text between believing and righteousness, and between confession and salvation. Paul says the sinner believes "unto (*eis*) righteousness" and confesses "unto (*eis*) salvation." *Eis* expresses purpose (and therefore result). I.e., the sinner believes for the purpose of receiving the gift of righteousness, and that is indeed the result of his faith. The sinner likewise confesses for the purpose of receiving the gift of salvation, and that is indeed the result of his confession.

When we understand that the two parts of this verse are parallel in form and that "righteousness" and "salvation" here have the same connotation, we can see why the faith-only approach to salvation cannot be true. This view assumes that righteousness or justification *by* faith means that one is justified *as soon as* he has faith, in the instant he has faith. Such simultaneity, however, is not inherent in the preposition "by" in the phrase "justified by faith," and this verse is evidence of it. The fact that another, separate act besides faith (i.e., confession) is also a condition for receiving salvation shows that one does not receive it *as soon as* the faith is present. This same logic also shows that justification by faith does not exclude from the salvation package the act of baptism, which in other texts is shown to be the precise *time* when the salvation is received (e.g., Col 2:12, "in baptism").

4. God's Righteousness Is Available Equally to Jews and Gentiles (10:11-13)

Why are so many Jews lost, while so many Gentiles are being saved? It all comes back to the question of righteousness, and *how* a person seeks to be accepted as righteous by God. The question has always been, "In whose righteousness do you trust?" Anyone who trusts in his own righteousness will come short of the glory of God and be put to shame on Judgment Day; but anyone who humbly, by faith, accepts the gift of God's own righteousness will be saved. This applies to Jews, covenant service notwithstanding; it also applies equally to Gentiles. In this New Covenant age, the focus of this trust must be Jesus Christ, whose saving work is the very source and essence of this gift of righteousness.

This brief section speaks of the universality of God's righteousness, and how it is intended for and available to every human being.

10:11 As the Scripture says, "Anyone who trusts in him will never be put to shame." Unlike v. 6, this is specifically identified as a quote from Scripture, namely, Isa 28:16b. This was quoted earlier in 9:33; see the comments there for its basic meaning.

"Will never be put to shame" means that those who meet God on the day of judgment wearing the free gift of the robe of Christ's righteousness (Isa 61:10; 2 Cor 5:21) will not be ashamed; those who refuse the gift (i.e., refuse to put their trust in Christ) will show up for the judgment wearing only their own filthy rags (Isa 64:6) and will be eternally ashamed. See Phil 3:9.

The "him" who is the object of trust is without question Jesus. In 9:33 this was implicit, but the context of 10:11 makes it explicit. He is the *Lord* of whom this whole passage speaks (vv. 9,12,13).

Paul cites Isaiah to once again provide OT confirmation for his teaching. His main point is righteousness by faith, and in vv. 8-10 Jesus Christ is the specific object of this faith. This is what Isa 28:16b means, he says.

Isaiah is quoted exactly the same in 9:33 and 10:11, except for the addition of one word in the latter. In each case the subject is a participle, "the one who believes/trusts" (ὁ πιστεύων, *ho pisteuōn*). Universality is implicit here, but in 10:11 Paul makes it explicit by adding the word πᾶς (*pas*), "all, everyone, anyone." Thus he emphatically affirms that God's offer of righteousness by faith is open to everyone. It is open to all Jews; those who refuse to accept it do so by their own choice. It is also open to all Gentiles, many of whom have accepted it (9:30). Those who exercise their freedom to trust in him constitute the true Israel, spiritual Israel, the remnant.

10:12 For there is no difference between Jew and Gentile . . . where the true Israel is concerned. Paul has already declared, in 3:22b, that "there is no difference" between these groups. In that verse his point was that there is no difference between them with regard to *sin*, "for all have sinned and fall short of the glory of God" (3:23); "Jews and Gentiles alike are all under sin" (3:9). In this verse, though, the statement sounds the joyful note that there is no difference between Jews and Gentiles with regard to *salvation*. The promise in v. 11 applies equally to all. As Peter learned through his encounter with Cornelius, "God does not show favoritism" when it comes to salvation (Acts 10:34). The Old Covenant distinction between Jews and Gentiles was a matter of the formers' election to service; faith-righteousness as the only way of salvation is offered to all. See 1 Cor 12:13; Gal 3:28; Col 3:11.

The all-inclusiveness of the gospel is grounded in the universality of the Lordship of the one Lord, Jesus Christ: **. . . the same Lord is Lord of all and richly blesses all who will call on him . . . .** In 3:29-30 Paul affirmed the unity of Jews and Gentiles by declaring that there is only one God who is the *God* of them both. The idea here is the same, with attention focusing specifically on Jesus as the one *Lord* who is over all. That "Lord" here refers to Jesus is clear from v. 9 (see 1 Cor 12:5; Eph 4:5; Phil 2:9-11). He is elsewhere declared to be "Lord of all" (Acts 10:36; see Rom 9:5; Eph 1:22).

"All" refers specifically to all *people*, Jews and Gentiles; but the reference to riches means he is also Lord over all *things*, especially the spiritual bounty of salvation. God is "rich in mercy" (Eph 2:4) and supplies all our needs "according to his glorious riches in Christ Jesus" (Phil 4:19).[104] This reminder that our Lord is rich assures us that there is an inexhaustible supply of grace; it will never run out, no matter how many heirs there may be. He is fully able to richly bless "all." Thus there was no need for the Jews to jealously seek an exclusive saving relationship with God. "The Jew had no reason to envy or begrudge the Gentiles their call, since it in no way impoverished him" (MP, 429).

Paul says that God richly blesses "all who call on him." We might have expected the Apostle to say, "all who believe in him," since his main emphasis thus far has been on faith (10:11). Why does he now change to "call on him"? Probably for two reasons. First, "calling upon the Lord" is a way of confessing him with our mouths; thus by using this language Paul reinforces the essentiality of confession as explained in 10:9-10. "Calling upon him" unites faith with the act of confessing. Second, Paul uses this word here to set up the quotation from Joel 2:32 in the next verse. To "call upon" (ἐπικαλέω, *epikaleō*) was a word widely used in biblical times in both secular and religious senses. In the middle voice (as here) it meant "to appeal to someone" for a favor or a blessing. It is the word Paul used when he "appealed" to Caesar (Acts 25:11-12,21,25; 26:32; 28:19). When used in reference to God it often had the sense of petitionary prayer (1 Kgs 18:24; Acts 7:59). To call upon the *name* of God was the same as calling upon God, as vv. 12 and 13 show.

Calling upon (the name of) the Lord – confessing his Lordship – has always been a distinguishing characteristic of God's people. Calling on the name of Yahweh set Israel apart from all the nations:

---

[104]Regarding spiritual riches see Rom 2:4; 9:23; 11:12; 1 Cor 4:8; 2 Cor 8:9; Eph 1:7,18; 2:7; 3:8,16; Col 1:27; 2:2; Titus 3:6. These riches are all Christians' family inheritance (8:16ff.), to which Jews and Gentiles are equal heirs (Gal 3:28-29).

"Pour out your wrath on the nations that do not acknowledge you, on the kingdoms what do not call on your name" (Ps 79:6; see v. 4). In the NT Christians are identified as the ones who call on the name of the Lord (Acts 9:14,21; 1 Cor 1:2; 2 Tim 2:22). To call upon the Lord is in essence a humble confession of his absolute, universal Lordship. As MacArthur (2:83) says, "To call upon the name of Jesus as Lord is to recognize and submit to His deity, His authority, His sovereignty, His power, His majesty, His word, and His grace."

10:13 Most important, calling upon the Lord is specifically related to salvation: **for, "everyone who calls on the name of the Lord will be saved."** In some contexts this may refer to praying for deliverance from temporal troubles, as in Ps 116:4, "Then I called on the name of the LORD: 'O LORD, save me!'" In other contexts, as here, it is an appeal to God for salvation from sin.

This verse (except for "for") is an exact quotation of Joel 2:32 (LXX, 3:5). In Acts 2:21 the Apostle Peter cites this as part of a Messianic prophecy that refers to calling on the name of the Lord Jesus Christ for salvation (Acts 2:36-38; see 4:12; 8:12). Here we see again how "calling on the name of the Lord" is equivalent to "confessing with your mouth that Jesus is Lord" (10:9), and how confessing with the mouth results in salvation (10:10).

The relation between calling on the Lord and salvation from sin also helps us to understand how baptism is related to the initial reception of salvation. In Acts 22:16, God's messenger Ananias tells the penitent but as-yet-unsaved Saul to do what Joel 2:32 says and call on the name of the Lord, i.e., for salvation. Do this, he says, while you are being baptized and washing away your sins. The very act of baptism is both a humble acknowledgment (confession) of the Lordship of Christ, and a prayer for him to save by washing away sins through his blood. The baptismal act should also be accompanied by a verbal prayer that "calls on his name," i.e., calls upon the Lord to keep his promises and wash away all sins. This is the sense of 1 Pet 3:21, which says that baptism saves us because it is "an appeal to God for a good conscience" (NASB; the NIV's "pledge" is incorrect). See Cottrell, *Baptism*, chs. 6 and 13.

One last point about 10:13 is that it is a clear affirmation of the deity of Jesus. There can be no question that "the Lord" here refers to Jesus, especially in view of the content of our saving confession in v. 9. Also, there can be no question that Paul is here quoting Joel 2:32 and applying it to Jesus. But in the original Hebrew of Joel 2:32, "Lord" is actually the tetragram, the name *Yahweh*. Thus Paul is identifying Jesus of Nazareth with Yahweh, the God of the OT. (This is not to say that Yahweh and Jesus are identical. Yahweh as known in the OT is actually all three persons of the trinity – Father, Son, and Holy Spirit – as known in the NT. See GRe, 127-128.)

The main point of this paragraph (10:4-13) is that Jesus Christ alone is the source of saving righteousness. The emphasis throughout has been upon him. Now, by climactically applying Joel's prophecy to Jesus, Paul shows why we can have such utter confidence in him: he is no less than God himself.

C. THE JEWS HAVE NOT BELIEVED IN CHRIST, AND THEIR UNBELIEF IS INEXCUSABLE (10:14-21)

How may we reconcile God's faithfulness with the Jews' lostness? In the first place, God's covenant with Israel never guaranteed that every Jew would be saved; it guaranteed only that the nation would serve God's redemptive purposes (9:1-29). In the second place, the lost condition of individual Jews is the result of their own choice of law rather than grace (9:30–10:21).

Regarding the latter point, the Jews have chosen to rest their case for salvation on their own righteousness, and not on the righteousness of God (9:30–10:3). But the only way anyone can be accepted by God is through the gift of God's own righteousness; the only basis for this gift is the work of Jesus Christ; and the only way to receive it is by faith in Christ (10:4-13).

This leads to the specific question now being discussed in this paragraph (10:14-21): it is true that the great majority of Jews have not believed in Jesus, but is their unbelief really their fault? Maybe they have not believed simply because they have never had the opportunity! "Perhaps the Jews have not had a fair deal? Perhaps the way has never been made clear to them?" (Morris, 389).

In response to such an idea, Paul makes it clear that the Jews have had every opportunity to believe, but have simply refused to do so. Thus they are without excuse and are personally responsible for their own lost state. As Fitzmyer says, "Paul stresses in this passage that God has done all that he could to bring Israel to faith. . . . Hence its 'ignorance' (10:3) is its own responsibility" (595, 596). Moo agrees: "Paul removes any possible excuse that the Jews might have for their failure to respond to God's offer of righteousness in Christ"; he shows that "Israel cannot plead ignorance" (662-663).

The flow of Paul's thought here is as follows. He has just asserted that everyone who calls on the name of the Lord will be saved (v. 13). But Israel has not called on his name (v. 16). Why not? Maybe it has something to do with the chain of contingencies that must precede the act of calling on the Lord's name, i.e., calling-on is contingent upon faith, which is contingent upon hearing, which is contingent upon preaching, which is contingent upon being sent (vv. 14-15a).

So maybe Israel's unbelief can be traced to one of these other contingencies, one over which they have no control. Faith can come only from hearing the message, which can come only through the word of Christ. So maybe the message has never been brought to them – which would not be *their* fault (v. 17). As Achtemeier says, the "logic of the passage" is that "perhaps the reason Israel had not responded properly was due to the fact that she had never heard the apostolic message" (174), at least in a way she could understand it.

In response to this idea Paul specifically affirms (in vv. 18-21) that the Jews have both heard and understood the gospel. In fact, their own Scriptures – including both the Law and the Prophets – should have prepared them for it. Therefore they have no excuse; their problem is not ignorance but stubborn, willful unbelief. See Smith, 2:27.

1. The Necessary Prerequisites to Saving Faith (10:14-15)

Even though their immediate application was to Paul's Jewish contemporaries, these two verses (along with v. 17) are general doctrinal principles with many other applications. For example, they have long been regarded – and rightly so – as crucial for such theological issues as the salvation status of the unevangelized, the necessity of missions, and the nature of conversion as such.

10:14-15a The four main verbs in this passage are third person plural with no subject specified; thus the general translation, "they." Though its scope is ultimately universal (see vv. 12-13), "they" refers specifically to the Jews. Though they are not expressly mentioned until v. 19,[105] they are the implicit subject all along.[106]

These four rhetorical questions are similar in form, beginning with "how" (πῶς, *pōs*) and a subjunctive verb. The sense is "How is it possible . . . ?" and the expected answer is, "It is impossible!"

The issue is, why have the Jews not called on the name of their Lord and Messiah, and thus received salvation? The question being explored is whether they may possibly have some excuse for not doing so. After all, a number of prerequisites must be in place before one can call on the Lord's name and be saved. These are listed here, in a kind of reverse order, as a chain of effects and causes. If any one of the links in the chain is missing, then it would be impossible for one to call on the Lord's name and be saved. This chain is summed up by Stott thus: "Christ sends heralds; heralds preach; people hear; hearers believe; believers call; and those who call are saved" (286).

How, then, can they call on the one they have not believed in? A genuine appeal for help presupposes a belief that the one to whom the appeal is made is able to comply. It is also a confession of need and dependence. Dunn rightly says (2:628), "To appeal to another is to put oneself in that other's power; and who would do that unless one believed in that other – believed that he could help, trusted oneself to him for that help?" As in vv. 9-10, mouth and heart are inseparably linked.

"Believed" is aorist and probably refers to the initial birth of faith in the heart. Believed "*in*" is εἰς (*eis*),[107] which is equivalent to ἐπί (*epi*) in v. 11. These expressions refer primarily to that element of faith usually called trust, which is a heartfelt surrender and commitment of the self to Christ. This involves a sense of dependence upon him, and a total confidence in his ability and willingness to keep his promises and to meet our needs.

---

[105]The NIV adds "Israelites" in v. 16; it is not in the original text.

[106]Paul proceeds the same way in ch. 2. Though the Jews are the subject from v. 1, they are not specifically mentioned until v. 17.

[107]This phrase is used in Paul's letters only here and in Gal 2:16 and Phil 1:29 (Col 2:5 has *pistis eis*). Contra Stott, 285-286.

In the discussion of 10:9 above, it was pointed out that the listing of both faith and confession as conditions for salvation disproves the common faith-only doctrine of salvation, which alleges that a person is saved the instant he believes. The question Paul asks here in v. 14a has the same effect. Paul's point is that these three things occur in a cause-effect sequence: believing, calling on the Lord's name, and being saved. One cannot contend that these events are only logically sequential while being in fact temporally simultaneous. The act of calling upon the Lord, as a public confession of one's faith, will almost never occur at the instant faith begins. The fact that Paul lists it here as an intermediary link between faith and salvation shows that salvation is not given at the moment one begins to believe. Faith is a prerequisite for calling upon the Lord, and calling upon him is a prerequisite for salvation.[108]

And how can they believe in the one of whom they have not heard? This is not a literal translation, because the Greek says neither "believe *in*" nor "*of* whom." It says literally, "How can they believe whom they have not heard?" As the next questions show, the one who is heard is actually the preacher of the gospel of Jesus Christ. But the previous question (indeed, the entire context) implies that the object of faith is Jesus himself. This has led many exegetes to suggest that "Christ is present in the preachers; to hear them is to hear him" (Morris, 389-390). This may well be true in the sense that the inspired message is the words of Jesus (John 16:12-15; see Luke 10:16), but the main point is surely as the NIV translates it.

Just as calling-on and faith are necessarily linked, so are faith and hearing. Hearing does not always produce faith; indeed, the main point of this paragraph is that the Jews have heard (v. 18), but have not believed. But on the other hand, there can be no faith without hearing (see v. 17). In other words, hearing is a *necessary* condition for faith, but not a *sufficient* one.

The hearing of which Paul speaks is more than mere sense perception; it is also an act of the mind. It involves at least a minimal level of understanding of the message heard, i.e., enough understanding to create culpability for failure to believe (see v. 19).

---

[108]Moo says that "calling on the name of the Lord is another way of saying 'believe'" (662). This is more consistent with faith-only soteriology, but it is quite implausible.

We must not underestimate the importance of hearing in the salvation process. On several occasions Jesus gave this exhortation: "He who has ears, let him hear" (Matt 11:15. See Matt 13:9,43; Mark 4:23; Luke 14:35; Rev 2:7,11,17,29; 3:6,13,22). This hearing is the responsibility not just of the messenger, but even more so of the listener, who is the one addressed in the exhortation. I.e., the listener is responsible for paying attention to the message, and for studying it and searching out its proper meaning.

And how can they hear without someone preaching to them? A proper hearing of the message of Jesus Christ presupposes and requires the work of a third party. God of course could speak his message directly to each individual, but instead he has chosen to use intermediaries to act as his messengers and ambassadors; and without their faithful preaching there will be no hearing.

"Someone preaching" is a form of the verb κηρύσσω (*kēryssō*), which means "to announce, to proclaim aloud, to preach, to herald abroad." Its noun form is κήρυξ (*kēryx*), a "*herald*, whose duty it is to make public proclamations" (AG, 432). We should remember that Paul wrote this long before the invention of the printing press and electronic media, in a time when the role of the herald was indispensable for spreading news. For our time we may properly assume that this "preaching" can be done via such media as printed material, television, and the internet.[109]

This question shows how important is the whole enterprise of evangelism, and specifically the office of evangelist (Eph 4:11) and the work of preaching the gospel. Murray says this verse refers to "the institution which is the ordinary and most effectual means of propagating the gospel, namely, the official preaching of the Word by those appointed to this task" (2:58-59). This includes both local evangelists and ministers, as well as missionaries engaged in world-wide evangelism.

Paul's point is not just that this heralding work is *important*; it is actually *necessary*. It is a prerequisite to the hearing that must precede faith. "Hence arises the necessity of proclaiming the gospel world-wide" (Bruce, 205). Some think that general revelation alone

[109]As we saw under 1:15, Paul considered his written letter to the Romans as a form of preaching the gospel (JC, 1:44-47, 101-102).

provides enough knowledge of God to enable pagans to believe and call upon God and be saved, but this text shows otherwise. The hearing that leads to salvation comes only through a personal, human messenger.

Since the hearing involves not just receiving but also understanding the message (as noted above), the heralding must include not just a bare speaking of the message but an earnest attempt to explain it as well. Hence the importance of sound exegetical and doctrinal training for those who proclaim the gospel.

And how can they preach unless they are sent? With this question Paul has traced the chain of prerequisites back to its beginning point: the *sending* of the heralds or preachers. At first glance this may seem to be out of place in a list of such obviously significant and interconnected events as preaching, hearing, believing, calling-on, and being saved. It may not appear to be on the same level with these other factors. Nevertheless, Paul through the Spirit has included it here. Therefore we must not weaken the connection between preaching and being sent; sending is just as necessary as the other elements in the chain.

The obvious question is, sent by whom? The first answer is, sent by *God*. This certainly applies to Paul himself, and to the other apostles, all of whom were commissioned and sent directly by Christ, who is God the Son. After his resurrection Jesus said to the Eleven, "As the Father has sent me, I am sending you" (John 20:21). Paul's commission came directly through Jesus and God the Father (Gal 1:1,15-16). In fact, the very word "apostle" is from ἀποστέλλω (*apostellō*), "to send," and means "one who is sent."

But God has sent more than these who are the "official" apostles. Jesus, God the Son, gave us his "great commission" (Matt 28:18-20), which most take to apply to all Christians. Even though it was spoken directly only to the apostles (28:16), Jesus told them to teach the rest of us to obey everything he commanded *them* to do (28:20). In the early church all Christians who were scattered abroad via persecution "preached the word wherever they went" (Acts 8:4). By the very fact that we possess the message, the word of the gospel, we have been inducted into the army of heralds who have been commissioned to take that word to the world. God himself has sent us.

The second answer to this question (sent by whom?) is, sent by *the church*, through the act of ordination. By ordaining an individual Christian to a specific ministry, the leadership of a local church acknowledges that servant's spiritual gift, puts an unofficial "stamp of approval" upon him (e.g., on his doctrinal soundness and his readiness for ministry), recommends him to the brotherhood at large, and establishes a relationship of encouragement and accountability. Various NT men and women were "apostles" – "ones who were sent" – in this generic sense, e.g., as missionaries (see Acts 13:1-3; Rom 16:7; 2 Cor 8:23). When we apply this verse to the sending of missionaries, we should think more in terms of ordination than financial support.

Such ordination does not create a "clergy class" that has a special access to God and an exclusive authority to interpret Scripture and "administer the sacraments." The key word is *accountability*. Via ordination an individual accepts his accountability to the ordaining body, and the ordaining body declares its accountability to the brotherhood for that individual's faithfulness in ministry. The goal and end result should be to see that the work of the ministry – in particular the preaching of the gospel – is imbued with the respect and importance warranted for it by its inclusion in this list of salvation prerequisites. See 11:13.

10:15b As it is written, "How beautiful are the feet of those who bring good news!" This quote is from Isa 52:7,[110] which was first of all a prophecy relating to the end of Israel's Babylonian captivity c. 536 B.C. It speaks of the herald "who brings good news as he runs on mountain ridges and announces to Jews left in ruined Jerusalem that deliverance from Babylonian captivity has come" (Fitzmyer, 597). But since that great event was itself an historical type of the Messiah's work of delivering his people from captivity to sin, Paul appropriately applies the prophecy to the work of preaching the gospel of Jesus Christ.

Why are the feet singled out? The implication is that the original messenger traveled from Babylon to Jerusalem on foot to bring his message of deliverance. His feet were responsible for bringing

[110]Some manuscripts expand the quote by adding another phrase from Isa 52:7, "and preach the gospel of peace" (KJV). See Fitzmyer, 597-598; Moo 661, n. 1.

him and his beautiful message to those set free from Babylon's oppression; therefore his feet were looked upon as sharing in the beauty of the message. Also, after such a long, hot, dusty journey, the messenger's feet would be the least attractive part of his appearance. But the messenger's news was *so good* that even his *feet* looked beautiful to those receiving his word!

Why exactly does Paul quote this text from Isaiah at this point? Some answer that it shows "the need for heralds"; it is "Paul's case for evangelism" (Stott, 286; see Moo, 664). This is at best a secondary point, however. The main reason for quoting Isa 52:7 is to affirm through OT testimony "that the 'gospel' has indeed been preached to Israel" (Fitzmyer, 597). Thus "the last condition for salvation listed by Paul in vv. 14-15a has been met: God has sent preachers" (Moo, 664). Paul knew this was true, because he himself was such a preacher.

2. Most Jews Have Not Believed the Gospel Message (10:16)

10:16 This verse states the obvious: **But not all the Israelites accepted the good news.** Literally this reads, "But not all obeyed the gospel." The context shows that the "Israelites" are indeed the subject, but this word is not in the original. "Not all" is rhetorical understatement, and simply highlights the fact that "only a few" Jews – a remnant – obeyed the gospel (9:6b, 27b).

"Accepted" is too mild a translation of ὑπακούω (*hypakouō*). Its root is ἀκούω (*akouō*, "to hear"; see vv. 14,18), but with the prefix ὑπό (*hypo*) it has the connotation "to heed, to submit, to be subject to, to obey." It means "to submit and yield to what is heard" (Lenski, 665).

To "obey the gospel" is a significant NT concept (2 Thess 1:8; 1 Pet 4:17), similar to "obeying the faith" (Acts 6:7; see JC, 1:81, on 1:5). It means submitting to God's instructions (meeting the conditions) for receiving the saving grace promised in the gospel. The primary (and representative) condition for salvation is faith, as v. 16b shows; that other conditions are also required has already been made clear in vv. 9-10 (confession) and vv. 13-14 (calling on his name).

To show that the Jews' rejection of the gospel was just part of a longstanding pattern of chronic unbelief, Paul quotes Isa 53:1 from the LXX: **For Isaiah says, "Lord, who has believed our message?"**[111] This was true in Isaiah's own day, when apostate Jews rejected God's words spoken through his prophets (see Acts 7:51-52). It was true of the Jews whom Jesus confronted during his earthly ministry. See John 12:37-38, where John quotes this same passage and declares that Israel's unbelief is the fulfilment of Isaiah's prophecy. And alas, much to Paul's dismay (9:1-3; 10:1-3), the prophecy was still being fulfilled in his own time.

That most Jews have not obeyed the gospel is just a restatement of v. 3b, which says "they did not submit to God's righteousness." In terms of the prerequisites for salvation listed in vv. 14-15a, they have not believed and have not called upon the Lord's name. The issue at hand is how to account for this, which is addressed in the next few verses.

3. The Jews' Problem Is Not Ignorance but Stubbornness of Will (10:17-21)

10:17 Consequently, faith comes from hearing the message, and the message is heard through the word of Christ. How this verse fits into the logical progression of Paul's argument is a bit puzzling. It is often taken as a summary of the salvation prerequisites listed in vv. 14-15a (Dunn, 2:623; Morris, 391; Hendriksen, 2:351). But it is not just a summary, since it focuses only on the middle of the chain (believing, hearing, preaching) and ignores its ends (calling-on, sending). Also, would not a summary have appeared immediately after v. 15? Why the awkward intrusion of v. 16?

Part of the problem is the transitional word, "consequently," at the beginning of the sentence.[112] How is v. 17 a result or consequence of v. 16? The truth stated in v. 16 is that Israel has not believed. But in order to respond to the charge that this unbelief represents some sort of failure on God's part, it is necessary to pursue the question of the *cause* of the Jews' unbelief. But to know

---

[111]The word for "message," is ἀκοή (*akoē*), which figures prominently in v. 17.

[112]Greek, ἄρα (*ara*), meaning "so, then, so then, as a result, consequently."

the cause of unbelief, we need to inquire as to the cause of belief itself, and at least a part of the answer to the latter question is found in the chain of prerequisites in vv. 14-15a.

The logic, then, is something like this: "Most Jews have not believed, even as Isaiah says. Consequently, in view of the chain of prerequisites listed earlier, some will say that Israel's unbelief must have something to do with that chain. There must be a breakdown in it somewhere. I.e., one of the necessary prerequisites for faith must be missing. Did we not say that faith comes from hearing, and hearing comes through the preaching of the gospel? Thus there must not have been any preaching or hearing, since if there had been, surely the Jews would have believed."

The NASB is literal and to the point: "So faith comes from hearing, and hearing by the word of Christ." The NIV is somewhat bulky in its attempt to account for the two different meanings of the word *akoē* in vv. 16 and 17. In v. 16 it means "the message that is heard," but in v. 17 it means "the act of hearing the message." Thus in v. 17 *akoē* is equivalent to the "hearing" in vv. 14 and 18.

We know that *akoē* means "hearing" and not "message" in v. 17, since it is distinguished from the "message" (ῥῆμα, *rhēma*) of Christ in 17b. It would not make sense to say that "the message comes through the message."

"The word of Christ" is the better textual reading, though some manuscripts have "the word of God."[113] Grammatically "the word of Christ" could mean either "the word Christ speaks" or "the word spoken about Christ." The latter is probably Paul's intent, since it is no doubt the same as "the word of faith" that he proclaimed (v. 8), i.e., the message about Christ's saving work.

The verse restates the important principle given in v. 14b, "And how can they believe in the one of whom they have not heard?" It also restates and expands v. 14c – "And how can they hear without someone preaching to them?" – i.e., preaching the word of Christ. It is exceedingly important that we acknowledge these necessary cause-and-effect connections. Faith must be preceded by hearing the word of Christ; it cannot arise under any other circumstances. The role of the word is indispensable. Also,

[113]On the textual issue see Dunn, 2:619, and Moo, 661, n. 2.

this "word" must be the word or message about *Jesus Christ.* Saving faith cannot arise in a context of general revelation only, which tells us nothing about Jesus.

We must not conclude, however, that wherever the word of Christ is present, faith will automatically follow. As said earlier, the word is a *necessary* condition for faith, but not a *sufficient* condition. Thus I cannot agree with Lard, who declares that this verse "settles the question as to how belief is produced" (340). True, it shows us an essential part of the picture, but it does not tell the whole story. We must be careful to avoid the fallacy of taking the part for the whole.

In fact, this very fallacy seems to be at the root of the attempt to excuse Jewish unbelief that Paul discusses in vv. 18-21. I.e., someone may try to say the following: "We grant that the Jews have not believed. But if it is true, as you say, that *faith comes from hearing,* then they must not have *heard* the gospel; because if they had heard it, they would have to believe it."

Paul's point is that this is fallacious thinking. The Jews have indeed heard the gospel, and have understood it. But hearing it is not the same as believing it, and does not automatically lead to saving faith. Such faith is a decision the individual must make, and a stubborn will may refuse to believe even in the face of clearly attested facts. Herein lies the real cause of the Jews' unbelief: they are simply "a disobedient and obstinate people" (v. 21).

Paul now discusses this point in detail.

10:18 So why has Israel not believed? Is it possible that they never really heard the word of Christ? Here is Paul's question, and his answer: **But I ask**, on behalf of all who may want to raise this question: **Did they not hear?** And I answer: **Of course they did.** It is true that no one can believe in someone of whom they have never heard (v. 14), but the Jews cannot use this excuse. In fact, the words of David in Ps 19:4 apply here: **"Their voice has gone out into all the earth, their words to the ends of the world."** (This is a verbatim quote from the LXX.)

Paul is not implying that these words from the Psalms are an actual prophecy of first-century evangelism. Thus he is not citing this passage to *prove* that the Jews have heard the gospel; the authority of his own words as an apostle is sufficient for this purpose.

In its original context this quote refers to the universal availability of general revelation (see also 1:18-20). The personified natural world is pictured as declaring the glory of its Creator to all people on earth. Paul's citation of the verse is by way of analogy: "The dissemination of the gospel is becoming as world-wide as the light of the heavenly bodies" (Bruce, 209). There is a "parallel between the universality of general revelation and the universalism of the gospel" (Murray, 2:61). See Moo, 667.

Lenski is right to take the two parts of the quote as synonymous (671). They are an example of Hebrew poetry's tendency to say the same thing twice in different words. Lard is wrong to identify "the earth" as the land of the Jews as distinct from "the world" as the Gentile countries (341). In NT times the Jews were scattered over most of the Roman Empire anyway.

When Paul said that the gospel had gone out into "all the earth" and "to the ends of the world," did he mean that this had already happened? Lard says, "At the time Paul wrote, the passage was literally true. . . . There is not the slightest exaggeration in the statement" (341). Others disagree and take this as an hyperbole (Dunn, 2:624, 630; Moo, 667; Stott, 288), limiting it at least to the lands included in the Roman Empire, variously called "the known world" and "the inhabited earth." As Godet says, "The voice of the preachers of the gospel has sounded in all countries and in all the cities of the known world" (388). When we remember that Paul is speaking here specifically of the Jews, we need not press his words beyond the scope of their scattered colonies. As Bruce says, Paul is affirming that "to every place where there is a Jewish community the gospel has been carried" (206).

The main point is that "the Jews had, indeed, gotten to hear!" (Lenski, 671). Thus ignorance cannot be cited as an explanation for their unbelief.

10:19 Paul now deals with one last attempt to excuse the Jews for their failure to obey the gospel: maybe they *heard* the message, but just did not *understand* it. He says, **Again I ask: Did Israel not understand?** As we saw above (v. 14), the concept of "hearing" in itself includes a basic understanding of the message received. Thus to distinguish here between hearing (v. 18) and understanding (v. 19) is grasping at straws, and Paul does not even consider the objection worthy of a direct answer.

The way Paul deals with this question shows that the Jews' "not knowing" in 10:3 was a *willful* ignorance (Stott, 289). As was the case with the Gentiles and general revelation in 1:18-25, knowledge of the gospel was there for the Jews but was willfully ignored or suppressed, the result being that there was no excuse.

Paul makes his point by quoting three passages from the Jews' own Scriptures (the OT). He implies that they should have understood from these texts that the Gentiles were ultimately going to be included within God's people, and the Jews excluded. But they also should have understood that in the final analysis God did not do the excluding; the Jews excluded themselves (v. 21). As Hendriksen says, the content of these prophecies, "though not a direct answer to this question [in 19a], implies the answer. It shows that not ignorance but unwillingness was the cause of Israel's lack of faith" (2:352).

Paul quotes first from Moses and then from Isaiah. **First, Moses says, "I will make you envious by those who are not a nation; I will make you angry by a nation that has no understanding."** This comes from Deut 32:21. Paul follows the LXX text closely, except he changes third person to second person so that the Jews are being addressed directly. The words are actually spoken by God; "Moses says" them in the sense that he is God's spokesman or prophet. (Paul here seems to assume the Mosaic authorship of Deuteronomy.)

The words are from Moses' final benediction to Israel just before his death. They are part of a warning that God will punish the Jews for their unfaithfulness. The whole verse says, "'They made me jealous by what is no god and angered me with their worthless idols. I will make them envious by those who are not a people; I will make them angry by a nation that has no understanding.'" As Moo sums it up, "Because Israel has made God jealous with 'what is no god' (v. 21a), God will make Israel 'jealous' with what is 'no people'" (668).

As quoted by Paul, "those who are not a nation" and "a nation that has no understanding" refer to the Gentiles in general. They are "not a nation" because God did not call them into a special covenant relationship with himself, the way he called Israel. Also, in contrast with Israel, they had "no understanding" (ἀσύνετος, *asynetos*) of God's redemptive purposes and plans. Paul uses this same word to describe the Gentiles in 1:21 ("foolish") and 1:31 ("senseless").

There may be a sense in which this prophecy was fulfilled in OT history in the various occasions when God used heathen nations to punish Israel (e.g., the Babylonian captivity), but its ultimate fulfillment lies in the NT era, in the continuing influx of Gentiles into the church in the face of Jewish unbelief. Thus Deut 32:21 is "a prophecy of the mission to the Gentiles," as Moo says (668).

The irony and the tragedy of these words in relation to Israel is this, that the nation that took such great pride in being God's chosen people and in being entrusted with God's special revelation would some day be humiliated by a "no-people" with "no understanding"! That is, the messianic blessings that were intended first of all for the Jews (1:16b) are being lavished upon the Gentiles, who are turning to Jesus the Messiah, calling upon his name, and being saved (10:11-13).

What are the implications of this for the Jews? First, Paul seems to be suggesting that Israel should have understood from this text that Gentile evangelism and conversion were part of God's plan. "Israel ought to have seen in the positive response of the Gentiles to the gospel of Messiah Jesus a fulfillment of Deut 32:21" (Dunn, 2:631). "From their own Scriptures, then, Israel should have recognized that God was at work in the gospel" (Moo, 668).

Second, the Deuteronomy text says that the conversion of the Gentiles would have the effect of arousing envy and anger in the hearts of the Jews. How so? "By letting Israel see the blessings which fall upon the Gentiles when they embrace Christ by faith." Israel then "asks why these same blessings should not even more rightfully be hers, and is assured that they will indeed be hers on the same basis – faith in Christ" (Bruce, 207).

Certainly God did not embrace the Gentiles just to make Israel jealous. He wanted to save the Gentiles for their own sake; Israel's jealous anger would be an indirect result of this (Lard, 341-342). Paul's earnest hope was that this jealous anger would then lead to Israel's own conversion (see 11:11-14).

10:20 And Isaiah boldly says, "I was found by those who did not seek me; I revealed myself to those who did not ask for me." After quoting from the Law, Paul now quotes from the prophets to make the same basic point. This verse is from Isa 65:1a, with the clauses being transposed. As in v. 19, the words of the prophecy are actually spoken by God. Isaiah, like Moses, is the prophet through whom he speaks.

One problem here is that Paul clearly applies this prophecy to the Gentiles (see v. 21), but in Isaiah it seems to have been originally spoken about Israel (see 9:25-26). Some disagree with the latter point. Lenski says Isa 65:1 refers to Gentiles, and 65:2-7 to Jews (676). Some think that 65:1b must be referring to Gentiles since it speaks of "a nation that did not call on my name" (Calvin, 405-406; MP, 440; see Moo, 669, n. 49).

It seems more likely, though, that when Isaiah wrote 65:1, he had the Jews in mind. Moo says, "This is the majority view among OT commentators," and he agrees (669), as do Bruce (211) and Cranfield (2:540). Paul sees in Isaiah's words "a principle which in the situation of his day is applicable to Gentiles" (Bruce, 211). "As he did with Hos. 1:10 and 2:23 in 9:25-26, Paul takes OT texts that speak of Israel and applies them, on the principle of analogy, to the Gentiles" (Moo, 669). See 10:18b.

Thus Paul takes Isa 65:1 as having the same general impact as Deut 32:21. Even if this were not Isaiah's original point, in view of the reality of widespread Gentile conversions, Israel should have been struck by the way these words precisely described what was happening among them. Thus, "as used by [Paul], the quotation from Isa 65:1 is parallel to the quotation in v. 19, and serves to confirm that Israel must have known, since God has actually been found by Gentiles who were not seeking Him" (Cranfield, 2:540-541). It is an argument from the lesser to the greater: if the Gentiles (who had no prior understanding based on special revelation) could understand the gospel and accept the Messiah through apostolic preaching, surely the Jews (with their long history of divine preparation) should be able to understand and obey the same gospel.

It is easy to see how these words apply to Gentiles. Paul's description of them in 1:18-32 shows emphatically that they do not seek God and do not ask for him. Nevertheless God "revealed" himself or "became manifest" to them through the word of Christ. This is the very nature of evangelism. In preaching the gospel we do not passively wait for people to come to us, but actively seek them where they are.

10:21 But concerning Israel he says, "All day long I have held out my hands to a disobedient and obstinate people." There is neither doubt nor disagreement that these words from Isaiah 65:2 apply to Israel; Paul expressly says so. His point goes back to 10:19: "Did Israel not understand?" He implies that the Jews of his day should have seen and understood how Isa 65:2 applied to their situation. They should have understood that the inclusion of the Gentiles in the messianic kingdom was not meant to exclude them. They should have learned from this text that they too were being invited into the kingdom, and that the only reason they were not included in it was their own stubborn refusal to believe in their Messiah, Jesus.

This image of God as one who constantly stands with welcoming arms outstretched toward rebellious sinners is one of the Bible's most graphic pictures of God as a God of grace. "All day long" indicates God's persistence and patience in his desire to save sinners. Stretched-out hands are a gesture of invitation, as God pleads with sinners and implores them to return to him. They are also "a gesture of appealing welcome and friendship" (Cranfield, 2:541). Thus it is clear that "God has never stopped reaching out to Israel, even in all its resistance" (Fitzmyer, 600).

Just as important is the verse's description of Israel as "a disobedient and obstinate people." Paul has already emphasized the Jews' refusal to obey the gospel (v. 16), and here he suggests the reason for it. Their failure to believe cannot be blamed on ignorance, as if no one had ever been sent to preach the gospel to them. No, their unbelief is due to their own obstinate will.

Cranfield (2:541) recalls vv. 9-10 and takes "disobedience" as the very opposite of believing, and "obstinate" as the very opposite of confession. "Obstinate" is a form of the verb ἀντιλέγω (*antilegō*), which means "to speak against, to contradict, to oppose, to refuse" (AG, 74). Instead of using their mouths to confess Jesus as Lord and to call upon his name, the Jews chose to speak against him, to oppose him, to deny him. Instead of welcoming their Messiah, "their response is negative, resistant, recalcitrant, dismissive," says Stott (289). "It is simply stubborn" (ibid., 288).

This is how this main section ends. Is Israel's lost state a reflection on God, evidence of his unfaithfulness, an indication that his word has failed (9:6)? No, God has faithfully kept his word to Israel in every way. He kept every promise he made to the nation relating to their covenant purposes and privileges (9:1-29). He has sent the Messiah and given them every opportunity to trust in him for personal salvation (9:30-10:21). Their refusal to accept him is their own fault. In summary, "The Apostle demonstrates the inexcusableness of Israel and does so by appeal to their own Scriptures" (Murray, 2:64).

Calvinists and others who take ch. 9 as teaching the sovereign, unconditional election of individuals to salvation find it difficult to reconcile this with the emphasis on Israel's willful unbelief in ch. 10. Stott's view is typical (289-290):

> So Paul concludes his second exploration into the unbelief of Israel. In chapter 9 he attributed it to God's purpose of election, on account of which many were passed by, and only a remnant was left, an Israel within Israel. In chapter 10, however, he attributes it to Israel's own disobedience. Their fall was their fault. The antinomy between divine sovereignty and human responsibility remains.

Morris likewise calls attention to the sharp contrast between this "predestinarian" understanding of ch. 9 and the emphasis in ch. 10 on "Israel's responsibility." He simply concludes, "If we are to understand what Paul is saying in Romans we must hold both truths at the same time, no matter how hard we find it to reconcile them to one another" (395).

This "antinomy" disappears, however, when we rightly see ch. 9 as discussing the unconditional election of Israel as a nation to a role of service, and ch. 10 as an explanation of how individual Jews are either saved or lost. There is no conflict between these chapters because they are discussing two different things, with the vindication of God's faithfulness being the main point in each case.

It is obvious that ch. 10 ends on a very negative, pessimistic note. Where does this leave the question of the Jews and their salvation? Murray puts it this way: "Verse 21 brings us to the terminus of the condemnation. We may well ask: what then? Is this the terminus of God's lovingkindness to Israel? Is verse 21 the last word?" (2:64). The answer, of course, is no. There is much more to be said – in ch. 11.

IV. THE SALVATION OF GOD'S TRUE ISRAEL (11:1-32)

Thus far in chs. 9–10 Paul has painted a very dark picture of Israel. He has implied that they are "cursed" (9:3). He has spoken of them as "vessels of wrath prepared for destruction" (9:22, NASB). They have pursued righteousness, but have not found it (9:31-32) because of their willful ignorance of what true righteousness is (10:3). Indeed, Israel is "a disobedient and obstinate people" (10:21).

At the same time Paul has stressed the fact that God is welcoming the Gentiles as "the objects of his mercy" (9:23-24), according to prophecy (9:25-26). The Gentiles found the very righteousness the Jews were seeking (9:30), again according to God's plan (10:19-20).

Such teaching naturally raises the question, "Did God reject his people?" (11:1). Has he simply given up on Israel, and turned his attention solely to the Gentiles? Romans 11 addresses this question and answers it with an emphatic No! God's desire and intention are still to save as many Jews as possible, even to the point when ultimately "all Israel will be saved" (11:26).

This chapter discusses not just the *fact* of Israel's salvation, but also the *means* by which God is accomplishing it. This involves intricate interrelationships between the Jews and the Gentiles, which God uses for the salvation of both. Even as Paul writes about this, he is overwhelmed with awe and amazement at the wisdom and mercy of God, and most appropriately closes out the chapter and the entire section with a hymn of praise to the Creator and Redeemer (11:33-36).

It is important to see that the question addressed here is different from that in ch. 9, which focuses on God's covenant faithfulness to ethnic Israel, i.e., how he kept his promises to them and how they fulfilled their purpose in God's plan. In ch. 11 the focus is not on the Old Covenant purpose for Israel as fulfilled in Jesus Christ (9:4-5), but on God's intended place for Jews as individuals under the *New* Covenant, in terms of salvation and eternal destiny. Throughout this chapter, the issue is *salvation*. What is God's plan for Israel with regard to salvation in this New Covenant age?

In this connection a major issue of interpretation is the place of Israel *as a nation* in this NT era. One main view is that God is still under obligation to save, restore, and preserve national Israel because of the covenant promises he made to the patriarchs. MacArthur states this position: "God cannot be finished with the nation of Israel – for the obvious reason that all of His promises to her have not yet been fulfilled" (2:92). "Because of God's promise to Abraham and to his descendants through Isaac . . . , the nation of Israel has always been and always will be divinely preserved. . . . God's character and integrity, His trustworthiness and faithfulness depend on His continued preservation of Israel" (2:93). "God's unqualified promises to Israel included the assurance that He would never completely forsake her." Even the Jews' initial rejection of their Messiah "could not abrogate the ultimate fulfillment of His promises to them. It is that glorious truth that Paul explains and clarifies in Romans 11" (2:95).

Another main view is the one defended here, i.e., that only the Old Covenant was made with Israel as a nation, that the essence of this covenant for Israel was service and not salvation, and finally that all God's covenant obligations to national Israel were fulfilled when Christ came into the world the first time. Under the New Covenant God is dealing with the Jews as individuals, not as a nation. He is now gathering together the remnant, the new Israel, the true spiritual Israel, from among both Gentiles and Jews. Those who believe the gospel and accept Jesus as their Messiah are added to this remnant. See Lard, 345; McGuiggan, 319-320.

The following exposition will show that Paul's teaching in Rom 11 is more consistent with the latter view.

A. GOD'S TRUE ISRAEL IS THE REMNANT CHOSEN BY GRACE (11:1-6)

Has God rejected Israel? The answer to this question is already obvious in chs. 9–10. In the first place, God has not rejected them; *they* have rejected *him*. "All day long I have held out my hands" to invite them to myself, God says (10:21), but "they did not submit" (10:3). See Matt 23:37.

In the second place, even if there is a sense in which God has "rejected" Israel, he has not rejected them all. Some Jews are still among "the objects of his mercy, whom he prepared in advance for glory" (9:23-24). These are "the remnant" of whom Isaiah spoke (9:27-29); they are the Jews who accepted God's righteousness on God's terms (10:1-17). They are still "his people," Israelites in the truest sense of the word.

Near the beginning of this main section (9:6b) Paul declares that "not all who are descended from Israel are Israel." This means in effect that there are two Israels. One is the physical nation descended from Jacob (renamed Israel, Gen 32:28), which was called as a group into covenant relationship with God to serve his redemptive purposes. The other is the remnant, the relatively small part of the nation who as individuals put their heartfelt trust in God's promises as the basis of their personal salvation. This remnant is "his people" in a double sense, both ethnically and spiritually.

The remnant is the subject of this paragraph. Paul's point is that God can never be accused of rejecting "his people," because there has always been a remnant from among the Jews who have accepted his way of grace and are thus in personal fellowship with him. Thus no matter what happens to the nation as a whole, "Israel" will never perish, because "the *real* Israel has always been less than the nation" (McGuiggan, 317).

1. God Has Not Rejected His People (11:1-2a)

11:1 I ask then: Did God reject his people?[114] **By no means!** The word "then" (οὖν, *oun*, "therefore") indicates that this question might naturally arise from the preceding chapters. Paul simply anticipates it and responds to it. The word for "reject" is ἀπωθέω (*apōtheō* – here in the middle voice). It means "to push away, cast away, or thrust away (from oneself); to repel; to spurn; to reject; to disown; to repudiate."

To be rejected or cast away by God is a terrible prospect for anyone, but for the Jews it was an absolutely unthinkable idea, given the facts that God had chosen them through Abraham (Gen 12:1-3), had established his covenant only with them at Sinai (Exod

[114]For the origin of the wording of this question, see v. 2 below.

19:5-6; see Deut 14:2), and thus had regarded them as his unique people for some 2,000 years. God described them as "my people, my chosen, the people I formed for myself" (Isa 43:20b-21a). "I will be your God and you will be my people," he promised them (Jer 7:23; see Lev 26:12).

But in view of 9:6b, we may ask, to which Israel does "his people" refer? Some think it refers only to the remnant, since "from Abraham onward only believing Israelites were 'his people'" (Lenski, 680). Others say it refers to "the *nation* as a whole" (Godet, 391; see MacArthur, 2:99). Strictly speaking neither view is correct. Contra Lenski, at this point "his people" is not spiritual but physical, as Paul's self-identification in v. 1b shows. But neither is it a reference to physical Israel as a whole, as if such a question ("Has God rejected the nation of Israel as such?") could be answered yes or no. Rather, Paul *is* thinking of ethnic Jews, but he is thinking of them *as individuals*. Has God rejected all of them?

The answer depends upon what is meant by "rejected." Does this "rejection" relate to Israel's role of service in God's redemptive plan, or does it relate to their personal, individual, eternal salvation? It cannot refer to the former, because such a question is irrelevant and meaningless. There is no sense in which God has ever rejected or will ever reject his nation Israel, either as a whole or as individuals, in reference to their role as the covenant people who prepared for the Messiah's coming into the world. God cannot *reject* them in reference to this role, because every purpose for which he thus chose them has already been fulfilled (9:4-5). Because of this it is true, to be sure, that there is no longer any rationale for Israel's continuing existence as a nation, or as Jews as distinct from Gentiles. Their existence as God's special, unique physical nation has thus come to an end (10:12; Gal 3:28; Col 3:11). But this is not the same as being "rejected." We may say, rather, that in full accordance with God's plan Israel as a nation has been honorably retired from service.

"Rejected" in this context must then refer to the question of personal salvation. Has God excluded his own people, the Jews, from salvation? Has he shut them out of heaven? Is the gospel invitation closed to Jews? Such a question does not (indeed, cannot) apply to Israel as a nation, but it does apply to all Israelites as individuals.

"Did God reject his people?" The question itself contains a Greek particle (μή, *mē*) which shows that a negative answer is intended. The question could thus be worded, "God has not rejected his people, has he?" Paul's answer is an emphatic and resounding NO! (μὴ γένοιτο, *mē genoito*; see 3:4; JC, 1:228). The very idea is unthinkable, and the evidence shows that it is not in fact the case.

The first bit of evidence that God has not rejected his people, the Jews, is Paul himself: **I am an Israelite myself, a descendant of Abraham, from the tribe of Benjamin.** Here Paul emphasizes his physical Jewishness. He is an "Israelite," which at the very least is equivalent to "Jew" (see 9:4). He is also "of the seed of Abraham" in the literal, physical sense (see 2 Cor 11:22), specifically of "the tribe of Benjamin," which along with Judah was one of the only two original tribes to be restored to their homeland following captivity and to remain intact into NT times. Thus "Paul shows that he is as firmly located within Judaism as anyone can be" (Dunn, 2:635).

Why does Paul make a big deal of his Jewish credentials? Some think he does so in order to make it clear that he is expressing "an authentically Jewish viewpoint" (Dunn, 2:635; see Fitzmyer, 603). I.e., he is showing that he, as a Jew, realizes just how repugnant is the whole idea that the Jews – the Jews, of all people! – could be rejected by God. He would thus be explaining why he recoils so vehemently from this suggestion (see Murray, 2:66). To paraphrase him, "I, too, am an Israelite, to whom the very idea of God's rejection of His people is an impious and incredible idea, to be repelled with horror" (Denney, 675).

This answer is possible, but more likely Paul thoroughly identifies himself as a Jew in order to give "living evidence" that God has not rejected "his people" (Moo, 673).[115] "How do I know that God has not excluded Jews from salvation? Because *I, Paul* am the most Jewish of Jews, and *I* am saved!" Thus Paul himself is "proof that God had not abandoned Israel" (Bruce, 211), proof that a remnant does exist. As Brunner says, Paul "himself is the strongest evidence

[115]Advocates of this view include Godet, 391; Bruce, 211; Hendriksen, 2:361; Lard, 346; Lenski, 678; MacArthur, 2:98; Brunner, 93; Stott, 292; and Achtemeier, 179. Dunn says this view "misses and cheapens the point" (2:635), but his explanation of it is a caricature (2:644).

for the fact that saving grace can even subdue a fanatical advocate of the righteousness of the law" (93).

11:2a God did not reject his people, whom he foreknew. Again Paul emphatically denies that God has rejected his people. The wording here (as in 11:1a) seems to be taken from 1 Sam 12:22 and Ps 94:14, which use the future tense to assert God's promise: "The LORD will not reject his people." Paul changes it to past tense and thus states it as a fact; God has kept his promise!

Why does Paul add the qualifier, "whom he foreknew"? This again raises the crucial question as to the essential meaning of προγινώσκω (*proginōskō*; see 8:29; JC, 1:505-511). Many, especially Calvinists, declare that it refers to an act of distinguishing, choosing love, and is thus the same as election or predestination. Those who take "his people" as referring only to spiritual Israel (the remnant) usually accept this meaning of "foreknew" here. Thus they take this passage as another reference to the unconditional salvific predestination of the elect remnant, especially among the Jews, similar to the Calvinist interpretations of 8:29 and 9:6-29.[116] In this context it becomes another reason why God has not rejected his people. How could he reject the very ones whom he has chosen ("foreknown") from all eternity for salvation? Thus "the 'foreknowing' is the guarantee that God has not cast off his people" (Murray, 2:67). "Foreknowledge and rejection are mutually incompatible" (Stott, 292).

Many of those who equate foreknowledge with predestination do not think it refers to the eternal salvation of the elect in this verse, however. This is because they take "his people" as referring to the Jewish *nation* as such. I.e., God cannot reject the nation of Israel, because he unconditionally chose it and set it apart with his electing love (i.e., his "foreknowledge"). Cranfield (2:545) takes this view: "We take it then that the relative clause refers to the general election of the people as a whole, and indicates a further ground for denying that God has cast off His people. The fact that God foreknew them (i.e., deliberately joined them to Himself in faithful love) excludes the possibility of His casting them off." Denney says, "Israel stood before God's eyes from eternity as His people, and in the immutableness of the sovereign love with which He made it His

[116]See Calvin, 410-411; Lenski, 679.

lies the impossibility of its rejection" (676). "Israel is the only *nation* God has foreknown and predetermined to be His people," says MacArthur. Because he has done so, "He can never totally reject them" (2:100). This is not a choosing of all Israel for salvation, though; it has to do only with the nation's irrevocable historical role as God's special people (see Moo, 674-675; Morris, 399).[117]

The problem with each of the above views is its erroneous understanding of foreknowledge as such. As I have shown earlier (JC, 1:505-511), foreknowledge means just that: knowing beforehand, in the sense of prior cognitive or mental awareness. "Foreknew" here could then mean the same as in 8:29, i.e., God did not reject those from among his people whom he foreknew would accept his grace through faith. The effect then would be to narrow the meaning of "his people" from the nation in general to the remnant. I.e., has God rejected his people? No, he has not rejected *all* of them. To be more specific, he has not rejected the ones foreknown to become believers, who by their very faith are the only ones who are truly "his people."

I do not think this is the point, however. I take "his people" in v. 2a to be the same as in v. 1a, i.e., it refers to all ethnic Israelites and thus to the nation of Israel; but it refers to them as individuals and not as a national unit. To say that God "foreknew" his people Israel means that even before he singled them out for a central role in his redemptive plan, he knew in advance the kind of people they would be all along the historical path to the Messiah and beyond. Nothing about them – their weaknesses, their failures, their unbelief, their idolatries – took him by surprise. He foreknew all these things and chose them anyway, because he also foreknew that there would always be a faithful remnant who would turn to him with believing hearts, who would keep the messianic hope alive, and who would turn to the Messiah when he came.

Thus God's foreknowledge of his people included a foreknowledge of their persistent rebellion (JC, 1:509), as well as a foreknowledge of a continuing, faithful remnant. The latter is the main point, as vv. 2b-5 show. Because he foreknew there would always be an

---

[117]Those who take this view tend to give the *nation* of Israel a continuing and even central role in God's plan for the end-times.

abiding remnant who is the true *spiritual* Israel, he did not abandon his ethnic people, even though he foreknew that most of them would never respond to his gracious invitation (10:21).

2. God Had a Remnant of Believers in the OT (11:2b-4)

11:2b-3 Don't you know what the Scripture says in the passage about Elijah – how he appealed to God against Israel: "Lord, they have killed your prophets and torn down your altars; I am the only one left, and they are trying to kill me"? In v. 1 Paul cited himself as evidence that God has not rejected his people; now he refers to a familiar incident from the OT as a further, more general proof (Godet, 392; Hendriksen, 2:361). In so doing he explicitly affirms the remnant concept introduced in 9:27-29.

"Don't you know" implies a positive answer: "You surely know, don't you?" "In the passage about Elijah" refers to 1 Kgs 17:1 through 2 Kgs 2:11. Students of Scripture in Paul's day would have known where to find this, even though they did not have chapter-and-verse divisions as we do today.

Paul refers to the specific place in the Elijah section where "he appealed to God against Israel." This is an unusual prayer, since most "appeals" to God regarding other people are intercessory, "a positive plea on behalf of someone," which is the way this same word is used in 8:27,34. But here Elijah is pictured as pleading with God *against* someone, in fact, against the people of his own nation (Moo, 675, n. 23).

Elijah's prayer grows out of his frustration and despair over Ahab's and Jezebel's success in introducing Baal-worship into Israel (1 Kgs 16:31-32). Despite the Lord's great victory over Baal and his prophets at Mt. Carmel (1 Kgs 18:16-40), Elijah was cowed by Jezebel and went into hiding in a cave at Mt. Horeb (1 Kgs 19:1-9). Here he was confronted by God, who twice asked him, "What are you doing here, Elijah?" (1 Kgs 19:9,13). Both times, Elijah answered (1 Kgs 19:10,14) with the complaint selectively paraphrased by Paul here in v. 3.

Elijah's words sum up his perception of the religious crisis facing Israel at that time. God's prophets were certainly being killed on Jezebel's orders (1 Kgs 18:4), and the altars were being demolished (1 Kgs 18:30-32).[118] Elijah's lament that he was "the only one left," even if it refers to prophets and not just true believers in general, is surely an exaggeration reflecting more his mood of despair than the facts as he knew them (see 1 Kgs 18:13,22).

The term translated "left" ("I am the only one left") is important because it ties in with several other words that represent the remnant concept. The word is the passive form of ὑπολείπω (*hypoleipō* – used only here in the NT), and means "to be left behind." Two other one-time words from this same family used in this context are λεῖμμα (*leimma*, 11:5) and ὑπόλειμμα (*hypoleimma*, 9:27). Both mean "the ones left behind," i.e., the remnant. In v. 4 a more common word meaning "to leave" καταλείπω (*kataleipō*) is used. Thus when Elijah complained, "I am the only one *left*," he was to the point of thinking he alone constituted the remnant of true believers (or at least true prophets).[119]

11:4 And what was God's answer[120] to him? "I have reserved for myself seven thousand who have not bowed the knee to Baal."[121] In order to shake Elijah out of his black mood, God gave him a demonstration of his solemn majesty (1 Kgs 19:11-13) and some concrete instructions (1 Kgs 19:15-17). He added the firm yet gentle reminder that Elijah was not alone; there were seven thousand other true worshipers of Yahweh in Israel (1 Kgs 19:18).

Many think the number "seven thousand" is not meant to be literal, but (since it involves the perfect number 7) is symbolic for

---

[118]There was one "official" altar associated with temple worship, but there were numbers of impromptu altars built to offer sacrifices to God. See Exod 20:24-25; Deut 27:5-6; Josh 8:30; Judg 6:24-26.

[119]Paul was in no way trying to draw a parallel between himself and Elijah. His mood was much more optimistic regarding the Jews, and he knew that many more besides himself were in the Lord's church.

[120]"God's answer" ("divine response," NASB) translates χρηματισμός (*chrēmatismos*), a word (along with the verb χρηματίζω [*chrēmatizō*]) loaded with heavy meaning. In secular contexts it referred to authoritative, official pronouncements; in religious contexts it meant a divine oracle, an utterance or warning from God. See the NT use of *chrēmatizō*, e.g., Matt 2:12,22; Luke 2:26; Acts 10:22.

[121]In the OT Baal is a masculine deity, but Paul uses the feminine definite article with the name. The reason for this is explained by many, e.g., Moo, 676, n. 25; Dunn, 2:638; Morris, 401.

the complete and perfect number of believers among Israel (see Cranfield, 2:547; Dunn, 2:638). Paul follows the LXX and adds the word ἀνήρ (*anēr*, "male") after "seven thousand," i.e., "seven thousand *men*." For a parallel see Acts 4:4. (The NIV translates *anēr* ["men"] in Acts 4:4, but leaves it out here.) If the number itself is symbolic and not literal, this is irrelevant. If not, then the total number of believers in Elijah's day were even greater than seven thousand, including women and youth (see Matt 14:21).

God's statement, "I have reserved for myself," uses the verb καταλείπω (*kataleipō*), another "remnant" term (see v. 3). Its usual meaning is "to leave." Those with Calvinist leanings see an oblique reference to unconditional predestination in this word. "Emphasis is placed on God's action; he had reserved these" through his "efficacious grace and differentiation," says Murray (2:69). The term refers to "the divine decision," says Cranfield (2:546).

But this is not the point. Certainly this is an act of God regarding these men, but God's act is conditioned on the fact that they "have not bowed the knee to Baal." God is telling Elijah, "There are more than just you who have remained faithful. Indeed, I have identified and singled out from the great majority of Israelites a group of seven thousand true worshipers. I have separated them from the rest; in my sight they are a different group, a remnant. These are the ones I have kept in my saving grace and in close fellowship with myself."

They are the ones, God says, "I have reserved *for myself*." They are "his people" in a special, spiritual sense. In this spiritual sense only these seven thousand belonged to God; the rest were Baal's. This remnant alone was the true Israel of 9:6b (McGuiggan, 319). "The seven thousand are Israel to Him" (Denney, 676). Thus God did not reject his people Israel. Though most rejected him, he still counted as his own those who sought him in faith. Though most abandoned him, these are still enough – a remnant to be sure – to constitute "his people."

3. Those under Grace Are God's New Covenant Israel (11:5-6)

11:5 Paul's reference to the Elijah incident is a good example of the remnant reality in OT times, but his main point is that this is an analogy of the Jewish situation in his own day. **So too, at the present time there is a remnant chosen by grace.** Paul uses three words to connect this verse with the preceding one: "so therefore also." He does not want us to miss the parallel, i.e., there is no difference between Elijah's day and "the present time."[122]

What is the nature of the parallel? The main point is the very *existence* of a remnant from among the people of Israel. God is no more rejecting his people in this gospel era than he was in Elijah's day. In the earlier time of national apostasy at least seven thousand remained true to God, "and so in Paul's day there was a faithful minority who had not rejected the gospel" (Bruce, 211). The existence of this remnant is sufficient to prove that God has not rejected his people, and thus that he is still faithful to his word and to his promises.

Many OT passages speak of the remnant concept. The immediate reference for most of them is the temporal deliverance of a remnant of survivors from the hands of oppressive enemies such as Assyria and Babylon (e.g., Ezra 9:8; Isa 1:9 [Rom 9:29]; 10:20-22 [Rom 9:27]; 11:11,16; 37:4,32; Jer 6:9; 23:3; 31:7; Ezek 9:8; 11:13; Joel 2:32; Amos 5:15; Mic 2:12; 4:6-7; 7:18; Zeph 3:13). Many refer to the end of the Babylonian captivity and the restoration of the remaining Israelites to their homeland. Because this event in itself is typological of spiritual deliverance from sin, many of these remnant references have clear messianic import. Thus it is appropriate that the remnant concept be used by Paul in a spiritual sense to represent those Jews delivered by the power of Christ from their bondage to sin. They are the true Israel, in contrast with the rest who still languish in such bondage.

The second part of the parallel has to do with the *means* by which the remnant of Israel is distinguished from the nation as a whole, i.e., the remnant is "chosen by grace." Literally Paul says that in this present time a remnant "has come into existence according to an election [or choice] of grace." Even though this was not stressed in the OT itself, by virtue of the parallel being drawn here we must conclude that the Old Covenant remnant, such as the

[122]"The present time" is the messianic or New Covenant era, "the period since Christ came" (Lenski, 682-683).

seven thousand in Elijah's day, were also established according to an election or choice of grace.

Paul says that the New Covenant remnant has "come into existence" or has "come to be" (NASB). The word is γίνομαι (*ginomai* – a word the NIV completely ignores), which basically means "come to be, become, originate" (AG, 157). The perfect tense of the verb may be referring to a single past historical event that brought the New Covenant remnant into existence, i.e., the establishment of the NT church (Acts 2).

Paul's statement that the remnant has come into existence "according to a choice of grace" is often interpreted as an affirmation of Calvinist unconditional election. It shows, says Murray, that the distinction between the nation as a whole and the remnant is due solely to "God's gracious election," i.e., to "the sovereign will of God" and not to "any determination proceeding from the will of man" (2:70). As such it is often equated with the election of 9:7-18 as interpreted by Calvinists (e.g., Moo, 677).

I reject this meaning for Paul's statement. For one thing, this election is *not* the same as that in ch. 9. The subject here is election to salvation; in ch. 9 it was election to service. Also, we have already seen in our discussion of 8:29 that election to salvation is based upon divine foreknowledge (precognition) of human choices. The remnant *is* a group chosen by God, but chosen according to his foreknowledge.

What does it mean to say that the remnant has come into existence according to a choice of grace? We must keep in mind that Paul is here explaining how the remnant is different from the nation as a whole, and I believe that he does intend for us to understand this by comparing it with the election in 9:7-13. In that passage Paul emphasizes that being chosen as an instrument for God's use in carrying out his redemptive purpose was not a matter of natural right based on natural birth, but was a matter of God's sovereign choice. It was "God's purpose in election" (9:11) that led him to select Isaac over Ishmael and Jacob over Esau. None of these sons had an inherent claim to the privilege.

Likewise, being part of the saved remnant (spiritual Israel) is not a matter of physical birth as a Jew; no ethnic Israelite has an inherent claim to salvation. Being a part of the remnant is a matter of God's choice, and he has the sovereign right to establish the basis or criterion by which he chooses some Israelites rather than others. Thus the remnant is according to choice, not birth. Here the election of 9:11 and that of 11:5 are similar.

But there is an important difference between these two elections. Since 9:11 was not election to salvation, it was not described as an "election of grace."[123] But in 11:5 the issue is salvation. The remnant consists of those within the nation of Israel who are saved, and the only way for sinners to be saved is by receiving God's gift of his own righteousness through faith (9:30–10:13) – in other words, by grace. This speaks to another main difference between the mass of ethnic Israel and the remnant. The former sought salvation by works or by their own righteousness (9:32; 10:3), while the latter sought it by faith in the righteousness of God. Thus to say that the remnant has come into existence according to an election of grace means that God chooses to save those Jews (and Gentiles, 9:30) who themselves choose his way of grace rather than the futile way of law. "God chose to elect all those who would choose to accept the grace extended through his son" (DeWelt, 176).

We must not lose sight of Paul's purpose for even mentioning the remnant here. His point is to show that God has not rejected his people; the existence of the remnant is evidence that he has not. The fact that he is willing to constitute this remnant according to the terms of grace rather than law shows how faithful he is, and just how determined he is to preserve "his people" in spite of their sin.[124]

11:6 And if by grace, then it is no longer by works; if it were, grace would no longer be grace.[125] This verse sums up some of the main conclusions concerning law and grace as ways of salvation that were discussed in chs. 1–5 (see also 9:30–10:4). It also reinforces the point made under 11:5 above, that the main difference between

---

[123]See the earlier discussion of the language in 9:10-18; the references to love and mercy in that context do not have salvation connotations.

[124]"The fact that there is a remnant, and one owing its existence to God's grace, is the proof that (in spite of the wholesale defection of Israel) God has not cast off His people" (Denney, 677).

[125]The ending to this verse included in older translations such as the KJV is now judged not to have been in the original text but to have been added in certain later manuscripts. See Moo, 670, n. 2.

ethnic Israel and remnant Israel is the latter's choice of grace instead of law as the only way to a saving relationship with God.

The first part of v. 6 has no stated subject in the Greek; translators usually supply "it." We may conclude from v. 5 that "being included in the remnant" is the understood subject.

The term "no longer" is used here in a logical sense, not temporal. I.e., Paul is not saying that in earlier times remnant membership was by works, but is so no longer. Rather, he is saying that once one sees that remnant membership is by grace, then he can no longer consider it to be by works.

Dunn notes that this is the first time Paul "brings 'works' and 'grace' into direct antithesis" (2:647). This is true of the terms themselves, but not of the concepts. The whole point of chs. 1–5 was the antithesis between law (works) and grace (faith) as ways of salvation. Since faith is a key element in the grace system, sometimes "faith" or "by faith" is simply shorthand for the system as a whole. Likewise, since works are a key element in the law system, sometimes "by works" or "from works" is just shorthand for the law system as a whole – which is the case here.[126] In 10:5-6 Paul contrasts "righteousness by law" and "righteousness by faith"; this is exactly the same contrast as that between "by grace" and "by works" in 11:6.

It is crucial that we correctly understand the meaning of "works," which is the same as "works of law" in 3:28. As explained there (JC, 1:268-271), "works" includes any response to the laws or commandments of the Creator given to human beings as creatures, without restriction as to dispensation (Old Covenant or New Covenant), form (written or innate), and motives (good or bad). Thus it is wrong to limit "works" to obedience to the Law of Moses. It is also wrong to expand the term to include "anything that human beings do" (contra Moo, 678; see 250), since it does not refer to the Redeemer's instructions on how to be saved, i.e., the conditions for receiving salvation. These are not a part of the Creator's law, and are not works in the Pauline sense. See JC, 1:270; MP, 449.

Those who wrongly expand the concept of works to include "anything a person does" usually then proceed to use v. 6 to

[126]See 3:20 (lit., "works of law"); 3:28 (lit., "by faith apart from works of law"); 9:30 ("by faith"); 9:32 ("by works"); 10:6 ("by faith").

support their Calvinist interpretation of v. 5. If "works" means *anything* a person does, this must include not only repentance, confession, and baptism, but even faith itself, insofar as it is a decision of man's will. Thus to Calvinists, even faith, regarded as something a person does as a result of his own choice, is a grace-canceling work. As Murray says, "If grace is conditioned in any way by human performance or by the will of man impelling to action, then grace ceases to be grace" (2:70). Grace cannot be conditioned on *anything* a person does, says Moo, for then grace would not be free: "For grace demands that God be perfectly free to bestow his favor on whomever he chooses. But if God's election were based on what human beings do, his freedom would be violated and he would no longer be acting in grace" (678). Moo acknowledges that Paul distinguishes works from faith, but declares nevertheless that "Paul's conception of God's grace . . . would seem to rule out anything outside God's own free will as a basis for his actions. To make election ultimately dependent on the human decision to believe violates Paul's notion of the grace of God. . . . God's grace is the efficient cause of salvation, human faith being not its basis but its result" (679, n. 43).

Using the same too-broad definition of works, Morris says 11:6 "rules out the idea that God foreknows *what people will do* and chooses the elect on the basis of this foreknowledge of their *works*" (402; emphasis added).

This whole approach to grace is a serious error, since it includes more in the category of works than Paul intends (as discussed above). Also, it is a false concept of the freedom that is inherently involved in grace. That grace is conditioned on certain human acts is not a violation of God's freedom in the bestowal of grace, since he himself is the one who freely chose to do it this way and the one who freely chose what the conditions shall be. Besides, the conditions he has chosen are completely consistent with the essence of grace.[127]

[127]See my discussion of these points in GRu, 184-186 ("Sovereign Grace"), 184-186 ("Unconditional Grace"); see the whole of ch. 5, "Special Providence and Free Will," 161-228. See also my discussion of these points in GRe, 383-389 ("The Freedom of Grace"), 389-399 ("Is Grace Conditional or Unconditional?").

Also, election according to foreknowledge does not contradict grace because the crucial object of God's foreknowledge is not the presence or absence of human works but the acceptance or rejection of God's free offer of grace in accord with the gracious conditions which he himself has laid down.

Paul's point in this verse is simply to sum up the main message of Romans, that the only way for a sinner to be saved is by grace through faith, not by the system of law. The two systems are mutually exclusive; one must choose either God's righteousness (grace) or personal righteousness (works) as the basis for his salvation. One must rely either upon himself or upon Jesus Christ; he cannot do both. Any trust in the worthiness of one's own achievements or the merit of one's own accomplishments is simply incompatible with grace. Trying to get to heaven by being "good enough" nullifies the way of grace.

As applied to remnant Jews, this means that they belong to the remnant not because they are essentially better than the rest, i.e., less sinful or more law-abiding, but because they have submitted to God's way of righteousness (10:3), which is grace. If everyone were to be accepted or rejected on the basis of his works, there would be no remnant. By its very nature the remnant is a grace entity. Though Paul is making this point specifically regarding the remnant of the Jews, it applies equally to the Gentiles, and thus to the church as a whole.

B. UNBELIEVING ISRAEL HAS BEEN HARDENED (11:7-10)

If only a remnant of Israel is saved, what has happened to the rest? Are they totally abandoned and forgotten by God? Having served their covenant purposes as a means of bringing Christ into the world, and paradoxically having refused to accept him as their Messiah, are they now to be completely ignored? Paul's answer is No, but exactly how they continue to be the object of God's attention is somewhat surprising. This is Paul's subject in this paragraph.

11:7 What then? What Israel sought so earnestly it did not obtain, but the elect did. The others were hardened, . . . The first part of this verse is a transitional statement that sums up the preceding thoughts in terms of a contrast between "the elect" on the one hand, and "Israel" ("the others") on the other hand.

Paul does not use the usual word for "the elect" (ἐκλεκτός, *eklektos*; see 8:33), but carries over the noun used in 11:5 (ἐκλογή, *eklogē*, "choice, election"). In this context it is synonymous with "the remnant." The term "Israel" here refers to the physical nation in general, or "Israel as a corporate whole," as Moo says (679). But strictly speaking, Paul is referring not to the totality of physical Israel, but only to unbelieving Jews, "the others" in contrast to the elect.[128]

What was Israel "so earnestly" seeking?[129] The answer can be found in 9:30–10:3; they were pursuing *righteousness*, a right standing before God (Denney, 677; Morris, 402; Moo, 680). In 9:30-31 Paul says the Gentiles found such righteousness though they were not seeking it, while Israel was pursuing it but did not find it. The reason they did not find it, he says (9:32; 10:3), was that they were seeking it in their own works and not in God's gift.

The NIV translates the verb as past tense ("sought"), which is consistent with the past tense of the verbs in 9:31-32; 10:3. But here the Greek is present tense ("that which Israel is seeking for," NASB), which implies that the Israelites in general were still seeking for this righteous standing before God.[130]

The emphasis, though, is not on the action of seeking, but on the result of the search. The good news is that the elect remnant did obtain the sought-for righteousness. The bad news is that the vast majority, Israel as a whole, did not (see 9:30). These are simply called "the others," or "the rest" (NASB), i.e., the rest of the Jews (not the rest of mankind in general, contra Morris, 403).

At this point Paul introduces a new and surprising thought: "the others," the unbelieving Jews, *were hardened*. This theme is a prominent part of the argument in the rest of this chapter, either implicitly

---

[128]See 9:30-32, where a similar contrast is drawn between Israel and the Gentiles. There as in 11:7, "Israel" is the physical nation in general, but strictly speaking only the mass of unbelieving Jews within it, as distinct from the remnant (9:27).

[129]The verb is ἐπιζητέω (*epizēteō*), which means to "search for, seek after" (AG, 292). The connotation of "*earnestly* seeking" is not inherent in the word.

[130]See the present tense in 10:2, "They have a zeal for God" (NASB).

or explicitly. Thus it is crucial that we understand it aright. The following facts concerning this hardening will emerge in the course of Paul's argument, but may profitably be summed up before we go any further. (1) Whatever the nature of this hardening, it is not the cause of anyone's unbelief. The only ones hardened are those who have already rejected God's righteousness in Christ. (2) Whatever the nature of the hardening, it is not irrevocable and final. Those hardened are still able to come to faith, as the next point indicates. (3) God's purpose for this hardening is to use it as a means of converting many Gentiles, which in turn will be a means of converting many of the hardened Jews themselves. Thus paradoxically the ultimate goal and result of the hardening is the salvation of those who are hardened! The sequence of events is as follows: the bulk of the Jews reject the gospel; they are hardened; as a consequence Gentiles are saved; as a consequence of this, many of the hardened Jews are made jealous and are saved; and as a consequence of this, even more Gentiles are saved!

The word for "hardened" is πωρόω (*pōroō*),[131] the noun form of which (πώρωσις, *pōrōsis*) is used in 11:25. (The meaning is the same as the verb used in 9:18, σκληρύνω [*sklērynō*].) The verb *pōroō* "is a medical term used in Hippocrates and elsewhere of a bone or hard substance growing when bones are fractured, or of a stone forming in the bladder" (SH, 314). Hence it means "to harden, to petrify"; in the NT[132] it is used in the figurative sense: "to make dull, obdurate, insensitive." It refers to "the heart becoming hardened or callous," i.e., to a state in which "a covering has grown over the heart, making men incapable[133] of receiving any new teaching however good, and making them oblivious of the wrong they are doing" (SH, 314).

In this verse the verb is passive, and the agent of the hardening is not identified. Some declare that the Jews hardened themselves. The hardening came about "through their own rejection, choosing

[131]Some manuscripts mistakenly substituted πηρόω (*pēroō*), "to maim"; in reference to the eyes, "to blind." Hence the KJV's "blinded."

[132]Outside Romans the verb is used of hardened hearts in Mark 6:52; 8:17; John 12:40, and of hardened minds in 2 Cor 3:14. The noun is used of hardness of heart in Mark 3:5; Eph 4:18.

[133]This is not absolutely so, as the following discussion shows.

rather to obey Satan . . . than the grace of God" (DeWelt, 176). Such self-hardening is certainly a biblically-attested reality (Exod 8:15,32; Heb 3:8,15; 4:7). Some identify Satan as the agent of the hardening, by God's permission (Lard, 351; MP, 451; Godet, 398). Others say the agent of the hardening is "intentionally left vague" and indefinite (Denney, 677; Morris, 403).

There is some truth in each of these views, but the context requires us to identify God himself as the main agent in the hardening of the Jews (see 9:18; 11:8; see Murray, 2:72; Moo, 680; Stott, 293). How he did so is not explained. It is very possible that he hardened them by allowing Satan a free hand to blind their eyes. Citing 1 Kgs 22:19-23, the book of Job, and 2 Cor 4:4, Godet says that "God proves or punishes by leaving Satan to act" (398). It is also possible that God hardened the Jews simply by diminishing or withdrawing his own positive influences toward them, as he did with the Gentiles when he "gave them over" to the destructiveness of their own sinful desires (1:24,26,28; JC, 1:149-150).

In any case there is general agreement that the Jews had already hardened themselves into a state of unbelief before God performed this act of hardening upon them. Thus the divine hardening is not the cause of their rejection of the gospel, but a punishment for it. They were hardened because they deserved it; it was retribution (v. 9) for their sin. It was "a judicial penalty for refusal to heed the Word of God" (Bruce, 215; see Lenski, 686). "God has judicially blinded those of His chosen people who willfully blind themselves to Him," says MacArthur (2:101). "God hardens only those hearts who, in rejecting His gracious offer of righteousness, harden themselves to His grace" (ibid., 103; see Hendriksen, 2:365; Morris, 403). Brunner says it well: "Hardening is being able no longer[134] to say anything but No. God permits them to become entangled in their own No." As with the Gentiles in ch. 1, "so he has now hardened the Jews after they have said their No. The hardening is not the original cause but God's punishment for their unbelief" (94).

What is the result of this hardening? Some interpret it as a final sealing of these Jews in a state of unbelief, and equate it with the eternal decree of reprobation that (in Calvinist thinking) predes-

[134]Again this is not absolutely the case.

tines some to hell, just as the eternal decree of election unconditionally predestines others to heaven (Calvin, 417; Murray, 2:72). We may conclude, says Moo, "that God's hardening permanently binds people in the sin that they have chosen for themselves" (681).

This view is a serious error, however, and must be vigorously rejected. Not even all Calvinists agree with it. Hendriksen (2:365) says, "To include Rom. 11:7 . . . in a list of passages proving reprobation is an error," because "even for the hardened ones there is hope," as the following context shows. Cranfield agrees: "The divine hardening is not God's last word for His rebellious people" (2:550). So whatever result this hardening has, it is something done only to unbelievers, and it does not ultimately prevent them from becoming believers. It is neither absolute nor irreversible. Hence it does not contradict the principle that God does not violate any individual's free will to choose his own eternal destiny.

The result of the hardening is Paul's subject in vv. 8-10. It certainly involves an insensitivity toward God's word, blinding one's spiritual eyes and deafening one's spiritual ears toward God's truth. In the act of hardening God takes away "from the heart the faculty of being touched by what is good or divine," and he takes away "from the understanding, the faculty of discerning between the true and the false, the good and the bad" (Godet, 395). In so doing God is simply confirming what is already present in the unbeliever's heart.

Why has God so hardened the Jews? As noted above, it is in the first place a judicial act, a recompense for unbelief. But there is an even deeper reason, a positive one that flows from the deepest and wisest recesses of God's loving heart. God has used many people, including the Jews as a nation, to carry out his redemptive purposes. Sometimes this can be done only by a limited and temporary hardening, as in the case of Pharaoh (9:18). So it is here, that by hardening "the rest" of the Jews, he can use them "as an instrument of his good pleasure" in bringing many people to salvation (see McGuiggan, 322). As Paul goes on to explain in 11:11ff., the hardening of the Jews is intended as a means by which the Gentiles may be saved, which in turn is a means by which the hardened Jews themselves may be brought to faith in their Messiah.

11:8 [A]s it is written: "God gave them a spirit of stupor, eyes so that they could not see and ears so that they could not hear, to

this very day." In this and the next two verses Paul draws from three OT passages to reinforce his assertion about the hardening of Israel. These texts are not treated as prophecies but as precedents. In v. 8 two passages are used. "God gave them a spirit of stupor" is from Isa 29:10a, "For the LORD has poured over you a spirit of deep sleep" (NASB). The last part of v. 8 is from Deut 29:4.[135]

The words from Isa 29:10 make it clear that God is the one who is responsible for the hardening in 11:7. The word for "stupor" suggests not so much a deep sleep as a state of numbness, of being bewildered and stunned. The word is κατάνυξις (*katanyxis*), and probably comes from κατανύσσω (*katanyssō*), which means "to strike violently, to stun" (Earle, 208).[136] Sometimes a person who has been struck on the head may seem to be fully conscious but is mentally confused and unaware of his surroundings. Just so, says Paul (as did Isaiah before him), God has enveloped Israel in a state of spiritual numbness, in "an attitude of deadness towards spiritual things" (Morris, 403), in a "mental and moral dulness [sic] or apathy" (Hendriksen, 2:364).

The word "spirit" probably means an attitude or a state of mind, but it is possible that it refers to a demonic spirit whom God permits to inflict Israel with this spiritual blindness. See 1 Sam 18:10 and 1 Kgs 22:20-23 for precedents. Whether this be the case or not, the result is God's intention: a "punitive hardening which follows after self-hardening has fully set in" (Lenski, 687). "The eyes of their souls are shut; they see nothing rightly" (Lard, 351).

So that there may be no mistake, the "spirit of stupor" is explained with the reference to Deut 29:4, "eyes so that they could not see and ears so that they could not hear." Again, Paul says *God gave* to Israel these nonseeing eyes and nonhearing ears.[137] The mass of Israel seemed to be spiritually conscious and God-fearing; indeed they had "a zeal for God," but it was "not in accordance

---

[135]An OT text with a similar meaning is Isa 6:9-10, which is used in Matt 13:14-15 (see Mark 4:12; Luke 8:10), John 12:40, and Acts 28:25-27.

[136]Another possibility is that it comes from κατανυστάζω (*katanystazō*), "to fall asleep," but this is less likely.

[137]Paul slightly alters the form of Deut 29:4, where Moses says of the Israelites of his day that God has *not* given them "eyes that see or ears that hear."

with knowledge" (10:2, NASB). God reinforced their own willful ignorance by covering their spiritual eyes and stopping up their spiritual ears.[138]

"To this very day" is part of the quotation from Deut 29:4. Moses' point was that after forty years of wilderness wandering the Israelites still had not come to understand and appreciate what God had done for them in delivering them from Egypt and giving them their own land, even on the very eve of their possession of that land. Paul seems to be saying that the Jews of his day were still laboring under the same spiritual blindness that caused them to crucify their Messiah (1 Thess 2:14-15), and that this blindness had not yet been lifted or counteracted as 11:11-32 suggests will some day happen.

11:9-10 And David says, "May their table become a snare and a trap, a stumbling block and a retribution for them. May their eyes be darkened so they cannot see, and their backs be bent forever." These two verses are taken from Ps 69:22-23. This is appropriate because Ps 69 is widely recognized as Messianic and is cited or alluded to frequently in the NT (e.g., Mark 15:23, 36 [69:21]; John 2:17 [69:9]; John 15:25 [69:4]; Acts 1:20 [69:25]; Rom 15:3 [69:9]; see Dunn, 2:642). As David wrote the Psalm, it was his prayer for God to deliver him from his enemies and to give those enemies the punishment they deserved. As Paul applies it to his time, he suggests that "what David prayed would happen to his persecutors, . . . God has brought upon those Jews who have resisted the gospel" (Moo, 683). "Paul takes it for granted that the doom invoked in these words has come upon the Jews," says Denney (678).

Paul's main point in citing these imprecations seems to be to reinforce the idea that the hardening affirmed in v. 7 is actually deserved by the unbelieving Jews. David's prayer was for three curses to come upon his enemies. The first is that "their table become a snare and a trap, a stumbling block." Here "table" may be an allusion to the OT law in general, and especially to its sacrificial system, which involved an altar and a table for eating the sacrificial meal (Denney, 678; Dunn, 2:642-643, 650). Or it may simply be a household table representing the food and fellowship of

---

[138]For the opposite action see Eph 1:17-18.

ordinary mealtime and earthly prosperity in general (Lenski, 689; Murray, 2:74).

In either case the prayer is "a wish that even the good things which these enemies enjoy may prove to be a cause of disaster to them" (Cranfield, 2:551). "Their table . . . is that in which they delight, and it is this which is to prove their ruin" (Denney, 678).[139]

The second curse is that "their eyes be darkened so they cannot see." This clearly ties in with the "spirit of stupor" in v. 8 and the hardening in v. 7, and indicates that Israel as a whole was blinded toward the truth of the gospel.

The third curse is that "their backs be bent[140] forever."[141] It is difficult to tell exactly what calamity this is supposed to represent. It may be a figure for the hard labor of slavery, the heaviness of a burden, a state of weakness, or the overwhelming effects of grief or fear. Any of these could apply to first-century Judaism. Paul may be saying, "May their backs be always weak and feeble under the burden that they bear because of their rejection of the gospel" (Fitzmyer, 607). Or he may be referring to "the state of slavish fear in which the Jews shall be held as long as this judgment of hardening which keeps them outside of the gospel shall last" (Godet, 397).

The main point, though, is expressed in v. 9b, where the wish is that their table may become "a retribution for them." The sense of this term is that of being repaid or paid back in kind. The implication is that all these curses are a recompense or retribution, a deserved penalty upon the Jews "rightly demanded by their wickedness" (Lenski, 690). It declares that "the evil which came upon the Jews was caused by their own fault and sin" (MP, 452); it "confirms the judicial character of their hardening" (Murray, 2:74).

---

[139]The words "snare," "trap," and "stumbling block" refer to three ways to hunt and ensnare animals. The "trap" is a net used for catching birds and other small game. The "stumbling block" is literally "the bait stick of a trap, the stick which triggers off the trapping mechanism when a bird or animal makes contact" (Morris, 404).

[140]The Hebrew text may be rendered "make their loins shake" or "tremble"; Paul follows the LXX.

[141]The expression rendered "forever" here does not mean "without end," but "constantly" or "continuously." I.e., as long as it lasts, may there be no relief. See Cranfield, 2:552; Fitzmyer, 607.

C. THE HARDENING OF UNBELIEVING ISRAEL BECOMES A BLESSING FOR BOTH THE GENTILES AND THE JEWS (11:11-16)

In this paragraph Paul is still developing his answer to the question in 11:1, "Did God reject his people?" He has supported his emphatic negative answer by pointing to the existence of the "remnant chosen by grace" (vv. 1-6). But what about the mass of unbelieving Jews not included in the remnant? They "were hardened" (11:7-10).

This leads to the question of the ultimate fate of hardened Israel. Are they simply and finally lost? Is there no place for them in the kingdom? Are they totally excluded from God's mercy and God's plan? "What about the sinning majority? Are they lost forever?" (Morris, 405).

Paul's answer is another emphatic No! It is true that this majority rejected their Messiah, and that God hardened them. But this is not the final word; it is not the whole story. In this section the Apostle shows how even hardened Israel is part of the larger picture of God's mercy, or "how Israel's failure fits into the salvific plan of God" (Fitzmyer, 608). God can use this unbelieving nation for his own redemptive purpose, and even his hardening of them furthers this purpose.

In essence, Paul explains that God's hardening of Israel (especially the withdrawing of direct evangelistic efforts to win them) is intended to start a chain reaction that leads back to the conversion of Jews by indirect means. In summary, the hardening of unbelieving Israel "is the occasion for the coming in of the Gentiles, which, in its turn, is to have the effect of awakening the unbelieving Jews to a realization of what they are missing and so to lead to their repentance" (Cranfield, 2:553). Thus "even the hardening of Israel serves the purposes of mercy" (Achtemeier, 181). As Hendriksen remarks, God's "purpose is ultimately one of grace, and this for the benefit of both Gentile and Jews" (2:366).

Nearly everyone agrees that this section shows that Israel's fall and hardening are not meant to be final. Just as vv. 1-10 show that her rejection is only partial, these verses show that it is intended to be only temporary. "God's punitive action against the majority" is "not his last word concerning Israel" (Dunn, 2:666). The Jews *can* be saved.

Unfortunately, many interpreters take Paul's basic message of hope for Israel and expand it into a veritable philosophy of history. They see in this paragraph the seeds of a complicated eschatology involving a renewed special role for the Jews as a nation.[142] I.e., they take Paul's statements about Israel's salvation as referring to a large-scale future conversion of the Jews *en masse*, and a restoration of the nation as such to their original status as the people of God. Many regard this as the key precursor to the end of this age and the final resurrection (v. 15). This theory will receive some attention in the following discussion.

11:11 Again I ask:[143] **Did they stumble so as to fall beyond recovery? Not at all!** Of whom is Paul speaking? Not Israel as a whole, as a corporate nation (contra Moo, 686), but only the individual Jews who rejected their Messiah and were subsequently hardened, i.e., "the others" of v. 7 (Cranfield, 2:554; Denney, 678).

The first verb, "stumble" (πταίω, *ptaiō*, "to stumble, to trip") is used in a figurative or moral sense, "to make a mistake, go astray, sin" (AG, 734; see Jas 2:10; 3:2; 2 Pet 1:10). The second verb, πίπτω (*piptō*), has a straightforward meaning: "to fall, to fall down, to collapse." In a moral sense it means "to fall into sin, to go astray," and may have an even stronger sense: to "fall from a state of grace, be completely ruined, perish" (AG, 665).

There is no question that hardened Israel stumbled (9:32-33), but did they *fall*? Despite Paul's emphatic No! (μὴ γένοιτο, *mē genoito*; see 3:4), the answer to this question is not as simple as it seems. The main reason is that v. 22 refers to these same Jews as "those who fell," and uses the same word as in v. 11 (*piptō*).

So what does Paul mean in v. 11? The most common approach is to give *piptō* an exceptionally strong meaning here, as in the NIV: "to fall beyond recovery." It means to be "finally lost" in the sense of "a complete and irrevocable fall," say Sanday and Headlam (320-321). It refers to a "fall without remedy" (Lard, 354), involving

---

[142]See Moo's contention that this section deals with "Israel as a whole and not the hardened 'remainder' only" (686). I disagree.

[143]Paul's opening words here are exactly the same as in 11:1, λέγω οὖν (*legō oun*), "I say then" (NASB).

"irretrievable spiritual ruin" (Moo, 687). Paul does imply that falling is more serious than merely stumbling, so this interpretation seems to fit. As Fitzmyer summarizes it, "Israel has stumbled over Christ, but it has not fallen down completely so that it cannot regain its footing" (611).

Is this interpretation acceptable? Yes. It surely fits the context, since one of Paul's main points is that fallen Israel can indeed be saved. A serious problem, though, is that it does not seem consistent with v. 22.

Thus out of concern for v. 22, some have suggested another understanding of v. 11.[144] The point of the question, they say, is this: did Israel stumble "merely for the purpose that they might fall" (Murray, 2:76)? Paul's No! is not intended to deny that they have fallen; it simply means that there is more to the story than this. They have not stumbled just for the purpose of falling, or with the simple result that they are now fallen and that's that. No, Paul's whole point is that God has incorporated Israel's stumbling and falling into a much larger and more glorious plan.

Is this interpretation acceptable? Yes, and in my opinion it is preferable. If anything, it fits the immediate context even better than the more common view, and it takes full account of v. 22. The main problem is that the concept of "merely" must be read into the question.

Another issue is the meaning of the word ἵνα (*hina*), which connects the two verbs ("so as," NIV). This word can imply either purpose or result. If Paul intends the former, he is asking whether hardened Israel stumbled "in order that they might fall" or "for the purpose of falling." If we read it in this sense, then Paul would be implying that God *caused* Israel to stumble (to reject their Messiah), and that he had a *purpose* for causing them to stumble. The issue then would be to identify that purpose, that "divinely intended outcome" (Dunn, 2:652). This of course assumes a Calvinist view of sovereignty and free will, as is the case with Murray, who speaks of "the overriding and overruling design of God in the stumbling and fall of Israel" (2:76).

Most interpreters, however (even among Calvinists), take *hina* as stating result rather than purpose. That is, has hardened Israel

---

[144]Murray, 2:75-76; Lenski, 692; McGuiggan, 323.

stumbled "with the result that" they have *fallen*? This meaning "makes excellent sense," says Dunn (2:653);[145] and this is so however one understands the concept of "falling."

The bottom line is that most Jews have indeed stumbled, i.e., have rejected Jesus and his grace, and consequently have fallen into a state of lostness and spiritual ruin. But that is not the whole picture; that is not the end of the story. The drama of Israel does not end on such a negative note. **Rather, because of their transgression, salvation has come to the Gentiles to make Israel envious.**

Paul refers here to "their transgression" (singular). Is this different from the stumbling and falling in v. 11a? It may be useful to bring together and analyze the variety of terms Paul uses to describe Israel's downfall. It seems that he distinguishes three steps in the process, the first two of which are attributable to the sinner's will and the last of which is an act of God. The first step is the sin of rejecting God's way of grace, most significantly the initial sin of rejecting Jesus as the only Savior. The second step is falling out of a saving relationship with God and into a state of lostness. The third step is God's placing those who have so fallen under his wrath and curse.

The first of these steps is what Paul means by "their transgression." It is the word παράπτωμα (*paraptōma*), which is "frequently used by Paul to denote 'trespass', 'sin' (in the sense of a particular sinful deed)," as Cranfield says (2:555). It is the same as the stumbling in v. 11a, i.e., their stumbling over Christ (9:32-33), their rejection of Christ as the Messiah. It is called "unbelief" in vv. 20,23, and "disobedience" in v. 30.

The second step is the Jews' "fall" in v. 11a (see v. 22), also called their "loss" in v. 12. This is not so much an *act* of the sinner as the natural result of the first step (the unbelief).

The third step is God's act of hardening (vv. 7, 25), which is his punitive response to the first two steps. This is also called his "rejection" of the Jews (v. 15), and his act of breaking off or cutting off the unbelieving branches (vv. 17,19-20,22).

In reference to the Jews' downfall, these three steps always go together; even when only one is mentioned, the other two are

[145]See also SH, 320; Cranfield, 2:554; Morris, 406; Lenski, 692. Lenski comments, "If purpose were intended, it certainly was not God's."

assumed to be a part of the total picture. Thus here when Paul says "because of their transgression," he does not mean the transgression alone, as distinct from the fall and the hardening. Rather, because of the transgression along with the consequent fall and the divine hardening, salvation has come to the Gentiles.

Herein lies the first element in God's plan that evokes Paul's extreme sense of awe and wonder at his wisdom (11:33-36), namely, that God has determined to use the Jews' unbelief and fall (along with his own act of hardening) as a means of bringing salvation to the Gentiles! I.e., "Israel's stumbling was the occasion for redemption to be opened to the gentiles" (Achtemeier, 180). Out of sin, salvation comes! Out of wrath, mercy comes!

This could refer to the fact that by delivering Jesus over to the Romans for crucifixion, the Jews were inadvertently helping to bring about the one great act of redemption that is the source of salvation for all. More likely, though, it refers to the ordinary process of evangelism reflected in the book of Acts. I.e., once Gentile evangelism finally began (Acts 10), the missionary strategy was still to preach to the Jews first. But when the Jews typically rejected the gospel message, attention was turned to the Gentiles. As Moo says, "Paul probably had in mind the way in which he and other preachers of the gospel would turn to the Gentiles after being spurned by the Jews" (687; see Cranfield, 2:556; Bruce, 212). See Acts 13:44-52; 18:1-6; 19:8-10; 28:23-28.

But even this is not the whole story. If it were, hardened Israel would still be abandoned in their lostness. But this is not God's plan. The other element in the divine strategy that evokes Paul's reverent amazement is that God intends the conversion of the Gentiles to arouse the hardened Jews to jealousy (or envy) and thereby cause them to turn at last to their Messiah (see v. 14). The language Paul uses here does indicate a "divine intention" (Cranfield, 2:556). I.e., "the salvation of the Gentiles was intended in the divine providence to arouse in Israel a passionate desire for the same good gift" (Morris, 407). "Thus that hardening of which v. 7 spoke has for its ultimate purpose the salvation of those who are hardened" (Cranfield, 2:556).

Paul has already introduced this theme of "provoking to envy" in 10:19, where he cites Deut 32:21. Some may be concerned that

God can speak of envy or jealousy as a motivation for accepting the gospel. Because they think of jealousy as always being sinful, it sounds to them like an "end justifies means" scheme. Some try to avoid this by using the word "emulation" instead (Lard, 355; MP, 454). But this misses the point. Emulation cannot be substituted for jealousy, since it is the effect of which jealousy is supposed to be the cause.

In the Bible jealousy is always the point of this word, but it is not always an evil attitude. God himself is often described as a "jealous God" (see GC, 409-416). Stott well says that "not all envy is tainted with selfishness, because it is not always a grudging discontent or a sinful covetousness." The essence of envy, he says, is the desire to have for oneself what is possessed by another. It is good envy or evil envy depending on the nature of what is desired and on whether one has a right to it (297). Surely in this case the salvation possessed by the Gentiles is something good and something God wants the Jews to have anyway, and the Jews' desire to have it will in no way diminish the Gentiles' possession of it. Thus it is not at all an unworthy motive for accepting the gospel.

In this verse three things are linked in a cause-and-effect chain: the Jews' transgression (their initial negative response to the gospel), Gentile salvation, and Jewish envy. It is significant that in the latter part of the verse there are no verbs, and thus no tenses (past, present, future). We know the first step has already occurred; we assume the second has at least begun ("salvation *has come*," NIV, NASB). Many assume the last step (Jewish envy) is still in the future, but our conclusion on this point must be based on the following verses.

11:12 But if their transgression means riches for the world, and their loss means riches for the Gentiles, how much greater riches will their fullness bring! Most of the content of this verse, rightly understood, has already been either affirmed or implied in v. 11 (Lard, 356; MP, 456-457). I.e., if the Jews' *transgression* (stumbling, unbelief) results in riches (salvation) for the world (the Gentiles), and if their *loss* (fall) similarly results in riches (salvation) for the Gentiles, then how much more likely it is that the *fullness* (salvation) of the Jews will result in spiritual riches for all.

We should note that in the Greek there are no verbs (and thus no tenses) in this entire verse; thus we should be cautious about assigning to any one of these three clauses an entirely past or entirely future enactment.

The first two clauses seem to be restating the link between the Jews' downfall and the Gentiles' salvation taught in v. 11. "Their transgression" is the same word used in v. 11 and has the same meaning, i.e., their stumbling over and rejecting their Messiah in unbelief. "Their loss" is equivalent to the "fall" in v. 11.

The word translated "loss" (ἥττημα, *hēttēma*) is seldom used and is quite difficult. Some give it a numerical connotation ("diminishing, fewness, diminutiveness, reduction to a small number"), mainly based on the assumption that the corresponding word in the next clause ("fullness") is also numerical.[146] But this is wrong, especially since "fullness" itself should not be understood numerically. Also, it does not fit the context. The subject here is not Israel *per se* but the hardened portion of Israel, which in comparison with the remnant is not few but many.

The basic meaning of *hēttēma* seems to be "defeat" (Isa 31:8, LXX; 1 Cor 6:7),[147] but the emphasis here seems to be more on the loss (e.g., of possessions, of freedom) that results from an actual defeat. "Loss" is thus a good translation. As a result of their rejection of their Messiah, the Jews suffered the loss of their relationship with God and of the spiritual riches of Christ's kingdom. Thus they exist in "a state of missed blessings" (McGuiggan, 324). This contrasts well with "riches." See Lard, 356; Murray, 2:78; McGuiggan, 323-324.

The point is that the Jews' trespass, along with their consequent loss, is a means of bringing spiritual riches upon the Gentiles, as pointed out in v. 11.[148] "Riches" refers to the spiritual riches of salvation and is equivalent to "salvation" in v. 11. See Eph 1:18, which refers to "the riches of his glorious inheritance in the saints" (See also 2:4; 9:23; 11:33; Eph 1:7; 2:7; 3:6, 8; Phil 4:19).

---

[146]So Barrett, 213-214; Godet, 400. Most oppose this, e.g., Cranfield, 2:557; Lenski, 695.

[147]So Hendriksen, 2:367; Moo, 688; Cranfield, 2:557. Cranfield says the Jews' rejection of their Messiah "is, though they do not yet recognize it as such, their defeat, discomfiture, rout, downfall."

[148]"World" (κόσμος, *kosmos*) here and in v. 15 is probably meant to be synonymous with Gentiles.

The last clause in this verse is extremely difficult. Literally it is very succinct: "by how much more their fullness" (no verb). How does this fit into the overall structure of the verse? The phrase "by how much more" (πόσῳ μᾶλλον, *posō mallon*) shows that some kind of comparison is being made between the first two clauses and this final clause. The common assumption is that "riches" is being compared with "more riches," i.e., if the Jews' transgression and loss bring *riches* to the Gentiles, their fullness will bring even *greater riches.*

I believe this misses the point, however. In six of its eight NT occurrences, the phrase *posō mallon* means "how much more likely it is that," and is usually part of an argument from the lesser to the greater. This meaning fits very well here. Thus the clause is not an argument from riches to more riches, but this: "If the Jews' *transgression* and *loss* mean riches for the Gentiles, *how much more likely it is that* the Jews' *fullness* [means riches for the Gentiles]."[149]

This conclusion will affect not only how we interpret v. 12, but also v. 15, where "life from the dead" is often identified with the alleged "greater riches" in v. 12. (E.g., see Moo, 689; DeWelt, 182.) Speculation then abounds. I.e., if the *riches* brought to the Gentiles by the Jews' sin is (rightly) understood as their *salvation* (v. 11), then the *greater riches* ("life from the dead") must be something even more significant than personal salvation; indeed, it must be something spectacular, such as a great future universal revival or the final general resurrection at the end-time. E.g., Denney posits some future "unimaginable blessing" (679), and Murray speaks of "unprecedented enrichment" (2:79).

But when we see that *posō mallon* is not really talking about "greater riches," the basis for such speculation is gone; and when we realize also that there is no verb (and thus no future tense) in this clause, the assumption that this word refers to some great eschatological event is also weakened.

This brings us to the difficult question, what is the nature of the Jews' "fullness" (πλήρωμα, *plērōma*)? There are two basic views. One is that this is a *quantitative* fullness, and refers to the ultimate

---

[149]The six occurrences are Matt 7:11; 10:25 (greater to lesser); Luke 11:13; 12:28; Rom 11:24 (greater to lesser); Heb 9:14. (The other two are Luke 12:25; Phlm 16.) Note especially Rom 11:24, where the phrase means exactly what I am saying it means here.

conversion of the "full number" of Jews; the other is that the fullness is *qualitative* and refers to the Jews' participation in the fullness of salvation.

The former view, that *plērōma* means "full and completed number," is, as Cranfield notes, "widely accepted"; and in his opinion it "seems very much more likely" than any other view (2:558). It refers to "the entrance of the full complement of the nation into the Messianic kingdom," say Sanday and Headlam (322). The TEV translates it "complete number." This is often paralleled with a numeric interpretation of *hēttēma* in the previous clause; see the NEB: "If their falling-off [*hēttēma*] means the enrichment of the Gentiles, how much more their coming to full strength!"

To what, then, would this refer? The most common idea is that it refers to a future large-scale conversion of Jews, in contrast with the present "remnant" situation. Israel's "diminishing to a small number," says Godet, will be reversed by a "national conversion" of "the totality of the then living members of the people of Israel" (400-401). "Paul cannot rest content in the thought of only a remnant saved," says Dunn (2:655). We must assume that the Apostle is referring to a future "conversion on a large scale," in line with 11:25, says Lard (357). See also Stott, 296; Moo, 689-690.

Some expand this idea to include the restoration of the Jews to their original status as God's chosen people. The word "fullness" means "a mass restoration of Israel is in view," says Murray. "Nothing else than a restoration of Israel as a people to faith, privilege, and blessing can satisfy the terms of this passage" (2:79, 80). This is often linked with the establishment of a millennial kingdom in the premillennial sense (e.g., MacArthur, 2:110-111).

Others agree that "fullness" means "full number," but interpret this (in a Calvinist sense) to mean the full number of elect Jews as they are gradually converted over the full course of Christian history. This is Hendriksen's view: "The salvation of the full number of Israelites who had been predestined to be saved (cf. 9:6) – hence, not just the salvation of a remnant at any *one* particular time (see 11:5) – would progressively bring an abundance of blessings to the entire world" (2:367).

The meaning of v. 12 would then be, in Cranfield's words, as follows: "If the present unbelief of the majority of Israel actually means the enrichment of the Gentiles, how much more wonderfully enriching must the situation resulting from the provoking to jealousy of this majority of Israel be!" (2:557-558).

The other view, and in my opinion the correct one, is that the *plērōma* of the Jews is meant in a qualitative sense and refers to spiritual fullness, or being filled with all the abundance of salvation. The word itself as used elsewhere in the NT does not refer to "full number" but to "completeness, abundance." See, e.g., John 1:16, "the fullness of his grace"; Rom 15:29, "the full measure of the blessing of Christ"; Eph 1:23, "the fullness of him [Christ]"; Eph 3:19, "that you may be filled to the measure of all the fullness of God"; Eph 4:13, "attaining to the whole measure of the fullness of Christ." (Compare the way the verb πληρόω [*plēroō*] is used in Rom 15:13-14; Eph 3:19; 5:18; Phil 1:11; Col 2:10.)

This meaning also fits the context. In v. 12 itself, "fullness" is in contrast with both "transgression" and "loss," words that sum up the lost state as opposed to salvation. This is an especially appropriate contrast with "loss," which as we have seen does not have a numerical connotation; the point is simply the lost state as compared with the saved state.

Also regarding context, this meaning is better in view of the connection between v. 11 and v. 12. Verse 11 describes a cause-and-effect chain: the Jews' transgression leads to Gentile salvation which leads to Jewish envy. The reference to Jewish envy implies Jewish salvation, since this is its intended result (see v. 14). As noted above, v. 12 is giving further reflection on the relations among these three items, especially the idea that the Jews' transgression results in riches (salvation) for the Gentiles. The one thought added in v. 12 is that the Jewish envy (and thus salvation) produced by the Gentiles' conversion would in turn lead to even more Gentiles being saved. Thus it is natural to take "fullness" in v. 12 as referring to the Jews' salvation, which in context corresponds to (since in fact it grows out of) their envy in v. 11.

As another contextual note, we shall see later that this meaning best corresponds to the meaning of *plērōma* in v. 25.

Thus I agree with McGuiggan when he says that the Jews' fullness is the "rich blessedness" they receive when they abandon their unbelief and accept their Messiah's salvation. "Israel by unbelief lost blessings, Israel by faith would be fully blessed." McGuiggan rightly says, "There is no ground in the text whatever for supposing that 'fulness' is somewhat equivalent to a conversion of Jews 'on a national scale' or 'on a scale commensurate with their rejection' (numerically speaking)." In fact, in v. 12 "there is no allusion to the number of Jews lost and (therefore, in the antithesis) there is no mention of the number of Jews (to be) saved. . . . 'Fullness' speaks of a rich state of blessedness as opposed to 'loss'" (324). See Lenski, 695.

We must also emphasize that the text does not project this conversion of the Jews to some distant future date; it does not preclude that it could already be happening at that very time. (Remember: the verse has no verbs and no tenses.) In fact, in vv. 13-14 Paul implies that his own ministry is already producing this result.

We must remember that the main point of v. 12 is not about the Jews but about the Gentiles, i.e., what will happen to the Gentiles as a result of the Jews' unbelief as well as their belief. If some Gentiles are saved as the result of the Jews' *rejection* of the gospel, then we have even more reason to expect Gentiles to be saved as the result of the Jews' envy-induced *acceptance* of the gospel.

11:13-14 I am talking to you Gentiles. Inasmuch as I am the apostle to the Gentiles, I make much of my ministry in the hope that I may somehow arouse my own people to envy and save some of them. Many think v. 13a shows that the Gentiles were in the majority in the church at Rome (e.g., Dunn, 2:655, 669; Moo, 691, n. 39), but Cranfield is right that such a conclusion cannot be drawn from this verse (2:559). Paul is simply saying that he wants the Gentiles among his readers to pay special attention to what he is saying, not just in what follows but in the preceding verses as well.

This is true for two reasons. One, in this whole main section, Israel has been the focus of attention; the Gentiles have entered the discussion only marginally. Thus the latter group "may well have been reasoning that all this about the Jews had little to do with them. They may have wondered why the apostle to the Gentiles should be spending so much time worrying about the Jews" (Morris, 408). Thus Paul stops to reassure the Gentiles that he has not forgotten the main focus of his ministry. He wants them to see "that this argument has an application to Gentiles as well as Jews." He is saying, in effect, "Do not think that what I am saying has nothing to do with you Gentiles. It makes me even more zealous in my work for you" (SH, 323-324). What he is showing them is that the welfare of the Jews and the Gentiles is entertwined.

Paul's other reason for addressing the Gentiles specifically is the possibility that what he teaches about Gentile salvation in vv. 11-12 may lead some to develop an attitude of arrogance toward the Jews (see v. 20). He does not want them to conclude that the Jews are merely a means to an end, that end being the salvation and exaltation of the Gentiles. Paul assures them of his own genuine concern for the Jews' salvation, and in the next section he shows them how much they owe to the Jews (vv. 17-24). He declares that even as God's Apostle to the Gentiles,[150] his work in that capacity has "an Israel-ward significance" (Cranfield, 2:559).

Paul says, "I make much of my ministry." It is possible that δια–κονία (*diakonia*, "ministry") here means "office" (KJV) in a special technical sense (see, e.g., Acts 1:25; 2 Cor 4:1; Col 4:17). More likely it means simply "ministry" or "area of service" or "mission," i.e., his specific assignment to be the apostle to the Gentiles. "Make much of" is δοξάζω (*doxazō*), which means "to honor, to praise, to glorify." It is usually used of giving glory to God, and is rarely used of men or anything human (see 8:30; 1 Cor 12:26; negatively, see Matt 6:2). Paul does not say that he honors or glorifies himself, but he glorifies his *ministry* as a task given to him by God. Thus he honors it not because of its fulfillment in himself but because of its origin in God.

Paul's point is that he has the highest respect for his calling, and approaches it with the utmost seriousness and diligence. "He honours and reverences his ministry to the Gentiles, and so fulfils it with all might and devotion" (Cranfield, 2:560).

To what end does Paul honor his ministry? It is taken for granted that he does so in order to win converts from among the Gentiles, but in view of the divine plan spelled out in v. 11, he knows that his ministry is also an indirect means of bringing his own kinsmen to faith in Christ. "My own people" is literally "my flesh" (see 9:3), i.e., the Jews, "Israel according to the flesh" (1 Cor 10:18, lit.). The relation between their envy and their salvation has already been implied in vv. 11-12 (see the explanation of "fullness" in v. 12

[150]See 1:5; JC, 1:98.

above). Thus he glorifies his ministry, because "the more Gentiles Paul converts, the more of this jealousy he creates, . . . which results in conversions of the Jews" (Lenski, 697).

Paul understands that this process will not be automatic and will not convert every Jew. He pursues his apostleship to the Gentiles "in the hope that" some Jews may be saved thereby. "In the hope that I may somehow" translates εἴ πως (*ei pōs*) plus the subjunctive case of the verb. This is "an expression of expectation," says Dunn (2:656), but as Moo says, it is a "hesitant expectation" (692, n. 46).

Why does Paul say "some of them"? Some interpreters think he says this because he knows that the number of Jews who will be saved through his own ministry will be few in comparison with the great ingathering and restoration of the Jewish people in the future. Thus his converts "are a precious foretoken of the salvation referred to in v. 26" (Cranfield, 2:561), or of the "fullness" in v. 12. As Moo says, "Paul does not see himself . . . as the figure whom God will use to bring Israel to its destined 'fullness'" (692).

I believe this misses the point, especially since the whole idea of a future large-scale conversion of Jews is far from certain. We must look elsewhere for the reasons why Paul says "some of them." First, he refers here only to the results of his own ministry, and he knew that Jews were being won to Christ by other evangelists and would continue to be won by others in later generations. Second, Paul knew from experience that the salvation of every individual Jew was too much to hope for. He knew that the unbelieving Jews of his own generation were hardened and strongly resistant to the gospel. But at the same time he knew that they still had the free will to believe, and that arousing them to envy was a means to this end. Thus by fulfilling his ministry to the Gentiles, he expected "some" of his ethnic brothers to be saved, but not all.

11:15 For if their rejection is the reconciliation of the world, what will their acceptance be but life from the dead? "For" indicates this verse is explaining something or giving a reason for something in the preceding context. Some take vv. 13-14 as a parenthesis, with v. 15 going back and picking up especially on v. 12 and repeating it in more specific terms (e.g., Fitzmyer, 612). Others see v. 15 as explaining the last clause in v. 14, i.e., as explaining why Paul is so enthusiastic about his ministry to the Gentiles (e.g., Lard, 358; Cranfield, 2:561-562).

I think it is best to see v. 15 as reaching back into both v. 12 and vv. 13-14, accomplishing both of the purposes named above at the same time (SH, 325). The key thought linking the end of v. 12 and the end of v. 14 with v. 15 is the salvation (fullness, acceptance) of some of the hardened Jews. In v. 15 Paul is stating why he wants to see as many as possible from this group come to salvation, because that is nothing less than "life from the dead."

We cannot ignore the fact that the form of this verse is very close to that of v. 12: if A leads to B, then surely C leads to D. "Their transgression" and "their loss" in v. 12 correspond to "their rejection" in v. 15. In both cases "their" refers to the unbelieving, hardened Jews. In v. 12 their transgression and loss refer to their unbelief and subsequent lost state. But what is the meaning of "rejection" in v. 15?

The word translated "rejection" is ἀποβολή (*apobolē*), which comes from the verb ἀποβάλλω (*apoballō*), which means "to throw away, to reject, to remove, to lose." Dunn is correct (2:657) that the contrast with "acceptance" in v. 15b means that *apobolē* refers to the deliberate act of throwing away or rejecting something, rather than the passive act of losing something. But the question is, who is rejecting whom?

Some say it is the Jews' rejection of Christ and the gospel of his grace. Thus it would be equivalent to "transgression" in vv. 11-12. Fitzmyer prefers this view since 11:1 specifically affirms that God has not rejected his people (612). However, in spite of v. 1, most take v. 15 to mean God's rejection of the Jews, "their temporary casting away by God" (Cranfield, 2:562; see Moo, 692-693). This is equivalent to God's hardening of Israel (v. 7), and his breaking off of some of the branches (vv. 17-20). It is "God's response to Jewish unbelief" (McGuiggan, 327).

But in v. 1 did not Paul emphatically deny that God has rejected his people? How then can he say here that they have been rejected? The Greek words are different, but the concepts seem to be the same. Is there a contradiction, then? The answer is No, and the reason for this is very important. In v. 1 the issue is whether God has rejected the Jews as such, just because they are Jews. I.e., has he rejected *every one* of "his people"? The answer is obviously No, because there is a remnant of true believers who have not been rejected. But in v. 15 Paul is talking only about the nonremnant Jews, the unbelieving Jews who rejected the gospel and whom God hardened. After their initial refusal to accept their Messiah, God rejected them (hardened them, broke them off the tree).

It is important to understand this so that we do not interpret v. 15 as referring to Israel *as a nation*. This verse says nothing about God's relationship with the nation as a whole. It refers only to those individual Jews who spurned the gospel and were consequently rejected by God, and to those individual Jews from among this group who later respond to the gospel and are consequently accepted by God – as individuals, on an individual basis. When we try to interpret v. 15 as referring to the Jews in general, or to the Jews as a corporate group, then we place it in conflict with v. 1.

God's rejection of the unbelieving Jews leads to the "reconciliation of the world." Here "world" must be taken in light of v. 12, where it refers especially to the Gentiles (Murray, 2:81; Lenski, 699-700). Thus the point is exactly the same as in the first two clauses of v. 12. "Riches for the world" (v. 12) and "the reconciliation of the world" (v. 15) both refer to the salvation of the Gentiles, with "reconciliation" being a specific aspect of that salvation (see 5:10; JC, 1:326-327). Reconciliation basically means the removal of hostility and the restoration of peace and friendship between two estranged parties. Some think this possibly refers to "the reconciliation of Jew and Gentile in one new people of God" (Barrett, 215; see Stott, 298). Others think it refers to the objective reconciliation of the whole world to God through Christ's propitiatory sacrifice, even if it is not accepted by all and applied to all (see 5:10-11; 2 Cor 5:19). This is Cranfield's view (2:562). Most probably, though, it refers to the actual subjective reconciliation of the believer to God, which is one aspect of individual salvation and the conversion process (see Lenski, 699; Moo, 693, n. 58). This reinforces the point made in the last paragraph, that Paul is thinking here of individuals rather than groups.

We now turn our attention to the second part of the verse, which is similar to the last clause in v. 12, both in its meaning and in its relation to the rest of the verse. I.e., if the assertion in the first part of the verse is true, then that gives us all the more reason to believe the second part.

"What will their acceptance be" is literally "what the acceptance." There is no verb, and no possessive pronoun ("their"). The latter should probably be understood, in view of the similarity to v. 12; but the insertion of the future tense ("will be") is based as much (if not more) on doctrinal presuppositions as on exegetical considerations. The word for "acceptance" is used only here in the NT, but the uses of its verb form[151] support the translation "acceptance." Other possibilities are "reception," "taking to oneself," "acquisition" (Dunn, 2:657), and "the act of welcoming" (Godet, 403).

As with v. 15a we must ask the question, who is accepting whom? Some take it as referring to the Jews' "acceptance or welcoming of the gospel" (Fitzmyer, 612), but most take it to mean God's acceptance of repentant Jews back into a saving relationship with himself (Moo, 693). God has rejected them because of their unbelief (15a), but he is just as eager to receive them back to himself if they will but turn to him.

What is this acceptance? Since it is the grammatical equivalent of "fullness" in v. 12, and since many interpret that fullness to mean a dramatic, large-scale, end-time conversion of the Jewish people, this is a common interpretation of "acceptance" as well. It is "God's final acceptance of what is now unbelieving Israel," says Cranfield (2:562). "Here again we supply *will be*, and make the Apostle assert the future conversion of the Jews," says Lard (358). It refers, says Murray, to "the reception of Israel again into the favour and blessing of God," i.e., "Israel as a whole," or "the mass of Israel" (2:81).

There is no reason other than a dogmatic one to interpret the acceptance thus, however. We have seen that "fullness" in v. 12 need not have this meaning, and more likely refers to the salvation of individual Jews, something that was already occurring even as Paul wrote. Also, the "rejection" in v. 15a refers to the unbelieving Jews as individuals, not to the Jews as a nation; the same must be true of their "acceptance." We must also remember that there is no future-tense verb in the original text. Thus it is altogether appropriate to interpret this acceptance of the Jews as referring to the ongoing conversion of individual Jews, something that was already happening in Paul's day (Lenski, 700).

---

[151]The verb is προσλαμβάνω (*proslambanō*). See, e.g., Acts 18:26; 28:2; Rom 14:1,3; 15:7; Phlm 17.

What happens when hardened Jews are converted? Well, says Paul, if God's casting away of the Jews results in the reconciliation of Gentiles to God, what can we expect as a result of their return and reception except "life from the dead"? This leads to our discussion of one of the most controversial expressions in this chapter, "life from the dead." Only v. 26 has "sparked more disagreement," says Moo (694).

What does it mean? Stott has identified three main answers: the literal, figurative, and spiritual views (298). Now, giving life to the dead in any sense is a marvelous event (see 4:17), but defenders of the first two of these views believe that in this case it must refer to some future, worldwide, awesome resurrection of unprecedented magnitude. This approach is based on their perception of Paul's lesser-to-greater arguments in both v. 12 and v. 15.

The common assumption is that in v. 12, the lesser element of the argument includes "riches," so the corresponding greater element must be "greater riches." Likewise it is assumed that in v. 15 the lesser includes "reconciliation," so the corresponding greater must be "life from the dead."[152] In both verses what is perceived as the lesser element is identified with the individual's present experience of salvation. Therefore the "greater riches" and "life from the dead" must be something greater than present salvation. Therefore since regeneration is part of this present salvation, then "life from the dead" cannot be regeneration but must refer to something of much greater magnitude. As Stott says, "*Much greater riches* demands to be understood as something new, even spectacular. To refer it to the new life in Christ which we already enjoy would be an anticlimax" (298). Cranfield agrees, declaring that "life from the dead" "must clearly denote something surpassing everything signified" by "salvation" in v. 11, by the "riches" in v. 12, and by "reconciliation" in v. 15. Therefore "it cannot denote the spiritual blessings already being enjoyed by the believing Gentiles" (2:562). Dunn agrees that it must be "something more wonderful" (2:658), as does Moo: "The logic of the verse shows that it must

---

[152]This equation of "life from the dead" with the "greater riches" in v. 12 is crucial, since v. 12 does not identify the "greater riches." But in v. 15 "the greater blessing is specified for us," says Murray (2:82).

refer to a blessing even greater or more climactic than the extension of reconciliation to the Gentiles." Why? Because "Paul argues from the lesser to the greater" (694).

What, then, is this greater "life from the dead"? The *literal* view says it refers to the final bodily resurrection of all the dead at the Second Coming of Christ, as preceded and signaled by the mass conversion of the Jews. This is Cranfield's view (2:563). It is clearly an eschatological event, says Dunn, i.e., "the final resurrection at the end of the age" (2:658). Moo agrees and gives a helpful listing of those holding to or sympathetic with this approach (694, n. 61). He also gives three main arguments for the view (695-696), citing the frequency with which the phrase "from the dead" is used of the final resurrection in the NT, the relation of this event to other parts of the total process described in ch. 11, and Paul's general apocalyptic tendencies.

The second view agrees that "life from the dead" must refer to some sort of sensational, unparalleled event, but interprets it in a *figurative* sense. It says that the Jews' fullness and reception will trigger some sort of "world-wide blessing which will so far surpass anything before experienced that it can only be likened to new life out of death" (Stott, 298). This will be "a great spiritual movement" (Morris, 411), "an unprecedented, semi-miraculous revival" (MP, 458), "an unprecedented quickening for the world in the expansion and success of the gospel" (Murray, 2:84), "a vast and intense revival of true religion from a state which, by comparison, was religious death" (Moule, 193). Since this is something triggered by the mass conversion of Jews, it must be a mass conversion of the Gentiles (Godet, 404), a "great spiritual harvest" from among the Gentiles (Lard, 359).[153]

The final view, the *spiritual* view, is that "life from the dead" refers to an element of the individual's present salvation experience, namely, regeneration (see 6:4,11; 8:10; Eph 2:1-5; Col 12:12-13). Thus it is part of the "salvation" and the "riches" mentioned in vv. 11-12, and is in the same category as the "reconciliation" named in v. 15a. This, I believe, is the correct view.

---

[153]Defenders of the previous view point out that this contradicts vv. 25-26, where mass revival ("fullness") among the Gentiles seems to precede the mass conversion of the Jews (Cranfield, 2:563).

But what about the common assumption that "life from the dead" must be something much different from and greater than this, in view of the fact that Paul is arguing from the lesser to the greater? In my judgment this is a major error based on a faulty understanding of the lesser-to-greater argument as Paul uses it here. As explained above in v. 12, the whole concept of "greater riches" misses Paul's point. There he is not arguing that if a lesser cause produces a significant effect ("riches"), then a greater cause will produce an even more significant effect ("greater riches"). Rather, he argues that if the lesser cause produces a significant effect, we have even *greater reason* to expect a greater cause to produce a similar effect. No greater effect is mentioned in the verse. The point is that the first two views above are based mainly on the assumption of an equivalence with the argument in v. 12, which itself is misinterpreted.

But what about v. 15? Indeed, there is a lesser-to-greater argument here, but the language is different from v. 12[154] and the logical force is weaker (Lenski, 701). But it is equivalent to v. 12 in the sense that the lesser-to-greater element in v. 15 (as in v. 12) lies only in the comparative *causes* in the two clauses, not in the effects. I.e., if the lesser cause (rejection of the Jews) produces a significant effect, then surely a greater cause (acceptance of the Jews) can be expected to produce a similarly significant effect. Thus the argument that "the logic of the verse" rules out the spiritual view is without foundation in fact.

Other considerations should be kept in mind. For example, we must remember that there are no verbs in this verse, and therefore no grammatical reason to think that "life from the dead" refers to some event that is only future. Also, the argument that the terminology "from the dead" refers only to the future bodily resurrection is offset by other linguistic data spelled out in detail by Murray (2:82-83). Also, apart from unfounded speculation regarding the meaning of "fullness" (vv. 12,25) the whole theme of eschatology simply does not appear in this context. The subject of personal salvation is dominant.

Thus we must see "life from the dead" as referring to the spiritual experience of regeneration, of passing over from the state of

[154]The key phrase *posō mallon* does not appear in v. 15.

spiritual death to the state of spiritual life (John 5:24; Col 2:12-13). Paul may be including the Gentiles within the scope of this statement, but its main application is to the Jews themselves. I.e., if the Jews' rejection results in reconciliation for the Gentiles, then the Jews' reception results in their own resurrection to new life in Christ. See Lenski, 701-702; Hendriksen, 2:369. As McGuiggan says, "The Jewish 'received' state is called 'life from the dead'. It is the return of the prodigal in Luke 15. The boy had been lost and was therefore miserably unblessed; he had been 'dead' and was now 'alive from the dead'" (327).[155] Referring to 4:17, Wright says that "the natural meaning of 11.15" is this: 'When a Gentile comes into the family of Christ, it is as it were a *creatio ex nihilo*, but when a Jew comes in it is like a resurrection'" (*Climax*, 248).

When we understand it this way, we see that v. 15 is just summing up what Paul has said thus far in this paragraph. Verse 15a focuses on the spiritual riches enjoyed by the Gentiles, brought about by the Jews' unbelief and rejection (vv. 11-12); and v. 15b focuses on the salvation of the Jews themselves, brought about by their own envy of the Gentiles (vv. 13-14).

11:16 If the part of the dough offered as firstfruits is holy, then the whole batch is holy; if the root is holy, so are the branches. Though many take this verse as starting the next paragraph, I agree with the NIV that it concludes the thought begun at v. 11. The general subject is still that there is hope for the salvation of the hardened portion of Israel. The main point is that God still has a special place in his heart for "his people," even those who have rejected their Messiah. This does not mean that they receive special treatment with reference to salvation (see 2:1–3:20), but it does mean that God still loves them and will make every possible effort to save them.

This verse uses two metaphors. The first is based on the fact of the divine ownership of all things. To reinforce this fact in the minds of the Jews, God required that the first portion of any product[156] be set apart (made holy) to him in a special way. Paul is

---

[155]Compare this with the concept of a lopped-off and dead branch being grafted back into its life-giving tree (vv. 23-24).

[156]E.g., the first [male] offspring of an animal (Exod 13:1,11-13; Num 18:15-17); the first grain of the harvest (Lev 23:9-14).

here alluding to one example of this general practice, i.e., presenting as an offering to God a portion of bread made from the meal ground from the first-harvested grain (Num 15:17-21). Though Num 15 does not specifically state this, based on the general practice it is assumed that the offering of the firstfruits "thereby consecrated to the Lord the entire grain harvest" (Hendriksen, 2:369), or all the flour and dough made from it.

The second metaphor is the relation of a tree's root to its branches. Since the root is the beginning of the pipeline through which the rest of a tree is watered and nourished, the condition of the root naturally affects the status of the branches as well. I.e., "if the root is holy, so are the branches."

The question is, what do these metaphors represent? In answering this question, two cautions must be observed. First, we should not assume that they are identical in meaning. Second, we should not assume that the point of the root-branches metaphor in v. 16 is the same as the point of the extended root-branches metaphor in vv. 17-24.

Some do take the metaphors to be parallel. For example, some have understood the firstfruits and the root to refer to Jesus Christ.[157] In view of the context, though, it is more probable that they refer somehow to the Jews. The most common view is that the firstfruits and root refer to the patriarchs, especially Abraham, while the "whole batch" or entire "lump" (KJV, NASB), as well as the branches, refer to all the Jews who have descended from them. According to most who hold this view, the Jews as a nation will always be treated in a special way because of their relation to "the patriarchs" (v. 28). Moo says, "Both of the metaphors in v. 16, then, assert that the 'holiness' of the patriarchs conveys to all of Israel a similar holiness" (700). See MP, 463; SH, 326.

What, then, would be the nature of this shared holiness? In a generic sense, to be holy means to be separated or set apart from all the rest; in a religious generic sense it means to be set apart for God or consecrated to God in a way that is special but does not necessarily involve salvation. Some interpret v. 16 thus, as God's

---

[157]Examples are several early church fathers, and Karl Barth. See Cranfield, 2:564-565, for further discussion.

promise that the nation of Israel will always be a distinct and special people, just as the patriarchs were set apart in the beginning. Many tie this in with the idea that God will one day restore the Jewish nation to its "original pre-eminence as leaders in the worship of Jehovah" (MP, 464). This does not assert "the salvation of every Israelite but the continuing 'special' identity of the people of Israel in the eyes of the Lord" (Moo, 701). As such this verse gives "support for the ultimate recovery of Israel," says Murray (2:85). Here Paul gives "the grounds of his confidence in the future of Israel" (SH, 326).

Some do interpret "holiness" in a salvific sense, however, and see this verse as a promise that all Israel will one day be saved (see v. 26). To some this means spiritual Israel only, i.e., "all the spiritual descendants" of the patriarchs (Lenski, 703). To others it is a promise that one day all (or a great majority of) ethnic Jews will be saved. In this verse, says Morris, "Paul proceeds to bring out the certainty that Israel will in due course enter salvation" (411; see MacArthur, 2:114).

I disagree with all of the above views. A key point is that the two metaphors are not parallel in their meaning, as if the firstfruits and the root refer to the same thing, and the lump and the branches refer to the same thing.[158] What do they mean, then? In other texts Paul uses the term "firstfruits" (ἀπαρχή, *aparchē*) to refer to the first converts in a particular context (16:5; 1 Cor 16:15). That is the point of the first metaphor here. The firstfruits are the early Jewish converts, the Jewish Christian remnant;[159] the "batch" is the Jews as a whole, especially the unbelieving and hardened ones.

Also, "holy" here does have the connotation of salvation. This does not imply, though, that just as the first converts *have been* saved, so ultimately all Jews *will be* saved.[160] It means this, rather: if *some* Jews can be saved, then *all* Jews can be saved. Lard says it

---

[158]Others holding this nonparallel view are Cranfield, 2:564-565; Dunn, 2:659; Fitzmyer, 614; Stott, 299.

[159]"Here the 'firstfruit' most probably comprises those people of Jewish birth who had, like Paul, accepted Jesus as Messiah and Lord" (Bruce, 217).

[160]Stott's interpretation is too positive: "When the first converts believe, the conversion of the rest can be expected to follow" (299).

right: "If the first Jewish christians were accepted of God, the whole nation is capable of being accepted. They are not irrevocably rejected" (360; see DeWelt, 183). It is the same hope that Paul holds out in this paragraph when he refers to the "fullness" and "acceptance" of the Jews (vv. 12,15).

The second metaphor is slightly different. The root includes the patriarchs but not them alone; it refers to the entire OT Israelite nation considered as a whole. The branches are all ethnic Jews living in the NT era, considered as individuals. Here the primary connotation of "holy" is the generic concept of "set apart" or "consecrated" to God, but its ultimate reference is still to salvation. The point is this: under the Old Covenant God chose the nation of Israel to be the instrument by which he worked his redemptive purpose in the world (9:6-29). Even though he no longer has a special purpose for Israel as a nation, nevertheless the love and concern he had for "his people" in OT times carries forward into the gospel era. Every branch, i.e., every individual Jew, is just as personally precious and special to him today as was the root, the nation of old. Thus the door of salvation is still open even to the hardened, unbelieving Jews. God is waiting to add them to the remnant.

The point of the verse, then, is not to promise that Israel as a nation will be restored to its OT prominence, nor to guarantee that all Jews actually *will* be saved. Rather, it is to stress the fact that any and all Jews *can* be saved (v. 16a), and that God *wants* them to be saved (v. 16b). Following up on this, the point of the next paragraph is to show exactly *how* they can be saved.

D. THE OLIVE TREE: A METAPHOR OF JUDGMENT AND HOPE (11:17-24)

Introduction

In this paragraph Paul stays with the metaphor of the olive tree, but he expands it considerably and uses it for different purposes. In brief, he uses it to show how the NT church is related to OT Israel, and how Jews and Gentiles are related to the church. The main point of vv. 17-22 is a double warning to Gentile Christians.

They are warned not to have an attitude of self-righteous superiority toward unbelieving Jews, and not to presume that they are any more immune to falling away than the Jews who fell. The main point of vv. 23-24, on the other hand, is an explanation of how the fallen and hardened Jews can be saved.

Why has Paul used the olive tree as a basis for making these points? For one thing, the OT compares God's people with an olive tree (Jer 11:16; Hos 14:6). Also, it was something his initial readers would have been very familiar with. Dunn notes that "the olive tree was the most widely cultivated fruit tree in the Mediterranean area" (2:660-661). Also, the common practice of grafting branches from one olive tree to another was a perfect illustration of the points he wanted to make.

Since Paul has just used the root-branches metaphor in v. 16, we would expect these two elements to have the same basic meaning in this new paragraph; and most agree that this is so. E.g., those who identified the root with the patriarchs in v. 16 do the same here. I agree that this is the best approach. Thus, as in v. 16, I identify the root with OT Israel as a national unit, and I identify the branches as (in part) including (some) individual Jews who live in this NT era.

In vv. 17-24, however, Paul has expanded the metaphor in at least three ways. First, the concept of the tree as a whole is important here. Whereas v. 16 was about the relationship between generic roots and branches, here a particular tree is in view. How the roots and branches of this tree are related is still important, but it is also important that we understand the character of the tree as a whole.[161] Second, the branches are not limited to individual Jews, but refer also to individual Gentiles. Finally, the grafting of branches is a central element of the metaphor in this paragraph.

---

[161]The main elements of the tree are still the root and the branches. We should not expand the metaphor to include other elements of a tree, such as trunk and limbs, and then speculate as to what these might represent. This will cause us to miss the point. The root and the branches are the only parts that matter for Paul's purposes. If anyone is troubled by the fact that branches are usually not directly attached to roots, then he may think of the root of the olive tree as including by implication the trunk and limbs.

The rest of this introduction will explain, first, the concept of the olive tree as a whole, and second, the imagery of the pruning and grafting of the branches.

The Meaning of the Olive Tree as a Whole

Exactly what does this olive tree stand for? It represents the people of God in a general sense, including both OT Israel and the NT church, the latter including both Jews and Gentiles (see Moo, 698). This tree cannot be limited to ethnic Israel alone, as some think (see Fitzmyer, 610, for examples).

In one sense the nation of Israel as it existed in the OT era was a kind of prototree, and was a precursor of Paul's olive tree. This is suggested by the references to the breaking off of some of the Jewish branches (vv. 17-21). If they were broken off, then they were already attached to something. Also, Paul calls his tree the Jews' "own olive tree" (v. 24). In this sense pre-Christian Israel was itself a tree, but this is not Paul's main point. Also, it is important to remember that the OT tree had no implications regarding the salvation of the individual Jews attached thereto as branches. The tree as a whole was an instrument by which God was working out his salvation purposes; some of the individual branches were saved and some were not.

Whatever the nature of this prototree which led to the existence of Paul's olive tree, we must recognize that it underwent a radical transformation in character and purpose with the coming of the NT era. In Paul's metaphor OT Israel is not identified with the tree as a whole, but only with its root. His focus is on the individual branches as they relate to this root. These branches themselves constitute an entirely new group: the NT people of God, the church. Most importantly, unlike the OT prototree, Paul's olive tree is a soteric metaphor. Its branches as a whole are the aggregate of all saved individuals in this new era.

We may now look more closely at the composition of the olive tree. As in v. 16, the root stands for OT Israel as a whole. Thus it includes but is not limited to the patriarchs. It represents the entire nation throughout its entire history from the patriarchs forward, not as the aggregate of saved individuals (the remnant), but as God's covenant servant. It represents Israel in its role of fulfilling

God's redemptive purposes, culminating in the coming of the Messiah. Thus the root includes all blessings enumerated in 9:4-5: the patriarchs, the covenants, the promises, and in a sense even the Messiah himself.

The branches of the tree, which are the focal point of the metaphor, are the saved individuals of the NT era. As such they are the new Israel. The olive tree as a whole represents the two Israels to which v. 9:6b alludes, "For not all who are descended from Israel are Israel." The root is OT ethnic Israel; the branches are NT spiritual Israel. When the Messiah came and the OT prototree was transformed into the olive tree, this transformation was a moment of crisis for all Jews. Prior to this time all individual Jews – unbelievers as well as believers – were part of the prototree as an instrument of service to God. But with the coming of Christ and the transformation of the tree, all unbelieving Jews as individual branches of the old tree were broken off. There are no unbelievers on the olive tree; its branches consist of believers only.

The olive tree metaphor teaches us that there is a definite *discontinuity* between OT Israel and the NT church. Paul's tree is not the same as the OT prototree. The latter was transformed at Pentecost (see MP, 464-465) into something different. What once was an entire tree is now just the root of a new tree. The church is as different from Israel as a tree's branches are different from its root.

But this fact in itself implies a *continuity* between OT Israel and the NT church. The old tree was not simply cut down and replaced with a completely new one.[162] The church by itself is not the entire tree, but only the branches that are growing from a root that is part of that same tree. The two parts of this one tree have never existed simultaneously but are sequential in time. I.e., the root and the branches represent two interconnected stages in salvation history. Though the root itself no longer exists, its prior existence was an essential preparation for the present reality of the branches. Herein lies the basis for one of Paul's main points in this section: the relationship of dependence between the two Israels. I.e., the church as

[162]Lard (362) correctly warns us against viewing the church as just an "outgrowth" of an "old Jewish church," but to assert that the former is totally "without genealogy, antecedent, or type" is too extreme.

the new Israel is dependent upon what was accomplished by old Israel. The NT branches would have no existence apart from their OT root, and they constantly reap the rich benefits of what God has done through the latter (vv. 17-18). This is one reason why Paul warns the Gentile Christians not to boast over the fallen Jews (v. 18a).

The Imagery of the Pruning and Grafting of the Branches

While the meaning of the olive tree as a whole tells us something about the relation between OT Israel and the NT church, the imagery of the pruning and grafting of individual branches tells us something about the salvation of Jews and Gentiles in the NT era. Unlike the root-branches illustration in v. 16, which dealt exclusively with Jews, the branches in the extended metaphor include both Jews and Gentiles.[54] While Jewish Christians are described as belonging naturally to the "cultivated" olive tree, Gentile Christians are pictured as belonging by nature to a "wild" olive tree and being grafted into the cultivated one (v. 24).

Paul's discussion of Jews and Gentiles in this paragraph is in terms of God's pruning some branches from the tree and grafting others into it. A crucial point is that, when the OT prototree was transformed into the present olive tree, some of the original branches (Jews) that were attached to the former were broken off, which is an indication of their lost state. Before the transformation some of these attached branches were already lost, since the prototree did not have a soteric significance. But when Christ came and the tree was changed, *all* Jews who refused to accept him as their Savior were removed from the tree. We have every reason to assume that this included some Jews who were previously in a saved state because of their faith in Yahweh as he was known through OT revelation, but who rejected Jesus as the promised Messiah. On the other hand, all Jews who did believe in Jesus remained as branches on the new tree.

At the same time, all Gentiles who accepted Jesus as their Savior were taken from the wild olive tree (the pagan world) and were

---

[163]In this paragraph Paul is still addressing Gentile Christians in particular (see v. 13).

grafted into the cultivated and transformed olive tree, alongside the believing Jews, in the community of salvation.

Some have raised questions about the accuracy of Paul's knowledge of the olive industry. It seems that the usual procedure for grafting olive branches is to take a shoot from a cultivated but depleted tree and graft it into a wild but vigorous tree, but here it is just the opposite. Some have concluded that Paul as a naïve city boy was just showing his ignorance. Others point to a few ancient sources which show that wild-to-tame grafts were sometimes made, just as Paul describes. Still others say that Paul knew wild-to-tame grafts were not a natural procedure, but he reversed the process in order to show that grace deliberately contravenes nature (v. 24).[164] Either of the last two explanations is acceptable.[165] The details of grafting as an agricultural practice are not crucial to Paul's point. He simply incorporates the general concept into his metaphor and adapts it for his own purposes; one does not have to be an olive tree expert to understand what he is saying.

Paul uses the practice of grafting to make two main points. One is that the Gentile Christians, as wild olive branches grafted into a cultivated tree, have absolutely no room for boasting or considering themselves superior to the Jewish branches that were broken off the tree (vv. 17-22). One reason is that they are dependent upon the Jewish root of the tree for their very salvation and sustenance (v. 18b). The other reason is that their being grafted into the tree is due to their faith in what Christ has done, not to some boastworthy achievement accomplished by their own hands. If they ever reach a point where they no longer believe in Jesus, they too will be broken off just as the unbelieving Jews were (vv. 20-21).

Paul's other point is a continuation of his theme in vv. 11-16, that the lopped-off Jews are not irrevocably lost but can still be saved, even though they are now in an unbelieving and hardened state. Here he is not just declaring that they *can* be saved, but showing *how* they can be saved, namely, by being grafted again into their own (transformed) olive tree, the church (vv. 23-24). This regrafting is done branch by branch, as individual Jews come to

[164]See Moo (703) for summary and sources. Also see Cranfield (2:565-566) and Stott (299-300) for details.

[165]Advocates of the last view include Lenski (703-704) and SH (328).

believe in their Messiah. It has absolutely nothing to do with a supposed "future restoration" of the Jewish nation (contra Godet, 404), or a time when "the natural descendants of Abraham will . . . once again be the Lord's chosen people of blessing" (contra MacArthur, 2:118). It is a possibility that is open to all Jews, any time, anywhere. The stated requirement is simply that they "not persist in unbelief" (v. 23). If they do not, then they will become branches on the tree, i.e., members of the church of Jesus Christ. This is the one hope of Gentiles and Jews alike; this is how "all Israel will be saved" (v. 26).

We should note Paul's emphasis on faith or the lack of it as the key to whether one is part of the olive tree or not. This is consistent with the main theme of Romans, that sinners are saved by grace through faith, and not by works of law (3:28), and consistent with his emphasis on faith in the previous main section (9:30–10:21).

1. Words of Warning to Gentile Christians (11:17-22)

The first part of this paragraph is a specific warning to Gentile Christians not to think of themselves as somehow superior to the Jewish branches that were broken off the tree. This may reflect some tension within the Roman church between Gentile Christians and Jewish Christians, and it may reflect a general cultural anti-Semitism carried over into the church by converted Gentiles. But these are matters of speculation and need not concern us, since the arrogant attitude of which Paul speaks could have been readily aroused just by unsound reflection upon Israel's history and the early decades of church history.

11:17-18a If some of the branches have been broken off, and you, though a wild olive shoot, have been grafted in among the others and now share in the nourishing sap from the olive root, do not boast over those branches. This is an "if-then" sentence in which the if-clause (the protasis, v. 17) is assumed to be true, with the then-clause (the apodosis, v. 18a) naturally following.

Paul keeps the root-branches metaphor introduced in v. 16 and begins to apply it to the way individual Jews and Gentiles are saved. He refers first to the Jews, who are compared with branches on a tree, some of which have been "broken off." This refers to the Jews who refused to accept Christ as their Messiah, and to God's punitive act of hardening and rejecting them (vv. 7, 15). That Paul says only "some" branches were broken off is a deliberate understatement reminiscent of 3:3. Actually the majority of Jews were in this category.

Next Paul refers to the Gentile Christians, whom he is addressing (v. 13). He uses the singular "you" to put his admonitions on a more personal level. This "you" is the typical Gentile Christian representing the whole group (Dunn, 2:673). Paul addressed the Jews in a similar way in 2:1ff.

The Gentile Christian is here described as "a wild olive shoot" (a branch cut from a wild or uncultivated olive tree) that has been grafted into the cultivated olive tree "among the others." The branches of this cultivated tree represent the NT church, and "the others" are the Jews who were the first converts to Christ and thus the first branches on the tree. That the wild branches were grafted in "among" them (beginning in Acts 10) means that they were placed alongside the Jewish Christians who had already been there from Acts 2 and following.

The last part of the protasis also speaks of Gentile Christians. It describes the result of their being grafted into the olive tree alongside the believing Jews. When this happened, says Paul, the Gentile Christians immediately became "fellow partakers" or "sharers together" (i.e., along with the Jewish Christians) of "the nourishing sap from the olive root." As seen in the introduction above, this root is OT Israel as it fulfilled its covenant purpose of bringing the Messiah into the world. In this sense OT Israel is the indispensable source of all the spiritual benefits that are absorbed by the branches, i.e., by each individual member of the church.

The Greek text for "the nourishing sap" is somewhat uncertain (see Moo, 696-697, n. 1). The best reading literally says "of the root of the fatness." This can be translated "in the root, that is to say, in the fatness (of the root)" (Cranfield, 2:567). The NIV follows this option, using "nourishing sap" to translate the word for "fatness" or "richness." The phrase can also be rendered "the rich root" (Moo, 702, n. 28; see the NASB). Either way the main point is that when a Gentile becomes a Christian, he immediately begins to draw upon all the spiritual blessings made possible by two millennia of Jewish history – blessings which are a natural inheritance for Jews who accept their Messiah. The Gentile Christian becomes a partaker in "the blessing of Abraham" (Gal 3:14, NASB); whether he realizes it or not, his "salvation is from the Jews" (John 4:22). See v. 18b.

In v. 18a Paul draws his conclusion from v. 17: "Do not boast over those branches." This is in the form of an exhortation, but its logical force is "you have no reason" to boast over them. Paul still addresses Gentile Christians (in the person of their typical representative); "those branches" are the Jews. Do these Jewish branches include both Jewish Christians ("the others") and the broken-off branches,[166] or do they include only the branches that were broken off? I agree with Murray (2:86) that the latter is probably the case, in view of v. 19.

Thus in this exhortation Paul warns Gentile Christians not to brag or boast over against the Jews who were broken off the tree, as if becoming a Christian were the result of some kind of competition between the two groups, with the Gentiles being the winners. You have no reason to boast, he says, as if being grafted into the tree were a sign of your superiority over those rejected Jews.

11:18b If you do, consider this: You do not support the root, but the root supports you. This is not an implicit permission to go ahead and boast. Rather, Paul is saying, "If you are still inclined to boast, or if you still have a boastful spirit, please remember this . . . ."

What Paul asks them to remember is very close in meaning to v. 17c, but here he is more forceful: "*You* [emphatic] do not support the root, *but* [emphatic] the root supports you." It is important to see that the root is not just the patriarchs, as many believe,[167] and especially not just "the covenant of salvation that God made with Abraham,"[168] but the entire scope of the Jews' covenant service

[166]So SH, 328; Cranfield, 2:568. If this is the case, Cranfield says it is likely that Paul is addressing "an anti-Semitic feeling within the Roman church reflecting the dislike of, and contempt for, the Jews which were common in the contemporary Roman world." We cannot be sure of this, though (Dunn, 2:662), and Moo doubts that anti-Semitism is the problem (703-704).

[167]Moo says the root is "the patriarchs as recipients and transmitters of the promises of God" (704).

[168]Contra MacArthur, 2:115. This is a serious yet common misunderstanding of the covenant.

from Abraham to Christ. Paul is thus asking the Gentile Christians, "What, historically, do the Jews owe to you? Which of their glorious blessings (9:4-5) came through you? Obviously, none; so your boasting is vain. The relationship of dependence is actually the other way around." In Denney's words, "You owe all you are proud of to an (artificially formed) relation to the race you would despise" (680). "Any merit, any virtue, any hope of salvation that the Gentiles may have arises entirely from the fact that they are grafted in a stock" that is fully Jewish (SH, 329). How can they ignore their Jewish heritage? "It is that very heritage upon which the Gentile Christians themselves depend for their own spiritual standing" (Moo, 704).

Moo notes that Paul uses present tense: this OT root "continues to be the source of spiritual nourishment that believers require" (704). "A church which is not drawing upon the sustenance of its Jewish heritage . . . would be a contradiction in terms for Paul" (Dunn, 2:662).

11:19 Wanting to drive this point home further, Paul puts a question in the mouth of the proud Gentile Christian: **You will say then, "Branches were broken off so that I could be grafted in."** The way Paul words the question highlights the egotism that he wants to turn aside: "Branches were broken off so that *I, even I,* could be grafted in!" The implication is that this person thinks God excluded some Jews from the church just to make a place for Gentile believers. "That surely involves some superiority in me," is the implied conclusion (Denney, 680). "I am surely better than those unbelieving Jews!" (Bruce, 218).

11:20a Granted. But they were broken off because of unbelief, and you stand by faith. Paul's opening word, "Granted" (καλῶς, *kalōs*), can be taken as "qualified agreement" (Moo, 705); it is "a form of partial and often ironical assent" (MP, 467). In other words, "There is some truth in what you are saying." Here Paul is probably referring to the point made in vv. 11-16, that "because of their transgression, salvation has come to the Gentiles" (v. 11), and "their rejection is the reconciliation of the world" (v. 15).

Paul's next statement can be paraphrased thus: "But this is not the whole story, and it is not even the most important part of the story. It's true that many Jews were broken off, and it's true that you, a Gentile, were grafted in.[169] But this is not a neat, self-contained cause-and-effect sequence, as if there were some sort of intrinsic connection between these two events. No, the important fact is this: the Jews were broken off *because of their unbelief*! They refused to believe in Jesus! Those who believed in him were not broken off; would that this had been true for all of them! And you: why have you been grafted into the tree? Not because the Jews were broken off, but only because you have put your faith in Jesus. Even if every Jew had believed, you would still have been grafted into the tree by virtue of your faith."

The implied conclusion, again, is that the circumstances of the Jews' rejection and the Gentiles' acceptance gave the latter absolutely no room for boasting against the former. This warning is reinforced by the reminder that the Gentiles stand, i.e., are saved, only by faith – a way of salvation that insistently excludes any reason for boasting (3:27; Eph 2:8-9).

11:20b-21 Do not be arrogant, but be afraid. For if God did not spare the natural branches, he will not spare you either. Here Paul tells the Gentile Christians the proper attitude to develop in place of arrogance: the fear of God. "Do not be arrogant" is literally "do not have high-minded thoughts" (see 12:16; 1 Tim 6:17), i.e., do not think so highly of yourselves. Instead, you should "fear" (NASB), or "be afraid" (NIV).

Either of these translations may be a proper rendering of the Greek φοβέω (*phobeō*), but they do not necessarily have the same connotation. The fear of God takes two different forms.[170] One is the healthy, reverential awe of the creature before his Creator. The other is the terror and dread of the sinner in the presence of the holy Lawgiver and Judge.

To which of these kinds of fear is Paul referring? Certainly to the first, which is always a main element of holy living. Also, there is no better antidote to arrogance, nothing more conducive to humility, than to come to a full realization of our creatureliness

---

[169]Here Paul actually says, "You are standing," or "You have been made to stand" (see 5:2). This term may be intended as a contrast to the references to *falling* in vv. 11,22.

[170]See GC, ch. 9, "The Fear of God."

before God Almighty. But what about the second, being afraid of the Judgment?[171] Certainly when it is truly felt, this kind of fear likewise cancels out arrogance as fire consumes tissue paper. As a rule, such fear is inappropriate for Christians, since we are free from condemnation thanks to justification by faith in the blood of Christ. But there is one context in which the fear of terror is still necessary even for Christians, namely, when we stand on the brink of apostasy or falling away. In such a situation, how can we not call to mind that "it is a dreadful thing to fall into the hands of the living God" (Heb 10:31)? In view of Paul's warning to the Gentile Christians in v. 21, I think he probably also has this kind of fear in mind in v. 20b, i.e., terror at the prospect of being cut off.

We should make no mistake: in v. 21 Paul holds before us all the real possibility of falling from grace and losing our salvation. This is another reason why Gentile Christians, and Jewish Christians as well, should realize the folly of arrogance regarding their salvation status. Here Paul uses an argument from the greater to the lesser. The "natural branches" are the Jews, who in view of their natal association with the root are inherently suitable for being attached as branches to the tree. But even so, when some refused to believe in Jesus, God did not spare them. I.e., he rejected them and broke them off the tree. This was true even if they were in a saved state before being confronted with the gospel. If they refused to convert their faith in Yahweh to a Trinitarian faith, they were broken off, and given no place in the transformed olive tree. And if God did not spare even these, he will certainly not spare the wild olive branches – Gentile Christians – that have no natural connection with the tree, if they return to their unbelief.[172]

11:22 Consider therefore the kindness and sternness of God: . . . This refers to what are rightly called "the two sides of the Divine character" (SH, 329). "Kindness" (χρηστότης, *chrēstotēs*; see 2:4) is an attitude of goodwill and generosity toward others, a goodness of heart or "kindly disposition" (SH, 55) that desires the happiness of

---

[171]The NIV translation, "Be afraid," emphasizes this kind of fear.

[172]Verse 21b does not say, "He *might not* spare you either"; nor does it say, "*Perhaps* he will not spare you." Such translations are based on questionable textual variations (see Moo, 697, n. 2). Paul's statement is a simple future tense: "Neither will he spare you."

others and especially their salvation. "Sternness" (ἀποτομία, *apotomia*; "severity," NASB) is an attitude of relentless and vigorous commitment to justice, including retributive justice; a strict upholding of the requirements of the law; an "inflexible hardness and severity" in judging (see Köster, "τέμνω," 107-108). Obviously, then, "the kindness and sternness of God" are "a fascinating contrast of attitudes, held simultaneously," as Morris says (416).

These two attributes are generally equivalent to God's love and God's holiness, which I believe are the two most basic and equally-ultimate moral attributes of God. God's love is his basic goodwill toward other moral beings. Other attributes within the sphere of his love are mercy, patience, grace, and kindness. God's holiness, on the other hand, is his perfect moral character, which is the basis of his work as Lawgiver and Judge. It embraces other attributes such as wrath and vengeance. See GRe, 238-239, 255-257.

Because these two sides of God's nature are equally ultimate, it is a serious misconception to think that they are just two different ways of expressing the same divine attribute. An example of this error is Cranfield's assertion that both kindness and sternness "are the expression of God's holy and faithful love" (2:569-570). There is probably no more widespread false doctrine in Christendom than this, and few with more serious consequences. See GRe, 303-314.

At the same time I will agree with Dunn's contention that these two aspects of God's nature are not of "equal weight," since in Scripture the "stronger emphasis is on grace and mercy" (2:665). This makes his holiness and wrath no less real, no less distinct, and no less ultimate, however. See GRe, 372-375.

Why does Paul admonish the representative Gentile Christian (and us) to "consider" or "observe" the kindness and sternness of God? Because these are the two basic attributes that God expresses toward sinners, depending on their response to the grace of his Son, Jesus Christ. In this context they are the attributes that lie behind the breaking off of the unbelieving Jewish branches and the grafting in of the believing Gentile branches: **sternness to those who fell,** i.e., the Jews who rejected Christ (v. 11),[173] **but kindness to you** as a Gentile who has accepted Christ.

[173]We should note that God's sternness did not cause their fall but was his response to it.

In v. 20 Paul stressed that the reason the Gentile Christians were grafted into the tree was their faith in the Messiah, not some merit on their part. Here he shows that God's willingness to accept someone on the simple basis of faith in Christ is a matter of his gracious kindness. There is no merit in faith itself.

Paul says all these things to set up his final warning to Gentile Christians, which also applies to all branches on the olive tree (all members of his church) in all times and places. I.e., the very fact that you are on the tree (and by implication saved) means that you have received the kindness of God. But be warned: you will remain on the tree as a recipient of God's kindness **provided that you continue in his kindness. Otherwise, you also will be cut off.**

"Provided that you continue" is ἐάν (*ean*) with the subjunctive, a form that expresses a contingency that may or may not be the case in the future. (For the same form see 13:4; 14:8.) God will continue to bestow his kindness upon you, *if and only if* you "continue in his kindness." To "continue in" God's kindness means to continue to *trust* his kindness and grace as embodied in the saving work of Jesus. What will happen if you *do not* continue to trust God's grace? Paul's answer is very clear: "you also," like the Jews who refused to believe, "will be cut off." You will lose your salvation.

This verse brings into sharp focus the issue of whether or not salvation is conditional, which includes the issue of "once saved, always saved." In general Calvinists believe that God's grace is sovereignly bestowed and maintained in an unconditional way, and non-Calvinists believe that it is conditional. But even some non-Calvinists hold that once a person believes by his own free choice, he will unconditionally continue to believe from that point on. This is the essence of the "once saved, always saved" doctrine.

In my judgment this verse unequivocally supports the view that salvation is conditional. Just as *becoming* saved is conditioned upon faith, *staying* saved is conditioned upon continuing to believe. You will remain as a branch on the olive tree "if you continue" (NASB) in God's kindness. (See Col 1:23 for the very same point.) More specifically this verse shows that falling from a saved state and thus losing one's salvation is possible. Dunn rightly says, "The possibility of believers 'falling away' . . . , apostatizing, is one which Paul certainly did not exclude." He adds, "Perseverance is a Christian responsibility rather than an unconditional promise" (2:664-665).

How do Calvinists handle this text? One may be surprised to see the strong Calvinist William Hendriksen conclude from this verse that God's kindness is "not unconditional. It requires genuine faith on man's part" (2:375). At the same time this verse does not imply "that those who truly belong to him will ever be rejected," as Stott explains (301).

But how could anyone believe that salvation is truly conditional, and at the same time deny the possibility of falling away? The answer, for the Calvinist, is as follows. First, God does require sinners to have faith in Jesus as a condition for being saved. Therefore, technically, salvation is conditional. But at the same time God sovereignly determines who will have faith and who will not. To those whom God has unconditionally chosen for eternal life, he unconditionally gives the gift of faith. Once the faith has been given, of course, it is the person who believes, and not God. Thus the person is fulfilling the condition for salvation. Hendriksen (2:375) says of 11:22 that it

> must not be understood in the sense that God will supply the kindness, man the faith. Salvation is ever God's gift. It is never a 50-50 affair. From start to finish it is the work of God. But this does not remove human responsibility. God does not exercise faith for man or in his place. It is and remains man who reposes his trust in God, but it is God who both imparts this faith to him and enables him to use it.

This, says Hendriksen, is the "sound, biblical sense . . . in which we can speak about salvation as being *conditional.*"

I sincerely believe that this and other such explanations are nothing but theological double-talk. To say that this is a "sound, biblical sense" in which salvation is conditional, and that such a system "does not remove human responsibility," is a sham. It is not enough just to say that God sets conditions for salvation. The Calvinist may begin with this premise, but then he declares that God unconditionally decides *who* will meet the conditions, and then unilaterally *causes* them to meet these conditions. In such a scenario there are no conditionality and human responsibility in any normal sense of these terms.

If persevering faith is a sovereign gift of God, what is the purpose of warnings in the Bible, such as the one in 11:22? Moule (197) grants that such passages imply "*contingency* in man's continuance in the mercy of God," but they are nevertheless in harmony with "sovereign and prevailing Divine grace." This is true because God both gives and preserves faith in the elect. The chosen will without fail persevere in faith, because God will infallibly enable them to do so. As Moule says, "Grace imparts *perseverance* by imparting and maintaining faith." And how does grace maintain faith? Among other things, "faith is properly animated and energized" through these warnings themselves.

In my opinion all such attempts to harmonize the "if" in 11:22 (or elsewhere) with Calvinism, or with any "once saved, always saved" belief, amount to more double-talk and reduce Paul's warning to a travesty. Unless there is a genuine possibility that this warning may be disregarded by a genuine believer, then it is not a warning at all, and its very presence in the Bible is deceptive.

Moo's attempt (707, n. 57) to reconcile 11:22 with a denial of the possibility of falling away is a little different but just as untenable. His view is that not every branch on the tree is a true believer in the first place. This must be true, he says, because the unbelieving Jews who were cut off the tree in reality were never part of the tree at all. It is only for the sake of his metaphor that "Paul presents them as if they had been. In the same way, then, those Gentiles within the church . . . who appear to be part of God's people, yet do not continue in faith, may never have been part of that tree at all."

This explanation fails for three reasons. One, it is an unwarranted assumption that *all* the Jews who were originally cut off from the tree were never truly saved to begin with. As I have already stated, it is quite likely that many Jews who had a faith adequate to save them in light of the limitations of the OT revelation refused to elevate their faith to the NT level when first confronted with the gospel. (Paul himself may have been in this category.) These would be among the branches that were broken off.

Second, Moo's explanation does not take account of the difference between the OT prototree and the olive tree as it has existed under the New Covenant dispensation. All Jews were branches on the former, but this had no soteric implications. The latter is occupied solely by those who are saved, Jews and Gentiles. Is this not the point of the breaking off of the unbelieving Jewish branches in the first place?

Third, the speculation that the Gentiles who do not continue in the faith may never have been part of the tree at all goes against everything Paul says in this paragraph. "You stand by faith," he says to the Gentile representative in v. 20. If the addressee is not saved – not truly part of the tree, then everything about this statement is false. God's kindness has been given to you, Paul says in v. 22, in contrast with the fallen Jews who received God's sternness. There is no way to reconcile this affirmation with a mere appearance of salvation.

The focus in vv. 23-24 will shift to the fallen Jews, but at this point we may note that the conditional promise about Jewish unbelievers in v. 23a is parallel in every way to the conditional warning about Gentile believers in v. 22b. If we cannot take the warning seriously, why should we take the promise seriously? If we say that v. 22 does not imply that an *actual* falling away can take place, must we not assume that v. 23 does not mean that any fallen Jews will *actually* be saved? But no one would ever consider the latter. Here is a statement by Stott (301): "After this warning to Gentile believers against pride and presumption, Paul is ready with his promise to Jewish unbelievers. His argument is that if those grafted in could be cut off, then those cut off could be grafted in again." Just so! But the "once saved, always saved" doctrine completely destroys the symmetry between the two conditions and leaves the latter open to doubt. Indeed, Stott himself says of the warning in v. 22, "Not that those who truly belong to him will ever be rejected . . ."! However, I have yet to see him or anyone else say of v. 23, "Not that those Jews who truly rejected him will ever be accepted . . . ."

2. Words of Hope for Hardened Jews (11:23-24)

In these last two verses about the olive tree, Paul returns to the main theme of the chapter, that God has not completely rejected the Jews. It is true that only a remnant accepted the Messiah in the beginning, and that the rest were hardened, rejected, and broken off the tree. But since v. 11 Paul has held forth the possibility and the hope that individuals in this latter group may still return to God. Here he reaffirms that hope as he shows how the rejected Jews may be saved.

11:23 And if they do not persist in unbelief, they will be grafted in, . . . The parallelism between v. 22b and v. 23a is obvious when we slightly reword 22b while keeping the same thought:

> If you [believing Gentiles] do not continue in God's kindness, you will be cut off the tree.
>
> If you [unbelieving Jews] do not continue in unbelief, you will be grafted back into the tree.

The subject here is obviously "those who fell" (v. 22), the Jewish unbelievers. Literally Paul says, "And those also," or, "Yes, and they too" (SH, 330). The verb translated "persist" is the same one translated "continue" in v. 22; and the conditional form is the same, *ean* with the subjunctive. The then-clause is just the simple future tense of ἐγκεντρίζω (*enkentrizō*, used in vv. 17,19), "they will be grafted in." To be grafted into the tree is the equivalent of "life from the dead" in v. 15.

This is a clear indication that God has not abandoned the Jewish people but is ready and willing to receive them back to himself at any time. "The door of opportunity for the entrance of Jews – even for initially hardened Jews – is standing open" (Hendriksen, 2:375).

It is also clear in this verse that the Jews' return to and acceptance by God is *conditional.* It is conditioned upon their change of heart concerning Jesus. They will be grafted into the tree *if* they do not continue in unbelief, but turn to Jesus in full faith and surrender. The promise that they will be grafted in is a promise that they will be saved.[174]

---

[174]This verse shows that being on the olive tree is equivalent to being saved. In view of everything Paul has said thus far in Romans about justification by faith, it is surely the case that unbelief implies lostness. But these Jewish branches were broken off the tree because of unbelief (v. 20); and if they do not continue in unbelief but come to faith instead, they will be grafted back into the tree. Thus there are no unbelievers on the tree, and all believers are on it. Thus only saved Jews (and Gentiles) are on the tree.

In spite of the clear and obvious conditional nature of this promise, some interpreters completely ignore the stated condition and take Paul's statement as an absolute promise that the Jews – all of them – will one day be saved. One writer says that Paul is here speaking of Israel's "glad future" when the whole nation ("all Israel") "shall be grafted in" and restored to "all their original privileges and rights." Even if vv. 23-24 reveal it only as a possibility, it is "established fully as a decreed event in the next section" (MP, 468). Another says of v. 23, "In the end, Israel will accept God's act for her in Christ and will return to her natural place within God's chosen people" (Achtemeier, 184). Commenting on vv. 23-24, MacArthur says, "The destiny of Israel can and will be reversed. Her return to the Lord not only is possible but certain" (2:122). Even though this promise is given here with a condition, "God had long beforehand assured His people that the condition would be met" (2:118).

What is happening here? Just as in reference to v. 22b, we are witnessing an inability – or an unwillingness – to take seriously the significance of Paul's "if." In v. 22, in the interest of preserving the "once saved, always saved" doctrine, some declare that the if-clause is something that *will not* happen, period. Here in v. 23, in the interest of supporting a particular view of the end-times, some declare that the if-clause is something that *will* happen, period. Paul might just as well have omitted the "if" in both cases.

We must take Paul at his word. He does not say "when"; he says "if." Hendriksen rightly reminds us that "the apostle does not say or imply that one day all unbelieving Jews are going to be grafted back into their own olive tree" (2:376). Or as Murray puts it, "No assurance is given in this verse that Israel will desist from unbelief" (2:89). Contrary to Fitzmyer, who says "Paul expects unbelieving Israel to be grafted once again" into the tree (616), McGuiggan rightly says that the tone of the verse suggests that he was *not* predicting "a national scale conversion of the Jews" (331).

We cannot say, of course, that this will never happen. But whether few or many Jews do come to faith in Christ, this verse shows *how* they will be saved and restored to God, namely, by being grafted into the olive tree, which is the church. There is absolutely nothing here about a restoration of the nation of Israel to its role as a separate and special people of God. The only thing Paul promises the Jews here, conditioned upon faith in Christ, is that they will be grafted into the olive tree. But this is not the same tree from which they were broken off in the first place. This is a transformed tree, only the root of which is OT national Israel. The branches are the new Israel, the church, and they consist of both believing Jews and believing Gentiles. To be joined to the tree is to be united with the Gentiles, not set apart from them again. To expect a national restoration to an OT-like special role is to go against the very essence of the olive-tree metaphor.

We must not allow such false hopes to blind us to the very real possibility Paul sets forth here. The Jews *can* become a part of the tree, **for God is able to graft them in again.** The promise does not depend on what was possible with regard to literal grafting practices; it depends on the supernatural power of God: "God is able." Denney says, "Even in the most hardened rejector of the Gospel we are not to limit either the resources of God's power or the possibilities of change in a self-conscious, self-determining creature" (681).

We should note that God's grafting the Jews into the tree is not the same as causing them to believe. The first part of this verse makes it clear that there is a difference between the believing and the grafting-in. God can and will graft them in, i.e., will add them to his church, but they must first meet the stated condition of not persisting in unbelief.

11:24 After all, if you were cut out of an olive tree that is wild by nature, and contrary to nature were grafted into a cultivated olive tree, how much more readily will these, the natural branches, be grafted into their own olive tree! This verse does not add anything new; it simply reinforces the last statement in v. 23, that *God is able* to graft the fallen Jewish branches back into the tree. It is an argument from the greater to the lesser. Paul says it is a lot easier to graft a broken-off branch back into its own olive tree than to graft wild and alien branches into that tree. Since God has already done the latter (in saving the Gentiles), we can be sure that the former (saving the Jews) will be no problem for him.

Using the singular, Paul still addresses the typical representative of all Gentile Christians. The first part of the verse sums up the Gentiles' situation in terms of the olive tree. The phrase "by nature" probably does not modify the wild olive tree itself (contra the NIV), but rather the branch that was cut out of it (see Cranfield, 2:571; Moo, 708, n. 63). I.e., it should read, "If you, who by nature belong to a wild olive tree, were cut off from that tree and contrary to nature were grafted into a cultivated olive tree . . . ."

This means that the Gentiles by nature belonged to the pagan world. This is where they were born and reared; this is where they learned and lived by the antibiblical worldview. This is where they were "at home," i.e., on the wild olive tree. But when they came to Christ they were cut off from this tree and grafted into the "cultivated olive tree," which is described as "cultivated" because of its Jewish root. The cultivation process includes all of God's dealings with the Jews from Abraham up to the first coming of Christ. Because of this background the earliest Jewish Christians – the first branches of the transformed olive tree – in a sense grew naturally out of this root. But when Gentiles were pried loose from their paganism and united with this OT root (Lenski, 712), this was definitely "contrary to nature," i.e., against everything they had thus far stood for.

On the other hand, v. 24b says that when unbelieving Jews ("these") are converted, this is like grafting broken-off branches back "into their own olive tree." Because of its Jewish root, even unbelieving, broken-off Jews have a natural affinity with the olive tree. Indeed, it is called "their own tree" for this very reason. OT ethnic Israel is not the tree as such, but it is the *root* of the tree. Thus when a Jew is converted to Christ he is being attached to his true roots; he is taking his natural place among the branches (the church) that were the divinely intended goal of the Israelite nation all along. What could be more natural than this?

Verse 24b is sometimes taken as an unqualified promise that the natural branches will be grafted in again, i.e., that they *will* be saved. E.g., Denney (682) says the future tense ("will be grafted in") refers to the "actual restoration of the Jews." In view of the "if-then" form of the verse, however, it is more reasonable to take this as a logical future. I.e., Paul is simply stating a greater-to-lesser argument: if A is true, then it is even more likely that B will also be true. Also, the condition in v. 23 must be carried over into v. 24; "will be grafted in" must be qualified with "if they do not persist in unbelief."

The main point is to show that from God's side, there is absolutely no obstacle to the Jews' salvation. Their hardening (v. 7) and their rejection (v. 15) need not be the final word concerning their eternal destiny. God is ready and willing to receive them back, if they will believe in their Redeemer. He has already added repentant, believing Gentiles to the church; and if he has done this, *how much more likely is it* that believing Jews will also be added? The key expression is πόσῳ μᾶλλον (*posō mallon,* "by how much more"), the same phrase used in v. 12 in a similar kind of argument. The purpose of the present argument is to give us confidence in God's power to save even fallen Jews.

Two implications from this olive tree metaphor must be emphasized. First, there is in this New Covenant age only one olive tree, only one chosen people, only one way of salvation. Any Jews who are saved will be saved by being grafted into this one tree. The Jewish branches and the Gentile branches are joined together into one aggregate of saved persons (the church), where the Jew-Gentile distinction is irrelevant. As Moo says, "Basic to the whole metaphor is the unity of God's people." There is only one olive tree, "whose branches include both Jews and Gentiles" (709). Hendriksen says (2:376), "For Jew and Gentile salvation is the same. . . . Remember: *ONE OLIVE TREE.*"

A second implication is that, contrary to a common misconception, *it is possible* for someone who has fallen from grace to be restored to full fellowship with God. Heb 6:4-6 is often misinterpreted as teaching the opposite, that it is impossible for a once-saved but now-fallen person to be brought back to a saved state. Some translations perpetuate this error by the way they translate Heb 6:6 (e.g., the word "because" in the NIV, and "since" in the NASB).

The olive-tree metaphor, however, shows that this interpretation of Heb 6 is false. This is true because we must assume that *some* of the Jews who were broken off the tree (v. 17) were believers in Yahweh as they knew him from the OT revelation and were thus in a saved state *until* they heard the gospel of Jesus and initially refused to accept it. E.g., Acts 2:41 says about 3,000 persons were baptized and added to the church on the day of Pentecost, when the church began. Unless this number includes the entire Pentecost audience, or unless it constitutes one hundred per cent of the pre-

Christian Jewish believers who were present, then we must assume that some believing Jews who were present at Pentecost "fell away" by not accepting Christ on that day. Since both of these possibilities are highly unlikely, we can assume that some of the "natural branches" being grafted back into the tree are fallen-away believers who are being restored to salvation. This means the alternative translation of Heb 6:6 given in the NIV and NASB margins ("while," i.e., "as long as") is the correct one.

In other words, Paul's teaching about the olive tree refutes both the "once saved, always saved" error, *and* the "once fallen, always fallen" error. Both are equally unbiblical.

E. GOD'S PLAN FOR ISRAEL'S SALVATION (11:25-32)

In this paragraph all eyes are usually focused on v. 26a, "And so all Israel will be saved." This is "the center of this paragraph," says Moo (712); the NIV makes this statement the heading for the entire section. What it means, though, is notoriously difficult, and is the subject of endless discussion. Every part of it is controversial. How extensive is the word "all"? Does "Israel" refer to ethnic or spiritual Israel? To what status is Israel "saved"?

One of the more common conclusions based on this text is that at some time in the future, at or near the end of this age, most living Jews will turn to Christ and be restored as a nation to a place of preeminence in God's kingdom. As Moule says, in this text Paul "now, in plain terms, reveals and predicts a great future Restoration" (197).

I cannot accept this interpretation, for reasons that will be made clear in the following exposition. At this point I will simply say that in v. 26a, emphasis is usually placed on the wrong word, namely, "all," with the verse being read thus: "And so *all* Israel will be saved." In my judgment the emphasis should be on the word "so," taken in the sense of "thus, in this manner." Thus we should read it: "And *in this way* all Israel will be saved." I.e., regarding Israel's salvation Paul's point is "How?" and not "How many?"

This does not mean that there is a question whether Israel's salvation will be by some means other than faith in Jesus. That issue has already been settled, especially in ch. 10. Rather, the question has to do with the interrelationship between Israel and the Gentiles, continuing the discussion begun in v. 11. Paul has already emphasized that Israel's sin and rejection have been used by God as a means to save the Gentiles; here he is emphasizing that the salvation of the Gentiles is God's means of bringing salvation to Israel.

This becomes clear when we view this paragraph in the perspective of ch. 11 as a whole. The discussion is still controlled by the question in 11:1, "Did God reject his people?" The answer is an emphatic No, for two reasons. First, there existed in the past, and there continues to exist "at the present time . . . a remnant chosen by grace" (11:5). What about "the others"? They were hardened (7b-10). Second, even those who are presently and hereafter hardened may still turn to Christ and be saved, because God has worked out a complex plan for showing mercy upon both Jews and Gentiles. This plan is spelled out in 11:11-32.

In the first step of his plan God uses the sin and hardening of Israel as a means of bringing the riches of salvation to the Gentiles. Paul emphasizes this in 11:11-16, while at the same time revealing that the salvation of the Gentiles will in turn be used to bring salvation to the Jews. The olive tree metaphor is an interlude meant to preclude Gentile Christian arrogance, especially by showing that the underlying reasons for being lost or saved are unbelief and belief respectively, for both Gentiles and Jews (11:17-24).

This leads to the present paragraph, where the main emphasis is on the climactic second step of God's plan, namely, that God will use the salvation of the Gentiles as a means of bringing salvation to the Jews. This is the way in which "all Israel will be saved." In v. 26a the word *all* is meant to be contrasted with the *remnant* saved "at the present time" (v. 5). I.e., in v. 5 Paul affirms that a saved remnant existed at the time of his writing. But what about "the others" – the mass of unsaved Jews, both present and future? They can be saved, too; and the burden of vv. 11-32 (vv. 25-32 in particular) is to show how this is done. I.e., *all* Israel, not just the presently-existing remnant, will be saved. But *how* will they be saved? In this way: by the *fullness of the Gentiles* (v. 25), *if* they put their *faith in Jesus Christ.* (v. 23).

These two main aspects of God's complex plan for showing mercy upon all are summed up in vv. 30-31: because of the Jews' disobedience the Gentiles have received mercy (v. 30; see vv. 11-16); and likewise because the Gentiles have received mercy, Israel will also receive mercy (v. 31; see vv. 25-32)!

What, then, is the purpose of this paragraph? Some think it is to reveal the mystery of Israel's future. For example, Dunn's heading for this section is "The Final Mystery Revealed" (2:675). Fitzmyer's heading is "The Mystery of Israel: It Will All Be Saved" (618). This can hardly be the purpose, however, since there is nothing in this paragraph that has not been stated or implied earlier.

Moo suggests that the purpose of vv. 25-32 is to resolve the tension present throughout chs. 9–11, i.e., the tension between "Israel's current hostile relationship with God" and "God's expressed and irrevocable promises to Israel" (712-713). But this issue as such was resolved in ch. 9, where Paul indicates that God's election of and promises to ethnic Israel related to their service and not to their salvation.

It is best to view this paragraph as presenting no new data, but as simply summing up the main points of ch. 11 with the main emphasis being on the way God uses the salvation of the Gentiles to bring mercy upon Israel. This serves as a fitting climax to chs. 9–11 as a whole,[175] in that God is shown to be not just fair and faithful in his relationship with the Jews, but much more than fair in that he offers them his undeserved grace and mercy.

1. The Mystery of Israel's Salvation (11:25-27)

First of all Paul declares the mystery of Israel's salvation: its reality, its means, and its nature. He begins with a word not translated in the NIV: γάρ (*gar*, "for, because"). This word links vv. 25ff. with the olive tree illustration. Especially, the imagery of grafting the broken-off natural branches back into the tree helps us to understand how Israel will be saved.

11:25 I do not want you to be ignorant of this mystery, brothers, so that you may not be conceited: . . . "I do not want you to be

[175]"But 11:25-32 is not only the climax of 11:11-32; it is also the climax to all of Rom. 9–11" (Moo, 712). Cranfield says it gathers together the whole of 9:1–11:24 (2:573).

ignorant" is a formula Paul sometimes uses to call attention to an important point (see on 1:13; JC, 1:96-97). "Brothers" is part of the formula. It indicates he is addressing the entire church, but the context shows he has Gentiles mainly in mind (see 11:13). In 11:17 he began using second person singular, addressing a typical representative Gentile Christian; but here he switches to second person plural. In this paragraph "you" and "they" still refer to Gentiles and Jews respectively.

Specifically, Paul does not want the Gentile Christians to be ignorant of "this mystery." The word "mystery" does not mean something that is and forever will be mysterious and incomprehensible. In the biblical context it refers to a truth once hidden in the mind of God and undiscoverable by human reason, but now made known by divine revelation and fully open to human understanding. Thus Paul is claiming that what he is teaching here is a revelation from God. We need not assume that it was revealed to Paul himself, though it probably was, nor that it was revealed only to him (see Eph 3:3-5). Nor should we assume that this was something revealed to him only at the moment he was writing these words (see Gal 1:11-18).

The reason Paul wants Gentile Christians to understand the mystery is "so that you may not be conceited," or "lest you be wise in your own estimation," as the NASB literally translates it. In vv. 18-20 Paul has already warned Gentile Christians against arrogant boasting in view of the fact that they were being gathered into the church while only relatively few Jews were being saved. Here he warns them again not to be "puffed up with self-importance" (Cranfield, 2:575), i.e., not to assume that God had permanently abandoned Israel and was now focusing his attention exclusively on them (see Morris, 419).

Exactly what is the content of the mystery that will nullify the Gentiles' pride? In the NT the word μυστήριον (*mystērion*) is often used in a general way for revelation concerning Christ and his church.[176] A mystery that was of special importance to Paul, though,

[176]See, e.g., Rom 16:25; 1 Cor 2:7; 4:1; Eph 6:19; Col 1:27; 4:3. In the NT the word has no special eschatological connotation, as if it necessarily refers to an end-time event. Thus the word itself does not imply that Paul is referring to an eschatological event in 11:25. The only time Paul clearly uses it for an end-time event is 1 Cor 15:51.

was the revelation that God had always intended to include Jews and Gentiles together in the church of Jesus Christ (Eph 3:3, 4, 9; see 2:11-3:11). In Eph 3 the emphasis is on the fact that God is bringing the Gentiles into the church; here in 11:25 the emphasis is on the fact that unbelieving Jews may still be brought into the church.

More specifically, in 11:25 the mystery focuses on "interdependence between the salvation of the Gentiles and that of Jews" (Hendriksen, 2:378). I.e., not only are the Jews and Gentiles united together in the one church, but in accordance with God's plan each group in part owes its inclusion to the other. This is spelled out in the rest of this verse and the beginning of v. 26 in three clauses: (1) "Israel has experienced a hardening in part"; (2) "until the full number of the Gentiles has come in"; (3) "and so all Israel will be saved." This is the mystery, once hidden and now revealed. Moo rightly points out that the mystery is not just the *fact* that "all Israel will be saved," but rather the *way* Israel will be saved, as expressed in v. 25b (716-717; see also Murray, 2:92; Stott, 302). Actually, vv. 25b-26a are a kind of summary of what has already been taught in vv. 11-24; thus we should not assume that "this mystery" refers only to what follows. It includes the content of the preceding verses as well.

The first element of the mystery is that **Israel has experienced a hardening in part . . . .** Paul has already referred to this hardening in v. 7. As we saw there, it is God's response to Israel's initial rejection of Jesus as their Messiah. In essence it is "a judicial process by which he hands people over to their own stubbornness" (Stott, 302).

Paul says that Israel's hardening was only "in part" (ἀπὸ μέρους, *apo merous*). Most seem to understand this phrase in a numerical sense, i.e., only a part of Israel were hardened. The NRSV translates it, "A hardening has come upon part of Israel"; see Murray, 2:92; Cranfield, 2:575. If this is the meaning, it is certainly not a new thought, in view of the clear distinction made in v. 7 between the elect remnant and "the others."

In my judgment, though, this is not what Paul means. The sentence says literally that "hardness from a part has happened to Israel," not "hardness has happened to part of Israel." The word "part" is not the object of the verb, nor does the phrase "from a part" modify Israel. It is possible that it modifies "hardness" itself, but more likely it modifies the verb, as it does in its other four NT occurrences.[177] Either way it means that even though Israel was hardened, the hardening was only partial; the unbelieving Jews were not completely hardened so as to preclude the possibility of repentance.[178] The NIV ("a hardening in part") reflects this view, as does the NASB ("a partial hardening").

Is this a new point, not made known until v. 25? Not really. That the hardening is only partial is clearly implied in the earlier references to Israel's salvation (vv. 12,14-15,23-24). Thus it would seem that there is nothing new in this statement in v. 25 about Israel's hardening. This part of the "mystery" has already been set forth.

The heart of the mystery is in the next clause, i.e., that the hardening will last **until the full number of the Gentiles has come in.** Combined with the preceding clause, and read in the light of vv. 11-12,15,18, this implies that the hardening of Israel has something to do with the coming of the full number or fullness of the Gentiles. At the same time, taken with the following clause (26a), and read in the light of vv. 11,13-14, it implies that the fullness of the Gentiles has something to do with the salvation of "all Israel." As said earlier, the "mystery" thus is how salvation of Jews and Gentiles is interrelated. It is important for the Gentile Christians to see this, in order to avoid thinking too highly of themselves.

The key question is the meaning of the expression "the full number of the Gentiles." The word translated "full number" (πλήρωμα, *plērōma*) is the same word the NIV translates as "fullness" in v. 12, where it refers to the fullness of the Jews. It seems that most interpreters favor the numerical connotation of the word, both here and in v. 12. It is said that Paul is referring to the "full destined number" of the Gentiles (Moule, 199); "the full completed number, the complement of the Gentiles, i.e., the Gentile world as a whole" (SH, 335); "the full number, totality, of the Gentiles" (Denney, 683); "numerical completion" (Moo, 719); "the full number of the saved Gentiles" (Lenski, 727). For some this refers to the total number of Gentiles saved over the whole course of church history up to the

[177]Rom 15:15, 24; 2 Cor 1:14; 2:5. See the use of the similar phrase, ἐκ μέρους (*ek merous*), in 1 Cor 13:9,12.

[178]This rules out any concept of total depravity based on this word. MacArthur (2:127) is totally wrong when he says that the majority of Jews were "totally hardened."

very end (e.g., Hendriksen, 2:378-379; Hoekema, *Bible*, 144). For others it refers to an unprecedented mass conversion of Gentiles near or at the end, "a greatly increased influx of Gentiles into God's kingdom" (Murray, 2:95; see Dunn, 2:680).

As was the case in v. 12, I cannot accept a numerical connotation for *plērōma*. Hence (contra the NIV) I do not see this as referring to the "full number" of Gentiles, but rather to the fullness of salvation as it was proclaimed to and accepted by the Gentiles, beginning in Acts 10. (See on v. 12 above.) The NT nowhere else uses *plērōma* in a numerical sense, but does use it for the fullness of salvation.[179] See John 1:16; Rom 15:29; Eph 3:19. See also Col 2:10, which uses the verb form of the word: "you have been given fullness in Christ" (NIV). Thus the "fullness of the Gentiles" is the "spiritual wealth with which God will make the Gentiles full" (McGuiggan, 332, quoting Beet), "the abundant nature of the blessings in Christ's gospel" (ibid., 333). Thus Paul is not saying anything basically different from v. 11: "Because of [the Jews'] transgression, salvation has come to the Gentiles"; or from v. 12: "Their loss means riches for the Gentiles"; or from v. 15: "Their rejection is the reconciliation of the world."[180]

In what sense does this full salvation of the Gentiles "come in"? This is εἰσέρχομαι (*eiserchomai*), the common word for "go in, enter." In the NT it is occasionally used for people entering the kingdom (e.g., Matt 5:20; 7:21; John 3:5) or entering eternal life (Mark 9:43,45). Thus many take it in v. 25 as referring to the full number of Gentiles entering the kingdom or the church. But on some occasions the word means simply to come or to appear (see Luke 1:28; Acts 10:3; 19:30). I take it in a similar sense here, i.e., "until the salvation of the Gentiles has appeared or arrived or come into the picture." Compare 5:12, where Paul uses this word to declare that *sin* entered or came into the world. Here he uses it to affirm that *salvation* came into the Gentile world.

---

[179]Arguments to the contrary often appear to be circular: "Why does v. 12 refer to the full number of the Jews? Because v. 25 refers to the full number of the Gentiles. But why does v. 25 refer to the full number of the Gentiles? Because v. 12 refers to the full number of the Jews."

[180]I do not see any connection between this verse and Matt 24:14 or Luke 21:24.

The point is that the hardening of the Jews was the occasion for the commencement of the preaching of the gospel to the Gentiles. Thus the Gentile Christians should not gloat over the Jews' lost state; in one sense they owe their very salvation to it.

The other side of this coin is that the partial hardening of Israel has happened (and by implication will persist) *until* the fullness of the Gentiles has come in.[181] This places a limit on the hardening of Israel. Once the Gentiles' participation in the blessings of salvation has become fully established, the period of Israel's hardening will be over.[182]

Those who interpret "fullness" as referring to a final ingathering of Gentiles at or near the second coming must naturally see this hardening as still present and as continuing up to or near the end. However, if we see the "fullness" as referring to the initial ingathering of Gentiles into the church, then the time of Israel's hardening was relatively brief and perhaps was coming to an end in Paul's own day. This is why he can say in v. 31 that the Jews "may *now* receive mercy as a result of God's mercy to you [Gentiles]."

Paul implies that the Gentiles' experience of the fullness of salvation in some way leads to the cessation of Israel's hardness (see the references to arousing the Jews' envy in vv. 11, 13-14). The further implication is that Gentile Christians, rather than feeling conceited because they are saved and most Jews are not, should instead be actively preaching the gospel to the Jewish community.

We may note again that what Paul affirms here in v. 25 has already been either stated or implied in vv. 11-24; hence this verse is not revealing anything new but is summarizing the "mystery" already set forth.

11:26a The last element in the mystery is this: **And so all Israel will be saved, . . .** This is the conclusion drawn from the first two

[181]Murray shows that the conjunction cannot mean "while," but must mean "until" (2:92, n. 45).

[182]Some say the ingathering of Gentiles will continue up to the very time of the Second Coming, at which time the hardening of the Jews will cease; but this does not imply a subsequent mass conversion of the Jews, since there will *be* no more Jews, the world having ended (Hendriksen, 2:378-379; Lenski, 720-722). Paul's whole point in this context goes against this idea, though, since he affirms that even the hardened Jews *can* be saved (vv. 12,15,16,24; see Moo, 717-718).

parts of the mystery, and in fact from 11:1-25 as a whole. Has God rejected his people? It is true that most of them were hardened. But in God's plan this hardening is instrumental in bringing the fullness of salvation to the Gentiles. Once the Gentiles have experienced this fullness, the Jews will be moved to envy and will be ready to receive God's mercy. Thus the hardening will last only until the fullness of the Gentiles has come in. After this they may be grafted back into the olive tree, if they accept the mercy offered to them through the gospel. And in this way, all Israel will be saved. So how can anyone say that God has rejected his people?

As we discuss this verse, three questions must be kept in mind at the same time. First, what does "Israel" mean? Also, how extensive is the "all"? Finally, what kind of salvation is Paul talking about? The key issue, of course is this: does this verse predict and thus guarantee the salvation of a large mass of Jews at some point in the future, or does Paul have something else in mind?

Before we examine the phrase "all Israel," it is important to have a proper understanding of the first two words in the verse, "and so." The word "and" clearly ties this sentence to the last two clauses, but the word "so" (οὕτως, *houtōs*) does so in an even clearer and more crucial way. Some take this word as indicating a temporal sequence between v. 25b and v. 26a: Israel has experienced a partial hardening until the fullness of the Gentiles has come in, and "when this is done"[183] all Israel will be saved. Bruce refers to the "well attested use" if *houtōs* "in a temporal sense" (222). But such a use is hardly well attested. Indeed, Fitzmyer argues that a temporal meaning is not found elsewhere in Greek (622), and Moo agrees with him (719-720). It is best to reject this meaning for the word.

Rather, *houtōs* here should be given its common meaning of "in this manner, thus, so" (AG, 602). The point is not *when* all Israel will be saved, but *how*. Cranfield says the word is emphatic: "It will be in this way, and only in this way," that all Israel will be saved (2:576). And what is this way? Here the term points us not to what follows but to what precedes. I.e., Israel will be saved by the coming of salvation to the Gentiles (v. 26b), which will arouse jealousy in the Jews themselves (vv. 11,13-14). Thus, "under the influence of

[183]This is Barrett's translation of *houtōs* (223).

the jealousy so excited – under the impression produced on the Jews by the sight of the Gentiles in their fulness peopling the kingdom – all Israel shall be saved" (Denney, 683). So also Godet (411), Dunn (2:681), and Moo (720).

But exactly what is meant by "all Israel"? The following discussion will seek to answer this question in two steps. First, the three major views will be explained. Second, the main arguments for and against these views will be presented, and one of the three will be identified as the best approach.

Of the three major views, the one most commonly held is that "all Israel" refers to *ethnic Israel as a whole.* (We shall call this view A.) The basic idea is that at some point in the future, once the fullness of the Gentiles has come in, there will be a mass conversion of Jews. This does not mean that every individual Jew will be saved, but it does mean that most Jews living at that time will become Christians. It is pointed out that the OT occasionally uses "all Israel" in this sense, e.g., 1 Sam 25:1; 1 Kgs 12:1; 2 Chr 12:1; Dan 9:11. Thus *all* Israel, and not just the present remnant (v. 5), will be saved. This view enjoys a "strong consensus," says Dunn (2:681).

This view has two versions, eschatological and noneschatological. The former says the future conversion of all Israel will be associated with Christ's Second Coming. Cranfield says it is probable "that Paul was thinking of a restoration of the nation of Israel as a whole to God *at the end*, an eschatological event in the strict sense" (2:577). It is clear, says Moo, "that Paul places this event at the end of time"; it will be "a large-scale conversion of Jewish people at the end of this age" (723-724). It will be "the climax of salvation-history," says Dunn (2:692). For some this will involve the restoration of Israel as a national entity, along with its repossession of the original promised land. This is a common feature in the dispensational premillennial view of end-time events. "All Israel," says MacArthur, means "the entire nation that survives God's judgment during the Great Tribulation" and thus prepares the way for the millennium (2:128-129; see Pentecost, *Things*, 504-507).

The noneschatological version of this view says there will be a future mass conversion of Jews, but not necessarily associated with the end-times and not involving a nationalistic restoration. "All Israel" will be saved by becoming a part of the church, alongside

Gentile Christians. As Moule puts it, Paul is "predicting the conversion of some generation or generations of Jews, a conversion so real and so vastly extensive that unbelief shall be the small exception at the most, and that Jews as such shall everywhere be recognized as true Christians" (199). Murray strongly defends this view (2:96-100), as does Stott, who says Paul promises that "the great mass of the Jewish people" will one day experience "salvation from sin through faith in Christ," but does not promise "a return to the land" as a "political entity" (303-304). See also Lard (370-371) and SH (335-336).[184]

The second major view is that "all Israel" means *the remnant portion of ethnic Israel,* or all believing Jews in all generations. (We shall call this view B.) Here the term "Israel" is taken in a slightly different sense in v. 26 as compared with v. 25 and elsewhere. I.e., it may be true that the mass of Israel has been hardened (v. 25), but all of true spiritual Israel will be saved (v. 26). They will be saved not in a single mass conversion but in the normal process of evangelism, being brought to faith in Christ and added to his church over the whole course of church history.

Hendriksen, a Calvinist, defends this view, saying that "all Israel" means "*the total number of elect Jews.*" It means that on the Judgment Day "not a single elect Israelite will be lacking" (2:381). Hoekema likewise says that v. 26a describes "the bringing to salvation throughout history of the total number of the elect from among the Jews" (*Bible,* 140). These are "the true Israelites," he says (141). What Paul means, says Lenski, is that "all God's true Israel, all of it that really deserves the name, will be saved" (719). This includes all true Israel "from the patriarchs onward until time ends" (724). As McGuiggan puts it, "Believing Jews are the real Israel. They are the Israel within Israel," of whom Paul speaks in 9:6 (335). Thus "all Israel" means "*every* Jew who is *truly* an Israelite" (336).

The third main view of "all Israel" is that it refers to *the whole of spiritual Israel,* including both believing Jews and believing Gentiles. (We shall call this view C.) In other words, it is God's new Israel, the church, which is identified in Gal 3:29 as "Abraham's seed," in

---

[184]Some who take this view do not specify whether they are opting for its eschatological or noneschatological form. E.g., Denney, 683; Bruce, 222; Godet, 411; Morris, 421.

Gal 6:16 as "the Israel of God," and in Phil 3:3 as "the circumcision." This view was common among the early church fathers (see Fitzmyer, 623-624), and was espoused by Calvin, who says, "I extend the word *Israel* to all the people of God" as gathered from among both Jews and Gentiles (437). See also Wright, *Climax* (250); and Smith (2:43).

We turn now to the second step of our discussion of "all Israel," which is to set forth and evaluate various arguments for and against these views. We shall begin by examining the main arguments for A, that "all Israel" means ethnic Israel as a whole. The best argument for this view is that it is consistent with the way the term "Israel" is used elsewhere in Romans, and especially in this context. In 9:1–11:25 the words "Israel" and "Israelite" occur eleven or twelve times (allowing for textual variations), and "in each case the reference is clearly to Jews, never to Gentiles" (Hendriksen, 2:380). Thus, it is asked, how can we possibly expect Paul, abruptly and without qualification, to use this same term in v. 26 with an entirely different meaning? Murray declares "that it is exegetically impossible to give to 'Israel' in this verse any other denotation than that which belongs to the term throughout this chapter. . . . It is of ethnic Israel Paul is speaking and Israel could not possibly include Gentiles" (2:96). Especially, since "Israel" in v. 25 undoubtedly means the whole nation, it is impossible that he would use it in a different sense in v. 26 (Bruce, 221-222). Thus, says Cranfield, that "all Israel" here "does not include Gentiles is virtually certain" (2:576).

A second argument for A is that it seems most consistent with the overall context of 9–11. I.e., one of the main issues in this whole section is the fate of the nation of Israel (Godet, 410). "The whole context shows clearly that it is the actual Israel of history that is referred to" (SH, 336). Thus, says Hughes, "there is no way 'Israel' here can be spiritualized, considering the context of chapters 9–11. It clearly refers to ethnic Israel, the Jewish people" (199).

A third argument for A is that the salvation of all ethnic Israel has already been affirmed several times in this chapter, especially in the reference to Israel's "fullness" in v. 12, her "acceptance" in v. 15, and her "grafting in" in vv. 23-24. Thus it is likely that v. 26 refers to the same thing, "because in vv. 15,25, we have had already a prediction of a restoration of Jews, *en masse*, to grace" (Moule,

199). It would be anticlimactic to refer v. 26 to anything less; indeed it would be "exegetical violence" (Murray, 2:97).

A final argument is that if "all Israel" is anything less than the whole nation of Israel, then this statement does not deserve to be called a "mystery" (v. 25) in the sense explained above. To say that all true/elect/spiritual Israel will be saved, whether in the sense of B or C, is called a truism or a tautology (Godet, 411), i.e., something true by definition. Only "the whole of ethnic Israel" does justice to the term "mystery" (Cranfield, 2:576-577; Morris, 421).

Do these four arguments rule out B and C, and establish A? The first argument is the strongest, and in my judgment makes C unlikely. I do not believe it rules out B, however, as will be seen below. The second argument likewise has merit and weakens the case for C, but again it does not rule out B. The third argument is altogether invalid because it is based on a false understanding of vv. 12,15, and 24-25. These verses do not refer to a future mass conversion of Israel. (See my explanation of them above.) Indeed, Hendriksen says that prior to v. 26 "the reader has not been prepared for the idea of a mass conversion of Israelites. All along Paul stresses the very opposite, namely, the salvation, in any age (past, present, future) of *a remnant*" (2:379). The fourth argument might have some merit if the emphasis in v. 26a were on the word "all." But since the emphasis is actually on the word "so," i.e., "in this way," the argument misses the point completely. The *how* of all Israel's salvation is surely worthy to be called a mystery. See Moo, 722.

The conclusion is that the arguments for A and against B and C are not as strong as one might expect, given the widespread acceptance of this view. The last two arguments are invalid in themselves; and the first two arguments, while making C unlikely, by no means rule out B. The issue then turns on whether a good case can be made for B.[185]

Before turning to B we shall briefly consider C, the view that "all Israel" means all spiritual Israel in general (the church), including both believing Jews and believing Gentiles. I have already indicated that I believe the use of the term "Israel" in 9–11 makes this

---

[185]Though from an exegetical point of view I do not accept A in any of its forms, its noneschatological form is not objectionable in itself.

view unlikely. One cannot appeal to 9:6 to support this meaning for "Israel" in v. 26a, since the "spiritual Israel" in 9:6 includes only Jewish believers and not Gentile believers. Thus I agree that it is unwarranted to say that "Israel" in v. 26a means "spiritual Israel" in the broadest sense of that term, the church.

The argument that the context as a whole militates against this view is not as strong, since the salvation of Jews and Gentiles together certainly has been considered in this main section (9:24; 10:12), and even in the immediate context (the olive tree). Moo makes a good point, though, when he says that this view would weaken "the hortatory purpose of Rom. 11:11-32," which is to counter the Gentiles' tendency to hold themselves above the Jews. In fact, "for Paul in this context to call the church 'Israel' would be to fuel the fire of the Gentiles' arrogance by giving them grounds to brag that '*we* are the true Israel'" (721).

While I do not accept this view (C) and believe that a good case cannot be made for it, I do not consider it to be an oddity or to be totally out of the question. As Wright (*Climax*, 250) points out, "Israel" *is* used in two different senses in a single verse (9:6) without warning or explanation. Can we rule out a similar tactic here? Also, in 9:24-29 Paul does speak of Jews and Gentiles together in the context of the remnant. In 10:12-13 he declares that no distinction can be made between Jews and Gentiles with regard to salvation. In 11:17-24 the olive tree contains both Jews and Gentiles, and even v. 25 refers to the salvation of both Jews and Gentiles, at least by implication.

This leads to our examination of the arguments for B, which I consider to be the correct view. When Paul says that "all Israel will be saved," he is speaking of all ethnic Jews who also belong to the true spiritual Israel. The first argument for this view is that it is consistent with the way Paul uses the term "Israel" in 9–11, and thus belies the criticism that A is the only view that interprets the term consistent with the context. To say that Paul uses this term elsewhere in this section only for ethnic Jews may be true; but that does not affect B, which agrees that v. 26a refers to ethnic Jews. The only issue is whether Paul uses the term only in the sense of the nation *as a whole*, and 9:6 shows that he does not. In 9:6 Paul uses the term "Israel" twice, first referring to the nation as a whole and then referring only to spiritual Israel, the remnant. In the Greek text of 9:6 these two uses are almost consecutive, being separated by only one Greek word. Thus 9:6 is more than enough justification for regarding "Israel" in 11:26a as referring to spiritual Israel, even though the same term in 11:25 refers to Israel as a whole.

The second argument for B is that it is totally consistent with the context in general. Proponents of A say that v. 26a must be talking about the nation as a whole, because the status of the nation as a whole is exactly what 9–11 is all about: How can we reconcile Israel's lostness with God's faithfulness? But this is not the whole picture. It is true that in 9–11 the unbelief of Israel in general is the *problem*, but it is also true that the existence of a remnant who believe is part of the *answer* to the problem. Hence the remnant concept is a prominent theme in the context as a whole. See especially 9:6,23-29; 11:1-7a.

Third, this view (B) is also consistent with the line of thought Paul is developing in ch. 11 specifically. Has God rejected his people? No. Though most are hardened, he has a remnant. But is there any hope for those who are hardened? Yes. Especially now that salvation has come to the Gentiles, all hardened Jews may believe in Jesus and *become a part of the remnant.* Paul has just declared that God can and will graft the broken-off branches back into the olive tree, conditioned upon their abandoning their unbelief (v. 23). In v. 24 Paul assures us that God *will* graft these natural branches back into the tree, but the condition of faith is obviously meant to be carried over from v. 23. The same is undoubtedly true in v. 26. When Paul says "All Israel will be saved," in view of v. 23 we must understand it as "all Israelites who believe in Jesus Christ – i.e., the remnant – will be saved." This shows the importance of translating *houtōs* as "thus, in this way." When Paul says "in this way" all Israel will be saved, he is referring not just to the summary statement in v. 25, but to the more complete explanation in vv. 11-24, including the emphasis on conditionality in vv. 23-24.

A fourth argument for B is that it does justice to the word "all" in "all Israel." One of the most serious flaws of A is that it really does not take the word "all" seriously. In practically every version of it, the only Jews who are saved are those who happen to be living at and possibly after a point of time still in the future, and for many it is only that final generation of Jews who are saved.[186] Most individual Jews in the scores of generations preceding that time are actually *not* saved. Thus the saved "will be just a fragment of the total number of Jews who have lived on the earth. How can such a fragment properly be called 'all Israel'?" (Hoekema, *Bible*, 144). Also, as McGuiggan points out, if the issue here is God's faithfulness to his promises to the Jews, how is the saving of just one generation evidence of such faithfulness? "Did he make these promises only to a coming generation of Jews? Did he not make them to past generations of Jews? . . . In what way does the salvation of a coming mass of Jews vindicate God's faithfulness?" (335-336; see Hendriksen, 2:379). But if "all Israel" means "the entire remnant of Jews," then this refers to *every* believing Israelite in *every* generation. *All* who meet the condition of v. 23 will be saved.

A fifth argument for B is that it is consistent with Paul's teaching in the following verses that "all Israel" is being saved *now*. As we shall soon see, the OT texts cited as confirmation of v. 26a refer to the *first* coming of Jesus and to the present salvation from sin by God's grace. They do not refer to the Second Coming and to some future national restoration (Hendriksen, 2:380). Especially, in v. 31 Paul says it is God's plan that the Jews "may *now* receive mercy as a result of God's mercy to you [Gentiles]." View A does not do justice to this "now," but B does. See Hoekema, *Bible*, 145-146.

Finally we may point out that Moo's criticism that C is not consistent with Paul's exhortations to the Gentile Christians (to not consider themselves better than the Jews) does not apply to B, since the remnant of which B speaks is from among the Jews only. In fact, though Moo accepts A, he declares that B "deserves consideration as a serious alternative" (723).

A final question in reference to "all Israel will be saved" is the meaning of "saved."[187] At stake is whether this salvation includes

---

[186]Moule says, "Israel in general, the Jews *of that day* as a great aggregate . . . , shall be saved" (199). Lard says that Paul speaks of "the future salvation of a great body of the Jews, *who shall then be alive*" (370). Moo says that "all Israel" means "the corporate entity of the nation of Israel *as it exists at a particular point in time*" (723). [Italics added.]

[187]Some have tried to interpret this to mean that Paul is envisioning a special way of salvation for the Jews apart from conversion to the gospel

something special for the Jews, or whether Paul is referring simply to the ordinary salvation from sin enjoyed by Gentile believers as well. Those who hold to the eschatological version of A usually take the former approach, saying that this salvation includes the restoration of Israel as a political entity to its original Palestinian homeland as a preparation for the millennium (see MacArthur, 2:128-129; Cranfield, 2:577-578). Almost everyone else, though, in view of vv. 26b-27, understands "saved" to mean the ordinary way of salvation which Paul has been expounding throughout Romans. As Stott says, it is "salvation from sin through faith in Christ. It is not a national salvation, for nothing is said about either a political entity or a return to the land" (304). Moo agrees that there is no evidence in Rom 11 that salvation includes restoration to the land (724, n. 59).

If this is the case, how does the salvation of all remnant Israel depend on the fullness of the Gentiles? The main thing is that the latter is an occasion for envy on the part of the Jews (11:12,13-14), but DeWelt reminds us also that it must involve "nothing short of the faithful preaching of the gospel by the Gentiles to the Jews" (188).

11:26b-27 . . . as it is written, "The deliverer will come from Zion; he will turn godlessness away from Jacob. And this is my covenant with them when I take away their sins." This is a brief OT confirmation that God is now saving "all Israel" through the gospel of Jesus Christ. These lines are taken from the LXX version of Isaiah. Verse 26b is basically the same as Isa 59:20; v. 27a is from Isa 59:21a; v. 27b is from Isa 27:9. In the last citation Paul changes "his sin" to "their sins." The phrase "from Zion" also represents a change. The Hebrew text here reads "*to* Zion"; the LXX has "*for the sake of* Zion"; but Paul says "*from* Zion." The fact that salvation comes "from Zion" is specifically mentioned in Ps 14:7; 53:6; 110:2. Paul chooses to incorporate this thought into his OT citation in order to make his point more clearly. (See Moo, 727-728.)

The word for "deliverer" is a participial form of the verb ῥύομαι (*ryomai*), which means "to save, to rescue, to deliver." The Hebrew text has גֹּאֵל (*go'el*), "Redeemer" (see GRe, 15-20). This originally would have been applied to Yahweh, but Paul's use of it here shows it

---

and for some even apart from Christ himself. See Moo (725) and Fitzmyer (619-620) for a summary of such views, which need not concern us here.

is definitely a messianic prophecy. The "deliverer" is Jesus Christ.[188] See 1 Thess 1:10.

"Jacob" of course was the original name of Isaac's favored son before it was changed to Israel. OT poetic and prophetic literature often used it as a synonym for Israel when referring to the Jewish people. That is its meaning here. It simply means "Israel" or "the Jews."

"Zion" was one of the hills on which Jerusalem was built. It was used in the OT as a poetic name for Jerusalem itself (e.g., Ps 48:2, 11-12; 51:18; 69:35), and often symbolically for the whole of Israel and the people of Israel (e.g., Ps 74:2; 78:68; 146:10; Isa 1:27; 46:13). Sometimes the nuance was Zion (Jerusalem) as the location of the temple and thus the dwelling place of God (e.g., Ps 76:2; 132:13; Isa 8:18; 18:7; 24:23; Jer 2:19; Joel 3:17,21). In this way "Zion" came to represent heaven itself as God's dwelling place (e.g., Ps 9:11; 14:7; 20:2; 50:2; 53:6; 110:2; 134:3).

In the New Covenant era "Zion" represents the new temple, the new people of God, the church. Messianic prophecies about Zion, such as Ps 2:6 and Isa 28:16 (see also Isa 2:3 and Micah 4:2) could be referring to the fact that the church was established in the earthly city of Jerusalem (Acts 2), from which the gospel then was taken into all the earth. But these texts could also be referring to the church itself, which seems more likely in view of Rom 9:33; Heb 12:22-23; and 1 Pet 2:6. See also Gal 4:26.

How does Paul intend for us to understand "from Zion" in this quote from Isa 59:20? Possibly it just means "Israel," i.e., Christ came forth from the people of Israel. Or it may mean "Jerusalem" in the sense that this is where the church and the preaching of the gospel originated. Most likely, though, it means Zion as God's heavenly dwelling place, i.e., God the Redeemer will come forth from heaven itself.

It makes a considerable difference whether this refers to the Messiah's first coming or his second coming. If it is the latter, this would give support to the eschatological version of view A above. Paul would be saying that all Israel will be saved when the Messiah

---

[188]This identification of Jesus with Yahweh is an indication of his deity; see on 9:33 above.

returns from heaven. Cranfield explains it exactly this way, then observes that this confirms that Paul is speaking of an eschatological salvation for the Jews (2:578). See also Bruce (222), Dunn (2:682, 692), and Moo (727-728).

I believe, on the contrary, that this refers to the first coming of Christ.[189] It is in future tense ("will come") from Isaiah's standpoint, not Paul's. Christ's first coming was just as much from the heavenly Zion as the second will be.[190] The strongest reason for taking it to be the first coming is the specific stated *purpose* for which the Redeemer comes from Zion. The redemptive acts mentioned by Isaiah and recited by Paul refer not to a political restoration of the Jewish nation but to the personal salvation of individuals. This is why Jesus came the first time: to die for the sins of his people, and thereby to establish a new covenant with them, a covenant to take away their sins.

Specifically the deliverer has come to "turn godlessness[191] away from Jacob" (v. 26b) and to "take away their sins" (v. 27b). This is the saving grace of forgiveness (justification), regeneration, and sanctification. It is a *spiritual* restoration, not a political one (Godet, 413; Denney, 684). This is the very thing Peter preached to the Jews in his second sermon in Acts: "When God raised up his servant, he sent him first to you to bless you by turning each of you from your wicked ways" (3:26). This taking away of sins, says Isaiah, is the purpose and result of God's "covenant with them."

Of which covenant is Isaiah speaking? Some assume it is the covenant God made with Abraham and his physical seed, the Jewish nation (e.g., Moo, 728-729). From this they conclude that God has promised salvation to the Jews as a nation (e.g., Fitzmyer, 625), and that for this covenant to be fulfilled God must ultimately bring about "the future restoration of Israel" (Murray, 2:100; see Moo, 729). This is completely off the mark, however. The covenant with Abraham *was* with the *nation* of Israel as a whole, but its promises were principally temporal blessings relating to Israel's role of bringing the Messiah into the world (9:4-5), not the spiritual

---

[189]Others taking this view include Moule, 200; Hendriksen, 2:383; Stott, 304; and Wright, *Climax*, 250-251.

[190]See on 10:6 above. See John 3:13,31; 6:33,38; 1 Cor 15:47.

[191]See on 1:18; JC, 1:135-137.

blessings of salvation as such. I.e., the Abrahamic covenant did not guarantee salvation to every Jew living under it. Also, the Abrahamic covenant was fulfilled with the first coming of Christ.

The covenant to which Isaiah's messianic prophecy refers is thus not the Abrahamic covenant, but the New Covenant prophesied in Jer 31:31-34,[192] and established through the death and shed blood of Christ (Luke 22:20; Heb 8:7-12; 10:15-17). The central promise of the New Covenant, as stated in Jer 31:34, is this: "For I will forgive their wickedness and will remember their sins no more." This is exactly what Paul is emphasizing in his quote from Isaiah: God covenants to take away the sins of "all Israel" through the blood of Christ if they will but trust in him. This covenant is conditional (11:23), and God gathers Jews into it one by one over the whole course of church history. This is how all true Israel will be saved.[193]

2. God's Continuing Love for Israel (11:28-29)

11:28 Speaking of the Jews, Paul continues to address the Gentiles, explaining the reason why God's salvation is offered to "all Israel." **As far as the gospel is concerned, they are enemies on your account; but as far as election is concerned, they are loved on account of the patriarchs, . . .** This verse reflects the tension within God's nature that sums up God's relation to all sin and all sinners, i.e., the tension between his holiness and his love.[194] This is seen in a special way in his attitude toward the Jews; they are at the same time his enemies and his beloved, the objects of both his hatred and his love.[195]

The word ἐχθρός (*echthros*) is usually translated "enemy" in the NT; it speaks of an attitude of enmity and hostility and hatred. The main point here is not the sinner's hatred of God, but God's hatred

---

[192]Agreeing are (e.g.) Stott, 304; Fitzmyer, 625; Dunn, 2:683; and Wright, *Climax*, 251.

[193]It is also how all willing Gentiles will be saved, but this is not Paul's point here.

[194]See GRe, 238-239, 313-314, 372-375, 408-409, 451.

[195]See on 11:22, which speaks of God's *sternness* and *kindness*. See Murray, 2:100; Stott, 306.

of the sinner,[196] in contrast with his love for the sinner in v. 28b (Morris, 422). To be hated by God is to be under his wrath, rejected by him, and shut off from him (SH, 337; Cranfield, 2:580). This divine hostility is not directed toward all Jews, but only toward those who have rejected the gospel. They are God's enemies "as far as the gospel is concerned," i.e., because they have refused to accept the gospel and to believe in Jesus as their Messiah (9:30-10:21).

Paul never ceases to remind the Gentile Christians, however, that God's enmity toward the Jews has been the occasion for bringing the gospel to them. The Jews are enemies, yes; but they are enemies "on your account," for your sake, "in order to open His kingdom wide to you" (Moule, 201). See vv. 11,12,15.

But this is only part of the picture, and the lesser part at that. Even though the hardened Jews have chosen to become God's enemies by rejecting the gospel, *God still loves them* because of the original relationship he established with them through the patriarchs (Abraham, Isaac, and Jacob). Thus he cannot forget them; he cannot pretend that this relationship never existed. Even if they no longer have a special role in God's ongoing plan, they still occupy a special place in his heart.

"As far as election is concerned" has been taken two ways. In vv. 5,7 Paul uses this same term (ἐκλογή, *eklogē*, "election, choice") for the elect remnant; some interpret it this way here,[197] saying that v. 28b refers only to the remnant within Israel, and thus limiting God's love to the elect alone. Others (correctly) interpret "election" here as referring to God's original choice of Abraham and through him of the entire nation of Israel. This is not an election of individuals to salvation, but the election of the Jews as a corporate body to covenant service, as in 9:11.[198]

Thus, whereas v. 28a reflects the reality of ch. 10 above, v. 28b reflects the reality of ch. 9. God chose Israel as a nation to serve his special redemptive purposes, and poured out upon them his special covenant blessings. Even though this relationship did not

---

[196]That God hates not just sin but sinners as well is seen in Ps 5:5-6; 11:5; Prov 6:16-19. See 5:10 above; JC, 1:326-327. See GRe, 286-287.

[197]E.g., Moule, 201; Lenski, 732; McGuiggan, 339-340.

[198]So also SH, 337; Denney, 684; Cranfield, 2:580; Dunn, 2:685; Moo, 731-732; Morris, 423.

automatically guarantee salvation to every individual Jew, God cannot help but regard every natural descendent of Abraham with a special affection. Thus for the Jews perhaps more than others, God is "not wishing for any to perish but for all to come to repentance" (2 Pet 3:9, NASB). That is why he wants to include them in his new covenant, the covenant of salvation (v. 27). God's enmity to the hardened Jews is real (v. 28a), but it does not cancel out his love for them.

That all Israel is loved by God "on account of the fathers" does not mean that the patriarchs did anything to merit or deserve this continuing love for their descendants.[199] Nor does it mean that God still has unfulfilled covenant obligations toward the fathers. This latter view is quite common, especially among those who believe there is just one covenant of salvation, beginning with Abraham and continuing through the NT era. According to this view, this is why God still loves the Jews and *must* save them, i.e., "for His covenant with Abraham, Isaac, and Jacob is sovereign and unchangeable" (Moule, 201; see Stott, 306; Dunn, 2:694). "When the Lord elected . . . the nation of Israel to be His own people, He bound Himself by His own promises to bring the Jews to salvation and be forever His beloved and holy people," says MacArthur (2:131). Murray says, "God has not suspended or rescinded his relation to Israel as his chosen people in terms of the covenants made with the fathers," and this is why he will save and restore them (2:101).

This view errs in thinking that the covenant with the patriarchs is the same as the covenant of salvation Jesus established on the cross. Thus it errs in thinking that the patriarchal covenant promised salvation to Jews as Jews in perpetuity. The truth is that every promise to Israel as a nation through the patriarchs was completely fulfilled when Jesus came into the world the first time (9:4-5; Acts 13:32-34).

11:29 This is not contradicted by what Paul says in the next verse: **for God's gifts and his call are irrevocable.** This refers still to God's original general election of the nation of Israel. The "gifts" are not the gifts of salvation (contra Moule, 201; Hendriksen, 2:384; MacArthur, 2:131). They are the benefits described in 9:4-5, which, though glorious in every respect, are still temporal and nonsalvific in themselves. The "call" likewise is not the salvific call to which

---

[199]See Cranfield, 2:580-581.

only the elect respond, as in 8:30 (contra Denney, 684; Hendriksen, 2:384; MacArthur, 2:132; Lenski, 734). It refers to the original call to Abraham and thus the call to Israel as a nation "to be His special people, to stand in a special relation to Himself, and to fulfil a special function in history" (Cranfield, 2:581).

These gifts and this call are "irrevocable," Paul says. This is the first word in the verse in the Greek text and therefore is in a place of emphasis. What does it mean? It comes from μεταμέλομαι (*metamelomai*), which means "to regret, to repent, to change one's mind." Here, with the negating alpha, the word is ἀμεταμέλητος (*ametamelētos*, "not to be regretted, not to be repented of." (See 2 Cor 7:10.) "Irrevocable" is not the best translation. The point is not that God must save the Jews because he has made an irrevocable promise to Abraham *et al.* to do so. Rather, it is that God does not regret his choice of Israel as the nation through whom he brought the Christ into the world. Despite the centuries of their heartbreaking unfaithfulness and idolatry in OT times, and despite their current rejection of the gospel, God does not regret all he did for them and through them to carry out his purposes.

This is why they are still beloved to him. Paul begins this thought with γάρ (*gar*), "for, because." The Jews are still beloved because of the patriarchs (v. 28b), because God has never regretted this Old Covenant relationship he established with them in the first place. As Lard says, "Their fathers were chosen and loved, and on their account their rejected descendants are still loved" (373).

3. God's Ultimate Purpose Is Mercy (11:30-32)

In describing God's dealings with the Jews and Gentiles, this chapter has strongly emphasized both sides of God's nature: his sternness and his kindness (v. 22), his enmity and his love (v. 28). It has not attempted to soften or disguise the wrath of God against the unbelieving Jews (vv. 7-10,19-22,28a). But this is not the main point of the chapter. The main point is that, in spite of the unbelief and disobedience of Gentiles and Jews alike, God wants the gracious side of his nature to prevail. His ultimate goal and purpose are *mercy*, not wrath. And the most marvelous thing of all is that

God can use the universal disobedience of mankind as a part of his plan to show mercy unto all. By explaining how this is so, this paragraph is a striking example of 8:28.

11:30-31 Just as you who were at one time disobedient to God have now received mercy as a result of their disobedience, so they too have now become disobedient in order that they too may now receive mercy as a result of God's mercy to you. The parts of these two verses are so carefully composed and so deliberately parallel that both must be printed together here. Dunn says this sentence is "the most contrived or carefully constructed formulation which Paul ever produced in such tight epigrammatic form, with so many balancing elements" (2:687). It may be diagrammed thus:

For just as YOU GENTILES
  then were disobedient to God, but
  now have received mercy
    by the JEWS' disobedience;
So also THESE JEWS
  now have become disobedient, so that
  now[200] they also may receive mercy
    by the mercy shown to you GENTILES.[201]

In a real sense this sentence sums up everything Paul has said in this chapter. As Godet puts it, "Ver. 30 describes the rebellion of the Gentiles, then their salvation determined by the rebellion of the Jews; and ver. 31, the rebellion of the Jews, then their salvation arising from the salvation of the Gentiles" (414).

The word ποτε (*pote,* "then, at one time") in v. 30a refers to the pre-Christian era when the Gentiles were limited to general revelation and were given over to the sinful excesses of their rebellion

---

[200]Some Greek manuscripts omit this "now," but the best reading is to include it. For details see Cranfield, 2:585-586; Dunn, 2:677; Moo, 711.

[201]There is a question as to the placement of this last phrase, which in the Greek is simply "by your mercy." Some take it as going with the first part of the sentence: the Jews have now become disobedient for the sake of mercy being shown to you Gentiles (Dunn, 2:688; Moo, 734-735). While this is true in itself, and may be a simpler reading of the original word order, I agree with the NIV and the many others who take the phrase with the latter part of the verse. Otherwise v. 31a would simply repeat v. 30b. Also, the parallelism is sharper this way.

against God (1:18-32). The word νῦν (*nyn*, "now") in v. 30b refers to the New Covenant era when Christ has commanded that the gospel be taken to all nations. Morris (424-425) points out that the contrast is not between disobedience and obedience, as if one could make up for his sins by beginning to obey the commandments of the law. As in 3:21–5:21, the only remedy for disobedience is the mercy and grace of God.

To say that the Gentiles have received mercy "as a result of their [the Jews'] disobedience" is simply to repeat vv. 11,12,15. God takes the Jews' rebellion against the gospel of Christ as an occasion for sending that gospel to the Gentiles.

These verses continue to undermine Gentile smugness in relation to the Jews. Paul reminds the Gentiles (1) that they too were once in a state of disobedience; (2) that in one sense they owe their present state of grace to the Jews' disobedience; and (3) that God's plan is for the Jews to ultimately receive the same mercy now enjoyed by the Gentiles, even though they will arrive at it by a slightly different route.

To say that the Jews "have now become disobedient" refers to their initial rejection of the gospel at the beginning of the New Covenant era.

The word translated "in order that" is ἵνα (*hina*). It usually denotes purpose, as the NIV chooses to translate it here. But if that is what it means here, this would suggest that somehow God *caused* the Jews to be disobedient, *so that* he might accomplish the stated purpose. Thus it is important to know two things about *hina*. First, it can denote simple result rather than purpose (AG, 378). Also, "contrary to regular usage" *hina* sometimes "is placed elsewhere than at the beginning of its clause, in order to emphasize the words that come before it" (AG, 379). I believe both of these points are in evidence here in v. 31b. We should especially note that, for emphasis, "by your [the Gentiles'] mercy" is placed at the very beginning of this clause, even before the word *hina*. Taken thus it reads quite naturally as follows: "The Jews have now become disobedient, with the result that, *by means of the mercy shown to you Gentiles*, they too may now obtain mercy."

This shows that God's ultimate goal, even for the hardened Jews, is that they may receive his mercy and be saved. It also emphasizes again that the salvation of the Gentiles is an instrument by which God will bring this about. This recalls the point about the Jews' being moved to envy by seeing the Gentiles enjoying the fruit of their own covenant service (vv. 11,13-14). It is also an incentive for Gentile Christians to evangelize the Jews. As Lard says, "The Gentiles have now to preach the gospel to the Jews, and induce them to obey it" (374).

The inclusion of the word "now" in v. 31b is very significant. It shows that the statement, "And so all Israel will be saved" in v. 26a does not refer to a mass conversion of ethnic Jews at some far distant point in the future (relative to the time of Paul's writing), but that it refers to the ongoing conversion of remnant Jews beginning even "now," in the first century (Hendriksen, 2:385). Those who take the former view give "now" some other meaning, such as "at any time" (Moo, 735), or "the eschatological now" (Cranfield, 2:586), i.e., sometime during this final messianic age, even if it is toward the end of it (Morris, 425). But the parallel with the "now" in v. 30b shows that Paul is thinking of the "now" in which he was living. Thus as Wright says, it indicates "a steady flow of Jews into the church, by grace through faith," from that very time (*Climax*, 249).

11:32 For God has bound all men over to disobedience so that he may have mercy on them all. In this final verse of the present section Paul emphasizes once again that God's goal and purpose are to bring mercy to all. The "all" in both clauses probably is not intended to refer to every individual as such, but to all in the sense of both *groups*, i.e., both Gentiles and Jews. To say God has bound all over to disobedience reflects Paul's emphasis in 3:9, that "Jews and Gentiles alike are all under sin" (see 3:9-20). The reference to God's "mercy on them all" does not teach universal salvation, but refers to the fact that he has poured out his mercy on Jews and Gentiles alike (10:12).

As a matter of fact, though, all individuals in both groups *are* bound over to sin (3:23). Also, there is a sense in which God has mercy on all individuals, in that his mercy is intended for all and is offered to all. It is not the case, though, that all will in fact accept it. "Whether the mercy will ever be actually realized or not, depends on belief in Christ" (Lard, 375).

The word translated "bound over" literally means "to enclose, to confine, to shut up, to imprison." How did God imprison the Gentiles in disobedience? This does not mean that he caused them to sin, or made it impossible for them not to sin. It refers to 1:18-32, and to God's decision to "give them over" to the sinful desires of their hearts (vv. 24,26,28). How did he imprison the Jews in disobedience? Again this does not mean he caused them to sin. It refers rather to 2:1-29, and to the conclusion that the law, in which the Jews trusted, has but one verdict for sinners: condemnation. It refers also to 11:7 and the hardening of Jewish unbelievers. All in all, as Moo says, this statement refers to "God's decision to 'confine' people in the state that they have chosen for themselves" (736).

From another standpoint, to say that God shuts up all men in their sin refers to the divine pronouncement that all have in fact sinned (3:23) and have become trapped in the consequences of their sin with no hope of escaping through any deeds or schemes of their own. "By the works of the Law no flesh will be justified in His sight" (3:20, NASB). For sinners this is what it means to be "under law" (6:14,15). For sinners the testimony of the law is a word of wrath. This word of wrath is like cords that bind sinners and leave them shut up in the dungeon of death, in the very vestibule of hell.

But this is not the last word, because God has provided a way of escape from this dungeon, this prison of sin. It is the way of mercy, the way of grace (3:21–5:21); and it is the *only* way. This is the whole point of Romans: "a man is justified by faith apart from works of the Law" (3:28, NASB). "We are not under law but under grace" (6:15). This is the point to which all of ch. 11 has been leading: that God can and will provide this mercy to all, Jews and Gentiles alike. "As they have been together in the prison of their disobedience, so they will be together in the freedom of God's mercy" (Stott, 307).

V. DOXOLOGY: GOD'S WAY IS RIGHT (11:33-36)

Godet rightly remarks regarding this paragraph, "Like a traveller who has reached the summit of an Alpine ascent, the apostle turns and contemplates. . . . The plan of God in the government of mankind spreads out before him," and his heart is filled with admiration and gratitude (416). His response to God's work is nothing less than a doxology (see 1:25; JC, 1:154), a hymn of highest praise to the one who is Creator, Ruler, and Redeemer of all the earth. Awe, wonder, and adoration fill his soul as he pens this "hymnic composition, a poem to the inscrutable wisdom of God" (Fitzmyer, 632). The very writing of it is an act of worship.

How does this doxology tie in with what precedes it? In a sense we may see it as "the conclusion to the whole of the doctrinal section of Romans (1:16–11:36)," as Fitzmyer says (633). It is more appropriate, though, to take it as the capstone for chapters 9–11,[202] where the overall subject is God's faithfulness in his dealings with Israel. The question has been, Does the combination of God's original covenant with the patriarchs and Israel's present lostness mean that God has been unfaithful and untrue to his word? In answer to this question, under divine inspiration, Paul has set forth a theodicy: God's way is right, especially his way with Israel. He has shown that the first covenant dealt with Israel's *service* as a *nation*, and that God has faithfully kept every promise he made to them under this covenant (ch. 9). He has also shown that the reason for Israel's lostness is not unfaithfulness on God's part but Israel's own unbelief (ch. 10). Finally he has shown that under the New Covenant God's redemptive plan incorporates Israel's unbelief in a way that leads ultimately back to her salvation (ch. 11).

These are the mysteries that fill Paul with wonder, and elicit from him this "hymn of admiration in honor of the divine plan" (Godet, 419), his "awesome plan" (Moo, 739). Paul no doubt has ch. 11 especially in mind, and particularly the summary statement in vv. 30-32, which emphasizes the mercy of God. Thus he marvels that God has vindicated his faithfulness in the face of Israel's unbelief in a way that glorifies both his holiness and his mercy.

A major theme of this doxology is the inscrutability of God's ways with mankind. Some say that Paul's purpose here is "to glorify God's incomprehensibility" (MacArthur, 2:134). As Morris puts it, this hymn "is prompted by what we do not know about God . . .

---

[202]As such it parallels the hymn of praise at the conclusion of the previous section, 8:31-39.

rather than by what we do know" (427). But this is misleading. Paul certainly emphasizes God's transcendent unsearchableness. But his wonder is evoked not by divine incomprehensibility as such, nor by things still hidden within its depths, but rather by the things that God has revealed to us and which are now open to us. To be sure, we could never have discerned on our own God's awesome plan for saving his people; but God has shown it to us, and that is why we are overwhelmed by the wisdom and mercy of it.

Godet long ago set us straight on this point. Against those who dwell on the divine incomprehensibility as if it were the last word, he rightly observes that Paul's hymn is evoked "not by the obscurity of God's plans, but . . . by their dazzling clearness." They are indeed unfathomable until revealed, but revealing them is exactly what Paul has been doing. "It is therefore in view of the *unveiled* mystery that the exclamation is raised" (417). Moo also makes this point (740), as does Murray (2:104): "What constrains the doxology is the revealed counsel."

11:33 Oh,[203] the depth of the riches of the wisdom and knowledge of God! There is disagreement over how this exclamation was intended to be structured. Some take "the depth of the riches" as a single idea, with "wisdom and knowledge" being its double object. See the NIV and NASB. Calvin says it refers to the "deep riches of wisdom and knowledge" (444; see Lenski, 739-740). According to this interpretation, the main emphasis of the whole section would be on God's wisdom and knowledge.

Others[204] take the three nouns, "riches and wisdom and knowledge," as three parallel objects of "depth." In my judgment this view is preferable (contra the NIV), since "the depth of the riches" as a single idea is redundant.[205] According to this view, then, the doxology is emphasizing not just God's wisdom and knowledge, but his *riches* as well. (The phrase "of God" goes with all three nouns.)

---

[203]This is an interjection that expresses strong emotion and thus sets the tone for the whole hymn.

[204]E.g., Lard, 375-376; Cranfield, 2:589; Fitzmyer, 634; Stott, 310; Moo, 741, n. 7.

[205]Either view is grammatically acceptable, and both are appropriate to the context (Murray, 2:106; Morris, 427-428).

The word "depth" is "a common Greek expression for inexhaustible fullness or superabundance" (MP, 479). The idea is that God is a bottomless, infinite resource of riches, wisdom, and knowledge.

Paul marvels first at the depth of God's *riches*. This word can mean material wealth (Matt 13:22; 1 Tim 6:17), but usually Paul uses it for spiritual riches, the riches of salvation (e.g., Eph 1:7,18; 3:8; Phil 4:19). This is the way he has used it thus far in Romans;[206] see especially 11:12, where it stands alone without a modifier as it does here in v. 33. The abundant references to God's superabundant mercy in vv. 30-32 are probably foremost in Paul's mind when he praises God for the depth of his riches (see Eph 2:4).

Paul refers next to the depth of God's *wisdom*, which is a common OT theme (see Dunn, 2:699). Generally speaking, wisdom "is the ability to choose the best possible end, and to choose the best possible means of achieving that end. It is not the same as knowledge, but is rather the ability to put one's knowledge to practical use" (GRu, 285; see 285-289). Here Paul has in mind the specific wisdom God has demonstrated in the way he has worked out the salvation of mankind (see 1 Cor 1:17–2:16), and especially in the way he has used the Jews and Gentiles to help each bring salvation to the other (ch. 11). As Godet puts it, wisdom is "the admirable skill with which God weaves into His plan the free actions of man, and transforms them into as many *means* for the accomplishment of the excellent end which He set originally before Him" (417).

Finally Paul extols the depth of God's *knowledge*.[207] God's knowledge is his constant, comprehensive, immediate consciousness or awareness of all facts – past, present, and future. This certainly refers to his omniscience, or his general knowledge of all things; and this includes his foreknowledge of man's free choices, of which he takes account and which he incorporates into his own plan of salvation.[208] Few truths about God are more awe-inspiring than his

[206]See 2:4; 9:23; 11:12. See also 10:12, where the verb form is used in the same sense.

[207]See GC (273-292) on the general subject of God's knowledge, including the concepts of omniscience and foreknowledge. On the latter see also GRu, 280-283.

[208]Godet, 417; Cranfield, 2:589-590; Dunn, 2:699; Fitzmyer, 632. On foreknowledge as it relates to predestination see on 8:29 (JC, 1:504-511).

foreknowledge of man's future free-will choices. It does not behoove us to reject the reality of such foreknowledge just because we do not understand how it is possible. Paul does not question the depth of God's knowledge; he simply bows before it.

How unsearchable his judgments, and his paths beyond tracing out! This basically says the same thing as v. 33a in different words. "Unsearchable" and "beyond tracing out" correspond to "depth," and are similar in meaning and implication. They convey the idea of "unfathomable, inscrutable, incomprehensible." I.e., the thoughts and ways of God are beyond our unaided ability to seek out and discover. The second word is especially vivid. It "literally refers to footprints that are untrackable" (MacArthur, 2:135). Thus Paul is saying that "even when God has gone and has done things we cannot discover the tracks and track his course" (Lenski, 741). We could never have seen in advance where he was going, nor understood how he would be able to accomplish his redemptive purposes. But he has done so, to his eternal glory!

This applies to both God's judgments and his paths. Stott rightly says that God's judgments are "what he thinks and decides," and his paths are "what he does and where he goes" (310). The word for "judgments" is κρίμα (*krima*), which often refers to a judicial decision to punish wrongdoers (e.g., 2:2-3; 3:8; 5:16). Here it probably is inclusive of all God's decisions as to how he will deal with mankind, and especially "his 'executive' decisions about the direction of salvation history" (Moo, 742; see Lard, 376). The word for "paths" is ὁδός (*hodos*), the common word for "road, way." A better translation here would be "ways" (NASB). The ways of God are simply his works or deeds, "the paths along which God moves in executing his plans and purposes" (Lard, 376). See Ps 95:10; Isa 55:8-9.

These two statements are a confession that the wisdom and the ways of God that work out our salvation surpass our knowledge and are beyond anything we can ask or imagine (Eph 3:19-20). Once they are explained to us, we may understand *what* God has done, but *how* he can do it and *why* he should even want to do it we will never fully comprehend. As finite creatures and sinners saved by grace, we can only do what Paul did and utter heartfelt expressions of praise.

11:34-35 "Who has known the mind of the Lord? Or who has been his counselor? Who has ever given to God, that God should repay him?" These three questions are based on texts from the OT (thus the NIV quotation marks). The first two (v. 34) are adapted from Isa 40:13, "Who has understood the [Spirit] of the LORD, or instructed him as his counselor?" The last (v. 35) is based on the Hebrew text of Job 41:11 (see 1 Chr 29:14; Job 35:7). The fact that Paul does not say "It is written" or "Isaiah says" indicates that he, under inspiration, is adapting these texts for his own purposes.

It is very likely that the three questions correspond, in reverse order, to the three elements in v. 33a. "Who has known the mind of the Lord?" refers to the depths of God's *knowledge*. God alone has access to the content of his own mind, but he graciously chooses to reveal some of this content to us through his inspired prophets and apostles (1 Cor 2:9-16). "Or who has been his counselor?" refers to the depths of God's *wisdom*. A counselor is one who gives advice on how to live and how to act, i.e., how to discern the best ends and the best means to achieve them. God needs no such advice; he does not need to ask anyone for help in devising his plan of salvation and in carrying it out.

The third question, "Who has ever given to God, that God should repay him?" corresponds to the depths of God's *riches*. The point is that we give nothing to God prior to his bestowing his riches upon us; therefore God's gifts to us are truly gifts and not just a repayment of something he owes to us. As the New Jerusalem Bible translates it, "Who has given anything to him, so that his presents come only as a debt returned?" It is impossible for us to perform some service for God that puts him in our debt. God is sovereign and thus free from any obligation, "except those He places on Himself" (MacArthur, 2:136).

This applies of course to the specific subject of God's dealings with the Jews. God placed himself under obligation to them when he entered into the covenant with their father Abraham. But the covenant itself was a gift and not an obligation; his promises both as made and as fulfilled were his free gift to them. And since those promises have now been fulfilled (9:4-5), the Jews can lay no claim upon God whatsoever, not even one based on the truth of his own word.

This also applies to the whole subject of salvation as a matter of grace rather than works. Only when salvation is by grace can it be a gift and not wages due (see 4:4). This is how God saves any sinner, Gentile or Jew. As far as salvation is concerned, "God is debtor to none, his favour is never compensation, merit places no constraints upon his mercy" (Murray, 2:107).

The answer to each question, of course, is "No one!" As finite sinners we all stand on equal footing before God; we are all helpless beggars who can only hold out empty hands to receive the gifts he earnestly desires to give us.

11:36 This verse first tells us why God is free from any obligation under which someone might try to place him: **For from him and through him and to him are all things**. In three succinct prepositional phrases the sovereign freedom and glorious supremacy of God are declared. He is related to all things as their *source*, originator, or Creator: "from him." He is related to all things as the *means* by which they came into existence and remain in existence: "through him." He is related to all things as the *goal* or purpose for which they exist: "to him," i.e., unto his glory and for his good pleasure. See Eph 4:6; Heb 2:10.

One should not take these three phrases as referring respectively to the three persons of the Trinity, as some ancient writers did. The Bible makes similar statements concerning Jesus Christ, God the Son (1 Cor 8:6; Col 1:16), but that is not the point here. Each phrase applies to all three persons of the Trinity.

To say that all things are "from God" does not mean that he makes them out of his own essence, a concept that would be equivalent to the false worldview called pantheism. This phrase refers rather to the act of creation *ex nihilo*, by which God in the beginning brought all things into existence out of nothing. See on 4:17 (JC, 1:300-301); see GC, 97-117.

The expression "all things" should not be limited. The statement is a general truth that applies to the whole of creation, even if the immediate application is to the establishment of the new creation through the work of redemption. We should not be surprised to find such a reference to God as Creator in this final verse of the theological portion of Romans. "In an argument which began with man's rebellion against God as creator (1:18-25), what could be more appropriate than a final acclamation of God the creator?" (Dunn, 2:704).

A final word of doxology closes this part of Romans: **To him be the glory forever! Amen.** The glory of God is his infinite and total greatness as it is manifested and as it shines forth for all to see (see GC, 446-452); it is "the reflection of all His perfections in all that exists" (Godet, 419). To ascribe glory to God ("to him be the glory") is not to give him anything or add anything to his nature, but simply to acknowledge and confess that he *is* glorious, and to call upon others to acknowledge this glory as well. Adding the word "forever" (lit., "unto the ages") intensifies the praise even further. On this and on "Amen," see 1:25 (JC, 1:154).

This brings us to the end of what may properly be called the theological section of Romans, namely, chs. 1–11. It is only fitting that it should end on a worshipful note, since, as Stott says, theology and worship should never be separated. He comments (311-312),

> . . . On the one hand, there can be no doxology without theology. It is not possible to worship an unknown god. All true worship is a response to the self-revelation of God in Christ and Scripture, and arises from our reflection on who he is and what he has done. It was the tremendous truths of Romans 1–11 which provoked Paul's outburst of praise. . . .
>
> On the other hand, there should be no theology without doxology. There is something fundamentally flawed about a purely academic interest in God. God is not an appropriate object for cool, critical, detached, scientific observation and evaluation. No, the true knowledge of God will always lead us to worship, as it did Paul. Our place is on our faces before him in adoration.

12:1–15:13 – PART FIVE

LIVING THE SANCTIFIED LIFE

There is definitely a break between ch. 11 and ch. 12, as Paul now begins a new section with an obviously different tone. Chapters 1–11 are usually labeled "doctrinal," and this new section is called "practical." It is the "application of doctrine to practice," says Moule (45). It is as if Paul were saying, "Because these things are true, this is the kind of person you should be" (Morris, 431).

We must be careful not to press this distinction too far, however. This is partly a matter of terminology. The word "doctrine" simply means "teaching"; thus even teaching about how to live, i.e., the so-called "practical" teaching, is still *doctrine*. For the sake of terminology we may distinguish theological doctrine (what is true or false) from ethical doctrine (what is right or wrong), but it is all doctrine.

Whatever terminology we use, the main point is that we cannot really separate these two categories. *All* doctrine is practical in the sense that it has implications as to how we ought to live; there is nothing more practical than sound theology. Also, all practical or ethical teaching is ultimately grounded in some theological truth such as the nature of God or the nature of man or the nature of salvation. As Moo puts it, the transition from ch. 11 to ch. 12 is not a transition from theology to practice, "but from a focus more on the 'indicative' side of the gospel to a focus more on the 'imperative' side of the gospel." And in the Christian life itself these are not two successive stages in our experience, but are two sides of one coin (745).

Here in the case of Romans, the specific theological foundation for ethical living is the doctrine of salvation: "In view of all that God has accomplished for His people in Christ, how should His people live?" (Bruce, 225). Specifically, Romans is intended to expound the fact that salvation is by *grace* rather than by works of law (see JC, 1:52-54). In this exposition Paul makes it clear that grace is not simply justification by faith in the blood of Christ, but also regeneration and sanctification by the power of the Holy Spirit. I.e., grace is a double cure (see JC, 1:248, 370). In chs. 6–8 the second part of this double cure (regeneration and sanctification) is set forth in a forceful way. The material here in Part Five is directly related to that.[1]

The exact nature of this relationship seems to be something like this. In chs. 6–8 Paul sets forth the reality of the new life in Christ (ch. 6) and the indwelling power of the Holy Spirit (ch. 8) in general theological terms. I.e., he tells us what God did for us when he saved us by grace. But now in chs. 12–15 he describes the character of this sanctified life in specific terms.[2] He has already said (1:5) that the goal of his preaching is to bring about the "obedience that comes from faith"; now he tells us exactly what that obedience should be. In 6:4 he tells us that in our baptism we were raised up from spiritual death so that we "may live a new life"; now he tells us in precise terms what the content of this new life should be.

The material in this section is divided into two main parts. The first (12:1–13:14) is a catalogue of virtues that does not seem to be in any particular order.[3] The important point is that these virtues have the character of law. They are rules for Christian living, laws to live by. They are nonnegotiable absolutes, not matters of opinion. This corrects any possible misunderstanding of 6:14-15, that we are "not under law but under grace." In that passage Paul means that we are not under law as a way of *salvation*, but he does not mean that law no longer applies to Christians in any sense. We are still under law – the moral law – as a way of life (see JC, 1:409-410). We may think of this present section as a good (but not necessarily complete) synopsis of God's moral law, the law that applies equally to all people in all times.[4]

---

[1]We should never approach this section of Romans as if it were simply a hortatory appendix having no integral relation to the preceding chapters. See Moo, 744.

[2]Murray says, "When Paul at 12:1 enters the sphere of practical application, he does so on the basis of his earlier teaching" (2:110).

[3]Fitzmyer observes that this is not intended to be a formal "ethical treatise, for it is quite unsystematic and somewhat rambling" (638).

[4]Some have pointed out Paul's many references and allusions to the teachings of Jesus as recorded in the Gospels and which were of course

The second main part is 14:1–15:13, the presupposition for which is that not everything in our Christian lives is regulated by law. There are many areas where there is no "Thus saith the Lord" and we are free to make our own decisions for daily living. The subject of this section is how Christians should handle these "matters of opinion," and how we must respect each other's freedom to decide on these matters according to our own consciences. The main point is that we must learn to live in unity and peace without being judgmental and without causing others to stumble.

Many commentators believe that this second part was directed against specific problems that existed in the Roman congregation and which had been reported to Paul (SH, 351; Fitzmyer, 638; Moo, 746-747). It is likely that these disagreements over matters of Christian liberty reflected differences between the Jewish and Gentile Christians in Rome (15:8-12), but were probably not limited to these.

I. A CATALOGUE OF VIRTUES (12:1–13:14)

As stated above, the instructions in this section have the essence of *law*. As Achtemeier says, this shows that "grace is not another form of total permissiveness," as if under grace anything goes. "Grace is thus the opposite of permissiveness"; it "brings with itself specific structures" (194). This should never be confused with legalism, however. As Morris points out, legalism says, "Do these things and live." Grace, on the other hand, says, "Live, and you will do these things" (431).

A. GRACE DEMANDS A TRANSFORMED LIFE (12:1-2)

This transitional passage asserts in a general way that the theology and the experience of grace as set forth in chs. 1–11 must necessarily bring about profound changes in every aspect of a believer's life. The very contemplation of the mercies of God, says Paul, compels us to offer up our bodies as living sacrifices to God (v. 1).

---

taught and circulated orally from the beginning. See the helpful chart in Stott, 318-319.

How is this accomplished? By refusing to conform our lives to the prevailing anti-Christian cultures of this age, and allowing ourselves to be transformed instead according to the standard of God's preceptive will (v. 2a). And how can this be done? Only by the renewing of the mind through initial regeneration by the Holy Spirit and continuing instruction from the written Word of God. As a result of this renewing we can discern which moral choices are in conformity with the will of God, i.e., the way of life that is truly good, truly pleasing to God, and truly fulfilling.

Three underlying themes are presupposed by the language of this brief passage. First, the language of worship, especially OT ritual worship, is prominent. This is seen especially in the expressions "offer," "sacrifices," and "act of worship," and to a lesser extent in the descriptions of the sacrifices in v. 1. Second, the theme of anthropological dualism is seen in the references to "bodies" (v. 1) and "mind" (v. 2), and to an extent in "spiritual" in v. 1. Paul's teaching in chs 6–8 is definitely in the background here (see JC, 1:372-374).

Third, contrary to the concept of sovereign or monergistic grace (as in Calvinism), the language of this passage reflects a synergistic concept of salvation, i.e., the basic and efficacious grace-works of God are joined with the human acts of submission and surrender in order to bring about the transformed life. The power of divine grace is presupposed throughout, but the reality of human responsibility is highlighted by the exhortations and imperatives that are the main content of the passage. As Dunn says, the text "deliberately indicates the balance necessary between personal commitment and divine enabling" (2:707).

12:1 Therefore, I urge you, brothers,[5] in view of God's mercy, to offer your bodies as living sacrifices, holy and pleasing to God – this is your spiritual act of worship. The word "therefore" links what follows not just to the immediately preceding verses, but to the entire message of the epistle thus far, which is summarized as "God's mercy." The word translated "mercy"[6] is οἰκτιρμός (*oiktirmos,*

[5]On the significance of "brothers," see 1:13 (JC, 1:96-97), and 10:1.

[6]The word is actually plural, "mercies," following OT usage. See Cranfield, 2:596; Dunn, 2:709.

"pity, mercy, compassion"); it is used only here in Romans. The more common word for mercy is ἔλεος (*eleos*); this word and its cognates are used in Romans only in 9:15-18 and 11:30-32. However, all the blessings of the grace of Jesus Christ described throughout chapters 1–11 are rightly included in "the mercies of God" (NASB).

The word translated "urge" has a number of meanings. The main question is whether Paul is using it in the sense of an authoritative command or a personal plea. It is certainly a plea on a personal level (they are "brothers"), one that is explicitly grounded in the mercies of God rather than in Paul's apostolic authority. I urge you, he says, "in view of" (διά, *dia*) God's mercies. When you truly understand and contemplate all that God has done to save you through Christ, how can you do less than offer your bodies as living sacrifices? You need no other motive than this.

Some would exclude the note of authority altogether, and limit Paul's appeal to that of a personal plea.[7] Others, however, interpret "I urge you" as an authoritative exhortation. Cranfield says it is an "authoritative summons" that includes "the note of authority" (2:597). See Moo, 748-749.

This is probably a false choice. Stott rightly remarks that "I urge you" is a "mixture of entreaty and authority" (320). The key is to distinguish obligation (why we *ought* to do something) from motivation (why we actually *do* something). As an inspired apostle, Paul always speaks with apostolic authority[8] unless he specifically suspends it (Phlm 8-10). Thus the authority of the writer imparts authority to what is written, and we who read are under obligation to obey. The main emphasis, though, is on motivation. By appealing to the mercies of God Paul wants to ensure that we offer our bodies as living sacrifices not just because he says we should, but because we are inwardly convicted that this is the only "appropriate and expected response to God's mercy as we have experienced it" (Moo, 749). As Stott says, "There is no greater incentive to holy living than a contemplation of the mercies of God" (321).

---

[7]Suggested translations are "I beg you" (McGuiggan, 347), "I ask you" (Lard, 379), "I beseech you" (Morris, 432). Dunn points out that "I beseech you" was a common formula used in correspondence between Greeks in that day (1:707-708).

[8]See 1:5; 11:13; 1 Cor 14:37; 1 Thess 2:13; 1 Tim 2:7.

Exactly what does Paul exhort us to do? Literally, "to offer your bodies as a sacrifice." The language here would have immediately reminded Paul's first readers of the common practice of offering up animals as sacrifices or burnt offerings to God in acts of worship. Ritual offerings were made in certain pagan religions, and of course were a central part of the Mosaic Law. The word "offer" (παρίστημι, *paristēmi*) is found also in 6:13,16,19, but it is not used there in the sense of offering up a sacrifice to God (see JC, 1:403). It does have this technical sense here, however (Cranfield, 2:598; Dunn, 2:709; Moo, 751). The word "sacrifice" (θυσία, *thysia*) is the common word for the animal or thing being offered up in such a ritual.

As Christians, says Paul, we must offer up our *bodies* (σώματα, *sōmata*) as sacrifices to God. At issue here is whether he really means bodies, or whether this is just shorthand for the entire self. Many take the latter approach, especially those who deny the reality of anthropological dualism. Here the NEB reads, "Offer your very selves." The TEV has "Offer yourselves." Moo says it means "the entire person, with special emphasis on that person's interaction with the world" (751). So also Cranfield, 2:589-590; Dunn, 2:709; Hendriksen, 2:401.

While it is true that we should offer our entire selves to God, this is not the point here. Paul knows how to say "offer yourselves" and to distinguish this from "offer your bodies." This is the very language he uses in 6:13. After he says "offer yourselves" (παραστήσατε ἑαυτούς, *parastēsate heautous*), in a separate exhortation he urges us to offer the members of our *bodies* to God (JC, 1:402-404). Here in 12:1 he means exactly what he says: offer your *bodies*. (So also Godet, 425; Lard, 380; Murray, 2:110-111; and Stott, 322.)

This exhortation shows the importance of the body in itself as an authentic part of our human nature, and shows how important it is to use the body to the glory of God. It also recalls especially the teaching of chs. 6–8, that in this present stage of our redemption only our souls/spirits have been renewed; the redemption of the body awaits the day of resurrection. In the meantime, our unredeemed bodies remain the seat of sin and the source of many temptations; thus they must be constantly and consciously offered up to God as part of the process of sanctification. This is how we fulfill the commands of 6:12-13. See Lard, 380; Murray, 2:110-111; and especially MacArthur, 142-144.

The nature of this bodily sacrifice is described with a string of three adjectives: "living," "holy," and "pleasing to God." In what sense is our sacrifice a "living" one? Some think this refers to the *new* life received in regeneration (6:4).[9] But if "bodies" literally means *bodies*, this cannot be, because the body as yet does not participate in this new life (8:10-11). It is better to take "living" as a deliberate contrast with OT sacrifices, in which the animals were killed in a one-time act. Under the New Covenant we no longer offer such sacrifices,[10] but instead offer up our bodies with all their vital energies in continuing, day-after-day worship (MP, 487; Moo, 751).

We offer our bodies also as *holy* sacrifices. "Holy" basically means "set apart in consecration to God." In this sense every true sacrifice is holy (Moo, 751), and so must we set our bodies apart from the world in daily service to God. Such separation from the world is not so much physical as it is ethical, i.e., refusing to use our bodies for participation in the defilements of sin (Murray, 2:112). This is the ethical equivalent of the OT requirement that sacrifices be without physical defects (e.g., Lev 1:3; 3:1,6).

Finally, the sacrifice of our bodies is described as "pleasing to God." It is pleasing to him just because it is living and holy. Such a sacrifice is a delight to God's heart. This is equivalent to the way the OT sacrifices provided "an aroma pleasing to the Lord" (e.g., Lev 1:9,13,17; 2:2,9,12; see Gen 8:21). Christ's sacrifice was likewise "a fragrant offering" (Eph 5:2), as are our acts of service to God (Phil 4:18).

The offering of our bodies as living, holy, and God-pleasing sacrifices is a "spiritual act of worship." The interpretation of the key words in this phrase – λογικός (*logikos*) and λατρεία (*latreia*) – is disputed. The issue regarding *latreia* is whether it means "service" to God of a general nature, as distinct from acts of worship as such, or whether it actually means "worship." The KJV and the ASV translate it "service"; this is often preferred by those who would make distinctions between formal worship settings and Christian service in our everyday lives.

---

[9]Cranfield, 2:600; Hendriksen, 2:402.

[10]As MacArthur says, under the New Covenant the only sacrifice that is literally put to death is Jesus Christ (2:146).

Whether or not this distinction between service and worship is valid, we cannot limit this word to the former concept only. *Latreia* and its cognate verb, λατρεύω (*latreuō*), often are used for ritual worship, as in 9:4. The imagery of ritual sacrifice in 12:1 leads us to interpret *latreia* here in that sense also; the NIV's "worship" is correct.[11] The point is that all Christian living is worship offered up to God. Public, corporate worship is special and must not be neglected, but that is not the only part of the Christian life that may be called "worship." Christians must do *everything* "for the glory of God" (1 Cor 10:31), and whatever is done for his glory is an act of worship. Thus Cranfield is correct: "The true worship which God desires embraces the whole of the Christian's life from day to day" (2:601; see Moo, 754; McGuiggan, 348-357).

The other key word in this phrase, the adjective *logikos,* can be interpreted several ways. The NIV and the NASB render it "spiritual," which seems to be its meaning in its only other NT use, 1 Pet 2:2. Some think Paul is describing the Christian's worship as "spiritual" in contrast with the external forms of worship prescribed in the OT (Bruce, 226; Barrett, 231). Such a contrast seems unlikely, since the Christian is sacrificing something external also, i.e., his body, and also since acceptable OT worship involved the spirit. If Paul is using *logikos* in the sense of "spiritual," his point is that even the way we use our physical bodies is a spiritual matter.

A second possibility is that *logikos* should be interpreted as "rational" in the sense of involving the mind, the reason, the intellect. The Greeks used this word to distinguish human beings from animals, and to distinguish reason-based worship from superstition (Dunn, 2:711-712; Moo, 752). Some see such a connotation here. I.e., offering our bodies as living, holy, and God-pleasing sacrifices is worship that is "worthy of thinking beings" (Jerusalem Bible; see Morris, 484; Murray, 2:112; Fitzmyer, 640). This is not too different from the previous view.

A third interpretation is that *logikos* means "reasonable" in the sense that offering our bodies as sacrifices to God is the only reasonable, logical thing to do once we understand the depths of his

[11]"*Act* of worship" is unfortunate, though, since Paul is not talking about a single act but an ongoing way of life.

mercies toward us in the work of Christ (Cranfield, 2:604-605; Lard, 380; MP, 485, 488; see the KJV, "reasonable service"). The word "therefore" at the beginning of the verse is consistent with this approach.

Any one of these views is possible in view of other biblical teaching, and is appropriate to the present context. I favor the first two views combined, because together they emphasize the internal nature of true worship, even when externals (e.g., the body) are involved. As the NEB puts it, this is "the worship offered by mind and heart." Jesus spoke of it as "worship in spirit and in truth" (John 4:24), i.e., worship that comes from the heart ("spiritual") and is consistent with reason ("rational").

12:2 Do not conform any longer to the pattern of this world, but be transformed . . . . How shall we go about offering our bodies as living sacrifices? This is explained in the two general exhortations in v. 2 (which in the best texts are present passive imperatives). We offer our bodies by refusing to be conformed to this world, and instead allowing ourselves to be transformed by the renewing of our minds.

In English these two verbs share a common root, "form," in the sense of "to form, to shape." The Greek words come from different roots, however. "Conform" comes from σχῆμα (*schēma*), and "transform" from μορφή (*morphē*). Some scholars (e.g., Trench, *Synonyms*, 261-267) make a sharp distinction between these two words, declaring that the former refers only to superficial or surface qualities, while the latter refers to the inner essence of a thing. Thus "conform" would imply only a superficial change, while "transform" would refer to a deep and abiding change from within. Paul is then read thus: "Be not outwardly conformed but be inwardly transformed" (Lenski, 749). I.e., "the demands of the world require no more than an outward, superficial conformity to its ways and customs," while "the Christ-life . . . demands that complete and fundamental inner change which fulfills and accomplishes regeneration" (MP, 488-489). See Hendriksen (2:405, n. 338) for a defense of this view. See also MacArthur, 2:149-150.

The biggest problem with this view is the idea that conformity to this world is only a shallow, external problem. In reality, as Barrett says, "conformity to this age is no superficial matter" (232-233).

Thus the "large consensus" (Dunn, 2:712) is that *schēma* and *morphē* are more or less synonyms, and that we should not read any significant distinction into the two verbs here in 12:2a (Cranfield, 2:605-607; Stott, 323; Moo, 756). The true contrast in this verse is not between two *kinds* of change, but between two totally different *models* according to which one may shape his life. These two competing models are "the pattern of this world" and "God's will" (12:2b). Paul emphatically commands us *not* to shape our lives according to the anti-Christian cultures of this world, but instead to continue allowing ourselves to be recreated according to God's will, a process which began in the act of regeneration (6:1-11) and which continues through the truth of his Word and the power of his Spirit.

The form of these verbs is as important as their meaning. They are *present* tense, which means that these are not one-time acts but are part of the ongoing process of progressive sanctification (see "living sacrifices," 12:1). They are also *passive* in form, which means that the change in view is not something we do or can do for ourselves; it is something that is done to us. Thus the transformation (and the renewing) can be accomplished by God alone. Finally, the verbs are *imperative*, which means that we have the responsibility of desiring the change and consenting to it and yielding ourselves up to the power of the Holy Spirit within us. Cranfield brings out all these nuances with the translation, "Continue to let yourselves be transformed" (2:607).

The negative command is literally, "Do not let yourselves be conformed to this age."[12] The term translated "world" in the NIV is αἰών (*aiōn*), which is better translated "age." The NT uses this term not just in the sense of a period of history, but as a period of history as marked by a certain ethical or spiritual character, or the world as understood in terms of a certain worldview or value system. In this sense, two "ages" can coexist, as they do now. "This age," the age to which we must not be conformed, is the world as fallen, the world as it has existed under the power of Satan, sin, and death since the Fall and as it will continue to exist until the Second Coming. Paul calls it "this present evil age" (Gal 1:4), since it is controlled by Satan, "the god of this age" (2 Cor 4:4; see 1 Cor 2:8).

[12]The NIV phrase "any longer" is not in the original text.

The new age or the "age to come" in one sense has already begun, being inaugurated through the death and resurrection of Christ; it will come in its fullness when Christ returns. (See Matt 12:32; Mark 10:30; Luke 18:30; 20:34-35; Eph 1:21; Heb 6:5.)

We are thus commanded not to be influenced by the false, anti-Christian religions and worldviews that are always springing up and embodying the spirit of "this age." We are admonished not to buy into the relativistic and sin-justifying value systems that exert constant pressure upon us. "Resist this process of being continually moulded and fashioned according to the pattern of this present age with its conventions and its standards of values" (Cranfield, 2:608). "Do not let yourselves be shaped by what everyone else does" (Achtemeier, 195). "Don't let the world around you squeeze you into its own mould" (Phillips translation). This means that we must consciously avoid, for example, "the use of dirty or offensive language, the singing of scurrilous songs, the reading of filthy books, the wearing of tempting attire, engaging in questionable pastimes, associating, on intimate terms, with worldly companions" (Hendriksen, 2:404).

The positive command, "Let yourselves be transformed," thus means by implication to shape your lives according to the biblical worldview, to orient your lives around the age to come, and to "set your hearts on things above, where Christ is seated at the right hand of God. Set your minds on things above, not on earthly things" (Col 3:1-2). "Live as those whose lives are governed by the principles and hopes of a holy eternity in prospect" (Moule, 206).

The means for accomplishing this ongoing transformation is **by the renewing of your mind.** This renewing has its beginning in the Spirit's work of regeneration that takes place in the moment of Christian baptism (6:3-5; Titus 3:5); and it continues as the ongoing process of sanctification, which is described in Col 3:10 as the renewing of the image of God in which we were originally created.

This is specifically a renewing of the *mind*. The "mind" is "the faculty by which the soul perceives and discerns the good and the true" (Godet, 427); it is "the seat of intellectual and moral judgment" (Fitzmyer, 641), the powers of our moral consciousness. Thus the renewing of the mind is the renewing of our ability to think correctly, especially about spiritual and moral matters.

But the mind is not just our formal intellectual and logical powers. It includes the inclinations and contents of our thought-life as well. It is our "inner disposition" (Hendriksen, 2:406); it includes our "inner thoughts, drives, and desires" (McGuiggan, 358). It involves the adoption of the Bible's comprehensive worldview, which usually requires a complete paradigm shift or reprogramming for most converts. As Moo says, "Christians are to adjust their way of thinking about everything in accordance with the 'newness' of their life in the Spirit" (756). It means to exchange the mind of the flesh for the mind of the Spirit (8:5-8).

Such a radical renewing is not something we can do by our natural powers; it can be accomplished only by the instrumentality of the Word of God and the Holy Spirit (Stott, 324). The Spirit renews our *ability* to think straight; this is part of his regenerating and sanctifying work (see chs. 7, 8). Then the Word of God, the Bible, renews the *content* of our minds (see Col 3:10, 16). "The transformed and renewed mind is the mind saturated with and controlled by the Word of God" (MacArthur, 2:151). The bottom line is that "the believer, whose life is that of the new age, does not think like an unbeliever" (Morris, 435).

What is the result of this renewing of the mind? **Then you will be able to test and approve what God's will is – his good, pleasing and perfect will.** "Test and approve" translates one Greek word, δοκιμάζω (*dokimazō*. It has several connotations: "put to the test, examine"; "prove by testing"; "accept as proved, approve" (AG, 201). The object of the verb is "God's will." The circumstance Paul is describing seems to be this. Like everyone else, Christians are confronted with a myriad of conflicting choices with regard to how to act and to live. But because they have been transformed by the renewing of their minds, they are able to subject all the options to the test of God's Word and are able to discern and distinguish the will of God from the false and demonic choices. The best translation is actually "discern," i.e., "so you can discern what conforms to God's will" (Achtemeier, 195). As MacArthur says, "When a believer's mind is transformed, his thinking ability, moral reasoning, and spiritual understanding are able to properly assess everything, and to accept only what conforms to the will of God" (2:151-152). See Cranfield, 2:609.

Moule says this renewing of the mind instills within us a "holy instinct" by which we "can discern, in conflicting cases, the will of God from the will of self or of the world" (207). Does this mean that we no longer will need the written Word of God? Not at all. The written Word is the very means by which this "holy instinct" is renewed and reprogrammed. As 2:15 indicates, the "requirements of the law" are written on the hearts of all human beings, by virtue of our being created in God's image. Sin corrupted this innate knowledge, but part of Christian salvation is the renewing of the image (JC, 1:201-203). This includes in part "being renewed in knowledge" (Col 3:10), i.e., knowledge of God's law and God's will.

Thus a mind that has been truly renewed can discern God's will in making moral decisions *just because* it has been saturated with the teachings of his Word. Moo is probably right, that Paul is talking about "Christians whose minds are so thoroughly renewed that we know from within, almost instinctively, what we are to do to please God in any given situation" (758). But such an instinct is thoroughly dependent upon the written Word. Paul himself shows that this is the case in the very next section of Romans. Immediately after making this remark about being able to discern the will of God because of the renewing of our minds, the Apostle proceeds to give us several chapters of moral instruction telling us in detail what the will of God consists of (12:3–15:13). Studying and digesting this material contributes to the renewing of our minds.

The will of God of which Paul speaks is his *preceptive* will, his commandments, as distinct from his purposive and permissive wills (see GRu, ch. 8). This preceptive will of God is declared to be equivalent to three things.[13] First, the will of God is the same as what is called "the good." This means primarily "good" in the sense of morally right (Cranfield, 2:610), since God himself is absolute goodness and since God's will is the verbalization of his good nature. Second, the will of God is defined as that which is acceptable or pleasing, i.e., pleasing *to God*. The phrase "to God" does not appear here, but it is used in v. 1 with this same word and is no doubt to be understood here. Third, the will of God is identified

---

[13]These are not adjectives modifying "will of God," but things with which the will of God is identified. They are in apposition to the will of God. See Murray, 2:115; Lenski, 752; Hendriksen, 2:406.

with "the perfect," i.e., with what is "ethically adequate and complete" (Denney, 688). It is all that we need to lead a life that is holy and fulfilled. The same word (τέλειον, *teleion*) is used in Matt 5:48.

The last part of v. 2, whether it expresses purpose or result, shows that a transformation that renews the mind is a necessary prerequisite for being able to discern God's will. An unsaved person cannot trust his "moral instinct." As Cranfield says, it is an illusion to think "that conscience, as such and apart from its renewal by the Spirit and instruction by the discipline of the gospel, is a thoroughly reliable guide to moral conduct" (2:609). I.e., 2:15 is true in principle, but only in a transformed and renewed Christian can this inward inscription of the law even begin to be a trustworthy moral guide.

B. USING THE GIFTS OF GRACE FOR UNSELFISH SERVICE (12:3-8)

Paul now begins to instruct us as to the specific nature of the transformed life. He tells us first of all that it is characterized by humble, unselfish service to our fellow believers. As in 1 Cor 12, he makes this point by using the metaphor of the human body.

Also as in 1 Cor 12, Paul teaches here that the functions performed by the various parts of the body are in accord with the different gifts or abilities bestowed upon us by God. Based on 1 Cor 12:1-11, we usually refer to these as spiritual gifts or gifts of the Spirit. In Rom 12 Paul calls them gifts of grace rather than gifts of the Spirit, but the point is the same. Other listings of such gifts are found in 1 Cor 12:8-10,28-30; Eph 4:11; and 1 Pet 4:10-11. Some gifts appear in more than one list; others appear in only one. No list is exhaustive in itself, and probably all taken together are not exhaustive.

In these verses Paul exhorts us to *evaluate* our gifts honestly and humbly (v. 3), to *dedicate* them to the good of the body as a whole (vv. 4-5), and to *activate* and use them conscientiously (vv. 6-8).

12:3 For by the grace given me I say to every one of you: . . . The spirit of this preface is "mildly imperative" (MP, 490), similar to "I urge" in v. 1. Moo calls it an "authoritative request" (760). The note of authority is found in the words "by the grace given me." Here the word "grace" refers not to salvation from sin but to the gift of Paul's apostleship (see 1:5; JC, 1:77-78). Thus the meaning is "I say to you in my capacity as an Apostle."

The exhortation is directed to the entire church, "to every one of you." The implication for the subject of spiritual gifts is that every Christian has a gift or a special ability of some kind that can be used to build up the body as a whole. See 1 Pet 4:10.

Identifying one's gift calls for honest and impartial self-examination: **Do not think of yourself more highly than you ought, but rather think of yourself with sober judgment, . . .** In v. 2 Paul has just indicated that the Christian's life is transformed by the renewing of his *mind*; here he gives one example of how the renewed mind must think. The key word is "think" (φρονέω, *phroneō*); it appears four times in this short statement, twice as such and twice in compound forms. It means "to set one's mind on, to have a specific opinion about or attitude toward" something (see 8:5; JC, 1:465). Though the words "of yourself" do not appear in the Greek text, it is generally agreed that this is the point. Paul is talking about how a person must view *himself*, "a man's estimation of himself" (Cranfield, 2:613).

The first (negative) side of this command is an exhortation to humility, an exhortation not to have too exalted an opinion of oneself, "not to over-think."[14] The context shows that this applies especially to the subject of spiritual gifts. The Christian "is not to overvalue his abilities, his gifts, or his worth but make an accurate estimate of himself" (MacArthur, 2:158).

The second (positive) part of the command is an exhortation to be sober-minded and to think clearly (σωφρονέω, *sōphroneō*), i.e., to examine oneself as honestly and objectively as possible with a view to assessing the gift with which one has been endowed by God. Such "sober judgment" not only excludes an exaggerated opinion of oneself, but also warns us not to *under*estimate the abilities God has given us. Sometimes a false modesty may be just as detrimental to the church as pride.

One's judgment is accurate when it is **in accordance with the measure of faith God has given you.** The NIV is not very precise here. Instead of "given," Paul actually says "divided, distributed,

---

[14]This translation by Moule (207) is on target; the word is ὑπερφρονέω (*hyperphroneō*). See the similar idea in 11:20b.

apportioned, allotted" (μερίζω, *merizō*). Instead of allotted to "you," he says "allotted to each." The NASB is better: "as God has allotted to each a measure of faith." The main point is that a person's sober estimate of himself must correspond with the "measure of faith" distributed to him by God.

The expression "measure of faith" is notoriously difficult. The word for "measure" (μέτρον, *metron*) can mean either an instrument or a *standard* by which something is measured, or it can mean the amount or *quantity* measured out in a particular situation. "Faith" could refer to the subjective faith by which a person is initially saved (Moule, 208; Cranfield, 2:615; Moo, 761), or the subjective faith by which a person lives the Christian life (Murray, 2:119; MacArthur, 2:161-162). Or "faith" could refer to objective faith, the doctrine or object in which we believe, especially Jesus Christ (Fitzmyer, 646). Or "faith" may be the special miracle-working faith which is one of the gifts of the Spirit (1 Cor 12:9; 13:2; Lard, 382-383; MP, 492).

One major view is that "the measure of faith" refers to *saving* faith as the *standard* by which each person must soberly evaluate himself (Cranfield, 2:615; Moo, 761). This standard forces every Christian "to concentrate his attention on those things in which he is on precisely the same level as his fellow-Christians" (Cranfield). "On this view God has not given a different measure to each Christian but has given to each Christian the same measure" (Moo). This interpretation is unacceptable for several reasons. First, it involves the Calvinist view of irresistible grace, which regards saving faith as an unconditional gift from God. Second and more to the point, the verb *merizō* ("has given," NIV) "is more naturally taken as apportioning of *different* measures," as in 1 Cor 7:17 and 2 Cor 10:13 (Dunn, 2:721). Finally and decisively, this view goes against the whole point of the passage, which is the *variety* (not the sameness) of what God has given to each Christian (see vv. 4, 6). We must honestly evaluate our own unique role in the body of Christ, as it corresponds to the personalized "measure of faith" given to each of us. There is no coherent way to explain how the *saving* faith held in common by all Christians could function as the standard by which our individual gifts might be measured.[15]

[15]These considerations also rule out the view that "faith" is the objective faith embraced equally by all (Fitzmyer, 646).

The point is that God has distributed to each Christian a particular gift. Some identify this gift with the faith itself. This could not be the miracle-working faith of 1 Cor 12:9, since that was given not to all but only to some (Cranfield, 2:614). But it could be a faith analogous to it but not necessarily connected with miracles, a faith which equips each Christian to function in his own unique way in the body of Christ. This is Bruce's view, that this faith is "the spiritual power given to each Christian for the discharge of his special responsibility" (227-228). This special kind of faith would then be the measure against which each Christian should evaluate himself.

This view is possible, but in my opinion, the specific gift God has distributed to each Christian is not the faith as such, but rather the "measure" itself. In this case *metron* does not have the sense of the standard by which we measure ourselves, but the sense of "quantity" or "limited amount." I.e., *God has given to each Christian a measured ability that is appropriate to or that corresponds to his own faith*. This, I believe, is the meaning of this difficult clause. As Murray points out (2:119), faith is involved not only in becoming a Christian but also in the day-by-day living of the Christian life (see 14:23; Phil 4:13). "In the church there is distribution of gift [sic] and each member possesses his own measure for which there is the corresponding faith by which and within the limits of which the gift is to be exercised" (Murray, 2:119). See also MacArthur, 2:161-162.

The main points of this verse are 1) *each* Christian has a gift; 2) these gifts are not all the same; 3) each one's gift has been given to him by God (1 Cor 4:7); and 4) one's gift is therefore no basis for feelings of superiority over others.

12:4-5 Just as each of us has one body with many members, and these members do not all have the same function, so in Christ we who are many form one body, and each member belongs to all the others. The analogy between the church and the body is also found in 1 Cor 10:17; 12:12-31; Eph 1:23; 4:4,11-16; 5:23-30; Col 1:18,24; 2:19; 3:15. Sometimes the point is the relation between the body as such and its head, Jesus Christ; sometimes it is the interrelations among the various members of the body. The latter is the point here. Like the human body, the one church has many members with different yet interdependent functions. I.e., there is *variety* in *unity*.

The unity of the "one body" is "in Christ." No matter how many members a local congregation may have, whether 50 or 5,000, and no matter how many Christians exist worldwide in the invisible church, we are all one body because we have the same Savior and Lord, Jesus Christ.

At the same time we are not an army of identical clones. Like the members of the human body, the members of the church do not all have the same "function" (πράξις, *praxis*, "activity, task, function").[16] As Bruce says, "Diversity, not uniformity, is the mark of God's handiwork," both in nature and in grace (227).

Rather than separating us from one another, though, the variety of gifts only brings us closer together when we see how much we depend on one another. "Each member belongs to all the others," says Paul (v. 5). "Christians, like the various members of a single body, although they differ from one another and have various functions, are all necessary to each other and equally under an obligation to serve one another, because they all belong together in a single whole" (Cranfield, 2:618). No matter how humble my gift may be (1 Cor 12:22-24), every other member of the body depends on it; and no matter how honorable my gift may be, I am dependent upon and blessed by even the humblest contribution of every other member.

12:6 The terseness of the material in vv. 6-8 makes interpretation difficult. Verse 6 begins with a participle ("having"). Some take this as dependent on "each member" in v. 5, with vv. 6b-8 being simply a descriptive listing of the different gifts (Dunn, 2:725, 728). The better and more common view (as in the NIV) is that the essence of vv. 6-8 is not descriptive but imperative, and that "having" in v. 6a begins a new sentence and is dependent on the imperative verbs in the clauses that follow. The problem is that the seven units comprising vv. 6b-8 are not really clauses and contain no verbs at all. These must be supplied.

The NASB supplies a whole imperative clause in the middle of v. 6, "let each exercise them accordingly," and intends for this to govern the seven units that follow, which it translates quite literally,

[16]The KJV translates this as "office," which is misleading. Paul is not referring here to church "offices," but simply to abilities or functions or tasks.

e.g., "if service, in his serving" (v. 7a). In terms of the NASB's supplied imperative the thought would then be, "If your gift is serving, then involve yourself in the work of serving."

The NIV takes a different approach, but the result is the same. Each of the seven units in vv. 6b-8 is converted into an exhortation. The imperative "let him" is added in each case, and the prepositional phrase that ends each unit is converted into a verb. Thus "if serving – in the serving" becomes "If it is serving, let him serve." Both the NASB and the NIV are acceptable; both convey the "underlying hortatory sense" of these verses (Moo, 764; see Murray, 2:121; Cranfield, 2:618).

The beginning of v. 6 emphasizes the *variety* of spiritual gifts: **We have different gifts, according to the grace given us.** On the word for gifts (χαρίσματα, *charismata*; singular, χάρισμα, *charisma*), see 1:11 (JC, 1:93-94). This does not refer to the gift of salvation as such, but to the gifts that endow the recipient with the right and the ability to render special service to the church. Likewise "grace" (χάρις, *charis*) here does not refer to saving grace, but is used in the more general sense of "a gift that brings joy or gladness" (see 1:5; JC, 1:77-78). In this sense *charis* is frequently used for the *charismata*; see v. 3, where Paul uses it for the gift of his own apostolic calling. See also 1 Pet 4:10, where "grace in its various forms" ("manifold grace," NASB) refers to the variety of spiritual gifts bestowed upon the church, or what Paul here calls "different gifts."

What follows is a series of (implied) exhortations urging conscientiousness in the exercise of the gifts discerned through the "sober judgment" mentioned in v. 3. In effect Paul is telling us: "Whatever your gift, be satisfied with it and use it diligently." The seven gifts which are named should be considered as a representative list, not an exhaustive one.

The first gift is prophecy: **If a man's gift is prophesying, let him use it in proportion to his faith** (lit., "if prophecy – according to the proportion of the faith"). The gift of prophecy was very important in the early church, being regarded as second only to the apostleship itself (1 Cor 12:28; Eph 2:20; 3:5).[17] It is named in other lists in

---

[17]Paul does not include apostleship in this list because he has already alluded to it in v. 3, "the grace given me."

1 Cor 12:10,28 and Eph 4:11. Paul stresses its preeminence in relation to other gifts, especially speaking in tongues (1 Cor 14:1,39).

Some equate prophecy in the NT with the ordinary proclamation of the Word. MacArthur calls it "the gift of preaching, of proclaiming the Word of God" (2:170). Lenski says the prophets were not inspired messengers, but simply "expositors of the Word and the will of God" (760). This view is quite unacceptable, however, in view of the lofty place given to this gift as noted above. The NT prophets performed the same function as the OT prophets, namely, they received revelation from God and spoke their revealed messages to God's people under divine inspiration.

Thus the gift of prophecy was a *miraculous* spiritual gift in the same category as speaking in tongues.[18] What a prophet proclaimed was "inspired speech, words given as from 'without' (by the Spirit) and not consciously formulated by the mind" (Dunn, 2:727). An apostle's personal authority was more general and abiding than that of a prophet, but the inspired words of a prophet were just as true and authoritative as the inspired words of an apostle. It is true that a prophet's words had to be weighed and tested (1 Cor 14:29; 1 Thess 5:20-21; see Stott, 327), but even an apostle's authority had to be substantiated by miraculous signs (2 Cor 12:12).

The implied exhortation is that if one does have the gift of prophecy, he must "use it in proportion to his faith." The Greek text does not say "*his* faith," but simply "the faith," with the definite article. This leads some to conclude that Paul is not talking about subjective faith (contra the NIV), but objective faith, i.e., "the faith" in the sense of the content of established biblical and gospel truth (see Jude 3). I.e., a prophet's message must be in a right relation to, or in true agreement with, established truth. (So Lenski, 761-762; Fitzmyer, 647-648; Stott, 327.)

This view is possible, but the very nature of prophecy makes it unlikely. I.e., if prophecy is the proclamation of revealed and inspired truth – which it is, then a prophetic message may in fact

---

[18]Thus if one believes (as I do) that miraculous spiritual gifts ceased to be given after the death of the apostles, then he will not expect anyone to possess the gift of prophecy after the second generation of the church. I see nothing in the contemporary church that is parallel to the NT gift of prophecy. (My view is based in part on 1 Cor 13:8-13.)

be adding completely new material to the existing canon and thus will not be measurable by that canon. I conclude, then, that Paul is referring to a prophet's subjective faith, in the sense explained above in v. 3b. I.e., one who has the gift of prophecy should allow himself to be used by God to the full extent of his faith in the power of God working through him. Thus Paul's exhortation has to do not with the content of the prophecy (over which the prophet has no control anyway), but with the spirit of complete submission with which a prophet must exercise his gift. Understood thus, this same exhortation may be applied to every other spiritual gift as well; and I believe this is Paul's intention, in view of the brevity of the six exhortations that follow.

12:7 If it is serving, let him serve . . . . (lit., "if serving – in the serving"). I.e., if your spiritual gift is serving, then apply yourself to the task of serving to the full extent of your faith in the power of God which is working through you. If God in his wisdom has assessed your faith and assigned to you the gift of serving, then devote yourself to it with all your heart.

The word for "serving" is διακονία (*diakonia*), which is the term for general service or ministry, as in 1 Cor 12:5; and it is similar to the term from which we get our word "deacon," as in 1 Tim 3:8. Some take it in the general sense here (Moule, 209; Morris, 441); see 1 Pet 4:10-11, where the verb form of the word is used inclusively. Many others take it in the more narrow sense of "deacon," not necessarily as the formal name of an office but as representing a specific function. A main reason for the latter view is that (unlike 1 Pet 4:10-11) the word is part of a longer list of specific gifts and therefore seems to be distinguished from them rather than to include them (see SH, 357; Moo, 766).

What specific function is in view? Some speculate that it refers to the ministry of the Word (Acts 6:4), a ministry of *spiritual* service, since it is listed between prophecy and teaching (Lenski, 762-763; see Murray, 2:123-124). Others, rightly concluding that the order of the list is not decisive, see it as referring to the ministry of meeting the *material* needs of the less fortunate in the congregation (Acts 6:1), "a ministry of mercy to the poor and infirm" (Murray, 2:124), or "church benevolence" (Hendriksen, 2:412). So also SH, 357; Moo, 766. I agree with the latter view. *Diakonia* here is probably similar to the "helps" listed in 1 Cor 12:28 ("those able to help others," NIV). In some ways it may be similar to the office of deacon as this is understood by many today (Lard, 385; MP, 494; Murray, 2:124; Hendriksen, 2:410; Cranfield, 2:622; Moo, 766).

[I]f it is teaching, let him teach . . . . (lit., "if one who teaches – in the teaching"). I.e., if you have been given the ability to teach, then apply yourself fully to the task of teaching.[19] This gift is also listed in 1 Cor 12:28-29 and Eph 4:11.

"Teaching" is best understood by comparing it with the gifts of prophecy and encouragement or exhortation (v. 8). Whereas prophecy is the gift of speaking messages directly inspired by God, teaching is the insightful exposition of the meaning and application of such inspired material, including OT Scripture and New Covenant revelation (Moule, 209; Cranfield, 2:623; Dunn, 2:729). A person with the gift of teaching thus is someone "divinely gifted with special ability to interpret and present God's truth understandably" (MacArthur, 2:172). As such the work of a teacher is directed toward the mind or the understanding, as compared with the work of an encourager (exhorter), which is directed mainly toward the feelings, the conscience, and the will (Murray, 2:125; see Godet, 432).

12:8 This leads us directly to the next gift: **if it is encouraging, let him encourage . . . .** The word is παρακαλέω (*parakaleō*), translated "I urge" in v. 1, and better translated here as "exhorting" (see the NASB). Literally it reads, "If one who exhorts – in the exhortation." I.e., if you have been given the ability to exhort, then apply yourself fully to that task.

The main work of an exhorter is to encourage and persuade Christians to act upon the knowledge received through prophecy and teaching, or as Cranfield says, "to help Christians to live out their obedience to the gospel" (2:624-625). One with the gift of exhorting knows how to touch the heart; he is able to deliver "a stirring appeal to men to do their duty" (Lard, 386).

[I]f it is contributing to the needs of others, let him give generously . . . . (lit., "the one who shares – in simplicity"). In the Greek

[19]The first two gifts are listed as nouns, "prophecy" and "service." This and the remaining four gifts are listed as participles, referring to the person thus gifted.

the word "if" is omitted here and in the next two items, but the thought is no doubt to be carried over from the preceding ones. Also, the prepositional phrase that forms the second part of each of these three last items does not simply repeat the action of the first part. By now, this part of the exhortation is to be understood. A prepositional phrase is still added, but it describes the *manner* in which the gift is to be used. Thus when this terse exhortation is fleshed out in view of carry-over elements from vv. 6-7, it has this sense: "If you have been given the gift of sharing, then apply yourself fully to this task to the full extent of your faith in the power of God at work within you; and do so with simplicity of motive."

The NIV interprets the single word, "sharing," to mean "contributing to the needs of others." This is no doubt Paul's point. Morris rightly says it refers to "those who had the gift of coming to the assistance of the poor" (442). Some have taken this to refer to the ability to administer the benevolent funds of the church in general (Calvin, 462-463), but most rightly see it as private benevolence, or the use of one's own funds to meet the needs of others. The essence of the gift includes the ability to earn significant amounts of money (or the simple possession of wealth), plus a "God-given inclination to give" (Cranfield, 2:625).

That it refers to private benevolence is supported by the fact that church benevolence has already been covered in the "serving" in v. 7 (Murray, 2:125; Hendriksen, 2:412), and by the sense of the qualifying phrase at the end ("in simplicity"; see Dunn, 2:730; Moo, 768).

The noun in this final phrase is ἁπλότης (*haplotēs*), the basic meaning of which is "simplicity [KJV], singleness, single-mindedness." When applied to actions it connotes pure motivation and thus sincerity (Eph 6:5; Col 3:22). But this noun also came to mean "generosity" or "liberality" in reference to giving. Either connotation is appropriate here. To give with simplicity means to give with the simple, unselfish purpose of wanting to help others, "and not with mixed motives, with the thought of ostentation or reward" (SH, 357), i.e., not with an ulterior motive. The connotation of generosity naturally goes with the gift of giving, though, and this is how most translations render it.

[I]f it is leadership, let him govern diligently . . . . (lit., "the one who leads – with diligence"). The verb translated "leadership" literally means "to stand before or in front of." This can mean "to stand before people for the purpose of protecting, aiding, or helping them,"[20] or "to stand before people for the purpose of leading, governing, or presiding over them." Here some retain the concept of leader but still take it mainly in the former sense, as referring to one who administers or directs the benevolent work of the church (Godet, 433; Cranfield, 2:626; Dunn, 2:731); see the RSV, "he who gives aid." This conclusion is based largely on the placement of this gift in the list, i.e., between two other forms of aid-giving. Also, it is near the bottom of the list; the theory is that if it refers to leadership, it should be nearer the top of the list.

I disagree with this reasoning; other than beginning with the gift of prophecy, the list does not seem to be ranked or arranged in any particular order.[21] Also, those who administer the benevolent work of the church have already been named ("serving," v. 7). Thus the NIV correctly gives it the connotation of leadership and governing (so also the NASB and NRSV). Some see this as referring to leaders of all kinds (SH, 358), or "anyone who is placed at the head of others" (Lenski, 765). Indeed, the term may be used for one who manages his household (1 Tim 3:4,5,12), but here it probably refers to those who are leaders in the church (as in 1 Thess 5:12 and 1 Tim 5:17), specifically the elders.[22] It is probably the same as "gifts of administration" in 1 Cor 12:28.

The elders are exhorted to "govern diligently," i.e., with eagerness, earnestness, zeal, and devotion. That is to say, elders must not approach their work with idleness and indifference (DeWelt, 200), because the very salvation of those under their care is at stake (Acts 20:28; Heb 13:17).

This brings us to the final gift: **if it is showing mercy, let him do it cheerfully** (lit., "the one who shows mercy – with cheerfulness"). Paul has already named the gift of serving (general church benevolence) and the gift of sharing (private benevolence). But there are

---

[20]See the meaning of the related word προστάτις (*prostatis*) in 16:2.

[21]If it is odd to list leadership so low on the list (Dunn, 2:731), it would be odder still to omit it altogether, which would be the effect of limiting the word to benevolent activity here.

[22]So also Calvin, 463; Lard, 387; DeWelt, 200; Murray, 2:128; Hendriksen, 2:412; Moo, 768-769. Compare Heb 13:17.

many acts of mercy that do not involve the giving of money or material goods, and these are probably what Paul refers to here. These include such things as visiting the sick at home or in hospitals, visiting and helping shut-ins, comforting the dying and the bereaved, visiting and corresponding with prisoners, and sending cards to or telephoning any of these.

Such acts of mercy do not emphasize the giving of money but rather the giving of one's heart in genuine love, caring, and sympathy. Money may be given anonymously and without personal involvement, but the gift of showing mercy is exercised through interpersonal, one-on-one, intimate contacts with people in need (see Murray, 2:127). Thus such a gift may be manifested in any Christian, rich or poor; and in many ways it is more vital than the giving of material goods. The one who has this gift is "divinely endowed with special sensitivity to suffering and sorrow," which includes the ability to notice when others are in misery and distress, and the desire to alleviate such distress (MacArthur, 2:177).

To show mercy "cheerfully" means to do so not from a sense of begrudging duty but from the desire of a joyful heart. This is necessary not just for the sake of the one showing mercy, but also for the purpose of unburdening the spirit of those being ministered to. As Godet says, a cheerful spirit makes the mercy-giver "a sunbeam penetrating into the sick-chamber and to the heart of the afflicted" (433).

C. MISCELLANEOUS MORAL TEACHING (12:9-16)

In this paragraph Paul continues to instruct us about the content of the sanctified life, with a slight change of direction. Whereas in the previous paragraph the exhortations about spiritual gifts apply individually only to those who have the particular gift in view, here the exhortations are general and apply equally to all Christians. This is not an exhaustive handbook on ethics, though, but rather a list of some of the more basic characteristics of the transformed life.

Though this teaching has a decidedly Christian flavor, for the most part it is not something newly revealed to and through Paul. Included are "maxims of traditional Jewish wisdom" rooted in the OT, and echoes of the teaching of Jesus as it was already being circulated among the churches (Dunn, 2:738, 745). Especially reflected here are the exceptionally high moral standards established by Jesus, representing a pattern of behavior regarded as foolish by the carnal mind and attainable only by the regeneration and renewing of the Holy Spirit.

As in the previous section, the moral maxims in this paragraph are set forth in a terse, no-nonsense style. As Moo says, "Paul fires off a volley of short, sharp injunctions with little elaboration" (771). These injunctions are mostly brief participial phrases, with a few infinitives and imperatives mixed in. It is generally agreed that they are all prescriptive and not just descriptive. I.e., they are "the equivalent of imperatives" (Fitzmyer, 653); they have the force of commandments. They are, as Bruce says, "the law of Christ" (228).

Some place vv. 9-21 under a common heading, e.g., "Love as the Norm for Social Relationships" (Dunn, 2:736); "Love and Its Manifestations," (Moo, 769). I think it is better to take vv. 17-21 as a separate unit, though, since it is a longer elaboration of a single theme and seems to be a preparation for 13:1-7. Also, some divide the material between verses 13 and 14, declaring that vv. 9-13 are about a Christian's relationships with his fellow believers, while vv. 14ff. are about his relationships with the unbelieving world (e.g., Cranfield, 2:629; Dunn, 2:738, 755). In my opinion such a division is forced. For example, v. 12 is more about our inner spiritual life than our relations with others, and vv. 15-16 are surely about our relations with other Christians.

There does not appear to be any logical order to this series of admonitions. They are a miscellany of mandates, a potpourri of prescriptions summing up the essence of the sanctified life.

A final introductory question is whether the first declaration, "Love must be sincere" (v. 9a), is intended to be a heading over the entire section, or whether it is just the first exhortation in the list. Many interpreters take it as a heading, and see what follows as an elaboration of what it means to love one another (e.g., Dunn, 2:738-739, 752; Moo, 774-775; Spicq, *Lexicon*, 1:135). "Each staccato imperative [in vv. 9b-16] adds a fresh ingredient to the apostle's recipe for love," says Stott (330).

There is an important truth here, since every command is always in a sense just a facet of the general commandments to love God and one's neighbor (Matt 22:36-40; Rom 13:8-10). I question the idea that the love command is the intended general heading for this paragraph, however. Actually it is not a command, and not even a full statement. It is a phrase which reads literally, "Love sincere." If it were meant to be a heading, we would expect the words to be reversed: "[This is] sincere love: . . . ." As it stands, it has the force of a commandment about the *character* of love, i.e., "[Let your] love [be] sincere." I agree with the judgment that love may be the "ruling thought" of the paragraph, "but the Apostle does not allow himself to be confined and pours forth directions as to the moral and spiritual life which crowd into his mind" (SH, 360).

12:9 Love must be sincere. Whether it be a heading or not, it is appropriate for this injunction to appear first, given the supreme importance of the virtue of love. Jesus singled it out as the essence of God's law (Matt 22:36-40) and as the central demand of the New Covenant (John 13:34-35); thus it "quickly became enshrined as the foundational and characteristic ethical norm of Christianity" (Moo, 775).

This applies primarily, of course, to the kind of love called ἀγάπη (*agapē*), which is the subject here. The Greeks knew several kinds of love, including a form of *agapē* (see Lewis, *Loves*; GRe, 327-328, 336-345); but the noun *agapē* was first used with "theological density" by the LXX (Spicq, *Lexicon*, 1:18), and was taken over and given a uniquely Christian meaning by Jesus and the NT writers (Dunn, 2:739; Moo, 775). This Christian meaning is drawn from the nature of God himself as displayed in his work of salvation through Jesus Christ, i.e., his selfless and sacrificial concern for the happiness and well-being of others (8:39; John 3:16; 1 John 4:10).

This is the essence of the *agapē* enjoined upon us as Christians. It differs from the other forms of love in that it does not depend upon some uncontrollable inner emotion or desire or need for fulfillment within the one who loves, but rather is a deliberately willed attitude of concern and good will based on the needs of the one who is loved.

The point of Paul's injunction is not that Christians should love one another, since this commandment should be something engrained on every Christian's mind from the beginning of his renewed life. Rather, the point is that the love we profess must be *sincere*; it must be from the heart and not be an external mask only.

The word for "sincere" is ἀνυπόκριτος (*anypokritos*), which means "unhypocritical, unfeigned, genuine, not counterfeit, without pretense or sham." Literally it means "without a mask." In the world of Greek drama "the *hypokritēs* was the 'play-actor' who projects an image and hides his true identity behind a mask" (Dunn, 2:740). Metaphorically and morally, a *hypokritēs* (a hypocrite) is anyone who pretends to be something he is not. Christians are commanded to be without hypocrisy not only in love (see also 2 Cor 6:6; 1 Pet 1:22) but also in faith (1 Tim 1:5; 2 Tim 1:5) and wisdom (Jas 3:17).

Murray notes that there is no vice worse than hypocrisy, just as there is no virtue surpassing love; thus hypocritical love is the ultimate moral contradiction (2:128).

Hate what is evil; cling to what is good. (See Amos 5:15, "Hate evil, love good.") Here good and evil are general terms, representing everything that is morally wicked and ungodly, and everything that is morally good and holy.

The verbs are very forceful. The word for hate "expresses a strong feeling of horror" (SH, 360), and implies loathing, abhorrence, and disgust. It means that Christians cannot just passively ignore evil, but must actively and aggressively oppose it and speak out against it (DeWelt, 200-201), and flee from it (1 Tim 6:11; 2 Tim 2:22). The hatred of sin, especially one's own, is the starting point for repentance.

The verb for "cling to" is likewise strong. In the active voice it means to join or glue two things together. Here in the middle voice it means "attach yourself closely" to everything that is good. The Christian must cleave to what is good and never let go of it; this begins by becoming united together with Jesus Christ (1 Cor 6:17).

The message here is clear: there can be no neutrality in the moral realm. We cannot hide behind some alleged moral or cultural relativism. Good and evil objectively exist in God's own nature and in God's law. Christians must take a clear and unequivocal stand against the evil and for the good.

12:10 Be devoted to one another in brotherly love. Here Paul moves from the general love (*agapē*) Christians must have for all people, to the more intimate love we must also have toward one another. He uses words compounded from two other Greek words for love, φιλία (*philia*) and στοργή (*storgē*). The former is used for the affectionate love between friends; the latter, the tender affection among family members.

"Be devoted" (φιλόστοργος, *philostorgos*) is a combination of both these terms, but has the nuance of *storgē*. It is a kind of instinctive affection, like that which parents and children feel toward one another.[23] It is "an attachment sealed by nature and blood ties," and especially represents "the mother's innate love, benevolence, and devotion toward her children" (Spicq, *Lexicon*, 3:462-463). It implies that the relationships among Christians should involve intimacy, understanding, and acceptance.

The other word is φιλαδελφία (*philadelphia*). It is a combination of φιλία (*philia*) and ἀδελφός (*adelphos*, "brother") and literally means "brotherly love."[24] As members of God's family and spiritual siblings of Jesus Christ (1:13; 8:12-17; 2 Cor 6:18), Christians truly have a sibling relationship with one another. Thus we are exhorted to develop the close and affectionate relationship that should exist among brothers and sisters.

The use of both of these words together does two things. First, it magnifies the importance of understanding the church as a family. In most cases the local congregation is like the immediate family, and the church universal is the extended family. Second, it intensifies the need to consciously seek to develop toward one another the tender affection and devotion appropriate among brothers and sisters.

Honor one another above yourselves. "Honor one another" is straightforward; it means to treat one another with genuine respect. This includes the general respect due to all Christians as members of the King's own household, and the specific respect and appreciation due to those who have made special contributions to the work of the kingdom. The same applies on a different level even to those outside the church (13:7b).

"Above yourselves" is not so easy. This is a rendering of the verb προηγέομαι (*proēgeomai*), which literally means "to go before,

---

[23]In 1:31 "heartless" (NASB, "unloving") is literally "without *storgē*," without natural family affection. See JC, 1:165.

[24]Other places where this word is used are 1 Thess 4:9; Heb 13:1; 1 Pet 1:22; 2 Pet 1:7. See 1 Pet 3:8, *philadelphos*.

to lead the way." Some thus take it to mean "set an example" (Lard, 389-390; MP, 498), or "show the way to one another" (Dunn, 2:741). I.e., in the matter of giving honor to others, each should try to set an example for all.

Others take this word to mean "to surpass, to outdo, to take the lead." I.e., "when it comes to bestowing honor, we are to take the lead" (McGuiggan, 368); we should try to "outdo one another in showing honor" (RSV; NRSV; Fitzmyer, 654; Moo, 777-778). "The thought can well be," says Murray, "that instead of looking and waiting for praise from others we should be foremost in according them honour" (2:129-130).

A third interpretation, reflected in the NIV, is that this verb can be translated "to prefer, to put first." This is the choice of the NASB also: "Give preference to one another in honor." I.e., give honor to your fellow believers "by putting them first" (MacArthur, 2:189). The main problem with this view is that this verb is not known to be used in this sense anywhere else (it appears only here in the NT). Many give it this meaning anyway, seeing a parallel between this verse and Phil 2:3b, "in humility consider others better than yourselves" (see Cranfield, 2:632-633; Hendriksen, 2:415). "The condition and result of true affection are that no one seeks his own honour or position, and every one is willing to give honour to others" (SH, 361).

Any one of these views is possible. Whichever we adopt, the main point is that we must exhibit toward one another the spirit of courtesy, unselfishness, and humility. See Murray, 2:130.

12:11 This verse is not a single neat sentence but a string of three short, sharp imperatival, participial phrases that express three basic Christian states of mind: "As to zeal – not slothful; as to the Spirit – on fire; as to the Lord – serving." The first appears in the NIV thus: **Never be lacking in zeal, . . .** The word for "zeal" (σπουδή, *spoudē*) is used in v. 8 in the expression "diligently" or "with diligence" (NASB).[25] Its verb form has the sense of "to apply oneself diligently to, to devote oneself to" a task. *Spoudē* itself means "fervor, zeal, eagerness, ardor, passion, enthusiasm."

[25]It has nothing to do with "business" (KJV) in the vocational sense of the word, but perhaps could be understood as "busyness."

"Never be lacking" is literally "not slow, not slothful, not lagging behind (NASB), not hesitant, not lazy, not complacent." The word for "lacking" describes "a person showing hesitation . . . through weariness, sloth, fear, bashfulness, or reserve" (Dunn, 2:741). It describes a loafer or a sluggard who is slow to get started, or who puts off fulfilling his Christian duties. See Prov 6:6-11; 21:25; 22:13; 26:13-16. As Cranfield says, Paul is warning us against "that attitude which seeks to get by with as little work and inconvenience as possible, which shrinks from dust and heat and resents the necessity for any exertion as a burden and imposition" (2:633).

It is interesting that in the LXX *spoudē* ("zeal") is almost always translated "haste." Spicq says, "The idea of 'haste, rapidity, alacrity' is in the forefront" of this word (*Lexicon*, 3:276-277). Thus Paul is making a kind of play on these words. In those matters of the Christian life that demand haste, do not be slow!

[B]ut keep your spiritual fervor . . . . (lit., "in the Spirit – on fire"). "Fervor" is from the verb *zeō*, "to bubble, to boil, to seethe, to burn." It is used of water boiling or of metal glowing with heat. Metaphorically it means to burn with desire or passion or rage (see Oepke, "ζέω," 2:875-876). In the context of Christian service (as here), it means "to be full of energy, to be on fire with zeal and enthusiasm." It is a warning against settling into comfortable, shallow ruts in our spiritual lives.

Paul says literally that we must be glowing or burning "in the Spirit." The issue here is whether he means our human spirit[26] or the Holy Spirit.[27] The same expression is used of Apollos in Acts 18:25, where it seems best to understand it as his own spirit, since he had not yet received the Holy Spirit in Christian baptism. But it is not necessary to interpret the phrase in the same way here. Indeed, the reference in the next phrase to "the Lord" gives us reason to see it as referring here to the Holy Spirit. The meaning would then be that "the Christian is to allow himself to be set on

---

[26]Advocates include Godet, 435; Lard, 390; Lenski, 769; Moule, 211; and Fitzmyer, 654. The NASB and NRSV translate it "in spirit." This view is implied by the NIV's "spiritual fervor."

[27]Supporters include Cranfield, 2:634; Dunn, 2:742; Hendriksen, 2:415; Bruce, 229; Stott, 331; and Moo, 778. The RSV translates it "aglow with the Spirit."

fire . . . by the Holy Spirit" (Cranfield, 2:634). Rather than depending on external stimulation (such as innovative worship programming), we must look to the Spirit within us to energize us and fire us up for Christian service.

. . . serving the Lord.[28] "The Lord" is specifically Jesus Christ. "Lord" (κύριος, *kyrios*) has the connotation of owner or master; "serving" (δουλεύω, *douleuō*) has the connotation of serving as a slave, a δοῦλος (*doulos*). This exhortation to serve the Lord as a slave refers not just to external obedience but also to the inner spiritual attitude of submission to the Lord's authority over us. We must be "obedient from the heart" (6:17). In other words it refers not just to individual acts of obedience, but to the willing acceptance of a certain identity. This is who we are: we are slaves, "serving the Lord." See 6:16,18,22.

12:12 Here is another triad of exhortations that are loosely related to each other, literally: "As to hope – rejoicing; as to affliction – patiently enduring; as to prayer – steadfastly persisting." The first appears in the NIV as **Be joyful in hope, . . .** Over and over the NT exhorts us to "Rejoice!" (e.g., Matt 5:12; Phil 3:1; 4:4; Rev 19:7). The word is χαίρω (*chairō*), which is related to the word for grace (χαρις, *charis*).

Paul indicates that one specific source of our joy as Christians is our *hope*, which of course is based on the grace bestowed upon us in Christ Jesus. Christian hope is not just a fond wish, but is an earnest and confident expectation of the full salvation awaiting us at the *eschaton*. See 4:18; 5:2 (JC, 1:301, 315). No matter what our present circumstances may be, when we think about the sure glory of heaven yet to come, we cannot help but be filled with joy! "Let hope keep you joyful," as Dunn puts it (2:742). "Hope of future salvation . . . stimulates present joy," says Hendriksen (2:415). It enables us to live our daily Christian lives with "the eagerness of a pilgrim going home" (DeWelt, 201).

---

[28]In some manuscripts *kyrios* ("Lord") has been replaced by *kairos* ("time"), yielding a meaning similar to Col 4:5, "redeeming the time" (KJV), or "making the most of every opportunity." Compare the contemporary maxim, "Seize the day." *Kyrios* is the preferred reading. See Cranfield, 2:634-636; Moo, 769-770.

The next admonition is to be **patient in affliction, . . .**[29] This follows naturally from the former; our hope-inspired joy gives us the courage to hold up under the afflictions of this age.[30] Afflictions include the various sufferings to which all men are susceptible because of the fallenness of this present world; they also include the opposition and persecution Christians can expect just because we are Christians (John 16:23; Acts 14:22; Rev 7:14).

"Be patient" is ὑπομένω (*hypomenō*). Cranfield says this translation is too weak; he suggests "hold out steadfastly" (2:637). The noun form (ὑπομενή, *hypomenē*) was used in 5:3-5; it means "patient endurance, steadfastness, the ability to bear up under whatever comes along" (JC, 1:317). These words have the nuance of "bearing up with courage" and "enduring what is hard to bear," i.e., "perseverance despite difficulties" (Spicq, *Lexicon*, 3:416-417, 419).

The next exhortation is related to this sort of situation but cannot be limited to it: be **faithful in prayer.** It is natural and proper to fall back on prayer in the midst of affliction or persecution, but we must not wait for trouble to befall us before we are moved to pray. The word translated "be faithful" is used with reference to prayer also in Acts 1:14; 2:42; 6:4; Col 4:2. It means "to continue steadfastly in, to persevere in, to persist in" prayer. "The idea is constant diligence, effort that never lets up, confident waiting for results" (Spicq, *Lexicon*, 3:193). See Luke 18:1; Eph 6:18; 1 Thess 5:17. The spirit or attitude of prayer, as well as regular times for praying, should be a major aspect of a Christian's life.

12:13 The two exhortations in this verse fall under the general heading of benevolence. They direct us to cultivate the spirit of giving, which befits those who are saved by grace. First, **Share with God's people**[31] **who are in need.**[32] This verse refers literally to "the needs of the saints," with physical needs such as food and clothing

---

[29]On the word for "affliction," see 5:3 (JC, 1:316).

[30]From another perspective, affliction can produce even more hope. See 5:3-5.

[31]"God's people" is literally "saints." See on 1:7 (JC, 1:85).

[32]Instead of χρεία (*chreia*, "need"), some manuscripts have μνεία (*mneia*), "remembrance." In this case the verse would be enjoining us to join together in remembering the saints. "Need" is the preferred reading. See Cranfield, 2:638; Dunn, 2:737.

being specifically in view. "To share with" is κοινωνέω (*koinōneō*), which is related to κοινωνία (*koinōnia*, "fellowship, sharing, participation (in)." These words are sometimes used for the gift or contribution of one's own money or material goods toward providing for the needs of the poor, or for the needs of gospel preachers.[33]

The idea is not just the outward act of giving, though, but sharing in one's own heart the burden of need felt by the needy, and the sense of a common ownership of those things that can meet these needs (Acts 4:32-35). In Murray's words, "We are to identify ourselves with the needs of the saints and make them our own" (2:133). Lard says, "When the children of God fall into want, take a part of their wants upon yourselves. Make their wants your wants to the full extent of your ability to relieve them" (391).

Some Christians are especially gifted to meet the needs of the saints, whether in a leadership capacity (12:7) or individually (12:8); but here Paul tells us that every Christian has a responsibility to participate in the church's ministry of benevolence to some degree. See Gal 6:10.

The Apostle zeroes in on a very specific kind of need when he says, **Practice hospitality.** "Hospitality" (φιλοξενία, *philoxenia*) is literally "love of strangers," or treating a stranger (ξένος, *xenos*) as a friend (φίλος, *philos*). It refers to the practice of hosting travelers. In NT times it was not nearly as easy for travelers to find safe and reasonable accommodations as it is today, so this would have been an important service. In most ancient cultures hospitality was a prized virtue, and it is identified as an important Christian virtue as well (see Matt 25:35; 1 Tim 3:2; Titus 1:8; Heb 13:2; 1 Pet 4:9; 3 John 5-8). It was especially necessary to care for itinerate preachers and Christians fleeing persecution.

"Practice" is an inadequate translation for the strong verb διώκω (*diōkō*; see v. 14). It means "to run after, to chase, to pursue, to strive for, to earnestly aspire to or seek after." In other words, we

---

[33]On the former see Heb 13:16; 1 Tim 6:18 (κοινωνικός, *koinōnikos*). On the latter see Phil 1:5; 4:15; Gal 6:6. In 15:26 and 2 Cor 9:13 Paul uses *koinōnia* for the churches' "contribution" for the poor saints in Jerusalem (see 2 Cor 8:4). Dunn thinks this is what Paul has in mind here (2:743), but this is probably not the case. This seems to be a general exhortation with general application (Lenski, 772).

should take the initiative in this matter of hospitality. Lenski says, "Hospitality is literally to be chased after as one hunts an animal and delights to carry the booty home" (773). Spicq relates the story of a pagan Greek citizen, Gallias of Agrigentum, who in the fourth century B.C. was so hospitable "that he posted his slaves at the city gates to welcome strangers when they presented themselves and ask them to his house" (*Lexicon*, 3:455). Some Christians have been known to build extra rooms on their houses in order to provide for traveling evangelists and missionaries on furlough.

12:14 Bless those who persecute you; bless and do not curse. This admonition may have been suggested to Paul by the fact that the word *diōkō* can mean both "pursue" (as in v. 13) and also "persecute" (as here). That Christians may expect to be persecuted, i.e., forced to suffer hurt and hatred and unjust treatment, is a common theme in the NT (Matt 5:10-11; John 15:20; 2 Tim 3:12).

Exactly what is God here requiring of us? Not just to endure persecution, not just to refrain from striking back at our persecutors, and not even just to refrain from wishing them harm. Rather, he is requiring us to pray a prayer of *blessing* for our persecutors. To "bless" in this sense is to ask God to bestow his favor upon someone. To "curse" would be the opposite, i.e., to call upon God to bring harm upon someone (Dunn, 2:744).

But how is this possible? As Murray says, the very fact that persecution is so unreasonable and unfair makes it seem inevitable and natural for its victims to have feelings of animosity and vindictiveness toward its perpetrators (2:134). Thus to *bless* those who persecute us seems to be the very opposite of the so-called "natural" response. This is what makes this admonition so striking and, on the face of it, so impossible to obey. Murray observes that "no practical exhortation places greater demands upon our spirits" than this (2:134). It surely "requires a powerful effort of the will," says Godet; and that is probably why it is repeated with such emphasis (436).

But this is the whole point of the renewing of the mind and the transformed life (v. 2): the regeneration of the Holy Spirit enables us to do what may seem impossible in the eyes of those still held captive by the powers of sin. God may require the "impossible," but he empowers us to achieve it! (See Cranfield, 2:640-641.) Jesus himself has shown us how to do this even in the most extreme circumstances (Luke 23:34), and the martyr Stephen has demonstrated that even an ordinary human being can follow Jesus' example (Acts 7:60).

We should note that Paul is not giving us a new teaching on this subject, but is just passing along commands already uttered by Jesus Christ: "Love your enemies and pray for those who persecute you" (Matt 5:44); and "bless those who curse you, pray for those who mistreat you" (Luke 6:28).

12:15 Rejoice with those who rejoice; mourn with those who mourn. Here is another requirement of love that will seem difficult for many, because it focuses on the emotional life. Many of us have enough difficulty "getting in touch with" our own feelings, but Paul exhorts us to get in touch even with the feelings of others! He calls for *compassion*, which literally means "suffering with"; and for *empathy*, which is the ability to identify with and actually experience the feelings and inner dispositions of others. See 1 Cor 12:26.[34]

To "rejoice with those who rejoice," to "share in one another's triumphs, joys, and successes," is probably the harder of the two commandments, as Fitzmyer observes (655). To see others succeed (especially where we may have failed) leads easily to negative feelings of envy, jealousy, and resentment. Through the renewing power of the Holy Spirit we must fight against such tendencies and be genuinely happy and filled with good will when others have cause to rejoice. MacArthur says, "It is distinctively Christian to rejoice in the blessings, honor, and welfare of others" (2:197).

To feel compassion toward others who are suffering may seem easier, but often it too requires deliberate, Spirit-assisted effort. It is easy to be indifferent toward the troubles and sorrows of others, especially when we ourselves are caught up in troubles of our own. Even worse, more often than we like to admit, we have a tendency to be glad when misfortune overtakes certain people. This is usually the case when their sufferings are the result of their own carelessness or sinful folly. Here we must guard against the urge to say, "It serves them right!"

---

[34]This probably refers to relationships among Christians, but Cranfield thinks it applies to a Christian's relations with unbelievers as well (2:641-642).

12:16 The final verse in this section is a series of exhortations condemning pride and enjoining humility. First Paul says, **Live in harmony with one another.** "Live in harmony" is a very loose translation of "think the same thing" or "think the same way." The word for "think" is φρονέω (*phroneō*; see 12:3); the idea is that we should all have the same attitude toward one another.

Some take this to mean that all Christians should have harmony and agreement in our doctrinal thinking, at least on the basics (see Cranfield, 2:643; Dunn, 2:746). Such doctrinal harmony is required of the church, to be sure (15:5-6; 1 Cor 1:10; Eph 4:13-15), but this is probably not Paul's point here. He does not just say, "Have the same mind," period. Nor does he say, "Think the same thoughts *along with* one another." Rather, he specifically says, "Think the same thing *toward* [εἰς, *eis*] one another." As Lard puts it, "Be of the same disposition one toward another; or have the same sentiments and feelings" (392). See Lenski, 775; Moo, 782-783. The NEB (first edition) captures this idea: "Have equal regard for one another." The TEV says, "Have the same concern for everyone."

This is the kind of harmony of which Paul is speaking, i.e., that we should all have the same attitudes and a common mindset toward one another. Exactly what is the content of this mindset? He has just been telling us: sincere love (v. 9a), family affection (v. 10a), mutual honor and respect (v. 10b), a spirit of sharing (v. 13), and empathetic joy and sorrow (v. 15).

What is the greatest hindrance to such harmonious attitudes? Putting oneself and one's own happiness ahead of that of others; having too high an opinion of oneself; in a word, pride. Thus in the interest of removing this barrier to harmony, Paul enjoins us thus: **Do not be proud, but be willing to associate with people of low position.** Literally he says, "Do not think high things," about yourself. This is basically the same as the admonitions in 11:20 and 12:3. We are to avoid self-aggrandizement, or thinking so highly of ourselves that the desires and opinions of others no longer matter.

The word for "associate with" should not be translated "condescend" as in the KJV, since this English word has a very unsavory connotation today. The word (in the passive voice) literally means "to be led along or carried away with" something or someone. The thought here is "to go along with, to be at home with, to associate comfortably with" the lowly.

A major question is whether "the lowly" (ταπεινός, *tapeinos*) here is masculine ("humble people") or neuter ("humble things").[35] Since this seems to be in contrast with "Do not think high *things*" (neuter), some take it as humble *things* (e.g., Lard, 392-393; Murray, 2:136; SH, 364). But since *tapeinos* is used elsewhere in the NT only for people, and since the main point of the verse seems to be interrelationships among Christian people, most take this as a reference to humble *people*, as in the NIV (e.g., Godet, 437; Cranfield, 2:644; Fitzmyer, 656). The NEB says, "go about with humble folk." Hendriksen puts it, "Do not be snobbish, but readily associate with humble folk" (2:419).[36]

The latter approach (as in the NIV) is to be preferred: Associate with people who are *tapeinos*. In the Greek world such a person was not "humble" in the sense of showing humility, but in the sense of having a position in life regarded as inferior because of his origin or occupation. The *tapeinos* person was "base, ignoble, of low birth . . . , servile . . . , working at a humble occupation . . . , held in low esteem" (Spicq, *Lexicon*, 3:370).

Paul's point is that, insofar as we are able, we must ignore the caste distinctions and social classes imposed by our various cultures, and look upon all people, especially our Christian brothers and sisters, in the same way. The Apostle does not tell us to associate *only* with "people of low position"; he tells us rather to include these folks in our circle of friends and not to discriminate against them. It would be appropriate, though, to pay special attention to those regarded as lowly in one's particular culture, since these are the ones more likely to be shunned by the world in general.

The final admonition in this paragraph is, **Do not be conceited**, or "Do not become wise in your own eyes" (see discussion on 11:25). "Wise" is φρόνιμος (*phronimos*), which is a positive attribute in itself ("sensible, thoughtful, wise"). The idea here, though, is not to let your wisdom become ingrown, or not to consider yourself to be the ultimate measure of wisdom. Paul thus forbids "that self-

---

[35]The dative case is the same for both genders, so this has to be settled by the context.

[36]Some think it may be deliberately ambiguous and refer both to lowly tasks and to people of low estate (Dunn, 2:747; Morris, 450; see Moo, 783).

sufficiency by which our own judgment is so highly esteemed that we will not have regard to wisdom that comes from any other source" (Murray, 2:137). As McGuiggan words it, "Don't take yourself too seriously. Others really *can* teach you something" (373).

D. PERSONAL VENGEANCE IS FORBIDDEN (12:17-21)

Paul is still explaining the essence of the sanctified life, but this is a new paragraph for two reasons. First, regarding form, the previous section (vv. 9-16) was basically a series of one-liners: short, terse exhortations in no particular order, handed to us like beads on a string. This section, though, seems to be a substantial development of a single theme. Second, for the most part, insofar as personal relationships are in view, vv. 9-16 tell us how Christians should relate to one another. In the present paragraph the emphasis is mainly on our relations with unbelievers, in particular those who in some way have caused us harm or injury.

Exactly what is the topic being discussed here? Our heading identifies it as personal vengeance. This is stated at the beginning in v. 17, "Do not repay anyone evil for evil," and is repeated in v. 19, "Do not take revenge." Sometimes these exhortations are equated with v. 14, "Bless those who persecute you"; but they are not exactly the same. Persecution is a specific kind of injury; it is injury inflicted upon a Christian just because he is a Christian ("because of me," Matt 5:11). Verses 17-21 are more general and speak of evil done to someone for *any* reason, including persecution but not limited to it.

What should a Christian do when harmed by another person,[37] i.e., when he is cheated, insulted, assaulted, cursed, robbed, or treated unjustly in any way? The almost-universal tendency is to personally strike back, to retaliate, to try to get even, to make the evildoer pay for the harm he has done, i.e., to seek personal revenge. Paul's point is that this tendency must be resisted. It is wrong for anyone to take it upon himself, personally, to exact vengeance upon someone who has harmed him.

[37]The other person could even be another Christian, but he is more likely to be an unbeliever.

This is not to say that vengeance as such, or seeing that the evildoer pays for his wrongdoing, is wrong. This is nothing more and nothing less than retributive justice, which as an ethical principle is just as eternally valid as mercy itself. The point is that there is an important limitation on who is permitted to be the instrument of retributive justice: vengeance is *God's* prerogative, not that of the person whose rights have been violated. Verse 19 states this clearly: "Never take your own revenge, beloved, but leave room for the wrath of God, for it is written, 'Vengeance is Mine, I will repay,' says the Lord" (NASB).

A crucial question, though, is *how and when* God pours out his vengeance upon evildoers. The answer is twofold. On the one hand, God's vengeance in the form of eternal wrath will be poured out upon all unbelieving evildoers at the final judgment (Heb 10:30). But on the other hand – and this is *extremely important* – God's vengeance in the form of temporal punishment is poured out *now* through his appointed servants, those who work in civil government.

The break between Rom 12 and Rom 13 is quite unfortunate, since it tends to obscure the deliberate connection between 12:17-21 and 13:1-7, which are two sides of one coin. Individuals (not just Christians, but *all* individuals) should not take their own revenge (12:17-21), because God has assigned the responsibility for exacting vengeance in his name here on earth to human government (13:1-7).

The proximity of these two passages, one forbidding personal revenge and the other affirming government's responsibility for retributive justice, shows the continuity between the Old Covenant ethic and the New Covenant ethic on this matter. Very often, Christian pacifists and others interpret Christ's teaching in Matt 5:38-48 as a repudiation of the OT ethic and a prohibition of vengeance in any form. Paul's teaching shows this is not the case. The key to understanding Christ's teaching is the distinction between personal vengeance, which is forbidden, and God's own vengeance rendered through civil government, which is necessary and right. Jesus was speaking only of the former, not the latter.

The Law of Moses included both teachings. On the one hand, it absolutely forbade personal vengeance: "Do not seek revenge or bear a grudge against one of your people, but love your neighbor as yourself" (Lev 19:18). Thus neither Jesus nor Paul was the first to teach this. On the other hand, Moses' Law required civil judges to measure out punishment to evildoers that fit the crime, no more and no less. This was the point of the *lex talionis*, the "eye-for-an-eye" principle. This principle is stated three times in the Mosaic Law: Exod 21:23-25; Lev 24:19-20; and Deut 19:21. In each case it is set forth as a rule to be applied only in a judicial context, not by individuals or by the injured parties themselves.

In Rom 12:17–13:7 Paul teaches the same two moral rules: no personal vengeance, and retributive justice only in the context of a court of law. The latter is the same as the "eye-for-an-eye" principle, which has *not* been repealed. Jesus does not repeal it in Matt 5:38-48. In that part of the Sermon on the Mount our Lord corrects rabbinic misinterpretations and misapplications of OT Law. One such misapplication was the wrongful use of the "eye-for-an-eye" principle as justification for personal revenge. This is what Jesus is repudiating. He is not contradicting the OT Law, nor is he setting this principle aside. He is simply saying, like Moses and Paul, that individuals do not have the right to take their own *personal* revenge. The *lex talionis* as it stood in the Law of Moses was never meant to apply to personal revenge; it was meant to be applied only by civil government. This is Paul's point in Romans. Jesus himself makes no reference to the role of civil government; he is concerned only with the way *individuals* should respond to those who have wronged them.[38] But Jesus does not contradict anything said by Paul. The following chart summarizes this:

	Law of Moses	**Jesus**	**Paul**
No personal revenge:	Lev 19:18	Matt 5:38-48	Rom 12:17-21
Governmental retribution:	Exod 21:23-25; Lev 24:19-20; Deut 19:21	[silence]	Rom 13:1-7

[38]Jesus and Paul did modify the OT prohibition in one respect. In view of God's plan to separate the nation of Israel from the unbelieving nations, Lev 19:18 limits the prohibition to one's fellow Israelites, "Do not seek revenge or bear a grudge against *one of your people*, but love *your neighbor* as yourself." Jesus and Paul expand this to include everyone, including one's *enemies* (Matt 5:43-45). The principle itself remains basically the same, however.

Clearly there are continuity and harmony among the Law of Moses, Jesus, and Paul on this subject. The prohibition of personal revenge and the approval of governmental retribution are not contradictory but complementary. Thus it is not wrong for governments to punish criminals, nor is it wrong for Christians to punish criminals when they are serving in an official capacity as representatives of civil government, e.g., as jurors, judges, or correctional workers. What is wrong is for *anyone*, Christians and unbelievers alike, to take justice into their own hands.[39]

12:17 Do not repay anyone evil for evil. By "evil" Paul means any injury or injustice, any situation in which someone "does you wrong." Our first inclination when we have been thus wronged is to strike back and "get even." This spirit of revenge, retaliation, and vindictiveness is what Paul is forbidding here.

As explained in the introduction above, this is not a condemnation of vengeance as such, but *personal* vengeance only, i.e., making oneself the instrument by which the wrongdoer is made to suffer. Vengeance is God's prerogative, and he has his own ways of working it out.

Paul's use of the word translated "anyone" (lit., "to no one") shows that this admonition applies to our relationships with all people and not just our fellow Christians. In fact, "to no one" is the first word in the sentence in the Greek, making it emphatic that this is a universal rule.

Other biblical references expressing this same rule include Lev 19:18; Matt 5:39-44; Luke 6:27-30; 1 Thess 5:15; and 1 Pet 3:9.

Be careful to do what is right in the eyes of everybody. "Be careful" is προνοέω (*pronoeō*), which literally means "to think about in advance." It means to give serious thought to something. "What is right" is καλά (*kala*; neuter plural of καλός [*kalos*]), "good things." In this context it refers to what is morally good or right; this is in direct contrast with "evil" (κακός, *kakos*) in v. 17a. In vv. 2 and 21 Paul uses another word for "good," ἀγαθός (*agathos*). As

[39]Thus we must reject such statements as this one by Lard, that although the *lex talionis* is "the very embodiment of naked justice, it is unchristian, because wholly unmixed with mercy" (393). The proper distinction is not between Christian and unchristian, but between personal and official.

Wuest explains it, *agathos* refers to intrinsic goodness, "and *kalos*, our word here, to exterior goodness, or goodness that is seen on the exterior of a person, the outward expression of an inward goodness" (218). Such exterior goodness is necessary because what we do as Christians is observed by those around us, and it is important that our conduct, which is open to "the eyes of everybody," brings honor to our God.

The main point is that, instead of reciprocating evil for evil, we should think out ahead of time how we will respond when others attack us or wrong us in some way. By taking forethought we can be ready to respond aright, with "good things," i.e., in such a way that we bear impressive witness before the world.

"In the eyes of everybody" is literally "before or in the sight of all men." Jesus taught that we should let our light shine before men, "that they may see your good deeds and praise your Father in heaven" (Matt 5:16; see 2 Cor 8:21; 1 Pet 2:12). This is a general principle and applies to all areas of our lives. The point is that we should always be sensitive to how our conduct is viewed by others, so as not to cause anyone to stumble or reject the gospel, and so as not to be an occasion for anyone to mock the God we profess to serve (1 Cor 10:32; 2 Cor 4:2; 1 Tim 3:7; 5:14; 1 Pet 2:15). Compare especially Rom 2:23-24. Phillips' translation of v. 17b reads, "See that your public behaviour is above criticism."

We must be careful not to misunderstand Paul here. He is not saying that we should do only what other people consider to be right, as if we are conforming to the world's norms after all, contrary to the command in v. 2. Nor is he saying that we should simply "live out the implications of the gospel" before the world, even if the world does not see the virtue of it (contra Cranfield, 2:646; Morris, 452). Rather, since the conduct of the law is written on the hearts of everyone (2:15), Paul assumes that there is a common core of decency acknowledged by all, or what Hendriksen calls a "public conscience" (2:420). Even if the world itself does not live up to such a standard, it is aware of it and is also keenly aware that Christians have openly subscribed to it. Thus the world is quick to notice when Christians' lives do not conform to this standard, and in such cases is even quicker to mock our faith and our Lord. See Dunn, 2:748; Fitzmyer, 656; Moo, 785.

12:18 If it is possible, as far as it depends on you, live at peace with everyone. See Matt 5:9; Heb 12:14; 1 Pet 3:11. As in v. 17, the admonition is about our relationships not just with other Christians but with everyone in general. As Murray sums it up, "Peaceableness in disposition and behaviour is a virtue to be cultivated in our relations with all men" (2:139). I.e., our goal should be to live in such a way that we would never antagonize anyone or give anyone an occasion for doing evil against us. We should never take the initiative in disturbing the peace (Morris, 452). In fact, we should go out of our way, doing all that is *possible*, to establish and maintain peaceable relations with others (see Matt 5:23-24). As Jesus says, we should *make peace happen* (Matt 5:9).

If it depended *only* on us, we could, through the power of the Holy Spirit working in us, be at peace with all men. But it does not depend just on us. Unfortunately, even after we have done everything in our power to live peaceably with others, sometimes they themselves simply will not allow it. Despite our best efforts they continue to perpetuate a spirit of hostility from their side.

In fact, if we live consistent, faithful lives, and if we take a firm stand for the truth of God's Word and for the uniqueness of Jesus Christ as the only Savior, we can expect to arouse enmity and be openly opposed and hated by those who hate Jesus (Matt 10:22, 34-36; John 16:33). The only way to avoid all such enmity is to compromise our commitment to Jesus, and this we cannot do. I.e., living at peace with others is not the highest virtue. Like Melchizedek, God is *first* King of righteousness, then King of peace (Heb 7:2). God's wisdom is *first* pure, then peaceable (Jas 3:17). Peace is nothing without holiness (Heb 12:14). See Murray 2:139-140.

12:19 Do not take revenge, my friends,[40] but leave room for God's wrath, . . . "Do not take revenge" is literally "not avenging yourselves." Unfortunately the NIV does not translate "yourselves"; the NASB is better: "Never take your own revenge, beloved." The issue is personal revenge, as explained in the introduction to this

[40]"My friends" is literally "beloved." In 1:7 (see JC, 1:85) Paul calls the Roman Christians "beloved of God." Here he uses the same word but does not add "of God," probably meaning they are beloved by him, Paul. "Beloved" is a term of endearment based on our family relationships in Christ (12:9-10).

section. Some see this verse as different from "Do not repay anyone evil for evil" in v. 17. If there is a difference, it is minimal. The verb here is ἐκδοκέω (*ekdokeō*), which means to avenge or punish. "Do not avenge yourself" means "Do not take it upon yourself to punish someone for some wrong he has done to you."

The alternative to personal vengeance is not *no* vengeance, but *God's* vengeance. Paul says, "Leave room for God's wrath." The expression "leave room" means the same thing as in Eph 4:27, i.e., "make room for, give place to." Here Paul means, "Get out of the way and allow God to handle the matter in his own way" (see Lenski, 780). Step aside, back off, and leave it up to the wrath of God.

The Greek text does not specifically say *God's* wrath; it just says "Give place to the wrath." Some (e.g., Moule, 213) have suggested this may mean the wrath of one's enemy, i.e., "Back off and let your enemy's wrath run its course without trying to retaliate." Others have suggested it refers to one's own wrath, i.e, "Slow down and count to ten and give your wrath room to dissipate; then you will not want to retaliate." Another possibility is that it means the wrath of human government. I.e., "Let the civil authorities handle it" (13:4). Almost everyone today agrees, though, that it refers to the wrath of *God*, even though it just says "the wrath" (as in 5:9; 1 Thess 2:16).[41]

Thus whenever we suffer harm or injustice, we must allow God to be our avenger. Wrath is his prerogative, and we must not attempt to usurp it.

[F]or it is written: "It is mine to avenge; I will repay," says the Lord. Here Paul lets us know immediately that he is referring to the wrath of God, by quoting an OT text in which God (the Lord, Yahweh) specifically says, "Vengeance is mine." This is a paraphrase of Deut 32:35, where the Hebrew text says, "To me belongs vengeance and recompense." This is also cited in Heb 10:30, where it refers to the final judgment.

The emphasis here is clearly on God's role as the one who exacts justice. The word order is emphatic: "*To me* belongs vengeance; *I* will repay." This shows that vengeance *per se* is not wrong. The moral issue is simply, who has the *right* to exact vengeance on evildoers; the answer is, God does.

---

[41]On these four views see Murray, 2:140-141.

We must ask, though, exactly when and how God inflicts his wrath upon these evildoers. As explained in the introduction, he does this in two ways. The ultimate expression of divine wrath, of course, is the eschatological wrath of *eternal punishment* in hell (Heb 10:30). Some think Paul is referring to this here (Fitzmyer, 657), or at least mainly to this (Morris, 454). I believe this is an error, though, because God has another means of inflicting his wrath on evildoers, and he is already in the process of doing so even now in this world. The means by which he is doing so is *civil government*, as Paul goes on to explain in this very context, in 13:1-4, especially v. 4. Thus it is a mistake to separate the wrath of government from the wrath of God; ideally they are the same thing.

Thus I believe God's wrath as expressed through civil government is Paul's primary reference here. I.e., "Leave room for God's wrath to work through his appointed servants, the civil rulers. When you try to take your own revenge, you are usurping the divinely-ordained role of government."

We may identify two reasons why God has not left vengeance in the hands of those who have been wronged, but has appointed civil rulers to take care of it instead. First, it is almost always impossible for the wronged party to be objective and even-handed in deciding on a proper punishment for the evildoer; the tendency will always be to go beyond what is warranted. Civil government as a third party (theoretically) can evaluate and decide on such matters objectively and fairly.

Second, some people who are wronged will not on their own have the power or the resources to see that justice is done and the evildoer punished. Thus it is necessary to have a civil government that is strong enough to take vengeance on even the most powerful wrongdoers.

12:20 On the contrary: "If your enemy is hungry, feed him; if he is thirsty, give him something to drink." The strong contrast between the world's tendency to seek personal revenge for wrongs suffered, and the response God demands and expects from those leading a transformed life, is seen in the opening phrase, "on the contrary" (ἀλλά, *alla*). Except for this phrase, this verse is a direct quote from Prov 25:21-22a (LXX).

In a circumstance crying out for revenge, it is not enough for us as individuals to passively refrain from retaliating while allowing

God's vengeance to prevail. Invoking the passage from Proverbs, Paul shows that the wronged party must also have a positive, loving attitude toward the wrongdoer, and must actively take steps to meet needs that he might have. Providing food and drink to satisfy his hunger and thirst are examples of the sort of kindness that must be shown; if these needs are not immediately present, we should look for other ways to give concrete expression to the love for our enemies that Jesus requires (Matt 5:44).

The rest of the quotation from Proverbs reads thus: **"In doing this, you will heap burning coals on his head."** The connecting word γάρ (*gar*, "for, because"), untranslated by the NIV, suggests that what follows is at least the result and possibly the motive for responding to our enemies with acts of kindness.

This is a very difficult clause, because we simply are not sure of the significance of heaping burning coals on someone's head. Two major approaches have been pursued. One interprets the burning coals negatively, as representing ultimate harm upon the enemy; the other takes the coals as a positive symbol representing a good result for the enemy.

The first view had adherents in the early centuries of the church, and has an occasional defender in modern times. In this view the burning coals represent the *wrath of God* (see Ps 11:6; 140:10). The idea is that the acts of kindness bestowed by a victim upon his enemy will in the final judgment only increase his guilt and thus intensify his eternal punishment, if he has not repented by then. Such action could thus be regarded as "a more noble type of revenge," as Fitzmyer puts it (658).

The biggest problem with this view is that it seems to suggest a motive for such acts of kindness that is the exact opposite of everything Paul is teaching about the transformed life. Deeds of kindness done for the express purpose of increasing an enemy's eternal punishment would not be more noble than tit-for-tat retaliation, but less noble. This is why most who have taken this view say that the increased punishment is just the *result* of showing kindness to an enemy, and should never be one's *purpose* or motive (Cranfield, 2:649; Moo, 788). But such a distinction, while clear in theory, would be difficult to maintain in practice, and would only create unnecessary ambiguities for the person who only wants to do the most loving thing for his enemy. Besides, the teaching from Proverbs as quoted by Paul seems to suggest that heaping coals on an enemy's head is the *very reason why* (*gar*) one should do such acts of kindness, and not just the result. Thus the context seems to be against this view. See Cranfield, 2:648-649; Morris, 454-455; Dunn, 2:750; Moo, 788-789.

The second view, rightly accepted by most modern scholars, is that the burning coals are meant to symbolize an *attitude* that may develop within the enemy's heart as a result of his victim's acts of kindness. This attitude is usually identified as the "burning pangs of shame and contrition" (Cranfield, 2:649), or "the vehement pangs and pains of conscience, the torments of shame, remorse, and self-reproach" (MP, 505). This is considered to be a positive result of the kind deeds, since burning shame and a tormented conscience may lead to genuine repentance.[42]

Why should the experience of shame, remorse, and repentance be symbolized by burning coals on the head? The answer to this is not clear. One speculation is that "heaping coals of fire is a figure derived from the crucible, where they were heaped upon the hard metal till it softened and melted" (MP, 505). Acts of kindness may have a similar effect upon a hardened heart. Another suggestion is that the writer of Proverbs was alluding to an Egyptian practice in which a penitent carried a container of live coals on his head as a sign of his contrition and repentance (Cranfield, 2:650; Moo, 789).

Whatever the origin of the metaphor, this view sees the acts of kindness as nothing but a positive expression of love, performed in order to influence the enemy to repent. As Moo says, "Acting kindly toward our enemies is a means of leading them to be ashamed of their conduct toward us and, perhaps, to repent and turn to the Lord whose love we embody" (789). In Stott's words, "The coals of fire this may heap on him are intended to heal, not to hurt, to win, not to alienate, in fact, to shame him into repentance" (337). Whether such repentance actually occurs is not the point;

[42]Some distinguish between the coals as a symbol of shame and the coals as a symbol of repentance (see Fitzmyer, 658; Lenski, 781; Morris, 455; Stott, 336). This is not appropriate, however, since the shame is meant to ultimately result in repentance.

what matters is that we have done for our enemy what our transformed life requires and makes possible. See Cranfield, 2:649-50; Dunn, 2:750-751; Moo, 788-789.

12:21 Do not be overcome by evil, but overcome evil with good. This could be an unlimited exhortation that applies to our battle against evil in general, but Paul more likely intends it to sum up his teaching about personal revenge in this paragraph.

"Do not be conquered by evil," or "Do not let evil gain the victory over you," means "Do not give in to the temptation to get even with your tormenter. Do not seek personal revenge." "Evil" (lit., "the evil") is not "the evil person," or the enemy himself. Rather, it refers to moral evil as a power that seeks to overcome us. We allow the power of evil to conquer us when we resort to acts of personal revenge.

To "overcome evil with good" means first to resist the temptation to retaliate in kind against one who has wronged us, and then to respond with acts of kindness instead. When we do this, we win the victory not only over the evil done against us by the enemy, but also over the evil we are tempted to do in retaliation.

E. THE RELATION BETWEEN CITIZENS AND GOVERNMENT (13:1-7)

In this section we have what appears to be an abrupt change of subject, as Paul turns his attention to the relationship between citizens and government. The main point, as Stott says, seems to be "conscientious citizenship" (338). The paragraph as a whole is "a coherent and well-organized argument about . . . the need for submission to governing authorities" (Moo, 790). But there is another side to the coin. While stating the citizens' responsibility toward government, Paul gives us very valuable information about the government's responsibility toward its citizens. Indeed, this passage presents the clearest biblical teaching concerning the divine origin and God-intended purpose of human government.

Why does Paul introduce this subject at this particular point? Some have argued that the passage has no logical connection with the context, and may even be an interpolation by someone other than Paul.[43] One reason some regard it thus is that there is nothing christological about the passage (see Cranfield, 2:651). Fitzmyer (663) says, "It is remarkable that Paul can discuss this topic in the absence of any christological consideration." Cranfield himself tries to discern an implicit christological element here, but the result is strained to say the least (2:653-655).

Some argue that Paul did not intend to state general truths here, but rather was addressing specific problems faced by the early church (especially in Rome).[44] Such an approach is highly speculative, however, since Paul does not allude to any particular circumstances facing the Roman Christians or the church in general (SH, 369). Lenski is correct to regard such speculation as going off on a tangent (784).

Another possibility is that Paul stresses obedience to civil government in view of "the danger of perverted notions of freedom" (Murray, 2:146). I.e., some might try to argue from "you are not under law, but under grace" (6:14) to a position of civil antinomianism or anarchy. Thus Paul shows that being free from law as a way of salvation does not relieve us of the obligation to obey either the laws of God (6:1ff.) or the laws of man.

Actually we do not have to go outside the immediate context to see how this paragraph fits into Paul's purposes in this section of his epistle. The subject here is the virtues required of those who are living the transformed life. Submission to authority is simply one aspect of God's will for us – "his good, pleasing and perfect will" (12:2; see Murray, 2:145). God's will for Christians includes not just specifically Christian duties such as the unselfish use of spiritual gifts (12:3-8), but also the laws of the Creator that apply to all human beings as his creatures. This passage falls into the latter category; its application is universal and applies to "everyone" (13:1). Dunn is correct: "The argument is theological, not Christological; it is expressed in terms of the normal circumstances of social order, not in terms of salvation-history" (2:772). This reminds us that Christianity is not just a "religion"; it is a *worldview*.

---

[43]See the discussion of such views in Cranfield, 2:651-655; and Moo, 791.

[44]The material is "context-specific," says Dunn (2:768). See the discussion in Fitzmyer, 662-663; and Moo, 792-793.

Without a doubt the most immediate contextual connection is with the preceding paragraph, 12:17-21. The teaching concerning the role of government in 13:3-4 deliberately complements the teaching about personal nonretaliation in 12:19.[45] These doctrines are in a sense just two sides of one coin, despite the unfortunate chapter division after 12:21. Paul wants to make it clear that the prohibition of personal vengeance does not mean that evildoers are free to do all the harm they please, without restraint and without fear of any kind of punishment at all. While individuals are not allowed to take their own vengeance against those who do them wrong, God has established civil government to be his earthly agent to see that such vengeance (i.e., justice) is carried out. We should never teach or preach from either of these paragraphs (12:17-21 and 13:1-7) without referring to the other.

Before turning to a detailed exegesis of this passage, I will give a brief systematic summary of its teaching. I must reemphasize that this instruction is not just a temporary expedient to be applied to some local problem only, but is "an important basis for a general theology of the state," contra Dunn (2:768). We are dealing here with "broad general principles" that apply to all times (SH, 369; so also Godet, 440; Lenski, 784; Fitzmyer, 664). We should also note that Paul is here describing the role or purpose of government in the *ideal*, as God intends for it to be carried out according to his preceptive will. This is "government as it *should* be" (Moo, 809), "the divine ideal, not the human reality" (Stott, 341).[46]

Paul's instruction on the one hand sets forth the responsibility of government toward its citizens; on the other hand it describes the responsibility of citizens toward their government. Regarding the former, the purpose of government is to *uphold justice*, which includes both the protection of the rights of all citizens, and the punishment of evildoers. It is important that these functions not be separated as if they were unrelated to one another. Actually they belong together as *means* and *end*.

---

[45]Murray denies that the sequence is deliberate (2:145-146), but Moo (792) grants that 12:19 may have been "the specific contextual trigger" for this teaching about government.

[46]See chs. 1–7 in Cottrell, *Questions, Part 2*, especially ch. 2, "The Purpose of Government."

The ultimate goal or purpose of government is a positive one, i.e., to protect the rights of its citizens. As such it is "the guardian of justice," as Godet puts it (439). This positive task is described in 13:4, "he is God's servant to do you good." It is stated in more detail in 1 Tim 2:2, which says we should pray for governing authorities to the end "that we may live peaceful and quiet lives in all godliness and holiness." The ultimate purpose of government is to make this possible.

The means by which government is meant to accomplish this is the punishment of those who do in fact violate the rights of others. This "punishment of evildoers" (1 Pet 2:14, NASB) is government's negative purpose. In one sense such punishment can be regarded as an end in itself, since the wrongdoer deserves it as a matter of retributive justice (wrath and vengeance – 12:19; 13:4). But in another sense punishment of criminals, functioning as a deterrant, is just a means of preserving the general state of peace and tranquility.

Thus ideally, government exists "to make justice reign by checking evil and upholding good" (Godet, 445). This is the reason why God ordained it in the first place. And we should not overlook this point: God is the one who has established human government and decreed its purpose. He has not prescribed any one particular *form* of government; any type that can accomplish his declared purpose is acceptable. But government as such is God's creation and God's servant. It is not inherently evil, and there is no inherent conflict between being a good Christian and being an instrument of the state.

We may now ask, what are the requirements of a good citizen, according to this passage? First and most important is the obligation to acknowledge and submit to the authority of civil rulers, and obey the various laws and regulations they impose on us in the interest of justice (13:1). We should remember that Paul's instruction here applies to the ideal situation. He does not go into the many "what if" circumstances that may require civil disobedience (see Cottrell, *Questions*, 2:33-35). Civil government is inherently good, but it can be corrupted just like any other institution. If it becomes perverted to the point that it requires us to do something contrary to God's revealed will, then "we must obey God rather than men" (Acts 5:29). Governmental authority is binding upon all citizens, but it is not absolute (see Stott, 342).

The second requirement of good citizens is that they must have an attitude of respect toward government and its representatives, insofar as the latter are functioning in their governmental roles as God's own servants (13:7b). A final requirement is that citizens must pay taxes to support those who devote themselves to the work of government, and to provide the equipment and programs that are necessary to uphold justice.

13:1 Everyone must submit himself to the governing authorities, . . . This exhortation reflects the most fundamental aspect of the relation between government and its citizens. Paul deliberately uses the universal terminology, "everyone" (πᾶσα ψυχή, *pasa psychē*), to show that what he is about to say applies to all people and not just to Christians (contra Cranfield, 2:656). The word *psychē* is the Greek word for "soul"; thus the KJV translation, "every soul." Here it does not mean the inner spiritual nature as distinct from the body (as in Matt 10:28; Rev 6:9), but refers rather to the whole person, body and spirit (see 2:9). This is a common meaning of the term. "Everyone" or "every person" (NASB) is a good translation.

"Authorities" is the plural form of ἐξουσία (*exousia*), the common word for "right, power, authority." The concept of authority includes the right to tell others what to do, and the right to enforce compliance through the exercise of power. In the plural, as here, it refers to the individuals who bear and exercise such authority. Sometimes the word is used for angelic beings, including the fallen angels who attempt to usurp authority (see Eph 3:10; 6:12; Col 1:16; 2:15; 1 Pet 3:22). This has led some to think that Paul is referring to angelic authorities here, or perhaps is making a double reference to human and angelic authorities; but this view is generally rejected today.[47] The context shows and most agree that Paul is referring to human rulers, or "duly constituted human governing authorities" (Fitzmyer, 666). See Luke 12:11 and Titus 3:1 for this use.

The word "authorities" is modified by a term (ὑπερέχω, *hyperechō*) that means "to surpass, to rise above, to be in a high position" (see the KJV, "higher" powers). Most agree that this word is used here

[47]See the lengthy presentations and refutations of this view in Murray (2:252-256) and Cranfield (2:656-659). See also Hendriksen (2:430-431) and Moo (796, n. 22).

not to distinguish higher-placed governing officials from lesser ones, but simply to distinguish government officials, who have authority, from ordinary citizens, who do not. In my judgment, though, the main point of the modifier is to distinguish *governmental* authorities from other kinds of authorities, as will be explained below. The NIV's "*governing* authorities" makes this point very well.

The basic relation between citizens and government is here summed up in one word: "submit." This is the Greek word ὑποτάσσω (*hypotassō*), which along with its noun form ὑποταγή (*hypotagē*) is used over forty times in the NT. It is used to describe creatures' submission to divine authority (e.g., 1 Cor 15:27-28; Eph 1:22; 5:24; Jas 4:7; 1 Pet 3:22); demons' submission to Christ's disciples (Luke 10:17,20); the submission of the incarnate Son to the authority of God the Father (1 Cor 15:28); and the submission of human beings to other human beings who are in positions of authority over them. The last category includes children submitting to parents (1 Tim 3:4), slaves submitting to masters (Titus 2:9; 1 Pet 2:18); Wives/women submitting to husbands/men (1 Cor 14:34; Eph 5:21-24; Col 3:18; 1 Tim 2:11; Titus 2:5; 1 Pet 3:1-5); and, as here, citizens submitting to government (also Titus 3:1; 1 Pet 2:13).

The verb *hypotassō* is formed by combining the preposition ὑπό (*hypo*) with the verb τάσσω (*tassō*). The basic meaning of *tassō* is "to appoint, to ordain, to determine, to arrange in order." The related noun τάγμα (*tagma*) refers to that which has been so ordered or fixed, either collectively (referring to a whole group such as a military troop) or individually (referring to the position or rank held by a particular member of the group (Delling, "τάσσω," 27-32). The preposition *hypo* means basically "under, below."

It is easy to see that the combination of these two words into *hypotassō* means "to place under, to subordinate, to arrange in order of rank." As Delling says, "Originally it is a hierarchical term which stresses the relation to superiors" ("τάσσω," 41; see 39-40). In our text it is in the middle voice, which usually means "to subject oneself, to be subservient, to submit, to surrender one's own rights or will, to acknowledge another's dominion, to obey" (ibid., 40). In the NT the term refers to an order or arrangement set in place by God himself, and the action in the middle voice refers to acquiescence to this divinely-willed order. "In *hypotassesthai* [submitting] to state, husband, and master the primary point is recognition of the existing relation of superordination" (ibid., 43-44).

One question is whether this word means or includes the concept of *obedience*. Some versions translate the word as "obey" (e.g., Phillips; TEV) or "be obedient" (Weymouth), and some exegetes use these terms in their explanation of the verse (Lard, 397; SH, 365; Barrett, 244-245; Newman & Nida, 244). Cranfield is reluctant to include the element of obedience in view of what he calls the "reciprocal obligation" in Eph 5:21.[48] But Murray is on the right track when he says the term includes but is not limited to obedience. "It implies obedience when ordinances to be obeyed are in view," as is the case with submission to government, but also includes an *attitude* of "willing subservience" to governmental authority (2:148).

We should note that "submission" and "authority" go together; Dunn correctly says that the one is the "natural correlative" of the other, "whatever the authority in question" whether of husbands, of parents, of masters, or of civil rulers (Dunn, 2:760).

[F]or there is no authority except that which God has established. The authorities that exist have been established by God. Most if not all commentators take these statements as referring to individual rulers and governments, and thus to God's sovereign choice and appointment of all such authorities. Now, it is true that God is in complete control of all the nations and rulers of this world. He appoints and arranges specific governments by his special providence as his purposes call for it, and his omnipotence and omniscience enable him to control all others within his general providence and permissive will. This is a common OT theme: Prov 8:15-16; Isa 45:1-7; Jer 27:5-6; Dan 2:21,37-38; 4:17,25,32; 5:21.[49]

The fact remains that if we take Paul to be referring here to individual governments and rulers, then we have no choice but to say that God has hand-picked and personally put into office every blood-thirsty tyrant, every genocidal dictator, every anti-Christian regime, every crooked politician and judge, every sadistic sheriff and police officer, and every immoral and bribe-taking public official

---

[48]Cranfield, 2:660-662. See my refutation of the common idea of "mutual submission" in the sense of reciprocity in *Feminism*, 301-307.

[49]See my thorough discussion of all that is at stake here in GRu, chs. 4–5, pp. 117-228.

who now exists, has ever existed, and ever will exist. Most take it exactly this way. As Cranfield says, "No one actually exercises ruling authority unless God has . . . set him up" (2:663). Moo says this is "a universally applicable truth about the ultimate origin of rulers"; it refers to "specific governmental officials" (798). "Thus the government in force and the ruler in power in any country at any given time are, *de facto*, God-appointed" (MP, 507).

It is easy to see how such an understanding can be used to justify every form of tyranny and to coerce citizens into blind obedience to the most degrading and antibiblical demands. It is no wonder that J.C. O'Neill has said of 13:1-7, "These seven verses have caused more unhappiness and misery in the Christian East and West than any other seven verses in the New Testament."[50]

In my opinion, this whole approach to 13:1b is wrong. I do not believe Paul is referring here to individual governments and rulers at all, but rather to the various *forms* or *spheres* of authority which God has established, including governmental authority along with all the others. In fact, I suggest that vv. 1b-2 are a parenthesis in which Paul is asserting the general truth that *all* forms of authority have been established by God, and that rebellion against *any* of them is rebellion against God himself and deserves his condemnation. In other words, vv. 1b-2 express the general principle, of which v. 1a is a specific application.

The second clause in v. 1 ("For there is no authority except that which God has established") begins with "for" and states a *reason* why everyone must submit to the governing authorities. The reason is that all valid human authority comes from God himself. He is the only one who has absolute, inherent authority. When he delegates authority to others, it is in a real sense still his own authority. Thus, because governing authorities are wielding authority given to them by God, we should be submissive to them.

In this second clause the word "authority," which is singular, should not be taken as referring to civil authority as such, but to authority of whatever type, i.e., "For there is no authority *of any kind* . . . ." The last part of the clause literally says, "except by God," and means, "except that which has been established by God." Thus

---

[50]Cited in Morris, 457, n. 1.

the entire clause reads thus: "For there is no authority of any kind except that which has been established by God."

The last clause in the verse is simply a positive restatement of the preceding one. "The authorities that exist" refers to all the existing authority relationships, including but not limited to governmental authority. All such authorities have been "established by God." The word for "establish" is *tassō*, which as explained above means "to ordain, to determine, to appoint." Since all authority ultimately comes from God, all existing authority-submission relationships have been ordained and arranged by God himself.

My contention, then, is that the word *exousia*, "authority," as used within the parenthesis (vv. 1b-2) means *authority in general*, authority in all of its forms. This is why *exousia* is modified by *hyperechō* in v. 1a – to specify *which* authority Paul has in mind. This word (especially as a participle), along with its noun form, ὑπεροχή (*hyperochē*), often refers to those in political or social positions, and especially to rulers (Delling, "ὑπερέχω," 523). "Οἱ ὑπερέχοντες is a fixed term for rulers," says Delling ("τάσσω," 43). See 1 Tim 2:2; 1 Pet 2:13.

Thus by qualifying the *exousiais* in v. 1a as *governing* authorities, Paul makes it clear that he is talking about *that* kind of authority in particular, as distinct from the other kinds. The use of the expression οἱ ἄρχοντες (*hoi archontes*, "the rulers") in v. 3 marks Paul's postparenthetical return to his discussion of *governing* authorities in particular.

What other kinds of human authority has God ordained, in addition to governmental authorities? We can easily determine this by examining the way the NT uses *exousia* and other words denoting authority, along with their "natural correlatives" (Dunn, 2:761), i.e., words denoting submission and obedience.[51] Having done this we may list without further comment the following authority-submission relationships:

1. Man/woman	1 Cor 11:3,10 (*kephalē, exousia*)
	1 Tim 2:11 (*hypotagē*)
2. Husband/wife	1 Cor 14:34 (*hypotassō*)
	Eph 5:21-24 (*hypotassō, kephalē*)

[51]The relevant words are *exousia*, "authority"; *kephalē*, "head" (see Cottrell, *Feminism*, 308-313); *peithō*, "obey"; *hypakouō*, "obey"; *hypeikō*, "submit"; *hypotagē*, "submission"; and *hypotassō*, "submit."

	Col 3:18 (*hypotassō*)
	Titus 2:5 (*hypotassō*)
	1 Pet 3:1,5,6 (*hypotassō, hypakouō*)
3. Parents/children	Luke 2:51 (*hypotassō*)
	Eph 6:1 (*hypakouō*)
	Col 3:20 (*hypakouō*)
	1 Tim 3:4 (*hypotagē*)
4. Elders/congregation	Heb 13:17 (*peithō, hypeikō*)
	1 Pet 5:5 (*hypotassō*)
5. Master/slave	Eph 6:5 (*hypakouō*)
	Col 3:20 (*hypakouō*)
	Titus 2:9 (*hypotassō*)
	1 Pet 2:18 (*hypotassō*)

13:2 Consequently, he who rebels against the authority is rebelling against what God has instituted, . . . According to the interpretation I am offering here, this continues the parenthesis and thus refers to rebellion against authority (*exousia*) of all kinds, but with special contextual reference to rebellion against civil authority.

The NIV term "rebel" translates two different Greek words. One is ἀντιτάσσω (*antitassō*), which refers to an attitude that is the very opposite of *hypotassō*, "submit," v. 1. The other is ἀνθίστημι (*anthistēmi*), which literally means "to take a stand against." "He who rebels against the authority" refers to anyone who opposes authority as such, or to anyone who resists a particular kind of authority or any individual who exercises that authority.

The opening word, "consequently," indicates that a conclusion is being drawn from the latter part of v. 1. Since all human authority ultimately derives from God, those who rebel against authority are really rebelling against God himself. Paul says they are setting themselves against "what God has instituted," literally, "the ordinance of God" (NASB). "Ordinance" is διαταγή (*diatagē*), which is directly related to *tassō* ("established") in v. 1. The use of this term again emphasizes the divine origin of all human authority.

. . . and those who do so will bring judgment on themselves. "Judgment" is κρίμα (*krima*), which usually stands for a negative judgment, i.e., punishment or condemnation (see 2:2-3; JC, 1:181-182). The main point is that those who refuse to submit to God's ordained authorities will bring his own divine condemnation upon themselves, to be meted out at the final judgment.[52] Since in this context the main reference is to governmental authority, it is possible that the *krima* also refers to the punishment exacted upon wrongdoers by civil rulers acting as agents of God's wrath (v. 4).[53]

13:3 For rulers hold no terror for those who do right, but for those who do wrong. After the parenthesis concerning authority in general, Paul now returns to the specific subject of *governing* authorities, calling them "rulers" (ἄρχων, *archōn*) to distinguish them from the other kinds of authority. He is answering the question, *why* should everyone submit to the governing authorities (v. 1a)? The parenthesis in vv. 1b-2 gives the most fundamental answer, i.e., because every authority including civil authority is ordained by God himself, and those who oppose authority of any kind must answer to God. Here he begins to give a more pragmatic answer: because (*gar*, "for") those who do not submit will be punished by the civil authorities themselves.

Paul presents this thought in terms of "terror," or fear (φόβος, *phobos*) in the sense of fear of punishment.[54] He states the principle thus (lit.): rulers are not a (cause for) terror to the good work (i.e., good conduct), but to the evil (i.e., bad conduct).[55] Since government exists to uphold justice by protecting the rights of its citizens, the evil deeds which should be forbidden by law and thus punished by rulers are those acts that violate the rights of others (e.g., disturbing the peace, theft of property, bodily harm).

Civil rulers have a divine mandate to punish evildoers; thus (ideally) anyone who contemplates breaking the law should be terrified by the thought of being caught and punished, and thus should decide to refrain from the evil deed. It is clear that fear of punishment is a proper motivation for obeying the laws of the land. As Dunn says, it is "something desirable for the good ordering of society" (2:763). This means that our legal systems should operate at least in part according to the principle of deterrence (see Deut 13:11; 17:13; 19:20; 21:21).

---

[52]So MP, 509; Cranfield, 2:664; Dunn, 2:762; Moo, 799.

[53]So SH, 367; Murray, 2:149; MacArthur, 2:221.

[54]See on 3:18; JC, 1:239. See also on the verb φοβέω (*phobeō*), 11:20.

[55]See 12:9,17,21 for other references to good (ἀγαθός [*agathos*], καλός [*kalos*]) and evil (πονηρός [*ponēros*], κακός [*kakos*]) together.

The obvious fact is that citizens have but two options in reference to civil laws: we may either obey them or disobey them. It is also clear that the system of civil law operates according to the very same rules as God's law for mankind: "Keep the commandments and escape the penalty; break the commandments and suffer the penalty" (JC, 1:128). Paul elaborates on these two points in the two parallel sections which follow, vv. 3b-4a and v. 4b.

First Paul explains the relation between government and law-abiding citizens. **Do you want to be free from fear of the one in authority? Then do what is right and he will commend you.** Up to this point Paul has been stating general principles in third person. Now he switches to second person singular, addressing each of us in a more intimate way. After asking us if we want to live without being afraid of civil authority, he tells us how to do this: "Do what is right," or what is "good." Since in this context "good" and "evil" are defined in terms of respecting the rights of other people, "doing right" is simply living in such a way that your conduct does not interfere with the rights of others.

If we do this, we not only should be free from the fear of punishment, but should also actually be commended or praised by our civil authorities (see 1 Pet 2:14). Exactly what this commendation or approval involves or should involve is not clear. Moo suggests that the reference may be to "the practice of Roman authorities of publishing on inscriptions the names of 'benefactors' of society," but is probably not limited to this (800-801, n. 50).

13:4 For he is God's servant to do you good. Paul is still speaking to "you" as the law-abiding citizen, the one who does what is right, whether Christian or non-Christian. He urges submission to the civil ruler on the basis of the fact that he is a servant or minister (διάκονος, *diakonos*) of God. "Of God" is in a position of emphasis in the Greek, i.e., he is a minister *of God!* The term *diakonos* was frequently used in secular Greek for civil officials and had no specific religious connotation (Dunn, 2:764; cf. "prime minister," "minister of defense"). Paul's point is that such "ministers" are not just servants of the people but are first of all servants *of God.* This is true because governmental authority as such has been established by God (v. 1); therefore anyone who functions as an enforcer of civil authority is serving God's purposes whether he acknowledges it or not (see Isa 45:1).

God's purpose is that the civil ruler exercise his authority "to you for good." I.e., he should do so for the benefit of you who want to live peaceably and abide by the laws of the land. Government exists not for its own sake, but for the sake of its citizens. It seeks their "good." This "good" should not be equated with the providential blessings promised to Christians in 8:28 (contra Cranfield, 2:666); it consists rather of the "civic well-being" which government provides by protecting us from unjust treatment from others (see 1 Tim 2:2).

Paul now switches gears and describes the relation between government and law*breakers*. He still uses direct address: **But if you do wrong, be afraid, . . .** The appeal is still to the fear of punishment, i.e., "As you are contemplating the carrying out of your intended evil deeds, you should be deterred when you remember the punishment you will receive at the hands of the civil authorities."

The next clause is a simple statement of fact: **for he does not bear the sword for nothing.** Outside the NT the word "sword" (μάχαιρα, *machaira*) was used for a wide variety of cutting instruments and weapons, including knives, daggers, and swords long and short (Michaelis, "μάχαιρα," 524-525). In the NT it is used quite frequently for a weapon of violence and death (Matt 10:34; 26:52,55; Luke 21:24; Rev 6:4; 13:10,14), including capital punishment (Acts 12:2; Rom 8:35; Heb 11:34,37). The form of the verb translated "bear" implies "repeated or habitual action," and thus can mean "wear" (Dunn, 2:764). In NT times the sword was worn as a symbol of governmental authority. To "wear the sword" meant to possess the right and the power to coerce obedience to law via threat of punishment, and to punish lawbreakers even unto death.

There can be no serious doubt that Paul is here sanctioning capital punishment as a legitimate instrument of the state (see Stott, 344-345).[56] In view of the way the sword is so frequently associated with death by execution, says Murray, to deny that it includes capital punishment in 13:4 "would be so arbitrary as to bear upon its face prejudice contrary to the evidence" (2:152-153). Those who argue that the transformed life replaces wrath with grace miss Paul's point altogether. God's purpose has always been that individuals

---

[56]See also Moule, 216; Lenski, 792; Dunn, 2:764; MacArthur, 2:225; Fitzmyer, 668; Moo, 802, n. 54.

respond to personal attacks with grace and forgiveness (12:17-21), but at the same time the government's job has always been – and still is – to punish evildoers according to the demands of justice, including the death penalty (Gen 9:6). This is why the evildoer should fear: because the government authorities wield the power of life and death, and they do not wield it "for nothing," in vain, to no avail. It is not – or *should* not be – an empty threat.

He is God's servant, an agent of wrath to bring punishment on the wrongdoer. Here for the second time the civil ruler is called God's servant, or "a minister of God." In the former instance (v. 4a) he is God's servant for the positive purpose of doing good for law-abiding citizens. Here he is God's servant for the negative purpose of bringing vengeance and wrath upon evildoers. *Both aspects of the government's task are equally valid and equally good.* As Murray says, "The same dignity and investiture belong to the ruler's penal prerogative as to his functioning in promoting good" (2:153).

The NIV's weak translation "agent of wrath" obscures the force of Paul's language and its deliberate connection with 12:19. The NASB is literally accurate: the civil ruler is "an avenger who brings wrath upon the one who practices evil." The references in both verses to vengeance and wrath make the connection obvious. "Avenger" is ἔκδικος (*ekdikos*), a noun form of ἐκδικέω (*ekdikeō*), "take revenge" (12:19). "Wrath" (ὀργη, *orgē*) is the same in both verses.

The point is clear: punitive wrath and vengeance are forbidden to individuals, but are delegated by God to civil authorities. When Paul in 12:19 commands us as individuals to "leave room for God's wrath," and refers to God's dictum, "It is mine to avenge; I will repay," he is laying the foundation for ascribing these tasks to the government in 13:4. Stott is correct: "It is important to hold Romans 12:19 and 13:4 together" (345). Taken together they show that the government's wrath and vengeance toward evildoers are no less than God's own wrath and vengeance. As a penal force the government is God's agent, God's servant. See Murray, 2:153; Lenski, 793; Moo, 802.

13:5 Therefore it is necessary to submit to the authorities, not only because of possible punishment but also because of conscience. "It is necessary" states our *obligation* to "submit" (*hypotassō* – see v. 1). The obligation is both hypothetical (pragmatic) and absolute. Regarding the former, submission is necessary (literally) "because of wrath." I.e., if we want to escape the penalty which the government imposes for wrongful acts, then we should obey its laws. Obedience thus is a "practical expedient" (Moo, 803).

Fear of the government's punishment in itself, however, is not the only reason to avoid civil disobedience. If it were, this would leave us morally free to break the law (e.g., zoning, tax, and speeding regulations) as long as we were reasonably sure we would not get caught or as long as we were willing to pay the penalty if caught. But Paul adds a second reason why it is necessary to submit, i.e., "also because of conscience." This means that our obligation to obey civil laws is absolute and unqualified. We must do it just because God says so, just because it is right. I.e., we must do it not just for our own sake (to avoid punishment) but also "for the Lord's sake" (1 Pet 2:13), "out of a sense of obligation to God" (Murray, 2:154). This requirement is for all citizens as God's creatures, and not just for Christians.

We should remember that Paul is here setting forth the *ideal* relation between citizens and government; it is not his purpose to comment on situations where a particular government has perverted its God-given mandate to uphold justice in accordance with God's moral law. In other places the Bible allows – even requires – civil disobedience where obedience to a human law would require us to break a divine commandment (e.g., Acts 5:29; see Cottrell, *Questions*, 2:33-35).

13:6 This is also why you pay taxes, for the authorities are God's servants, who give their full time to governing. The first clause is not an imperative (contra the KJV); Paul is simply referring to paying taxes as a fact of life. His main point is to explain the *reason* why we pay taxes. What exactly is this reason? Some think he is referring back only to v. 5b, "because of conscience." I.e., you pay taxes in order to have a clear conscience (e.g., Hendriksen, 2:431; Cranfield, 2:668; Moo, 804). Others (correctly) think Paul is referring back to the general teaching of vv. 1-4, i.e., you pay taxes in order to support the government's divinely-mandated program of protecting law-abiding citizens and punishing evildoers (e.g., Godet, 445; Lenski, 794; MacArthur, 2:230).

The latter view is supported by the second clause in the verse, which alludes to the civil ruler's task as set forth in vv. 1-4. Here the governmental authorities are again called "God's servants," though Paul uses λειτουργός (*leitourgos*) instead of *diakonos*. Some think this term has a more inherently religious connotation (see Bruce, 239, 260; Hendriksen, 2:436-437), but in fact it was used in the secular Greek world simply to refer to "public servants" or public officials (Cranfield, 2:669; Dunn, 2:767). The religious nature of their service is again connoted by calling them servants *of God.*

Paul says we pay taxes because the authorities are servants of God who (literally) "devote themselves constantly to this very thing." "Give their full time to" (NIV) is a good translation of the verb here. But what is the meaning of "this very thing"? Some think it refers back to government's work of collecting taxes[57], but this can hardly be called the task to which government devotes its full time. Collecting taxes is a means to an end, and that end is the *governing* itself, i.e., the twofold purpose of government as set forth in vv. 1-4.[58] The NIV interpretation ("to governing") is thus correct.

13:7 Give everyone what you owe him . . . , or "Render to all what is due them" (NASB). This *is* an imperative, and thus makes the payment of taxes (along with other things) a divine command, an obligation we owe not only to the government but also to God himself. The word for "give" is the same as in Mark 12:17, in Jesus' command to "*render* to Caesar the things that are Caesar's" (NASB). The similarity of the language and subject matter make it very likely that Paul is consciously thinking of Christ's teaching on this topic.

Because of the context it is probable that "everyone" here means "every governmental authority." The words for "give" and "owe" both include the connotation of obligation or debt. "Give" is ἀποδίδωμι (*apodidōmi*) and here has the sense of "give back, repay, pay a debt." "What you owe" is ὀφειλή (*opheilē*; cf. *opheilēma*), or "obligation, duty, debt." The idea is that, because of their position as servants of God and their purpose as ordained by God, civil authorities are *owed* certain things by their citizens; and as conscientious citizens we are obligated to give them these things.

"What you owe" is followed by four short phrases listing what citizens owe to their government: taxes, revenue, respect, and honor.

---

[57]Lard, 401; Murray, 2:155; Cranfield, 2:669; Dunn, 2:767; Fitzmyer, 669.

[58]Godet, 445; SH, 368; Lenski, 794-795; Barrett, 247.

Each phrase is governed by "what you owe" and has the same compact form, literally, e.g., "to the one taxes, taxes," i.e., "to the one [to whom you owe] taxes, [give him your] taxes." The NIV renders the phrases thus: **If you owe taxes, pay taxes; if revenue, then revenue; if respect, then respect; if honor, then honor.** Actually the Greek text does not make these obligations conditional ("if"). The sense is more of an imperative: "Pay taxes to the one to whom you owe taxes," etc.

Paul uses two different words in order to stress our obligation to pay taxes of all sorts. The first word ("taxes") is φόρος (*phoros*), which in NT times included tribute paid to foreign rulers in the form of property taxes and per capita (poll) taxes. The second word ("revenue") is τέλος (*telos*), which in this context refers to various forms of taxation such as customs or tariffs on imported and exported goods, sales and business taxes, and tolls (Weiss, "φέρω," 80-81). These commands to pay taxes clearly show that tax fraud is a sin, that refusing to pay taxes is an act of direct disobedience to God. This is true even of taxes levied by pagan governments such as Rome.

The other two things Paul says citizens owe to civil authorities are respect and honor. The word for "respect" is *phobos*, the same word translated "terror" in v. 3, where it was something to avoid if possible. We must remember that *phobos* can be used in either sense, depending on the context. Most agree that it is used here in the sense of veneration or respect (see Eph 5:33; 1 Pet 2:18).[59] It refers to "the respectful awe which is felt for one who has power in his hands" (SH, 368). The contrast is well stated by Murray: in vv. 3-4 the *absence* of the fear of *terror* is good; in v. 7 the *presence* of the fear of *respect* is good (2:156).

Paul says finally that "honor" should be paid to rulers. This is not greatly different from respect. One possibility is that respectful fear is internal, an attitude of the heart, while honor is the overt expression of respect toward its object. A complementary possibility is that the former is a constant attitude toward those in government simply because of the nature and divine origin of their roles

---

[59]E.g., Murray, 2:156; Hendriksen, 2:437; Morris, 466; Fitzmyer, 670; MacArthur, 2:240.

as such, while the latter is contingent upon the actual accomplishments of individuals.

F. THE RELATION BETWEEN LOVE AND LAW (13:8-10)

Paul cannot draw his discussion of Christian virtues to a close without returning to the most important virtue of all, namely, love (see 12:9-10). His main point is to show the relation between the love command and all other commands, which he does in two correlative statements: "Love is the fulfillment of the law" (vv. 8b, 10b); and, all commandments "are summed up" in the rule of love (v. 9b).

The "law" here is not just the Law of Moses, contrary to the approach of many interpreters, but is the totality of the moral law as such, the sum total of all the commands that apply to those living in the New Testament era. In this context this "law" includes the very instructions Paul has been setting forth since 12:1. Since most of these have to do with interpersonal human relationships, Paul focuses here only on the second greatest commandment, the one enjoining neighbor-love.

After setting forth his definitive teaching that sinners are justified by faith apart from works of law (chs. 1–5), Paul knew that some would erroneously conclude that the principle of faith negates the necessity of obeying God's commands. Thus, beginning in 6:1, he shows that this is definitely not the case. Now, in view of the prominence given by Jesus himself to the command of love (Matt 22:34-40; Mark 12:28-34; Luke 10:25-28; John 13:34-35), Paul knows that some might erroneously conclude that the principle of love makes all law obsolete. Thus in this brief paragraph he shows that this is not the case, either.

It is true that the love command is special. As Godet says, "Love is not in the law a commandment *side by side* with all the rest; it is itself the essence of the law" (446). It is the *general* commandment; all the others are just the specific ways in which it is expressed. Love is like a finely cut diamond; all the other commandments are its various facets. Love and law are like two sides of a single coin. One entire side is composed of love; the other side is divided into all the other commandments. To truly love one's neighbor is to keep these other commandments.

13:8 Let no debt remain outstanding, except the continuing debt to love one another, . . . The concept of debt or obligation is the bridge between this and the previous paragraph. In v. 7 Paul says, "Give everyone what you owe him"; "what you owe" is the noun *opheilē*. He begins this verse with the verb ὀφείλω (*opheilō*, "to owe, to be indebted, to be obligated"). The result sounds almost like a contradiction. "Pay what you owe," and (lit.) "Owe nothing to anyone" (NASB).

Now, it is obvious that v. 7 is talking not about obligations entered into voluntarily, but about duties inherent in the relation between citizens and government. We have no choice about such "debts." Does v. 8a, then, forbid voluntarily entering into debt? Does it rule out car loans, house mortgages, and credit cards? No, this is not the point. Other Scriptures show that borrowing and lending on reasonable terms (e.g., no interest charged to the poor) are not prohibited; see Exod 22:25; Lev 25:35-37; Ps 37:26; Matt 5:42; Luke 6:35. The point rather is that when you enter into a loan agreement, the payments must be submitted promptly and honestly and in accordance with the terms of the contract.[60] The NIV captures the intent of the command quite well.

The command not to owe anyone anything is actually just a way of leading into the main commandment, "to love one another." By saying we should have no unpaid debts *except* to love one another, Paul says that love itself is a *debt,* in the sense of a moral or spiritual obligation; he is also saying that (unlike other debts) it can never be completely paid off.[61] Of course we should be making every effort to discharge this obligation; but no matter how diligently we express our love, it remains "an unlimited debt which we can never be done with discharging" (Cranfield, 2:674). As Moo says, "We will never be in a position to claim that we have 'loved enough'" (810).

The love of which Paul speaks is *agapē*; see 12:9 above.

---

[60]See Lard, 403; Lenski, 797; Hendriksen, 2:439; MacArthur, 2:246; Moo, 812.

[61]Murray says "except" should be read as "but," i.e., "Owe no one anything; *but* – you ought to love one another." This allows us to think of love as a debt (a "perpetual obligation"), but not as an *unpaid* debt (2:159). This distinction is not crucial.

What is the scope of "one another"? Some say this expression in Paul's writings always refers to one's fellow Christians, which must be the primary application here. However, they point out that the rest of the paragraph uses universal language ("his fellowman," 8b; "your neighbor," 9-10), which means that our debt of love ultimately extends to all human beings (Murray, 2:159-160; Moo, 813). It is generally agreed that the scope is unlimited. Even in this context personal enemies (12:14,17-21) and government officials (13:1-7) would seem to be included. See Matt 5:44; Luke 10:25-37; Gal 6:10.

It is necessary to love one another, **for he who loves his fellowman has fulfilled the law.** "His fellowman" is literally just "the other." It is possible to attach this to "law" and thus read it as "the other law," i.e., as the second commandment (Matt 22:39) of the Mosaic Law;[62] but the general agreement is that it is the object of "to love" as in the NIV. Loving "the other" is open-ended; Paul does not specify any particular "other." As Morris says, it refers to "any other person whatever" with whom we have anything at all to do (468).

Many take "the law" to be the Torah or Mosaic Law,[63] but this is usually based on the assumption that νόμος (*nomos*, "law") is the Mosaic Law throughout Romans, which itself is a fallacy. "Law" should be understood here as the moral law as it governs interpersonal relationships, in whatever form one may possess it (see Lard, 403; Lenski, 798).

How does neighbor-love fulfill the law? It is absolutely not the case that love fulfills the law by taking its place and making it unnecessary. Moo (814-815) says that "Christians who love others have satisfied the demands of the law *en toto*; and they need therefore not worry about any other commandment." Of course, he says, this is true only of *perfect* love; and since we do not have perfect love, we still need other commands to guide us. This thinking is unacceptable, however, since Paul knows he is addressing imperfect people, and he is telling us that our *imperfect* love fulfills the law.

How does it do this? We can sum it up thus, that love fulfills *the requirements of* the law. The one who loves *will* do the things required by all the other commandments regarding interpersonal

---

[62]See the discussion of this in Cranfield, 2:675; Moo, 813, n. 19.

[63]E.g., Dunn, 2:776; Fitzmyer, 677-678; Moo, 814. Morris says the same, but then says that Paul's point is true of any law.

relationships, because these other commandments are simply the contents of love, or the verbalization of the various expressions of love. This applies even to negative commandments such as those in v. 9a; the one who loves will *not* do such things because they are the very opposite of love.

One can obey the commands outwardly without love, in which case the commands are not fully obeyed (i.e., fulfilled); but one cannot love the other without obeying the commandments and thus fulfilling the law.

13:9 The commandments, "Do not commit adultery," "Do not murder," "Do not steal," "Do not covet," and whatever other commandment there may be, are summed up in this one rule: "Love your neighbor as yourself." This verse is intended to explain v. 8b. The commandments in v. 9a are *examples* of the law Paul has in mind, and are not intended to be an exhaustive list, as v. 9b shows. These are, of course, four of the "ten commandments," nos. 6, 7, 8, and 10.[64] They are listed in the order of the LXX in Deut 5:17-21. Though originally appearing in the Law of Moses, they are not limited to that particular law code. Paul condemned the Gentiles for covetous desires (ἐπιθυμία, *epithymia*, 1:24) and murder (1:29). These commands are all repeated as binding on people today: no adultery (Jas 2:11; 1 Cor 6:9; Heb 13:4), no murder (Jas 2:11; 4:2; Rev 9:21; 21:8; 22:15), no stealing (Eph 4:28; 1 Cor 6:10; Titus 2:10), and no covetousness (Col 3:5; 1 Tim 6:9; Jas 4:2; 1 Pet 2:11; 4:3).[65]

The actions represented in these and other such commands are simply the opposite of love and are prohibited for that very reason. To deride and disparage such commands because they are negative in form ("Thou shalt not . . .") demonstrates a failure to understand the nature of love. True love does demand positive action (1 Cor 13:4a,6b,7), but just as validly rules out nonloving deeds and attitudes (1 Cor 13:4b-6a).

Paul's reference to "whatever other commandment there may be" shows these four to be just a few examples to which many more could be added, from both the Law of Moses and the NT

---

[64]Some manuscripts have "Thou shalt not bear false witness" (KJV), but this is usually taken to be a later addition. See Cranfield, 2:677.

[65]See also Matt 5:21,28-29; 15:19; 19:18; Mark 7:21; 10:19; Luke 18:11,20; Rom 2:21-22; 7:7-8; 1 Pet 4:15.

revelation.[66] He seems to have in mind just those commands that cover interpersonal relationships, though (Lard, 405; Murray, 2:160; Moo, 815). These are all included in the "law" in v. 8b.

All such commands, he says, are summed up in the one rule or command,[67] "Love your neighbor as yourself." This is not an exclusively NT command, being taken directly from Lev 19:18; but Jesus identified it as one of the two greatest of all commands (Matt 22:34-40) and declared mutual love to be the identifying mark of his disciples (John 13:34-35). Paul cites this command again in Gal 5:14 as the fulfillment of the entire law, and Jas 2:8 calls it "the royal law." See also Matt 5:43; 19:19.

All other commands, says Paul, are "summed up" in this one rule. The word for "summed up" is used in the NT only here and in Eph 1:10. Literally it means "to bring together under one head," or (in literary terms) under one heading. I.e., the love commandment is the category heading, and all the other commands are listed under love as part of it or expressions of it. This helps to explain how these other commands ("the law") are fulfilled by love.

In Lev 19:18 "neighbor" probably meant one's fellow Israelite (see "one of your people," v. 18a); but by NT times the Jews themselves had begun to give it a wider meaning (see Dunn, 2:779-780), and Christ's illustrative parable of the Good Samaritan definitely gives it a universal scope (Luke 10:25-37). MacArthur rightly defines one's neighbor as "anyone with whom we have contact, especially if he is in need" (2:251).

Does this command justify self-love ("Love your neighbor *as yourself*")? Yes, there is nothing wrong with self-love as long as it is of the *agapē* type (see Eph 5:28-29). As Murray correctly points out, not all self-love is *selfish* love (2:163). We can and must have the same kind of concern for our basic well-being, including our temporal health and our eternal salvation, as God does. Not to care about ourselves in this sense is to deny God's own purposes for us.

---

[66]Concerning the "commandments" (ἐντολή, *entolē*) of the NT, see 1 Cor 7:19; 14:37; Eph 6:1-2; 1 Tim 6:14; 2 Pet 2:21; 3:2; 1 John 2:3-4; 5:2-3; 2 John 6; Rev 12:17; 14:12.

[67]"Rule" is λόγος (*logos*, "word"). In Deut 10:4 (LXX) the "ten commandments" are called the "ten words," the δέκα λόγους (*deka logous*), from which we get the term decalogue.

Stott perceptively states, "We are to affirm all of ourselves which stems from the creation, while denying all of ourselves which stems from the fall" (350).

The main point, though, is not self-love, however pure, but a love that embodies an equally deep concern for the well-being of others.

13:10 Love does no harm to its neighbor. Therefore love is the fulfillment of the law. This verse basically recapitulates the point of the paragraph. "Love does no harm" is simply the converse of "Love seeks the neighbor's well-being." It sums up the essence of the negative commands given in v. 9a. Adultery, murder, theft, and covetousness all cause great harm to other people. Thus if we truly love others, we will not do these or any other harmful things. Loving action and law keeping are thus the same thing; they are but two sides of the same coin. (See the introduction to this paragraph, and the comments under v. 8.)

G. WALKING IN THE LIGHT (13:11-14)

This main section ends as it began, with an appeal to believers to lead the sanctified life. In 12:1-2 the appeal is based upon the mercies of God, which include his saving work *for* us through Jesus Christ, and his saving work *in* us in justification and regeneration, the latter being specifically cited ("by the renewing of your mind," 12:2). In 13:11-14 the appeal is based more on the reality of an already-accomplished, external, cosmic change, i.e., the transition from the old age (old creation) to the eschatological new age (new creation).

This brief paragraph abounds in temporal references to these contrasting ages and our relationship to them: "the present time," "the hour," "salvation is nearer," "the night," "the day," "darkness," "light," "the daytime." The following chart will prepare us for a brief discussion of the significance of these terms:

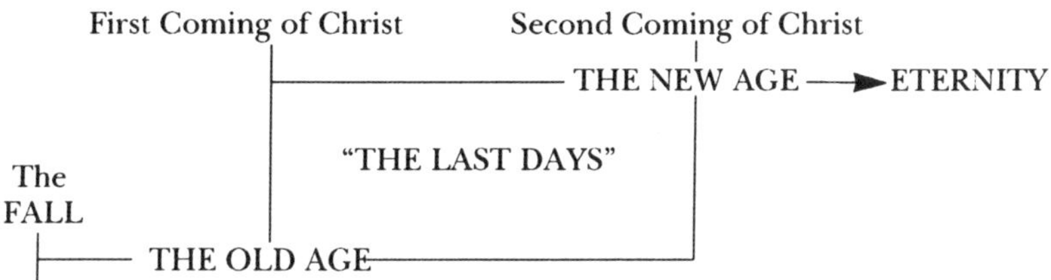

In our text the "old age" is the "night," the time of "darkness." It is the sphere of the old, fallen creation. It is the same as "this world" in 12:2, and "this present evil age" in Gal 1:4. Christ's first coming, in particular his death and resurrection, brought judgment (*krisis*) upon this world (John 12:31). Its end is certain. At the time of the Second Coming it will be burned up and replaced by "new heavens and a new earth" (2 Pet 3:10-13, NASB). Between the first coming and the second coming of Christ, the status of this old age resembles that of a murderer who has been condemned to death. They are both existing between the time of sentencing and the time of execution.

What is called the "new age" on our chart is in our text the "day," the time of "light." It is the sphere of the new, redeemed creation, which is an eschatological reality that has already begun. It was inaugurated by the death and resurrection of Jesus, and now exists in embryo form alongside the old age. Its reality consists mainly in the presence of the Holy Spirit, who is a foretaste and pledge of the future fullness of the new age. This "day" will unfold in its fullness at the Second Coming, which will bring into being our resurrection bodies, the new heavens and new earth, and eternal life.

The "last days" on the chart is the church age, the period when the old age and the new age coexist temporarily side by side. As Stott says, "At present the two ages overlap" (351). The "last days" concept is well established in Scripture; see Acts 2:17; 2 Tim 3:1; Heb 1:2; 1 Pet 1:20; 2 Pet 3:3; 1 John 2:18; Jude 1:18. The phrase has a double meaning. It refers at the same time to the final period of the old age and to the initial period of the new age. With reference to the former meaning, these "last days" are indeed the last stage of the old creation; the very next step in God's plan is the Second Coming itself. This is one sense in which we can say that the Second Coming is "near," regardless of the actual temporal length of the "last days."

"Understanding the present time" (13:11) simply means understanding this scheme and its terminology, and where we are in the scheme. "The hour" in 13:11 refers to the opportune time for the Christian to recognize that he has experienced his own personal transition from the old age to the new age (John 5:24; 2 Cor 5:17). That is, it is time to recognize that we are already, now, living in the *eschaton*, and should thus awaken from our apathetic indifference and begin to live the kind of life that belongs to the light of day.

This section thus is a call for Christians to live the lifestyle that is appropriate to the new age. We are a part of that age (vv. 11-12a); therefore ("so") we should live like it (vv. 12b-14).

Most agree that Paul presents this old-age-to-new-age transition in order to motivate Christians to live a holy life. This is called the "eschatological motivation of Christian obedience," i.e., an "appeal to eschatology as an incentive to moral earnestness" (Cranfield, 2:679-680; see also Murray, 2:166; Fitzmyer, 681-682; Stott, 351).

Most interpret Paul as basing this appeal on *future* eschatology. I.e., because Christ's coming is "near," we must devote ourselves to holy living in order to be prepared for him when he returns. As one writer puts it, Paul exhorts us "with an appeal to the *future reward* of God" (MP, 517). Paul is "encouraging Christians to look at the present in the light of the future," says Moo (818-819). Dunn labels this paragraph "The Imminence of the End as Spur" (2:783).

I agree that Paul's appeal is eschatological, but I believe his emphasis is not so much on future eschatology as on *present* eschatology. I.e., his exhortation to holy living is based not on something that is yet to come,[68] but on the eschatological reality of the new age that has *already begun*. He does not say, "Live right, so that you will be ready for Christ's return and so you will be rewarded in heaven." He says rather, "Live right, because this alone is consistent with the new age which was inaugurated by Christ's death and resurrection, and in which you are already participating by virtue of your conversion." The *eschaton* has already begun and we are a part of it; therefore our lifestyle must be consistent with it; we must "live a life in tune with the new aeon" (Fitzmyer, 681).

13:11 And do this, understanding the present time. "This" could be just the preceding paragraph about neighbor-love (Murray, 2:165), or more likely the entire section on holy living, chs. 12-13 (Cranfield, 2:680; Moo, 820). The verb "do" is supplied; the Greek simply has the idiomatic "And this." The NIV and a few other translations (e.g., NASB, TEV, NAB) make it an imperative by adding

[68]Such an appeal is quite valid, and is made in other places. See Mark 13:33-37; Luke 12:35-40; 1 Thess 5:1-11,23 (which has much of the same terminology as our present text); Heb 10:23-25; Jas 5:7-11; 1 Pet 4:7-11.

"do." There are other possible renderings,[69] but the NIV's approach probably captures the meaning best (Fitzmyer, 682; Moo, 819).

This simple phrase gathers together "all the Apostle has just been enjoining" (Lard, 407) and introduces the main point of the paragraph, i.e., the immediate motivation for doing all these things. We should do them, he says, because we understand the significance of the time in which we live. "Time" is καιρός (*kairos*), which refers not to clock time or a calendar date, but to an era or epoch of a certain character or significance, e.g., a welcome time, a critical time, an opportune time, the right moment (AG, 395-396). As we saw in the introduction above, the time in which Christians live is "the last days," the epoch immediately preceding our Lord's return. Paul's point is that we should be all the more diligent in living the transformed life in view of the nature of the time in which we live.

The hour has come for you to wake up from your slumber, because our salvation is nearer now than when we first believed. These clauses explain the nature of the *kairos* in more detail. "The hour has come" (literally, "the hour is now," or "it is already the hour") emphasizes the urgency of the situation. You know, says Paul, that the moment for action has arrived. Specifically, it is time to wake up, to get out of bed, and to apply yourselves to the business of holy living as if there were no tomorrow.

The metaphor of sleep is used in the NT to represent a state of inattention and unpreparedness (Matt 25:1-13; Mark 13:35-37; Rev 16:15). It also stands for a state of spiritual apathy, lukewarmness, complacency, and indifference, in short, "a lethargic Christian life" (Morris, 471; see Eph 5:14-16; 1 Thess 5:4-8; Rev 3:2-3). Both of these ideas are present here, especially the latter. It is time, says Paul – and you *know* it is time, to shake off your complacency and get serious about living the transformed life.

The urgency of the time – the fact that "our salvation is nearer now than when we first believed" – is the reason why we should awake from our slumber. Paul refers again to the eschatological *now*, i.e., the "last days," and to the nearness of the end. Every passing day brings us closer to our salvation. This is true, of course,

[69]E.g., "Besides this" (RSV, NRSV); "Live thus" (Weymouth); "In all this" (NEB); "Why all this stress on behaviour?" (Phillips).

whether we are thinking of the moment of our death (MP, 519-520) or the Second Coming of Christ (Murray, 2:165; Moo, 822; see Titus 2:11-13). The latter is probably the case, since "our salvation" most likely refers to our full and final salvation (5:9-10; 8:23; 1 Thess 5:8-9; 1 Pet 1:5), our state of glorification. We receive such salvation not at our death, but at the time of the Second Coming (Hendriksen, 2:445).

Our final salvation is nearer to us now than when we began to believe. Fitzmyer (682) thinks this refers to Christians collectively, i.e., to the beginning of the Christian era when people first began to believe in Jesus. Others rightly take it as a reference to individual Christians, and to the time when we as individuals "first confessed our faith in the Lord Jesus Christ and were baptized" (Hendriksen, 2:441). See v. 12 below for an explanation of this nearness.

13:12 The night is nearly over; the day is almost here. This contrast between night and day is a key concept. "Night" is a negative image, being associated with indifferent sleep (v. 11), darkness (v. 12b), and evil deeds (v. 13). "Day" is a positive image, representing light (v. 12b) and decent living (v. 13). Here they stand for the two eras of salvation history. "Night" is the *old* age, "this present evil age" (Gal 1:4), the sphere of the old creation as it stands under God's curse and Satan's dominion. "Day" is the *new* age, the sphere of the new creation, the eschatological age, the kingdom age, the era of truth and power and freedom in the Holy Spirit.

As explained in the introduction, these two ages overlap in what are called "the last days." The old age (the "night") still exists and will exist until the Second Coming, but its power is broken and it is "nearly over," "far spent" (KJV), or "almost gone" (NASB). The new age (the "day"[70]) will not fully arrive until the Second Coming; but it has already been inaugurated by the saving death and resurrection of Jesus, and its light is already shining over the horizon (1 John 2:8; Rev 22:16).[71]

A serious question arises in reference to Paul's assertion that this "day" is "almost here" (literally, "has drawn near"). If this "day"

[70]For the eschatological use of the term "day" or "the day" in the NT, see Murray, 2:167.

[71]"The day of Christ, though not yet come, is nevertheless throwing its light backward upon the present" (Murray, 2:169).

will begin in its fullness only at the Second Coming of Christ, in what sense can Paul say, just decades after the first coming, that it "has drawn near"? Some have taken this reference to the nearness of the day as an indication that Paul and other early Christians believed Christ would return in their own generation. Since this did not happen, they were obviously wrong – according to this view.

If we believe that Paul's inspired writing cannot be wrong (as I do), then how may we explain the *nearness* of the Second Coming, especially from the perspective of the first century, since over 1,900 years have now passed since then? There are three main points. First, the Second Coming was near, even then, in the sense that its spiritual power had already been unleashed via Christ's death and resurrection, and Christians had already begun to taste of its power and glory (2 Cor 1:22; Eph 1:13-14; Heb 6:4-5), as we still do today. Second, Christ's first coming and the redemptive events associated with it began the final stage of history ("the last days") leading up to the Second Coming, and left nothing more to be accomplished but the Second Coming itself. Thus the latter is near in the sense that it is "the next great epochal event" (Murray, 2:168), whether the actual lapse of time between the two comings is 20, 200, or 2,000 years.[72] Third, God's way of counting time is not necessarily the same as ours. "But do not forget this one thing, dear friends: With the Lord a day is like a thousand years, and a thousand years are like a day. The Lord is not slow in keeping his promise, as some understand slowness" (2 Pet 3:8-9a; see Hendriksen, 2:446-447).

In view of these considerations, we should never say, "Christ *is* coming soon"; but we should always think and say, "Christ *may be* coming soon." The final day is "always imminent – its coming certain, its time incalculable" (Moo, 822). See Matt 24:36; Acts 1:7; 1 Thess 5:1-2.

So let us put aside the deeds of darkness and put on the armor of light. Paul now turns from the eschatological presence of the new age (vv. 11-12a) to the consequent necessity of living the kind of life that is consistent with it. The rest of this paragraph is

---

[72]This is the most commonly accepted explanation of the language of "nearness" (Phil 4:5; Heb 10:35-37; Jas 5:8; 1 Pet 4:7; Rev 22:12, 20). See Murray, 2:168; Cranfield, 2:683-684; Moo, 822. "God [has] nothing left on his calendar before the parousia" (Stott, 352).

governed by the word "so" (οὖν, *oun*, "therefore"). I.e., because we have in fact experienced the transition from the age of night to the newly-dawning day (Acts 26:18; 1 Pet 2:9b), let us live like it. Let us completely abandon all deeds that are associated with the darkness and devote ourselves wholly to a lifestyle suited to the light of day, so that we may be free from shame and reproach and accusations of hypocrisy.

The contrast between darkness and light is parallel to that between night and day (v. 12a). "Darkness" relates to the old, evil age; "light" is characteristic of this new age of salvation in Christ.

"Deeds of darkness" are evil, sinful deeds (e.g., v. 13), "the deeds that are done under the cover of night" (Fitzmyer, 683), "the sort of things which were frequently indulged in during the night in a pagan city" (Cranfield, 2:686). The word for "put aside" was often used for taking off garments. It was used figuratively for getting rid of or laying aside sinful deeds (Eph 4:22,25; Col 3:8; Heb 12:1; Jas 1:21; 1 Pet 2:1).

The "armor of light" is equivalent to the "full armor of God" in Eph 6:13-17 (see 1 Thess 5:8). The word for "armor" is ὅπλον (*hoplon*), which can mean either "an instrument" in general (6:13), or "a weapon" in particular. The military connotation seems to be intended here. The implication is that the Christian life is a state of spiritual warfare against the forces of evil; thus we must be dressed for battle so that we may fight off and defeat the lingering enemies of the night.

Our battle gear is called the armor of *light* because it consists largely of truth (Eph 6:14a) and holiness (Eph 6:14b; 1 Thess 5:8), which are the principal forms of light associated with God. Truth and holiness are the main weapons with which we are able to defeat the forces of darkness. The word for "put on" is used for putting on garments; in the NT it is often used in the figurative sense of incorporating works of holiness into one's character and lifestyle (13:14; Eph 4:24; 6:11,14; Col 3:12; 1 Thess 5:8).

The message is clear: we as Christians have passed from the sphere of darkness and death into the sphere of light and life. Therefore we must at once cast away from us everything associated with darkness and evil, and wrap ourselves completely and exclusively in the lifestyle of moral purity and truth (Eph 5:8-9).

13:13 Let us behave decently, as in the daytime, . . . This basically says the same thing as v. 12b; it is repeated to set up the examples of "deeds of darkness" in v. 13b. "Behave" is the word περιπατέω (*peripateō*), which literally means "to walk around" but is often used figuratively for daily conduct (e.g., 6:4; 8:4; 14:15). "Decently" refers to conduct that "would generally be regarded as decent, proper, presentable in responsible society" (Dunn, 2:789). "As in the daytime" refers to the fact that in Christ we have already passed from darkness to light and are therefore expected to "walk in the light, as he is in the light" (1 John 1:7).

The rest of this verse gives examples of the dark deeds that must be abandoned if we are serious about walking in the light: **. . . not in orgies and drunkenness, not in sexual immorality and debauchery, not in dissension and jealousy.** Though six specific sins are mentioned, they clearly are meant to be taken as three related pairs, with each pair referring to things closely associated with each other.

The first works of darkness are "orgies and drunkenness," or drunken revelry. The former term (κῶμος, *kōmos*) was originally used for "a festal procession in honor of Dionysus, then a joyous meal or banquet" (AG, 462), but came to have the negative connotation of excessive, uninhibited revelry, carousing, wild partying, or boisterous brawls and riots. Since such revelry usually was accompanied by excessive drinking, Paul couples with it a word for drunkenness (μέθη, *methē*). The two words are listed together also in Gal 5:21 as works of the flesh. Either by itself is a sin; together they denote "a noisy drunken frolic" (Lard, 409) or a drunken spree (Lenski, 807).

The second pair is "sexual immorality and debauchery." The former is the word κοίτη (*koitē*), which literally means "bed," but was used as a euphemism for sexual intercourse, either in a good sense (Heb 13:4) or bad (as here). As used here in the plural it refers to sexual promiscuity, sexual excesses, and harlotries. The second word (ἀσέλγεια, *aselgeia*) refers to sensual excesses of all kinds, but especially sexual excess, lewdness, licentiousness, or "uninhibited and unabashed lasciviousness" (MacArthur, 2:267). See Mark 7:22; 2 Cor 12:21; Gal 5:19; Eph 4:19; 1 Pet 4:3; 2 Pet 2:18. The two terms taken together, both in the plural, refer to a lifestyle of unrestrained sexual promiscuity.

The final pair refers to sins of a different kind, but deeds of darkness nevertheless. "Dissension" is ἔρις (*eris*), the same word translated "strife" in 1:29. It refers to a quarrelsome disposition, a spirit of contention and bickering. MacArthur describes it well: "It reflects a spirit of antagonistic competitiveness that fights to have its own way, regardless of cost to itself or of harm to others" (2:267). This sin pairs up well with jealousy (ζῆλος, *zēlos*), since the latter is often the source of the former. *Zēlos* can mean "zeal" in a good or neutral sense (10:2), but is usually used in the negative sense of envy or jealousy, or "the various forms of venomous and hateful feelings leading to discord" (MP, 521). When used together (as they are here and in 1 Cor 3:3; 2 Cor 12:20; Gal 5:20), these two words refer to "envious rivalry" (Dunn, 2:792) or "party quarrels" (Godet, 451), or "a determination to have one's own way, a self-willed readiness to quarrel" (Morris, 473).

Many other deeds of darkness could be added to these examples. What is striking is that the ones chosen here are certainly some of the ugliest and most detestable sins we can imagine, yet Paul deems it necessary to warn *Christians* not to engage in them! This suggests that even Christians are not completely immune to temptation regarding such behavior. As Lenski says, Paul "does not operate with illusions and assumptions, he knows human nature. How many 'excellent' church members have been caught in vice and crime and been stained with utter disgrace!" (807).

13:14 Rather, clothe yourselves with the Lord Jesus Christ, and do not think about how to gratify the desires of the sinful nature. Paul closes this section with a positive and a negative exhortation, which together sum up the moral instruction presented in it. "Clothe yourselves" is the same word translated "put on" in v. 12b, where the "clothing" was the "armor of light" or Christian virtues in general. Here the clothing is a person, the Lord Jesus Christ. As Christians we have already been clothed with Christ in one sense (Gal 3:27). When we were immersed into Christ, we received the robe of his own righteousness (Isa 61:10; Phil 3:9), i.e., his blood shed in payment of the penalty for our sins. We have been "wearing" Christ in this sense from the moment of our baptism, and this has been the basis for our continuing justification before God.

But in this verse Paul *exhorts* Christians to "put on Christ," implying a reference to something not yet completed. Thus it is generally agreed that he must be using this metaphor in a sense different from Gal 3:27, i.e., that here he is talking about *sanctification* rather than justification, which is what we would expect in this context. Thus "putting on Christ" is here equivalent to being transformed by the renewing of our minds (12:2). It is the same as putting on "the new self," which is the process of the recreation of the image of God within us (Eph 4:24; Col 3:10). Thus to clothe ourselves with Christ in this sense means to gird ourselves outwardly and inwardly with the same holy character exhibited by the sinless Christ during his earthly sojourn.[73] As Lard says, "Let your whole exterior life, as seen by the world, be but a reproduction of the temper and conduct of Christ" (409).

The concluding negative exhortation is parallel in meaning to "put aside the deeds of darkness" (v. 12b), such as those named in v. 13. "Do not think about how to gratify" translates words that literally mean "take no forethought for," or "make no provision for." I.e., we should not try to hold on to certain sins, planning our lives and our daily schedules in such a way that we have time and opportunity to indulge ourselves in them (see Ps 36:1-4).

"Desires" (ἐπιθυμία, *epithymia*) here means sinful desires or "lusts" (NASB), as in 1:24 and 6:12. "The sinful nature" is literally "the flesh" (σάρξ, *sarx*). As explained earlier (JC, 1:373-377), I believe that faithful exegesis leads us to reject the prevalent understanding of *sarx* as "sinful nature" (contra the NIV), and see it as referring to the unredeemed physical body. Thus, what the NIV calls "the desires of the sinful nature" here are the same as the lusts or "evil desires" of the "mortal body" in 6:12 (see JC, 1:401-402).

Thus I reject Cranfield's definition of "flesh" here as "the whole of our human nature in its fallenness" (2:689), and I think Lenski is on the right track when he says it is "the body we all have, through which so much sin tries to invade us" (809).

This verse in no way prohibits us from taking care and forethought for the health and well-being of our bodies (see the reference to self-love in 13:9). It is concerned only with those propensities

[73]We must be careful not to regard the incarnate Christ as the final, complete, and exclusive norm for conduct, though. This is a common error in the area of ethics, one I call the "christological fallacy." See GC, 170-171; GRe, 263.

toward sin that still lurk without our unredeemed bodies. All in all, in attending to the needs of the body, we must be careful to distinguish its genuine needs from its sinful lusts. Thus we "must, as it were, go on tiptoe, and be exercised with extreme caution, so as not to waken in us those slumbering dogs of lust which, if aroused, will tear our spiritual life to pieces" (MP, 523).

II. CHRISTIAN LIBERTY IN MATTERS OF OPINION (14:1-15:13)

In this main section (12:1–15:13) the general subject is "living the sanctified life." A Christian's sanctified life is basically divided into two areas, corresponding to the two parts of the slogan, "Where Scripture speaks, we speak; where Scripture is silent, we are silent." The former is the area of the Christian life governed by God's law, i.e., the specific commandments and general principles he has spoken to us through his inspired apostles and prophets in the pages of the Bible. Such are the "good, pleasing and perfect" will of God (12:2), which was the subject of the previous subsection (12:1–13:14). In matters where God has spoken, we are not free to decide what is right and what is wrong; we are free only in the sense of having the free will to choose whether to obey God's law or not.

In this subsection (14:1–15:13), Paul turns his attention to areas of Christian living corresponding to the second part of the slogan, i.e., matters upon which Scripture is silent. These are the issues and aspects of our daily life that are not addressed by any "Thus saith the Lord." That Scripture is silent about these things means that it neither commands (requires) them nor forbids them. They are called the "adiaphora," or indifferent matters;[74] they are also called "matters of opinion," i.e., issues for which opposite viewpoints or opinions are equally valid.[75]

---

[74]"Adiaphora" comes from the Greek noun *diaphora* ("difference") or adjective *diaphoros* ("different"), plus the negating alpha. Thus it means "things that make no difference."

[75]We should not use "nonessentials" in this context, since this term most commonly refers to things that are not essential for *salvation*, and that is not the issue with respect to matters of opinion. Equating "opinions" with

Here is where the expression "Christian liberty" applies. In matters of opinion individual Christians are free to choose whichever course of action seems best to them, whether it is a mere preference or a matter of conscience. In this connection it is important to remember that Christians are *not* free from law as such (see chs. 6–8). Paul's point here is not "the problem of law versus freedom" (contra Fitzmyer, 687), as if the Christian must choose between law and freedom. It is not a question of either/or, but both/and. Some aspects of the Christian life are governed by law; some rightly fall under the heading of freedom of opinion. Paul is discussing the latter category here.[76]

Paul's point here is not to give us a complete list of those things which are matters of opinion and therefore of Christian liberty, though he does cite three issues as examples: eating meat (14:2-3,6,14-15,20,23), keeping special days (14:5-6), and drinking wine (14:21). His point is to tell us how to manage our Christian liberty, and to warn us not to sin against each other in these matters. The implication is rather ironic if not paradoxical, i.e., that how we use our *liberty* is a matter of *law*!

Paul indicates that there are two basic approaches to matters of opinion: the way of the *weak* and the way of the *strong* (14:1; 15:1). The weak are those who tend to include too much under the heading of law. Because of their weak understanding of Scripture, they treat issues that are actually matters of opinion as if they were matters of law. This group is especially warned against the sin of condemning those who do not agree with them on such issues (14:3,10). By implication, i.e., by the very fact that they are called "weak," they are encouraged to pursue a more mature approach to these matters.

The strong, on the other hand, are those who better understand how to distinguish matters of opinion from matters of law. This is not a question of having a stronger faith in Christ, nor is it a question of having a better or more sophisticated view of biblical authority. Both the strong and the weak may be in agreement on

---

"nonessentials" leads to serious confusion and weakens the concept of truth. See Cottrell, *Fundamentals*, 16-22.

[76]This seems to be generally agreed upon. E.g., see Lard, 412-414; Lenski, 811, 816; MacArthur, 2:279; Stott, 358.

these points. Rather it is a question of hermeneutics, or how to interpret and apply God's revealed will. The hermeneutical issues that are especially relevant here are the nature of the distinction between the covenants, the implications of biblical silence, how to make proper inferences from general principles, and how to distinguish between eternal principles and cultural expressions thereof. In general, the strong are those who have a better grasp of these points, and therefore are able to distinguish which elements of God's revealed will are binding as law upon Christians throughout the church age, and which are not. Because of this better understanding, the strong are able to do certain things (e.g., eat meat) with a clear, biblically-informed conscience, whereas weak Christians doing the same things would be violating their consciences.

Although the strong have a better understanding of matters of opinion than do the weak, the former are not without responsibilities. First, they are commanded to accept the weak without looking down on them for their weakness (14:1-3,10). Second, they must be ready to sacrifice their freedom if it appears that the exercise of it could become a stumbling block to the weak (14:13-15,21).

It is interesting that Paul condemns neither the weak nor the strong as such. Though he clearly considers himself to be one of the strong (15:1), he nevertheless "expresses himself in a very gentle and subdued manner" toward the weak (Hendriksen, 2:455). This indicates that the weak brethren, unlike the Judaizers in Galatia, were not attempting to impose their convictions upon others as conditions for salvation.[77] I.e., the issue between the weak and the strong is not justification by faith as such, but what truly constitutes the sanctified life.

It is generally agreed that the Roman congregation was experiencing a conflict between weak and strong Christians, and that Paul had heard about it and was thus specifically addressing the situation here. There is no general agreement, however, as to the exact nature of the problem and the exact identity of the weak.[78] The most widely accepted view is that the weak brethren were mainly

---

[77]See Lenski, 816; Hendriksen, 2:455; Murray, 2:172-173; Cranfield, 2:690-691; Moo, 830.

[78]See Cranfield (2:690-697) for an excellent analysis of the possible views.

some converted Jews, and perhaps some converted God-fearing Gentiles who had come under Jewish influence, who were unable to let go of certain crucial aspects of OT ceremonial law, especially the rules regarding diet and special days.[79]

Another major approach is simply to say that we cannot be sure who the weak Christians were, and that they probably came from not just one but several backgrounds. Some converted Jews were probably included, but all of Paul's references to the weak do not neatly apply to this group.[80] Also, the teaching here is similar to 1 Cor 8:1-13; 10:23-33, where the weak were converted pagans who could no longer conscientiously eat meat that had been offered to idols. Though Paul does not specifically mention this problem in Romans, a similar situation probably existed in the Roman church, thus accounting for the vegetarianism mentioned in 14:2.[81] I believe this latter approach helps us to explain more of the data more reasonably.

In any case it is not crucial that we know the exact identity of the weak in Rome. The teaching is clear enough and general enough to be applied to similar problems regarding Christian liberty, whether it be in the first or twenty-first century. In fact, we must not think that Paul's treatment of this subject was solely occasioned by a problem in Rome, and that it has no inherent connection with his overall topic. As we saw at the beginning of this introduction, instruction on how to handle matters of silence follows naturally and logically upon the section dealing with issues governed by God's law.

In this section Paul first speaks to both the strong and the weak, and instructs them not to sit in judgment upon one another (14:1-12). He then addresses the strong in particular, admonishing them to respect the conscience of the weak and not to do anything that would cause the latter to go against their own convictions (14:13-23). Finally he urges all Christians to live in unity and peace with one another (15:1-13).

---

[79]E.g., see Cranfield, 2:694-697; Dunn, 2:800-801; Fitzmyer, 687-688; Stott, 355-357; and Moo, 827-831.

[80]E.g., vegetarianism (14:2) and abstaining from wine (14:21) were not requirements of the Mosaic Law.

[81]E.g., see Achtemeier, 215; Lenski, 812; Murray, 2:172-174; MacArthur, 2:273-274; Morris, 475.

A. DO NOT JUDGE OTHERS IN MATTERS OF OPINION (14:1-12)

As Morris observes, there will always be differences within the church, since "Christians are not clones" (476). When it comes to matters of opinion, however, these differences will not lead to divisions unless we perversely allow them to do so. Paul now tells us how we can have acceptable differences without divisions, namely, by not sitting in judgment upon other Christians who do not agree with us on specific matters of opinion.

Paul begins this paragraph by admonishing us to accept in full fellowship and unity all whom God has accepted (vv. 1-3). He then reminds us that we are all servants of the same Lord, and we all answer to our Lord rather than to each other (vv. 4-9). He concludes by assuring us that a final judgment will occur, and that each of us will indeed be judged by God (vv. 10-12).

1. We Should Accept All Whom God Has Accepted (14:1-3)

14:1 Accept him whose faith is weak, without passing judgment on disputable matters. Precisely what Paul means by "faith" in this and the next verse is not easy to determine. It may help to recall that faith has two basic elements, assent and trust (see JC, 1:107-108). Saving faith includes "believing that" the facts of the gospel are true, and "believing in" or trusting specifically in Jesus for one's salvation.

Some scholars locate the weakness in the *trust* element of faith. Dunn says that "to be 'weak in faith' is to fail to trust God completely and without qualification." The weak Christians in Rome were not trusting in God alone, but trusting "in God *plus* dietary and festival laws" (2:798). What was at stake, then, was the very principle of justification by faith apart from works of law.[82]

[82]See Barrett, 256-257; Fitzmyer, 688. "'Weakness in faith,' means an inadequate grasp of the great principle of salvation by faith in Christ; the consequence of which will be an anxious desire to make this salvation more certain by the scrupulous fulfilment of formal rules" (SH, 384).

I disagree with this approach, since nowhere in this section does Paul relate this problem to justification by faith as such. The emphasis is not on trusting in Jesus as Savior, but on conscientious submission to him as Lord (vv. 4-9). Also, if this weakness were somehow a challenge to justification by faith, we would expect Paul to vigorously expose and condemn it as such; but he does not do this.

The problem, then, would seem to be related to the *assent* element of faith. Assent is that act by which the mind or intellect acknowledges the truth of a statement. I.e., it means believing the content of the Christian faith, or accepting the truth of "the faith that was once for all entrusted to the saints" (Jude 3). This is how some understand "faith" here. In v. 1 it actually has the article, "*the* faith." Thus Lenski says the "weak in faith" are those who do not understand and thus do not accept (assent to) what the Christian faith teaches. This does not mean they are doubting the saving facts of the gospel, but simply are failing to comprehend "what Christian doctrine involves in regard to food, observance of days, etc." (814). See MacArthur, 2:275.

A similar approach says that "weak in faith" means a failure to understand all the implications of believing in Jesus as Savior. According to Moo, Paul is not saying that these weak brethren have a faulty trust in Jesus. "Rather, he is criticizing them for lack of insight into some of the implications of their faith" (836; see Morris, 477). "Weak in faith" means they lack the assurance that their faith permits them to do certain things, as Cranfield puts it (2:700).

This understanding of "weak in faith" is consistent with Paul's similar teaching in 1 Cor 8:7-12; 9:22, where the weakness is located in the conscience and consists in a *lack of knowledge* about the true nature of God and idols.

It is possible, of course, for such a weakness to be associated with a compromised view of justification by faith; but this need not be the case and does not seem to be so here. A person may understand fully what it means to be justified by faith in Jesus, and at the same time be overly strict in his Christian practice simply out of a strong but uninformed desire to please God in every possible way. The problem is not a shaky trust in Jesus, nor an overly conscientious motivation for serving him. As noted in the introduction, the problem is faulty hermeneutics, i.e., an inability to properly determine what conduct is actually pleasing to God.

Paul does not specifically address this command to "the strong"; this term is not used until 15:1. He just addresses it to the church in general, which suggests that "the weak" were a minority in the congregation. To "accept" the weak brother means not just to formally receive him into church membership, but to warmly welcome him into one's heart in the spirit of affection and true fellowship. For other uses of the same verb see John 14:3; Phlm 17.

The last part of this verse is quite difficult. Its structure tells us that Paul is laying down a qualification as to the *motive* for accepting the weak brother into close fellowship. It begins with the words μὴ εἰς (*mē eis*), literally, "not unto." The preposition "unto" denotes purpose. The NASB rightly translates this as "but not for the purpose of." The next word (the object of the preposition) is διακρίσις (*diakrisis*), which means "decision, judgment, quarrel, dispute." The NIV rendering, "passing judgment," is good.

The last word in the verse is διαλογισμός (*dialogismos*), which basically means "a thought, an opinion," and can mean "a doubt, a dispute." The best translation in this context is simply "opinions," which is after all the subject of the whole section. The NASB says it best: "but not for the purpose of passing judgment on his opinions." I.e., accept the weak brother as one of the group, but not just so you can stand in judgment upon him and pick him apart for his sincere but faulty convictions about practices that are neither required nor forbidden in themselves.

What Paul is trying to eliminate through this qualification, says Dunn, is a situation where a "strong" majority welcomes weak brethren simply as an opportunity to debate the disputed issues and settle them in their own favor (2:798). The implication, he says, is that a congregation "should be able to embrace divergent views and practices without a feeling that they must be resolved or that a common mind must be achieved on every point of disagreement" (2:799). This applies, of course, only to things that are truly matters of opinion.

14:2 One man's faith allows him to eat everything, but another man, whose faith is weak, eats only vegetables. Here Paul introduces an example of an issue where either side is acceptable, i.e., eating "all things" (including meat), or eating only vegetables. This does not mean that both sides are equally correct in their thinking, since the one who practices vegetarianism is described as "weak." I.e., his conviction and practice are based on a faulty understanding of the implications of his faith. He could actually eat meat without sinning, but he does not see it that way. Thus, since it is no sin *not* to eat meat, it is perfectly acceptable for him to restrict his diet to vegetables; and the rest of us should not make a fuss about it.

On the other hand, "we who are strong" (15:1) eat everything, because our "faith allows" it. Literally, we "believe to eat all things." Some say "to believe" in this verse means "to have confidence, to have assurance" (Cranfield, 2:697-698; Fitzmyer, 689; Lenski, 815). Moo says that it means to "believe that something is legitimate" (836, 838). The implication, though, is not just that we *believe* it, but that we *rightly* believe it. Thus the Christian who eats all things is the one who has correctly sorted out the relation between faith in Jesus and the kinds of food one may eat. See 14:14,20; 1 Tim 4:3-5.

What sort of circumstances in NT times would cause some Christians to practice vegetarianism as a matter of conscience? For one thing, certain pagan beliefs forbade the eating of meat (see Cranfield, 2:693, n. 5; Dunn, 2:799-800; see Col 2:16-23); therefore some Gentile Christians from this background may have found it difficult to change their habits. Also, much of the meat sold in the ancient markets came from animals that had been offered as sacrifices to idols. Some converted pagans still could not in their minds separate this meat as such from the idolatrous use that had been made of it, and thus violated their consciences if they ate it (1 Cor 8:4-13). The uncertain source of meat sold in the market caused them to avoid meat altogether.

This same course of action was followed by many converted Jews. Even though the Mosaic Law did not forbid the eating of all meat, it did distinguish between the clean and the unclean (see 14:14,20), and prescribed that even clean meat be prepared in a certain way (see Lev 7:22-27; 17:10-16). Some Jewish Christians apparently could not bring themselves to eat what God's own law had forbidden for 1,500 years. And since it was next to impossible to verify the "clean" status of meat sold in the markets or served in someone else's home, many of them apparently renounced the eating of meat altogether rather than risk unwittingly eating something unclean (see Dan 1:8-16).[83]

---

[83]See Dunn, 2:801; Hendriksen, 2:456; MacArthur, 2:278; Moo, 837.

Any one of these would have qualified as an early Christian who "eats only vegetables" because his "faith is weak." Paul was probably not thinking of any one of them in exclusion of the others.

14:3 The Apostle's point is that within the Christian community both strong and weak should be allowed to follow their consciences on this matter without being hassled by the other side. It is, after all, a *matter of opinion*. To enforce this point, Paul has an exhortation for each group, speaking of them in the representative singular. First he instructs the strong, **The man who eats everything must not look down on him who does not, . . .** "Look down on" is ἐξουθενέω (*exoutheneō*), a strong word meaning "despise, disdain, regard with contempt." The more liberated Christian must guard against the temptation to feel superior toward the less enlightened Christian. It is easy for the former to regard the latter as legalistic and nit-picking, and perhaps narrow-minded and a bit dense. All such temptations must be resisted. The strong must have full respect for the integrity and the conscience of the weak.

On the other hand, the weak are not without their own temptations to sit in judgment on the strong, whom they may regard as morally lax or at least inconsistent. Thus Paul exhorts the weak Christian: **. . . and the man who does not eat everything must not condemn the man who does.** "Condemn" is κρίνω (*krinō*), which can mean either "pass judgment on," or the stronger "condemn." It probably has the latter connotation here, and not just "criticize" (contra Lenski, 817). Dunn is right to point out that Paul's command implies that (sometimes at least) the weak Christian looks upon the strong as "not actually to be reckoned as a Christian" (2:813). As Lard says, he "is sure to adjudge the strong a sinner" and is "ready to refuse him fellowship" (415). Not all weak Christians may go this far, but at least they will be tempted to condemn the *conduct* of the strong (e.g., eating meat) as being sinful and unacceptable to God. Because of such a "holier-than-thou," censorious attitude, Morris observes that "not infrequently the weak is the greater tyrant" (479).

In the last part of v. 3 Paul gives the reason why the strong should not despise the weak, nor the weak condemn the strong: **for God has accepted him.** It is possible that "him" here refers only to the one who eats meat (and thus by implication to any strong Christian), as some argue (Murray, 2:176; Cranfield, 2:702; Moo,

839). In my judgment, though, "him" refers to both the strong and the weak. In 15:7 Paul exhorts both groups to "accept one another," using the same verb. In 14:1 he begins this paragraph by urging the strong to "accept" the weak (same verb). Thus it is reasonable to conclude that the acceptance in v. 3c applies not just to the strong eater in v. 3b but to the weak noneater in v. 3a as well (Moule, 224; MacArthur, 2:279). Thus the strong should not despise the weak, *for God has accepted him.* Neither should the weak condemn the strong, *for God has accepted him.*

The bottom line is this: "How dare we reject a person whom God has accepted?" (Stott, 361). Acceptance by God thus becomes the basis for all genuine Christian fellowship. We cannot accept as brothers and sisters in Christ a smaller group than God himself has accepted as his children.

2. We Answer to Our Lord and Not to Each Other (14:4-9)

Another reason why Christians, both weak and strong, should not judge one another in matters of opinion is rooted in the nature of the servant-Lord relationship. Only the owner (lord) of a slave has the right to sit in judgment on the slave's conduct. In the church the only Lord is Jesus Christ (10:9); all Christians are equally his slaves. He alone is our arbiter and judge; we answer only to him. See Matt 7:1; 1 Cor 4:3-5.

14:4 Paul states this as a general principle, with obvious application to the church: **Who are you to judge someone else's servant? To his own master he stands or falls.** "Judge" is *krinō*, the same Greek word translated "condemn" in v. 3; "servant" is οἰκέτης (*oiketēs*) or house-slave, the kind of servant who was usually close to his master.

Since in v. 3 "judging" ("condemning") is the act of the weak toward the strong, some think the question in v. 4a is directed only toward the weak (Cranfield, 2:702). But in v. 13 the same word (*krinō*) is applied to both sides, and it is better to apply it to both here in v. 4a.

Paul's question is a strong rebuke, and it reveals the presumptuousness of any Christian who either ridicules the weak or condemns the strong for following his conscience in the area of opinions. We must not think Paul is ruling out honest and respectful discussions about such issues, however; he is especially not ruling out loving attempts to lead the weak to a better understanding of the implications of Christian belief, and thus into freedom from unnecessary prohibitions.

"Master" is the word for "lord" (κύριος, *kyrios*). In an ordinary master-slave relationship it means "owner." This meaning carries over into the relationship of each Christian to Jesus Christ; he has bought us with a price (1 Cor 6:20) and therefore is our Lord or owner. It is to him alone ("his *own* master") that each Christian, as his slave, stands or falls.

"Stands or falls" refers to the Master's acceptance or nonacceptance of his slave's conduct.[84] I.e., it is the Lord's place either to approve him and lift him up for his conscientious service, or to condemn him for his wrongdoing. The implication is that in matters of opinion any course of action (e.g., eating meat, or eating vegetables only) offered in good conscience to God is accepted by him (v. 3c), and the conscientious servant stands before his Lord with the latter's full approval and without guilt. Moo says, "It is the Lord, not the fellow Christian, whom the believer must please and who will ultimately determine the acceptability of the believer and his or her conduct" (841).

And he will stand, for the Lord[85] is able to make him stand.[86] Even if your fellow Christian's conduct makes it appear to you that he has stumbled and fallen (because he does not agree with you), as long as he is true to his conscience on indifferent matters (14:22-23), he will stand approved by the Lord. "The Lord is able to make him stand" may mean only that the Lord has accepted him; or it may refer to the Lord's gift of the Holy Spirit (Acts 2:33-39), whose sanctifying power enables the Christian to remain true to his conscience.

14:5 One man considers one day more sacred than another; another man considers every day alike. Here Paul introduces a

---

[84]Moule, 224; Dunn, 2:804; Moo, 841; contra Cranfield, 2:703.

[85]"Lord" in this context probably refers to Jesus (see v. 9). So Godet, 455; Murray, 2:176.

[86]This is not a reference to standing acquitted on the Day of Judgment (contra Lard, 416), but the Lord's approval of our daily conduct (Murray, 2:177).

second example of an issue that is a matter of opinion, i.e., whether or not to observe special days. The one who considers some days to be more holy than others is equivalent to the one who makes distinctions among foods; he is therefore presumed to be the weak brother on this issue. The one who considers every day alike is thus equivalent to the strong brother who eats any kind of food.

Interestingly, the word for "considers" is *krinō*, the same word translated "condemn" and "judge" in vv. 3 and 4. Here in v. 5 it obviously has the neutral meaning of "judge between, distinguish, decide." "More sacred" is the NIV's (probably correct) interpretation of the preposition παρά (*para*), which here means "above, beyond, more than, rather than" (see 1:25; 12:3; Luke 13:2,4). Literally Paul says the weak Christian judges "a day more than a day," i.e., one day to be more important or more sacred than another day.

What is the issue here? Most likely it is the question of whether Christians must continue to honor the special days set apart under the Old Covenant. Dunn observes that the "problem arose because many Jewish Christians (and Gentile Christians influenced by Jewish tradition) regarded the continued observance of the special feast days of Judaism (particularly the sabbath) as of continuing importance" (2:805). Most agree with this (e.g., Godet, 456; Cranfield, 2:705; Moo, 842). As Fitzmyer says, "Such days as sabbaths, new moons, feasts, and jubilee years are probably meant" (690). In other texts (Gal 4:10; Col 2:16) Paul is very clear that observing such days is no longer a matter of law, and that insisting that all Christians do so is a kind of legalism that destroys Christian liberty. His point here, though, is that a Christian may continue to observe these special days as a matter of personal conviction, as long as he does not condemn those who decide otherwise.

The latter (the strong) are those who judge "every day alike." The word "alike" is not in the original but is properly inferred. From the Christian point of view, to consider every day alike does not mean to regard them all as *secular*, but rather to consider "every day to be equally high and excellent" (Lenski, 820), or to see "every day as equally to be dedicated to the service of God" (Bruce, 245). The main point is that the one who judges all days alike is no less Christian than the one who feels that some days are special.

Each one should be fully convinced in his own mind. Whichever of these acceptable views one chooses, he should do so only after examining the case for both sides and coming to a conclusion he judges to be reasonable. To "be fully convinced" is to have "a settled conviction . . . that the pattern of conduct followed is in accord with the will of God" (Dunn, 2:806). Our opinions may be personal ("his *own* mind"), but we must believe they are adequately supported by good evidence ("his own *mind*"). This applies to both the strong and the weak. Thus in matters of opinion it is not wrong to believe we are right, even if we are wrong – which is exactly the situation of those who hold the "weak" side in such issues.

Is the teaching of this verse meant to be applied to the observance of the first day of the week (Sunday) as a special day in the church age? Most Christians have traditionally regarded Sunday observance as a matter of law (based on apostolic precedent) rather than a matter of opinion (see Acts 20:7; 1 Cor 16:2). Therefore they see this verse as applying only to the holy days of the Mosaic Law, not to the Christian Sunday.[87] Others take this verse to mean that even the observance of Sunday is a matter of opinion, and therefore they have no problem with Thursday communion and Saturday night worship. I personally am "fully convinced" that a better case can be made for the former position.

14:6 In this verse Paul again shows how the servant-Lord relationship is the reason why it is wrong to judge one another in matters of opinion. He makes his point in reference to both special days and dietary preferences. **He who regards one day as special, does so to the Lord.** By implication the same can be said of the one who treats all days alike.[88] Also, **He who eats meat, eats to the Lord, for he gives thanks to God; and he who abstains, does so to the Lord and gives thanks to God.**

The main point is that whatever convictions a Christian has about these and similar matters, he lives out (or *should* live out) his

---

[87]See Moule, 223-224; Murray, 2:257-259; Hendriksen, 2:458; Lard, 417. Lard says that Sunday is no *better* than any other day, but still has been set apart for a special use or purpose.

[88]Some manuscripts add at this point, "and he that regardeth not the day, to the Lord he doth not regard it" (KJV). A copyist probably added this later in the interest of symmetry.

convictions "to the Lord." In other words, it is a matter between him and his Lord, and he is motivated by a conscientious desire to bring honor and glory to his Lord. "Both alike do what they do with the intention of serving the Lord" (Cranfield, 2:706). This is a warning to both the weak and the strong not to regard those of differing opinions as being impious or selfishly motivated.

Paul notes that both the eat-anything Christian and the vegetarian Christian are equally diligent in giving thanks to God for their food, each regarding his meal as a gift from God. Paul himself identified with the former, saying that "nothing is to be rejected, if it is received with gratitude; for it is sanctified by means of the word of God and prayer" (1 Tim 4:4-5, NASB). At the same time he respected the conscience of the vegetarian and regarded him as being equally grateful to God for his more limited fare.

This verse probably refers to "the blessing spoken at meals" (Dunn, 2:807), and thus supports the common practice of "saying grace" before eating. It "indicates that grace before meals was the universal practice of Christians in Paul's day" (MP, 527). See Matt 15:36; John 6:11,23; Acts 27:35; 1 Cor 10:30; 1 Tim 4:4.

14:7 For none of us lives to himself alone and none of us dies to himself alone. Even in the most general sense, "no man is an island" because human beings are social creatures who exist in a web of interdependence. This is especially true of Christians, "for we are members of one another" (Eph 4:25b, NASB). But Paul's point here is not our connections with other people, but our continuing relationship with our Lord, as v. 8 shows.

14:8 If we live, we live to the Lord; and if we die, we die to the Lord. I.e., none of us lives and dies to himself alone, *because* we all live and die "to the Lord" (see Phil 1:21-24). This basically reinforces the point of v. 6, that every Christian, no matter what position he takes on matters of opinion, is doing so in his capacity as a servant of Jesus Christ. This is true, because *everything* we do is done "in the name of the Lord Jesus" (Col 3:17) and for his sake. The reference to both living and dying emphasizes the all-inclusiveness of this principle. No part of our life or death, not even our seemingly insignificant opinions about matters of indifference, is outside the boundaries of our responsibility to our Lord.

How does one "die to the Lord"? It may mean that at death our bondservice to Christ does not end; rather, we simply pass into another sphere or form of service to him (Moule, 226; Morris, 482). More likely, though, it refers to the circumstances of one's death. Whatever the mode of our bodily death, as Christ's servants we are determined to fully trust his promises and be fully surrendered to his purposes. Whether it be a peaceful transition while asleep or a martyr's violent death, we will bring glory to our Lord by confidently praying, "Lord Jesus, receive my spirit" (Acts 7:59).

So, whether we live or die, we belong to the Lord. He is our owner; we are his slaves, his possessions. We live (and die) to serve him, not to please ourselves.

14:9 For this very reason, Christ died and returned to life so that he might be the Lord of both the dead and the living. The servant-Lord relationship between Christians and Jesus Christ is the key to harmonious relationships within the church in the area of opinions. But this servant-Lord relationship is not something we should take for granted. Jesus is Lord only because, in his role and nature as the incarnate Christ, he met and defeated his enemies through his glorious death and resurrection. It was unto this end, or "for this very purpose," that he died and returned to life.

The word for "returned to life" is not the usual word for "raised up," but the word ζάω (*zaō*), which means simply "to live." Some may conclude from this word that Paul is referring just to Christ's earthly life ("he lived") and his death ("he died"). But if that were the meaning, the verbs would have been reversed. Paul says Jesus "died and lived." There is no doubt that he means "lived again, came back to life, returned to life," as the NIV has it.[89]

As the result of his death and resurrection, Jesus is "Lord of both the dead and the living." This unusual order – we would expect "the living and the dead" – is probably determined by the reference to Christ's death and resurrection in the first part of the verse. It is not that Christ's death made him Lord of the dead, and his resurrection made him Lord of the living. Rather, his death and resurrection together made him Lord over all people, whether they have already died or are still living (see Cranfield, 2:708).

There is a cause-and-effect relation between Christ's death and resurrection on the one hand, and his Lordship (sovereign ownership

[89]This unusual terminology led to a number of textual emendations and variations at this point. See Moo, 834, n. 28, for a summary.

and rule) on the other hand. The eternal Logos was by nature the sovereign Lord over all things, but the God-man Jesus Christ earned his right to Lordship by means of his victorious work of death and resurrection. As the risen Redeemer he could rightly lay claim to all glory and power and honor, and exercise his Lordship over all. See Matt 28:18-20; Acts 2:36; Rom 1:3-4; Phil 2:7-11; Col 2:15; Heb 2:14-15; Rev 1:18; 5:9-12.

The point is that this is why *Jesus*, and no one else, is the Lord over all Christians. Unless we can say that *we* have died and come back to life by our own power in direct triumph over sin and death and Satan, we have no right to sit in judgment on our fellow Christians and their conscientious decisions in matters of opinion.

3. Each of Us Will Be Judged by God (14:10-12)

Here is the final reason why Christians should not judge one another in matters of opinion, namely, because each of us will one day *be* judged in the final accounting before God's judgment seat. The emphasis is on the exclusive right of God to judge others, which is a corollary of his sovereign Lordship over all.[90] We who are servants do not have this right. Instead, we will all one day stand alongside one another before the same Lord and Judge.

14:10 You, then, why do you judge your brother? Or why do you look down on your brother? The emphatic "You, then!" gets our attention. Reminding us that we are brothers only magnifies the inconsistency and presumptuousness of sitting in judgment on one another: "These are your *brothers and sisters* in Christ! Why are you so eager to condemn them and belittle them?" Paul returns to the terminology used in v. 3, where "judge" (*krinō*) is the act of the weak toward the strong, and "look down on" (ἐξουθενέω, *exoutheneō*) is the act of the strong toward the weak.

[90]In this passage Paul assumes a relationship of equality between God the Father and Jesus Christ his Son. That Christ is Lord (vv. 4-9) and that God is Judge (vv. 10-12) are perfectly consistent in view of the divine nature of Christ, and in view of the biblical teaching that the Father judges with and through the Son. See John 5:22,30; Acts 10:42; 17:31; Rom 2:16.

"Why do you judge or look down on your brother?" Paul has already given two reasons why this is wrong, i.e., because God has accepted the brother (v. 3), and because we are all servants together of one Lord, Jesus Christ (vv. 4-9). Now he adds a third reason: **For we will all stand before God's judgment seat.** Anticipation of our own judgment should cause us to think twice before judging a brother. It should remind us that we too are sinners whose only hope in that day will be God's abundant grace, gratitude for which should even now cause us to regard our fellow Christians with a gracious spirit.

"Judgment seat" is βῆμα (*bēma*), a word used for the platform upon which a judge's chair might rest, and thus for the chair or seat itself (see Matt 27:19; John 19:13; Acts 12:21), and also for the tribunal before which one was judged ("the court" – see Acts 18:12,16,17; 25:6,10,17). *Bēma* is also used in 2 Cor 5:10 for "the judgment seat of Christ." This is not different from the "great white throne" of Rev 20:11.

A main emphasis is on the universality of this event: *all* will stand before God's *bēma*. This is true even of Christians, as 2 Cor 5:10 confirms: "For we must all appear before the judgment seat of Christ, that each one may receive what is due him for the things done while in the body, whether good or bad." See 1 Cor 3:13. Some mistakenly think that Christians will not be brought into the judgment, or that their sins will not be made manifest there; but these ideas are incorrect. God "remembers our sins no more" (Heb 8:12; 10:17) in the sense that they are forgiven and will never condemn us, but the Bible is clear: "The judgment embraces not only all persons but also all deeds" (Murray, 2:184).

14:11 Paul reinforces the universality of the final judgment by citing the OT: **It is written: "'As surely as I live,' says the Lord, 'every knee will bow before me; every tongue will confess to God.'"** Most of this quote is from Isa 45:23, but the introductory words ("'As surely as I live,' says the Lord") are found in a number of texts as a solemn preface to a prophetic word from God (e.g., Isa 49:18; Jer 22:24; 46:18; Ezek 5:11; 14:16; Zeph 2:9). By including them in his quotation, Paul leaves no doubt as to the identity of the "me" before whom every knee will bow, namely, the Lord (Yahweh) himself.

To bow the knee before God is an act of submission, and to confess God with the tongue is to acknowledge that he and he alone is truly God. The word for "confess" is ἐξομολογέω (*exomologeō*), which in the middle voice means "to acknowledge, to confess, to admit." As an act of worship it can also mean "to praise," as in 15:9. This does not refer to confessing sins to God (contra Fitzmyer, 692), but rather to confessing or acknowledging his sovereign Lordship, his worthiness to be worshiped, and his right to bring us into judgment. See Phil 2:9-11.

The emphasis again is on the universality of this homage: *every* knee will bow; *every* tongue will confess. Some will do so in terror and grudging resentment, having rebelled against God in their lifetime. Others will do so with the same sincere and willing worship they offered up to him while on the earth. Only the latter will receive the gift of eternal life.

14:12 So then, each of us will give an account of himself to God. This restates the point already made in vv. 10-11. "So then" indicates that this is the logical conclusion from the preceding affirmations. "Each" reaffirms the universality of the judgment. No one, not even Christians, are exempt from it. "Of us" makes this prospect very personal. All of us Christians, including the strong who are tempted to belittle the weak, and the weak who are prone to condemn the strong, will experience our own personal judgment.

We "will give an account" of all our deeds, including our sins (2 Cor 5:10). We will have to answer for how we have despised our weak brethren, or condemned fellow Christians who are stronger than we are, in matters of indifference.

Each will give an account "of himself," not of someone else. We will answer for what *we* have done, not for what others do. Finally, this account will be given "to God." We will answer only to him, not to our fellow Christians.

All of these points together emphasize the folly of judging others, and provide the material basis for the transitional exhortation in v. 13a, "Therefore let us stop passing judgment on one another."

B. THE STEWARDSHIP OF CHRISTIAN LIBERTY (14:13-23)

The subject of this general section is how Christians are to deal with matters of opinion. The preceding paragraph (14:1-12) presumes that some (the strong) are able to discern these issues as truly being matters of opinion, while others (the weak) are unable to separate them from matters of law. Paul addresses both groups and admonishes them not to sit in judgment on one another.

The present paragraph is addressed to the strong, i.e., those who understand the nature of Christian liberty and whose conscience allows them to choose as they please in matters of opinion. Paul's message to this group is that such freedom is not absolute, and that one must not insist upon exercising his rights in such matters if this should prove harmful to the weaker brother and to the cause of Christ. As Achtemeier says, the Apostle emphasizes "the priority of responsibilities over rights within the Christian community" (214). Specifically, in the spirit of Christian love the strong must be willing to sacrifice their liberty, if necessary, where there is a danger that the weak may imitate them and thereby sin against their own consciences. Christian liberty is important, but even more basic is "the rule of Christian charity, and this demands, above all, consideration for the feelings and consciences of others" (SH, 390).

The motto of the strong, in matters of opinion, must be Paul's rule in 1 Cor 10:23, "All things are lawful, but not all things are profitable. All things are lawful, but not all things edify" (NASB).

Paul's thought in this paragraph proceeds as follows. First, we must be willing to sacrifice our liberty for the sake of the weak brother (vv. 13-15). Second, our behavior must not cause outsiders to despise God's kingdom on earth (vv. 16-18). Third, we must do only those things which build up the church rather than tear it down (vv. 19-21). Finally, each Christian must be true to his own convictions (vv. 22-23).

1. We Must Sacrifice Our Liberty for the Sake of the Weak (14:13-15)

14:13 Therefore let us stop passing judgment on one another. This is addressed to both the strong and the weak, and basically is a transitional statement that sums up vv. 1-12. "Let us stop" implies that such judging was occurring in the church at Rome. See Matt 7:1.

Instead, make up your mind not to put any stumbling block or obstacle in your brother's way. From this point on the paragraph seems to be directed mainly to the strong. "Make up your mind" is *krinō*, the same word translated "condemn" in vv. 3,22; "judge" in vv. 4,10; "pass judgment" in v. 13a; and "consider" in v. 5. Here its meaning is "make a decision about," or "let this be your decision."

The strong Christian is warned not to place a stumbling block (πρόσκομμα, *proskomma*) or an obstacle (σκάνδαλον, *skandalon*) in a brother's path. These words are very similar in meaning and refer to an obstacle which causes someone to stumble and fall. See 9:32-33, where the same words describe Jesus as a stone over which the Jews stumbled, to their destruction. The stumbling in this verse is spiritual, not physical; it refers to stumbling and falling *into sin*.

It is important that we understand that the stumbling to which Paul refers is not just becoming offended or having one's feelings wounded. It refers to real spiritual harm (see 9:33; 11:9), a true "spiritual downfall" (Moo, 851). The cause for such spiritual stumbling would be an act on the part of the strong brother that is not wrong in itself, but which is perceived as wrong by a weak brother. Such an act becomes a stumbling block when the weak brother observes it and is influenced thereby to do the same thing, *even though in his heart he believes it is wrong*, which is sin (v. 23). In this way the strong brother has inadvertently influenced the weak brother to "fall into sin and potential spiritual ruin" (Moo, 852), just by exercising his Christian liberty (see 1 Cor 8:9). The point is that we must be sensitive to how our conduct is affecting others, and we must be willing to forgo perfectly legitimate behavior if it has the potential of causing someone to sin against his conscience. Verses 14 and 23 in particular show how this may happen.

14:14 The main example of such behavior is the eating of certain kinds of food (see 14:2). **As one who is in the Lord Jesus, I am fully convinced that no food is unclean in itself.** The word "food" actually does not appear in this verse; literally Paul says that "*nothing* is unclean in itself." By "nothing" he means "nothing in the created world"; the following context shows that he has food in mind as a primary example of this.

Under the Old Covenant certain foods were declared to be "unclean," but they were not inherently so. For Old Covenant purposes God simply pronounced them ceremonially unclean and forbade the Jews to eat them; but this restriction does not apply under the New Covenant (Mark 7:15; Acts 10:9-16; 1 Tim 4:4-5; Titus 1:15). That Paul at least has in mind this OT distinction between clean and unclean foods is shown by his use of the term "unclean."[91] He may also have in mind meat offered to idols, which is not inherently polluted for those who know the difference between the true Creator-God and vain idols (1 Cor 8:4-6; 10:23-33).

Paul is very emphatic in his conviction that no food is unclean in itself. "Fully persuaded" is actually two verbs, "I know" and "I have been persuaded." The source of this conviction is "the Lord Jesus." The Greek phrase (ἐν κυρίῳ Ἰησοῦ, *en kyriō Iēsou*) probably means "by the Lord Jesus," with Paul thus referring to a special revelation given to him in his capacity as an apostle (MP, 529; MacArthur, 2:291) or perhaps to Christ's public teaching as recorded in Matt 15:10-11,15-20; Mark 7:15-23 (see Cranfield, 2:712-713; Hendriksen, 2:462; Moo, 852-853). The NIV translation reflects another common view, that the phrase indicates that Paul's conviction is based in a general way on "his status as a Christian" and "his association with the risen Christ" (Fitzmyer, 695; see Lard, 423; SH, 390; Murray, 2:188). I.e., "Everything I know about Jesus tells me that this is true."

That "no food is unclean in itself" is the fundamental principle from which the rest is deduced. Thus "in principle the 'strong' are right" (Morris, 486). Idols are nothing, so idol-meat is not really polluted; and Christ has abolished the clean/unclean distinction of the Mosaic Law.

But what if someone does not fully understand these points? What if, because of his weak understanding, he still regards eating OT foods and idol-meat as wrong? In this case, says Paul, another principle applies: **But if anyone regards something as unclean, then for him it is unclean.** And because he truly thinks of it in his heart as unclean according to God's own law, his conscience tells him that it would be wrong to eat it. And if he does in fact eat it, contrary to what his conscience tells him, he is guilty of sin. In such a case the sin is not in the eating *per se*, but in the violation of the conscience.

---

[91]The word is actually κοινή (*koinē*), "common," which in the biblical context may have the connotation of "unclean." In Acts 10:14; 11:8 it is translated "impure" and treated as a synonym for ἀκάθαρτος (*akathartos*), "unclean."

This is the principle that applies to the weak. See also 1 Cor 8:7.

Since no object is in itself evil or unclean, sin is always in the heart, mind, and actions of a person. Some acts and mental states are always sinful (e.g., murder, greed), but some are wrong only because a person mistakenly thinks they are (see Lenski, 834). In the former case moral standards are absolute; only in the latter case are they relative, and these have to do only with things that are in reality matters of opinion.

Where a weak conscience thus exists, the ideal approach, as Moule indicates, would be "*correction by better light*" (229); but in the meantime the weak believer must follow his mistaken conscience on such matters or else be guilty of sin.

14:15 If your brother is distressed because of what you eat, you are no longer acting in love. The NASB is more literal here: "For if because of food your brother is hurt . . . ."

It seems best to consider the statement of principles in v. 14 as a parenthesis, with this verse linking up directly with v. 13. In v. 13 Paul urges the strong Christian not to put a stumbling block in the way of the weak; here in v. 15 he gives one *reason*[92] for this, i.e., it is not consistent with love (*agapē*; see 12:9). As Stott says, "Love never disregards weak consciences" (365). To the one who loves, a weak brother's spiritual well-being is always more important than indulging the right to eat whatever one likes.

A crucial question is the meaning of "distressed" ("hurt" in the NASB). The word is λυπέω (*lypeō*), which in the passive means "to be grieved, distressed, hurt" (AG, 482-483). The issue is whether Paul is referring simply to hurt feelings, or to actual spiritual harm. If the former, then he is saying that one must sacrifice his Christian liberty even if its use merely *upsets* the weaker brother or is offensive to his feelings. Godet, for one, says it refers to "the painful and bitter feeling produced in the heart of the weak by the spectacle of the free and bold eating of the strong" (461; see Lard, 424). Thus "even to grieve a brother, to make him feel bad," is contrary to love, says Lenski (836; see Hendriksen, 2:462; MacArthur, 2:293). Since "the weak are always with us," this interpretation would seem to seriously limit if not practically eliminate Christian liberty.

---

[92]The verse begins with γάρ ("for, because"), which the NIV does not translate.

The other view, that *lypeō* here refers to actual spiritual harm, is more in keeping with the context and thus appears to be the right interpretation. The meaning would then be that one is not acting in love if his exercise of liberty influences a weak brother to follow his example and thus fall into sin by violating his own conscience. Murray (2:190-191) gives convincing arguments for this view and against the idea that the "distress" here is merely annoyance or displeasure at seeing the strong partake of certain foods. This latter view, he says, does not do justice to the reference to the stumbling block (v. 13), nor to the word "destroy" in v. 15b, nor to many elements in vv. 20-23. Dunn agrees; he says Paul is referring to "an actual wounding of conscience . . . which destroys the whole balance of the brother's faith" (2:820; see also Cranfield, 2:714; MP, 530; Moo, 854).

The rest of the verse supports this interpretation: **Do not by your eating destroy your brother for whom Christ died.** The Greek word for "destroy" is ἀπόλλυμι (*apollymi*), a very strong word which means "to ruin, destroy, kill, put to death, cause to perish" (AG, 94). It is not intended here to be something at the other end of the spectrum from "distressed" (contra Lenski, 837), but as something close to the kind of distress Paul has in mind. This is not to say that distress and destruction are here equivalent; rather, there seems to be an increasingly stronger description of the harmful results of the insensitive exercise of Christian liberty: the weak are caused to stumble (v. 13); they are gravely hurt (v. 15a); they are destroyed (v. 15b).

What are the implications of this warning? Just how serious is this destruction? Is Paul referring to loss of salvation, and condemnation to hell? Those committed to Calvinism and especially to "once saved, always saved" of course deny that Paul has this in mind. They must rule this out since Paul is talking here about "brothers" (vv. 13b, 15a) who have already been saved; and (according to their view) once they have become saved, they can never be lost.[93] Thus the destruction is limited to "loss of spiritual well-being" and "utter devastation" in the area of Christian

[93]See Murray, 2:191-192; MacArthur, 2:293-294; Stott, 365-366; and Moo, 854-855.

growth (MacArthur, 2:294). It refers only to serious damage to Christian discipleship, says Stott (366). Though this could potentially lead to "eternal perdition" if not corrected, Paul is not implying that it actually will do so; he uses this dire language only to show the strong brother how serious his offense is (Murray, 2:192; see Moo, 854).

I must conclude, though, that this strong warning does imply that the careless and unloving exercise of Christian liberty can lead to actual loss of salvation for a weak brother. *Apollymi* is frequently used in the sense of eternal destruction in hell (e.g., Matt 10:28; Luke 13:3; John 3:16; Rom 2:12). The reference to the fact that Christ died for these weak brethren supports this meaning here. I.e., the destruction in view would negate the very purpose of Christ's death, which is to save them from eternal condemnation.

Stott is correct to point out that a weak Christian's single sin against his conscience does not in itself bring him under eternal punishment (365-366), but here Paul is not referring to a single act of stumbling. He has in mind the ultimate outcome to which a single act of this kind could potentially lead. By violating his conscience the weak brother is weakened even further and could ultimately give up his faith altogether and return to idolatry (Lard, 425). The weak brother's destruction is thus his "actual and complete ruin" (Lenski, 837), his "final eschatological ruin" (Dunn, 2:821; see Cranfield, 2:715). The verse cannot be reconciled with "once saved, always saved."

We must remember that this passage is addressed to the strong brother. By showing him the potential disastrous consequences of the indiscriminate use of his Christian liberty, Paul attempts to motivate him to a discreet and even sacrificial use of it. Just what is your weak brother's eternal life worth to you? he asks. To Jesus, it was worth his very life. If Jesus was willing to give up his life to save your brothers, surely you can give up meat! "Shall we set a higher value on our meat than Christ did on his divine life?" (MP, 530). Do you love your freedom more than you love your brother or sister for whom Christ died? See 1 Cor 8:11.

2. Do Not Allow What You Consider Good to Be Spoken of as Evil (14:16-18)

In these three verses Paul gives another reason for the strong to be discerning in his use of Christian liberty. I.e., he must never insist upon his "rights" if exercising them creates a situation within the church that gives outsiders a bad impression of Christ, Christianity, or the kingdom of God. I.e., we must be sensitive to how the kingdom of God is perceived by those who are not a part of it.

14:16 Do not allow what you consider good to be spoken of as evil. The "good" could be the Christian faith in general (Lenski, 839), or the gospel as such (Cranfield, 2:717; Morris, 488). Others take it to refer generally to the principle of Christian liberty, or more specifically to the Christian's freedom from OT ceremonial law (SH, 391; MP, 530; Murray, 2:193; Moo, 855). But Paul does not refer to "the good" in either an absolute or a general sense, but rather to "the good of you," or "your good." Thus he seems to be referring to the good conduct of the strong brother, i.e., conduct which in accordance with the principle of Christian liberty (v. 14a) is inherently good.

Paul thus exhorts the strong Christian not to use his liberty in such a way that it is "spoken of as evil." This is the word "to blaspheme, to speak against" (see 2:24; JC, 1:214). What would cause someone to speak evil of the practice of Christian liberty? When that liberty is used in such a way that others are harmed thereby.

Those who are led to thus blaspheme the conduct of the strong are not the weak (contra SH, 391; Moo, 855), but those outside the church (see 2:24 for a parallel). As Hendriksen observes concerning conflict between the strong and the weak, "Open quarrels between the two groups would certainly result in slanderous talk on the part of outsiders" (2:463). Thus strong Christians are admonished to consider "the impact of [their] insensitive conduct upon any onlooking or visiting unbelievers" (Dunn, 2:831).

14:17 For the kingdom of God is not a matter of eating and drinking, but of righteousness, peace and joy in the Holy Spirit, . . . In most places where Paul speaks of the "kingdom of God," he refers to "the future inheritance of the people of God" (Bruce, 252; see, e.g., 1 Cor 6:9-10; 15:50; Gal 5:21; Eph 5:5), but here (and in 1 Cor 4:20) he speaks of God's kingdom as it presently exists. The most basic meaning of the "kingdom" (βασιλεία, *basileia*) of God is the *reign* or *rule* of God; in a secondary sense it refers to the realm over which God reigns, and specifically to that body of people who acknowledge and submit to his dominion. In the NT era, this is the church.

Paul's point is this: when outsiders observe God's church, what characteristics or phenomena should they immediately see as a demonstration of the true essence of God's reign on earth? What is the primary evidence that God is truly ruling in the hearts of Christians and in the midst of his church? Or as Moo puts it (856), "What is truly important in the kingdom of God?" What can Christians do to show the world "what the kingdom of God is all about?"

No wonder people have nothing good to say about Christians when they see the latter fighting over such trivial things as "eating and drinking." Are rules about food and drink the essence of the kingdom of God? Does true Christianity consist of getting one's way with regard to eating and drinking? *No*, says Paul; the kingdom of God is not about such ultimately unimportant matters (see Matt 15:11-20), *but*[94] is rather about "righteousness, peace and joy in the Holy Spirit."

Some take these three elements to mean the private and personal gifts of grace that characterize the Christian's (vertical) relationship with God, i.e., the "states wrought by grace" (Lenski, 841; see Moule, 230; Stott, 366-367). "Righteousness" is thus the gift of a righteous status before God; "peace" is the gift of personal reconciliation with God; and "joy" is the inner fruit of the Spirit that comes from personal assurance of salvation. See Cranfield, 2:718; Lenski, 840; Hendriksen, 2:464.

In this context, however, the main point seems to be how the church appears before the world, so that it is either spoken against (v. 16) or "approved by men" (v. 18). Thus the righteousness, peace, and joy that are the true essence of the observable church are better understood in a horizontal or "social sense" (Godet, 461), i.e., as having to do with how Christians get along with each other (SH, 392; Murray, 2:194; MacArthur, 2:298; Moo, 857).

---

[94]This is ἀλλά (*alla*), indicating a very strong contrast.

"Righteousness" thus is the daily righteous conduct of Christians, especially in the right use of Christian liberty. "Peace" is the state of loving harmony among all the members of the church (see v. 19), of "the loving, tranquil relationship of believers" (MacArthur, 2:298). "Joy" is the happy and cheerful spirit that always is obvious among people who enjoy being together. Godet calls it "that individual and collective exultation which prevails among believers when brotherly communion makes its sweetness felt" (461).

The phrase "in the Holy Spirit" goes especially with joy (Acts 13:52; 1 Thess 1:6), but the Spirit's presence is rightly the source of all three of these virtues (see Gal 5:22-23).

Paul's point is that the very nature of the kingdom of God is another reason why the strong brother should not make an issue of his liberty to eat meat or to take any other stand on things that are just matters of opinion anyway. For the sake of the kingdom of God and its impact on the world, he will surely be willing to forgo his rights.

14:18 . . . because anyone who serves Christ in this way is pleasing to God and approved by men. The verb in "serves Christ" is δουλεύω (*douleuō*), which means to serve as a slave, a δοῦλος (*doulos*; see 1:1; JC, 1:59-60). It is important when thinking of Christian *liberty* to remember that such freedom is not absolute; we are still subject to Christ's will for us.

To what does "in this way" refer? No doubt it means doing those things that bring about righteousness, peace, and joy in the life of the church (Lard, 426; SH, 392). When we do those things we not only please God, but earn the approval or respect of our fellow men, who expect to see these virtues exhibited in the church. This is the counterpart to living a life of strife and hypocrisy, which elicits the contempt and blasphemy of the world (v. 16).

This section makes it clear that we Christians cannot be indifferent to others' observations and opinions about the church (see Matt 5:16). Everything about matters of opinion is not a matter of opinion. We are free to decide either way in such matters, but *how* we decide concerning them, and how we perceive them in relation to the kingdom of God, are *not* matters of indifference. Rather, these things are a part of serving Christ as his slaves.

3. We Must Do Only Those Things Which Build Others Up (14:19-21)

14:19 Let us therefore make every effort to do what leads to peace and to mutual edification. This exhortation is based especially on the foundational principle in v. 17, and generally upon the entire teaching of vv. 13-18. It is a call to action,[95] urging all Christians, but especially the strong, to deliberately work to maintain peace and harmony among all believers.

This is accomplished when Christians do and say only those things which lead to "mutual edification," or "the building up of one another" (NASB). Here Paul invokes the familiar image of God's saving work as a construction project. The main emphasis is on the building up of individuals, i.e., causing them to grow and be strengthened in Christ. See, e.g., 1 Cor 8:1; 2 Cor 12:19; 1 Thess 5:11. This of course contributes to the building up of the church as a whole. (For the metaphor of the church itself as a building, see Matt 16:18; Rom 15:20; 1 Cor 3:9-10; 2 Cor 10:8; 13:10; Eph 2:19-21; 1 Pet 2:5.)

This is just another way of describing the limit which love places on our Christian liberty. Love must constrain us to curb our own freedom, and to forgo even good behavior if indulging in it is actually destructive rather than edifying to others.

14:20 Do not destroy the work of God for the sake of food. "The work of God" is the work God is doing, the work he is in the process of accomplishing. Some think this refers specifically to God's building up of the church as a whole.[96] While this cannot be ruled out, the main emphasis again (as in v. 19) seems to be upon the individual Christian viewed as God's "new creation" (2 Cor 5:17) or as "God's workmanship" (Eph 2:10).[97]

This "work of God" is the weak Christian in particular, and Paul is again admonishing the strong not to bring spiritual harm to the

[95]The NIV rightly takes the verb as an imperative (Cranfield, 2:720-721; Moo, 849), though some manuscripts have it in the indicative (SH, 392; Dunn, 2:816).

[96]Lard, 427; Barrett, 265; Dunn, 2:825; Stott, 367; Moo, 860.

[97]Lenski, 846; Murray, 2:195; Hendriksen, 2:466; Cranfield, 2:723; Fitzmyer, 698; MacArthur, 2:299; Morris, 490.

weak by insisting on his right to eat any food he pleases, any time he pleases. The thought is exactly parallel to v. 15b: *destroying the work of God* for the sake of food is equivalent to *destroying the brother for whom Christ died* by the same careless act. A moment's sober reflection should show the strong brother how disastrously absurd this would be.

The word for "destroy" is not the same as in v. 15b; here it is καταλύω (*katalyō*), which has the connotation "to tear down, to demolish." It is used in direct contrast with the work of edifying or building up in v. 19. Do what it takes to build a brother up, says Paul; do not do anything that will tear him down. We are in the construction business, not the demolition business.

The word "destroy" in this verse is thus a very strong word, as is the word in v. 15b. Again it includes the possibility that the strong believer can cause the weak believer to stumble in a way that leads to his ultimate loss of salvation.

All food is clean, but it is wrong for a man to eat anything that causes someone else to stumble. "All food is clean" is a positive restatement of the basic principle given negatively in v. 14a. The rest of the sentence is a clear statement of the ethical principle that underlies all the exhortations to the strong in this paragraph. Although all food[98] is clean, there is at least one circumstance where eating even clean food is wrong, i.e., if it causes a brother to stumble.

"It is wrong" (κακός, *kakos*, "evil") is meant to be in contrast with "it is better" (καλός, *kalos*, "good") in v. 21a. To cause the weak to stumble by what one eats is a moral evil on the part of the strong, and at the same time it has evil or injurious consequences for the weak.

The sentence structure in the Greek is quite terse and leaves open the possibility that the "man" in this sentence is the *weak* brother, who by eating in violation of his conscience commits a sin.[99] This would make the sentence equivalent to vv. 14b, 23. Most agree with the NIV, though, that the "man" is the strong brother

---

[98]Lit., "all things," i.e., all created things. See v. 14a.

[99]See Godet, 463; Murray, 2:195; and the Phillips NT (1958 edition). (Phillips changed his mind about this interpretation before the 1972 edition was published.)

who commits sin by using his freedom in such a way that his eating becomes a stumbling block to the weak. The use of "stumbling block" (πρόσκομμα, *proskomma*) recalls the exhortation to the strong in v. 13b, "not to put any stumbling block" in a brother's way.

The same would be true, of course, for all matters of opinion. Lenski (848) states the general principle well: "Any use of Christian liberty which disregards the damaging effect it may produce upon a weak brother is a bad one."

14:21 The next verse does in fact extend the principle beyond the example of eating certain foods: **It is better**[100] **not to eat meat or drink wine or to do anything else that will cause your brother to fall.** This is, as Moo (861) says, "the basic practical point" of the whole paragraph. This is the way of unselfish love (v. 15a).

Being free to eat any kind of meat is the main example of Christian liberty in this whole section, though this is the first specific reference to "meat" in the Greek text. It is clearly implied in v. 2, however, which says that the strong eats "everything" while the weak eats "only vegetables."

This verse also uses drinking wine as an example of Christian liberty. The reference to "drinking" in v. 17 alludes to this, but it is not mentioned anywhere else in Paul's discussions of the subject of liberty. In biblical times wine was commonly drunk with meals, though it was usually diluted considerably with water. The fact that Paul uses this practice as an example of Christian freedom shows that we cannot say that drinking wine in and of itself is wrong.

We are not sure what circumstances would have required the strong brother in NT times to abstain from drinking wine. Idol worship sometimes involved the pouring out of wine as a sacrifice to the gods; some converted pagans may have thus associated wine with idol worship as they did meat. Thus their overly-sensitive consciences may have prevented them from drinking wine altogether.[101] In such a situation the strong Christian is under obligation not to drink wine, just as he is under obligation not to eat meat, if his

[100]The Greek does not have the comparative "better," but simply, "It is good." The NIV is thus misleading. There is no comparison between *good* and *better* in this context, but between evil (*kakos*) in v. 20, and good (*kalos*) in this verse.

[101]See MP, 531; Dunn, 2:827; Moo, 861.

eating or drinking carries the risk of causing the weak brother to imitate him and thus sin against his own conscience.

"Or to do anything else" leaves the category of opinions open so that this principle may be applied according to our informed Christian wisdom in all times and cultures. The strong Christian must always be sensitive to what the tender conscience of the weak regards as sinful behavior, and must lovingly avoid doing anything that would lead the weak to go against his conscience. When the strong ignores this responsibility in such a situation, two sins are committed: the weak sins[102] by violating his conscience, and the strong sins by becoming a stumbling block to the weak. These are the circumstances that turn an action that is right in itself into a sin.

We should note that the prohibition against meat and wine is not absolute, but must be applied only when such eating or drinking would be a stumbling block for the weak (see Lenski, 849-850; Moo, 861).[103] This means that the strong Christian must conscientiously use his best judgment as to when the exercise of his freedom might lead another into sin. If he cannot be sure, then total abstention would be the loving decision. See 1 Cor 8:13.

4. Each Christian Must Be True to His Own Convictions (14:22-23)

14:22 So whatever you believe about these things keep between yourself and God. "Whatever you believe about these things" is literally "the faith which you have." Since Paul is addressing the strong, the meaning of "faith" here is similar to the faith in v. 2a, in contrast with the faith of the weak in vv. 1,2b. Thus the Apostle is not really talking about "whatever" faith one happens to have; he is rather referring to the correct faith of the strong Christian, who is strong *just because* he has a right understanding of the implications of Christian faith with reference to matters of opinion.

---

[102]The verb "to fall" in this verse is προσκόπτω (*proskoptō*), which is related to the noun πρόσκομμα (*proskomma*), "stumbling block" (vv. 13, 20). Here it refers to stumbling and falling *into sin*.

[103]Some base this conclusion on the aorist tense of these verbs (e.g., Barrett, 266), but the context would suggest it in any case (Morris, 491).

I do not take the word "faith" (πίστις, *pistis*) in itself to mean "conviction," contrary to a common understanding of this verse.[104] As in vv. 1-2, it refers to the content of the Christian faith along with the implications thereof, to which we must give assent and which we must seek to understand. This *understanding* is what is at issue here. The strong have a proper understanding; the weak do not.

Paul's point is that those who have this proper understanding should not flaunt it or wave it in the face of the weak. Rather than make a big issue of it, it is better just to keep it "between yourself and God." As Lard paraphrases it, "Keep your belief, or the knowledge and freedom it gives you, to yourself, as something known only to you and to God" (428). Even if you cannot exercise your freedom when you are in the presence of the weak, you can do so when you are alone before God. Dunn says, those who understand their freedom "can rejoice in the liberty they have in matters of personal conduct before God without having to parade that liberty before others" (2:834).

Blessed is the man who does not condemn himself by what he approves. To be "blessed" is to have inward happiness. Κρίνω (*krinō*) here is properly rendered "condemn" by the NIV.

This beatitude has been understood in two ways. Some take it thus: Blessed is the strong Christian who does not bring God's condemnation upon himself by flaunting his freedom regarding those things he rightly regards as acceptable, in such a way that a weaker brother is caused to stumble (Lard, 428; Moule, 232; Hendriksen, 2:467-468). This meaning is possible, but the second interpretation sets up a better contrast with v. 23, namely: Blessed is the strong Christian who does not condemn himself or feel guilty about his understanding that there is nothing wrong with eating meat, drinking wine, or doing other things about which the revealed will of God is truly silent. He is blessed because he can do these things with a clear conscience.

14:23 But the man who has doubts is condemned if he eats, . . . On the word "has doubts," see 4:20 (JC, 1:304). Here it means "to be uncertain, to waver between two judgments" (Lenski, 853). This

[104]E.g., Bruce says faith here is "a firm and intelligent conviction before God that what one is doing is right" (253). See also MP, 531; Fitzmyer, 698; Moo, 861.

refers to the weak Christian who does not understand the true implications of Christian belief in this area of opinions. It is not a sin to have this inadequate understanding or to have doubts about such things as eating meat offered to idols, though it would certainly be better to come to a right understanding of such things. But it *is* wrong, in the presence of these doubts, to go ahead and eat the meat anyway. The one who does so is "condemned." This word is κατακρίνω (*katakrinō*), an intensified form of *krinō*; it leaves no doubt that eating or doing anything else contrary to one's conscience is condemned by God as a sin.

This verse makes it clear that stumbling or falling on the part of the weak, which the strong are warned not to cause, is not just an inward disapproval of the strong's eating, or an inward distress caused by just witnessing it. It lies rather in being led to actually partake of the disapproved food: "if he eats."

Such an act is wrong for the weak Christian **because his eating is not from faith . . . .** As in vv. 1-2, the "faith" here is not one's inner trust, as if the weak Christian's faith in God and in Jesus Christ for salvation are somehow in question (contra Dunn, 2:835). Rather, it has to do with the weak brother's understanding of the content and implications of Christian faith as such. His understanding is faulty to begin with, but the problem is compounded when he yields to temptation and goes against what he believes his faith requires. His action therefore is not consistent with Christian faith as he understands it; thus he is violating his own conscience, to his own condemnation. Even though the action is not wrong in itself, he *thinks* it is wrong; therefore if he does it anyway, for him it is a sin.

[A]nd everything that does not come from faith is sin. It is tempting to take "faith" here in the specific sense of "trust in Jesus Christ," and to make this a general principle affirming that literally everything an unbeliever does is a sin before God. This may well be true,[105] but most likely this is not Paul's point in this verse. The context limits the "everything" to the debate about matters of opinion.[106]

---

[105]See Moo, 863.

[106]See Lard, 428-429; SH, 393-394; Murray, 2:196; Cranfield, 2:728; Fitzmyer, 699-700. Taking the former view are Lenski, 853-854; Hendriksen, 2:468; and Dunn, 2:828-829, 835.

Thus the point is to extend the statement in v. 23a about *eating* contrary to one's conscience, to cover *all* acts that violate one's convictions about what Christian faith requires. This again is the meaning of "does not come from faith," as in v. 23a. Thus we may paraphrase Paul thus: "Every act that is in fact a matter of opinion but is nevertheless inconsistent with one's (even faulty) understanding of Christian faith is a sin."

C. LIVING IN UNITY AND HOPE (15:1-13)

These verses form the conclusion of the larger section on Christian liberty in matters of opinion (14:1–15:13). The language in both 15:1 and 15:7 shows that Paul still has this subject in mind. The main concern seems to be how the church's handling of such matters affects its internal unity and the integrity of its witness to the watching world. The foundation and the example for such unity, says the Apostle, have been supplied by the redeeming work of Christ.

These verses conclude not only the section on Christian liberty, but also the entire unit on the application of the theological doctrine of the gospel to practical Christian living ("Living the Sanctified Life," 12:1–15:13). It likewise brings to an end the main body of the letter as a whole, and prepares the way for Paul's concluding personal remarks (15:14–16:27).

1. Selfless Service Produces a Unified Witness (15:1-6)

Like much of this section on Christian liberty, these verses are addressed mainly to the strong, which leads Dunn to comment that the primary responsibility for maintaining harmony in the church regarding matters of opinion lies with the strong (2:841). The main hindrance to harmony is the spirit of selfishness, and the key to achieving harmony is to imitate the example of Jesus Christ. Thus Moo sums up these verses as "basically a call to the 'strong' in Rome to follow Christ's example of loving service of others as a means of bringing unity to the church" (865).

15:1 We who are strong ought to bear with the failings of the weak and not to please ourselves. The contrast is still between the weak and the strong, and these terms are still limited to the one issue of Christian liberty regarding opinions. The "weak" were described with a different term in 14:1-2, but the basic concept is the same. This is the first time Paul has used any specific term for the strong. (By saying "we who are strong," Paul includes himself in this group.)

The contrasting terms are δυνατός (*dynatos*, "able, empowered, possible, strong") and ἀδύνατος (*adynatos*, "without power, unable, impossible, weak"). The "strong" are those who, because of their better understanding of the implications of Christian faith, are *able* to do various things (in the category of opinions) with clear consciences. The "weak" are those who are *unable* to do these same things without violating their consciences.

The word "ought"[107] introduces a moral obligation on the part of the strong, a debt which the strong owe to the weak. Stated positively, the strong "ought to bear with the failings of the weak." The term translated "bear with" (βαστάζω, *bastazō*) can mean "to bear with, to tolerate, to put up with, to endure," as the NIV renders it here (see also the RSV; NRSV; SH, 394; Barrett, 269). Most of the time in the NT, however, it means "to bear, to carry," as the NIV translates it in Gal 6:2. Most scholars believe it has this latter connotation here, too. Also, the term translated "failings" in the NIV is simply "weaknesses"; the word "failings" has a negative connotation not evident in the Greek.

All in all the NASB translation is better here: the strong "ought to bear the weaknesses of those without strength." This is a specific instance of the general principle in Gal 6:2, "Carry each other's burdens." I.e., the strong should not merely tolerate the weaknesses of the weak, but should help them carry the burden of their scruples. How may we – the strong – do this? By trying to understand the weak, and by putting ourselves in their place. We may support the weak, as MacArthur says, "by not being critical or condescending and by showing respect for sincere views or practices that we may not agree with" (2:308). As Godet says, "The strong ought to show his strength, not by humiliating the weak and triumphing in the feeling of his superiority, but by bearing the burden of his

[107]This is the verb ὀφείλω (*opheilō*), "to owe a debt, to be under obligation, to be bound by duty."

weakness with love and tenderness" (468). (See also Hendriksen, 2:469; Moo, 866.)

Why should the strong be the ones required to make this sort of concession? Because, as Lard says, the strong can do so without violating their consciences, but the weak cannot (431).

The negative aspect of the moral obligation of the strong is "not to please ourselves." Here Paul identifies the real key to unity, harmony, and peace within the body of Christ, i.e., *selflessness*, or the willingness to sacrifice one's personal rights and personal happiness in order to meet the needs of others. This does not mean that we must avoid pleasing ourselves altogether, and it is not a condemnation of pleasure as such. It is rather a condemnation of the hedonistic attitude that puts personal pleasure ahead of everything else, regardless of how this affects others, especially our fellow Christians. (See Hendriksen, 2:470; Cranfield, 2:731.)

The teaching of this verse is exactly the opposite of any kind of "survival of the fittest" doctrine. It is contrary to the general tendency in the fallen world for the strong (at best) to ignore the weak, and (at worst) to exploit them and take advantage of them. As Cranfield points out (2:730-731), our true obligation before God goes against "the tendency of our fallen human nature, which – so far from being to help those weaker than oneself with their burdens – is for the strong to seek to compel the weak to shoulder the burdens of the strong as well as their own."

15:2 Each of us should please his neighbor for his good, to build him up. "Each of us" could refer to all Christians (Morris, 497-498), but most likely it refers still to strong Christians, the "we" in v. 1 (Moo, 866-867). Thus "each of us should please his neighbor" is simply the same obligation as v. 1b, stated positively. In this case the "neighbor" is the weak Christian.

The rest of this verse – "for his good, to build him up" – identifies and limits the kind of neighbor-pleasing to which Paul is referring. First, this description distinguishes "neighbor-pleasing" from the sinful "man-pleasing" condemned elsewhere by Paul (Gal 1:10; 1 Thess 2:4; see Eph 6:6 and Col 3:22, NASB). In the latter the contrasting choices are pleasing *men* and pleasing *God*; in such circumstances "man-pleasing" means trying to win someone's favor for one's own personal, self-serving purposes. But here in 15:1-2 the contrasting choices are pleasing *ourselves* and pleasing *others*, where "neighbor-pleasing" means that we sacrifice our own desires for the good of the other.

Second, this description – "for his good, to build him up"[108] – limits the extent to which we should go in pleasing our neighbor. Such neighbor-pleasing is not absolute, as if "we are always to defer to the whims and wishes of others" (Murray, 2:197-198). The context shows that Paul is talking about pleasing one's neighbor in areas of opinion where his conscience is threatened by his weak faith. Pleasing the weak "for his good" means "for his spiritual profit or spiritual advantage." It means doing what is necessary to help him maintain a clear conscience in these areas. This includes making an effort to lead the weak out of his unnecessary scruples. As Morris wisely says (498), this verse

> . . . does not mean that the weak control the church – that they have only to express a scruple and all rush to conform. That would mean that the church would be permanently tied to the level of the weak and that life and growth would cease. . . . A genuine concern for the weak will mean an attempt to make them strong by leading them out of their irrational scruples so that they, too, will be strong. . . .

15:3 For even Christ did not please himself . . . . Here Jesus is cited as a model for the virtue of selflessness, one which we should imitate. This is also the main point of Phil 2:5-11, which declares that the selfless attitude of the eternal Logos is exhibited in the incarnation, in his accepting the role of a servant, and especially in his submission to the cross. In every way the Logos put the needs and the interests of the lost human race before his own. It was the Father's will that Jesus undergo an unimaginably agonizing death to save us from our sins, and Jesus surrendered his will to that of his Father. (See Heb 10:7; Matt 20:28 [Mark 10:45]; Matt 26:39 [Luke 22:42]; John 4:24; 5:30; 6:38.) When we as Christians relate to one another in this same spirit of selfless service (Phil 2:5), unity and harmony will surely follow (Phil 2:1-4).

---

[108]"To build him up" uses the same word as in 14:19, and (as there) refers primarily to the spiritual growth of the individual Christian, the weak brother in particular. See also 14:20.

Paul cites just one OT prophecy concerning Jesus to illustrate and confirm his spirit of unselfishness: **. . . but, as it is written: "The insults of those who insult you have fallen on me."** This is taken directly from Ps 69:9b,[109] where David is lamenting that God's enemies are also his enemies and are taking out their hatred of God on him. Paul in effect puts David's words in the mouth of Christ, thus making David's suffering a type of Christ's suffering on the cross. Christ thus declares that, in his submissive life and especially in his substitutionary death, the insults (reproaches, blasphemies) that sinners direct against God are being borne by him. "All the enmity of men against God was directed to Christ" (Murray, 2:199). See Ps 22:6-8; Matt 27:39-44.

The point is that Jesus willingly and unselfishly chose to walk this path of humiliation and suffering for the sake of helpless and ungodly sinners. And if Jesus himself made such a selfless choice, we should all the more be willing to do so for the sake of our weak brothers. Paul is thus making an argument from the greater to the lesser: if the incarnate Son of God went to such an extreme in not pleasing himself, then surely we can "renounce our self-gratification in so unimportant a matter as the exercising of our freedom with regard to what we eat or whether we observe special days" (Cranfield, 2:733). See also Hendriksen, 2:470; Murray, 2:199; Dunn, 2:842-843; Moo, 869.

15:4 The next verse is a parenthesis in which Paul reminds us of the validity of citing OT texts as a basis for ethical exhortation to Christians: **For everything that was written in the past was written to teach us, . . .** "Everything that was written" refers to OT Scripture, and declares that every part of it has meaning and value for those living under the New Covenant. It was written not just to teach us theological truths, but also to be a source of practical instruction for Christians concerning how to live. Paul was thinking mainly (but not exclusively) of OT Scripture when he said, "All Scripture is God-breathed and is useful for teaching, rebuking, correcting and training in righteousness, so that the man of God may be thoroughly equipped for every good work" (2 Tim 3:16-17). See 1 Cor 9:10; 10:6,11; Rom 4:23-25.

---

[109]This is Ps 68:10 in the LXX, which is quoted exactly. Paul has already quoted Ps 69:22-23 in 11:9-10, confirming its Davidic authorship.

In particular, says Paul, the OT was written **so that through endurance and the encouragement of the Scriptures we might have hope.** "Endurance" (ὑπομονή, *hypomonē*) is the same as "perseverance" in 5:3; it indicates patient endurance, steadfastness, the ability to bear and to bear up under whatever comes along (see JC, 1:317). "Encouragement" (παράκλησις, *paraklēsis*) has the connotation of "exhortation" in 12:8, but here it means "comfort, consolation, encouragement." "Hope" (ἐλπίς, *elpis*) for Christians is the confident and joyful expectation of the future possession of full salvation, as explained under 4:18 and 5:2 (JC, 1:301, 315).

This is a purpose clause, introduced by ἵνα (*hina*, "so that, in order that"). I.e., God intends for us to be taught by the OT Scriptures, to the end that "we might have hope." How does the study of the OT give hope to Christians? Paul says it does so specifically "through endurance and the encouragement of the Scriptures."

Interpreters are divided as to whether the phrase "of the Scriptures" is meant to modify both endurance and encouragement. Some think it modifies only the latter, which would yield a translation something like this: ". . . so that, with patient endurance, we might have hope by means of the encouragement received from the Scriptures" (see Cranfield, 2:735-736; Dunn, 2:839; Morris, 500). The grammatical structure (a repetition of the preposition διά (*dia*) before "encouragement") supports this view but does not require it. In my judgment the context (Paul's explanation for citing the OT) favors the other view, that "of the Scriptures" refers to both endurance and encouragement. Moule (235) says it means "the patience and comfort taught by the Scriptures." See also Lard, 433; Lenski, 860; Murray, 2:200.

The point is that when we read the OT accounts of and testimony to God's just and faithful dealings with Israel, this reinforces our confidence in God's promises to us through the New Covenant, and thus gives us patience and encouragement in times of personal spiritual doubt and distress. The result of such endurance and encouragement is that our hope – our assurance of salvation – is in turn strengthened. This hope is fortified even further by "reading the OT and seeing its fulfillment in Christ and the church" (Moo, 870). On the relationship between endurance and hope, see 5:3-4; 1 Thess 1:3.

15:5-6 The next two verses are a prayer[110] for God to bless the church with the spirit of unity: **May the God who gives endurance and encouragement give you a spirit of unity among yourselves as you follow Christ Jesus, so that with one heart and mouth you may glorify the God and Father of our Lord Jesus Christ.**

The Greek text speaks literally of "the God of endurance and encouragement"; the NIV rightly takes this to mean that God is the *source* of these blessings in the Christian life. The idea is that God by his words and deeds gives us every reason to have patient endurance and to be encouraged even in the bleakest of circumstances, and he gives us knowledge of and access to these words and deeds through his Spirit-inspired Scriptures (see v. 4).

The heart of Paul's prayer is that God "will give you[111] a spirit of unity among yourselves." Just what is the nature of the unity for which Paul prays? "A spirit of unity" (v. 5) and "with one heart" (v. 6) suggest something similar to "live in harmony " (12:16). "With one heart" ("with one accord," NASB) especially points to a harmony on the inward level, a harmony of spirit and attitude that binds the hearts of all Christians together in mutual love and esteem and in a solidarity of spirit and purpose. See Phil 2:2.

But Paul's language here shows that the unity for which he prays is not just a harmonious spirit, but also a unity of faith, i.e., an agreement as to the *content* of what is believed. "A spirit of unity" is literally "to be of the same mind." This phrase does not necessarily refer to intellectual agreement, since it occurs in the same or similar form in 12:16 and Phil 2:2, where it refers to the general unity of love and purpose. But the reference to the "mind" does leave the door open for the concept of intellectual agreement; and the expression "with one mouth" in v. 6 definitely shows that this is part of what Paul is praying for.

"With one mouth" shows that the church's unity must be on a verbal level, which certainly involves a unity in worship (SH, 396; Dunn, 2:841); but this presupposes a unity of *what we believe* about the one whom we worship. Lenski says it involves outward agreement wherein all confess "the one same gospel truth" (863).

---

[110]Some call it a "prayer-wish." See Cranfield, 2:736; Dunn, 2:840; Moo, 871.

[111]"You" refers to all Christians, not just the strong.

This prayer for unity regarding what we believe certainly does not prescribe total agreement regarding matters of opinion, since matters of opinion by definition to not require agreement. In reference to opinions, the most Paul can be praying for is that all Christians have the same understanding of the *nature* of *adiaphora* or opinions, and of how to *handle* them with mature faith. But at the very least this prayer is instructing us to seek basic agreement concerning the fundamental truths about God and the gospel,[112] over against the idea that "each man may have . . . the right to his own personal views" about the truths affirmed in God's Word (Lenski, 864).

Paul prays that the church will have such unity "as you follow Christ Jesus," or better, "according to Christ Jesus" (NASB). Some take this to mean "according to Jesus' example" (SH, 396; Murray, 2:201; Dunn, 2:840); others "according to Jesus' will" (Cranfield, 2:737). Paul may have both of these in mind (Lard, 433; Hendriksen, 2:473), but the main point is that Christ Jesus must always be the touchstone of the church's unity. That is, we must never pursue unity just for the sake of unity. God is not interested in unity at all costs, especially at the cost of truth. Those things on which the church is united must correspond to Christ's way, Christ's will, Christ's gospel, and Christ's word as we know it through inspired Scripture.

What is the purpose of seeking this inner harmony and this unity of confessed faith? So that "you may glorify the God and Father of our Lord Jesus Christ." To glorify God is to acknowledge and declare his greatness before others, and to lead them to do the same (see 1:21; JC, 1:144-145). A church with internal dissensions and conflicting beliefs brings dishonor to God and to Jesus its Head. A church united in heart and mind brings glory to both. See 1 Cor 1:10; Eph 4:11-15.

Some may raise questions about the description of God as "the God and Father of our Lord Jesus Christ." No one will have a problem with calling God "the *Father* of our Lord Jesus Christ." But since Jesus himself is divine, i.e., God the Son, how can we speak of "the *God* of Jesus Christ"? The KJV translates it "God, even the

---

[112]Or as Stott says, unity regarding the "essentials" (371). See my treatment of this whole issue in *Faith's Fundamentals*.

Father of our Lord Jesus Christ"; Lard agrees (434). But there is no problem with the language as it stands in the NIV. In his incarnate state as Jesus of Nazareth, the human nature of Jesus was in full submission to God the Father as *his God.* In John 20:17, speaking to Mary, Jesus refers to God the Father as "my God and your God." Eph 1:17 uses the very phrase, "the God of our Lord Jesus Christ." See also Matt 27:46 (Mark 15:34) and Heb 1:9. There is no conflict between this concept and the divinity of Christ.

2. Through Christ's Selfless Service, Jews and Gentiles Glorify God Together (15:7-12)

Some see this paragraph as standing alone and serving as a conclusion to the doctrinal body of the letter (Dunn, 2:844). Most, however, see it as belonging to the section on Christian liberty. The main emphasis still seems to be on the unity of the body of Christ, which was being threatened by false approaches to matters of opinion.

The main point is the way the saving work of Jesus has united two groups, the Jews and the Gentiles, into one body and into one voice singing praises to God. This is significant because in the ancient world these two groups would surely have been regarded as the least likely to be reconciled. In the immediate context this serves as another argument from the greater to the lesser. If Christ's selfless service can succeed in unifying such disparate groups as the Jews and the Gentiles, surely we as Christians can do what is necessary to establish accord among strong and weak believers within the church. As Bruce sums it up, we must "follow the example of Christ, who welcomed us without discrimination, and make room for one another without discrimination" (255).

Paul's bringing together of Jews and Gentiles in this paragraph serves other purposes, too. It means that Paul has come full circle in his presentation of the gospel, which in the introduction was announced to be God's way of salvation, "first for the Jew, then for the Gentile" (1:16). It calls attention again to the fact that God's faithfulness to the Jews has always involved his intention to save the Gentiles as well (chs. 9–11). Finally, Paul's citation of OT prophecies concerning the salvation of the Gentiles serves as a transition to his personal remarks about his own mission to the Gentiles (15:14-33).

Some think the reference to Jews and Gentiles at this point supports the view that the weak and the strong in the church at Rome were divided mainly along these lines, with the weak being mainly from the Jews and the strong mainly from the Gentiles (SH, 397; Cranfield, 2:740-741). Others are rightly reluctant to draw this conclusion (Lenski, 866; Murray, 2:204). Even if we think there is a hint in this direction, this discussion of Jews and Gentiles is better explained by the points mentioned above (see Dunn, 2:852).

15:7 Accept one another, then, just as Christ accepted you,[113] **in order to bring praise to God.** It seems clear that this paragraph is meant to be the conclusion to the section on Christian liberty (Moo, 874). This verse begins with the conjunction διό (*dio*, "wherefore, then"), indicating that the following exhortation is an inference from the preceding discussion (14:1-15:6). The exhortation to "accept" one another also ties this paragraph to this same discussion, since 14:1 uses the same verb to exhort the strong to "accept" the weak. Another link is the stated bases for the two exhortations: accept the weak, "for God has accepted him" (14:3); accept each other "as Christ accepted you" (15:7).

While this exhortation is parallel to 14:1, it also goes beyond it by addressing the entire church and not just the strong. In fact, it has the nature of a general principle that applies to all potential causes of division in the church. The fact that Christ has united Jews and Gentiles together serves as a paradigm for the healing of all divisions. His acceptance of both groups is the reason why we should embrace all believers in full fellowship despite differences that do not affect our common salvation. Paul's point is "that all are to accept those who differ from them" (Morris, 503).

The verse closes with a phrase of purpose: "to the glory of God" (see NASB). The NIV translation, "in order to bring praise to God," captures the general sense. One question is whether this phrase modifies "accept one another," thus in effect giving us a motive for

[113]Some manuscripts have "us," but "you" is the preferred reading. It follows most naturally from the imperative "accept," which is second person ("accept ye"). See SH, 397; Murray, 2:203; Cranfield, 2:739; Dunn, 2:844; Moo, 872.

obeying this command (Godet, 470; Cranfield, 2:739-740; Moo, 875), or whether it modifies "as Christ accepted you," indicating the glorious result of his accepting us (SH, 397; Lenski, 867; Murray, 2:204). The word order favors the latter view; but this in effect makes the former true also, since our acceptance of one another is patterned after ("just as") Christ's acceptance of us.

15:8a For I tell you that Christ has become a servant of the Jews on behalf of God's truth, . . . Here Paul begins to explain how Christ has "accepted you" through the redeeming work performed in his role as the Jewish Messiah. The words "I tell you" introduce "a solemn doctrinal declaration" (Cranfield, 2:740). "Servant" is διάκονος (*diakonos*), which can mean "deacon" or "minister," but is rightly translated here with its basic generic sense, "servant." "Has become" is in the perfect tense, indicating past action (perhaps the incarnation but certainly the atonement and resurrection) with a lasting result; Christ is still "a servant of the Jews" (Morris, 503). "Jews" is literally "circumcision," a term often used for the Jews as a nation (see 3:30; 4:12; Gal 2:8-9). This emphasizes the fact that the Jews were under the covenant God made with Abraham, of which circumcision was the covenant sign (Gen 17:1-14).

That the Logos entered the world in the role of a servant is clear; see v. 3 above, and see Phil 2:7-8, where he is called a "slave" (δοῦλος, *doulos*). Jesus says that he "did not come to be served, but to serve" (Matt 20:28; Mark 10:45; see Luke 22:27). He was primarily a servant of the Father himself (Isa 52:13), but in that role he served the lost world by giving "his life as a ransom for many" (Matt 20:28).

Most specifically Jesus performed his redeeming work as "a servant of the Jews." This refers to his role as the Jews' Messiah (the Christ). In order to fulfill this role Christ Jesus came into the world *through* the Jews (John 4:22; Rom 9:4-5) and *for* the Jews, i.e., so that the Jews themselves might be the first to receive the gospel of salvation (Matt 15:24; Rom 1:16; 2:10; Gal 4:4-5).

Paul affirms that Jesus became a servant of the Jews "on behalf of God's truth." "Truth" (ἀλήθεια, *alētheia*) here refers to an attribute of God and may better be rendered "truthfulness" (Lard, 434), "fidelity" (Godet, 471; Fitzmyer, 706), or "faithfulness" (Cranfield, 2:740; Dunn, 2:847; Moo, 877). The specific reference is to God's faithfulness to his covenant promises. Everything Christ did as the

Jewish Messiah was in fulfilment of what God has been promising to do for his people (both Jews and Gentiles) from the very beginning of his covenant with Abraham (Gen 12:1-3).

15:8b-9a The rest of this section shows how Christ's Jewish Messiahship has affected not only the Jews but the Gentiles as well. Christ was a servant of the Jews **to confirm the promises made to the patriarchs so that the Gentiles may glorify God for his mercy, . . .** Interpreters disagree over the syntax of this segment. All agree that Paul is making two parallel statements, one about the Jews and the other about the Gentiles. The question is, where does the first statement begin? One view is that it begins immediately after "I tell you" in v. 8a, and the two statements are parallel objects of "I tell you." Thus Paul would be saying, "I tell you first that Christ has become a servant of the Jews on behalf God's truth, to confirm the promises made to the patriarchs. And I also tell you that the Gentiles are glorifying God for his mercy" (see Godet, 471; Cranfield, 2:742-744). This view is attractive because it allows the two phrases "on behalf of [ὑπέρ, *hyper*] God's truth" and "for [*hyper*] his mercy" to be regarded as parallel.[114]

The other view is that the first of the two parallel statements begins with the words "to confirm" in v. 8b. Thus the two statements are parallel objects of the preposition *eis* (translated "to" but better rendered "in order to"), indicating a *double purpose* for Christ's Jewish Messiahship. Thus Paul is saying that Christ became a servant of the Jews first of all for the purpose of confirming the promises made to the patriarchs, and also so that the Gentiles may glorify God for his mercy (see SH, 398; Lenski, 868; Stott, 372; Moo, 876).

The point of the second view, which I accept, is to emphasize the obvious fact that the messianic work of Jesus Christ was intended all along to have redemptive results not just for the Jews but also for the Gentiles.

The first intended result of Christ's Messiahship was "to confirm the promises made to the patriarchs" (Abraham, Isaac, and Jacob). This reference to the patriarchs (or "fathers"; see 9:5), along with the very phrase "servant of the Jews," shows that Paul is here referring to

[114]Dunn shows the weaknesses of this view, but is ambiguous as to his own preference (2:847-848).

promises concerning the Jews themselves. See Gen 12:1-3; 13:14-17; 15:1-5; 17:1-8; 18:19; 22:15-18; 26:3-4; 28:13-15.

Paul has already affirmed that God in his faithfulness has fulfilled all his promises to the Jews as a nation (9:4-5) and as a believing remnant (see the entire discussion in chs. 9–11). Here he says that Christ's work as the Jews' servant has *confirmed* these promises. This means that he has proved the promises to be reliable and trustworthy, but it means more than this. Christ has confirmed the promises by fulfilling them, by establishing them, by bringing them to realization. What was in the beginning just a promise is now a reality for the Jews.[115]

The second intended result of Christ's Messiahship, and the one Paul emphasizes, was to enable the Gentiles to "glorify God for his mercy." This purpose is seen in the fact that the covenant promises made to the patriarchs included the blessing of salvation for all peoples and nations on earth (Gen 12:3; 17:3-5; 22:18; 26:4; 28:14; Rom 4:13, 16-17). Though Christ's earthly ministry was conducted almost entirely among the Jews, his "great commission" directs that the gospel be preached to all nations (Matt 28:19; Luke 24:47; Acts 1:8). By thus including the Gentiles within the scope of his salvation, Christ causes them to glorify God (see v. 6), specifically for having mercy upon them (see 11:30-32).

As Stott summarizes the Messiah's two-fold purpose, "It was in mercy to the Gentiles, as it was in faithfulness to Israel, that Christ became a servant for the benefit of both" (372).

15:9b The rest of this section is a series of four quotes from the OT showing that God all along intended to bring the Gentiles within the scope of his mercy, thus uniting Jews and Gentiles together into one harmonious chorus of praise to God.

The first quote is as follows: **. . . as it is written: "Therefore I will praise you among the Gentiles; I will sing hymns to your name."** This is a direct quote from Ps 18:49 (LXX, 17:50) and 2 Sam 22:50, except for the omission of "O LORD." In this Psalm David is praising God for giving him victory over his enemies and for making the nations subject to him. In verse 49 he announces that he will sing hymns of praise to the Lord among these nations (i.e.,

[115]See Moule, 236; Lenski, 868; Murray, 2:205; Dunn, 2:847; Moo, 877.

Gentiles), so that the Gentiles may know the true God and join in the praise.

Paul sees in this Psalm an indication of God's plan to include the Gentiles in the Messiah's people. As Cranfield notes (2:795), it is possible that the Apostle sees David's words as foreshadowing his own mission to the Gentiles, a subject he is just about to expand upon (15:14ff.).

The word for "sing hymns" is simply ψάλλω (*psallō*), which Morris says "referred originally to plucking the strings of a musical instrument; later it appears to have been used of singing with accompaniment and then simply of singing. There is nothing in the Greek to correspond to NIV's *hymns*; the translators have assumed (not unreasonably) that it is hymns that would be sung to God" (505, n. 51).

15:10 Again, it[116] says, "Rejoice, O Gentiles, with his people." This next quotation is the first line of Deut 32:43 (LXX). Deut 32 is a song of Moses celebrating the righteousness of God that takes vengeance on his enemies and saves his people. In this line Moses invites the nations (Gentiles) to join with God's people (the Jews) in rejoicing over this. The key phrase is "with his people," which contemplates Jews and Gentiles praising God with a single voice. Paul sees this as an expression of God's plan to unite the two groups.

15:11 And again, "Praise the Lord, all you Gentiles, and sing praises to him, all you peoples." This is a close paraphrase of Ps 117:1 (LXX, 116:1). The main point again is the reference to the Gentiles, and the fact that they are invited to sing praises to the Lord, the God of Israel. This is another indication that the work of the Messiah was intended to bring Jews and Gentiles together into one body, so that "his people" (v. 10) along with "all you peoples" (v. 11) may glorify God together for his mercy.

15:12 And again, Isaiah says, "The Root of Jesse will spring up, one who will arise[117] to rule over the nations; the Gentiles will hope in him." This is taken from Isa 11:10, and is closer to the LXX than to the Hebrew text. It is a specific messianic prophecy, "the Root of Jesse" being a title for Jesus. Jesse was David's father; thus this title is equivalent to "the Root of David" in Rev 5:5; 22:16,

---

[116]The "it" is Scripture (4:3; 9:17; 10:11; 11:2).

[117]Though the word for "arise" sometimes means resurrection from the dead, here it probably means "appear," referring to the incarnation.

which refers to Christ. The word translated "root" is ῥίζα (*rhiza*), which can mean either the root itself or a shoot or sprout that comes forth from the root. In this case "Jesse," standing for the family and dynasty of David (see Luke 2:4), is the root itself; Jesus is the shoot or sprout that springs up from that root (Isa 11:1; 53:2).

The main point is that when "the Root of Jesse" rises up, the Gentiles will rally around him and submit to him and find their salvation in him. The Hebrew text of Isa 11:10 says that "the Root of Jesse will stand as a banner for the peoples." The LXX interprets the banner or ensign as a symbol of command and authority; thus when the Gentiles rally around this banner (which is Jesus himself), they are submitting to him and he is ruling over them.

The messianic rule of which Isaiah speaks is not a military conquest of rebellious and unwilling foes, but a benevolent embrace of willing subjects for the purpose of bestowing mercy upon them. As a result, "the Gentiles will hope in him," i.e., they will find their salvation in him. The startling thing about this is that the *Gentiles* will be saved by submitting to the Messiah of the *Jews*!

Paul has already said as much in vv. 6-8, where he says Christ has become a servant of the Jews "so that the Gentiles may glorify God for his mercy." The OT quotations are designed to reinforce this point by showing that it has always been God's purpose to include the Gentiles within the Messiah's kingdom. More specifically, now that the Jews' Messiah has come, both Jews and Gentiles together have been accepted by Christ into his own body, to the praise and glory of God and his mercy. In view of God's majestic and glorious program for uniting all believers into a single ensemble of praise, how can we refuse to obey the simple command to "accept one another" (15:7)?

3. A Prayer That All Believers May Abound in Hope (15:13)

15:13 May the God of hope fill you with all joy and peace as you trust in him, so that you may overflow with hope by the power of the Holy Spirit. This last verse of the main body of the letter expresses Paul's desire that all Christians may experience the fullness of the spiritual benefits that come from knowing, understanding, and receiving the gospel of God's grace. As such it draws together many of the main threads that the Apostle has woven into the carefully designed pattern of his doctrinal essay about this gospel. Specifically mentioned are faith, joy, peace, hope, and power.

The first and primary benefit that comes from knowing the gospel is faith itself (10:17). All the other blessings come only "as you trust in him," or literally, "in connection with believing." At the outset Paul emphasized the key role of faith in receiving salvation (1:16-17). Jesus Christ died for our sins and was raised for our justification (3:24-26; 4:25), but we cannot receive this justification without faith (3:25-28; 10:9-10). In this verse Paul is reaffirming the central and essential role of faith in the gospel plan of salvation.

Paul prays that we as believers may be filled with joy, peace, and hope, all of which come from knowing that we are justified by faith in the blood of Christ (5:1-2). *Peace* is first of all the objective state of being reconciled to God (5:1, 10). It is also an attitude of inward tranquility and freedom from worry about salvation (1:7; 8:6); this is the main point in view here. Finally peace is the corporate harmony that exists among brethren (14:17).

Joy is the inward delight and jubilance that keep us excited about being Christians, about being under the blood of Christ, and about living the sanctified life (5:2-3,11; 12:12,15; 14:17). Joy and peace together are "two of the great human desirables," as Dunn says (2:853), and they are available to mankind only through the gospel of Jesus Christ.

The last of this trio of related blessings is *hope*, which is a key aspect of assurance and in many ways is equivalent to it. Assurance is first of all a peaceful confidence about our *present* relationship with God through Jesus Christ; second, it is a joyful expectation of the *future* fullness of glory to be received when Christ returns. The latter is the essence of hope.

Knowing that we are justified by faith is the key to such hope or assurance (5:1-2), which is certainly the climactic benefit of the gospel and a frequent subject in Romans (4:18; 5:2-5; 8:20,24-25; 12:12; 15:4,12). That God is here called "the God of hope," i.e., the source of everything that gives us hope, shows how important hope is in the context of the gospel.

Paul's prayer and wish are not just that believers might *possess* joy, peace, and hope, but that we might be *filled to overflowing* with these blessings. Since they are linked to faith, they will increase as our faith increases (Luke 17:5). Faith consists of *assent* and *trust* (1:16; JC, 1:107-108). Assent increases as we grow in our understanding of what we believe about Jesus and the gospel, and trust increases as we grow in our love for Jesus and in confidence in his promises.

The ultimate means of our being filled to overflowing with joy, peace, and hope is the fifth blessing mentioned in this verse, i.e., *power* – "the power of the Holy Spirit." Paul has made it clear in Romans that all spiritual growth comes from the power of the indwelling Spirit (2:29; 5:5; 8:3-16,26-27; 14:17; see Gal 5:22-23). Here he prays that the Spirit's power may work within our hearts to make us abound in hope. There could hardly be a more appropriate conclusion to the didactic body of the Epistle to the Romans!

15:14–16:27 – PART SIX

PERSONAL MESSAGES FROM PAUL

The main body of the Epistle to the Romans (the doctrinal essay, 1:18–15:13) has now been concluded. What follows is a kind of epilogue containing many of the same elements found in the conclusions of Paul's other letters, e.g., personal greetings to individuals, his travel plans, a request for prayer, a wish for peace, a reference to the holy kiss, warnings and exhortations, and a concluding benediction or doxology.[1]

All of these elements are communicated on a very personal level, as Paul addresses the Roman Christians not just in his role as an Apostle (15:15), but also on the level of warm brotherly fellowship (15:14,30; 16:17).

I. PAUL'S MINISTRY AS THE APOSTLE TO THE GENTILES (15:14-33)

As he begins his conclusion, Paul first of all expresses his confidence in the spiritual maturity of the Christians at Rome, and suggests that the sternness of some of his exhortations is not meant to imply weakness on their part (14-15a). All of his ministry, including the writing of this letter, is carried out in his specific role as the Apostle to the Gentiles, which he regards as a kind of priesthood in which he offers up converted Gentiles as sacrifices pleasing to God (15b-16).

Paul realizes that his work has produced significant results, but he gives God all the glory (17-19a). Up to the time of this writing, he has concentrated his efforts in the geographical area ranging from

[1]See charts comparing the material in the conclusion of Romans with that in Paul's other epistles in Dunn (1:854) and Moo (884).

Jerusalem to Illyricum, using the strategy of starting new churches in unevangelized areas (19b-21). This has kept him so busy that he has been unable to fulfill his dream of visiting Rome (22).

But the situation is different now. He has accomplished his purpose for this eastern area and is now ready to travel west, stopping off to visit the Christians in Rome on his way to evangelize Spain – an endeavor for which he hopes to enlist the aid of the church in Rome (23-24).

But before he can begin to carry out this plan, he has one other very important task to complete. He must journey to Jerusalem, and deliver the contributions he has collected from the Gentile churches for the poor saints in the Jerusalem church (25-27; see JC, 1:35-36). Then he will head directly to Rome and on to Spain (28-29).

The side trip to Jerusalem is anything but routine, however. Paul anticipates the possibility of serious problems there, including attacks upon him personally from non-Christian Jews, and a reluctance on the part of the Jewish Christians to accept gifts from Gentile Christians. Therefore he urges the Roman brethren to join him in praying that the Jerusalem trip will go well, so that he may subsequently go on to Rome in a joyful spirit (30-32). He prays for God's peace to be with them (33).

Some see this section as the key to Paul's purpose for writing Romans in the first place, or at least the key to "the content and emphases of the letter" (Moo, 885). Some think Paul's long essay is intended to demonstrate his doctrinal orthodoxy to the Roman Christians, showing them the gospel he would preach in Spain as part of his effort to persuade them to back his mission there. Others think Paul is rehearsing the defense he will give in Jerusalem, in case his orthodoxy is challenged in connection with the delivery of the Gentile Christians' gifts to the Jerusalem church. (See JC, 1:40-42; see Dunn, 2:884.)

In my opinion, though, these factors are secondary in Paul's mind as he writes this letter. His main purpose, as explained earlier (JC, 1:44-45), stems from his eager desire "to preach the gospel also to you who are at Rome" (1:15).

While the themes of this section definitely overlap the contents of the introduction to the epistle (1:1-17; see Moo, 886), there is significant new information here, as the above summary indicates. We may break it down into paragraphs dealing with Paul's past service (14-22), his future plans (23-29), and his request for prayer (30-33).

A. REFLECTIONS ON HIS PAST SERVICE (15:14-22)

This paragraph gives us important insights, first into Paul as a person, and then into his self-understanding of his apostolic ministry. The former is manifest in vv. 14-15, in the way he deals with his concern that the Christians in Rome might misunderstand the occasionally serious tone of his letter. He has uttered some rather stern rebukes and strong exhortations along the way, and now he wants to make sure that the brethren in Rome do not take these to mean that he had a low opinion of their Christian faith and life. Thus he expresses his own confidence in them and compliments them on their personal maturity as Christians (see 1:8; 16:19). At the same time he wants them not to see him as insensitive and presumptuous but to understand that it is his duty as the Apostle to the Gentiles to address them with authority. (See MacArthur, 2:326; Stott, 377.)

These two verses (14-15), says Hendriksen, thus show us what kind of person Paul was. Specifically, they show Paul to be a man of tact, modesty, prudence, humility, and concern for the feelings of others (2:484).

The other major insight we glean from this paragraph has to do with the way Paul understood the nature of his apostleship. First, as to essence, he saw it in terms of *priesthood* (v. 16). Second, as to strategy, he saw himself called to be a *church planter*. I.e., his task was to be a pioneer preacher, commissioned to carry the gospel into the centers of Gentile population, plant churches, and move on (vv. 19-21).

It was this self-understanding that had shaped his past service, and was now shaping his plans for the immediate future.

15:14 I myself am convinced, my brothers, that you yourselves are full of goodness, complete in knowledge and competent to instruct one another. We must not forget that the just-completed essay on the doctrine of salvation was not written just for the sake of the church at Rome, but was intended by the Holy Spirit to apply to the entire body of Christ in all ages. At times Paul's admonitions seem rather severe, e.g., 6:1-3,15-16; 11:17-22; 13:12-14; 14:1-4,10-16; and in the church as a whole some Christians will feel their sting more than others will.

This is why Paul wants the Christians in Rome to know that he is not necessarily implying that they are personally lacking in these areas. "I myself" translates an emphatic phrase, as does "you yourselves." "As far as I personally am concerned," Paul says, "I am persuaded that you personally are Christians of solid maturity." He knew their good reputation (1:8; 16:19), and he knew some of them on a personal basis. His praise is neither insincere flattery nor oily diplomacy, nor is he apologizing for anything he has said.[2] Dunn rightly notes, though, that the language is "exaggerated, in the way that courteous compliments in the East tend to be" (2:866).[3]

Paul compliments the Roman Christians in three areas. First, he says they are "full of goodness" (ἀγαθοσύνη, *agathosynē*). This basically refers to a morally upright character, a general goodness of the heart that loves righteousness and opposes all that is evil. "This would be first of all goodwill or the intention to do that which is good," says Spicq (*Lexicon,* 1:3). It is not just obedience (16:19), but an obedient heart as well (6:17).

That the Romans were *full* of goodness is hyperbole, since perfection eludes all. It means, says Morris, that they had a "plentiful supply" of goodness and not just an occasional episode of it (509). The sense is this: "I am fully aware of your spiritual maturity and moral virtue, and I commend you for it" (MacArthur, 2:327). This is indeed a high compliment; at the opposite end of the spectrum would be a church like the one at Corinth as reflected in 1 Corinthians.

Paul next praises the church at Rome for being "complete in knowledge," or "filled with all knowledge" (NASB). This again is hyperbole, since omniscience belongs to God alone. Also, Paul is not saying they had knowledge of every possible topic; his comment is "limited by the subject in hand" (Lard, 439), i.e., the gospel or the Christian faith. Paul is saying that they have a solid and practical understanding of Christian teaching. (The very depth of the

---

[2]Some think Paul's words here have a "semiapologetic tone" (Fitzmyer, 710), or an "almost apologetic tone" (Moo, 887).

[3]See "*full of* goodness," and "*filled* with *all* knowledge" (NASB).

essay on salvation which is the heart of this letter shows Paul's confidence in the mature level of their understanding; this is no doctrinal primer!)

Paul's commendation of the Romans' *goodness* and *knowledge* together is a rebuke to those Christians who deliberately deemphasize doctrine and focus entirely on loving interpersonal relationships as the essence of Christianity. Virtue and truth are inseparable, as MacArthur says (2:327). The issue is not either-or, but both-and.

In his third compliment Paul declares that the Romans are "competent to instruct one another." Νουθετέω (*noutheteō*) means literally to put something into someone's mind, i.e., "to instruct"; but it often means instruction in the sense of "admonish, warn, reprimand, rebuke," especially with reference to moral training (see Col 1:28; see Spicq, *Lexicon*, 2:548-551). Paul is basically saying that the Roman Christians do not need for him to admonish them, for they are fully capable of admonishing one another.

15:15 I have written you quite boldly on some points,[4] as if to remind you of them again, because of the grace God gave me . . . . In what sense is this letter somewhat *bold* (audacious, daring)? Paul is probably referring to those places mentioned above where his admonitions are rather severe. Some think he is being "slightly apologetic" in view of the fact that he was not the one who founded the church in Rome and did not even know most of them (Cranfield, 2:752-753; Bruce, 260; Dunn, 2:857). Such an "apology" is not necessary, however, in view of Paul's general apostolic authority, to which he appeals in v. 15b.

Some may think that Paul had to speak forcefully at times because the Roman brethren's spiritual immaturity made it necessary. But we have just seen that Paul regards them as being not immature but "spiritually strong and well-equipped" (MacArthur, 2:330). Indeed, this is the very point: he has addressed them boldly just because their maturity makes them able to handle such admonitions and to profit from them.

Paul says he is *reminding* them *again* of these things, implying the prior knowledge mentioned in v. 14. This "diplomatic exaggeration" (Moo, 888) does not necessarily mean that they already knew

---

[4]The NIV rightly takes ἀπὸ μέρους (*apo merous*, "in part") as referring to "some points" in the letter.

everything Paul writes in this letter, but probably means that they knew the fundamental facts of the gospel, the deeper implications of which he is here setting forth. In any case it teaches us this, that although Christians are not supposed to keep focusing on the basics to the neglect of deeper doctrine (Heb 5:11–6:3), there is still a need for us to be periodically reminded even of fundamental truths (2 Tim 2:8-14; Titus 3:1; 2 Pet 1:12; 3:1).

In the last part of this verse Paul declares that he has reminded them of these things somewhat boldly on account of "the grace God gave to me." This grace is the gift of apostleship, his commission to be the Apostle to the Gentiles (see 1:5; JC, 1:77-78). His apostolic authority and apostolic duty are thus the basis or justification for what he has written in this letter and for the authoritative manner in which he has written it.

15:16 Paul now explains the essence of his apostleship. God gave me this grace, he says, **to be a minister of Christ Jesus to the Gentiles with the priestly duty of proclaiming the gospel of God, so that the Gentiles might become an offering acceptable to God, sanctified by the Holy Spirit.** Three words in this verse show that Paul viewed his ministry as a (metaphorical) *priesthood*. First, he says God's grace has made him a "minister" (λειτουργός, *leitourgos*; see 13:6). This word does not always have a religious connotation, but along with its cognates it sometimes refers to priestly service. (This is the word group from which we get the term "liturgy.") The present context, especially the other two words discussed below, shows that Paul has this priestly connotation in mind here.[5] He thus identifies himself as a priestly minister serving Jesus Christ "to the Gentiles," or for the sake of the Gentiles. OT priests interceded with God on behalf of the Jews, but under the New Covenant that service is now performed on behalf of the Gentiles as well.

The second religious or cultic word used here is the verb ἱερουργέω (*hierourgeō*), translated "priestly duty" in the NIV. (See the words ἱερός [*hieros*, "holy"] and ἱερόν [*hieron*, "sanctuary, temple"].) Most agree that it means "to serve or act as a priest" (AG, 374; Murray, 2:210; Dunn, 2:860; Moo, 890).

---

[5]See Bruce, 260; Dunn, 2:859; Moo, 889. Cranfield's theory (2:755, following Barth), that the term implies the ministry not of a priest but of a Levite, is (in Dunn's words) "too strained."

Thus Paul says that his specific work as a minister of Christ is to perform the work of a priest, and to do so with reference to "the gospel of God." The latter phrase can mean "by proclaiming the gospel," i.e., by using the gospel as an instrument.[6] Or it can mean "for the cause of the gospel," i.e., to bring about the ultimate purpose sought by the gospel: the salvation of sinners (or in Paul's case, *Gentile* sinners).

The third word identifying Paul's ministry as a priesthood is "offering," or προσφορά (*prosphora*), which in this case means the *thing* offered or sacrificed to God (see Acts 21:26; Eph 5:2; Heb 10:5, 8). The main work of a priest is to offer sacrifices to God on behalf of sinners, in order to restore them to a proper relationship with God.[7] This is why Paul was called to his priestly ministry, i.e., for the purpose of presenting an offering before God.

What offering does Paul the priest present to God? Literally, "the offering of the Gentiles," i.e., the offering that consists of the Gentiles. As the result of Paul's ministry, converted Gentiles are themselves offered up to God as sacrifices that are well-pleasing and acceptable in his sight (Lenski, 880; Cranfield, 2:756; Dunn, 2:860). This does not mean simply that he leads them to *offer themselves* as living sacrifices (12:1); in his role as priest, Paul is the one who presents them to God (Stott, 379; contra Morris, 511). Though he does not quote it, Paul may have had in mind the prophecy in Isa 66:19-21, where God says he would scatter the Jews to proclaim his glory to the nations, so that the latter might be brought back to Jerusalem "as an offering to the Lord."

Paul says that this offering is "acceptable to God" because it is "sanctified by the Holy Spirit." Just as OT temple sacrifices had to be ritually clean and acceptable to God, so must NT sacrifices be acceptable to him. In the eyes of the Jews, the Gentiles were considered to be unclean and therefore unacceptable by nature, just because they were not Jews (Acts 10:9-16,28,34-35; 11:1-18). But

---

[6]A priest's main duty was to offer sacrifices, requiring him to kill animal sacrifices with a knife. Calvin likens the gospel to a knife or "sword, by which the minister sacrifices men as victims to God" (527).

[7]See the discussion of the priesthood, especially the High Priesthood of Jesus, in Heb 7–10. Fitzmyer says, "The *finis* of all sacrifice is to bring about in some way the return of sinful human beings to God" (712).

God makes the Gentiles acceptable to him by *sanctifying* them through the Holy Spirit. This was done symbolically for all time when God poured out his Spirit on Cornelius and his household (Acts 10:44-47; 11:15-17; 15:8-9); and it is done for every individual Gentile convert when he receives the gift of the indwelling Spirit in Christian baptism (Acts 2:38,39; 1 Cor 12:3). At this point he is initially sanctified or set apart unto God "by the Spirit" (1 Cor 6:11).

Thus the essence of Paul's apostolic ministry is priestly service. The same can be said also of all those who preach the gospel. Paul's priestly offerings were specialized (the Gentiles), but in a real sense "all evangelists are priests because they offer their converts to God" (Stott, 379). Actually, every Christian is a priest and has some sort of sacrifice to offer. The Protestant Reformers rightly spoke of the "priesthood of all believers." The church, says Peter, is "a holy priesthood, offering spiritual sacrifices acceptable to God through Jesus Christ" (1 Pet 2:5; see 2:9; Rev 1:6; 20:6). These "spiritual sacrifices" are the "sacrifice of praise," or *good words* (Heb 13:15), and also the sacrifices of *good works* (Heb 13:16). The purpose of all such sacrifices is to impress others with the saving love of God and to lead them to surrender to him (Matt 5:16; 1 Pet 2:9-12).

15:17 Therefore I glory[8] in Christ Jesus in my service to God. "I glory" is literally "I have a reason for boasting." In terms of both the quantity and the quality of of his service – winning converts, starting churches, writing books of the Bible! – Paul certainly could have put together a very impressive resume. But he was not interested in bringing glory to himself. He knew that his apostleship as such was a gift of grace (v. 15b), that the gospel is the real power that saves (1:16; 10:17), and that he owed his accomplishments to God's power working through him (v. 19a).

Thus Paul's boasting is not for himself, but for the Lord. He glories only "in Christ Jesus," and only regarding "things pertaining to God" (NASB). In 1 Cor 1:31 and 2 Cor 10:17, citing Jer 9:24, Paul states his philosophy of boasting: "Let him who boasts boast in the Lord."

15:18 I will not venture to speak of anything except what Christ has accomplished through me in leading the Gentiles to obey God

---

[8]On the verb form of this word, see 2:17 (JC, 1:208).

by what I have said and done . . . . Christ certainly accomplished many things through Paul, resulting in obedience on the part of many Gentiles.[9] But here Paul reiterates and explains the determination expressed in v. 17, not to call attention to himself or to speak of his accomplishments as if they were his own. He will talk about them, but only as things that Christ has done through him, using him as an instrument. "Not I, but Christ" is his theme. See Acts 15:1-2; 21:19.

Some think Paul's emphasis is on what Christ has accomplished "through *me*, rather than through *someone else*" (Moule, 239; SH, 406; Murray, 2:212). This does not seem to be the point, though. The emphasis is on "what *Christ* has done *through* me."

Verse 18 ends with the short phrase, "by word and deed" (NASB). The NIV interprets this, as do most scholars, as modifying "accomplished," i.e., as referring to *Paul's* words and deeds. In this case it is a brief but comprehensive reference to his total ministry. "By word" refers to his preaching and teaching; "by deed" refers to his journeys, his sufferings, his miracles, and his many labors. See 2 Cor 10:11.

It is also possible to take this phrase as modifying "the obedience of the Gentiles," in which case it would mean that Paul's priestly ministry is intended to lead the Gentiles into a life of total obedience, in word and deed. See Col 3:17; 2 Thess 2:17.

15:19a *How* did Christ accomplish the evangelization of the Gentiles through Paul? He did it **by the power of signs and miracles, through the power of the Spirit.** He did it first of all by "the power of signs and wonders" (NASB).[10] All three of these words are used elsewhere to refer to miracles (Acts 2:22; 2 Cor 12:12; Heb 2:4; see 2 Thess 2:9; see GRu, 229-231). "Signs" refers to miracles in terms of their purpose, namely, to function as proof or evidence for the validity of an accompanying truth-claim (see GRu, 231-240). They can function thus because they are also "wonders."[11] I.e., because miracles are observable events that are outside the laws of

---

[9]This last phrase is εἰς ὑπακοὴν ἔθνων (*eis hypakoēn ethnōn*), "unto obedience of Gentiles." It is a shortened version of the important expression, "unto obedience of faith among all the Gentiles" in 1:5 (JC, 1:78-82).

[10]"Signs and *miracles*" (NIV) is a bad translation, since the "signs" are miracles also.

[11]This word, τέρας (*teras*), is used in the NT (16 times) only in the phrase, "signs and wonders."

nature (GRu, 244-261), they elicit awe and wonder in those who observe or hear of them. Miracles are also called "powers," referring to their source in the mighty power of God. (Here in 15:19a the word "power" is not referring to the miracles as such, but to the divine power from which they come.)

As an Apostle, Paul had the ability to perform miracles, and used it to attest to the truth of the message he proclaimed. See Acts 14:8-10; 16:16-18; 20:9-12; 28:3-9. These miracles confirmed the authenticity of his apostleship (2 Cor 12:12).

"Through the power of the Holy Spirit" could be saying only that the signs and wonders were done through the Spirit's power, but most (rightly) take it as setting forth a more general reason for the success of Paul's work among the Gentiles. I.e., *everything* Christ did through Paul was accomplished through the power of the Spirit working in him. This is a comprehensive explanation, since the Spirit's power was indeed the source of the miracles, but was also the source of Paul's inspired preaching and writing, and the source of his apostolic activity in general. (See Murray, 2:213; Cranfield, 2:759; Moo, 893.)

15:19b Having reflected on the source of, essence of, and power behind his ministry as the apostle to the Gentiles, Paul now tells us (in vv. 19b-22) something of the *strategy* behind it, and how that strategy has affected and is still affecting his choices of *where* to serve. He says, **So from Jerusalem all the way around to Illyricum, I have fully proclaimed the gospel of Christ.**

Here he sums up where he has preached the gospel thus far, i.e., within the boundaries of an arc-like span around the northeastern portion of the Mediterranean Sea, reaching from Jerusalem in the southeast to Illyricum in the northwest. "All the way around" translates a single word which literally means "in a circle." Some think this refers to the area surrounding Jerusalem, i.e., "the other countries lying around that city" (Lard, 442; see Godet, 480; Moule, 240). Recent interpreters agree that it refers to the geographical arc (which looks like part of a circle) mentioned above, as the general area within which Paul had thus far traveled and evangelized.

Illyricum (also called Dalmatia, 2 Tim 4:10) was a Roman province consisting of the area lying east of Italy across the Adriatic Sea, and northwest of Macedonia and Achaia. Moo notes that it corresponds roughly to the modern areas of northern Albania, much of Yugoslavia, and Bosnia-Herzegovina (894).

Some have questioned the accuracy of this statement, since the NT does not specifically mention Paul's journeying into either Jerusalem or Illyricum on any of his preaching tours. His ministry did include some time in Jerusalem (Gal 1:17-19; 2:2; Acts 9:26-29; 26:20), although he probably was not preaching to Gentiles there. Also, Acts 20:1-2 states that he traveled throughout the general area of Macedonia, which could have included an excursion into Illyricum.

In any case it is not necessary that we interpret Paul's statement to mean that he pursued his Gentile mission *inside* the borders of either Jerusalem or Illyricum. He may mean only that these are in general the boundaries *up to which* he carried the gospel (Cranfield, 2:761-762). Also, it is important to see that he is not talking about a single, chronologically-ordered trip. I.e., he is not saying he *started* in Jerusalem and *wound up* in Illyricum. He is speaking rather of the general geographical arc within which he worked. The statement is not a "detailed itinerary, but simply a grand design" (Dunn, 2:869).

What does Paul mean when he says he "fully proclaimed the gospel of Christ" in this area? Literally he says he "fulfilled the gospel" there. This could possibly refer to the *content* of his preaching, indicating that he left nothing out of his message (see Acts 20:20,27); but that does not seem to be his point here (see Murray, 2:214; Cranfield, 2:762). In this context he is focusing on the *places* where he preached.

Is he affirming, then, that he has already preached the gospel in every city, town, and village within the Jerusalem-Illyricum arc? No, this would have been physically impossible. The reasonable consensus is a little different, namely, that he "fully proclaimed the gospel" in the entire area named, but only according to the strategy explained in vv. 20-21. I.e., he preached in all the strategic cities and population centers in these provinces, going where no one had yet carried the gospel, and planting new churches which could then take up the task of spreading the Word to the surrounding regions. Thus in terms of his special mission as a trail-blazing, pioneer preacher, he had indeed "fulfilled the gospel" within the described arc.[12]

---

[12]See SH, 409; Bruce, 261; Murray, 2:214; Cranfield, 2:762; Fitzmyer, 713; Stott, 382; Moo, 896.

15:20 It has always been my ambition to preach the gospel where Christ was not known, so that I would not be building on someone else's foundation. This verse begins with Greek words unfortunately not translated by the NIV, οὕτως δέ (*houtōs de*).[13] *Houtōs* means "thus, in this way." It connects v. 20 with v. 19 by explaining *how* Paul was able to fully proclaim the gospel from Jerusalem to Illyricum. I.e., he was able to complete this task because it was his policy always to be covering new ground. As Dunn says, this strategy was "a calculated policy on Paul's part, judged by him to be the most effective way of carrying the message of the gospel as far as he could throughout the gentile world" (2:869).

Paul states his strategy in two ways. First, his goal has been to preach "where Christ was not known," or literally, "not named." That is, he wanted to go into virgin territory where the Gentiles had not yet heard about Jesus and had not had the opportunity to name him as their Savior and Lord (10:9-13; 2 Tim 2:19).

Second, he has made it his practice to concentrate on unevangelized areas "so that [ἵνα, *hina*] I would not be building on someone else's foundation." This was exactly how he had worked in Corinth: "By the grace God has given me, I laid a foundation as an expert builder, and someone else is building on it" (1 Cor 3:10). Stated in a different way: "I planted the seed, Apollos watered it, but God made it grow" (1 Cor 3:6).

The consensus is that Paul understood himself to be called "to be a trail-blazer for the gospel, a pioneer missionary, a founder of churches" (Hendriksen, 2:490). His ministry was that of "establishing strategic churches in virgin gospel territory" (Moo, 896). By following this policy, says Dunn, Paul was able "to achieve the greatest missionary expansion with the greatest economy of missionary effort" (2:869).

While this was his general strategy, it was not an absolute rule and did not prevent him from making certain exceptions under special circumstances. For example, he was planning an immediate trip to Jerusalem to deliver the Gentile Christians' offering to the poor saints there (15:25-27). Also, he had long desired to visit Rome (1:9-15; 15:23), and was planning to go there as soon as he completed his business in Jerusalem (15:24,28).

---

[13]See the NASB, "And thus."

While his planned visit to Rome would clearly be an exception to his usual policy, it was at the same time subordinated to it. The main reason he had not visited there earlier, he says (vv. 22-23), is that he was concentrating on the unevangelized regions in the East. Also, his visit to Rome would be part of a larger plan to begin a pioneer gospel mission in the West, specifically, in Spain (vv. 24,28). Finally, the visit to Rome would be just that: a brief visit (vv. 24,28).

15:21 Paul now cites an OT text which he sees as validating his pioneer-preacher policy. **Rather, as it is written: "Those who were not told about him will see, and those who have not heard will understand."** (The quote is from Isa 52:15, LXX.) This text is about the Servant of Yahweh and is undoubtedly messianic; it prepares the way for the great prophecy of Christ's propitiatory death in Isa 53. Paul cites this verse because the first part of it clearly indicates that Isaiah is talking about the Gentiles: "So will he [the Suffering Servant] sprinkle many nations" (i.e., to purify them; see 15:16).

The Gentiles are the ones "who were not told" about the Messiah, and "who have not heard." The point of the prophecy, however, is that they *will* see, and they *will* understand. Paul clearly implies that his own work as the Apostle to the Gentiles is a fulfillment of this prophecy, in that he is the means by which the nations are seeing and understanding.

If Paul derived his self-understanding as the Apostle of the Gentiles from this text, it is easy to see how he made it his policy "to preach the gospel where Christ was not known" (v. 20), since Isaiah speaks of nations "who were not told" and "who have not heard."

15:22 This is why I have often been hindered from coming to you. Paul has already indicated in 1:13 that he had planned many times to visit Rome, but had been prevented from doing so until now. While other factors were also responsible (see JC, 1:97), the main reason why he had not yet been able to go to Rome was the urgent need to preach the gospel to the unevangelized in the Jerusalem-Illyricum arc. "His concern for place after place in that eastern area preoccupied him so that he could not come to Rome, no matter how often he thought of doing so" (Fitzmyer, 716).

B. HIS PLANS FOR THE FUTURE (15:23-29)

But this is all about to change, because Paul sees himself as having completed his trailblazing work in the eastern area. Having done so, he has now formulated a plan for a totally new phase in his missionary work, one that will definitely allow him to spend a short time in Rome. In this paragraph he explains it to the Roman church.

The plan Paul outlines is no small undertaking. His ultimate goal is Spain, in the far western regions of southern Europe. But instead of traveling directly there from Corinth (his location when he wrote this letter; see JC, 1:31), he felt the need to personally present the Gentiles' offering to the Jerusalem church. Only then would he go back westward to Spain, stopping at Rome on the way. Stott (384) calculates that this itinerary would require Paul to travel (mostly by boat) about 3,000 miles: c. 800 from Corinth to Jerusalem, c. 1,500 from Jerusalem to Rome, and c. 700 from Rome to Spain. Such a trip would be long, perilous, and uncomfortable.

15:23-24a But now that there is no more place for me to work in these regions, and since I have been longing for many years to see you, I plan to do so when I go to Spain. Here Paul names two basic factors that have shaped his upcoming travel plans. The first has to do with the completion of his missionary work in the eastern area. "Place" is τόπος (*topos*), which can also mean "opportunity," a meaning that fits well here. "These regions" are the area described in v. 19b. Paul is simply saying that now that he has laid the foundation for the church there, he is ready to move on to a totally new area. In terms of the strategy affirmed in v. 20, there is no more opportunity for him to pursue his calling here.

The second factor shaping his itinerary is his long-standing desire to visit Rome itself, as described in 1:9-15. "Having been longing" is a rather rare noun that suggests a very strong desire.

The two parts of v. 23 are literally two participial phrases: "no longer having an opportunity" and "having a desire." The NIV properly translates them as dependent clauses. What we would expect next is a main clause in which Paul specifically asserts his intentions, e.g., "I am now planning a trip." But unfortunately (from a grammatical point of view, at least), that main clause never appears. In v. 24a Paul adds one more dependent clause (lit., "whenever I journey to Spain"), and breaks off his sentence without giving us a main clause of any kind.

Some later manuscripts added a main clause ("I will come to you," KJV), but this is not in the original text. Obviously Paul knows that we will understand his point even without a main clause, which we can indeed easily surmise in view of the context. Lard (445) suggests that at the end of v. 23 we can insert, "I purpose doing so"; this completes the thought. The NIV has done the same thing, adding a main clause at the beginning of v. 24, "I plan to do so." But this is not in the original; the next clause, "when I go to Spain," is actually how v. 24 begins. (See the NASB for a literal rendering of vv. 23-24a.)

Verse 24a and v. 28 are Paul's only references to his intention to evangelize Spain. We do not know if he was ever able to do this. The Bible says nothing more about it, but this does not rule out the possibility. Two statements from early Christian writings are sometimes interpreted as affirming that Paul did get to Spain, but these cannot be verified.[14]

The main part of Paul's plan is to go to Spain; his visit to Rome will be but a brief stopover in his journey farther west. Spain, thought to be the location of Tarshish (Jonah 1:3; see 1 Kgs 10:22), was growing in significance as a cultural and commercial area of the Roman empire. This is no doubt why Paul saw it as a logical next step in his plan to evangelize those who had not yet heard.

15:24b In the rest of v. 24 Paul explains to the Christians at Rome the place of his intended visit there in relation to his overall plan. **I hope to visit you while passing through and to have you assist me on my journey there, after I have enjoyed your company for a while.** First, he says he will just be stopping by "to visit you" as he is "passing through." Both of these terms indicate that his stay in Rome will be "not much more than a stop on his way to his ultimate destination, which is Spain" (Moo, 898). Second, he says he will be able to stay only "for a while," literally, "in part." I.e., it will only be a partial visit compared with what he would prefer.

But even though his visit in Rome will be brief, he hopes to accomplish two things. First, he will attempt to persuade the church in Rome to assist him in his mission to Spain. The word

[14]For details see Murray, 2:217, n. 27.

translated "assist me on my journey" is προπέμπω (*propempō*), which could mean just "accompany, escort" (Acts 20:38; 21:5); but it more likely means "help on one's journey with food, money, by arranging for companions, means of travel, etc." (AG, 716). It is used several times in the NT in the latter sense (Acts 15:3; 1 Cor 16:6,11; 2 Cor 1:16; Titus 3:13; 3 John 6). It suggests at least that Paul was expecting the Roman Christians to give him substantial aid for the remainder of his journey to Spain. It may be that he was even hoping they would become a "supporting church" for his mission there, perhaps by providing him with a missionary recruit to help him in his work, as Philippi had sent Epaphroditus (Phil 2:25-30).

The other thing Paul hoped to accomplish by his visit with the Roman Christians was to "enjoy their company" in Christian fellowship. The word used here literally means "to be filled full"; it is appropriate to interpret it (as does the NIV) to mean something like "filled full with the pleasure of your company." He has already said (1:12) that he knows a visit with the brethren at Rome would be an encouragement to him (JC, 1:95-96). This is true even though he could be there only "for a while."

15:25 Now, however, I am on my way to Jerusalem in the service of the saints there. Here Paul informs his Roman brothers that there is still one more thing he has to do before making his journey to Rome and Spain. He is just now beginning[15] a trip to Jerusalem (Acts 19:21; 20:16), to deliver money collected from the Gentile churches during his third missionary journey, to help the poor Christians in the Jerusalem church. In this way he would be "serving the saints" (NASB).

The word for "serving" is διακονέω (*diakoneō*), the verb form of διακονία (*diakonia*). These words can have the general sense of serving or ministering to others' needs (see 16:1), or they can signify a more specific kind of service. As we have seen, *diakonia* in 12:7 probably refers to benevolent work in the church, just as *diakoneō* refers here to the collection taken for the poor in Jerusalem.[16]

---

[15]Paul uses the present tense of πορεύομαι (*poreuomai*), "I am going," indicating that he will be departing for Jerusalem at any moment. "I am on my way" says it well.

[16]These two words are used for the collection in the following texts also: Acts 11:29; 12:25; Rom 15:31; 2 Cor 8:4,19-20; 9:1,12-13.

"Saints" is a word used for all Christians (see 1:7; JC, 1:85); here it refers specifically to the poor saints in Jerusalem (v. 26).

Ten or eleven years earlier, Paul (along with Barnabas) had already carried an offering to the Jerusalem church, sent by the church at Antioch (Acts 11:28-30; 12:25). The occasion then was a famine, and the motivation was simply Christian love.

What was the purpose of this present offering? First, there is no doubt that Paul encouraged this offering simply as an act of benevolence, as a way of helping the poor (Gal 2:10) in the spirit of Christian love (2 Cor 8:8,24). There is no indication that there was another widespread famine in the Jerusalem area at this time, but there did seem to be quite a number of poor saints there who needed continuing help.

Second and more significantly, Paul apparently regarded this offering as a concrete symbol of the unity and interdependence of Gentiles and Jews under the banner of the gospel of Christ. He has already written at length about this interdependence in ch. 11, and he will refer to it again in v. 29. By encouraging the Gentile Christians to contribute to this collection, Paul was hoping to get them to acknowledge their dependence on the Jews for salvation and to give them a token of their gratitude in return. In this way he "intended to establish good relations between the Jewish Christian mother-community in Jerusalem and the newly founded Gentile Christian churches" (Fitzmyer, 720).

15:26 After the initial general reference to his Jerusalem trip in v. 25, Paul now states its purpose explicitly: **For Macedonia and Achaia were pleased to make a contribution for the poor among the saints in Jerusalem.** "Macedonia and Achaia" refer, of course, to the *churches* in these two areas. Other areas had also participated in the collection,[17] but these are the ones he had been working with most recently.

Macedonia lay southeast of Illyricum, across the Adriatic Sea from Italy's boot heel. It was bordered by the Aegean Sea on the east and Achaia on the south. Its main cities included Berea,

[17]As Bruce (264) points out, 1 Cor 16:1 shows that the Galatian churches were participating. Also, the presence of Tychicus and Trophimus (Acts 20:4; 21:29) shows that the churches in Ephesus and elsewhere in Asia were sharing in it.

Philippi, and Thessalonica (the capital). Achaia lay south of Macedonia as the end of a peninsula jutting out into the Mediterranean Sea. Athens and Corinth were its major cities. Both Macedonia and Achaia were part of pre-Roman Greece.

The Christians in these areas, says Paul, were "pleased" or delighted to participate in Paul's collection for the poor in Jerusalem. Though Paul had urged them to give (1 Cor 16:1-4; 2 Cor 8:7,24), he made it clear that it was not a matter of necessity but of free and cheerful choice (2 Cor 8:8; 9:5,7). This free and cheerful spirit in which the gifts were given is indicated in the word "pleased"; Paul thinks this point is important enough to repeat the word in v. 27a. As v. 31b indicates, he hopes the gifts will be received by the Jerusalem church in a similar spirit.

The word translated "contribute" is κοινωνία (*koinōnia*), which literally means "fellowship, participation, sharing in." The same word is used for this collection in 2 Cor 8:4; 9:13, where it is translated "sharing." Since money earned as salary or wages is indeed "coined life," when one gives his money to help meet the needs of others, it is truly an act of fellowship, of sharing one's very life with the recipient of the gift. Thus the very nature of benevolent giving (as an act of fellowship) made Paul's collection an ideal means of drawing the early Jewish and Gentile Christians closer together.

"The poor *among* the saints" rightly indicates that only *some* of the Christians in Jerusalem were poor. This had been true from the beginning, and the other Christians in the church there had always been ready to help them (Acts 4:34-37; 6:1). What is significant here is that so many *Gentile* Christians were willing to do the same.

15:27 This verse indicates *why* the Gentile Christians were so eagerly pleased to help the poor saints in Jerusalem: **They were pleased to do it, and indeed they owe it to them. For if the Gentiles have shared in the Jews' spiritual blessings, they owe it to the Jews to share with them their material blessings.** Here for the first time Paul indicates that the main thing at stake in this collection was the relation between Jews and Gentiles in the church. The Gentile Christians were happy to share with the Jewish Christians (at Jerusalem), because they felt they *owed* it to them. Literally Paul says "they are debtors," using the same word he used of himself in 1:14 (JC, 1:99-100). This is not a legal debt but a moral obligation, a debt of gratitude. The Gentiles owed this debt to the Jews because of what the latter had done for them.

Paul explains the debt in the rest of the verse. The Gentiles, he says, "have shared in the Jews' spiritual blessings." The "spiritual things" of which Paul speaks are the blessings of salvation, and his point is that the Gentiles must remember that "salvation is from the Jews" (John 4:22; see Rom 11:11,17; 15:8). It was through the Jews that the Savior came into the world (9:5), and in this sense all Christians owe an unpayable debt to the Jews. Also, it was from Jerusalem, through the early Jewish Christians, that the gospel was first proclaimed and from which it spread into all the earth (Acts 1:8; see Isa 2:3-5; Micah 4:2-5). This resulted in "an obligation on the part of the gentile churches to those through whom the stream of salvation-history blessings had flowed to them" (Dunn, 2:873). As MacArthur says (2:347), "On the human level, all Gentile Christians owe their spiritual lives to the Jewish apostles, prophets, teachers, and evangelists who first proclaimed the gospel of salvation in Jesus Christ."

Although the collection obviously could never begin to be equivalent to the spiritual gifts the Gentile Christians had received through and from the Jewish Christians, it was nevertheless fitting and proper for the former to give back a gift of material[18] things as a way of expressing their gratitude. Indeed, they *ought* to do so; they "owe" it to them – again in terms of moral obligation.

The word translated "share" is λειτουργέω (*leitourgeō*) (the verb form of *leitourgos* in 15:16), which indicates that the collection was an act of servanthood and an act of worship. See 2 Cor 9:12, where Paul refers to this contribution as "the ministry [*diakonia*] of this service [*leitourgia*]" (NASB).

15:28 So after I have completed this task and have made sure that they have received this fruit, I will go to Spain and visit you on the way. Having explained his imminent trip to Jerusalem (vv. 25-27), Paul now returns to the main point he was making in v. 24, about his planned trip to Rome and then to Spain. He will make the latter

[18]"Material" is literally "fleshly," which refers to the body in contrast with the spirit of man. The point is that the money in the collection will buy food and clothes for the body.

trip only after he has finished the business about the collection, i.e., after he has delivered it to the Jerusalem church in person.

At this point Paul adds a participial phrase that most find difficult to understand. It explains what, to Paul, was involved in completing the task of delivering the collection. He describes this act as, literally, "having sealed to them this fruit." "This fruit" is the collection itself, but in what sense is it "fruit"? This may mean that it was the fruit of Paul's own labor, i.e., of the effort he expended in raising these gifts. More likely Paul means it was the fruit produced among the Gentiles as a result of the spiritual blessings sent forth to them by the Jerusalem Christians (Cranfield, 2:775; Murray, 2:219).

The difficult question is, what does Paul mean when he says that he will *seal* this fruit to the Jerusalem church?[19] To place one's seal upon something means to put one's unique identifying mark upon it in order to guarantee its authenticity. The NIV interprets Paul's sealing action here in terms of safe delivery. I.e., Paul travels along with the collection in order to *make sure* that the Jerusalem church receives it. This is probably not the point, since Paul had many trusted helpers who could have done this. Thus the NIV translation is off the mark.

Some take the concept of the seal here in its most basic sense, i.e., as a mark of identification. Sometimes an image taken from tenant farming is cited: "When the tenant farmer delivered the harvested fruit or produce to the owner, the sacks were marked with the farmer's seal as an identification of its source." Thus "the seal was an official mark of ownership used in deliveries, and sealing was the last act before delivery" (Fitzmyer, 723). Lenski rejects such an explanation, saying that ownership of the collection is not the issue (893).

The most likely meaning is that Paul put his seal on the collection in the sense that he attested and certified to the Jewish Christians in Jerusalem that this money was a gift of genuine love from their Gentile brethren. He made this long and arduous trip to Jerusalem just to make sure that the Jewish Christians understood the significance of the gift as an instrument that was meant to join them and their Gentile brothers together in a bond of Christian fellowship.[20]

---

[19]See the discussion of the noun, "seal," in 4:11 (JC, 1:291).

[20]Supporters of this view include Murray, 2:220; Lenski, 893; Cranfield, 2:775; and Moo, 906-907.

Once this has been accomplished, Paul says, "I will go on by way of you to Spain" (NASB). The NIV's "visit you on the way" is literally "through you," i.e., through Rome. This is another indication that his visit to Rome was going to be brief and was secondary to his purpose of taking the gospel to Spain (see v. 24).

15:29 I know that when I come to you, I will come in the full measure of the blessing of Christ. Here Paul expresses a measure of confidence that he will finally be able to fulfill his longing to visit Rome, once the Jerusalem task is completed. "I know," he says; "I will come," he says. We know from the book of Acts that he did indeed go to Rome, though not exactly according to his original plan.

In any case, he was sure that when he came, it would be with the full blessing of Christ. That is, he knew that Christ's blessing would be upon him, and he knew that he would be able to bestow the fullness of Christ's blessing upon them (see 1:12).

C. HIS REQUEST FOR PRAYER (15:30-33)

Despite the confidence expressed in v. 29, Paul is still somewhat apprehensive about his trip to Jerusalem, especially about how he and the contribution would be received there. Thus he closes this section of the letter with a request for prayer concerning his announced itinerary.

15:30 I urge you, brothers, by our Lord Jesus Christ and by the love of the Spirit, to join me in my struggle by praying to God for me. This is surely more a personal plea than an authoritative command (see 12:1). It is an urgent plea; the word for "urge" (παρακαλέω, *parakaleō*) often has the connotation of pleading and begging. The language shows that Paul feels a serious need for the intercessory prayer of his brethren.

Paul names two bases for his appeal. First, he pleads for prayer "by [διά, *dia*] our Lord Jesus Christ." This may be a reference to the authority by which he makes his request (Moo, 909), but more likely he is just appealing to the fact that he and his Roman brethren both worship the same Lord ("*our* Lord"): "I urge you, as one Christian to another . . . ."

The other basis for his appeal is "the love of the Spirit." This is no doubt the Holy Spirit, but it is not clear just how the Spirit and the love (ἀγάπη, *agapē*) are related. Grammatically it could mean the Spirit's love for us: "The Spirit's love should incite to prayer" (Murray, 2:221). Also, it could mean our love for the Spirit (MacArthur, 2:350). Most likely, though, it means the love which the Holy Spirit imparts to us as part of his sanctifying work, and which is one aspect of the fruit of the Spirit (Gal 5:22).[21] It is "that love between Christians which is the effect of the Holy Spirit's indwelling" (Cranfield, 2:776; see Morris, 523; Dunn, 2:878; Moo, 909). I.e., Paul is saying, "If you really love me – and Spirit-filled Christians should love one another – you will pray for me."

Paul beseeches his brethren not just "to pray," but to strive or struggle along with him in prayer. The word for "struggle" is συναγωνίζομαι (*synagōnizomai*, cf. "agonize"). This is a combination of *agōnizomai*, which means "to engage in a contest, to fight, to struggle, to wrestle, to strive"; plus *syn*, "along with" (AG, 15, 791). Paul's use of the term here does not necessarily imply struggling *against* someone or something, though we may be tempted to think of Jacob's wrestling with God (Gen 32:24-30) and of every Christian's struggle against evil powers (Eph 6:10-12).

To what struggle does Paul refer? Quite possibly he is thinking of the struggle he anticipates in Jerusalem, where he expects to meet with resistance from both his unbelieving Jewish enemies and the Jewish Christians (see v. 31). The NIV suggests this meaning; it pictures Paul beseeching the Christians at Rome to march alongside him in this struggle, not by their physical presence but by their prayers for him (see Dunn, 2:878).

The other possibility, which is more likely, is that the struggle to which Paul refers is the praying itself, in which case he is not talking about ordinary, casual prayer but earnest, forceful, and persistent prayer like that of Jesus in Gethsemane (see Cranfield, 2:777). Thus he "calls for prayers into which one puts his whole heart and soul as do the contestants in the arena" (Lenski, 895).

It may be incidental, but there is a Trinitarian framework in this verse. Paul pleads with the Romans to pray (1) to God the Father,

---

[21]This probably does not refer to the love *of God* which the Spirit pours into our hearts as mentioned in 5:5 (JC, 1:318-320).

(2) through the Lord Jesus Christ, and (3) through the love of the Holy Spirit (see also vv. 18-19). It should be noted that the prayer is directed to God the Father, not to the Son nor to the Spirit.

15:31 Now Paul instructs the saints at Rome to pray for two things in particular: **Pray that I may be rescued from the unbelievers in Judea and that my service in Jerusalem may be acceptable to the saints there, . . .** The "unbelievers[22] in Judea" are the unbelieving, unconverted Jews in Jerusalem and the whole surrounding area. Paul was well known to them as a former leader among the Jews (see JC, 1:27-28) and was considered to be a betrayer of his people and his religion, and the Apostle was well aware of their hostility toward him (Acts 13:45,50; 17:5-8,13; 18:12-17; 19:9; 20:3). They had already tried to kill him (Acts 9:29; 14:19), and would do so again (Acts 23:12-15). Thus "Paul realized fully that he was walking into a den of lions" (Lenski, 895). He was not afraid to die, but he wanted to live in order to fulfill his plans to evangelize Spain (Acts 20:24; see Phil 1:21-25).

Paul specifically requests that his brethren pray that he might "be rescued" from the unbelieving Jews. The word for "rescue" (ῥύομαι, *rhyomai*) can mean "to protect or preserve from harm," but often it has the connotation of delivering or rescuing someone from a peril that has already come upon him. At the time Paul wrote this letter he may already have known that he was going to be captured and bound by the Jews in Jerusalem; it was certainly made clear to him shortly after this (Acts 20:22-23; 21:10-14). Thus he may be requesting prayer that God will literally rescue him out of this certain captivity.

As a matter of fact, this *is* the way it happened. If Paul was praying and asking for prayer that he not be captured at all, then his prayer was not answered. If he was praying and asking for prayer that he be delivered from his Jewish enemies after they had captured him, then this prayer was definitely answered – but not necessarily in any way that Paul could have anticipated. He was in

[22]This word is actually the "disobeying" ones. The point is that many Jews disobeyed God by refusing to believe in their Messiah. This does not imply, though, that unbelief and disobedience are interchangeable terms; neither are belief and obedience.

fact rescued from his Jewish captors, but only by becoming a prisoner of the Roman government.

Paul's other specific prayer request is that the Jewish Christians in Jerusalem ("the saints," vv. 25, 26) would accept the offering[23] he was bringing to them. This is not just a prayer that all will go well in a general way (contra Cranfield, 2:778), but a prayer that the existing tension between Paul and his Gentile converts on the one hand, and the Jewish Christians in Jerusalem on the other hand, would not lead to a rejection of the offering but instead would break down that very tension and unite them all in true brotherhood. Many of the Jewish Christians still could not get used to the idea that God would accept the Gentiles (unless they first submitted to the Law of Moses; Acts 15:1-5); and they were suspicious of Paul's gospel, regarding it as negative toward Jews and the Law (see Acts 21:20-21). Therefore they might think that accepting the contribution would be an endorsement of Paul's gospel and thus a compromise of their beliefs. Paul requests prayer that none of this will happen, and that the offering will be accepted in the right spirit.

15:32 [S]o that by God's will I may come to you with joy and together with you be refreshed. While Paul's main concerns were his safety and a congenial acceptance of the offering, he did have a secondary concern, one relating to his planned trip to Rome. If the first prayer was not answered, Paul knew that he might not get to Rome at all; and even if that one was answered but the second one was not, his heart would be heavy and his visit to Rome would be tainted with melancholy. Thus he requests fervent prayer for these two things, "so that" (ἵνα, *hina*) he may indeed be able to come to Rome, and to come with joy.

If this does happen, says Paul, it will be "by God's will." This does not mean the decretive will of Calvinist determinism (contra Murray, 2:223), according to which God unconditionally and unilaterally decrees and determines everything that happens. It may refer only or at least partly to the *permissive* will of God (GRu, 313-317), by which God in his sovereignty allows historical events to unfold according to human free will choices. Or it may refer to God's *purposive* will (GRu, 304-310), according to which God intervenes via

[23]Lit., "the service" (διακονία, *diakonia*); see v. 25.

his special providence in order to accomplish certain purposes, particularly in answer to prayer (see GRu, 376-378).

Paul knew that his itinerary was subject to God's will in these senses (Acts 16:6-10; 18:21; Rom 1:10; 1 Cor 4:19; 16:7). So in this case, he knew God either could allow his adversaries' evil purposes to unfold as they may, or could intervene in the historical process in answer to prayer and cause positive results to occur. Either way, he knew it would be God's will – either permissive or purposive. And either way, he knew it would all work together for good (8:28).

The fact is that Paul did get to go to Rome and visit with the brethren there (Acts 28:15), but not according to his own plan. His plan was to stay there for a short time and "be refreshed" by his visit with the brethren, in a kind of "R & R" mode. He was looking forward to Rome as being "like a lovely, quiet harbor; he sees himself storm-tossed and battling during the period ahead of him and longs to reach Rome, the quiet haven, to drop anchor there for a while and – come to rest" (Lenski, 896). It did not happen this way, though. Instead, he came to the city as a prisoner of the Roman government, and was under house arrest for two years (Acts 28:16,30).

We are not specifically told what happened after these two years, but it is almost certain that he was released (see Gaertner, *Acts*, 429-431). Perhaps at that time he was at last able to "be refreshed" with the Roman Christians.

15:33 After his request for prayer in his own behalf by the church at Rome, Paul cannot close this section without himself uttering a prayer on their behalf. Thus he says, **The God of peace be with you all. Amen.**

Paul has just recently spoken of God as the God of endurance and encouragement (v. 5), and the God of hope (v. 13). Now he calls him the "God of peace" (see also 16:20; 2 Cor 13:11; Phil 4:9; 1 Thess 5:23; Heb 13:20), i.e., the God who bestows upon believing sinners a state of peace and reconciliation with himself (5:1), a feeling of peace and tranquility within (8:6; 15:13), and a relationship of peace and harmony among brethren (14:17).

In view of his own anticipated tensions in Jerusalem, Paul has just requested prayer from the Roman brethren that God would make his trip to Jerusalem a peaceful one. Thus it is appropriate that he should pray for the same "God of peace" to be with the saints in Rome also. For God to "be with" someone means that he is present to them in all his loving power in order to bless and to protect. On "Amen," see 1:25 (JC, 1:154).

II. PAUL AND HIS FELLOW WORKERS (16:1-23)

Some critics have speculated that Rom 16 was not part of the original letter to the Romans. One suggestion is that it was a separate brief letter sent to the church at Ephesus, and only later added on to the end of the Roman letter. This issue will not be discussed here. It is enough to note that such an idea is inconsistent with both the internal and the external evidence,[24] and it is thoroughly refuted by Morris, 24-31; and Lampe, "Romans 16," 217-221.

This section is almost altogether about specific personalities, many of them Paul's fellow workers. First comes a brief word of commendation for Phoebe (vv. 1-2), followed by a long list of personal greetings to Christians living in Rome (vv. 3-16). These warm and encouraging words to sincere Christian workers are followed by a solemn warning to be on guard against false teachers (vv. 17-20). Finally, some of Paul's coworkers in Corinth send their greetings to the Roman Christians (vv. 21-24).

A. COMMENDATION OF PHOEBE (16:1-2)

Paul is writing this letter from Corinth and is just about to depart for Jerusalem. At this same time a Christian woman from the nearby town of Cenchrea is about to leave on a trip to Rome. Apparently Paul has asked her to carry this letter with her and deliver it to the church at Rome. In these two verses he provides

---

[24]E.g, regarding internal evidence, the particle *de* at the beginning of v. 1 (often untranslated) indicates continuation from a previous thought and would not appear at the beginning of a document (Cranfield, 2:780; Dunn, 2:884). An example of external evidence is that no extant manuscript of Romans ends with ch. 15 (Lampe, "Romans 16," 217).

her with a statement of introduction and recommendation, ensuring that she will be well received by the Roman Christians.

16:1 I commend to you our sister Phoebe, a servant of the church in Cenchrea. The word "commend" (συνίστημι, *synistēmi*) was the usual term, a "technical epistolary expression," for introducing and recommending a friend to other acquaintances (Fitzmyer, 728; Cranfield, 2:780). Letters of introduction were very useful in the ancient world. Travel was hazardous, and public accommodations were scarce and somewhat risky; and such letters could secure private hospitality. They also gave some assurance to potential hosts (such as the Christians at Rome) that they were not being defrauded by pretenders (MacArthur, 2:361; Morris, 528). See Acts 18:27; 2 Cor 3:1.

Phoebe is not mentioned anywhere else in the NT. Her name (which means "bright, radiant") indicates that she was probably a Gentile by birth, since *Phoibē* was the name of a pagan goddess.[25] Paul calls her "our sister," meaning our sister[26] in Christ, a part of the family of God, one of "our own."

Paul also describes her as "a servant of the church in Cenchrea." Cenchrea was the eastern seaport for Corinth,[27] and obviously a church had been established there, perhaps by Paul himself. This is the first use of the word "church" (ἐκκλησία, *ekklēsia*) in Romans, and (as it does most of the time in Paul's writings) it refers to the local congregation, the collective body of Christians in a particular area.

What does Paul mean when he calls Phoebe a *servant* of the church in Cenchrea? This is a matter of considerable controversy. Paul uses the Greek word διάκονος (*diakonos*), a word which is masculine in form but was used for both men and women. Its basic connotation is "servant, helper, one who carries out the will or purpose of another, one who ministers to the needs of others." The NT usually uses it in this generic sense for Christian workers (and others). In this case the English word "servant" is most appropriate.

---

[25]Φοίβη was a Titaness, the daughter of Uranus (Heaven) and Gaea (Earth).

[26]"Sister" (ἀδελφή, *adelphē*) is not used in this spiritual sense very often: 1 Cor 7:15; 9:5; Phlm 2; Jas 2:15.

[27]In Acts 18:18, when Paul left Corinth on his way to Ephesus, he set sail from Cenchrea. It was about eight miles southeast of Corinth.

But on at least three occasions (Phil 1:1; 1 Tim 3:8,12) this word seems to be used for a more or less "official" role of service in the church – "official" in the sense that the individual is selected and appointed by the local congregation to be responsible for a specific task within or on behalf of that congregation. In this latter case the English word "deacon" is used.[28]

In what sense does Paul call Phoebe a *diakonos*? To answer this we must see how the term is used elsewhere. A study of the word *diakonos* and its related words, *diakonia* ("ministry, service") and *diakoneō* ("serving, helping, ministering"), yields the following conclusions. First, in the most general sense, every Christian is (or should be) the *diakonos* or servant of all other Christians (Matt 20:26; 23:11; Mark 9:35; 10:43). Ministry (*diakonia*) is something every Christian should be involved in (Eph 4:12; Rev 2:19).

Second, there are many different ways in which one can serve (1 Pet 4:10,11; *diakoneō*); there are many different *kinds* of ministry (1 Cor 12:5; *diakonia*). The important point here is that the terms in question are not limited to any one kind of ministry, but are used for all of them. These include the ministry of the Word (Acts 6:4), the ministry of the evangelist (2 Tim 4:5), the ministry of benevolence (Acts 6:1; 11:29; 12:25; Rom 12:7; 15:31; 2 Cor 8:4; 9:1,13), and the ministry of apostleship (Acts 1:17,25; 20:24; 21:19; Rom 11:13; 1 Tim 1:12; 2 Tim 4:11).

Third, in the great majority of cases, these terms – especially *diakonos* – are used in the generic sense of "servant" or "service, ministry." As such they are used for *any* Christian worker, "official" or not, no matter what his or her speciality might be. Paul the Apostle calls himself a *diakonos* many times.[29] Other Christians described as *diakonoi* are Apollos (1 Cor 3:5), Tychicus (Eph 6:21; Col 4:7), Epaphras (Col 1:7); and Timothy (1 Tim 4:6).[30] The *diakonia* of

[28]The English word "minister" should be avoided in translations, since it has a limited modern cultural connotation with no real parallel in the NT. "Ministry" as a translation for the related word *diakonia* is appropriate, though, since its connotations can be more general.

[29]1 Cor 3:5; 2 Cor 3:6; 6:4; Eph 3:7; Col 1:23,25. Several times he refers to his *diakonia*: Acts 20:24; 21:19; Rom 11:13; 1 Tim 1:12; 2 Tim 4:11; and many times in 2 Cor.

[30]Also called *diakonoi* in a general sense are civil rulers (13:40), Christ

Archippus is also mentioned (Col 4:7). What this shows is that *any* Christian who is carrying out a specific task or filling a specific role in the church is a *diakonos*, in the general sense of "servant."

Fourth, none of these ministries or individuals seem to have anything to do with the "office" of a deacon in the local church. To say it another way, we do not know enough about the so-called "office" of deacon in the first-century church to know if it relates to the above ministries and servants or not.

What, then, was Phoebe? First, there is no warrant whatsoever for referring to her as a "minister" of the church at Cenchrea,[31] in the sense of the modern-day "senior minister" or pulpit minister. But was she a deacon(ess), implying some sort of official leadership status in the church at Cenchrea? Many so affirm. "Deaconess" is the way the word is translated in the RSV, the NAB, and Phillips; the NRSV says "deacon." Cranfield says it is "virtually certain" that she was a deacon in the sense of Phil 1:1; 1 Tim 3:8,12 (2:781). Phoebe is thus "the first recorded 'deacon' in the history of Christianity," says Dunn (2:887). Lard (452) and Lenski (899) call her a deaconess.

Dunn (2:886-887) and others cite as evidence for this view the presence of the participle, "being" (οὖσαν, *ousan*, untranslated in the NIV): "*being* a servant of the church" (see also Lenski, 899; Walters, "'Phoebe,'" 181). This argument loses its force, though, when we notice that a similar participle is used in v. 11b ("*being* in the Lord"). It is merely one way to introduce an identifying phrase.

The strongest argument for this view is the fact that Phoebe is called a *diakonos* of a specific congregation (Spencer, *Curse*, 115; Walters, "'Phoebe,'" 181; Moo, 914). Such a phrase appears nowhere else in the NT. But such phrasing does not necessarily imply that Phoebe held the *office* of deacon in the Cenchrean church (contra the NEB, "who holds office in the congregation at Cenchreae"). There is no reason to think that Paul is doing anything more than specifying where Phoebe came from, i.e., where her home church was, for the simple purpose of identifying her to the Roman church.

(15:8; see Gal 2:17), Paul's challengers (2 Cor 11:23), and Satan's servants (2 Cor 11:25).

[31]Contra Spencer, *Curse*, 115; Bilezikian, *Roles*, 305; and Schüssler Fiorenza, *Memory*, 170, 181.

The most we can say with any confidence is that Phoebe was a *servant* of the church in Cenchrea (see KJV, NASB, NIV), in the sense that she had a significant ministry there. She was a *diakonos* like Paul, Timothy, Epaphras, Tychicus, and Archippus, i.e., someone who faithfully carried out a specific task in service to others. I agree with Murray, that there is "neither need nor warrant to suppose that she occupied or exercised what amounted to an ecclesiastical office comparable to that of the diaconate" (2:226).

Two more things need to be said. First, to deny that Phoebe was a deacon(ess) in the church at Cenchrea in no way detracts from her service and influence in the church there, nor from her stature as a role model for Christian women today. Phoebe was a woman whom Paul was able to commend in the highest terms – not because she held some (rather nebulous) "office," but because of the important service she rendered to the church.

Second, even if we grant that Phoebe was a deacon(ess) in the Cenchrean church, this in no way violates the clear teaching of 1 Tim 2:12, that women may not teach men or have authority over men in the church. The "office" of deacon is neither a teaching office nor an office of authority. Thus if anyone feels compelled to speak of Phoebe as a deacon(ess), he should not fear that he is in any sense capitulating to egalitarianism (feminism); nor should egalitarians assume that this would be some sort of victory for their cause.

The NT never specifies what the duties of a deacon are, nor does Paul state specifically what service Phoebe rendered to the church at Cenchrea. Verse 2 does give us a clue as to the latter, though, when Paul says that she has been "a great help" to many, including himself. This will be discussed below.

16:2 In v. 2 Paul makes two specific requests of the church at Rome: **I ask you to receive her in the Lord in a way worthy of the saints and to give her any help she may need from you, . . .** "Receive her" is not the same word used in 14:1 and 15:7, where the issue was potential division over matters of opinion. Here the idea is something like, "Welcome her into your midst with the open arms of fellowship" (see Phil 2:29). To receive her "in the Lord" means to receive her as a fellow-believer in the Lord, as a "sister" in Christ (v. 1). Because of the blessed tie that binds our hearts in

Christian love, Christians can find instant communion and rapport with other Christians who show up even as strangers at our doors. To receive her "in a way worthy of the saints" means to do so in a manner one would expect from a follower of Jesus, i.e., with loving respect, unselfish generosity, and a cheerful heart.

The second request is for the Roman church to assist Phoebe in any way that she might need help. It is unlikely that Paul was requesting financial aid for her, since she was probably well-to-do in her own right. However, she would be in need of hospitality from trusted people. Also, she was traveling to Rome for some specific purpose, perhaps relating to some business or legal matter. Some think the latter was the case, based on Paul's use of the word πράγμα (*pragma*),[32] which basically means "matter, task, affair, thing," but which can mean "a matter of law, a lawsuit, a legal dispute" (see 1 Cor 6:1). We cannot be sure of this, though. In any case, whatever her purpose, the Roman Christians would be able to advise Phoebe as to "how things worked" in business and legal circles in Rome. On the other hand, Paul may not have had anything specific in mind beyond general hospitality.

At this point Paul says there is a reason to help Phoebe besides the general obligation of Christian love. You should help her in any way you can, he says, **for she has been a great help to many people, including me.** The noun used to describe Phoebe is προστάτις (*prostatis*).[33] It has two possible meanings. It can mean "helper, benefactor, patron, protector," as in the NIV's "a great help." Or it may mean "leader, director, ruler, presider."

Sensing a victory for the egalitarian cause, some adopt the latter meaning and flatly declare that Paul calls Phoebe a ruler and perhaps an elder in the church. Spencer says the verb form of the word means to "help by ruling." "Therefore, the most likely significance of *prostatis* is its common meaning of a leader and ruler." Phoebe thus was "a woman set over others," an explicit example of "a woman set in authority over a man, in this case, the great apostle Paul" (*Curse*, 115-116).

---

[32]This is untranslated in the NIV. See the NASB: "Help her in whatever matter [*pragma*] she may have need of you."

[33]This is the feminine form; the masculine form is *prostatēs*. The former occurs only here in the NT; the latter not at all.

It is true that the verb form of this word in the NT most often means "to lead, rule, direct, manage, be over" (see Rom 12:8; 1 Thess 5:12; 1 Tim 3:4,5,12; 5:17), but the word also can mean "to assist, help, protect, care for" (see Reicke, "προΐστημι, 700-701). The key to the meaning of the noun *prostatis* here must be the context; and in every way, the context excludes the concept of ruler and supports the connotation of helper.

Here are three contextual considerations. First, Paul says Phoebe became a *prostatis* of "many." This suggests, says Moo (916), that "the term here does not denote an official, or even semiofficial, position in the local church." If she were something like an elder, she would be a *prostatis* of the whole church, not just of "many."

Second, she was a *prostatis* of Paul himself. There is simply no acceptable sense in which we may think of Phoebe or any other Christian, even a man, as having authority over Paul or any other apostle. We may easily think of Phoebe as Paul's helper, but not his ruler.

Finally, we get back to the reason Paul asks the Roman Christians to be of assistance to Phoebe. *You* should help *her*, he says, because *she herself* has been a helper to many, even to me. This is why she deserves your help. As Murray says, "There is exact correspondence between the service to Phoebe enjoined upon the church and the service she herself bestowed upon others. The thought of presidency is alien to this parallel" (2:227, n. 1).

The two words for helping are slightly different, but they convey the same general sense. The verb "give [her any] help" is *paristēmi*, literally, "stand by or beside." The verb form of *prostatis* is *proistēmi*, literally, "to stand before, stand in front of." Thus Paul is saying something like this: "You stand by her, because she has stood up for many."

The concept of a *prostatis* in the sense of a helper, especially a *patron*, was well established in Paul's day.[34] A patron (*prostatis* or *prostatēs*, woman or man) was usually a prominent, well-to-do person who used his or her position, wealth, and influence for the public good. They sometimes helped the whole community, sometimes groups within the community, and sometimes individuals, e.g., by opening their homes to travelers and taking care of their needs.

[34]See the good discussion of this by Walters, "'Phoebe,'" 169-180.

Since many women performed such a service, it is easy to see how Phoebe could belong to this category. She was no doubt "a figure of significance, whose wealth or influence had been put at the disposal of the church at Cenchreae" (Dunn, 2:889). Walters concludes, "By virtue of wealth and status, she was able to make connections that benefitted Paul and other Christians residing in or passing through Corinth. Hospitality was likely a key element of her patronage" ("'Phoebe,'" 179). Since the Cenchrean church was in the eastern seaport town for Corinth, it would have the occasion to host many travelers. This was probably Phoebe's special ministry, and the nature of her work as a *diakonos* of that church. In this sense she was a helper to many, including the traveler Paul; and the Roman Christians are asked to reward her in kind.

B. GREETINGS TO INDIVIDUAL ACQUAINTANCES (16:3-16)

Sending greetings to specific individuals in his letters is something Paul seldom did. In Col 4:15 he greets Nympha; in 2 Tim 4:19 he greets Prisca and Aquila. But here at the end of Romans he sends greetings to 24 named individuals, two specific but unnamed individuals (vv. 13,15), and several groups. The groups include two households and (apparently) three house churches.

Who are these individuals whom Paul specifically names? Most of them are completely unknown to us except for what we are told in this list. We know Prisca and Aquila for sure (v. 3). We probably know Rufus (v. 13) from one other NT reference. It is possible that the men whose names are attached to the two households (Aristobulus, v. 10; Narcissus, v. 11)[35] can be identified with prominent individuals known from secular sources, but this is less certain than the identification of Rufus.

The fact is that the other 21 individuals whom Paul greets by name are simply otherwise unknown. In view of this, it is rather amazing that so much space is devoted to discussing them in the commentaries! In most cases the only thing we can do with these

---

[35]Paul's greetings are sent to the households, not to these individuals as such. This indicates that either these men were dead but their households were still intact, or they were not Christians.

brothers and sisters is to analyze what Paul says about them and compare their names with lists of the same names compiled from contemporary inscriptions and other sources from ancient Rome.[36] But even then, there is no sure way to connect any of the individuals here with any individuals mentioned on inscriptions.

We can, however, draw some basic general conclusions about the Christians in this list, including the unknown individuals. First, Paul obviously knows some better than others. He takes pains to say something complimentary[37] about the first 16 persons listed (vv. 3-13), but then greets ten others without elaboration (vv. 14-15). Some in the group of 16 he obviously knew quite well; others he may have known only casually. The last ten were known to him, but perhaps only through communications he had received from friends in Rome, such as Prisca and Aquila. See Lampe, "Romans 16," 220; Moo, 917-918.

Concerning the ones Paul knew personally, since he had never been to Rome, he would have met them somewhere during his missionary work in the eastern regions before they migrated to Rome.

Second, we know for sure that several of these individuals are Jewish, some because we know them otherwise (vv. 3,13), and some because Paul calls them his "kinsmen" (vv. 7,11, NASB). The rest, obviously the majority, are most likely Gentiles, since their names were used by Gentiles of that day. This does not necessarily prove that the church as a whole was predominantly Gentile, but it points in that direction (see Moo, 918).

Third, many of the names on the list are otherwise found to be common among slaves and former slaves (freedmen, freedwomen). Many of these names were prominent among slaves in the emperor's household. According to Lampe ("Romans 16," 227-228), only the names Urbanus, Rufus, Prisca, and Aquila "do not indicate any affinity to people born into slavery." Of the rest, ten are most probably slave names; the rest cannot be determined one way or the other. (The households of Narcissus and Aristobulus no doubt would also include slaves.)

---

[36]E.g., see the analysis by Lampe, "Romans 16," 222-230.

[37]Three are called "fellow workers" of Paul (vv. 3,9; see v. 21). He refers to four as "beloved" (v. 12) or "my beloved" (vv. 5,8,9). Four are called hard workers (vv. 6,12), and three are Paul's kinsmen (vv. 7,11; see v. 21).

Fourth, the prominence of women in the list is noteworthy. Nine of the 26 individuals are women.[38] Of these, Prisca is described as Paul's fellow worker; Junia is praised for her outstanding missionary work; and four others are praised for their labor for the Lord (Mary, Tryphena, Tryphosa, and Persis). Only three men are complimented in these same terms (Aquila, Urbanus, and Andronicus). (See Lampe, "Romans 16," 222-223.) This shows that faithful Christian women had important roles in the church in the apostolic era, and should have the same today. This, along with the reference to Phoebe in vv. 1-2, shows that women can have high-profile ministries in the church without violating the limitations imposed in 1 Tim 2:12. (See Moo, 927; Cottrell, "Priscilla," 4-5.)

Since such a long list of names is unusual in Paul's letters, we may ask why he went into such detail here in Rom 16, even regarding people he probably did not know or know very well. The answer no doubt lies in the fact that Paul had never been to Rome and was not the founder of the church there, but he was on the verge of paying them a visit and seeking aid from them for his mission to Spain (15:23-24). A list like this would impress not only those who are named, but those who are not mentioned as well. This would prepare the way for a positive reception by and fruitful relationship with the whole congregation, once he arrived in Rome (Moo, 918). "Common friends build a first bridge of confidence between people who do not know each other," says Lampe. Thus Paul's list would make the following statement: "Look at these many and honorable personal friends of mine in the midst of your church – and you will find that I, too, am trustworthy" (Lampe, "Romans 16," 218).

16:3 Greet Priscilla and Aquila, my fellow workers in Christ Jesus. That "greet" should be an imperative plural is not unusual in an epistle like this. Paul is just asking the church as a whole to make sure these individuals in particular are made aware of the letter and of these greetings. It was a standard epistolary way of saying "Greetings to . . ." (Dunn, 2:891; Moo, 919).

That Prisca and Aquila should be greeted first is no surprise, given their prominence in the NT in relation to Paul's ministry.

---

[38]These are Prisca, Mary, probably Junia, Tryphena, Tryphosa, Persis, Rufus's mother, Julia, and Nereus's sister.

Paul first met them in Corinth on his second missionary journey (Acts 18:1-2). They had been living in Rome, but had to leave when Claudius expelled the Jews, c. A.D. 49 (JC, 1:33-34). Aquila was a Jew (Acts 18:2), and his wife Prisca probably was, too. We do not know if they were already Christians while in Rome, or if they were converted after leaving there, perhaps by Paul in Corinth. The latter is more likely, since Acts 18:2 describes Aquila as simply "a Jew" when Paul first met him and Prisca.[39] Paul's first attraction to them was their common trade as tentmakers; apparently he stayed in their house (Acts 18:3).

Later when Paul left Corinth, Prisca and Aquila went with him. When they came to Ephesus, Paul continued on but Prisca and Aquila remained (Acts 18:18-19). In Ephesus they met "a Jew named Apollos," who was preaching about Jesus but was not yet a Christian, since he knew only the baptism of John. Prisca and Aquila took him into their house, explained the full gospel to him, and converted him (Acts 18:24-26). When Paul later returned to Ephesus, he worked alongside Prisca and Aquila for a time (1 Cor 16:19). Later, after Claudius died in A.D. 54 and his edict against the Jews was no longer enforced, Prisca and Aquila obviously returned to Rome; and Paul knew they were there and thus now sends greetings to them. Sometime after this, they apparently returned to Ephesus (2 Tim 4:19).

This husband-wife team is mentioned three times by Paul (16:3; 1 Cor 16:19; 2 Tim 4:19), who always calls the wife Prisca; and three times by Luke (Acts 18:2,18,26), who always refers to her as Priscilla, the diminutive form of Prisca. The woman is mentioned first in four of these six references (Acts 18:18,26; Rom 16:3; 2 Tim 4:19). This is somewhat unusual, and speculation abounds as to why it is so. It is suggested, for example, that Prisca was from a higher social position, that she had a more dominant personality, or that she was converted first and was therefore more prominent in the church. Lampe says she was apparently "more outstanding in her work for the church than was Aquila" ("Romans 16," 223). "Her superiority is evident," says Lenski (903).

In my judgment such speculation is just that: speculation. To affirm that Prisca was "superior" or "more outstanding" in any

[39]So Godet, 489; and Lenski, 903; contra Dunn, 2:891.

sense is precarious, since if this were true, it would be difficult to explain why she is not mentioned first all six times. It seems that either order of the names was acceptable, with no message being sent either way.

There is no doubt, though, that Prisca's service in the church was *just as significant* as that of her husband. They were both involved in evangelism (Acts 18:24-26), and Paul was certainly impressed with the work of both, judging from his other references to them and from what he says about them here. Dunn says they were "two of the most important people in Paul's missionary enterprise" (2:981). They may well have been his best friends, and were surely his best liaison with the church at Rome.

Thus it is not surprising that Paul has more to say about this couple than anyone else on the list. In what ways does he commend them? First, he calls them his "fellow workers in Christ Jesus." In his letters Paul refers to a number of other individuals as his fellow workers,[40] but does not say what specific work they were doing. Since Paul's work specifically was missionary in nature, focusing on evangelism and church planting, we can assume that all these fellow workers were associated with him in some way in this kind of ministry. Since new converts must be gathered together into local congregations, one thing associated with missionary work is organizing and providing for these newly-established congregations. By hosting "house churches" (v. 5; 1 Cor 16:19) Prisca and Aquila were very much involved in this aspect of missions.

Paul calls them his fellow workers "in Christ Jesus." He is not talking about their common secular trade of tentmaking (Acts 18:3), but about "gospel work" (Lenski, 903). They and Paul served a common Savior and Lord.

16:4 Paul's second commendation of Prisca and Aquila is this: **They risked their lives for me. Not only I but all the churches of the Gentiles are grateful to them.** "Risked their lives" is literally "risked their neck." At some point in their laboring together, these two friends of Paul put their lives on the line for his sake. Paul suffered

---

[40]Urbanus (16:9); Timothy (16:21); Titus (2 Cor 8:23); Epaphroditus (Phil 2:25); Euodia, Syntyche, and Clement (Phil 4:2-3); Aristarchus, Mark, and Jesus/Justus (Col 4:10-11); Philemon (Phlm 1); and Mark, Aristarchus again, Demas, and Luke (Phlm 24).

many perils in his many years of service (2 Cor 11:23-29), but we do not know the specific event he has in mind here. The episode in Corinth recorded in Acts 18:12-17 does not seem to be a serious threat to Paul. The later riot at Ephesus (Acts 19:23-41) was more dangerous for him; Prisca and Aquila may have intervened for him there at their own peril (see v. 30), but Luke does not mention it. In any case, at some point they put themselves in jeopardy for Paul's sake.

Because of this especially, and no doubt for countless other reasons, Paul says he gives thanks to God for Prisca and Aquila. In fact, he says, all the Gentile churches thank God for this great servant couple. Why? Probably, because if they had not saved his life, his mission to the Gentiles would have been cut short, and many of these Gentile churches may never have existed (Lard, 454; MP, 546).

16:5a Paul adds one more item to his greeting to Prisca and Aquila: **Greet also the church that meets at their house**. In the apostolic era, in some times and places, it may have been possible for the whole church in an area to meet together (1 Cor 11:18; 14:23), but church buildings as such did not exist, and often the Christians just met together in smaller groups in the houses of individual Christians (Acts 12:12; Col 4:15; Phlm 2). Prisca and Aquila hosted house churches both in Ephesus (1 Cor 16:19) and in Rome (indicated here). Verses 14,15 also seem to refer to such house churches, though the specific expression is not used. Also, the two households in vv. 10-11 may have been nuclei for house churches.

16:5b Paul now turns his attention to other saints in Rome. **Greet my dear friend Epenetus, who was the first convert to Christ in the province of Asia.**[41] Otherwise unknown to us, Epenetus must have been well known to Paul, who refers to him literally as "my beloved." This probably means that he was Paul's "dear friend" (NIV), though this is an interpretation and not a translation.[42] Cranfield says Epenetus may have been no more special to Paul than any of the other acquaintances named; the Apostle just wanted

[41]Some manuscripts have "Achaia," and older translations sometimes say this (KJV). But the better reading is "Asia."

[42]Verse 8 has the same phrase, but the NIV translates it there as "whom I love."

to say something nice about all of them, and this was his compliment for Epenetus (2:786-787). This is unlikely, though, since Paul already has something else quite unique to say about this man, namely, he was the first convert from Asia. Thus "my beloved" probably indicates a special affection between the two.

Paul says Epenetus was literally the "firstfruit" of Asia for Christ, a term that was used for the first converts in a particular context (see 8:23; 11:16; 1 Cor 16:15). It is possible that he was a convert of Prisca and Aquila (Acts 18:18-19), and that this is why he is mentioned just after them.

16:6 Greet Mary, who worked very hard for you. There is no reason to equate this Mary with any other Mary in Scripture. It was a common name in Rome and was used among both Jews and Gentiles, more commonly among the latter (Lampe, "Romans 16," 225). Whoever this Mary was, Paul gives her a high compliment when he says she "worked very hard for you."

The verb for "worked hard" is κοπιάω (*kopiaō*), "to toil, labor, struggle, strive, work hard." The adverb "very" translates πολλά (*polla*), "many things, much," which intensifies an already strong verb. Some have argued that *kopiaō* was a kind of technical term for Christian missionary work, but this is unlikely (Moo, 921, n. 28). Paul uses it, as well as the noun *kopos*, to describe the essence of the Christian life and work in general. Living as a Christian is not a bed of roses; it is *hard work.*

In a note of praise such as this, though, this verb indicates that Mary and others (v. 12) have probably devoted themselves to some "voluntary, laborious activity on behalf of the gospel" (Fitzmyer, 737). The language may be used of those in leadership roles (1 Thess 5:12; 1 Tim 5:17), but is not limited to this.[43] Laudably laboring for the Lord is something that can be done by both men and women. In this list of greetings Paul uses the term only for four women and no men.

16:7a Greet Andronicus and Junias, my relatives who have been in prison with me. These individuals, along with Herodion (v. 11), Lucius, Jason, and Sosipater (v. 21), are called Paul's "relatives." This

[43]For *kopiaō* see Acts 20:35; 1 Cor 16:16. For κόπος (*kopos*) see 1 Cor 15:58; 1 Thess 1:3; Rev 2:2; 14:13.

is a misleading translation, because Paul almost certainly means not "close relatives," but "fellow Jews," "those of my own race" (9:3, same word).

These two disciples are also called "my fellow prisoners." Paul uses this term also for Aristarchus (Col 4:10) and Epaphras (Phlm 23), who were with him during his Roman imprisonment. We do not know when Andronicus and Junia(s) were fellow prisoners with Paul. The Apostle says he was "frequently" in prison (2 Cor 11:23), but the only such episode recorded in Acts prior to this writing is Acts 16:24. Whether Andronicus and Junia(s) were in the same prison at the same time as Paul, or whether they had simply suffered the same kind of imprisonment for Christ as Paul did, we cannot tell.

A major question is whether the individual called "Junias" was a man or a woman. In the Greek text *Junian* is the accusative case either for a man named Junias or a woman named Junia. Prior to the thirteenth century it was generally assumed that the person was a woman and that her name was Junia (see references in Fitzmyer, 737-738). From the thirteenth century up to the mid-twentieth century, it was generally assumed that the person was a man, and that his name was Junias or something similar.[44] In more recent decades interpreters have been returning to the view that Junia was a woman, e.g., Cranfield, 2:788; Dunn, 2:894; Moo, 923 (see NRSV).

The main reason some have argued that the name must be masculine is that v. 7b describes these two workers as "outstanding among the apostles," and gender-role considerations rule out the possibility that a woman could be an apostle. But since egalitarianism has changed many people's thinking about gender roles, it is fairly easy for modern interpreters to accept the fact that Junia was a *woman*, indeed, a woman *apostle*.

Apart from preconceptions about gender roles, what evidence can be adduced one way or the other on this issue? The deciding factor seems to be the existence or nonexistence of these two names in contemporary Roman inscriptions. The facts are that the feminine name Junia has been found about 250 times in such

[44]So translated in the RSV, NASB, and NIV. See Godet, 491; Lard, 455; Moule, 248; Lenski, 905; Hendriksen, 2:504.

inscriptions, while the masculine form Junias has thus far been found *nowhere* (Lampe, "Romans 16," 223, 226). The reasonable conclusion, then, is that Junia was a woman, and that Andronicus and Junia were husband and wife.

16:7b With this conclusion, the rest of the verse now presents a major problem. It says of Andronicus and Junia, **They are outstanding among the apostles, and they were in Christ before I was.** The latter statement is not difficult. That they were "in Christ" before Paul just means they were converted to Christ before Paul was, which must have been within the first few years after Pentecost. Thus they had been laboring for Christ for over 20 years, and possibly for as long as 25 years.

The problem lies in Paul's statement that Andronicus and Junia are "outstanding among the apostles." If this means what it appears to mean, then Paul is affirming not only that Junia, a woman, was an apostle, but that she was one of the *very best* apostles.[45] One way to avoid this conclusion is to interpret this statement to mean that Andronicus and Junia were outstanding *in the eyes of* the apostles. This is grammatically possible, and has some support among scholars (see MP, 547; Moule, 248; Lenski, 906-907; Murray, 2:230). I believe it is a reasonable interpretation.

Most conclude, however, that the much less awkward and more natural interpretation is that Andronicus and Junia were outstanding members in the group known as apostles. If this is the case, how does the fact that Junia is called an outstanding apostle affect our view of gender roles in the church?

The answer depends on what is meant by "apostle." If we think that the word always refers to someone on or near the level of the original twelve apostles, the ones (like Paul) upon whom (along with the prophets) the church is built (Eph 2:20; see JC, 1:62-63), then Paul is saying that a woman, Junia, held the highest authoritative office in the NT church, thus obliterating all gender-role distinctions and vindicating egalitarianism. Dunn defends this view. He declares that this verse strongly suggests "that Andronicus and Junia belonged to the large group (larger than the twelve) of those

[45]"Outstanding" is ἐπίσημος (*episēmos*), which means "splendid, prominent, notable, esteemed, outstanding."

appointed apostles by the risen Christ in 1 Cor 15:7." I.e., "they belonged most probably to the closed group of apostles appointed directly by the risen Christ in a limited period following his resurrection." Thus "we may firmly conclude . . . that one of the foundation apostles of Christianity [in terms of Eph 2:20] was a woman and wife" (2:894-895). Agreeing with this view, Spencer says that "Junia (and her male colleague Andronicus) would be Paul's counterpart in Rome" (*Curse*, 102).

This is by no means the only possible, nor even the more likely, understanding of "apostle" in this verse, however. As we saw earlier (1:1; JC, 1:62), the word ἀπόστολος (*apostolos*) comes from the common verb ἀποστέλλω (*apostellō*), "to send (on a mission)." Thus the noun *apostolos* is sometimes used in the NT in the general (generic) sense of "someone sent on a mission," i.e., an ambassador, a messenger, or (in the context of Christian work) a missionary. When it is used in this sense it has no connotation of "an authoritative leadership position" (Moo, 923).

This is the sense in which Jesus himself is called an apostle, i.e., he was someone sent on a mission (Heb 3:1). The word is applied to Saul and Barnabas in this sense in Acts 14:4,14, because they were sent out as missionaries by the church at Antioch (Acts 13:1-3). In Phil 2:25 Epaphroditus is called the *apostolos* (NIV, "messenger") of the church at Philippi, because they had sent him to help Paul in his work. In 2 Cor 8:23 Paul speaks of several unnamed brethren who are "*apostoloi* of the churches," i.e., messengers (NASB) or representatives (NIV) sent out by the churches. In modern terms, they were *missionaries*.

There are good reasons for the word "apostles" here in v. 7 to be taken in this latter, generic sense. One is that this is consistent with a proper understanding of 1 Tim 2:12.[46] Another is that if Andronicus and Junia were "outstanding among the apostles" in the sense of authoritative leaders in the church (equivalent to Paul himself), it is very strange that we have no other references to them anywhere in the NT.

The best understanding of Paul's laudatory statement about this couple is that they were "outstanding missionaries" (Stott, 396),

[46]See my treatment of this text in "1 Timothy 2:12" and "Response."

"commissioned itinerant evangelists" (Fitzmyer, 739), a "married missionary couple" (Lampe, "Romans 16," 224). While women missionaries would be most effective in witnessing to other women, there is no biblical reason why women cannot proclaim the gospel to unsaved men as well. First Timothy 2:12 prohibits women from teaching only *Christian* men within the context of the church (1 Tim 3:15). (See Cottrell, "Priscilla," 4-5.)

16:8 Greet Ampliatus, whom I love in the Lord. We know nothing for sure about this man, other than the fact that Paul loved him in the Lord. Paul calls him (lit.) "my beloved," using exactly the same phrase the NIV translates "my dear friend" or "dear friend" in vv. 5,9,12. The point is that he was a personal friend of Paul (see v. 5).

Cranfield points out that in a burial chamber in the Catacomb of Domatilla in Rome, there is a late first-century or early second-century tomb with the inscription AMPLIAT[I], belonging to "someone who was specially esteemed" (2:790; see SH, 424). Whether this is the person Paul mentions we have no way of knowing.

16:9 Greet Urbanus, our fellow worker in Christ, and my dear friend Stachys. Urbanus (otherwise unknown) apparently worked with Paul somewhere before coming to Rome. That Paul says "our" fellow worker, not "my" fellow worker," I judge to be insignificant. He had worked with Paul. On the term "fellow worker," see v. 3.

Stachys, also otherwise unknown, is another of Paul's "beloved" friends (see v. 5).

16:10 Greet Apelles, tested and approved in Christ. Apelles is otherwise unknown. The interesting thing is the word Paul uses to describe him, δόκιμος (*dokimos*), translated "tested and approved." It is possible that Paul intends this in the same general sense that *all* Christians are "approved in Christ," i.e., approved by God because Christ has taken away the guilt and penalty of our sins.

But this term is part of a word group that speaks of being put to the test and thus being approved as the result of specific testing. See the use of δοκιμή (*dokimē*), "proven character," in 5:4 (NASB); see JC, 1:317. Paul more than likely means something like this. Thus it may be that Apelles had been subjected to the kind of serious suffering that produces proven character (5:4), or that he had been entrusted with an important work for Christ which he had successfully completed (see 2 Cor 8:22). Whatever the nature of his test or trial, he proved to be faithful; and Paul commends him for it.

Greet those who belong to the household of Aristobulus. This greeting is not sent to Aristobulus himself, which means either that he was dead, or that he himself was not a believer. In any case a good portion of his household (family and servants) were Christians; these are the ones Paul greets.

We do have knowledge of an important man bearing this name who was a part of the Herod family at this very time. Aristobulus was the grandson of Herod the Great and the brother of Herod Agrippa I. Though he himself was not a public official, his family was close to the Emperor Claudius. This Aristobulus died around A.D. 48. It is quite possible that those whom Paul greets here belonged to his household, which Cranfield says were probably united with the imperial household after his death (2:791).[47] Dunn says there is "strong plausibility" for this identification (2:896).

16:11 Greet Herodion, my relative, i.e., "my kinsman, my fellow Jew" (see v. 7). The name indicates most likely a slave or freedman in the service of someone in the Herod family, possibly a prominent member of the household of Aristobulus.

Greet those in the household of Narcissus who are in the Lord. Narcissus, like Aristobulus, must have been either dead or an unbeliever; the greeting goes to his household, or more precisely, to those of his household who are "in the Lord," i.e., Christians.

We know that there was a wealthy and well-known freedman with this name who served the Emperor Claudius. After Claudius was murdered and Nero became emperor, Nero's mother Agrippina forced this Narcissus to commit suicide. This happened in A.D. 54, shortly before Paul wrote Romans. Again, his household would probably have been absorbed into that of the emperor. It is possible that this is the household to which Paul refers (Dunn, 2:896); Cranfield says it is "quite probable" (2:793).

16:12 Greet Tryphena and Tryphosa, those women who work hard in the Lord. The similarity of these names indicates that these women were probably sisters. Both names are based on the noun

[47]This would partly explain the greeting in Phil 4:22, "All the saints [in Rome] send you greetings, especially those who belong to Caesar's household."

τρυφή (*tryphē*, "softness, delicacy, daintiness"). Some think they may be twins, and that their names would be equivalent to "Delicate" and "Dainty." It is ironic that women with such names would be praised for their hard work! "Work hard" is again *kopiaō* (see v. 6). The nature of their work is not known, since we know nothing else about them.

Greet my dear friend Persis, another woman who has worked very hard in the Lord. The name "Persis" indicates a woman from Persia, possibly a slave or freedwoman who came from that region (Moo, 925). She is otherwise unknown to us. Paul calls her "the beloved" (see v. 5), indicating again a possible personal friendship between them. He does not call her "*my* beloved" (as he does for men in vv. 5,8,9), possibly because referring to a woman in this way might have been misunderstood.[48] She also is praised for working "very hard." Again, as in v. 6, Paul uses both *kopiaō* and *polla*. He also uses past tense, which may indicate that Persis is now elderly or disabled.

16:13 Greet Rufus, chosen in the Lord, and his mother, who has been a mother to me, too. In his gospel (15:21) Mark identifies Simon of Cyrene as "the father of Alexander and Rufus." He probably did this because of the prominence of Simon's sons in the early church. Since Mark was probably writing his gospel especially for the Roman Christians, it is likely that these men were active in or known by the church at Rome. Thus it is quite probable that this Rufus and Simon's son are the same man. It is "very plausible," says Dunn (2:897; see Cranfield, 2:794). We cannot be certain about this, of course, since Rufus was a very common name, occurring about 374 times on Roman inscriptions from this era (Lampe, "Romans 16," 226).

Paul declares that Rufus is "chosen" (elect) in the Lord. This might be just a general "commendatory expression" that could apply to any Christian, since all Christians are among "the elect" (so Cranfield, 2:794; see Moo, 926). But most of the things Paul says about the Christians on this list seem to refer to something extraordinary about their lives and service. Thus it is likely that "chosen" here means something more specific. Some say it means he was chosen

[48]"It might have been indelicate," says Murray (2:231).

for a particular task of some importance (Dunn, 2:897). Others say the term should be taken in the sense of "choice." I.e., Rufus was an outstanding, choice, distinguished Christian servant (e.g., Lard, 458; Bruce, 274; Murray, 2:231; Fitzmyer, 741; Morris, 536).

Paul also sends greetings to Rufus' mother, who, he says, was his mother, too. He surely does not mean this literally. All we can say is that "on some occasion Rufus' mother had befriended Paul in a motherly way" (Cranfield, 2:794).

16:14 Greet Asyncritus, Phlegon, Hermes, Patrobas, Hermas and the brothers with them. These men are simply not known to us. It may be, since Paul says nothing about them, that he himself did not know them personally but only by reputation. The "brothers with them" may refer to a house church to which they all belonged.

16:15 Greet Philologus, Julia, Nereus and his sister, and Olympas and all the saints with them. This group, again unknown to us, may have constituted another house church. Some speculate that the first two were husband and wife, and the next two were their children; but there is no way to verify this. Of interest is the fact that the name Julia appears on over 1,400 inscriptions in Rome, which makes it by far the most common name of those in this list (the next most frequent is Hermes, 640 times). See Lampe, "Romans 16," 226.

16:16a Greet one another with a holy kiss. A chaste kiss as a form of greeting – the "osculatory salutation" (MP, 548) – and also parting, was simply a part of the culture of the ancient world in general, including Judaism (see Luke 7:45; 22:47; Acts 20:37).[49] Ordinarily Paul would not have to exhort Christians to greet one another with a kiss, since that was the normal practice. A kiss of greeting was given to anyone for whom there was fondness or affection or even respect, and was not intended to be romantic or erotic.

The emphasis in Paul's exhortation thus must be upon the word "holy." It may be that some Christians were reluctant to use this greeting for fear of rousing suspicions in non-Christians or even erotic feelings within themselves. We know that this was true in

---

[49]The word for "kiss" is φίλημα (*philēma*), from φιλέω (*phileō*), "to love." See the lengthy *TDNT* article on the subject by Stählin, "φιλέω [etc.]," especially 121-122, 126-127.

some areas of the church in later times (Stählin, "φιλέω," 143). Thus Paul may be telling the Christians at Rome not to be afraid to use the kiss of greeting, but to make sure that it is given (and received) in a holy (i.e., chaste, nonerotic) manner. As Pendleton says, "Paul is not teaching the Roman church a new custom, but is purifying an old one" (MP, 548).

But is there more to it than this? This verse is not the only place where Paul exhorts the church to "greet one another with a holy kiss"; see also 1 Cor 16:20; 2 Cor 13:12; 1 Thess 5:26.[50] Does the frequency with which this exhortation appears suggest that the holy kiss was instituted by the apostles as an obligatory part of public worship? My answer is, yes, but not as a kiss as such.

Though the holy kiss was incorporated into Christian liturgy over the next few centuries (Stählin, "φιλέω," 142-145), in my judgment its culture-relative character puts it into the same category as foot-washing as a Christian practice. That is, its essence, not its form, is what is binding upon us. Its essence is that of fellowship and brotherhood; it is a concrete expression of the familial bond that exists among all Christians. It is thus a "kiss of fellowship" (Lenski, 912-913), a "sign of brotherhood" (Godet, 494). Other cultural expressions of affection, fellowship, and brotherhood will serve the same purpose, e.g., a warm handshake or a hug.[51] With the understanding that such cultural substitutes are permissible, we are still left with the exhortation to use them, and yes, very likely as a part of the public assembly.

16:16b All the churches of Christ send greetings. By "all" the churches, Paul no doubt means all the churches in the eastern region, the Jerusalem-Illyricum arc, which he had established and with which he was still associated. Even as he writes, he is about to embark for Jerusalem with these Gentile churches' offering for the poor in Jerusalem, and he has a whole company of representatives of some of these churches with him (Acts 20:3-4). Speaking on behalf of their churches, these men are no doubt sending greetings to Rome through Paul.

---

[50]In 1 Pet 5:14 Peter exhorts us to greet one another with a "kiss of love," using both φίλημα and ἀγάπη.

[51]Phillips offers this translation: "Give each other a hearty handshake all round in Christian love."

Some believe that this verse gives us *the* proper name for individual churches, and that every local congregation should therefore be called a "church of Christ." This phrase is probably not intended to constitute an official name, however; it is descriptive, just as the phrase "church of God" is descriptive.[52] It is appropriate, though, to refer to a congregation and to the whole church as "the church of Christ," since he is the Head and Savior of that church (Eph 5:23).

By sending this general greeting from all the eastern churches, Paul identifies himself with them and them with himself, indicating to the Roman Christians that he has the backing of these churches in his general work and in his upcoming mission to Spain. This is another subtle way of recommending himself to the congregation in Rome and winning their support for his mission. (See Dunn, 2:899; Lampe, "Romans 16," 218.)

C. WARNINGS AGAINST FALSE TEACHERS (16:17-20)

Some writers believe this section could not have been authored by Paul, or at least was not part of the original letter to the Romans.[53] One argument for this idea is that the tone of these verses is supposedly much more harshly polemical than anywhere else in Romans. Käsemann (419) calls this paragraph a "wild polemic." Even those who accept its integrity speak of its "fierceness" (Dunn, 1:901) and call it a "vehement outburst" (SH, 429). Such language is surely exaggerated, however. Paul is in no sense here reproving or rebuking the Roman Christians for internal and personal sins or weaknesses (in contrast with, e.g., 1 Cor). Rather, he gives them a serious yet loving warning of dangers from without. As Godet says (495), this paragraph is "a simple putting on their guard in the most affectionate and fatherly tone." See Acts 20:28-32 for a similar warning.

---

[52]It is interesting that while this is the only verse which speaks specifically of "churches *of Christ*," there are at least eleven references to the "church/churches *of God*." See Acts 20:28; 1 Cor 1:2; 10:32; 11:16,22; 15:9; 2 Cor 1:1; Gal 1:13; 1 Thess 2:14; 2 Thess 1:4; 1 Tim 3:5.

[53]See Moo on this point (928), and Dunn (2:901-902).

Some think that such a strong admonition would have been inappropriate to a church that Paul himself had not founded. Fitzmyer says (745), "It is strange that Paul, writing to a community that he did not found or evangelize, would undertake to admonish it." But this is a groundless objection. After all, Paul was an Apostle appointed by Jesus himself, an Apostle who spoke for Christ and with the authority of Christ to the *whole* church. Besides, even before this point Paul has already included some stern exhortations and warnings (e.g., 6:1-2,15; 12:1-2; 13:1; 14:1-3,13).

Others think it is odd that Paul would interrupt his section on greetings and interject this warning about false doctrine, which seems so completely unrelated to the context. But this paragraph is not as unrelated as it may seem at first. For one thing, the greetings which it separates are of two different kinds. Verses 3-16 focus on the Christians in Rome to whom greetings are being sent, while vv. 21-23 name those with Paul who are sending greetings. Also, there *is* a definite connection between this paragraph and the previous verse. In v. 16 the references to the holy kiss and to "all the churches" call attention to the unity, harmony, and love that are God's ideal for his churches; and Paul knew that false teachers and their false doctrines were one of the greatest threats to this unity (Lenski, 914-915; Hendriksen, 2:510).

In summary, Paul knew from experience that false teachers could devastate a church, and he did not want this to happen to Rome. He was always conscious of this problem. Since he has not yet in this letter said anything about this danger, he sees this as an opportune moment to insert this warning.

16:17 I urge you, brothers, to watch out for those who cause divisions and put obstacles in your way that are contrary to the teaching you have learned. Keep away from them. "I urge you, brothers" is identical with 15:30, which is a personal plea; it is also identical (except for the conjunction *oun*) with 12:1, where "urge" has the double sense of personal appeal and authoritative command. The latter is the case here also; Paul is invoking his apostolic authority.

The reference to the holy kiss (v. 16) may have reminded Paul of the hypocritical kiss with which Judas betrayed Jesus (Luke 22:47-48), which in turn would remind him of the Judas-like kiss of betrayal with which false teachers doom the church. Thus he warns the church against "the unholy kisses of those who would attach themselves to the church's fellowship insincerely, remaining all the time alien from it in doctrine or life" (Cranfield, 2:797).

Paul exhorts the church to "watch out for" such false teachers. This could mean "keep your eye on" such teachers as may already be among you and "mark them" (KJV) so as to avoid them (MacArthur, 2:372; Cranfield, 2:798). More likely, though, it means "be on the lookout for, keep your eyes open for" such teachers, so that you will be sure to spot them if and when they show up (in Rome). Paul's unqualified praise for the Roman congregation suggests that these false teachers were not yet present within it (1:8; 16:19a).[54]

It is significant that Paul does not refer directly to the false teaching propagated by these false teachers, but speaks of the "divisions" and "obstacles" they cause in the church. "Divisions" are a work of the flesh according to Gal 5:20, where the word is translated "dissensions." It refers to anything that separates one group of brethren from another group. "Obstacles" is hardly a strong enough translation for the Greek word σκάνδαλον (*skandalon*) (see 9:33; 14:13), which is an occasion not just for stumbling, but for falling into ruin and destruction (see Lenski, 915).

What, then, is this potential danger, one so serious that it is able to separate brother from brother, and to lead them to destruction? The answer is *false doctrine*. How do we know this? Because Paul specifically says that what these outsiders may bring into the church is "contrary to the teaching [διδαχή, *didachē*, "doctrine"] you have learned." This implies that the Roman Christians have already learned good solid teaching, not just from Paul himself but from those leaders who started the church in Rome. Thus he warns them to be on the lookout for anyone who teaches something contrary to basic Christian belief, because false doctrine leads to division and destruction (see Moo, 930).

What Paul says here is directly opposed to the "peace at any price" approach to Christian unity, which often maligns all emphasis on sound doctrine as being divisive. But Paul is very clear. It is not *doctrine* that divides the church, but *false* doctrine. We do not

---

[54]So SH, 429; Lenski, 915; Murray, 2:234; Moo, 929.

have to choose between doctrinal truth and unity. Rather, we must pursue unity through sound doctrine, and "watch out for" the false doctrine that causes divisions and destruction. In and of itself, standing for the truth is not divisive in any negative sense; error is the true cause of division (see MacArthur, 2:372).

What shall we do with such false teachers, if we spot them? "Keep away from them," says Paul. Shun them, avoid them, stay out of their way. Since these men were probably not in Rome at this time, Paul is probably not talking about withdrawal of fellowship (as he seems to be in 1 Cor 5:11), but about refusing to give them any opportunity to spread their false teachings (2 John 7-11). The elders of the church should not allow them access to the congregation, but should themselves expose and refute their false teaching (Titus 1:9-11).

16:18 For such people are not serving our Lord Christ, but their own appetites. By smooth talk and flattery they deceive the minds of naive people. In this verse Paul says all that he wants to say about the false teachers of v. 17. The main question is whether he has any particular false teaching in mind, or whether this verse is just a generic description of false teachers of all kinds.

For those who take the former view, the next question is whether we can tell from v. 18 *which* false teaching he has in mind. Several possibilities have been suggested, with no one view gaining a consensus. The one thing we have to go on is Paul's statement that "such people" do not serve Christ but "their own appetites." "Serve" is δουλεύω (*douleuō*), which means to serve as a slave, to be a slave. We are supposed to be slaves of Christ (14:18), but these false teachers are slaves (lit.) to their own bellies or stomachs.

Being a slave to one's stomach, taken literally, could refer to gluttony, but gluttony as such was not the main point of any system of false doctrine which Paul confronted on a regular basis. Barrett suggests that it refers to "preoccupation with food laws" (285). However, those "preoccupied" with food laws were usually concerned with *denying* themselves certain foods, whereas Paul's phrasing suggests the opposite.

Some link this phrase with Paul's earlier teaching about the weak and the strong, and thus about opinions as to what a Christian is permitted to eat (ch. 14). The false teachers in this case would be the strong who insist on eating whatever they desire, even if it places a *skandalon* (14:13) in the weak brother's way (see Donfried, "Note," 51-52). This is unlikely, however, since Paul counted himself among the strong, and since the description of the strong in ch. 14 was far less severe than what is said of the false teachers in this paragraph. E.g., in ch. 14 Paul urged full acceptance of the strong; here he says to avoid the false teachers.

A more common approach is to take "belly" as a symbol for physical appetites in general (as in the NIV and other translations). Thus Paul would be referring to those who are dominated by their animal appetites (Dunn, 1:903), perhaps "antinomian libertines" (Murray, 2:235) or incipient Gnostics who misinterpreted the gospel as setting them free from all laws restricting their appetites (Phil 3:19; see Bruce, 277-278).

Still others take "belly" as a symbol for the even more general concept of the self as such. Being a slave to one's belly thus has "the sense of serving oneself, of being the willing slave of one's egotism," which is in essence walking according to the flesh (8:5-8) and not the Spirit (Cranfield, 2:800; see Hendriksen, 2:511; Murray, 2:235). If the sense is this general, it could refer to almost any kind of false teaching; and some who take it this way think Paul is talking about the Judaizers, as in Acts 15:5; Phil 3:2 (Godet, 496; SH, 429; Murray, 2:235).

Probably the best approach is to take the phrase in this most general sense, and to acknowledge that we simply are not sure if Paul had any specific group in mind, or to acknowledge that if he did we cannot identify it with any certainty. In this case we may take the warning as speaking generically about all false teachers, who by definition are no longer serving Christ but are slaves to their own egos. See Cranfield, 2:802; Dunn, 2:903-904.

One reason Paul issues such a strong warning about these false teachers, whoever they may have been, was their ability to teach and defend their false doctrines with such fluent and persuasive speech. They used "smooth talk," speech that sounds so good and plausible and beneficial, speech that creates the illusion of truth based on its form alone, regardless of its content. The Apostle thus reminds us that many a lie is hidden behind eloquence and personal charisma. We must never accept teaching as true just because of the packaging it comes in, but must "search the Scriptures" daily to see if the content of what we are being taught is indeed true (Acts 17:11). We must discipline ourselves to remember that form and style are secondary to content.

Those who are especially vulnerable to being taken in by fancy talk and flattery are described as ἄκακος (*akakos*), "innocent, simple, unsuspecting, unwary, naïve." They are "innocent of evil and easily duped" (Godet, 498). They are "not given to the wiles of deceit" and thus are "not suspecting the same in others" (Murray, 2:236). While a certain kind of simple innocence is good (v. 19), that of which Paul speaks here is not necessarily so. In Christian infancy it may be excusable, but we are supposed to outgrow it as we mature in Christ (Heb 5:11-14). To be called simple-minded in the sense of being easy prey for false teachers is by no means a compliment.[55]

16:19 Everyone has heard about your obedience, so I am full of joy over you; . . . In this verse Paul lets the Roman Christians know that he is not implying that their congregation is itself the origin of these false teachers.[56] He speaks again of their universal reputation for faithfulness (see 1:8), and declares that they are the source of much joy for him personally.

But, he says, this universal good reputation is the very reason why he must warn them about the false teachers. The NIV does not translate the word γάρ (*gar*), with which this verse begins. It means "for, because." It connects with v. 17: "I urge you to watch out for false teachers, because (*gar*) you have a widespread reputation for being a strong and obedient church; and false teachers seem to be attracted to such churches, to try to draw them into their own counterfeit orbits. Your reputation is so stellar that not only are you sure to be a target of false teaching, but also your fall would have a tragic and devastating effect on all who look up to you" (see Murray, 2:236).

---

[55]Spicq says the word *akakos* in the LXX took on the meaning of "almost foolishly simple." This trait is found in people whose simple-minded credulity makes it easy for hypocritical people to take advantage of them. "These are the credulous simpletons who are in view in Rom 16:18," he says (*Lexicon*, I:54-55).

[56]As Stott says, this comment shows that this false teaching has not yet arrived in Rome (430).

How may Christians guard against false teachers? Paul gives this instruction: **but I want you to be wise about what is good, and innocent about what is evil.**[57] Being "wise about what is good" presupposes a *knowledge* of what is good, i.e., being thoroughly familiar with sound doctrine with regard to both theology[58] and ethics. But wisdom is more than just knowing these truths; wisdom is knowing how to use them and apply them to life. It is knowing how to live by them, and especially how to distinguish between truth and falsehood and between good and evil. It means to know all about the good, not just in terms of book knowledge but by experience as well. Such wisdom replaces the simple-mindedness that makes us vulnerable to false doctrine.

At the same time, says Paul, the Christian must retain a real innocence with respect to what is evil (including both false beliefs and immoral deeds). The adjective for "innocent" here is ἀκέραιος (*akeraios*), not *akakos* as in v. 18. *Akeraios* literally means "unmixed, untainted," and thus "pure, innocent, guileless." I.e., keep your doctrine (the teaching you believe to be true) unmixed with false teachings; do not let yourself get "all mixed up" in your thinking (see Eph 4:14). Also, keep your moral life unmixed with sin and even the appearance of sin; stay as far away from evil as possible. Be so sensitive to it that the moment you suspect something is evil, flee from it at once.

Phillips's translation sums this thought up well: "I want to see you experts in good, and not even beginners in evil."

16:20 The God of peace will soon crush Satan under your feet. This promise is still connected with vv. 17-19. The implication is that Satan is the ultimate source of all lies and false doctrines (John 8:44; 1 Tim 4:1), and thus is the "author of discord" (Bruce, 278). Paul does not hesitate to say that "false teachers are under the influence of Satan, as in 2 Cor 11:14-15" (Fitzmyer, 746-747; see Godet, 489-499).

But Paul's promise is that if we follow his instructions in vv. 17-19, Satan will not ensnare us with false doctrine but will instead be defeated by the power of God and the power of his truth.

---

[57]For similar statements see Matt 10:16; 1 Cor 14:20; 1 Thess 5:21-22.

[58]The context requires that the "good" in this verse must include *doctrinal truth*, or sound doctrine. See Lenski, 922.

The imagery here seems to be taken from Gen 3:15 (Hebrew text), where God promised that the seed of the woman (Jesus) would crush the head of the serpent (Satan). This refers to the work of Jesus in his death and resurrection, by which the Devil was decisively defeated (Heb 2:14, NASB; 1 John 3:8). Paul's point is that the followers of Christ in every way will share in the Messiah's victory over the Devil. The power that wins this victory is God's power; he is the one who actually crushes Satan. But the enemy is crushed *under our feet*, i.e., in our own experience. The word for "crush" (συντρίβω, *syntribō*) is very strong; it means "shatter, smash, crush" (AG, 801), leaving no doubt as to who is the winner in this battle.

This *will* happen; it is God's promise. But *when* will it happen? Many think this refers to "the final, eschatological victory of God over Satan" at the Second Coming (Hendriksen, 2:512-513); see Cranfield, 2:803; Dunn, 2:905). Such a victory is certainly assured, but that is probably not Paul's main point here. "Under your feet" does not fit very well with the eschatological defeat of the Devil, which is altogether God's doing. But it does fit the daily victories we experience in the battles of truth against falsehood, and good against evil. As Morris says (541), "It is better to see [this as] the promise of a victory over Satan in the here and now." Such victories are won by the power of God's Word in inspired Scripture (John 8:32; Rom 1:16; Heb 4:12), and the power of God's Spirit indwelling our bodies (8:13).

The word "soon" is not the best translation of ἐν τάχει (*en tachei*), which is better rendered "quickly, swiftly, speedily, rapidly." Even if this promise referred to the Second Coming, it would not imply that this event was supposed to happen "soon" after Paul wrote. It would only mean that Christ's coming would occur quickly, "in a flash, in the twinkling of an eye" (1 Cor 15:52); see Rev 22:20 (NASB). But the promise refers mainly to our present battle against the Devil, and Paul is assuring us that the victory is not only certain but swift. "When the believer fights with the armor of God . . . , the conflict is never long" (Godet, 499). The truth quickly squelches error (Lenski, 923).

It is somewhat paradoxical to say that the God *of peace* (see 15:33; Heb 13:20) will quickly *crush* Satan under our feet. God is truly a God of peace and will establish peace, but he will not do so until his enemies have been defeated in decisive battle. True peace cannot exist in the presence of falsehood and evil. As in the case of Melchizedek (Heb 7:2), the Lord God is first of all King of Righteousness, and then King of Peace. He does not want "just peace," but "a just and righteous peace."

The grace of our Lord Jesus be with you. This is Paul's standard way of concluding his letters, with the same or a similar blessing appearing at the end of every one of them. In every other letter except 1 Corinthians, it is or is part of the last verse; in 1 Corinthians it is the next to the last verse. Here in Romans it is not at the very end because Paul has a few more greetings to add, and because he wants to conclude this magnificent epistle with a more majestic doxology.

On grace as a greeting and blessing, see 1:7. It is appropriate that Paul should mention grace both at the beginning and at the end of this letter, since the letter is about salvation by grace apart from works of law. This is in a sense incidental, though, since grace is Paul's standard greeting.

For the grace of Jesus to "be with" us means that we are existing within the shelter of his goodness and are enjoying the gifts of his love, especially the gifts of salvation.

This same blessing is repeated as 16:24 in older translations, but at that point it is generally regarded as a later addition; thus v. 24 is not included in most modern translations.

D. GREETINGS FROM PAUL'S COMPANIONS (16:21-24)

16:21 At this point Paul adds greetings from those who are with him in Corinth, beginning with Timothy. **Timothy, my fellow worker, sends his greetings to you, as do Lucius, Jason and Sosipater, my relatives.** Timothy joined Paul on the latter's second missionary journey (Acts 16:1-3) and apparently had been his traveling assistant for about eight years; he is mentioned in all of Paul's letters except Galatians, Ephesians, and Titus. He was very close to Paul (1 Cor 4:17), and Paul praised him as his most unselfish and dependable worker (Phil 2:19-23). Here Paul calls him his "fellow worker" (see 16:3), which Hendriksen calls "an understatement" (2:514). He was with Paul in Corinth at this time (Acts 20:4).

Paul refers to the next three men as his "relatives," by which he does not mean close family members but fellow Jews (see 16:7). We cannot with any certainty identify these men with anyone else mentioned in the NT, though possibilities exist and speculations abound.

Most agree that the Lucius named here is not the one mentioned in Acts 13:1. A more tantalizing suggestion is that "Lucius" (Λούκιος, *Loukios*) is a variation of the name "Luke" (Λουκᾶς, *Loukas*), and that this is actually the physician who authored Luke and Acts, and Paul's occasional traveling companion. This is not likely, though, since Luke was a Gentile, and Paul's reference to these men as his fellow Jews ("relatives") most likely includes all three. Thus we consider this Lucius to be otherwise unknown.

Although we cannot be sure, it is "quite possible" (Cranfield, 2:805-806) or even "very likely" (Moo, 934) that the Jason mentioned here is the same as Paul's harrassed host in the city of Thessalonica (Acts 17:6-9).

Some think Sosipater is the same as Sopater in Acts 20:4, since the latter was probably with Paul when he wrote Romans. Fitzmyer says this identification should "undoubtedly" be made (749), and Moo says it is "almost certainly" the case (934). Morris doubts it, though, since Sosipater is Paul's fellow Jew, and the Sopater in Acts 20:4 would more likely be a Gentile since he was helping to transport the collection from the Gentile churches to the church in Jerusalem (543).

16:22 I, Tertius, who wrote down this letter, greet you in the Lord. Tertius is otherwise unknown, but we know from this verse that he was Paul's amanuensis or scribe, the one who was actually writing down the words of this epistle as Paul dictated them. Comments made by Paul in other letters suggest that he usually used a scribe (1 Cor 16:21; Gal 6:11; Col 4:18; 2 Thess 3:17), but this is the only one who is named.[59]

Having a scribe take down his words by dictation compromises neither the integrity of Paul's authorship of this letter, nor the Holy Spirit's inspiration of it. We can reasonably assume that Paul read the finished product and gave it his apostolic "seal of approval."

---

[59]See Cranfield, 1:2-5, for a detailed discussion of Tertius' role as the amanuensis for Romans.

This one verse, though, was obviously not dictated by Paul, but was Tertius' own greeting to the Romans, perhaps at Paul's suggestion.

Tertius greeted them "in the Lord," i.e., in the name of the Lord Jesus, as a fellow Christian.

16:23 Gaius, whose hospitality I and the whole church here enjoy, sends you his greetings. Though this was a very common name, it is generally agreed that this Gaius is probably the same one listed in 1 Cor 1:14 as one of the few converts Paul personally baptized. Not quite as certain, but still possible, is Gaius' identification with Titius Justus in Acts 18:7. There is reason to think that Titius Justus was not his complete name; Gaius would have been his "first name." Also, this Titius Justus is mentioned along with Crispus (Acts 18:8), who is also linked with Gaius in 1 Cor 1:14. Finally, the Titius Justus in Acts 18:7 opened his house up to Paul and his company when they were run out of the nearby synagogue; here in 16:23 Paul speaks of Gaius's hospitality. (See Bruce, 280; Murray, 2:238; Dunn, 2:910; Moo, 935.)

In any case the Gaius named here had a house in Corinth, which he was sharing at this time not only with Paul but with "the whole church." This may mean that he had a large house and allowed it to be used by the entire church *in Corinth* when they wanted to have a combined gathering of the smaller house churches in the city (Dunn, 2:911; Fitzmyer, 749-750). Or it may mean that he provided hospitality for any Christians who were traveling through Corinth (Lenski, 925; Hendriksen, 2:515). Moo says it could have been either, but more likely the latter (935).

Erastus, who is the city's director of public works, and our brother Quartus send you their greetings. There was an Erastus who traveled with Paul (Acts 19:22; 2 Tim 4:20); for this reason some assume the one mentioned here cannot be the same person, since this one was a city official in Corinth and could hardly have traveled at will. Not everyone agrees with this, however. Fitzmyer says the two are "almost certainly" the same (750; see Moo, 935). Again, we cannot be sure.

Nor can we say one way or the other whether this Erastus is the same as a city official whose name (Erastus) appears on an inscription in Corinth from this very period. Everything fits except the fact that the title on the inscription (something like "commissioner of public works," says Bruce, 280) is not the same as the title given here, i.e., "city treasurer" (NASB; the NIV translation is imprecise and presumptuous). It is possible that Erastus held both positions at different times, holding one office when Paul wrote and another when the inscription was made. (See Cranfield, 2:807-808; Fitzmyer, 750; Moo, 935-936.)

The last name is Quartus, called "the brother" (NASB), which probably just means that he was a fellow Christian. Nothing else is known about him.

16:24 As stated earlier, this verse as it appears in the Textus Receptus, from which the KJV was translated, was probably not in the original text of Romans and thus is not included in most modern translations, including the NIV. (See Moo, 933, n. 1, for the textual data.) Its content is the same as v. 20b.

III. CONCLUDING DOXOLOGY (16:25-27)

The textual evidence regarding the integrity of this passage (i.e., whether it should be accepted as part of the original Roman letter) is mixed. In a long footnote Moo summarizes its "checkered textual history" and other problems, then gives a lengthy list of many who regard this doxology as "a post-Pauline addition to Romans." Then he summarizes the arguments, textual and otherwise, for including it in the original, and lists many who support its inclusion. His own view is stated thus: "A decision is very difficult; but we are slightly inclined to include the doxology as part of Paul's original letter" (936-937, n. 2).

I agree with this conclusion and will proceed with the assumption that this is Paul's own inspired conclusion to his letter. It is unthinkable that he would have ended this awe-inspiring composition with nothing more than "and Quartus, the brother" (16:23, NASB; see Godet, 502). Also, the themes which appear in these closing verses echo the themes of the opening verses, 1:1-16 (see Moo, 937-938). All in all these words of praise magnify and glorify the God of grace. It is only fitting that a doxology so "elaborate and grand in thought and in form" should close this great epistle (Lenski, 927).[60]

[60]For other lengthy doxologies see 11:33-36; Heb 13:20-21; Jude 24-25. On the concept of a doxology, see 1:25 (JC, 1:154).

One problem with this passage is that its syntax is not easily decipherable, especially since it appears to be "one long incomplete sentence" (Moo, 938; see v. 27). It may be helpful to set forth at this point a schematic of these verses, showing how the parts are related to the whole. (In what follows, the order of the words and phrases does not always follow the Greek, nor do the order and wording always conform to the NIV.)

I. Now to him who is able to establish you
  A. By my gospel, yea,
  B. [By] the proclamation of Jesus Christ –
    1. [Which is] according to the revelation of the mystery
      a. [Which was] hidden for long ages past,
      b. But now [is]
        (1) Manifested, and
        (2) Made known –
          (1) Unto all the Gentiles,
          (2) Through the prophetic writings,
          (3) By the command of the eternal God,
          (4) For the purpose of obedience of faith;
II. To the only wise God;
III. To him [I say]
  – BE GLORY FOREVER, THROUGH JESUS CHRIST! AMEN!

16:25 Now to him who is able to establish you by my gospel and the proclamation of Jesus Christ, . . . As a doxology these words constitute an act of worship and praise offered up to God, but they are not addressed directly to God. They are formulated in third person, not second person. The actual declaration of praise is in v. 27b, "[To him] be glory forever through Jesus Christ!" The verses which precede these words (vv. 25-27a) are identifying the one who is being praised, and explaining (in part) why he should be praised.

That one, of course, is God; and here he is described as the one who is able (δύναμαι, *dynamai*, has the power) "to establish you." One reason Paul wanted to visit the Roman Christians was to impart to them a spiritual gift that would "make [them] strong" (1:11). The word used here and in 1:11 is the same, i.e., στηρίζω (*stērizō*), "to strengthen, confirm, establish upon a firm foundation" (see JC, 1:95).

As explained earlier (JC, 1:94-95), the spiritual gift Paul wanted to give the Romans, the gift that would establish them, was the gospel itself. Now that he has completed this epistle, he has in effect given them the gift of the gospel. Thus he can say here in 16:25 that God has the power "to establish you *by*[61] *my gospel*," i.e., the gospel that was revealed and entrusted to him (1 Cor 15:1-4; Gal 1:11-12), and the gospel which he has just proclaimed in the words of this grand epistle. This gospel has already been identified as the power by which God brings salvation (1:16), including the initial gift of justifying grace and also the subsequent sanctifying and glorifying grace that will lead us home.

"The proclamation of Jesus Christ" is not different from "my gospel," but is an explanation of it. "Proclamation" is κήρυγμα (*kērygma*), which can be either the act of preaching (Matt 12:41) or the message preached (2 Tim 4:17; Titus 1:3). Here it is the latter, and thus identifies the content of the gospel, namely, Jesus Christ (see 1 Cor 15:1-4).

Paul now describes this gospel further. The gospel by which God establishes us, he says, is **according to the revelation of the mystery hidden for long ages past, . . .** This phrase could be taken as parallel with "by my gospel," and thus as giving a second means by which God establishes us. More likely, though, it introduces a more complete description of the gospel. My gospel, says Paul, is in accordance with or in conformity with the revelation of the mystery. Everything from here through the end of v. 26 is part of one long description of this mystery.

Paul says his gospel is in accord with "the revelation of the mystery." In biblical terminology a "mystery" is a truth hidden in the mind of God and undiscoverable by human reason, and thus known only through divine revelation (see 11:25). Thus the word can apply to many things, but for Paul the mystery that seemed to awe him the most was God's plan to include Jews and Gentiles together in the church of Jesus Christ in this New Covenant age (see 11:25 again).[62] This is the mystery that has now been revealed

---

[61]This word is κατά (*kata*), which can mean "in accordance with, in agreement with," but can sometimes mean "on the basis of" (AG, 408), indicating means (Moo, 938; MacArthur, 2:383), as in the NIV ("by").

[62]See Bruce, 283; Hendriksen, 2:517; MacArthur, 2:387.

especially to Paul, the Apostle to the Gentiles (Eph 3:3-11); it is the mystery according to which his gospel took shape.

Paul now says three main things about this mystery. First, it was "hidden for long ages past." "Hidden" is σιγάω (*sigaō*), "keep silent, keep secret." I.e., for a long time God kept this a secret; it truly was a mystery. What are these "long ages past"?[63] Some think this refers only to the time preceding the OT prophets (Lard, 467), since the next verse says the mystery is made known "through the prophetic writings." Another view, which I accept, is that these "long ages past" include the OT dispensation and came to an end only with the first coming of Christ and the proclamation of New Covenant revelation. How, then, could this mystery still have been a *mystery* in OT times if it was made known through the prophetic writings? This is explained in the next verse.

16:26 [B]ut now, says Paul, this mystery is **revealed and made known through the prophetic writings by the command of the eternal God, so that all nations might believe and obey him –** Here is the second fact about the mystery: it is "now revealed" or "manifested" (NASB). "Now" refers to this New Covenant era. "Revealed" is φανερόω (*phaneroō*), the word which is also used in 3:21: "But now a righteousness from God . . . has been made known." The initial and decisive revelation of the mystery was accomplished through the incarnation, ministry, and saving work of Jesus Christ (Morris, 547). But further explanation was necessary. Thus, following Jesus' ascension into heaven, the full meaning of "the mystery of Christ . . . has now been revealed by the Spirit to God's holy apostles and prophets" (Eph 3:4b-5; see 1 Cor 2:6-16).[64] Their revealed and inspired message is given to us in the form of the NT writings.

The third thing about the mystery is that it has been "made known" (γνωρίζω, *gnōrizō*). In Ephesians Paul uses this word five times in referring to the mystery (1:9; 3:3,5,10; 6:19). Here it could be a simple synonym for *phaneroō*, but its placement at the opposite end of the verse (in the Greek) suggests a different connotation. The mystery of Christ has now not only been revealed inwardly to

[63]Murray thinks the "long ages past" might extend into eternity past, into the eternal counsels of God (2:241).

[64]The prophets to which this passage refers are NT prophets. See Eph 2:20; 4:11.

the prophets and apostles, but has been and is being outwardly and publicly made known through the preaching of the gospel to all the world (Godet, 504). See Eph 6:19.

The rest of this verse consists of four prepositional phrases that modify "made known" and thus describe the preaching of the gospel, especially the essence of Paul's ministry as the Apostle to the Gentiles. First, the mystery is made known "to all the nations" (NASB), i.e., to the Gentiles.[65] The unveiled mystery is not a secret to be jealously guarded by an inner circle of gnostic priests, but is a message meant to be proclaimed to everyone.

Second, the mystery is made known "through the prophetic writings." This presents a problem. If the mystery was not revealed and made known until the New Covenant era, how could it be made known *through the prophets*? Does this not imply that it was "made known" even in the OT era? Some say the "prophetic writings" are those of the *New* Covenant prophets mentioned in Eph 2:20; 3:5 (Godet, 505), but most rightly agree that the OT prophets are in view here. How may we explain this?

The answer is simple. Many things revealed to the OT prophets were not capable of being fully understood until the first coming of Christ (1 Pet 1:10-12). But now that Christ has come, the full meaning of these prophetic writings has been made clear. Until Jesus came, the prophecies were there, but their meaning was veiled. Now they are being properly interpreted and clarified in relation to Jesus Christ and his saving work. See 3:21. (See Murray, 2:242; Cranfield, 2:812; Stott, 404-405.)

Paul's point, though, is that the prophetic writings, now understood as applying to Christ and his church, are a *means* of making the mystery known to all the nations. Early Christian preaching was thus heavily dependent upon the OT, and modern preaching could no doubt make better and more frequent use of the "prophetic writings."

Third, the mystery is made known "by the command of the eternal[66] God." This refers first of all to the Great Commission (Matt 28:18-20; Luke 24:47; Acts 1:8), but also refers to Paul's singular

---

[65]This phrase, which is actually the last of the four in the Greek text, is totally obscured by the NIV.

[66]On God's nature as eternal, see GC, 250-264.

commission to be the Apostle to the Gentiles (Murray, 2:242-243). It is the express will and command of God that the now-explained mystery be made known to all.

Finally, the purpose of proclaiming the mystery of Jesus Christ is to bring about "obedience of faith." Paul used this same phrase in 1:5 to explain the ultimate purpose of his apostleship (see JC, 1:78-82). It is fitting that he should refer to it again here at the end of his epistle. The goal of all Christian preaching and witnessing, including the goal of this very letter to the Romans, is to bring about heartfelt obedience that springs from faith in Jesus as Savior and Lord.

16:27 [T]o the only wise God be glory forever through Jesus Christ! Amen.[67] Paul began this doxology by referring to God as the one who is able to establish and strengthen us by the gospel, and then he went into detail about this gospel and the marvelous plan by which God has made it known. Here in v. 27 he catches his breath, so to speak, and refers once more to the God whom he is about to bless. But now he refers to him as "the only wise God."

One question is whether Paul is emphasizing two things about God – his singularity ("the only God"[68]) and his wisdom ("the wise God"[69]) – or whether he is simply emphasizing the uniqueness of his wisdom. Most agree that the latter is the case. Paul has already blessed God for his wisdom in an earlier doxology (11:33). Elsewhere he declares that the message of the cross of Christ is the epitome of God's wisdom (1 Cor 1:18-25,30), and in Eph 3:10 he refers to the unveiled mystery as "the manifold wisdom of God."

His point here, then, is that the God who has devised such a marvelous plan of salvation, has worked it out in the arena of history, has in this present age accomplished it through Jesus Christ, and has made it all known through the gospel – such a God is truly the essence of wisdom! Everything that Paul has written up to this point in this awesome letter causes him to praise and adore God for his wisdom. This is truly a fitting theme with which to close the epistle.

[67]On "Amen," see 1:25 (JC, 1:154).

[68]On the Bible's extensive teaching that God is truly the one and only God, see GC, 250-264.

[69]On God's wisdom see GRu, 285-289.

The very last phrase presents a translation problem. As noted earlier, this whole doxology is an incomplete sentence. As is typical of doxologies, it lacks a main verb. Most translations, including the NIV, simply and appropriately add the verb "be." The more difficult problem, though, is the presence in the Greek text of the relative pronoun ᾧ (*hō*, "to whom"), which makes the text read literally, "to the only wise God, through Jesus Christ, *to whom* [be] the glory forever." Grammatically "to whom" could refer to Jesus Christ, which would be doctrinally appropriate, to be sure. Most agree, though, that it refers to God, who has twice been designated as the object of this statement of praise (vv. 25a, 27a). The relative pronoun *hō* would then serve what is called a "resumptive" purpose and would be translated, "To him, I say" (Lenski, 933). The NIV and the NASB simply ignore this pronoun, but they retain the proper meaning.

The phrase "through Jesus Christ" immediately follows "to the only wise God," but is properly interpreted by the NIV as modifying "be glory forever." The eternal glory that we creatures must ascribe to God is obviously warranted by his mighty works of creation and providence, which are distinct from the redemptive work of the incarnate Christ (GRe, 27-43). But the glory that surpasses all other, and elicits from God's saints the highest possible praise, is the glory that is due him for what he has done through our Lord and Savior, Jesus Christ. Amen!